D1563946

INTERNATIONAL TRADE AND RESOURCE ALLOCATION

ADVANCED TEXTBOOKS IN ECONOMICS

VOLUME 19

Editors:

C.J. BLISS

M.D. INTRILIGATOR

Advisory Editors:

L. JOHANSEN

D.W. JORGENSON

M.C. KEMP

J.-J. LAFFONT

J.-F. RICHARD

NORTH-HOLLAND PUBLISHING COMPANY
AMSTERDAM · NEW YORK · OXFORD

INTERNATIONAL TRADE
AND RESOURCE ALLOCATION

A.D. WOODLAND

University of Sydney, Australia

1982

NORTH-HOLLAND PUBLISHING COMPANY
AMSTERDAM · NEW YORK · OXFORD

© NORTH-HOLLAND PUBLISHING COMPANY – 1982

ISBN 0 444 86370 2

Publishers

NORTH-HOLLAND PUBLISHING COMPANY
AMSTERDAM · NEW YORK · OXFORD

Sole distributors for the U.S.A. and Canada

ELSEVIER SCIENCE PUBLISHING COMPANY, INC.
52 VANDERBILT AVENUE
NEW YORK, N.Y. 10017

Library of Congress Cataloging in Publication Data

Woodland, A. D.
    International trade and resource allocation.

    (Advanced textbooks in economics ; v. 19)
    Includes bibliographies and index.
    1. Commerce. 2. Economics. I. Title.
II. Series.
HF1411.W59 1982   382   82-8045
ISBN 0-444-86370-2 (Elsevier Science Pub. Co.)
                            AACR2

PRINTED IN THE NETHERLANDS

INTRODUCTION TO THE SERIES

The aim of the series is to cover topics in economics, mathematical economics and econometrics, at a level suitable for graduate students or final year under-graduates specializing in economics. There is at any time much material that has become well established in journal papers and discussion series which still awaits a clear, self-contained treatment that can easily be mastered by students without considerable preparation or extra reading. Leading specialists will be invited to contribute volumes to fill such gaps. Primary emphasis will be placed on clarity, comprehensive coverage of sensibly defined areas, and insight into fundamentals, but original ideas will not be excluded. Certain volumes will therefore add to existing knowledge, while others will serve as a means of communicating both known and new ideas in a way that will inspire and attract students not already familiar with the subject matter concerned.

The Editors

TO

Narelle

and Lisa, Nicole and Todd
who are pleased that my "story" is finished

CONTENTS

PREFACE

This book is a substantial revision and extension of lecture notes prepared for a graduate course in the theory of international trade at the University of British Columbia. The primary aim of the book is to present the essence of the modern theory of international trade within a unified framework, which emphasizes the generality of the results obtained and which treats the traditional two-dimensional model as an interesting special case of a more general model.

It has often been remarked that international trade theory is difficult since there are so many different models and theories that do not seem to hang together. I have found such remarks rather strange since I have always thought of international trade theory as having a very consistent framework fashioned by the general competitive equilibrium model. Yet there is some validity to the remark since the literature has not, until recent years perhaps, emphasized the general framework, relying as it did on a mixture of diagrammatic and algebraic techniques and a preoccupation with two-dimensional models and simple generalizations thereof. This book attempts to overcome these difficulties for students of international trade theory by presenting a general and unified analysis. Such a general analysis is made easier by the extensive use of modern duality theory. Thus, the analysis is cast in terms of cost, expenditure, indirect utility and gross national production functions which have very useful properties rather than production, direct utility and transformation functions.

Duality theory is not new to the economics literature, being used by Hotelling in the 1930s and by Shephard and Samuelson in the early 1950s. Nevertheless, it is only during the last few years that its power has been appreciated and its use has spread. This book has been written under the firm conviction that the use of duality theory will soon become standard practice. It is hoped that it will be useful for students and researchers who wish to study the theory of international trade and/or wish to see how duality can be used in this area.

The book is directed towards graduate students with a sound background in microeconomic theory. The mathematical prerequisite is that the student be familiar with differential calculus, elementary set theory, optimization and linear algebra. This appears to be consistent with the level of preparation of first-year graduate students in most North American graduate schools. Since students may not be well prepared in the duality approach, a full chapter is devoted to its exposition and use in the theory of the producer and consumer.

While the emphasis is on the theoretical aspects of international trade, one chapter has been allocated to the task of relating the theory to some of the empirical research that has taken place. The intent is not to provide a comprehensive account of all empirical work that has been undertaken, but to select those empirical works that bear a strong relationship to the economic theory dealt with in this book. This should help the student to appreciate the theory and its connection with the real world.

Of further aid to the reader are the "notes on the literature" at the end of most chapters. These are not intended to be comprehensive but to give some guidance for further reading. Also, each chapter has a selection of problems for solution. These include proofs of assertions within the text, consideration of special cases, and extensions of the analysis.

My debt to those who have helped me in the task of writing this book is large indeed. The existence of this book owes much to the encouragement of Erwin Diewert to whom I am most grateful. I also wish to thank those who have read individual chapters and have contributed many valuable comments. These include W. Chang, A. Dixit, D. Donaldson, W. Ethier, M. Kemp, U. Kohli, P. Lloyd, D. Ryan, W. Schworm and L. Svensson. Thanks also go to the many graduate students who contributed suggestions regarding the substance and presentation of the lecture notes upon which the book is based. Finally, I wish to express my appreciation to the typists, too numerous to mention individually, but especially to Cathy Sevil who cheerfully handled the final revisions.

CHAPTER 1

INTRODUCTION TO THE THEORY OF INTERNATIONAL TRADE

1.1. Introduction

Although international trade is simply an extension of domestic trade beyond political boundaries it has been a very old tradition in the economics literature to provide a special treatment and analysis of international trade. There are at least two reasons for this. First, it is sometimes argued that there may be some factors of production and goods which are less mobile internationally than they are intranationally. This argument has been reflected in the traditional models which make the extreme assumption that factors are perfectly mobile intranationally but are completely immobile internationally, in contrast to goods which are perfectly mobile everywhere. Consequently, international trade deserves special attention because the basic framework is special. The second reason is that there are many questions that arise with regard to international trade simply because of the existence of political boundaries. For example, the effects of trade taxes such as import duties or of import quotas or of taxes on the earnings of foreign-owned capital constitute interesting avenues for enquiry that arise because of the fact that international governments can and do impose such restrictions on international trade.

Despite the fact that the study of international trade is given special treatment it is nevertheless true that the basic economic principles which govern domestic trade also govern international trade. Trade between individuals within an economy exists because they find it to their mutual benefit. Individuals in different nations also trade with one another because each finds it beneficial.

1.2. Scope and nature of international trade theory

There are two types of questions that can be asked about international trade. The first concerns *normative* economics, and involves the welfare consequences of international trade or of changes in the economic environment. For example, does the opening up of trade between two previously closed economies benefit the citizens of each nation? If not, can one devise appropriate tax policies which can be used in conjunction with trade to raise the welfare of all citizens? How are the benefits and losses from a change in the tariff structure distributed across individuals? Does the formation of a customs union or free trade agreement between two nations benefit the citizens of each nation? These, and many more, are questions that are concerned with the welfare consequences of changes in the economy.

The second type of question concerns *positive* economics, and is involved simply with the nature of international trade. For example, what are the reasons for international trade? How does the pattern of commodity trade relate to the relative factor endowments of trading nations? What is the effect of a change in the tariff structure upon the domestic prices of commodities, output levels, consumption levels, the pattern and volume of trade, the allocation of factors amongst the industries, the distribution of income, and the level of tariff revenue? How will the distribution of capital between nations be affected, both in the short and long runs, by a change in the economic environment such as a change in tariffs or technology? One has only to recall the after-effects of the sudden increase in the price of oil produced by OPEC (Organization of Petroleum Exporting Countries) to realize that the internal structure of economies and international distribution of capital and incomes can be vitally affected by changes that occur in the international market place.

In order to answer the types of questions posed above, it is necessary to construct a theoretical framework within which to work. This framework is dictated by the state of technology in the economics discipline and by the desirability to keep the analysis sufficiently simple for purposes of exposition. The framework taken is that of a perfectly competitive equilibrium model, and mostly it will be static in nature. In the competitive model there exist consumers, producers and traders each of whom makes decisions on the assumption that prices are given and beyond the individual's control. They are price-takers. Each consumer has given preferences described by a utility function and decides on a consumption vector which maximizes utility subject to the budget constraint. Each producer maximizes his profit subject to the constraints imposed by the available technology. There is freedom of entry and exit to any industry, such entry and exit being motivated by profit. Traders take prices as given and buy and sell to maximize their profits. In short, whenever there exists the possibility of a profit in the economy, someone will seize the opportunity and by so doing in large numbers will eventually remove further opportunities for profit. That is to say, in a competitive equilibrium profit-seeking activities ensure that profits are eliminated.

Several remarks concerning the chosen framework deserve attention. First, the framework does not involve the concept of money and therefore implies a separation of the "real" and monetary aspects of international trade. Thus, the analysis is exclusively within the tradition of the "real" or "pure theory" aspect of the international trade literature. Secondly, most of the analysis is static in nature and time plays no essential role. While time could be introduced at the outset, as in Debreu (1959), by assuming the existence of futures markets for all goods, or using Hicks' (1946) temporary equilibrium framework in which point expectations about future variables are formed, a treatment of time is postponed until the static model has been thoroughly analysed. This has pedagological value and, moreover, many interesting questions can be posed and answered without involving time.

Thirdly, there is no treatment of models involving non-competitive behaviour. This is not because such behaviour is not viewed as being important theoretically or empirically, though its importance is sometimes exaggerated, but because of limitations of space and because its theoretical treatment is still in its infancy.

Despite the limitations of the theoretical framework, the competitive equilibrium model is a very useful vehicle which enables the analysis of many interesting questions in international trade. Nevertheless, its limitations should be kept in mind.

Two important characteristics of the international trade literature arc its concentration upon simple two-dimensional models and upon the diagram as a tool of analysis. While the diagram can be a very powerful tool it loses its power as the complexity of the questions being asked is increased and when interest extends to dimensions greater than two. In this regard, it is noteworthy that much of the recent literature has been concerned with the question of whether propositions established for two-dimensional models carry over to multi-dimensional models. As a consequence, mathematics has almost completely replaced the diagram as a research tool since mathematics is more efficient for multi-dimensional problems.

Where possible the analysis in this book deals with multi-dimensional models (many products, factors and consumers) and it treats the two-dimensional model as an interesting special case which generally has considerably more structure. The diagram is often used, not to prove results necessarily but to provide a geometric interpretation of the nature of the problem or proposition involved. Thus, the diagram and mathematics are viewed as complements.

If mathematics is chosen as the tool of analysis because it is more efficient than the diagram, then the type of mathematics should be chosen accordingly. With this in mind much of the analysis involves the use of *duality theory*. The use of duality theory to formulate and analyse competitive models is efficient in that it minimizes the number of variables in the model (pushing unwanted variables behind the scenes and concentrating attention upon the important ones), often yields results in a simple way, and emphasizes the economic assumptions in, and basic structure of, the model. Thus, when dealing with the firm it is convenient to define the minimum cost function, indicating the minimum factor cost attainable given the technology as a function of the output and factor price vectors, rather than dealing with the conditions for cost minimization expressed in terms of the production function. Similarly, the consumer's constrained utility maximization problem is dealt with in terms of the minimum expenditure function or the indirect utility function rather than the (direct) utility function itself.

At the aggregate level dual functions can also be used. On the production side, it is well known that competitive behaviour leads to maximum gross national product (GNP). Thus, it is useful to define the GNP function which gives the maximum GNP attainable as a function of the product prices and factor endowments. The GNP function is *dual* to the production possibility set in the sense that each one contains enough information to reconstruct the other exactly. They are, therefore, equivalent representations of the technology. On the consumption side, one can define an aggregate minimum expenditure function which is the minimum expenditure required to attain a given utility vector under a given price vector. If expenditure is required to be less than or equal to income, the utility possibility set, depending upon prices and income, is thereby defined.

Different dual functions can be defined for a particular problem. For example, as mentioned above, for the consumer problem one can work with the expenditure function or the indirect utility function. The latter is a "pure" dual function in that it does not contain any variables endogenous to the consumer's problem and depends only upon exogenous prices and income. The expenditure function, however, is only a "partial" dual since, while the consumption vector has been optimized out, the level of utility remains as an argument and it is endogenous to the consumer's problem. Both functions are dual to the utility function and hence are equally good characterizations of preferences. However, for some purposes it is more convenient to use the expenditure function and for others it is more convenient to use the indirect utility function. Duality theory enables the researcher to switch from one characterization to another to suit his purpose. One is not restricted by a particular model formulation.

1.3. An overview[1]

The following is intended to indicate the structure of the book and to provide an overview of the theory of international trade developed, the models used and questions asked.

Because of the extensive reliance upon duality theory, Chapter 2 is devoted to an elementary explanation of duality within the context of the theory of competitive consumer and producer theory, which underlies the competitive model of international trade. Here we introduce the unit cost function

$$c(w) \equiv \min_{x} \{wx: \ f(x) \geqslant 1, \ x \geqslant 0\}, \tag{1}$$

which is the minimum of all factor costs wx that are consistent with the production of 1 unit of output, where w is the factor price vector, x is the factor input vector and $f(x)$ is the linearly homogeneous production function. Duality theory is concerned with the properties of $f(x)$ and $c(w)$. Under appropriate conditions f and c are dual in the sense that each contains enough information to be able, in principle at least, to reconstruct the other exactly. If linear homogeneity is not assumed one can define the cost function $C(w, y)$, where y is the level of output.

On the consumer side the expenditure function is defined analogously to the cost function as

$$E(p, \mu) \equiv \min_{z} \{pz: u(z) \geqslant \mu, \ z \geqslant 0\}, \tag{2}$$

where $u(z)$ is the utility function, μ is the level of utility and z is the consumption vector. The indirect utility function is defined either directly or indirectly in terms of the expenditure function as

$$V(p, m) \equiv \max_{z} \{u(z): pz \leqslant m, z \geqslant 0\} \equiv \max_{\mu} \{\mu: E(p, \mu) \leqslant m\}. \tag{3}$$

The expenditure and indirect utility functions are dual to the direct utility function under weak conditions.

The value of such dual functions stems primarily from their curvature and slope properties. In particular,

---

[1] Since this section presents an overview of the modelling of international trade, the notation and functions are only briefly defined. Section 4 below gives a summary of the main notation used throughout the book.

(a) $x^0 = c_w(w^0),$

(b) $z^0 = E_p(p^0, \mu^0) = -V_p(p^0, m^0)/V_m(p^0, m^0),$ $m^0 = E(p^0, \mu^0),$ (4)

where $c_w(w^0)$ denotes the gradient (derivative) vector of c with respect to w evaluated at w^0 and similarly for E_p, V_p and V_m. Thus, (4) states that the quantity solutions are easily obtained from the dual functions by differentiation. This means there is an economy in that the quantity variables do not have to be explicitly considered.

In Chapter 3 a competitive model of the production sector of the economy is formulated. Each industry produces a single product with a technology described by a production function or, equally well, by a cost function. There is a fixed factor endowment v of factors and the product price vector is given. The profit-maximization behaviour of producers and the competitive factor market combine to determine the levels of industry outputs and the factor prices. In terms of cost functions the model is written as

(a) $c^j(w) - p_j \geqslant 0 \leqslant y_j,$ $j = 1, \ldots, M,$

(b) $\displaystyle\sum_{j=1}^{M} c_{ij}(w) y_j - v_i \leqslant 0 \leqslant w_i,$ $i = 1, \ldots, N,$ (5)

where j denotes the industry, $c_{ij}(w) \equiv \partial c^j(w)/\partial w_i$, and the double inequalities imply complementary slackness.

Many interesting questions of international trade theory can be asked within the context of (5). For example, how will a change in world prices for goods affect the output levels, the factor prices (hence the functional distribution of income) and resource allocation? Also, as a prelude to wider questions, how are factor prices and industry outputs affected by factor endowments? These questions are raised in Chapter 4, and give rise to the famous Rybczynski, Stolper–Samuelson and factor price equalization theorems of international trade theory. Similar questions are asked in Chapter 5 within the context of more general models involving intermediate inputs and joint outputs.

In the models of Chapters 3–5 competitive behaviour determines the value of production (GNP) as a function of the product price and factor endowment vectors. It is also true that the competitive and centrally planned solutions are identical so that the GNP function may be written as

$$G(p, v) \equiv \max_{y} \{py : y \in Y(v)\}, \tag{6}$$

where $Y(v)$ denotes the (net) production possibility set. This function is dual to

$Y(v)$ and has special properties which completely characterize the competitive solution, including the convenient property

$$y^0 = G_p(p^0, v^0); \quad w^0 = G_v(p^0, v^0). \tag{7}$$

That is to say, the derivative of G yields the output supply and factor price functions. Thus, in a formal sense, Chapters 3–5 are really concerned with the properties of $G(p, v)$ under various special assumptions regarding the technology, e.g. with no intermediate inputs or joint outputs, as in (5) above. For many purposes it is desirable to establish propositions which are as general as possible and not restricted by special assumptions, in which case it is appropriate to use the GNP function $G(p, v)$ defined for a general production possibility set $Y(v)$. For example, we can simply require that it be non-empty, closed and convex, an assumption consistent with a whole range of possible technological models. Of course, it is also desirable at times to deal with specific models, such as (5), which impose added structure on $G(p, v)$. This added structure can then be exploited in the analysis being undertaken. Chapter 5, in addition to dealing with intermediate inputs and joint outputs, establishes the general properties of $G(p, v)$ and obtains *general* propositions regarding the effects of p and v upon y and w.

The task of Chapter 6 is to complete the model of international trade for a small open economy (price-taker) by introducing the consumption sector. For a given distribution of ownership of the factor endowments among individuals, (7) determines the factor price vector and hence the distribution of income. The aggregate demand vector clearly depends upon the income distribution as well as prices. For expositional purposes it is sometimes convenient to assume that the consumption sector behaves as if it were an individual, an assumption which pervades the literature. Chapter 6 is primarily concerned with the conditions under which such modelling is valid and, not surprising, the conditions are fairly strict. However, in such cases the net export function can be defined as

$$x(p, v) \equiv G_p(p, v) - E_p(p, V(p, G(p, v))) = G_p(p, v) - \phi(p, G(p, v)), \tag{8}$$

where $\phi(p, m) \equiv E_p(p, V(p, m))$ is the vector of demand functions and income is $m = G(p, v)$. The net export functions indicate how trade depends upon prices and factor endowments (and income distribution if the model is generalized) and Chapter 6 analyses this dependence.

The model of international trade is completed in Chapter 7 by explicitly introducing a foreign nation and specifying the international market equilibrium condition for goods as

$$X(p, v, v^*) \equiv x(p, v) + x^*(p, v^*) = 0, \tag{9}$$

where the asterisk (*) denotes the foreign nation. This determines, up to a factor of proportionality, the equilibrium price vector p under free trade. This is a full general equilibrium since not only do the international markets for goods clear, but within each nation all consumers and producers are in equilibrium and the factor markets clear. Once the equilibrium price vector is established (8) indicates the net export vector as well as the production and consumption vectors. Also, the factor price vector is determined as in (7). If one wants to go back to the allocation of resources between industries, then the specific model underlying $G(p, v)$ can be consulted, e.g. (5). Most of Chapter 7 is concerned with the nature of free trade between nations with emphasis on the Ricardian theory of comparative advantage, the Heckscher–Ohlin–Samuelson theory of relative factor endowments, and attempts to generalize these theories when there are many goods and factors.

Chapter 8 deals with the model extended to take account of non-traded goods and variable factor supplies. These phenomena are formally equivalent but have, nevertheless, been given separate treatments. Non-traded goods, for example, create complications because when the price of a traded good changes there will generally be a change in the prices of non-traded goods which have to be taken into account in establishing the effects of the change in the price of the traded good. Chapter 8 considers the extent to which the main results from Chapters 3–7 are affected by the presence of non-traded goods and variable factor supplies.

The welfare aspects of international trade are developed in Chapter 9. Emphasis is on a comparison of free trade, restricted trade and autarky (no trade) from the viewpoint of the welfare of consumers. If $E(p, \mu)$ denotes the minimum expenditure required to attain a *vector* of individual utilities, μ, then a necessary and sufficient condition for free trade at price vector p to be *potentially* superior to autarky (with utility vector μ^0) is that

$$G(p, v) > E(p, \mu^0). \tag{10}$$

When (10) holds there is more than sufficient income under free trade for there to exist a distribution of income so that μ^0 is available. The gain is potential in that it is conditional upon the redistribution being socially feasible and undertaken. Restricted trade is also considered in Chapter 9, as is the question of whether free trade is optimal for a single nation when it is known that it is Pareto optimal from the point of view of the world. Here the concept of a trade tax structure, which is Pareto optimal from the point of view of the nation, is developed.

Chapter 10 deals with the positive theory of international trade under various policy interventions in the form of unilateral transfers of incomes, taxes on international trade and internal taxes on consumption and production. These involve changes to the model by redefining disposable income, m, to take account of the transfer payments and the net tax revenue and, in the case of taxes, by imposing tax wedges between and hence distinguishing producer, consumer and world prices for goods. Interest centres on the effects of these policy interventions upon world and domestic prices, income distribution and also welfare. The concept of effective rates of tariff protection is also analysed.

Chapter 11 continues the discussion of government intervention in international trade. First, the equivalence of trade taxes and quotas is considered, as is the question of the optimal tax policy required to satisfy quantitative restrictions on production, consumption and trade. Piecemeal tax policies designed to improve welfare from a given initial situation, as opposed to tax policies designed to maximize welfare, are discussed. The remainder of the chapter is concerned with welfare effects for a subset of countries which form a club or association and agree to co-ordinate their tax policies. The optimality of free trade areas is considered under various restrictions and the positive theory of economic clubs is outlined.

A review of some of the more pertinent empirical research that has been undertaken in international trade is provided in Chapter 12. The review is not meant to be exhaustive or comprehensive, but is designed to illustrate the relationship between the theory of international trade, as developed here, and empirical studies. Thus, emphasis is on those studies which are closely related to the theory. They include empirical estimations of net export functions, consumer preferences, production and cost functions; studies of the causes of trade and calculations of effective rates of tariff protection; and various attempts to calculate the general equilibrium effects of tariff and other changes.

Chapter 13 uses the comparative statics technique to analyse the effects of changes in technology and factor endowments, and deals with the international mobility of capital and labour. Hitherto, technology and endowments were assumed to be fixed. In the case of internationally mobile capital a distinction is made between the capital owned by domestic residents and the capital employed domestically, and disposable income has a foreign component to it. From a formal viewpoint trading in capital services is just like trading in goods, and a similar analysis applies. For example, the optimal tax policy involves taxes on the earnings of foreign capital.

Chapter 14 is devoted to the extension of the static model to a dynamic framework in which saving and investment in capital can occur. Both optimal or rational saving and the ad hoc fixed saving assumptions are considered. The dynamics of the equations of motion are dealt with, as are the comparative statics of the stationary state solutions. In particular the effects of trade taxes are considered. Trade taxes in a static model cause domestic and foreign (if the nation has market power) prices to alter. In the steady state these changes will induce the capital stock to change so there is not only a movement around the production possibility curve but a shift of this curve as well. The question of the gains from trade in an intertemporal framework is also discussed.

Chapter 15 continues the analysis of the dynamics of trade and growth. The first topic is an examination of endogenous technical change within the context of dynamic externalities created by "learning by doing". This is the basis of the famous infant industry argument for tariff protection. The second topic concerns an analysis of the dynamics and steady-state solutions in a model with many capital goods. Finally, a model in which consumers can invest in foreign as well as domestic capital is developed and analysed.

The final chapter provides a brief introduction to a number of topics that have not been covered elsewhere in the book, but which form obvious extensions of the analysis. These are topics which are not at the core of international trade theory and so have not been covered in detail. Nevertheless they are of sufficient importance that some mention is necessary. Accordingly the discussion is brief, consisting mainly of an outline of the problem, the relationship to the core theory and an indication of appropriate references. The topics include uncertainty; distortions in production due to externalities, monopolistic behaviour and institutional rigidities; and trade and growth with exhaustive resources.

The preceding overview of the contents of this study of international trade theory has been rather brief. Its intention was to indicate the formal structure of the competitive model of trade considered, and to indicate how each chapter deals with a particular aspect of the model. General reviews of the theory of international trade already exist in the literature. These offer a broader view of the literature and form an invaluable complement to the present treatment. Readers are particularly referred to the surveys by Bhagwati (1964), Chipman (1965a, 1965b, 1966), Kemp (1975) and Mundell (1960).

1.4. Summary of notation

The following is a listing of the principal notation used throughout the book. The notation is also explained on its first occurrence in subsequent chapters. Notations which are not extensively used are explained in the text but are not mentioned here.

$p = (p_1, ..., p_M)$	=	vector of prices for M goods
$y = (y_1, ..., y_M)$	=	vector of net outputs for M goods
$z = (z_1, ..., z_M)$	=	vector of consumer demands for M goods
$g = (g_1, ..., g_M)$	=	vector of gross outputs for M goods
$x = (x_1, ..., x_M)$	=	vector of net exports for M goods
$t = (t_1, ..., t_M)$	=	vector of taxes for M goods
$w = (w_1, ..., w_N)$	=	vector of factor prices for N factors
$v = (v_1, ..., v_N)$	=	vector of endowments for N factors
$\mu = (\mu^1, ..., \mu^L)$	=	vector of utilities for L individuals
$G(p, v)$	=	gross national product (GNP) function
$C^j(w, y_j)$	=	cost function for product j
$c^j(w)$	=	unit cost function for product j
$E(p, \mu)$	=	expenditure function
$V(p, m)$	=	indirect utility function
$\phi(p, m)$	=	vector of consumer demand for functions for M goods
$S(p, u, v) \equiv G(p, v) - E(p, \mu)$	=	net revenue (balance of trade)
m	=	income
$u(z)$	=	(direct) utility function
$U(x, v)$	=	trade utility function
$H(p, b, v) \equiv V(p, G(p, v) + b)$	=	indirect trade utility function

An asterisk (*) denotes functions and variables for the foreign nation

The notation is not completely uniform and consistent throughout the book. Sometimes the same symbol is used with several different meanings. However, this (hopefully) does not occur within the same chapter and so there should be little possibility of confusion. For example, x_j is used as a vector of factor inputs in industry j in Chapter 3 and as the quantity of net exports of product j from Chapter 7 onwards.

Subscripts are used to denote derivatives. For example,

$$G_p(p, v) \equiv \partial G(p, v)/\partial p = [\partial G(p, v)/\partial p_j]$$

is a vector of derivatives of the function $G(p, v)$ with respect to vector p. Often the jth element of $G_p(p, v)$ will be written $G_j(p, v)$ when there is no possibility of confusion (as might arise if $\partial G(p, v)/\partial v_j$ was also being used in the discussion). Second derivatives are written with two subscripts. For example,

$$G_{pp}(p, v) \equiv \partial G_p(p, v)/\partial p = [\partial^2 G(p, v)/\partial p_i \partial p_j] \tag{11}$$

and

$$G_{pv}(p, v) \equiv \partial G_p(p, v)/\partial v = [\partial^2 G(p, v)/\partial p_i \partial v_j]. \tag{12}$$

Again, the ijth element of $G_{pp}(p, v)$ is often written as $G_{ij}(p, v)$ with the same qualification as above.

In general row and column vectors are not distinguished to reduce notation. Thus, for example,

$$py \equiv \sum_{j=1}^{M} p_j y_j \tag{13}$$

is the inner product between p and y. Where the distinction is important the standard notation where all vectors are column vectors and for example, p^T, the transpose of p, is a row vector, is explicitly used. Generally, however, there should be no confusion and the notation is considerably simplified. For example, it should be clear that

$$pG_{pv}v = \sum_{j=1}^{M} \sum_{i=1}^{N} p_j \frac{\partial^2 G(p, v)}{\partial p_j \partial v_i} v_i. \tag{14}$$

Vector inequalities are given by

$$
\begin{aligned}
&x = 0,   &&\text{implies } x_j = 0,   &&j = 1, ..., M,\\
&x > 0,   &&\text{implies } x_j > 0,   &&j = 1, ..., M,\\
&x \geqslant 0,   &&\text{implies } x_j \geqslant 0,   &&j = 1, ..., M,\\
&x \gtrsim 0,   &&\text{implies } x_j \geqslant 0,   &&j = 1, ..., M \text{ and } x_k > 0
\end{aligned}
\tag{15}
$$

for one or more k.

A convention used throughout is that, for any pair of conformable vectors, the double inequality

$$x \geqslant 0 \leqslant y \quad \text{or} \quad x \geqslant 0 \geqslant -y \tag{16}$$

is equivalent to

$$x \geqslant 0; \quad y \geqslant 0; \quad xy = 0. \tag{17}$$

The expression $x \geqslant 0 \leqslant y$ is never used to mean $x \geqslant 0, y \geqslant 0$. Expression (17), and hence (16), is sometimes referred to as the complementary slackness condition.

Reference to equation numbers in a different chapter is indicated by (x. y) where y is the equation number in Chapter x.

References

Bhagwati, J.N. (1964) "The pure theory of international trade: A survey", *Economic Journal* 74, March, 1–84.

Chipman, J.S. (1965a) "A survey of the theory of international trade: Part 1, The classical theory", *Econometrica* 33-3, July, 477–519.

Chipman, J.S. (1965b) "A survey of the theory of international trade: Part 2, The neoclassical theory", *Econometrica* 33-4, October, 685–760.

Chipman, J.S. (1966) "A survey of the theory of international trade: Part 3, The modern theory", *Econometrica* 34-1, January, 18–76.

Debreu, G. (1959) *Theory of Value* (New York: John Wiley).

Hicks, J.R. (1946) *Value and Capital*, 2nd edition (London: Oxford University Press).

Kemp, M.C. (1975) "The pure theory of international trade", in: M.J. Beckmann, G. Menges and R. Selten (eds.) *Handwortenbuch der Mathematischen Wirtschaftswissenschaften* (Westdeutscher Verlag).

Mundell, R.A. (1960) "The pure theory of international trade", *American Economic Review* 50-1, March, 67–110.

CHAPTER 2

PRODUCER AND CONSUMER THEORY: A DUALITY APPROACH

2.1. Introduction

The model of international trade to be developed and analysed in subsequent chapters assumes the existence of price-taking firms and consumers. Accordingly, it will be useful to review the theories of the firm and the consumer. This review is all the more important because the approach to international trade theory taken in this book is to make extensive use of modern *duality theory*. While duality theory has proved useful in economic analysis, many readers may not be familiar with it. A second purpose of this chapter is, therefore, to introduce the concept of duality theory and to argue its usefulness and desirability in the analysis of the behaviour of price-taking firms and consumers.

2.2. The price-taking firm

We begin with the theory of the firm. Consider a firm which produces a quantity y of a single product using N inputs in quantity $x = (x_1, ..., x_N)$ per period. The state of the technology available to the firm is assumed to be given and may be described by a production function $f(x)$ which indicates the maximum output attainable when the input vector is x. The firm can sell as much of the product as it wishes at the given price p, while it may purchase as much of the inputs as it wishes at the given input price vector $w = (w_1, ..., w_N)$. This means that this producer is sufficiently small that it cannot perceptibly affect the market prices for the product and the inputs.

The firm is assumed to maximize profit, equal to revenue py minus cost $wx = w_1 x_1 + ... + w_N x_N$, subject to the technology constraint.[1] It is clear that

---

[1] Except where it would be confusing, no distinction is made between column and row vectors. Thus, wx denotes the inner product between vectors w and x.

whatever output level maximizes profit, the corresponding input vector is the one which minimizes the input cost of producing that output. Following the standard treatment of profit maximization the problem is decomposed into two parts. In the first part inputs are chosen to minimize the cost of producing a given level of output. In the second, the output level is chosen to maximize revenue minus the minimum cost.

The cost-minimization problem defines the cost function

$$C(w,y) \equiv \min_{x} \{wx: f(x) \geqslant y, \ x \geqslant 0\}. \tag{1}$$

The right-hand side of (1) is interpreted as follows. The brackets { } denote a set, while the colon means "such that" or "with the property that". Thus, the right-hand side of (1) defines the problem of choosing the vector x to minimize the set of input costs wx such that the input vector is non-negative and is consistent with the production function.[2] For each choice of $w \geqslant 0$ and $y \geqslant 0$ this problem may be solved for the minimum cost. $C(w, y)$ defined by (1) denotes the solution to this problem and is, therefore, the minimum cost of producing output level y when the input price vector is w. It summarizes the cost-minimization problem.

With the cost function in hand, the firm's profit-maximization problem becomes

$$\Pi(p, w) \equiv \max_{y} \{py - C(w,y): \ y \geqslant 0\}, \tag{2}$$

where $\Pi(p, w)$ denotes the maximum profit attainable when the product price is p and the input price vector is w. Intermediate microeconomics textbooks invariably treat the theory of the price-taking firm in this manner, albeit less formally, except that, in order to concentrate on y, they usually do not make the dependence of the cost upon the input price vector w explicit. As will become evident below, the role of w is crucial in developing demand functions for inputs.

One reason why the cost function is given prominence in our treatment of the theory of the firm is that, under constant returns to scale, the profit function does not have nice properties. In this case it is either zero or infinity, as will be shown in section 2.5 below. The cost function, however, is well behaved and has properties which have interesting economic interpretations.

---

[2] The convention used for vector inequalities is as follows. A vector $x = (x_1, ..., x_N) \geqslant 0$ if each element is non-negative; $x = 0$ if each element is equal to zero; $x > 0$ if each element is positive; and $x \gtrsim 0$ if each element is non-negative and at least one element is positive. If $x \geqslant 0$, then x is said to be non-negative, while if $x \gtrsim 0$ it is said to be semi-positive.

2.3. The duality between production and cost functions

In the present context duality theory is concerned with the properties of the cost function $C(w, y)$ and with its relationship to the production function. While a significant body of literature has grown around the concept of duality theory in recent years, based on the early work of Hotelling (1932), Shephard (1953), Samuelson (1953) and Uzawa (1964), the present treatment attempts to examine those results of most interest for the purposes of this book and, in addition, to show that these results may be obtained using quite simple arguments.

2.3.1. Production function

Let the production function satisfy the following conditions:

> The production function $f(x)$ is defined for all $x \geqslant 0$. It is non-negative for $x \geqslant 0$ and positive for $x > 0$, continuous, quasi-concave, weakly increasing in the sense that $x^1 > x^0$ implies $f(x^1) > f(x^0)$, and is defined such that for any $y \geqslant 0$ there exists an x such that $f(x) \geqslant y$. (3)

What do these properties mean from an economic viewpoint? First, for each feasible input vector there exists a maximum output attainable and if something of all inputs is used then output is positive. The continuity property is for mathematical convenience and rules out sudden jumps in output. The increasing property indicates that more output can always be obtained by using more inputs. It also means that more of any one input cannot reduce output, sometimes referred to as the property of free disposal of inputs. To see this let $x^2 \gtrsim x^1 > 0$, i.e. x^2 has at least one element greater than the corresponding element of x^1 while all elements of x^2 are at least as great as those in x^1, which in turn are all positive. Suppose that $f(x^2) < f(x^1)$ and that $f(x^2) = f(x^0)$, where $x^0 < x^1$. (Such an x^0 can always be found by the increasing property.) But this contradicts the increasing property since $x^2 > x^0$ requires $f(x^2) > f(x^0)$. Thus, the assumption that $f(x^2) < f(x^1)$ is false, and so $f(x^2) \geqslant f(x^1)$ when $x^2 \gtrsim x^1 > 0$. The assumption that $f(x)$ is quasi-concave means that the set of input vectors which will produce at least y units of output, namely the level set $X(y) \equiv \{x: f(x) \geqslant y, x \geqslant 0\}$ is a convex set.

> A set X is convex if $x^0 \in X$, $x^1 \in X$ and $0 \leqslant \lambda \leqslant 1$ implies that $x^\lambda \equiv \lambda x^0 + (1 - \lambda) x^1 \in X$, where λ is a scalar. (4)

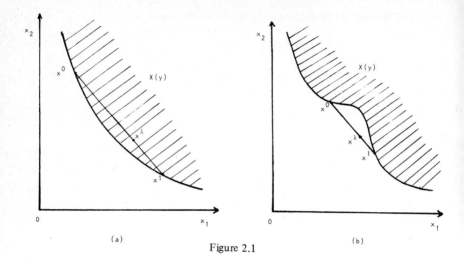

(a)   (b)

Figure 2.1

   This means that if x^0 and x^1 can separately produce output level y, then the input vector x^λ, which is a convex combination of x^0 and x^1, can also produce output level y. This property is illustrated in fig. 2.1 (a). Fig. 2.1 (b) illustrates a case where $X(y)$ is not a convex set since x^λ is not in $X(y)$. The convexity of the level set implies non-increasing marginal rates of substitution between inputs around the isoquant (boundary of $X(y)$). That is to say, the isoquant defines any one component of x as a function of the remaining ones, and this function is convex. The final property of the production function ensures that any non-negative output level can be produced if enough of the inputs are used. It is worth noting that the isoquants may consist of several linear segments and hence that differentiability of $f(x)$ is not assumed.

2.3.2. Cost function

Having specified and discussed the properties of the production function, attention is now turned to the cost function $C(w, y)$. The first question which arises is whether the cost function is defined for all $w \geqslant 0$ and $y \geqslant 0$. In example 2, presented at the end of this section, it will be shown that if one input price is zero, it may be that the minimum cost does not exist. In this example, the firm can always reduce costs by using more of the free factor and less of the other factors. The cost approaches a finite limit called the infimum, however, so the cost function may be redefined as an infimum rather than a minimum solution,

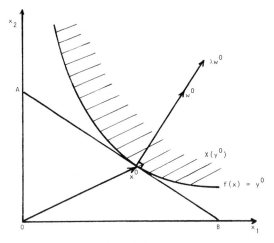

Figure 2.2

thus allowing it to be defined for all $w \geqslant 0$ and $y \geqslant 0$. While this technical diffi-culty could be avoided by assumption, it arises in the case of popular functional forms such as the constant elasticity of substitution (CES) production function and accordingly should not be overlooked.

Clearly the cost function is non-negative since $w \geqslant 0$ and $x \geqslant 0$ is required. Also, if all factor prices are multiplied by a scalar $\lambda > 0$, then the cost-minimizing choice for x will not change so that cost will be multiplied by λ. That is, $C(\lambda w, y) = \lambda C(w, y)$ for $\lambda > 0$, which means that C is homogeneous of degree one in w. This is illustrated in fig. 2.2, where the minimum cost solution is presented. Here, the level set $X(y^0)$ is the shaded area. The price vector w^0 determines a family of iso-cost lines drawn at right angles to w^0, with the minimum iso-cost line con-sistent with production of y^0 being AB.[3] This iso-cost line is tangent to or sup-ports $X(y^0)$ at the input solution x^0. For factor price vector $w^1 \equiv \lambda w^0$ the mini-mum iso-cost line consistent with producing output y^0 is again AB and the opti-mal solution remains at x^0.

If $w^1 \gtrsim w^0 > 0$, then $C(w^1, y) \geqslant C(w^0, y)$, meaning that the cost function is non-decreasing in w. To see this let x^1 be a solution when w^1 occurs and let x^0

---

[3] This geometric construction is used extensively. If $wx = k$ defines a line where k is some constant, it follows that $w(x^1 - x^0) = 0$ for any two points x^0, x^1 on that line. But this is simply the statement that w and $(x^1 - x^0)$ are orthogonal or at right angles. This means that the vector w is at a right angle to the line joining x^0 and x^1 which is the line de-scribed by $wx = k$. See, for example, Hadley (1961, pp. 32–33).

be a solution when w^0 occurs. Then $w^0 x^0 \leqslant w^0 x^1$ since $x^1 \in X(y^0)$ and hence is feasible when w^0 occurs. Also, $w^1 x^1 \geqslant w^0 x^1$ since $w^1 \gtrsim w^0$. Putting these inequalities together yields $C(w^1, y) \equiv w^1 x^1 \geqslant w^0 x^1 \geqslant w^0 x^0 \equiv C(w^0, y)$.

If x^0 and x^1 are solutions when input price vectors are w^0 and w^1, respectively, then $w^0 x^0 \leqslant w^0 x^1$ (as shown above), and similarly $w^1 x^1 \leqslant w^1 x^0$ since x^0 is feasible when w^1 occurs. Adding these inequalities yields

$$(w^1 - w^0)(x^1 - x^0) \leqslant 0. \tag{5}$$

This inequality indicates in a general way the limits placed upon the response of the solution for x to a change in w. For example, if w^1 and w^0 differ only in the ith element, then (5) becomes $(w_i^1 - w_i^0)(x_i^1 - x_i^0) \leqslant 0$ which indicates that x_i cannot increase if w_i increases. Of course, in many instances a strict inequality will hold, in which case less of input i is used to produce a given output if its price increases.

The inequalities which give rise to (5) may be used to show that $C(w, y)$ is a concave function of w. That is, if $w^\lambda \equiv \lambda w^0 + (1 - \lambda) w^1$, where $0 \leqslant \lambda \leqslant 1$, then

$$C(w^\lambda, y) \geqslant \lambda C(w^0, y) + (1 - \lambda) C(w^1, y), \quad w^0, w^1 \geqslant 0. \tag{6}$$

This property is illustrated in fig. 2.3, where w is interpreted as a scalar. The cost function never lies below the line segment between any two points on the func-

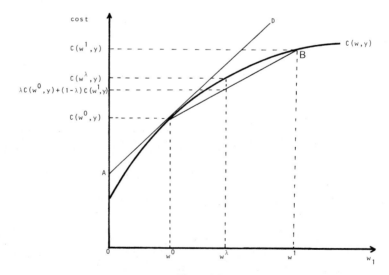

Figure 2.3

tion, such as E and B. Below an alternative characterization of concavity will be provided. The proof of concavity is quite simple and proceeds as follows. First note that $w^\lambda \geqslant 0$ since it is a weighted average of non-negative factor price vectors. If x^* is a solution when w^λ occurs, then $C(w^0, y) \leqslant w^0 x^*$ and $C(w^1, y) \leqslant w^1 x^*$ from the definition of $C(w, y)$ as the minimum cost on the set $X(y)$ which contains x^*. From the definition of w^λ and the fact that $0 \leqslant \lambda \leqslant 1$ it follows that

$$C(w^\lambda, y) = w^\lambda x^* = [\lambda w^0 + (1 - \lambda) w^1] x^*$$
$$= \lambda w^0 x^* + (1 - \lambda) w^1 x^* \geqslant \lambda C(w^0, y) + (1 - \lambda) C(w^1, y).$$

Since this is the same as (6) the cost function is concave in w.

The cost function is non-decreasing in y if $w > 0$. If $y^1 > y^0$, then $X(y^1)$ is a subset of $X(y^0)$ and so $C(w, y^0) \leqslant C(w, y^1)$. Finally, the cost function $C(w, y)$ will also be continuous in y.

The above properties of the cost function are summarized as follows:

The cost function $C(w, y)$ is a non-negative, continuous function defined over $w > 0$ and $y \geqslant 0$. It is (a) homogeneous of degree one in w, (b) non-decreasing in w, (c) concave in w, and (d) non-decreasing in y. If defined as an infimum, its domain is extended to $w \geqslant 0, y \geqslant 0$. $\hspace{2cm}$ (7)

2.3.3. *Input demand functions*

Another property of the cost function which gives it considerable importance in theoretical and empirical analysis is that the optimal (cost-minimizing) solution for the input vector can be simply derived from the cost function. Let the cost function $C(w, y)$ be differentiable with respect to w at w^0 and let x^0 be the solution when w^0 occurs. Then for any $w > 0$, the definition of $C(w, y)$ as the minimum of wx on the set $X(y)$ which contains x^0 implies that $C(w, y) \leqslant wx^0$ with equality holding for $w = w^0$. Thus, the function $g(w) \equiv C(w, y) - wx^0 \leqslant 0$ for $w > 0$ and it attains its maximum value of zero for $w = w^0$, which must satisfy the first-order conditions for a maximum, namely $\partial g(w^0)/\partial w_i \equiv \partial C(w^0, y)/\partial w_i - x_i^0 = 0$ for $i = 1, ..., N$. This shows that $\partial C(w^0, y)/\partial w_i = x_i^0$ and hence that the optimal input vector can be obtained by differentiating the cost function with respect to prices. Since this result will be used extensively, it is stated formally as follows:

Shephard's lemma. If $C(w, y)$ is differentiable with respect to w at w^0, and x^0 is the solution when w^0 occurs, then $C_i(w^0, y) \equiv \partial C(w^0, y)/\partial w_i = x_i$, $i = 1, ..., N$. That is, $C_w(w^0, y) = x^0$, where $C_w(w^0, y)$ is the vector of derivatives with respect to w. (8)

The importance of this result is that, while the cost function subsumes the details of the calculation of the optimal solution for the inputs, the latter may be obtained very easily from the cost function by differentiation. Also, if we wish to calculate the effect of a change in w and/or y upon the optimal input vector, this can be done by differentiating $\partial C(w^0, y)/\partial w_i$ with respect to w and/or y. Thus, the assumption that C is twice continuously differentiable with respect to (w, y) is the assumption required to carry out a differential comparative static analysis. This is done below. The assumption that C is differentiable with respect to w implies that the solution for x is unique. If the isoquant contains flat segments this is not necessarily true, in which case the derivatives in (8) do not exist. However, left- and right-hand derivatives will exist for all $w > 0$ and it is easily shown that

$$C_w(w^0, y)^+ \leqslant x^0 \leqslant C_w(w^0, y)^-, \tag{9}$$

where the superscript plus and minus signs denote the right- and left-hand derivatives, respectively.[4]

If C is differentiable with respect to w at w^0, then another convenient characterization of concavity is possible. Since $w^1 x^1 \leqslant w^1 x^0 = w^0 x^0 + (w^1 - w^0) x^0$ it follows that

$$C(w^1, y) \equiv w^1 x^1 \leqslant C(w^0, y) + (w^1 - w^0) x^0. \tag{10}$$

Since x^0 is the gradient of $C(w^0, y)$, (10) indicates that $C(w, y)$ is never above the tangent plane through any point such as w^0, thus providing another charac-

---

[4] If $\Delta w \equiv w^1 - w^0$ has zero elements except for the ith, then the right-hand derivative is defined as:

$$\frac{\partial C(w^0, y)^+}{\partial w_i} \equiv \lim_{\substack{\Delta w_i \to 0 \\ \Delta w_i > 0}} \frac{C(w^0 + \Delta w, y) - C(w^0, y)}{\Delta w_i}.$$

The left-hand derivative is defined in the same way except that $\Delta w_i < 0$ is assumed. The set of vectors between the vectors of right- and left-hand derivatives is called the supergradient. Thus, the set of solutions to the cost-minimization problem is the supergradient, this result being a generalization of Shephard's lemma.

terization of concavity. This is illustrated in fig. 2.3, where the support plane is AD. If there was no response by x to a change in w, the cost function would be $C^*(w, y) = wx^0$, which is the line AD. However, for $w^1 \neq w^0$ substitution amongst inputs may permit the cost to be reduced below $w^1 x^0$ to the point B. Thus, the cost function is never above its tangent planes.

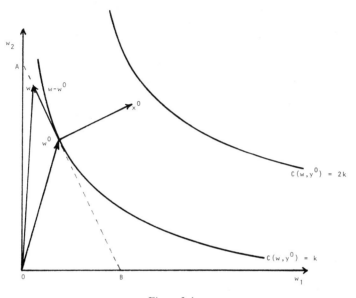

Figure 2.4

A geometric interpretation of the properties of the cost function and of Shephard's lemma (7) is provided in fig. 2.4, where two iso-cost curves for $C(w, y^0)$ are drawn between w_1 and w_2 for a given level of output y^0. Each curve is downward-sloping since the cost function is non-decreasing in w_1 and w_2 (actually increasing in the figure). Because the cost function is concave in w the level set $\{w: C(w, y) \geqslant k, w \geqslant 0\}$ is a convex set and hence the iso-cost lines are convex.[5] Since $C(w, y)$ is linearly homogeneous in w the iso-cost curve for cost $2k$ is everywhere twice as far from the origin as the curve for cost k. Furthermore, if y were to increase, the two curves for cost k and $2k$ corresponding to the higher output level would lie towards the origin from the curves in fig. 2.4. This is be-

---

[5] To prove this choose any w^0 and w^1 such that $C(w^0, y) = C(w^1, y)$. Then the definition of concavity (6) implies that $C(w^\lambda, y) \geqslant C(w^0, y) = C(w^1, y)$ for any $w^\lambda \equiv \lambda w^0 + (1 - \lambda) w^1$, where $0 \leqslant \lambda \leqslant 1$.

cause the factor prices would have to fall if the cost of producing a higher level
of output were to remain constant.

Shephard's lemma says that the gradient of $C(w, y)$ is precisely the optimal
input vector. Let the price vector be w^0 and the output level be y^0, as in fig. 2.2.
In fig. 2.4 Shephard's lemma requires x^0 to be perpendicular to the support
plane AB of $C(w, y^0) = k$ at w^0. To see why this is so, totally differentiate
$C(w, y^0) = k$ with respect to w at w^0 to get $dC = C_w (w^0, y^0)\, dw = x^0\, dw = 0$.
The tangent line is described by $C_w(w^0, y^0)\, (w - w^0) = 0$, where w is another
point on the tangent line. Thus, $x^0 (w - w^0) = 0$, which means that x^0 is orthogonal (at right angles) to the tangent line AB. Note the symmetry between figs.
2.4 and 2.2. In fig. 2.2 w^0 is perpendicular to the support plane AB of $f(x) = y^0$
at x^0, which is simply a geometric representation of the first-order conditions for
cost minimization. The first-order conditions are that the marginal products be
proportional to factor prices, which means that the gradient vector (marginal
products) points in the same direction as w^0 which is orthogonal to the iso-cost
line AB in fig. 2.2.

2.3.4. Duality

There is a fundamental duality that exists between the production function and
the cost function. Various economists have produced duality theorems under
different conditions on the production function, but the purpose here is simply
to indicate the nature of these theorems under present assumptions.

One part of the duality is that the cost function alone may be used to reconstruct the production function from which it was originally derived. This means
that the cost function retains all the information contained in the production
function, so there is no loss of information in using the cost function. It will
have occurred to the alert reader that the proofs of the properties of the cost
function provided above did not use all the properties (3) of the production function, e.g. quasi-concavity and increasingness. These apparently redundant assumptions are, however, needed to establish the above duality result. The reason why
quasi-concavity is important for duality is as follows. The essence of the duality
between production and cost functions is that every input vector x is optimal for
some choice of w and y and hence by fixing y and varying w one can construct
a locus for $x = C_w (w, y)$ which coincides with the isoquant defined by $y = f(x)$.
It should be evident from fig. 2.1 (a) that any point on the isoquant is optimal
for some w, whereas in fig. 2.1 (b) the point x^2 can never be optimal for any w
since the level set is non-convex, i.e. $f(x)$ is not quasi-concave at x^2. The non-
quasi-concave part of $f(x)$ cannot be reconstructed from the cost function alone.

A second duality result is that if some function $C^*(w, y)$ satisfies properties (7) then there exists a function $f^*(x)$, which satisfies conditions (3) and which therefore may be interpreted as a production function. Furthermore, its cost function is precisely $C^*(w, y)$. Hence, in empirical and theoretical work one can dispense with the production function and carry out the analysis completely in terms of the cost function, provided, of course, that the cost-minimization assumption is valid.

These results may be formally stated, without proof, as[6]

Duality theorem.

(a) Let $f(x)$ satisfy conditions (3). Then (i) the cost function defined by (1) satisfies condition (7). Moreover, (ii) $f(x) = \max_y$ $\{y: C(w, y) \leqslant wx$ for every $w \geqslant 0\}$ for all $x > 0$, where $C(w, y)$ is extended to $w \geqslant 0$.

(b) Let $C^*(w, y)$ satisfy condition (7) and be extended to $w \geqslant 0$. Then (i) $f^*(x) \equiv \max_y$ $\{y: C^*(w, y) \leqslant wx$ for every $w \geqslant 0\}$ satisfies condition (3) over $x > 0$. Moreover, (ii) $C^*(w, y)$ is the cost function for production function $f^*(x)$. (11)

2.3.5. *Constant returns to scale*

A special assumption which is often made about the production function is that it is linearly homogeneous. This means that there are constant returns to scale in production because $f(\lambda x) = \lambda f(x)$ for all $x \geqslant 0$ and $\lambda > 0$. That is to say, if all inputs are increased by a given percentage, then output will increase by the same percentage. As a consequence of constant returns to scale (CRS) the cost function has the special form

$$C(w, y) = y\, c(w), \tag{12}$$

where $c(w) \equiv C(w, 1)$ is called the *unit (output) cost function*. Property (12) may be proved as follows:

---

[6] For a detailed treatment of the duality between production and cost functions, including the CRS case dealt with below, see Diewert (1974, 1978) on which these statements are based. The extension of $C(w, y)$ to $w \geqslant 0$ can be achieved by redefining it as an infimum rather than a minimum.

$$C(w, y) \equiv \min_{x} \{wx: f(x) \geqslant y, \ x \geqslant 0\}$$

$$= \min_{x} \{y \ wx/y: f(x/y) \geqslant 1, \ x/y \geqslant 0\}, \quad \text{by CRS}, \ y > 0$$

$$= y \min_{a} \{wa: f(a) \geqslant 1, \ a \geqslant 0\}, \quad a = x/y$$

$$= y \ C(w, 1) = y \ c(w).$$

It is evident from (12) that $c(w)$ is both the average and marginal cost of production and, although it depends upon w, it is independent of the level of output.[7] It is worth noting that (12) implies that all of the properties of $C(w, y)$ with respect to y are inherited by $c(w)$. These consequences of CRS will be used extensively below.

Had CRS been assumed at the outset, the conditions (3) on the production function could have been simplified to read:

The production function $f(x)$ is positive, linearly homogeneous, and concave for $x > 0$. (3′)

In this case, the unit cost function $c(w)$ can be shown to satisfy these same properties, and the production function may be recovered from $c(w)$ as

$$f(x) = 1/\max_{w} \{c(w): wx = 1, \ w \geqslant 0\}, \tag{13}$$

where $c(w)$ is extended to $w \geqslant 0$.

In subsequent chapters it will be assumed that the technology exhibits CRS. However, the more general analysis has been presented above for several reasons. The first is to indicate clearly that duality theory does not depend upon CRS. Secondly, the general analysis will allow the interested reader to formulate and analyse trade models in which CRS are not assumed. Finally, the more general analysis is required for the theory of the consumer developed below.

---

[7] A less strict assumption is that the production function is *homothetic*, which means that $f(x) = \phi(h(x))$, where h is linearly homogeneous and ϕ is a positive, increasing function. In this case it can be shown that $C(w, y) = \phi^{-1}(y) \ c(w)$, where $c(w)$ is the unit cost function for $h(x)$, so the marginal and average cost functions depend upon the output level. However, factor *ratios* do not depend upon the output level as can be seen by applying Shephard's lemma and taking ratios. Clearly, homogeneity of degree r is a special case of homotheticity, occurring when $\phi(h(x)) = [h(x)]^r$.

2.3.6. *Examples*

The following two examples are intended to show concretely how cost functions may be derived from production functions, and then illustrate their properties.

Example 1. Leontief production function. The Leontief or fixed coefficients production function is

$$f(x) = \min\{x_1/a_1, ..., x_N/a_N\}, \qquad a_i > 0. \tag{14}$$

The unit isoquant for this linearly homogeneous production function is illustrated for $N = 2$ in fig. 2.5 (a). In this case the cost-minimizing problem is trivial

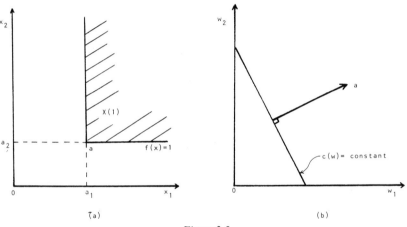

Figure 2.5

with solution $x = a = (a_1, ..., a_N)$ for all $w > 0$. Thus, $c(w) = wa$ is the unit cost function and $C(w, y) = y\, c(w)$. The cost function is linear in w and so the factor demand functions are

$$C_i(w, y) = a_i y, \qquad i = 1, ..., N, \tag{15}$$

which are independent of w. The cost function is concave in w (a linear function is both convex and concave), increasing in w (since $a_i > 0$), and is linearly homogeneous (linear) in w. It is illustrated in fig. 2.5(b).

Example 2. Constant elasticity of substitution (CES) function.   The production function is

$$f(x) = \left[\sum_{i=1}^{N} a_i x_i^{-b} \right]^{-1/b}, \qquad a_i \geqslant 0, \quad 1 + b > 0. \tag{16}$$

It is homogeneous of degree 1 (it can be made homogeneous of degree r by raising it to the power r), is non-decreasing in x, and is concave. The marginal products are $f_i(x) = a_i(x_i/f(x))^{-(1+b)}$. The first-order conditions for cost minimization are

$$f_i(x)/f_1(x) = w_i/w_1,$$
$$\qquad\qquad\qquad i = 2, ..., N, \tag{17}$$
$$f(x) = 1,$$

where 1 unit of output is to be produced and $w > 0$ is assumed. That is,

$$a_i x_i^{-(1+b)}/a_1 x_1^{-(1+b)} = w_i/w_1,$$
$$\qquad\qquad\qquad\qquad i = 2, ..., N$$
$$\left[\sum_{i=1}^{N} a_i x_i^{b} \right]^{-1/b} = 1.$$

Raising both sides of the ith equation to the power $-1/(1+b)$ we obtain the optimal input ratios as $x_i/x_1 = (a_1 w_i/a_i w_1)^{-\sigma}$, where $\sigma \equiv 1/(1+b)$. Substituting for x_i in the production function yields:

$$1^{-b} = \sum_{i=1}^{N} a_i x_i^{-b} = a_1 x_1^{-b} + \sum_{i=2}^{N} a_i \left(\frac{a_1 w_i}{a_i w_1} \right)^{b\sigma} x_1^{-b}$$

$$= x_1^{-b} \left[\sum_{i=1}^{N} a_i \left(\frac{w_i}{a_i} \right)^{b\sigma} \right] \Bigg/ \left(\frac{w_1}{a_1} \right)^{b\sigma},$$

whence

$$x_1 = \left(\frac{w_1}{a_1} \right)^{-\sigma} \Bigg/ \left[\sum_{i=1}^{N} a_i \left(\frac{w_i}{a_i} \right)^{b\sigma} \right]^{-1/b}.$$

Similarly,

$$x_j = \left(\frac{w_j}{a_j} \right)^{-\sigma} \Bigg/ \left[\sum_{i=1}^{N} a_i \left(\frac{w_i}{a_i} \right)^{b\sigma} \right]^{-1/b}, \qquad \text{for } j = 1, ..., N.$$

These are the factor demand functions per unit of output. Hence, the unit cost function is

$$c(w) = \sum_{i=1}^{N} w_i x_i = \sum_{j=1}^{N} a_j^\sigma w_j^{1-\sigma} \bigg/ \left[\sum_{i=1}^{N} a_i^\sigma w_i^{1-\sigma} \right]^{-1/b}.$$

Since the numerator and the term in square brackets are the same, and $1 + 1/b = 1/(1-\sigma)$, the unit cost function is

$$c(w) = \left[\sum_{j=1}^{N} a_j^\sigma w_j^{1-\sigma} \right]^{1/(1-\sigma)}, \qquad \sigma = 1/(1+b). \tag{18}$$

This function also belongs to the family of CES functions since it has the same structure as (16). However, this "self-duality" is not a general property of production and cost functions.

The above derivation of the cost function from (17) assumes that $w > 0$. If not, then the Lagrangian technique may be used directly. The Lagrangian is

$$L = \sum_{i=1}^{N} w_i x_i + \lambda[1 - f(x)]$$

and the first-order conditions for an interior solution are

$$\frac{\partial L}{\partial x_i} = w_i - \lambda f_i(x) = 0,$$

$$i = 1, ..., N,$$

$$\frac{\partial L}{\partial \lambda} = 1 - f(x) = 0,$$

from which (17) is obtained if $w > 0$. The first condition becomes $w_i - \lambda a_i x_i^{-(1+b)} = 0$ which has no solution for x_i when $w_i = 0$ and $\lambda > 0$. The Lagrange multiplier λ can be interpreted as the marginal cost of production, and will be positive.[8] Thus, the cost function for the CES production function is not defined when an element of w is zero. It is well defined as an infimum since the lower bound on cost is zero.

---

[8]   See Intriligator (1971, pp. 36–38, 60–62) for this interpretation of λ.

2.4. Comparative statics for the firm

This section is concerned with the calculation of the response of the firm to changes in the prices of the inputs of production and to changes in the output level, assuming that the firm minimizes its input cost. A local approach assuming differentiability is taken, though a more general treatment based upon (5), for example, is also possible. The comparative statics results follow directly from the properties of the cost function $C(w, y)$. It will be recalled that this function is non-decreasing, linearly homogeneous and concave in w and non-decreasing in y.

Since $C_w(w, y)$ is the vector of factor demand functions by Shephard's lemma (8), the properties of the demand functions are determined by the properties of the cost function. Thus, the non-decreasing property of $C(w, y)$ in w becomes

$$0 \leqslant \partial C(w, y)/\partial w_i \equiv C_i(w, y), \quad i = 1, ..., N, \quad \text{i.e. } 0 \leqslant C_w(w, y), \quad (19)$$

or that input demands are non-negative. The fact that $C(w, y)$ is homogeneous of degree one in w implies that the input demand functions are homogeneous of degree zero, and the Euler relations[9]

$$C(w, y) = \sum_{i=1}^{N} w_i \partial C(w, y)/\partial w_i \equiv \sum_{i=1}^{N} w_i C_i(w, y) = w C_w(w, y) \quad (20)$$

and

$$0 = \sum_{j=1}^{N} w_j \partial^2 C(w, y)/\partial w_i \partial w_j \equiv \sum_{j=1}^{N} w_j \partial C_i(w, y)/\partial w_j,$$

$$i = 1, ..., N, \quad \text{i.e. } C_{ww}(w, y) w = 0, \quad (21)$$

where

$$C_{ww}(w, y) \equiv [C_{ij}(w, y)] \equiv [\partial^2 C(w, y)/\partial w_i \partial w_j]$$

is the Hessian of the cost function. Finally, the concavity of $C(w, y)$ with respect to w implies that the matrix of second derivatives, $C_{ww}(w, y)$, is a negative semi-definite matrix.[10] From the definition of the latter, it follows that

$$z C_{ww}(w, y) z = z \frac{\partial C_w(w, y)}{\partial w} z \leqslant 0, \quad \text{for all } z = (z_1, ..., z_N). \quad (22)$$

---

[9]   See, for example, Allen (1938, p. 317) for a discussion of Euler's relationships for homogeneous functions.

[10]   See, for example, Lancaster (1968, p. 333).

As is evident from (22), the diagonal elements of the Hessian must be non-positive, meaning that the input demands cannot rise (and will generally fall) when the price of the input rises. Of course, (22) provides other constraints which are, however, less intuitive.

Conditions (21) and (22) together indicate the constraints upon the response of input demands to changes in input prices, when output is fixed. With respect to output, the only constraint is that $C_y(w, y) \equiv \partial C(w, y)/\partial y \geqslant 0$.

2.4.1. Elasticity formulae

Often it is desirable to express the effect on the input quantities of changes in prices in terms of elasticities. The elasticity of demand for input i with respect to the price of input j, ϵ_{ij}, and the Allen–Uzawa elasticity of substitution between i and j, σ_{ij}, are the most commonly used elasticity concepts and are defined by

(a) $\quad \epsilon_{ij} \equiv \partial \ln C_i(w, y)/\partial \ln w_j = w_j C_{ij}/C_i,$

$$(23)$$

(b) $\quad \sigma_{ij} \equiv C_{ij} C/C_i C_j = \epsilon_{ij}/\theta_j,$

where $C_i = C_i(w, y)$, $C_{ij} = C_{ij}(w, y)$ and $\theta_j \equiv w_j C_j/C$ is the cost share of factor j. The Euler conditions (21) may be rewritten in terms of these elasticities as

$$\sum_{j=1}^{N} \epsilon_{ij} = \sum_{j=1}^{N} \sigma_{ij} \theta_j = 0, \quad i = 1, ..., N. \tag{24}$$

It is further noted that the matrix $[\sigma_{ij}]$ is symmetric and negative semi-definite.

2.4.2. Comparison of production and cost function approaches

It is constructive to compare the derivation of these comparative static results with the traditional derivation. The latter is based upon the first-order conditions for cost minimization, which are expressed in terms of the derivatives of the production function. These are

$$f_i(x)/f_1(x) = w_i/w_1,$$
$$i = 2, ..., N, \tag{25}$$
$$f(x) = y,$$

where $f_i(x)$ denotes the marginal product for input i and $w > 0$. The approach here is to totally differentiate the N equations in (23) and to solve the resulting equations for dx in terms of dw and dy. Then theorems concerning the signs of various bordered Hessians for the production function, which follow from the second-order conditions for a minimum, are used to provide comparative statics results.

The cost function approach seems more desirable in several respects. First, it avoids dealing with the first-order conditions and the theory of bordered Hessians. Secondly, the comparative static results follow directly from the properties of the cost function and these follow directly from the act of minimizing a linear function. Thirdly, the cost function is a natural concept for an economist to work with since it embodies the economic behaviour of the firm. Finally, the analysis is slightly more general in that it easily handles the case of the Leontief technology, which violates the differentiability assumptions required for the first-order conditions approach.

2.5. Profit maximization

If the output level is to be chosen to maximize profit the problem facing the firm is (2). If a positive output maximizes profit and $C(w, y)$ is differentiable with respect to y, then this requires the well-known rule for profit maximization, namely that price equals marginal cost, i.e. $p = \partial C(w, y)/\partial y$. In subsequent chapters it will be assumed that the production function exhibits CRS so the cost function has the special structure (11). Hence, the maximum profit is

$$\Pi(p, w) \equiv \max_y \{y[p - c(w)], \ y \geqslant 0\} = \begin{cases} 0, & c(w) \geqslant p, \\ \infty, & c(w) < p. \end{cases} \tag{26}$$

That is to say, profit is either zero or infinite (strictly, it is undefined) depending on the relative magnitudes of p and $c(w)$. If $c(w) > p$, then production yields a loss so the optimal output is $y = 0$. If $c(w) = p$, then any output $y \geqslant 0$ will yield the maximum profit of zero. Thus, the solution for y is not unique and is indeterminate in this case. In the next chapter, the solution is made determinate once the complete set of conditions for a competitive equilibrium for the production sector is specified.

2.6. The consumer

The traditional neoclassical theory of the consumer assumes that the vector $z = (z_1, ..., z_M)$ of consumption of M goods is chosen to maximize a utility function $u(z)$ subject to the budget constraint $pz \equiv \Sigma_{i=1}^{M} p_i z_i = m$, where income and the price vector $p = (p_1, ..., p_M)$ are given. The utility function is an indicator of the preferences of the consumer, with a higher level of utility representing a preferred consumption.

The maximum level of utility attainable is

$$V^*(p/m) = V(p, m) \equiv \max_{z} \{u(z): pz \leqslant m, z \geqslant 0\}, \tag{27}$$

which is called the *indirect utility function*.[11] Again, as with the cost function, the technical details of the solution to the problem in (27) are avoided. The solution for the consumption vector z, if unique, is the vector $\phi(p, m)$ of demand functions whose properties need to be found. Fortunately, a completely new analysis is unnecessary since the material of section 2.3 on the duality between production and cost functions may be applied to the present context in a straightforward manner.

The utility function $u(z)$ is assumed to have the same properties as the production function $f(x)$, as given by (3). In particular, it is non-negative, continuous, quasi-concave and increasing. For any given level of utility μ and vector prices p, the minimum expenditure function may be defined as

$$E(p, \mu) \equiv \min_{z} \{pz: u(z) \geqslant \mu, z \geqslant 0\}. \tag{28}$$

This definition corresponds exactly to that for a cost function provided in (1) and, since $u(z)$ has the same properties as $f(x)$, all the results established concerning the relationship between $f(x)$ and $C(w, y)$ also apply to the relationship between $u(z)$ and $E(p, \mu)$. Shephard's lemma, for example, yields the Hicksian or "compensated" demand functions:

$$z = E_p(p, \mu). \tag{29}$$

These functions have the same properties as the factor demand functions $C_w(w, y)$; properties which constitute the basic results of the theory of the consumer.

---

[11] This function is clearly homogeneous of degree zero in (p, m) for $m > 0$, since the budget constraint can be written as $(p/m) x \leqslant 1$. Hence, it is sometimes written as $V^*(p/m) \equiv V(p/m, 1)$ in terms of the "normalized" vector of prices p/m.

How does the expenditure function relate to the indirect utility function, and how do the Hicksian demand functions relate to the ordinary demand functions $\phi_i(p, m)$? Under the assumption that the utility function is increasing, it is evident that the consumer will spend all his income m. If he did not then a new consumption with more of all goods could be found to satisfy the budget constraint, yielding higher utility by (3). Also, it is evident from (27) that the consumer will minimize the expenditure on goods for any given level of utility which he might choose. Thus, the optimal level of utility may be found by solving

$$E(p, \mu) = m \tag{30}$$

for $\mu = V(p, m)$. The ordinary demand functions are found by substituting the solution for μ into the Hicksian demand functions (29) to obtain:

$$\phi(p, m) = E_p(p, V(p, m)). \tag{31}$$

Alternatively, (30) may be substituted into the ordinary demand functions to obtain the compensated demand functions as

$$E_p(p, \mu) \equiv \phi(p, E(p, \mu)). \tag{32}$$

The Slutsky decomposition for the effect of a price change upon the demand quantities can easily be obtained using (32). Differentiating the identity $E_i(p, \mu) \equiv \phi_i(p, E(p, \mu))$ with respect to p_j yields:

$$E_{ij} = \phi_{ij} + \phi_{im} E_j, \quad i, j = 1, ..., M, \tag{33}$$

where $\phi_{ij} \equiv \partial \phi_i / \partial p_j$ and $\phi_{im} \equiv \partial \phi_i / \partial m$. Hence,

$$\partial \phi_i(p, m)/\partial p_j \equiv \phi_{ij} = E_{ij}(p, \mu) - \phi_{im}(p, m) E_j(p, \mu),$$
$$i, j = 1, ..., M, \tag{34}$$

where $m = E(p, \mu)$. Thus, the price effect consists of the pure substitution effect, $E_{ij}(p, \mu)$, which corresponds to the movement around an indifference curve, and the real income effect, $-\phi_{im}(p, m) E_j(p, \mu)$, which is the movement to a new level of utility due to the increase in real income of $-E_j(p, \mu)$.

The income effect on demand for good i may be expressed as

$$\partial \phi_i(p, m)/\partial m \equiv \phi_{im}(p, m) = E_{i\mu}(p, \mu) V_m(p, m) = E_{i\mu}(p, \mu)/E_\mu(p, \mu),$$
$$i = 1, ..., M, \tag{35}$$

where $m = E(p, \mu)$. This is obtained by differentiating (30) and the ith identity in (32) with respect to m.

2.6.1. Homothetic preferences

If the utility function is homothetic the demand functions have special properties. Without loss of generality the utility function may be assumed to be linearly homogeneous, since utility functions are only unique up to a monotonic transformation. Hence, the expenditure function has the special structure $E(p, \mu) = e(p)\mu$, where $e(p) \equiv E(p, 1)$ is the unit (utility) expenditure function. Hence, using (30), the indirect utility function takes the special form:

$$V(p, m) = m/e(p). \tag{36}$$

The function $e(p)$ may be interpreted as a price index, so that V becomes real income. The Hicksian and ordinary demand functions simplify to

$$E_p(p, \mu) = e_p(p)\mu,$$
$$\phi(p, m) = me_p(p)/e(p) = m\beta(p). \tag{37}$$

The main consequence of the homogeneity assumption is that the consumption ratios are independent of the level of utility or income. This can be seen by taking ratios of the Hicksian or ordinary demand functions yielding $\phi_i(p, m)/\phi_j(p, m) = e_i(p)/e_j(p)$.

2.6.2. The indirect utility function

The preceding discussion has concentrated upon the expenditure function. However, the indirect utility is also an important concept and will often be used in subsequent chapters. It too is dual to the direct utility function, although a formal duality theorem will not be presented here. It is simply noted that the indirect utility function can be used to generate the ordinary demand functions as

$$\phi(p, m) = -V_p(p, m)/V_m(p, m), \tag{38}$$

a relationship known as Roy's identity. Also, the indirect utility function satisfies the following conditions if the direct utility function satisfies condition (3):

The indirect utility function $V^*(p^*) \equiv V(p, m)$, where $p^* = p/m$, is a (i) continuous and finite, (ii) non-increasing, and (iii) quasi-convex function of $p^* > 0$. (39)

For further details and proofs the reader is referred to Diewert's (1974) survey.

2.7. Extensions and notes on the literature

It should be clear to the reader that duality theory simply exploits the general properties of optimization problems and writes down the solution in terms of the parameters. In doing so it avoids, or rather subsumes, the technical problem of actually performing the optimization. It has been illustrated and used above in the formulation and analysis of the theories of the firm and consumer, obtaining results which will be used extensively in subsequent chapters.

In general one might formulate an economic problem as maximization of a function $F(x, w)$ subject to the constraint that $x \in X(y)$, where $x = (x_1, ..., x_N)$, $w = (w_1, ..., w_L)$ and $y = (y_1, ..., y_M)$. The solution is summarized by

$$G(w, y) \equiv \max_x \{F(x, w): \ x \in X(y)\}. \tag{40}$$

The function G summarizes the solution to the maximization problem. Duality theory is concerned with its properties given those of F and X, and with the question of whether F and X can be recovered from G. When the objective function is linear, $F(x, w) = wx$, the problem simplifies. It will be clear from the proofs provided above that if $F(x, w) = wx$ and continuity holds, the function G will be homogeneous of degree one in w. Furthermore, it will be convex in w (maximization yields convexity, minimization yields concavity) and, if differentiable, Shephard's lemma will hold. Thus, these properties, which were established for the cost function $C(w, y)$, occur in many and more general contexts. They follow simply from optimizing a linear function on a constraint set.

Many of the applications of duality theory in economics assume a linear objective function, as did the theory of the consumer and the firm above. Some obvious extensions to these formulations are possible. For example, in the theory of the firm there might be a vector of outputs y rather than a single output, in which case $G(w, y)$ is a joint cost function; or some of the factors might be fixed, in which case it is a variable cost function. In the theory of the consumer some of the consumptions might be fixed due to contractual obligations. In the following chapter the gross national product function which is introduced may be regarded as a solution to a constrained maximization problem and therefore as a special case of (40).

Recently two excellent surveys of duality theory have been published by Diewert (1974, 1978) and these provide a comprehensive view of the area, the latter survey being directed towards microeconomic theory. Textbook treatments of the theory of the firm and the consumer, which make some use of duality theory, are Baumol (1977), Dixit (1976) and Varian (1978). Also of interest is Gorman (1976) who discusses various applications of duality and separability, and Diamond and McFadden (1974) who consider the expenditure function and its use in public finance.

Problems

1. Let the production function be $f(x) = a\, x_1^{b_1} x_2^{b_2} \dots x_N^{b_N}$, where $a > 0$, $b_i \geqslant 0$ (a Cobb–Douglas function when $\Sigma_{i=1}^{N} b_i = 1$).
   - (a) Derive the factor demand functions for given factor prices $w_1, \dots, w_N$ and output level y.
   - (b) Using these functions, calculate the cost function.
   - (c) Verify Shephard's lemma.
   - (d) Derive the marginal cost function, and show that it is also the average cost function if $\Sigma_{i=1}^{N} b_i = 1$.
2. Let $c(w) = \min \{w_1/b_1, w_2/b_2\}$ be the unit cost function where $b_1, b_2 > 0$.
   - (a) What is the production function?
   - (b) Is $c(w)$ differentiable? Why or why not?
3. Let $c(w) = \Sigma_{i=1}^{N} \Sigma_{j=1}^{N} a_{ij} (w_i w_j)^{1/2}$ be the unit cost function.
   - (a) Derive the input demand functions (per unit of output).
   - (b) What conditions on the a_{ij}'s imply a Leontief technology? (This function was introduced by Diewert, 1971.)
4. The Allen–Uzawa elasticity of substitution between inputs i and j around an isoquant is defined as $\sigma_{ij} = C_{ij}(w, y) C(w, y)/[C_i(w, y) C_j(w, y)]$, where the $C_{ij}(w, y)$ are the second derivatives of C with respect to factor prices.
   - (a) If the share of factor i in the cost of production is $\theta_i \equiv w_i C_i(w, y)/C(w, y)$, show that $\partial \ln \theta_i/\partial \ln w_j = (\sigma_{ij} - 1)\theta_j$ for $j \neq i$.
   - (b) For the cost function of example 2 of the text, show that $\sigma_{12} = \sigma$.
   - (c) Prove that the matrix of σ_{ij}'s is negative semi-definite.
5. If the utility function is linearly homogeneous, show that the income elasticities of demand are all unity.
6. Roy's identity is $\phi(p, m) = -V_p(p, m)/V_m(p, m)$.
   - (a) Prove Roy's identity. (*Hint*: use the identity $\mu \equiv V(p, E(p, \mu))$.)
   - (b) Derive the right-hand-side in terms of $V^*(p/m)$.
   - (c) Specialize the identity for the case of homothetic preferences.

References

Allen, R.G.D. (1938) *Mathematical Analysis for Economists* (Macmillan).

Baumol, W.J. (1977) *Economic Theory and Operations Analysis*, 4th edition (Prentice-Hall).

Diamond, P.A. and D.L. McFadden (1974) "Some uses of the expenditure function in public finance", *Journal of Public Economics* 3, 3–21.

Diewert, W.E. (1971) "An application of the Shephard duality theorem: A generalized Leontief production function", *Journal of Political Economy* 79-3, May/June, 481–507.

Diewert, W.E. (1974) "Applications of duality theory", in: M.D. Intriligator and D.A. Kendrick (eds.), *Frontiers of Quantitative Economics*, vol. II (North-Holland), pp. 106–171.

Diewert, W.E. (1978) "Duality approaches to microeconomic theory", in: K.J. Arrow and M.D. Intriligator (eds.), *Handbook of Mathematical Economics* (North-Holland).

Dixit, A.K. (1976) *Optimization in Economic Theory* (Oxford University Press).

Gorman, W.M. (1976) "Tricks with utility functions", in: R. Artis and R. Nobay (eds.), *Essays in Economic Analysis. Proceedings of the Association of University Teachers of Economic Annual Conference, Sheffield, 1974* (Cambridge University Press).

Hadley, G. (1961) *Linear Algebra* (Addison-Wesley).

Hotelling, H. (1932) "Edgeworth's taxation paradox and the nature of demand and supply functions", *Journal of Political Economy* 40, 577–616.

Intriligator, M.D. (1971) *Mathematical Optimization and Economic Theory* (Prentice-Hall).

Lancaster, K. (1968) *Mathematical Economics* (Macmillan).

Samuelson, P.A. (1953) "Prices of factors and goods in general equilibrium", *Review of Economic Studies* 21, 1–20.

Shephard, R.W. (1953) *Cost and Production Functions* (Princeton University Press).

Shephard, R.W. (1970) *Theory of Cost and Production Functions* (Princeton University Press).

Uzawa, H. (1964) "Duality principles in the theory of cost and production", *International Economic Review* 5, 216–220.

Varian, H.R. (1978) *Microeconomic Analysis* (Norton).

CHAPTER 3

THE PRODUCTION SECTOR

3.1. Introduction

In order to ask questions about the effect upon a nation of changes in exogenous variables, such as a change in world market conditions, a change in the tariff structure, or a change in factor endowments or technology, it is necessary to have a model of how the economy operates. The model used throughout this book draws heavily upon the concept of a perfectly competitive economy operating in a static framework, where money, time and uncertainty play no essential role. While these are important aspects of international trade, the model used here provides a very useful vehicle for the analysis of the major issues of international trade, and in addition is the one on which most of the literature is based.

In this chapter a competitive model of the production sector of an economy is formulated and discussed. The consumption sector will be introduced in a subsequent chapter. There are two reasons for proceeding in this manner. The first is that from the point of view of exposition it is convenient gradually to build up the complete model of the economy, beginning with the production sector. Once this is done the model of the trading world will be formulated. The second reason is that many interesting questions concerning the effect of changes in world prices, the tariff structure and factor endowments can be answered using the model of the production sector alone, provided the economy is a price-taker in the world market. To be able to do this, it is necessary to assume that the decisions taken in the production sector are independent of those taken both in the consumption sector and in foreign nations. Thus, all goods that enter or leave the production sector do so at a fixed price, while the amounts of the primary factors of production (resources) available to the production sector are fixed. By making this assumption, attention is focused upon the production sector without having to explicitly consider the consumption sector or the rest of the world.

3.2. A model of the production sector

The production sector is assumed to produce M final goods using N factors of production. Each product j is produced according to the production function $y_j = f^j(x_j)$, where $x_j = (x_{1j}, ..., x_{Nj})$ is a vector of inputs of the factors. Thus, there is no joint production and there are no intermediate inputs, i.e. inputs which are used by one industry but produced by another. These possibilities will be introduced in a later chapter. The product prices facing the producers are fixed and are given by the vector $p = (p_1, ..., p_M)$. If the economy is a "small open economy" then p is given by world market conditions which cannot be perceptibly influenced by any decision taken by domestic producers. The vector of resource endowments is fixed and is given by $v = (v_1, ..., v_N)$. This means that the amounts of buildings, machinery, equipment, land, and labour of all types are given and not influenced by, for example, their prices. The case of endogenous factor supplies will also be taken up in a later chapter.

The production sector determines, endogenously, the market prices for the N factors of production and the output levels for the M products as well as the allocation of the resources amongst the producers. The vector of industry outputs is denoted $y = (y_1, ..., y_M)$, while the vector of factor prices is $w = (w_1, ..., w_N)$. Thus, it is being assumed that f^j is the industry production function and the industry will be treated as the decision-maker. Also, it is assumed that there is perfect mobility of factors between industries and that the factor market is perfectly competitive. Thus, individual industries take factor prices as given.

If each of many firms in an industry has the same non-increasing-return-to-scale production function and there is perfect freedom of entry and exit at zero cost, then the industry behaves as if it has a constant-returns-to-scale technology. This is because if one firm produces a particular output y_j with a given input vector x_j any number of firms (λ) can do the same, so that the industry produces λy_j output with λx_j input. Thus, the CRS production function for the industry is a good approximation of the relation between industry output and inputs.[1]

Accordingly, the industry production function $f^j(x_j)$ is assumed to satisfy conditions (2.3') which are that $f^j(x_j)$ is a positive, linearly homogeneous, concave function of $x_j > 0$. From Chapter 2 it is known that the cost function for the industry is $C^j(w, y_j) = c^j(w) y_j$, where the unit cost function $c^j(w)$ satisfies condition (2.3') also. Each industry j maximizes profit $y_j[p_j - c^j(w)]$ subject to $y_j \geqslant 0$, as discussed in Chapter 2. Clearly, if $p_j - c^j(w) > 0$, then profit can be increased without limit by increasing output y_j. This possibility is inconsistent with a competitive equilibrium, since an attempt to increase output in this man-

---

[1] See Debreu (1959, p. 41) for a formal treatment.

ner would cause the prices of the factors to be bid up in an attempt to obtain the requisite resources. Thus, in competitive equilibrium positive profits are not possible and hence $p_j - c^j(w) \leqslant 0$ is required. Clearly, if $p_j - c^j(w) < 0$, the profit-maximizing output is $y_j = 0$, while if $p_j - c^j(w) = 0$, any $y_j \geqslant 0$ will maximize profits. These conditions may be written as

$$y_j \geqslant 0; \quad p_j - c^j(w) \leqslant 0; \quad y_j[p_j - c^j(w)] = 0; \quad j = 1, ..., M. \tag{1}$$

A convention used throughout this book is to write conditions such as (1) in the form

$$p_j - c^j(w) \leqslant 0 \leqslant y_j, \quad j = 1, ..., M. \tag{2}$$

Thus, whenever conditions such as (2) appear (with a double inequality) they imply that the two terms, which have the inequality constraints, when multiplied together yield zero, as indicated in (1). This is a convenient convention which will also be used for vectors when every pair of elements in two vectors obeys conditions such as (1). It is worth noting that conditions such as (1) correspond to the Kuhn–Tucker conditions for the solution to a constrained optimization problem, which will be dealt with below.

In addition to the profit-maximization conditions (1), the factor market equilibrium conditions are needed to complete the model of the production sector. To do this the demand functions for the factors are needed. It was shown in Chapter 2 that the factor demand functions for a cost-minimizing industry facing the factor price vector w and producing output y_j are given by Shephard's lemma as the vector of derivatives of the cost function with respect to the factor prices. That is, the demand for factor i is $\partial C^j(w, y_j)/\partial w_i$ which, because of CRS, is

$$\partial C^j(w, y_j)/\partial w_i = c_{ij}(w)y_j, \quad \text{where } c_{ij}(w) \equiv \partial c^j(w)/\partial w_i. \tag{3}$$

Since $c^j(w)$ is the unit cost function, $c_{ij}(w)$ is the demand for factor i per unit of output j or the optimal input–output coefficient. The demand for factor i when y_j is produced is then $c_{ij}(w)y_j$ due to CRS. Thus, demand functions for the factors are easily determined from the cost functions. The vector of demands by industry j is $c_w^j(w)y_j$, where $c_w^j(w)$ is the vector of derivatives of $c^j(w)$.

The market equilibrium conditions for the factors are

$$\sum_{j=1}^{M} c_{ij}(w)y_j - v_i \leqslant 0 \leqslant w_i, \quad i = 1, ..., N, \tag{4}$$

which is written in accordance with the convention discussed above. Thus (4) says that the production sector's total demand for factor i must be less than or equal to the available supply v_i, and that the factor price w_i must be non-negative. Furthermore, if $w_i > 0$, then the left-hand side of (4) must be zero, i.e. demand equals supply, and if supply exceeds demand then the factor price must be zero. Thus, an excess supply is only consistent with equilibrium if the factor is free. In vector form (4) may be rewritten as

$$\sum_{j=1}^{M} c_w^j(w)y_j - v \leqslant 0 \leqslant w. \tag{4}$$

The above discussion may be summarized by defining what is meant by an equilibrium for the production sector.

The production sector is in equilibrium if (y, w) satisfies (2) and (4). $\tag{5}$

Thus, production sector equilibrium requires all industries to be maximizing profits, which must be non-positive, and all factor markets must be in equilibrium. These conditions are conveniently formulated in terms of the industry unit cost functions which, by their duality with production functions, describe the technology.[2,3]

The equilibrium solution obeys the national income accounting identity that gross national product py equals national income wv. To see that this is true multiply the left-hand side of eq. (2) by y_j and sum to get:

$$py = \sum_{j=1}^{M} c^j(w)y_j,$$

---

[2] Note that the cost functions and their derivatives are assumed to be defined for all $w \geqslant 0$. In Chapter 2 it was shown that the cost function may not be defined when an element of w is zero. However, if the unit cost function is defined as $c^j(w) \equiv \inf_{x_j} \{wx_j \colon f^j(x_j) \geqslant 1, x_j \geqslant 0\}$, where inf means infimum, rather than as a minimum, then it will be defined for all $w \geqslant 0$. The derivative may approach infinity as w_i approaches zero, in which case the derivative is not well defined. However, an equilibrium could never occur at $w_i = 0$ *in such a case*, since the demand for factor i would exceed the finite supply. This technical difficulty is ignored in order to streamline the exposition.

The infimum is the greatest lower bound or the limit of the function being minimized. For example, if unit cost is always positive, but can be reduced arbitrarily close to zero by using more of a free factor and less (but still positive) amount of other factors, the limit of cost is zero. This is the infimum which in this case cannot be attained.

[3] If the cost function is not differentiable, then the equilibrium conditions can be reformulated so that (4) reads $\sum_{j=1}^{M} a_j y_j - v \leqslant 0 \leqslant w$, where the vector $a_j \in c_w^j(w)$ and $c_w^j(w)$ is now defined as the set of gradients of $c_w^j(w)$ at w, which will exist. This $c_w^j(w)$ is then the set of solutions to the cost-minimization problem.

and multiply the left-hand side of eq. (4) by w_i and sum to get:

$$wv = \sum_{j=1}^{M} y_j \sum_{i=1}^{N} c_{ij}(w) w_i = \sum_{j=1}^{M} y_j c^j(w).$$

These equalities together show that $py = wv$.

Given the cost functions (hence the technology), the product price vector p and the endowment vector v the equilibrium conditions (2) and (4) may be solved for the endogenous vectors w and y. It is sometimes convenient to write these solutions in vector form as $w = w(p, v)$ and $y = y(p, v)$. In the following sections and in the next chapter, attention is focused on the properties of these functions and their relevance to international trade.

3.3. Diagrammatic representation of equilibrium

The above model of the production sector may be given convenient diagrammatic representations in the case where there are $N = 2$ factors of production. Two different diagrams will be used here. The first is the famous "Lerner diagram" (Lerner, 1952) which is in the factor quantity space, while the second is formulated in the factor price space and therefore corresponds more closely to the mathematical formulation of eqs. (2) and (4).

3.3.1. Lerner diagram

Before presenting the Lerner diagram, the equilibrium conditions (2) and (4) are rewritten in terms of a new output variable. If industry j produces output y_j at price p_j then the revenue is $r_j \equiv p_j y_j$. Let the number of dollar's worth of output produced, r_j, be the decision variable for industry j rather than y_j. What then is the cost function for producing one unit (dollar's worth) of revenue? If $p_j > 0$ the production of $1/p_j$ units of output is worth \$1 and the cost is $c^j(w)/p_j$. Since $c^j(w)$ is linearly homogeneous in w it follows that $c^j(w/p_j) = c^j(w)/p_j$ is the cost of producing \$1 worth of output. Also, if $p_j > 0$, then r_j and y_j have the same sign. Thus, the equilibrium conditions (2) and (4) may be reformulated in terms of w and r as

$$1 - c^j(w/p_j) \leqslant 0 \leqslant r_j, \qquad\qquad j = 1, ..., M, \qquad\qquad (6)$$

$$\sum_{j=1}^{M} (c_{ij}(w)/p_j)\, r_j - v_i \leqslant 0 \leqslant w_i, \quad i = 1, ..., N. \qquad\qquad (7)$$

Condition (6) says that if the cost of producing $1 worth of j exceeds $1, then none of j will be produced, and that if j is produced, then $c^j(w)/p_j = 1$. Condition (7) has the same interpretations as (4) except to note that the quantity of factor i used to produce $1 worth of output is $c_{ij}(w/p_j)$. This formulation is convenient if interest centres on the "real wage" vectors w/p_j, and corresponds to the Lerner diagram to which attention is now turned.

The Lerner diagram is presented as fig. 3.1 for the case $M = 3$ and $N = 2$. The axes refer to the quantities of the two factors. Drawn in are the unit value iso-

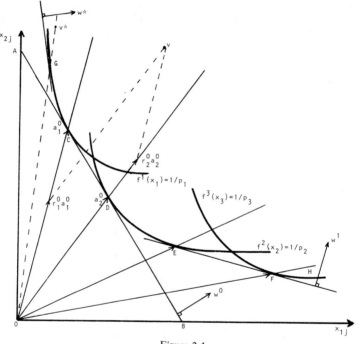

Figure 3.1

quants, which indicate the set of inputs which can produce $1 worth of output, for each of the three goods. To find an equilibrium we have to find a factor price vector $w = (w_1, w_2)$ such that each industry maximizes profits (which can be at most zero) and the factor markets clear (if $w > 0$). The straight lines through C and D and through E and F are the $1 isocost lines for price vectors w^0 and w^1, respectively. Thus, if w^0 prevails, industries 1 and 2 obtain zero profits while industry 3 makes a loss.

Are w^0 and w^1 candidates for the equilibrium price vector? If w^0 prevails, industry 1 will be anywhere along the ray through C, industry 2 will be anywhere along the ray through D and industry 3 will be at the origin since it does not produce. To see this first note that C is at the point $a_j^0 = (a_{1j}^0, a_{2j}^0)$, where $a_{ij}^0 \equiv c_{ij}(w^0)/p_j$ denotes the optimal input of i per \$1 output of j. Secondly, note that if r_j dollar's worth of output is produced then, by constant returns to scale the factor demand by industry j is $a_j^0 r_j$. The scale factor r_1 moves the factor demand vector for industry 1 out along the ray OC, while r_2 moves industry 2's demand vector out along the ray OD. Because each industry earns a zero profit at a_1^0 and a_2^0 by construction, they continue to earn zero profits for all $r_1, r_2 \geqslant 0$. If the endowment vector v is in the cone formed by COD, as in fig. 3.1, then it is possible to find $r_1^0, r_2^0 > 0$ such that $a_1^0 r_1^0 + a_2^0 r_2^0 = v$. This can be done by forming a parallelogram with slopes of OC and OD and end points O and v, as in fig. 3.1. Thus, w^0 and $r^0 = (r_1^0, r_2^0, 0)$ solve (6) and (7) and therefore constitute an equilibrium.

Of course, the endowment vector v need not occur in the cone COD. If it occurs in the cone EOF then it is easy to show, using the above argument, that w^1 is the equilibrium factor price vector and that equilibrium revenue vector $r^1 \geqslant 0$ can be found with $r_1^1 = 0$. The cones COD and EOF are called "cones of diversification". Each cone, defined for a factor price vector which allows two industries to produce, is the set of endowment vectors for which the factor market equilibrium conditions will be satisfied.[4]

If v is not in either diversification cone, the economy must specialize in the production of one good. For example, if v^* is the endowment vector it can be verified that only good 1 will be produced, that the vector a_1 is the point G, and that the factor price vector is normal, i.e. at right angles to the unit value isoquant at G. The verification is left to the reader.

3.3.2. *Factor price diagram*

Now consider an alternative diagrammatic treatment in terms of the factor price space. In fig. 3.2 the three curves indicate the set of factor prices for which unit cost equals price for the three industries. They are downward-sloping since $c^j(w)$ is non-decreasing (increasing here) in w, and convex to the origin since $c^j(w)$ is a concave function. The curves intersect at w^0, w^1 and w^2, the first two vectors

---

[4] Diversification usually refers to the situation where as many products are produced as there are factors (in this case two), although the concept can be generalized to deal with situations involving the production of fewer products. Diversification cones play an important role in the discussion of the factor price equalization theorem in Chapter 4 below.

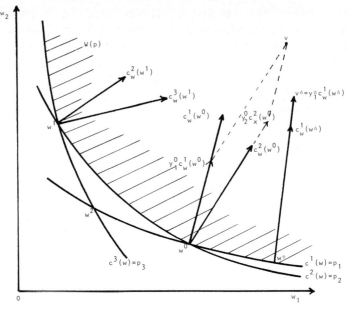

Figure 3.2

corresponding to w^0 and w^1 of fig. 3.1. At w^0 industries 1 and 2 are profitable while 3 is not, and at w^1 industries 2 and 3 are profitable while 1 is not. Shephard's lemma indicates that the input vectors per unit of output are $c^j_w(w)$ which are normal, i.e. at right angles, to the isocost curve $c^j(w) = p_j$ at w. Thus, if w^0 prevails the optimal input vectors are as shown in fig. 3.1 for $j = 1,2$. Industry 3 does not produce since $c^3(w^0) > p_3$. To see this note that the $c^3(w) = p_3$ curve passes below and to the left of w^0, so each factor price would have to be reduced from w^0 if industry 3 was to be made profitable. Alternatively, since the cost of producing one unit of good 3 is exactly p_3 along the iso-cost curve $c^3(w) = p_3$, the cost at w^0 must be greater than p_3 since the cost function is increasing in w. Thus, at w^0 industry 3 does not produce. The cone formed by $c^j_w(w^0) \, j = 1,2$ corresponds to *COD* of fig. 3.1. If v is drawn in with origin at w^0 output levels y^0_1 and $y^0_2 > 0$ can be found such that $c^1_w(w^0)y^0_1 + c^2_w(w^0)y^0_2 = v$ so w^0 and $y^0 = (y^0_1, y^0_2, 0)$ is an equilibrium. The points $c^1_w(w^0)y^0$ and $c^2_w(w^0)y^0$, and hence y^0_1 and y^0_2, are found by forming a parallelogram with vertices w^0 and v and slopes of sides given by the vectors $c^1_w(w^0)$ and $c^2_w(w^0)$, as shown in fig. 3.2.

If v is not in the diversification cone with origin w^0, then it is either in the diversification cone formed at w^1 or is in neither cone. If it is in the cone formed by w^1, then w^1 is the equilibrium factor price vector. If the endowment vector is in neither cone, then only one good will be produced in equilibrium. For example, if the endowment vector is v^* the factor price vector will be w^* and product 1 will be the only one produced. The vector w^* is such that v^* is normal to industry 1's iso-cost curve at w^*. The optimal input vector $c_w^1(w^*)$ is proportional to v^* so $y_1^* > 0$ can be found such that $c_w^1(w^*) y_1^* = v^*$, which means that the factor markets clear.

Why is w^2 not an equilibrium factor price vector? The answer is that while industries 1 and 3 make zero profits at w^2, industry 2 makes a positive profit since $c^2(w^2) < p_2$. This violates the zero profit condition for industry equilibrium. In fig. 3.1, w^2 would correspond to a \$1 iso-cost line drawn tangent to the unit value isoquant for industries 1 and 3.

Figure 3.2 provides a very convenient diagrammatic representation of the production sector, since our mathematical formulation is in terms of unit cost functions. Not only does the factor price diagram directly depict the profit-maximization conditions in the factor price space, but the factor market equilibrium conditions are easily depicted also. This is because of Shephard's lemma which states that the optimal input–output vectors are normal, i.e. at right angles, to the iso-cost curves. These input–output vectors can then be drawn in the factor price diagram with origin at the factor price vector as can the endowment vector.[5] In other words, the diversification cones of the Lerner diagram can be constructed, using Shephard's lemma, on the factor price diagram to indicate the optimal input–output vectors and derive the optimal output levels. In short, the factor price diagram provides all the necessary information about equilibrium in the production sector in a simple way and, moreover, corresponds directly to our mathematical formulation.

An interesting feature of the model that can be easily illustrated in the factor price diagram is that in equilibrium the number of products actually produced need be no greater than the number of fully used factors. For simplicity assume an equilibrium in which all N factors are fully employed and all M products are produced. Then the N factor markets clear, and the equilibrium output vector $y^0 > 0$ solves the equation set

$$\sum_{j=1}^{M} c_w^j(w^0) y_j = v, \qquad y = (y_1, ..., y_M) \geq 0, \tag{8}$$

where $w^0 > 0$ is the equilibrium factor price vector. This is a set of N linear equations in M unknowns $y_1, ..., y_M$. Consider the case where $M > N$. A fundamental

---

[5] The fact that the axes are factor prices while the input–output vectors and the endowment factors are quantities is of no importance. Simply let the axes refer to both quantities and prices.

result in the theory of linear programming is that if the matrix $A = [c_w^1(w^0), ..., c_w^M(w^0)]$ has rank N and if the equation set (8) has a solution $y^0 > 0$, then there exists another solution y^* with at most N positive elements.[6] This solution is called a non-negative basic solution.

Figure 3.3 illustrates a situation where three products can be produced at zero profits with two factors of production. This situation requires a special configuration of product prices to ensure that all three iso-cost curves intersect at the

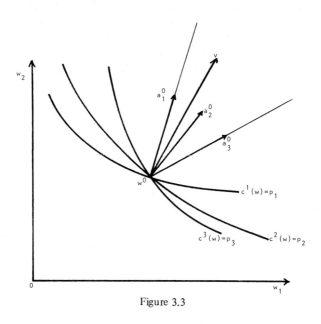

Figure 3.3

point w^0. The reader may verify that all three goods can be produced, and that there exists an infinity of solutions for y_1, y_2 and y_3. While all three goods can be produced, it is possible to satisfy the equilibrium conditions with only two goods being produced, since the optimal input vectors a_1^0 and a_2^0 span v^0 as also do a_1^0 and a_3^0. Evidently a_2^0 and a_3^0 do not span v^0 so it is not possible to find $y_2^0, y_3^0 > 0$ such that $y_2^0 a_2^0 + y_3^0 a_3^0 = v$.

If p is arbitrarily given then it is highly unlikely that it will be profitable for more goods to be produced than there are factors. This is because the product price vector has to be special in order for the M cost equations in $N < M$ un-

---

[6]   See Hadley (1962, pp. 80—82) for a statement and proof of this result.

knowns to have a solution $w \geqslant 0$.[7] In fig. 3.3 if p_3, say, were to decrease then good 3 would not be produced, and if p_3 increased then good 2 would become unprofitable.

3.4. Equilibrium and optimization

It is a rather remarkable fact that the equilibrium for the production sector may be obtained as the solution to two different but equivalent optimization problems. This result is rather important and so this section is devoted to the presentation of these optimization problems and to the discussion of their relationship to the production sector equilibrium.

The optimization problems are as follows. The first is defined on the factor price space and is

$$m(p, v) \equiv \min_{w} \{wv: \ w \in W(p)\}, \tag{9}$$

where

$$W(p) \equiv \{w: \ c^j(w) \geqslant p_j, \ j = 1, ..., M; \ w \geqslant 0\} \tag{10}$$

is the factor price set. $W(p)$ is the set of all non-negative factor price vectors for which no industry can make a positive profit. Its boundary is called the factor price frontier. The problem defined is to choose a factor price vector in the factor price set which minimizes the total payment to the factors. The minimum factor payment function is $m(p, v)$.

The second optimization problem is defined in the product quantity space and is

$$G(p, v) \equiv \max_{y} \{py: \ y \in Y(v)\}, \tag{11}$$

where

$$Y(v) \equiv \left\{ y: \ y_j \leqslant f^j(x_j), \ x_j \geqslant 0, \ j = 1, ..., M; \ \sum_{j=1}^{M} x_j \leqslant v; \ y \geqslant 0 \right\} \tag{12}$$

[7] Of course unless the economy is small and open, p is not arbitrarily given but is determined by market conditions. For example, if the economy is closed and demand conditions are such that there is a positive demand for each good at any price vector (as with Cobb–Douglas preferences) then all goods will be produced even if there are fewer factors. The same applies if there is trade between two nations with the same technology.

is the production possibility set. $Y(v)$ is the set of all output vectors which can be produced given the technology and the factor endowment. Its boundary is called the production possibility frontier or curve or the transformation frontier. Thus, problem (11) is to choose a feasible output vector which maximizes the total value of production or gross national product (GNP). The maximum GNP function is $G(p, v)$. This is the problem that a central planner would attempt to solve given a vector of prices p and the endowment vector v. It is shown below that the solution for y is precisely the equilibrium output vector obtained by solving conditions (2) and (4). Thus, the production sector made up of a multitude of individual firms operating under perfect competition acts as if it was controlled by a central planner. This is, of course, the proposition of Adam Smith (1776) that individual self-interest leads to the best situation for the whole economy.

It will also be shown that the solution for w to problem (9) is precisely the equilibrium factor price vector obtained by solving conditions (2) and (4). Moreover, it turns out that $m(p, v) = G(p, v)$, i.e. the minimum factor payments exactly equal the maximum GNP for every choice of p and v. These results together imply a duality between the two problems. The fact that the equilibrium y and w may be obtained as solutions to optimization problems is rather important for international trade theory, especially for the demonstration of the gains from trade, and provides a very useful way of calculating equilibrium solutions. In this book the latter point will be exploited from a diagrammatic viewpoint, although appendix B is devoted to the presentation of an algorithm for the numerical solution of problem (11).

These optimization problems may be illustrated diagrammatically in figs. 3.4 and 3.5 for the case where $M = N = 2$. In fig. 3.4 the shaded area is the production possibility set and the highest iso-GNP line is drawn tangent to $Y(v^0)$ at y^0 which therefore solves problem (11). Since the solution y^0 is the equilibrium output vector, fig. 3.4 provides a very convenient way of showing the response of outputs to changes in product prices.

In fig. 3.5 the factor price set is the shaded area lying above the $c^j(w) = p_j$ curves. For a given v there is a family of iso-factor payments lines. The lowest iso-factor payments line touching the set $W(p)$ passes through w^0, which therefore solves problem (9). That the factor price vector which solves problem (9) is indeed the equilibrium factor price vector, can easily be verified by examining fig. 3.5 and recalling the earlier discussion of fig. 3.2 (which is the same as fig. 3.5 if product 3 is ignored). Evidently, at w^0 both industries make zero profits so the profit-maximization conditions hold if positive outputs occur. That each industry produces a positive output can be verified by observing that v is between $c_w^1(w^0)$ and $c_w^2(w^0)$ and hence there exist output levels $y_1^0 > 0$ and $y_2^0 > 0$ such

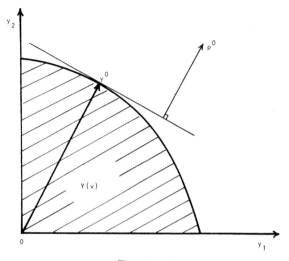

Figure 3.4

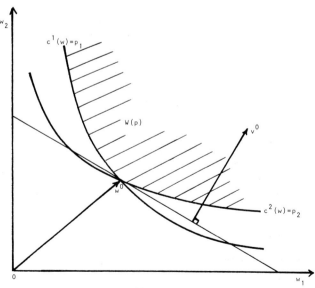

Figure 3.5

that $c_w^1(w^0) y_1^0 + c_w^2(w^0) y_2^0 = v$. That is, (w^0, y^0) constitute a competitive equilibrium. Thus, w^0 is both the solution to problem (9) and the equilibrium factor price vector.

Because of the importance of the production possibility set in international trade theory, some of its properties are now presented and derived:

> If the production functions $f^j(x_j)$ satisfy conditions (2.3'), then the production possibility set $Y(v)$ defined by (12) is non-empty, convex and compact for $v \geqslant 0$. (13)

That $Y(v)$ is non-empty simply means that some $y \geqslant 0$ is possible. Since $v \geqslant 0$, it is clearly possible to choose all $x_j = 0$ and $y_j = 0$ so that $y = 0 \in Y(v)$. If $v > 0$, then a positive input vector, $x_j > 0$, can be chosen for each industry j and so by (2.3') $y_j > 0$. Thus, when $v > 0$ then some $y > 0$ is feasible.

The production possibility set in fig. 3.4 is drawn as a convex set with a concave frontier. To prove that this must be the case it is necessary to show that if productions $y^0, y^1 \in Y(v)$, then the production vector $y^\lambda \equiv \lambda y^0 + (1 - \lambda) y^1 \in Y(v)$, where $0 \leqslant \lambda \leqslant 1$. That is, the line joining any two points in the set must also be in the set. If y^0 is possible using input vectors $x_j^0, j = 1, ..., M$, then by the CRS assumption λy^0 is possible if each industry j uses input vector λx_j^0. In this case the total factor use is $\lambda \Sigma_j x_j \leqslant \lambda v$ for $0 \leqslant \lambda \leqslant 1$. Similarly, if y^1 is possible using input vectors x_j^1, then $(1 - \lambda) y^1$ is possible if input vectors $(1 - \lambda) x_j^1$ are used in which case the total factor use is $(1 - \lambda) \Sigma x_j^1 \leqslant (1 - \lambda) v$. Adding these productions together yields output vector $\lambda y^0 + (1 - \lambda) y^1 = y^\lambda$ which is certainly non-negative since both y^0 and y^1 are non-negative, and which is feasible since the total factor use is $\lambda \Sigma_j x_j^0 + (1 - \lambda) \Sigma x_j^1 \leqslant \lambda v + (1 - \lambda) v = v$. Thus, the production possibility set is convex.

A set is compact if it is closed, meaning that it contains its boundary, and bounded, meaning that it can be contained in a "box" of finite size. The set $Y(v)$ is bounded below since $y \geqslant 0$ is required and is bounded above since $y_j \leqslant f^j(v)$, $j = 1, ..., M$. That is to say, if all resources are put into one industry a finite production of that good would occur, and if production of another good was required some resources would have to be released from the former industry. Closedness follows from the continuity of the production functions and will not be discussed.

3.5. Equilibrium and optimization – derivations

The formal relationships between the competitive equilibrium for the production sector and the solutions to problems (9) and (11) are developed in this section.

To do this some fundamental results from the theory of nonlinear programming are required. Appendix A below contains these results in the form of the saddle-point theorem and the Kuhn–Tucker theorem.

3.5.1. The minimum factor payments problem

The minimum factor payments problem satisfies all of the assumptions of the Kuhn–Tucker (1956) theorem (A4). The objective function is $-wv$ (converting to a maximum problem) which is linear and hence concave in w. The functions $c^j(w) - p_j \geq 0$ are concave in w and since the unit cost functions are increasing there must exist some $\bar{w} \geq 0$ such that $c^j(\bar{w}) > p_j$. Thus, theorem (A4) may be applied. The Lagrangian is

$$L(w, y) = -wv + \sum_{j=1}^{M} y_j [c^j(w) - p_j], \tag{14}$$

where $y = (y_1, ..., y_M)$ is the vector of Lagrange multipliers. The choice of y here anticipates a result which will allow the vector of Lagrange multipliers to be interpreted as the output vector. Applying theorem (A4), the necessary and sufficient Kuhn–Tucker condition for w^0 to solve (9) is that there exists a y^0 such that

$$\frac{\partial L(w^0, y^0)}{\partial w_i} = \sum_{j=1}^{M} y_j^0 c_{ij}(w^0) - v_i \leq 0 \leq w_i^0, \quad i = 1, ..., N,$$

$$\frac{\partial L(w^0, y^0)}{\partial y_j} = c^j(w^0) - p_j \geq 0 \leq y_j^0, \quad j = 1, ..., M. \tag{15}$$

Recognizing that $c_{ij}(w^0)$ is the demand for factor i per unit of output of product j, by Shephard's lemma, and interpreting y_j as the output of product j, it is evident that (15) is simply the set of equilibrium conditions for the production sector written above as (2) and (4). Thus, solving problem (9) yields the same solution as the equilibrium conditions (2) and (4) for w.

3.5.2. The maximum GNP problem

It is now shown that the solution for y in problem (11) is precisely the equilibrium output vector obtained from (2) and (4). One way to do this is to assume that the production functions are differentiable, apply the Kuhn–Tucker theorem

(A4) to problem (11), and show that the resulting Kuhn–Tucker conditions yield the same solution for y as (2) and (4). This approach is left to the reader and is the subject of one of the problems at the end of the chapter. A more direct approach, which does not assume differentiability, is to apply the saddlepoint theorem (A2) directly to problem (11) and show that this saddlepoint problem is identical to that for problem (9).

Thus, problems (11) and (9) have the same saddlepoint problem and so the Kuhn–Tucker conditions are the same for both problems. But we have already shown that the Kuhn–Tucker conditions for a solution to problem (9), or, equivalently for a solution to the saddlepoint problem, are precisely the equilibrium conditions for the production sector. Hence, we will have proved that the solution y^0 to problem (11) is the equilibrium output vector. Moreover, we will have proved the duality between problems (9) and (11) by showing that they have identical saddlepoint problems and Kuhn–Tucker conditions.

The Lagrangian for problem (10) is

$$L(y, x_1, ..., x_M, \mu, w) \equiv py + \sum_{j=1}^{M} \mu_j[f^j(x_j) - y_j] + w\left[v - \sum_{j=1}^{M} x_j\right], \quad (16)$$

where $\mu = (\mu_1, ..., \mu_M)$ and $w = (w_1, ..., w_N)$ are vectors of Lagrange multipliers. The choice of w here anticipates the interpretation of these multipliers as factor prices. Can the saddlepoint theorem be applied? Since the production functions are concave and the objective function and the factor endowment constraints are linear, the concavity requirement is satisfied. If $v > 0$, then a positive input vector $\bar{x}_j > 0$ can be allocated to industry j so we can choose $\bar{y}_j < f^j(\bar{x})$, by assumption (2.3′), and still have $\sum_{j=1}^{M} \bar{x}_j < v$. Hence, all the assumptions of the saddlepoint theorem are satisfied, and it may be applied.

Let $(y^0, x_1^0, ..., x_M^0, \mu^0, w^0)$ be a saddlepoint for (16). Then by the definition of a saddlepoint $L(y^0, x_1, x_2^0, ..., x_M^0, \mu_1, \mu_2^0, ..., \mu_M^0, w^0)$ is maximized with respect to x_1 and minimized with respect to μ_1 at (x_1^0, μ_1^0). That is, (x_1^0, μ_1^0) is a saddlepoint of the function

$$\phi_1(x_1, \mu_1) \equiv -w^0 x_1 + \mu_1[f^1(x_1) - y_1^0], \quad (17)$$

since this contains all of the terms of L involving (x_1, μ_1). But this is the Lagrangian for the cost-minimization problem for industry 1, written as

$$\max_{x_1} \{-w^0 x_1 : f^1(x_1) - y_1^0 \geq 0, \quad x_1 \geq 0\}. \quad (18)$$

Clearly, the maximum of $-w^0 x_1$ is minus the minimum of $w^0 x_1$. Thus, the maximum of $-w^0 x_1$ in (18) is minus the cost function $C^1(w^0, y_1^0)$ which factors as $C^1(w^0, y_1^0) = c^1(w^0) y_0^1$ due to CRS. Since (x_1^0, μ_1^0) is a saddlepoint of (17):

$$\phi_1(x_1^0, \mu_1^0) = \min_{\mu_1 \geqslant 0} \{-w^0 x_1^0 + \mu_1 [f^1(x_1^0) - y_1^0]\}$$

$$= -w^0 x_1^0 + \begin{cases} 0, & \text{if } f^1(x_1^0) - y_1^0 \geqslant 0, \\ -\infty, & \text{if } f^1(x_1^0) - y_1^0 < 0. \end{cases}$$

Since it is assumed that the saddlepoint for (16) and hence (17) exists, it cannot be the case that $\phi_1(x_1^0, \mu_1^0) = -\infty$. Hence, $f^1(x_1^0) - y_1^0 \geqslant 0$ holds and

$$\phi_1(x_1^0, \mu_1^0) = -w^0 x_1^0 = -c^1(w^0) y_1^0. \tag{19}$$

The same argument applies for each j so that $\phi_j(x_j^0, \mu_j^0) = -c^j(w^0) y_j^0$, $j=1,...,M$.

Rewriting the Lagrangian (16) in terms of $\phi_j(x_j, \mu_j)$, substituting the expression $\phi_j(x_j^0, \mu_j^0) = -c^j(w^0) y_j^0$, and rearranging terms yields:

$$L(y_1^0, x_1^0, ..., x_M^0, \mu^0, w^0) = w^0 v + \sum_{j=1}^M y_j^0 [p_j - c^j(w^0)] \equiv L^*(w^0, y^0). \tag{20}$$

The Lagrangian $L(y, x_1, ..., x_M, \mu, w)$ has a saddlepoint $(y^0, x_1^0, ..., x_M^0, \mu^0, w^0)$. We have just "concentrated" this saddlepoint by solving for the x_j^0's and μ^0 in terms of the remaining variables by carrying out the maximization with respect to the x_j's and the minimization with respect to μ. Thus, by solving out these variables the original saddlepoint problem reduces to finding a saddlepoint of the "concentrated" Lagrangian $L^*(w, y)$. The concentrated Lagrangian $L^*(w, y)$ has a maximum with respect to y and a minimum with respect to w at (w^0, y^0). Clearly, $-L^*(w, y)$ is the Lagrangian (14) for problem (9). Thus, the saddlepoint problems for (9) and (11) are identical. Accordingly, in view of the saddlepoint theorem, (9) and (11) have exactly the same necessary and sufficient conditions which, by the Kuhn–Tucker theorem, were shown to be precisely the competitive equilibrium conditions (2) and (4). Finally, conditions (2) and (4) yield the result that $py^0 = w^0 v$, as shown above in section 3.2.

These results may be summarized as:

Optimization theorem. Let the production functions satisfy conditions (2.3′) and $v > 0$. Then (y^0, w^0) is a competitive equilibrium if and only if y^0 solves the maximum GNP problem (11) or, equivalently, w^0 solves the minimum factor payments problem (9). Also, $G(p, v) = m(p, v)$ holds identically for all p, v.[8] (21)

This is a very important result. In particular it indicates that the production sector behaves in such a way that GNP is maximized on the production possibility set. This justifies the usual diagrammatic treatment of equilibrium in the production sector, as illustrated in fig. 3.4.

3.6. Traditional formulation in terms of production functions

If the concept of cost functions had not been used, the equilibrium conditions for the production sector could have been formulated directly in terms of the production functions. In this section this formulation is outlined and related to the cost function formulation.

Assuming the differentiability of the production functions $f^j(x_j)$, the profit maximization and factor market equilibrium conditions are

$$p_j f^j_x(x_j) - w \leqslant 0 \leqslant x_j, \quad j = 1, ..., M, \tag{22}$$

$$\sum_{j=1}^{M} x_j - v \leqslant 0 \leqslant w, \tag{23}$$

where x_j and w and $f^j_x(x_j)$ are N-dimensioned vectors and $f^j_x(x_j)$ is the vector of marginal products in industry j. Eqs. (22) are the Kuhn–Tucker conditions for the problem of maximizing profit $p_j f^j(x_j) - wx_j$ subject to $x_j \geqslant 0$. They state that the value of the marginal product for a factor must be equal to the factor price if that factor is used, and if the factor price exceeds the value of the marginal product the factor is not used. Condition (23) is the factor market equilibrium requirement that demand cannot exceed supply and that a zero factor price is only consistent with an excess supply.

Conditions (22) and (23) are a set of $NM + N$ "equations" in $NM + N$ unknowns, namely the N-vectors $x_1, ..., x_M$, and w. The cost function or duality approach is to solve eqs. (22) for x_j explicitly in terms of w and p_j and thus eliminate x_j from the equilibrium conditions. Actually, x_j is obtained in terms of w and y_j and then the profit-maximization conditions are written in terms of y_j. This is most easily seen by rewriting profit as $p_j x_j - wx_j$ and maximizing it

---

[8] No mention is made of the differentiability of cost functions in this theorem since it is valid without differentiability. Also, the $v > 0$ assumption is required to ensure a solution to problem (8) as well as to satisfy the conditions of (A2). If an element of v, say $v_1 = 0$, then it is possible for wv to have no minimum if the boundary of $W(p)$ is asymptotic to a line parallel to the w_1 axis. The infimum, however, would exist.

with respect to $y_j \geqslant 0$ and $x_j \geqslant 0$ subject to the condition $y_j = f^j(x_j)$. Using theorem (A4) this yields the Kuhn–Tucker conditions:

$$p_j - \mu_j \leqslant 0 \leqslant y_j, \qquad\qquad\qquad j = 1, ..., M, \qquad\qquad (24)$$

$$\mu_j f_x^j(x_j) - w \leqslant 0 \leqslant x_j, \quad y_j = f^j(x_j), \qquad j = 1, ..., M, \qquad (25)$$

where μ_j is a Lagrange multiplier. When $p_j = \mu_j$, as is the case when $y_j > 0$, (25) is the same as (22). The cost function approach is to solve (25) for the cost minimizing x_j and for μ_j in terms of w and y_j. Multiplying the first expression in (25) by x_j yields $\mu_j = w x_j / x_j\, f_x^j(x_j)$. Because the production function is linearly homogeneous, Euler's theorem implies that $x_j\, f_x^j(x_j) = f^j(x_j)$. Consequently, $\mu_j = w x_j / f^j(x_j)$ is the average or unit cost of production and can be written as $\mu_j = c^j(w)$. Substituting this expression for μ_j in (24) yields the profit-maximizing condition (2). Using Shephard's lemma, x_j can be replaced by $c_w^j(w) y_j$ in (23) to get (4).

The cost function approach used in the formulation provided by (2) and (4) has several advantages over the production function approach in (22) and (23) (or in (24) and (25)). First, it has the advantage of reducing the number of equilibrium conditions from $MN + N$ to $M + N$. It achieves this by solving for the cost-minimizing vector of inputs x_j and hence eliminating explicit consideration of x_j in the equilibrium conditions. Secondly, the differentiability assumption on the cost function is less restrictive than on the production function. Finally, it permits the *structure* of the equilibrium conditions to be exposed more clearly and simplifies their analysis.

Jones (1965) introduced a formulation of the equilibrium conditions which almost coincides with that used here except that he does not explicitly consider the cost function. He denotes the optimal input–output vectors as $a_j(w)$ and notes that the unit cost in industry j is $w a_j(w)$. Here the latter is explicitly written as $c^j(w)$ and the former as $c_w^j(w)$ in view of Shephard's lemma. Thus, the correspondence between the cost function formulation and that of Jones is very close.

The correspondence between Jones' approach and the cost function approach may not be clear from reading Jones' paper. In obtaining comparative static results he totally differentiates the unit cost to obtain:

$$dc^j(w) = d \left[\sum_{i=1}^{N} a_{ij}(w) w_i \right] = \sum_i a_{ij}(w)\, dw_i + \sum_i w_i\, da_{ij}(w).$$

The first-order conditions for cost minimization ensure that the second term in this expression is zero, and hence $dc^j(w) = \sum_i a_{ij}(w)\, dw_i$. This result is quoted

as an example of the famous Wong–Viner envelope theorem. The same result
is obtained *directly* by the application of Shephard's lemma. In other words,
Shephard's lemma and the Wong–Viner envelope theorem are really the same.

3.7. Properties of the GNP function

The GNP function $G(p, v) \equiv m(p, v)$ summarizes the solution to the problem of
maximizing py on $Y(v)$ or, equivalently, minimizing wv on $W(p)$. Recalling the
discussion of cost functions in Chapter 2, it should be evident that $G(p, v)$ is
dual to both $Y(v)$ and $W(p)$. In this section the properties of $G(p, v)$ are presented
and briefly discussed.

   Problem (9) is to choose w to minimize the linear function wv on the factor
price set $W(p)$. This is formally the same as the problem of choosing x to minimize
the linear function wx on the set $X(y)$, which was dealt with in Chapter 2. Thus,
$G(p, v) \equiv m(p, v)$ will be a non-decreasing, linearly homogeneous, concave function of v just as the cost function was shown to be a non-decreasing, linearly homogeneous, concave function of w.

   Problem (11) is to maximize the linear function py on the production possibility set $Y(v)$. Using the same line of proof as used in Chapter 2 to derive the
properties of the cost function, it is readily shown that $G(p, v)$ is a non-decreasing,
linearly homogeneous, and *convex* function of p.[9] The convexity in p occurs because problem (11) is a maximization problem, whereas concavity in v occurred
because problem (9) is a minimization problem.

   Thus we have that:

   $G(p, v)$ is a non-negative function of $p > 0$, $v > 0$, which is non-
   decreasing, linearly homogeneous, and concave in v, and non-
   decreasing, linearly homogeneous, and convex in p.   (26)

   Just as with the cost function, these properties of the GNP function have a
very simple interpretation. More of any factor cannot reduce GNP and will increase it if that factor is productive at the margin, so G is non-decreasing in v.
Similarly, an increase in the price of a good will not decrease GNP and will increase it if the good whose price has risen is actually produced, so G is non-decreasing in p. Doubling the factor endowment will allow the production of all
goods to double, by CRS, and hence GNP will double. Thus, G is linearly homo-

---

[9]   A function $G(p, v)$ is convex in p if $-G(p, v)$ is concave in p. Equivalently it is con-
vex if $G(p^\lambda, v) \leqslant \lambda G(p^0, v) + (1 - \lambda) G(p^1, v)$ where $p^\lambda \equiv \lambda p^0 + (1 - \lambda) p^1$ and $0 \leqslant \lambda \leqslant 1$.

geneous in v. Doubling all product prices allows GNP to double, so G is also linearly homogeneous in p. If the price of a good increases and production does not change, then G will be a linear function of the price. However, the production mix may be able to be altered to improve GNP further, meaning that G is a convex function of prices. Similarly, if an endowment increases and factor prices do not change, then G will be a linear function of v. However, the price of the factor may decrease so the factor payments (which equal GNP) may be reduced from this higher level, meaning that they are a concave function of v.

Furthermore, the derivation of Shephard's lemma carries over to the present context so that if $G(p, v)$ is differentiable at (p^0, v^0) then

$$y^0 = \partial G(p^0, v^0)/\partial p \equiv G_p(p^0, v^0) \tag{27}$$

and

$$w^0 = \partial G(p^0, v^0)/\partial v \equiv G_v(p^0, v^0), \tag{28}$$

where (y^0, w^0) are the solutions to (9) and (11). This result, together with the curvature conditions on $G(p, v)$, permit an easy development of comparative static results. In Chapter 5 below these properties of $G(p, v)$ will be discussed further in the context of a more general model of the production sector and general comparative static results will be developed.

3.8. Notes on the literature

The traditional formulation of the equilibrium conditions for the production sector, written in terms of production functions and the marginal productivity conditions for profit maximization, may be found in Kemp (1969) and Takayama (1972). These authors are mainly concerned with the two-product, two-factor model, as was most of the literature in the journals until fairly recently.

The papers by Samuelson (1953, 1967) contain a mixture of the production function and cost function approaches. Indeed, the duality approach has been used in various degrees in the literature, especially in the discussions of the factor price equalization theorem. Jones' (1965) formulation in terms of input–output coefficients has become extremely popular. As pointed out in section 3.6, the cost function approach used in this book extends Jones' formulation by explicitly dealing with the cost function and exploiting its properties directly. This chapter draws heavily upon Woodland (1977). Dixit and Norman (1980) make extensive use of duality theory including the GNP function which they term the "revenue function".

Appendix A: Theorems in non-linear programming

Here we present and briefly discuss some useful theorems in non-linear programming, which is concerned with maximizing a function of variables subject to constraints. This optimization problem may be expressed as:

$$\max_{x} \{ f(x): g_i(x) \geqslant 0, \ i = 1, ..., I; \ x = (x, ..., x_J) \geqslant 0 \}. \tag{A1}$$

The following theorems characterize the solution of this problem:

Saddlepoint theorem (Uzawa, 1958). Let $f, g_1, ..., g_I$ be concave. Let there exist a vector $\bar{x} \geqslant 0$ such that $g_i(\bar{x}) > 0$, for all $i = 1, ..., I$. Then a vector x^0 solves problem (A1) if an only if there exists a vector $u^0 \geqslant 0$ such that (x^0, u^0) is a saddlepoint of the Lagrangian $L(x, u) \equiv f(x) + \Sigma_{i=1}^I u_i g_i(x)$, i.e. such that (A2)

$$L(x, u^0) \leqslant L(x^0, u^0) \leqslant L(x^0, u), \quad \text{for all} \ \ x \geqslant 0, \ u \geqslant 0. \tag{A3}$$

Another important result based upon differentiability is as follows:

Kuhn–Tucker (1956) theorem. Let $f, g_1, ..., g_I$ be differentiable and concave. The vector x^0 solves the maximization problem in (A1) if and only if there exists a vector u^0 such that the Kuhn–Tucker conditions (A5) below are satisfied: (A4)

$$\frac{\partial L(x^0, u^0)}{\partial x_j} = \frac{\partial f(x^0)}{\partial x_j} + \sum_{i=1}^I u_i \frac{\partial g_i(x^0)}{\partial x_j} \leqslant 0 \leqslant x_j^0, \quad j = 1, ..., J,$$

$$\frac{\partial L(x^0, u^0)}{\partial u_i} = g_i(x^0) \geqslant 0 \leqslant u_i^0, \quad i = 1, ..., I. \tag{A5}$$

These theorems are extremely useful in economic analysis. The artificial variables $u_1, ..., u_I$ introduced to define the Lagrangian are called Lagrange multipliers and they have a very convenient interpretation as shadow prices. This is because it can be shown that the increase in the optimal value of the objective function $f(x^0)$ due to the relaxation of the ith constraint by one (small) unit is precisely the value of the ith Lagrange multiplier u_i^0. Thus, u_i^0 represents the "value" or shadow price of the constraint at the margin. Theorem (A2) indicates that the constrained optimization problem can be reformulated as a saddlepoint problem. The Kuhn–Tucker theorem (A4) characterizes the saddlepoint in terms of derivatives. The Kuhn–Tucker conditions can be used to describe the solution and often have a clear economic interpretation.

The nature of a saddlepoint and the interpretation of the Kuhn–Tucker conditions are perhaps not widely known and hence deserve some discussion. If (x^0, u^0) is a saddlepoint of $L(x, u)$, as defined by (A3), then $L(x^0, u)$ attains its minimum with respect to $u \geqslant 0$ at u^0 and $L(x, u^0)$ attains its maximum with respect to $x \geqslant 0$ at x^0. Thus, $L(x, u)$ is being minimized with respect to $u \geqslant 0$ and maximized with respect to $x \geqslant 0$. The role of the Lagrange multipliers in the Lagrangian is to get rid of the constraints by putting them in the objective function.

The Kuhn–Tucker conditions (A5) are written in accordance with our convention regarding double inequalities. If $x_j^0 > 0$, then the first set of equations in (A5) says that $\partial L(x^0, u^0)/\partial x_j = 0$, which is the classical first-order Lagrangian condition for a constrained maximum without the inequality constraint on x_j. Also, if at the solution $\partial L(x^0, u^0)/\partial x_j < 0$, then $x_j = 0$ must be true. The same applies to the second set of equations in (A5). If the ith constraint is ineffective at the solution, i.e. $g_i(x^0) > 0$, then it must be true that $u_i^0 = 0$. On the other hand, if $u_i^0 > 0$, then $g_i(x^0) = 0$ so the constraint must be effective. These statements are intuitively reasonable since they imply that the shadow price of a constraint is zero if it is ineffective, and if positive the constraint must be effective.

When no constraint is effective and $x^0 > 0$, the solution x^0 is in the interior of the constraint region. In this case $u^0 = 0$ and so (A5) indicates that $\partial f(x^0)/\partial x_j = 0$, $j = 1, ..., J$, which are the classical first-order conditions for an unconstrained maximum. When each constraint holds with equality and $x^0 > 0$, (A5) reduces to the classical first-order conditions for a maximum subject to equality constraints. The Kuhn–Tucker conditions are therefore generalizations of these more familiar conditions to deal with the non-negativity of x and inequality constraints. For further details and discussion on Lagrangians and the theory of constrained optimization the reader is referred to Intriligator (1971, ch. 2–4) who provides a clear exposition with applications to economics and Mangasarian (1969) for a more thorough mathematical treatment.

Appendix B: Computation of equilibria

In this appendix we briefly present a numerical algorithm for solving for the equilibrium output quantity and input price vectors. The algorithm is based upon Van Slyke (1968) and is discussed in more detail within the context of a more general model by Diewert and Woodland (1977). For details on linear programming see Hadley (1962) and Intriligator (1971, ch. 5).

If the production functions are all of the Leontief, fixed-coefficient type, then the maximum GNP and minimum factor payments problems are linear programming problems. In this case the equilibrium solutions can be found by applying any one of a number of linear programming algorithms to either problem (9) or (11).

The linear programming procedure can be used to solve more general problems provided that the production functions exhibit constant returns to scale. The algorithm is iterative and proceeds as follows.

B.1. Algorithm

(a) Initiate the algorithm by choosing $w > 0$ and computing $a_j = c_w^j(w)$, $j = 1, ..., M$.

(b) Solve the restricted master problem:

$$P = \max_{y} \left\{ py: \sum_{j=1}^{M} a_j y_j \leqslant v, \ y \geqslant 0 \right\}$$

or its dual

$$D = \min_{w} \{wv: wa_j \geqslant p_j, \ j = 1, ..., M; \ w \geqslant 0\}.$$

Thus, we have the restricted solutions (y, w).

(c) Solve the subproblems. That is, using the solution for w from (b) compute $c^j(w)$, $j = 1, ..., M$.

(d) Check for convergence. (i) If $c^j(w) \geqslant p_j, j = 1, ..., M$, then a solution has been obtained – the restricted solution for (y, w) from (b) is the equilibrium solution. (ii) If $p_j > c^j(w)$ for some j, then proceed to (e).

(e) Alter the restricted master problem by introducing a new activity into P, or a new constraint into D. To do this find h such that $p_h - c^h(w) \geqslant p_j - c^j(w)$, $j = 1, ..., M$, and calculate $a_h = c_w^h(w)$. Then introduce a new activity with vector a_h into P, or introduce a new constraint $wa_h \geqslant p_h$ into D. Solve the new restricted master problem as in (b), continue to (c), and so on until convergence is achieved.

Several remarks are in order. First, the algorithm converges to a solution to (9) or (11) since the addition of a new activity cannot reduce the value of P, and will increase it if $p_j > c^j(w)$ for some j in step (e). Secondly, as a practical matter one can simply replace the old a_h by the new a_h rather than include a new activity in P (or constraint in D) since, if necessary, the old one can be reintroduced at a later stage. This prevents the size of the linear programming problem from increasing at each iteration of our algorithm. Thirdly, another variation in step (e) is to replace a_j by (or add) the new $c_w^j(w)$ vectors for all j such that $p_j > c^j(w)$, and this may speed up convergence in some problems. Fourthly, if the restricted solution for w contains zero elements and $c^j(w)$ is not defined for such w, then the appropriate procedure is to perturb w to make it positive, whence steps (d) and (e) can proceed. Fifthly, convergence may only be asymptotic so the appropriate convergence criterion, which yields an approximate solution, is that $p_j - c^j(w) \leqslant \epsilon$, for all j, where ϵ is some small positive number, e.g. 0.0001.

B.2. *Example*

Let $c^1(w_1, w_2) = w_1^{0.75} w_2^{0.25}$, $c^2(w_1, w_2) = w_1^{0.25} w_2^{0.75}$, $p = (1 \quad 1)$, and $v = (1.5 \quad 1.5)$. It may be verified that the equilibrium is $y = (1 \quad 1)$ and $w = (1 \quad 1)$. The factor demand functions per unit of output are $c_{11}(w) = 0.75(w_2/w_1)^{0.25}$, $c_{21}(w) = 0.25(w_2/w_1)^{-0.75}$, $c_{12}(w) = 0.25(w_2/w_1)^{0.75}$ and $c_{22}(w) = 0.75(w_2/w_1)^{-0.25}$.

Let $w = (1 \quad 3)$ be the initial choice for the factor price vector. Then the sequence of solutions to the restricted master and subproblems for a number of iterations of the algorithm are as indicated in table 3.B.1. The algorithm yields a rapid convergence to the solution.

Table 3.B.1

Iteration	w_1	w_2	$c^1(w)$	$c^2(w)$	y_1	y_2	P, D
1[a]	0.9204	0.8344	0.8981	0.8597	2.6322	0	2.6322
2	0.8988	1.0283	0.9296	0.9943	1.1063	1.7841	2.8907
3	0.9981	0.9989	0.9983	0.9987	1.4901	1.5055	2.9955
4	1.0006	0.9981	1.0000	0.9987	1.5617	1.4363	2.9981
5	1.0000	1.0000	1.0000	1.0000	1.5009	1.4991	3.0000
Solution	1.0	1.0	1.0	1.0	1.0	1.0	3.0

[a] The solution for w is not unique.

This problem is, of course, rather trivial but was chosen to illustrate simply the working of the algorithm. The reader may wish to illustrate the sequence of "solutions" on the factor price diagram. The more adventurous may wish to solve problems involving several goods and factors.

Problems

1. Consider a production sector which produces two products using capital and labour. While labour is perfectly mobile between industries, capital is not and therefore can only be used in the industry in which it was installed. Using cost functions, write down the equilibrium conditions.

2. Write down the equilibrium conditions for a production sector which produces two products using labour and capital, when the rate of tax on the earnings of capital is different in the two industries.

3. Let the unit cost functions for a two-product, two-factor economy be linear.
    (a) Derive the production functions.
    (b) Write down the dual optimization problems (9) and (11). Note that they are dual linear programming problems.
    (c) Derive the production possibility frontier.

4. It was shown in the text that the production possibility set is convex when the production functions exhibit CRS.
    (a) The proof showed that the line joining any two points in the production possibility set is in the set. This does not prove that the set has a *strictly* concave frontier as is usually drawn. Verify that to obtain a strictly concave frontier requires the existence of a more efficient allocation of resources than the one used in the proof to produce a point on the line joining two production points.
    (b) Verify that the proof in the text is unaffected by decreasing-returns-to-scale production functions.
    (c) If the production functions exhibit increasing returns to scale, will the production possibility set be convex? What if one industry has increasing returns to scale and the other industries have CRS?

5. Consider a production sector with three products and two factors.
    (a) Show that if three products can be produced in equilibrium, the solution for output levels is multi-valued. That is, there is a set of solutions for y.
    (b) Hence show that the production possibility surface is "ruled", i.e. it is formed by an infinite family of non-parallel straight lines.

6. Let $c^1(w) = w_1 + 2w_2$, $c^2(w) = 2w_1 + w_2$, and $p_1 = p_2 = 1$.
    (a) Draw the factor price set $W(p)$.
    (b) If $v = (2,2)$ calculate the solution to the minimum factor payments problem (9) and hence calculate the equilibrium. Check all equilibrium conditions.
    (c) Now let v vary and derive the function $m(p, v)$ for $v \geqslant 0$ and $p = (1,1)$.

7. Prove that $G(p, v)$ is a non-negative, non-decreasing, convex function of $p \geqslant 0$.
8. Using the type of argument used immediately following (18), show that the saddlepoint for $L^*(w, y)$ satisfies the conditions for equilibrium *without* assuming differentiability. (Recall footnote 3.)
9. Apply theorem (A4) directly to problem (11) of the text to obtain the first-order conditions for a solution. Show that these conditions yield the competitive equilibrium conditions.

References

Debreu, G. (1959) *Theory of Value* (New York: John Wiley).

Diewert, W.E. and A.D. Woodland (1977) "Frank Knight's theorem in linear programming revisited", *Econometrica* 45-2, March, 375–398.

Dixit, A.K. and V. Norman (1980) *Theory of International Trade* (J. Nisbet/Cambridge University Press).

Hadley, G. (1962) *Linear Programming* (Reading, Mass.: Addison-Wesley).

Intriligator, M.D. (1971) *Mathematical Optimization and Economic Theory* (Englewood Cliffs, N.J.: Prentice-Hall).

Jones, R.W. (1965) "The structure of simple general equilibrium models", *Journal of Political Economy* 73-6, December, 557–572.

Kemp, M.C. (1969) *The Pure Theory of International Trade and Investment* (Englewood Cliffs, N.J.: Prentice-Hall).

Kuhn, H.W. and A.W. Tucker (1956) "Nonlinear programming", in: Neyman, J. (ed.), *Proceedings of the Second Berkeley Symposium on Mathematical Statistics and Probability*, vol. 5 (Berkeley; University of California Press), pp. 481–492.

Lerner, A.P. (1952) "Factor prices and international trade", *Economica* 19, 1–15.

Mangasarian, O.L. (1959) *Nonlinear Programming* (New York: McGraw-Hill).

Samuelson, P.A. (1953) "Prices of factors and goods in general equilibrium", *Review of Economic Studies* 21-1, 1–20.

Samuelson, P.A. (1967) "Summary on factor-price equalization", *International Economic Review* 8-3, October, 286–295.

Smith, A. (1776) *An Inquiry into the Nature and Causes of the Wealth of Nations*; reprinted in 1937: E. Cannon (ed.) (New York: Random House).

Takayama, A. (1972) *International Trade* (Holt, Rinehart and Winston).

Uzawa, H. (1958) "The Kuhn–Tucker theorem in concave programming", in: K.J. Arrow, L. Hurwicz and H. Uzawa (eds.), *Studies in Linear and Nonlinear Programming* (Stanford: Stanford University Press), pp. 32–37.

Van Slyke, R.M. (1968) "Mathematical programming and optimal control theory", *Operations Research Center Report* 68-21, University of California at Berkeley, July.

Woodland, A.D. (1977) "A dual approach to equilibrium in the production sector in international trade theory", *Canadian Journal of Economics* 10-1, February, 50–68.

CHAPTER 4

COMPARATIVE STATICS OF THE PRODUCTION SECTOR

4.1. Introduction

The previous chapter was devoted to the formulation of a competitive model of the production sector of an economy which uses primary factors or resources to produce final goods using a constant-return-to-scale, non-joint production technology. The purpose of the present chapter is to examine the effects of changes in the exogenous variables — prices of output and quantities of resources — upon the endogenous variables, namely the industry outputs and the factor prices. This will involve a discussion of several famous theorems which are central to the theory of international trade. These include the factor price equalization, the Stolper–Samuelson, and the Rybczynski theorems.

The model is formulated in terms of the industry cost functions as

$$c^j(w) - p_j \geqslant 0 \leqslant y_j, \qquad j = 1, ..., M, \tag{1}$$

$$\sum_{j=1}^{M} c_{ij}(w) y_j - v_i \leqslant 0 \leqslant w_i, \quad i = 1, ..., N, \tag{2}$$

where the product price vector $p = (p_1, ..., p_M)$ and the resource endowment vector $v = (v_1, ..., v_N)$ are exogenous, and the output vector $y = (y_1, ..., y_M)$ and factor price vector $w = (w_1, ..., w_N)$ are endogenous. The solutions for y and w, given p and v, may be written as

$$y_j = y_j(p, v), \quad j = 1, ..., M,$$

$$w_i = w_i(p, v), \quad i = 1, ..., N, \tag{3}$$

or in vector notation as:

$$y = y(p, v),$$

$$w = w(p, v),$$

(3′)

where $y(p, v)$ and $w(p, v)$ are vector valued functions. The function $y_j(p, v)$ is referred to as the supply function for good j while $w_i(p, v)$ is the factor price function for resource i. From a mathematical viewpoint the purpose of this chapter is to discuss the properties of these functions.[1] First, we ask how the output levels and factor prices respond to uniform percentage changes in product prices and endowments. Then attention is focused upon the effects of non-proportional changes in the factor endowments upon factor prices, giving rise to the factor price equalization theorem. The effects upon output supplies are then examined and the Rybczynski theorem is discussed. The next two sections are devoted to an examination of the effects of changes in product prices upon factor prices, yielding the Stolper–Samuelson theorem, and upon industry outputs, respectively. Finally, a general treatment of the comparative statics of the model is presented, which shows the importance of the relationship between the number of produced products and the number of factors.

4.2. Scale effects

The first question to be asked is how y and w respond to a proportional increase or decrease in the prices of all goods. Economic intuition suggests that the "real variables" such as the industry outputs and "real incomes" (w_i/p_j) will not be affected but the (nominal) factor prices will increase or decrease by the same proportion. That is,

$$y_j(\lambda p, v) = y_j(p, v), \qquad j = 1, ..., M,$$

$$w_i(\lambda p, v) = \lambda w_i(p, v), \qquad i = 1, ..., N,$$

(4)

for all $\lambda > 0$. In other words, the output supply functions are homogeneous of degree zero in prices, while the factor price functions are homogeneous of degree one. Below it is shown that (4) holds for all $\lambda > 0$; hence, we may choose $\lambda = 1/p_1$

---

[1]   To be technically correct, they should be referred to as correspondences rather than functions since they may be set valued. For example, it has been shown in the previous chapter that when there are more goods than factors, and in particular more goods which are profitable to produce than fully employed factors, then there is a set of solutions for the output vector.

if $p_1 > 0$ and so $y_j(p/p_1, v) = y_j(1, p_2/p_1, ..., p_M/p_1, v)$, indicating that output supplies depend upon relative and not absolute prices.

To prove (4) simply replace p and w in (1) and (2) by λp and λw, leaving y and v unchanged, and show that these equilibrium conditions continue to hold. For example, since $c^j(w)$ is linearly homogeneous in w it follows that $c^j(\lambda w) - \lambda p_j = \lambda c^j(w) - \lambda p_j = \lambda[c^j(w) - p_j]$ which has the same sign as $c^j(w) - p_j$. Thus, if output j was produced under p, then it will continue to be produced when the price vector is λp. Since the input demand functions per unit of output are homogeneous of degree zero $c_{ij}(\lambda w) = c_{ij}(w)$, meaning factor demands depend only upon relative factor prices, condition (2) will hold replacing w by λw.

Now consider what happens to the equilibrium if endowments are increased or decreased proportionately. It is demonstrated below that

$$y_j(p, \lambda v) = \lambda y_j(p, v), \quad j = 1, ..., M,$$

$$w_i(p, \lambda v) = w_i(p, v), \quad i = 1, ..., N,$$

(5)

for all $\lambda > 0$. This means that all outputs increase or decrease by the same proportion so that the output supply functions are homogeneous of degree one in v. Also, the factor prices are not affected so the factor price functions are homogeneous of degree zero in v.

To prove this simply replace v and y in (1) and (2) by λv and λy leaving w unchanged and, as in preceding case, show that the equilibrium conditions continue to hold. Because of the CRS assumption each industry is able to produce λy_j output with $c_{ij}(w) \lambda y_j$ input of factor i, so total demand for factor i is now λ times what it was before the endowment change. Thus, excess supplies are now λ times their previous levels and so those factors with positive prices continue to have zero excess supplies while others continue to have positive excess supplies. Condition (1) continues to hold when y_j is replaced by λy_j. Thus, it has been shown that the new solution to (1) and (2) is provided by w and λy.

Figure 4.1 illustrates the effect of a proportionate increase in factor endowments. With the CRS assumption, the production possibility set expands proportionately by the factor λ along every ray through the origin. Thus, the new set is $Y(\lambda v^0) = \lambda Y(v^0)$. Along the ray OR the slopes of the two production possibility frontiers are the same, so the point $y^1 = \lambda y^0$ is the solution for the output vector when the endowment vector is $v^1 = \lambda v^0$.

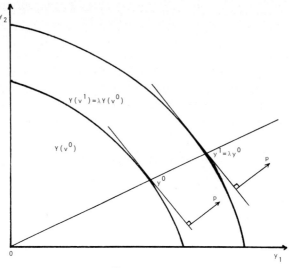

Figure 4.1

4.3.   Effect of a change in endowments upon factor prices

A Swedish economist, Heckscher, raised a very intriguing question about the relationship between factor endowments and factor prices, which was studied by
one of his students Ohlin and more recently by Samuelson, McKenzie and many
others. The question is: If two or more nations, trading with each other with
zero transport costs and no tariffs or other impediments to trade, face the same
product prices in the world market, will they also have the same prices for the
factors of production? If the answer is "Yes", then we have a rather remarkable
result. It would mean that, despite vast differences in resource endowments such
as labour, land, capital and natural resources like oil and minerals, the nominal
and real returns to each resource would be the same in all nations as long as goods
were freely traded at the same prices. Thus, trade would indeed be a substitute
for factor mobility. The factors would be indirectly mobile via the products they
helped to produce. Thus, under these conditions it would not matter that Japan
had little land and a large population and that Canada had the reverse: land rents
and wage rates would be the same in both nations and standards of living would
be equal.

   But is the answer "Yes"? It is certainly not true unless some special assumptions are invoked. Even within the context of our model it is evident that there

is no reason for factor price equalization if the cost functions are different from one nation to another (i.e. they have different technologies) or if each nation produces a different selection of goods. As will be seen below, even more stringent conditions have to be met to attain factor price equalization.

A feel for the development of the literature surrounding the factor price equalization theorem can be obtained by examining the equilibrium conditions (1) and (2). Notice that v does not appear directly in (1). Now suppose that M^* $\geqslant N$ products are positively produced so that price equals unit cost for these products. That is,

$$c^j(w_1, ..., w_N) = p_j, \quad j = 1, ..., M^* \geqslant N, \tag{6}$$

where it has been assumed, without loss of generality, that the goods are labelled so that the first $M^* \leqslant M$ are produced. Then these cost equations should be enough to determine w without giving any consideration to v. Thus, so the argument might go, those nations which produce these M^* products at the same prices using the same technology (i.e. cost functions) will have the same factor prices despite possible differences in their endowment vectors.

There are two difficulties with this argument. The first is that the equation set (6) may not have a unique solution for the factor price vector w, in which case factor price equalization may not occur. Recognition of this possibility has led many economists to seek conditions on the cost function which ensure that (6) has only one solution, i.e. conditions under which the cost functions are globally univalent or invertible. The second difficulty is that, while the endowment vector is not explicitly mentioned in the argument, it is very important in determining the goods which are produced. Moreover, if more than one solution exists for (6), then the endowment vector is important in determining which of the several possible solutions will occur for a nation. Thus endowments cannot be ignored.

4.3.1. Diversification cones and factor price equalization

If unit cost equals price for $M^* \geqslant N$ goods and exceeds price for the remaining $M - M^*$ goods, then (6) may be solved for w. As indicated above there may exist multiple solutions for w. If w^0 is a solution to (6), under what conditions will it be an equilibrium factor price vector for the production sector? Clearly, the profit-maximization conditions are satisfied so it remains to see if there exist output levels $y_1^0, y_2^0, ..., y_{M^*}^0 \geqslant 0, y_{M^*+1}^0 = ... = y_M^0 = 0$ such that the factor market equilibrium conditions (2) are satisfied. To simplify the discussion, suppose that $w^0 > 0$, in which case equilibrium in the factor market requires that all factors be fully employed. The optimal input vectors $c_w^1(w^0), c_w^2(w^0), ..., c_w^{M*}(w^0)$ form a cone defined as [2]

$$K(w^0, p) \equiv \left\{ u = (u_1, ..., u_N): \sum_{j=1}^{M*} c_w^j(w^0) y_j = u, (y_1, ..., y_{M*}) \geqslant 0 \right\}. \quad (7)$$

This is the set of factor endowments which can be fully used by industries $1, 2,$ $..., M*$ and is called a *diversification cone*. If v is in the *interior* of $K(w^0, p)$, then by definition there exist output levels $y_1^0, ..., y_{M*}^0 > 0$ such that $\sum_{j=1}^{M*} c_w^j(w^0) y_j^0 = v$ which means that the factor market clears. Thus, w^0 is an equilibrium factor price vector such that all $M*$ industries produce. In other words, if $v \in$ interior $K(w^0, p)$, then the production sector is "diversified" in equilibrium.

If v is on the boundary of $K(w^0, p)$, then less than $M*$ output levels will be positive. Nevertheless, w^0 is an equilibrium factor price vector, although we cannot be sure that it is the only one. It is easy to construct an example (see problem set) where $w^1 \neq w^0$ and $K(w^1, p)$ and $K(w^0, p)$ have boundaries which are common along a ray through the origin. Thus, if v is on this ray, i.e. on the boundary of both diversification cones, then w^0 and w^1 are both equilibrium factor price vectors. Thus, knowledge that two endowments are elements of a particular diversification cone is not sufficient to be able to say that both nations will have the same factor price vector. All that can be said is that both can have the same factor price vector.

The condition under which two nations will have the same factor price vector, given that they face the same product prices and have the same cost functions, is now clear. They will have the same factor price vector if their endowment vectors lie in the interior of the same cone of diversification. This result is summarized as a theorem:

> **Factor price equalization theorem.** If two or more nations have the same cost functions (technology), face the same product prices, produce the same $M*$ products, and have their endowment vectors in the interior of the same cone of diversification, then each nation will have the same factor price vector. (8)

Figures 4.2 and 4.3 illustrate the discussion for the case where $M = M* = N = 2$. Fig. 4.2 depicts the iso-cost curves for the two industries in the factor price space.

---

[2]   Recall that $c_w^j(w^0)$ is the N-dimensional vector of partial derivatives of the jth cost function with respect to the factor prices, evaluated at w^0. For simplicity we assume that the cost functions are differentiable. The argument could be adjusted to accommodate non-differentiability.

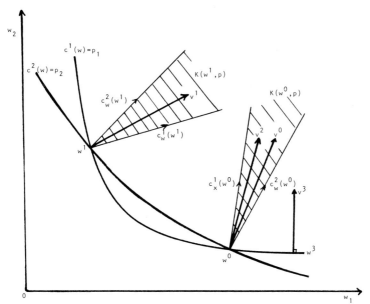

Figure 4.2

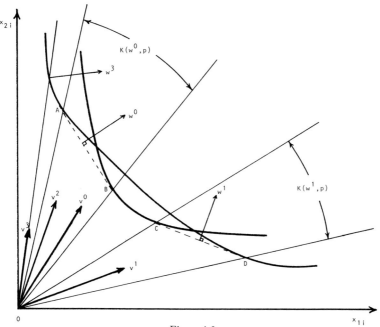

Figure 4.3

They cross twice, indicating that there are two solutions, w^0 and w^1, to the cost equations (6). The optimal input vectors are drawn perpendicular to the iso-cost curves at w^0 and w^1, because of Shephard's lemma, and form the diversification cones $K(w^0, p)$ and $K(w^1, p)$. Knowledge that a nation produces both goods is not enough to determine which factor price vector is the equilibrium factor price vector. If $v^0 \in$ interior $K(w^0, p)$, then w^0 prevails. If another nation has its endowment vector $v^1 \in$ interior $K(w^1, p)$, then it will have w^1 as its factor price vector, not w^0. However, if another nation has endowment v^2 in cone $K(w^0, p)$ it will have the same factor price vector, w^0, as the first nation. If the endowment vector is in neither cone, then both products cannot be produced and the factor price vector is neither w^0 nor w^1. For example, v^3 is in neither cone and it is only consistent with w^3 as the equilibrium factor price vector and the production of good 1 alone. Fig. 4.3 illustrates the same situation as fig. 4.2 but in the factor quantity space. The \$1 cost lines corresponding to w^0 and w^1 are drawn as tangents AB and CD to the unit value isoquants for the two products. The diversification cones are AOB and COD which are the cones $K(w^0, p)$ and $K(w^1, p)$, respectively, in fig. 4.2. The endowment vectors $v^0 - v^3$ are also depicted. It is evident that both figures contain the same information.

4.3.2. Remarks on the factor price equalization theorem

Several features of the factor-price equalization (FPE) theorem are worthy of note. First, it is important to recognize that the assumptions of the theorem imply a rather special relationship between the product prices, technology and the endowments. This is because the production of the same M^* products in each nation is assumed, and because it is required that the endowment vectors lie in the same diversification cone. Since the selection of products which are produced (the pattern of production) is endogenous to the model of the production sector, the FPE theorem may be regarded as a conditional theorem, i.e. conditional upon a certain degree of diversification. This begs the question of the conditions required to ensure equal diversification in several nations, and suggests that the FPE problem should be looked at in a general equilibrium setting in which product prices are endogenous.[3] Secondly, early statements of the theorem did not mention factor endowments or say the conclusion held despite differences in factor endowments. For example, Samuelson (1953–54, pp. 5–6) states that:

---

[3]   For an analysis of the FPE problem within a general equilibrium setting see Dixit and Norman (1980, pp. 110–125).

... without mentioning factor endowments of the country or the scale of production of any good, we have uniquely determined its factor prices from knowledge of its commodity prices alone.

Although endowments may not have been mentioned, they should have been since they determine whether diversification occurs and, if more than one cone exists, they determine which factor price vector will occur.

Thirdly, it should be recognized that while most discussions in the literature have concentrated upon the case where $M^* = N$, the statement in theorem (8) imposes no restrictions on the number of products produced, M^*. When $M^* \geqslant N$ it is evident from (6) that the cost equations are sufficient in number to determine the vector of factor prices w, which has $N \leqslant M^*$ elements. The cone $K(w^0, p)$ has an interior in N-space if the M^* input vectors are linearly independent, so variations of v within such a cone clearly yield factor price equalization.[4] The production of $M^* \geqslant N$ goods is what is usually meant by "diversification". However, the FPE theorem is valid, as stated, for any M^*, including the case where $M^* < N$. In this case the cost equations (6) are insufficient in number to determine w, so the factor market equilibrium conditions are explicitly needed. Thus, in general, w will depend upon v.

However, this does not necessarily mean that two nations with different endowment vectors will have different factor price vectors. Let $w^0 > 0$ be the equilibrium price vector for (p, v^0) with $M^* < N$ goods produced. Then for $K(w^0, p)$ defined in (7), it is still true that if $v \in K(w^0, p)$, then w^0 will be the equilibrium factor price vector. The only difference is that $K(w^0, p)$ is a cone constructed from M^* optimal input vectors in an N-dimensional space, where $M^* < N$. Thus, the cone is degenerate. For example, if $N = 3$ and $M^* = 2$, then the cone is on a plane in 3-space, while if $M^* = 1$ it is a ray. The smaller is M^* relative to N the "more degenerate" is the cone and the lower is the chance that an endowment vector will be in it.[5]

Fourthly, it is important that the same M^* products be produced by the nations in question if factor price equalization is to hold. Fig. 4.4 illustrates the case $M = 3$, $N = 2$ in which $M^* = 2$ goods are produced, but the pair of goods produced depends upon the endowment vector. It is clear from a comparison of

---

[4]   The vectors $c_w^j(w^0)$, $j = 1, ..., M^*$, are linearly independent if there do not exist scalars $\lambda_1, ..., \lambda_{M^*}$, not all zero, such that $\Sigma_{j=1}^{M^*} \lambda_j c_w^j(w^0) = 0$. If they are independent they form a basis for N-space, in that any vector in N-space can be expressed as a linear combination of the vectors in the basis. The basis is said to span the N-space. Evidently, to do this they must form a cone with an interior. For further details see Hadley (1961, pp. 39–41).

[5]   That is to say, if v has a continuous probability distribution over $v \geqslant 0$, then the event that $v \in K(w^0, p)$ has density but does not have a positive probability when $M^* < N$. In such a case we say that this event has probability of measure zero.

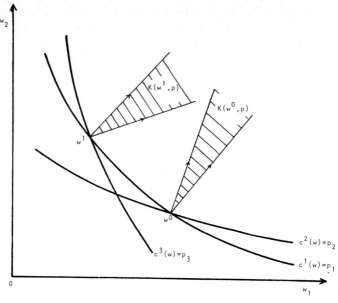

Figure 4.4

figs. 4.2 and 4.4 that there is no fundamental difference between having two solutions, w^0 and w^1, to the cost equations when there are more goods than factors and when they are equal in number.

4.3.3. Global univalence of cost functions

The question of whether eqs. (6) have a unique solution for w when $M^* = N$ led to considerable debate in what became known as the factor price equalization controversy. Whether or not these equations can be locally inverted to yield a unique solution for w is determined by the implicit function theorem.[6] This controversy was concerned with the conditions required to ensure that the cost equations (6) have a unique solution for w, given the product price vector p. If there exists just one solution for w, there is just one cone of diversification so that if two nations are observed to produce the same M^* products their endowment vectors must be in the same diversification cone and, hence, they must have the same

---

[6] See, for example, Chiang (1967, p. 211), or Apostol (1957, p. 147) for a discussion of the implicit function theorem.

factor price vector. The question of whether the solution is unique, i.e. whether the cost functions are univalent or invertible, can be asked in a local or global context. In the present context and with $M^* = N$ this theorem states that a solution w^0 to the cost equations (6) is unique in a small neighbourhood of w^0 if the Jacobian $J_c(w^0)$ does not vanish, i.e. $J_c(w^0) \neq 0$, where

$$J_c(w^0) \equiv |A(w^0)|, \tag{9}$$

and $A(w^0) \equiv [c_w^1(w^0), ..., c_w^N(w^0)].$[7] When $M^* = N = 2$, this condition is that $|A(w^0)| = a_{11} a_{22} - a_{12} a_{21} \neq 0$, where $a_{ij} \equiv c_{ij}(w^0)$ is the optimal input of i per unit output of j. If $a_{11}, a_{12} \neq 0$, this may be expressed as $|A(w^0)| = a_{11} a_{12}(a_{22}/a_{12} - a_{21}/a_{11}) = a_{11} a_{12}(k_2 - k_1) \neq 0$, where $k_j \equiv a_{2j}/a_{1j}$ is the factor ratio or intensity in industry j. Hence, the condition $|A(w^0)| \neq 0$ means that factor ratios or intensities must be different in the two industries.

The question of whether the cost functions are globally (i.e. on $w \geq 0$) invertible is answered by a theorem due to Gale and Nikaido (1965). In the present context the sufficient (but not necessary) conditions for global invertibility are that $|A(w)| > 0$ and all other principal submatrices of $A(w)$ have non-negative determinants for all $w > 0$. When $M^* = N = 2$, these conditions are that $|A(w)| = a_{11} a_{22} - a_{12} a_{21} > 0$ and $a_{11}, a_{22} \geq 0$, where $a_{ij} \equiv c_{ij}(w)$, which are the same as those for local invertibility since $a_{ii} \geq 0$ anyhow, and since the columns of A can always be ordered to obtain a positive determinant if the determinant is non-zero. When the elements of A are positive, the condition that $k_2(w) > k_1(w)$, for all $w > 0$, or $k_1(w) > k_2(w)$, for all $w > 0$, where $k_j(w) = c_{2j}(w)/c_{1j}(w)$, is called the "Samuelson intensity condition".

To illustrate the possibility of factor intensity reversals it is instructive to consider an example involving the popular constant elasticity of substitution (CES) cost function.

Example. Suppose the unit cost function for industry j is

$$c^j(w) = [\alpha_{1j} w_1^{-\beta_j} + \alpha_{2j} w_2^{-\beta_j}]^{-1/\beta_j}, \quad \alpha_{1j}, \alpha_{2j} \geq 0, \quad 1 + \beta_j > 0,$$

where there are $N = 2$ factors. Using Shephard's lemma the optimal input–output coefficients are obtained by differentiating $c^j(w)$ with respect to w to get:

$$c_{ij}(w) = \alpha_{ij}[w_i/c^j(w)]^{-(1+\beta_j)}.$$

---

[7] When $M^* > N$ uniqueness occurs if for some selection of N cost equations the Jacobian does not vanish.

The factor ratios or intensities are

$$k_j(w) \equiv c_{2j}(w)/c_{1j}(w) = (\alpha_{2j}/\alpha_{1j})\,(w_1/w_2)^{1+\beta_j},$$

which in logarithmic form are

$$\ln k_j(w) = \ln(\alpha_{2j}/\alpha_{1j}) + (1+\beta_j)\ln(w_1/w_2).$$

This relationship is linear in natural logs with slope given by $1+\beta_j$. Fig. 4.5 illustrates this relationship for $j=1,2$ in which $\beta_2 > \beta_1$. The two lines intersect at $\ln w^*$ so for $w_1/w_2 > w^*$ it follows that $k_2 > k_1$, while for $w_1/w_2 < w^*$ the reverse inequality, $k_2 < k_1$, holds. In other words, there is a factor intensity reversal at $w_1/w_2 = w^*$.

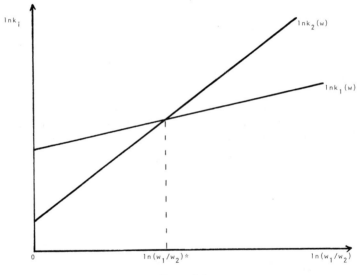

Figure 4.5

4.3.4. Summary

Let us summarize the discussion. It has been shown that if the production sector has an equilibrium (w^0, y^0) such that M^* goods are produced, then a change in the endowment vector will not alter factor prices as long as the new factor price vector remains in the same cone of diversification, $K(w^0, p)$. When $M^* < N$, this may require very special changes in v since the cone is degenerate. However, when $M^* \geqslant N$ and the matrix of input–output coefficients $A(w) \equiv [c_w^1(w),$ ..., $c_w^{M^*}(w)]$ has rank N, the cone is not degenerate. In this case if $v \in$ interior $K(w^0, p)$, it follows that sufficiently small changes in v in any direction will leave factor prices unaltered. This means that if the factor price functions $w_i(p, v)$ are differentiable, then

$$\partial w_i(p, v)/\partial v_j = 0, \quad i, j = 1, ..., N, \quad \text{if } v \in \text{interior } K(w^0, p). \tag{10}$$

In general, it seems intuitive that an increase in the endowment of a factor will not raise its price and will usually lower it. This is indeed true and falls out of a more general comparative static result as a special case. Recall from the previous chapter that the equilibrium w can be found as the solution to a minimization problem. For a given p let w^0 and w^1 be the equilibrium factor price vectors when the endowment vector is v^0 and v^1, respectively. Then $w^0 v^0 \leqslant w^1 v^1$ and $w^1 v^1 \leqslant w^0 v^1$ since w^0 minimizes wv^0 on the set $W(p)$, and w^1 minimizes wv^1 on the same set. Subtracting these inequalities yields:

$$(w^1 - w^0)(v^1 - v^0) \leqslant 0 \quad \text{or} \quad \Delta w \Delta v \leqslant 0, \tag{11}$$

where Δ denotes "change in", which indicates the general restrictions on changes in w due to a change in v. It applies to *all* changes, not just those within a cone of diversification. For example, if only the ith elements of v^0 and v^1 differ (11) states that $\Delta w_i \Delta v_i \leqslant 0$ or that w_i cannot go up when the endowment of factor i increases.

4.4. Effect of a change in endowments upon outputs

To examine the effect of changes in factor endowments upon industry outputs it is convenient to consider separately three cases: $M^* > N, M^* = N,$ and $M^* < N$. In the first case more goods are produced than there are factors and consequently the output levels are indeterminate. This can be seen as follows. If the equation system

$$\sum_{j=1}^{M^*} c_w^j(w) y_j = v \quad (y_1, ..., y_{M^*}) \geqslant 0, \tag{12}$$

has a solution $(y_1, ..., y_{M^*}) > 0$ and the $N \times M^*$ matrix $A \equiv [c_w^1(w), ..., c_w^{M^*}(w)]$ has rank N, then it is always possible to rewrite (12) as

$$\sum_{j=1}^{N} c_w^j(w) y_j = v - \sum_{j=N+1}^{M*} c_w^j(w) y_j, \tag{12'}$$

and solve for $y_1, ..., y_N$ in terms of v and $y_{N+1}, ..., y_{M*}$. The first N goods can always be chosen such that $c_w^1(w), ..., c_w^N(w)$ form a cone K which spans v, because of the rank condition. Thus, if $y_{M*+1}, ..., y_N = 0$ there is a positive solution for $y_1, ..., y_{M*}$ when $v > 0$. By making the output of the last $M* - N$ goods positive but sufficiently small, the vector of factor quantities left over for the first N industries (the right-hand side of (12')) will remain in the cone K so there will be a positive solution for the outputs of the first N goods. Since the choice of $y_{N+1}, ..., y_{M*}$ is not uniquely given, the solution for outputs is non-unique. Because the solution for outputs is indeterminate there is little point in attempting to establish the effect of a change in v upon the output levels.[8] The case where $M* < N$ is the most complicated of the three cases and will be dealt with in section 4.7 below.

Consider the case where $M* = N$. If the N factors are fully employed at the equilibrium (w^0, y^0), then the factor market equilibrium conditions may be written as:

$$A(w^0) y_*^0 = v^0, \tag{13}$$

where $y_*^0 \equiv (y_1^0, ..., y_{M*}^0) > 0$ and v^0 is the initial endowment vector. If v changes to v^1 such that it remains in the interior of the cone of diversification $K(w^0, p)$, then the same $M* = N$ products will continue to be produced and, by the FPE theorem, the factor price vector will remain at w^0. Thus, the new output vector y_*^1 will satisfy

$$A(w^0) y_*^1 = v^1. \tag{14}$$

Subtracting (13) from (14) yields:

$$A(w^0)(y_*^1 - y_*^0) = v^1 - v^0, \tag{15}$$

so that if $A(w^0)$ has full rank N, this set of N linear equations in N unknowns may be solved as

$$\Delta y_* \equiv y_*^1 - y_*^0 = A(w^0)^{-1} \Delta v, \tag{16}$$

---

[8]   The above argument shows that the solutions are set valued, i.e. there is a set of solutions with more than a single element. We could, of course, attempt to establish the effect of a change in v upon the solution sets, but this approach is not pursued.

where $\Delta v \equiv v^1 - v^0$. Eq. (16) provides a formula for calculating the effect of a change in v upon industry outputs. An alternative formula may be expressed in terms of percentage changes in outputs and endowments. For each factor i eq. (15) states that

$$\sum_{j=1}^{M^*} a_{ij}(w^0)\,\Delta y_j = \Delta v_i. \tag{16'}$$

Multiplying and dividing each term in the sum of the left-hand side of (16') by y_j^0 and dividing both sides by v_i^0 for each i yields:

$$\sum_{j=1}^{M^*} \lambda_{ij}\,\hat{y}_j = \hat{v}_i, \qquad i = 1, ..., N, \tag{17}$$

where $\lambda_{ij} \equiv a_{ij}(w^0)\, y_j^0 / v_i^0$ is the percentage of factor i employed in industry j before the endowment change and the cavet ($\hat{\ }$) denotes "percentage change", i.e. $\hat{y}_j = (y_j^1 - y_j^0)/y_j^0$. Expressing (17) in matrix notation as $\lambda \hat{y}_* = \hat{v}$, the solution to this system of equations may be written as

$$\hat{y}_* = \lambda^{-1}\,\hat{v}, \tag{18}$$

where $\lambda = [\lambda_{ij}]$ is the matrix of industry shares. Given the matrix λ (18) may be used to compute elasticities of outputs with respect to endowment changes, these elasticities being the elements of λ^{-1}.

4.4.1. General results

An examination of (17) provides some general results regarding the effect of endowment changes upon industry outputs. To obtain the desired results, the very weak assumption that A, hence λ, is a semi-positive matrix is made. The matrix λ is said to be a semi-positive matrix if every row and every column contain at least one positive element. This means that each industry uses at least one factor input (this follows from the assumptions on the production functions) and that each factor is used by at least one industry. With this assumption at hand, let us now consider the effects of a change in the factor endowment such that the new endowment vector is in the same cone of diversification. Suppose that the ith endowment changes by percentage $\hat{v}_i > 0$, while all other endowments remain unchanged. Then since λ is semi-positive, at least one output must rise to use the additional quantity of factor i.

If the first L industries expand then

$$\sum_{\ell=1}^{L} \lambda_{h\ell}\,\hat{y}_\ell = \hat{v}_h - \sum_{\ell=L+1}^{M^*} \lambda_{h\ell}\,\hat{y}_\ell \geq \hat{v}_h, \qquad h = 1, ..., N, \tag{17'}$$

where the left-hand side is the percentage increase in the use of factor h by all expanding industries, $\hat{v}_h$ is the exogenous percentage change in the endowment of factor h ($= 0$ for $h \neq i$), and $-\Sigma_{\varrho=L+1}^{M^*} \lambda_{h\varrho} \, \hat{y}_\varrho$ is the amount of factor h released by the "contraction" of industries $L+1$, ..., M^*. If the expanding industries use only factor i then the LHS of $(17')$ is zero for all $h \neq i$ and so no industry will contract. If, however, the expanding industries use at least one other factor the LHS of $(17')$ will be positive for some h and hence $(17')$ indicates that some industry, say j, must contract. In either case, for $h = i$ $(17')$ indicates that at least one industry, say k, must expand by a percentage at least as great as $\hat{v}_i$ since the $\lambda_{i\varrho}$ shares cannot exceed unity. Thus, it has been shown that if the endowment of factor i increases, then there exist industries j and k such that

$$\hat{y}_k \geqslant \hat{v}_i > 0 \geqslant \hat{y}_j. \tag{19}$$

This is a general result relying upon the fact that λ is semi-positive. It indicates that at least one industry, k, will expand at least as much as the endowment of factor i in percentage terms. It is possible to strengthen this result by imposing more conditions on λ (or A). It has already been shown that one industry, j, will contract if the expanding industries use factors in addition to i. If the expanding industry k is not the only user of factor i, then examination of $(17')$ shows that at least one industry, k, must have $\hat{y}_k > \hat{v}_i$, since the shares $\lambda_{i\varrho}$ are strictly less than unity. Thus, under these strengthened conditions, it follows that if the endowment of factor i increases, there exist industries j and k such that

$$\hat{y}_k > \hat{v}_i > 0 > \hat{y}_j. \tag{19'}$$

A sufficient condition for these conditions to hold is that every row and column of λ contain at least two positive elements, i.e. that each industry uses at least two factors and each factor be used by at least two industries. If λ (or A) satisfies these conditions they will be said to be strictly semi-positive.[9]

---

[9] Actually, if λ is strictly semi-positive (19) follows from an even simpler argument. Since $\Sigma_{j=1}^{M} \lambda_{hj} \hat{y}_j = \hat{v}_h$, where each row of λ is strictly semi-positive and sums to unity, it follows that $\hat{v}_h$ is a strictly convex combination (weighted average) of $\hat{y}_1$, ..., $\hat{y}_M$, which therefore span $\hat{v}_h$. That is, unless $\hat{y}_1 = ... = \hat{y}_M = \hat{v}_h$ we can always find j and k, depending upon h, such that $\hat{y}_k > \hat{v}_h > \hat{y}_j$. The situation $\hat{y}_1 = ... = \hat{y}_M = \hat{v}_h$ for all h is ruled out since $\hat{v}_i > 0$ and $\hat{v}_h = 0$ for $h \neq i$ by assumption. When $h = i$, therefore, there is a k such that $\hat{y}_k > \hat{v}_i > 0$. For each $h \neq i$ there is a j, depending upon h, such that $0 = \hat{v}_h > \hat{y}_j$. Thus (19) follows.

4.4.2. *Special results*

While (19) is a general result, it does not indicate which industries will expand and which will contract. This depends upon the nature of A^{-1} or λ^{-1}. When $M^* = N = 2$, a very clear result is obtained by examining the solution (18) which is

$$
\begin{bmatrix} \hat{y}_1 \\ \hat{y}_2 \end{bmatrix} = \frac{1}{|\lambda|} \begin{bmatrix} \lambda_{22} & -\lambda_{12} \\ -\lambda_{21} & \lambda_{11} \end{bmatrix} \begin{bmatrix} \hat{v}_1 \\ \hat{v}_2 \end{bmatrix} , \tag{20}
$$

where $|\lambda| = \lambda_{11}\lambda_{22} - \lambda_{12}\lambda_{21} = |A| y_1^0 y_2^0 / v_1^0 v_2^0$. Since the elements of λ are all $\geqslant 0$, the elements of λ^{-1} have signs which depend upon the sign of $|\lambda|$, which has the same sign as $|A|$. It has already been shown that

$$
|A| = a_{11} a_{22} - a_{12} a_{21} = a_{11} a_{12} (a_{22}/a_{12} - a_{21}/a_{11}), \quad a_{11}, a_{12} > 0. \tag{21}
$$

Industry 2 is said to use factor 2 relatively intensively if its ratio of factor 2 to factor 1 is greater than in industry 1, i.e. if $a_{22}/a_{12} > a_{21}/a_{11}$. Thus, $|A| > 0$ ($|\lambda| > 0$) signifies that industry 2 is relatively factor 2 intensive, while $|A| < 0$ ($|\lambda| < 0$) means that it is relatively factor 1 intensive. Consequently, the signs of the elements of λ^{-1} and A^{-1} depend upon which industry uses factor 2 most intensively. An important result, due originally to Rybczynski (1955), is provided in the following theorem:

Rybczynski's theorem. If $\hat{v}_2 > 0 = \hat{v}_1$, $\lambda > 0$ and $|\lambda| > 0$, then
$$
\hat{y}_2 > \hat{v}_2 > 0 > \hat{y}_1. \tag{22}
$$

In other words, (22) states that if the endowment of a factor increases, then the industry which uses that factor relatively intensively will expand more than proportionately to the increase in endowment, while the other industry will contract.

This result is illustrated in figs. 4.6 and 4.7. In fig. 4.6 the increase in the endowment of factor 2 causes the production possibility frontier to shift out since more of each product can now be produced. The shift outwards is greatest along the y_2-axis since industry 2 uses factor 2 relatively intensively and hence its production is enhanced more than is the production of good 1, so much so that the new production possibility frontier is steeper along every vertical line than the original frontier. Consequently, given the same product prices, GNP is maximized at a higher level of output for good 2 and a lower output level for good 1 in accordance with (22). The straight line passing through points y^0 and y^1 is the locus

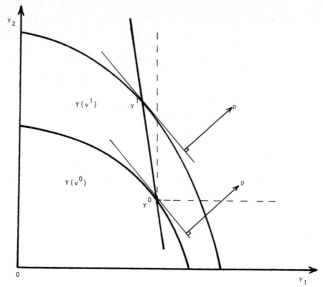

Figure 4.6

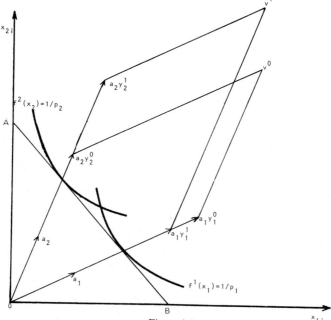

Figure 4.7

of solutions for all values of v_2 such that v remains in the cone of diversification. The proof of this statement is left to the reader as an exercise. In fig. 4.7 AB is the \$1 iso-cost line tangent to the unit value isoquants. The original endowment vector v^0 is in the cone formed by a_1 and a_2 and the points $a_1 y_1^0$ and $a_2 y_2^0$ are obtained by forming the parallelogram on v^0. When v changes to v^1, the new parallelogram requires y_2 to rise and y_1 to fall, again in accordance with (22).

Subtracting $\hat{y}_1$ from $\hat{y}_2$ and recognizing that $\lambda_{i1} + \lambda_{i2} = 1$, we obtain:

$$\hat{y}_2 - \hat{y}_1 = (\hat{v}_2 - \hat{v}_1)/|\lambda|. \tag{23}$$

In the special case where the percentage changes are very small, $\hat{y}_2 - \hat{y}_1 = (y_2/y_1)$ is the percentage change in the ratio of outputs. In this case (23) gives the formula for the percentage change in y_2/y_1 due to a given percentage change in v_2/v_1.

Finally, (20) may be used to obtain Jones' (1965) "magnification effect" which is:

$$\text{if } \hat{v}_2 > \hat{v}_1, \ \lambda > 0 \text{ and } |\lambda| > 0, \text{ then } \hat{y}_2 > \hat{v}_2 > \hat{v}_1 > \hat{y}_1. \tag{24}$$

To prove this, write the solutions (20) explicitly as

$$\hat{y}_1 = (\lambda_{22}\hat{v}_1 - \lambda_{12}\hat{v}_2)/|\lambda| = \hat{v}_1 - \lambda_{12}(\hat{v}_2 - \hat{v}_1)/|\lambda|,$$
$$\hat{y}_2 = (\lambda_{11}\hat{v}_2 - \lambda_{21}\hat{v}_1)/|\lambda| = \hat{v}_2 + \lambda_{21}(\hat{v}_2 - \hat{v}_1)/|\lambda|, \tag{20'}$$

where $|\lambda| = \lambda_{11}\lambda_{22} - \lambda_{12}\lambda_{21} = \lambda_{22} - \lambda_{12} = \lambda_{11} - \lambda_{21}$ (to be proved as an exercise). If $\hat{v}_2 - \hat{v}_1 > 0$, $\lambda_{12} > 0$, $\lambda_{21} > 0$ and $|\lambda| > 0$ it follows directly from (20') that $\hat{y}_2 > \hat{v}_2$ and that $\hat{y}_1 < v_1$, thus proving (24).

The result contained in (24) indicates that the percentage changes in outputs span the percentage changes in factors or, equivalently, that the effects of changes in factor endowments are "magnified". Clearly, the Rybczynski theorem (22) is a special case of this result when $\hat{v}_1 = 0$.

Considerable effort has been expended by many economists into finding conditions on A or λ when $M^* = N > 2$ which would generalize the Rybczynski result. One approach is to find conditions on λ such that λ^{-1} has diagonal elements all greater than unity and off-diagonal elements all less than zero (strong Rybczynski property). In this case, if the endowment of factor 1 increased, for example, then $\hat{y}_1 > \hat{v}_1$ and $\hat{y}_2, ..., \hat{y}_{M*} < 0$, which is a very strong result. A weaker condition is simply that the diagonal elements of λ^{-1} are greater than unity (weak Rybczynski property). A difficulty with this approach is that the conditions on λ are not easily interpreted. Moreover, it is not clear why one would expect that there should be such a one-to-one connection or relationship between factors and products. Consequently, this approach will not be pursued here.

4.5. Effect of a change in product prices upon factor prices

The relationship between product and factor prices is not only of theoretical interest but it is of considerable interest from policy viewpoints. In general when product prices alter due to changes in foreign market conditions, changes in the home nation's tariff policy, or changes in domestic demand conditions, various industries expand while others contract, altering the demand for factors. This in turn alters factor prices and hence income distribution. Thus, it is of considerable interest to consider the effects of changes in product prices upon the factor prices and hence income distribution. It will be shown that when product prices change, some factors will gain in real income while others will lose and hence become worse off. This raises the question as to whether certain factors of production gain when the prices of certain goods rise and lose when those prices fall. Stolper and Samuelson (1941) showed in a two-product, two-factor model that the factor used intensively in the industry which experienced a product price increase would unambiguously gain in real income, while the other factor would unambiguously lose. Below we establish this result as part of a more general enquiry into the relationship between product and factor prices.

This section considers the case where there are $M^* = N$ goods produced in equilibrium. The case where $M^* < N$ is more complicated and will be dealt with in section 4.7 below. If $M^* > N$, then an arbitrary price change, however small, will cause $M^* - N$ industries to become unprofitable, resulting in just N industries producing. For M^* industries to remain profitable the price change would have to be very special.[10] Once the list of goods that continue to be produced is known, the effect upon factor prices can be obtained as in the $M^* = N$ case.

If $M^* = N$ goods are produced, then the cost equations

$$c^j(w_1, ..., w_N) = p_j, \quad j = 1, ..., M^* = N, \tag{25}$$

have a solution w^0 when $p_* \equiv (p_1, ..., p_{M^*}) = p_*^0$. If there is a sufficiently small change in p_*, the same M^* goods will continue to be produced and so the effect

---

[10]   This can be seen from fig. 3.3 in Chapter 3 for the case where $M^* = 3, N = 2$. If p_1 increases, p_2 and p_3 will have to change in a special way to ensure a new solution for w to all three cost equations.

upon w can be obtained by totally differentiating (25) and solving the resulting linear equations. The total differential of (25) is:

$$\sum_{i=1}^{N} c_{ij}(w^0)\,dw_i = dp_j, \quad j = 1, ..., M^*, \tag{26}$$

which may be written in matrix notation as

$$A^T dw = dp_*, \tag{27}$$

where $A \equiv [c_w^1(w^0), ..., c_w^{M^*}(w^0)]$, A^T is the transpose of A, and dw and dp_* are vectors.[11] It is assumed that A is of full rank N and hence has an inverse. Thus, (27) may be solved as:

$$dw = (A^T)^{-1} dp_*. \tag{28}$$

An alternative expression in terms of percentage changes in prices may be obtained. Multiplying and dividing each term on the LHS of (26) by w_i^0 and dividing both sides by $p_j^0 = c^j(w^0)$ yields:

$$\sum_{i=1}^{N} \theta_{ij}\,\hat{w}_i = \hat{p}_j, \quad j = 1, ..., M^*, \tag{29}$$

where $\theta_{ij} \equiv c_{ij}(w^0)\, w_i^0 / c^j(w^0)$ is the share of factor i in the cost of producing product j and the caret ($\,\hat{}\,$) denotes percentage change. In matrix notation (29) is written as $\theta \hat{w} = \hat{p}_*$ and the solution for $\hat{w}$ is:

$$\hat{w} = \theta^{-1} \hat{p}_*, \tag{30}$$

where $\theta = [\theta_{ji}]$ is the matrix of factor shares.

4.5.1. General results

Some general results regarding the effect of changes in product prices upon factor prices can be obtained by examining (29). It is assumed that A, and hence θ, is a semi-positive matrix so each column and row of θ has a non-zero element.

---

[11] While we have previously not distinguished explicitly between column and row vectors, it now becomes important to do so for the remainder of this chapter. Thus, all vectors will be assumed to be column vectors, and the transpose notation such as x^T will be used to obtain row vectors.

Thus, if $\hat{p}_j > 0$ and all other product prices remain unchanged, at least one factor price must rise to maintain the equality of price and unit cost in industry j. If the first L factor prices rise, then

$$\sum_{\ell=1}^{L} \theta_{\ell h}\, \hat{w}_\ell = \hat{p}_h - \sum_{\ell=L+1}^{N} \theta_{\ell h}\, \hat{w}_\ell \geqslant \hat{p}_h, \qquad h = 1, ..., M^*, \tag{31}$$

where the left-hand side is the percentage increase in the unit cost in industry h caused by the increase in the factor prices, $\hat{p}_h$ is the exogenous increase in the price of product $h (= 0$ for $h \neq j)$, and $-\Sigma_{\ell=L+1}^{N} \theta_{\ell h}\, \hat{w}_\ell$ is the reduction in unit cost caused by the "reduction" in the prices for factors $L+1, ..., N$. If the only constraint is that θ be semi-positive, it can be shown, using the same argument used in the derivation of (19), that there exist factors i and k such that

$$\hat{w}_k \geqslant \hat{p}_j > 0 \geqslant \hat{w}_i. \tag{32}$$

This means that at least one factor k will experience an increase in return which will be at least as great as $\hat{p}_j$ in percentage terms. Thus, this factor cannot lose welfare even if it consumes only good j. In addition factor i cannot gain and will indeed lose welfare if it consumes product j.

   This is a weak result relying only upon the assumption that θ is semi-positive. If one of the factors whose price rises is used by an industry other than j, then (31) indicates that the price of some other factor, say i, must actually fall. Thus, factor i unambiguously loses real income since its income falls, while no product has fallen and one has risen. If product j uses more than one factor the shares $\theta_{\ell j}$ will be strictly less than unity and so (31) indicates that there must be some factor, say k, whose price rises by a greater percentage than $\hat{p}_j$. Thus, under these strengthened conditions it has been shown that, if p_j increases, then there exist factors k and i such that

$$\hat{w}_k > \hat{p}_j > 0 > \hat{w}_i. \tag{32'}$$

This is a general result, a sufficient condition for which is the assumption that each industry uses at least two factors and each factor is used in at least two industries, i.e. that θ (or A) be strictly semi-positive. It indicates that factor k will experience an increase in real income expressed in terms of any good since its money income has increased by a greater percentage than any price. On the other hand, factor i suffers a loss in real income expressed in terms of any good since its money income has gone down. As a result the budget constraint for factor k as a consumer will shift outwards implying that he is better off, while the budget constraint for factor i shifts inward implying that he is worse off. Thus (32) shows that at least one factor will gain and at least one factor will lose in terms of real income or welfare if a product price changes.

4.5.2. Special results

What (32) does not indicate is how to identify the factors that gain and those that lose, and whether there are ambiguous cases. This depends upon the nature of A^{-1} or θ^{-1}. When $M^* = N = 2$, clear-cut results may be obtained by examining the solution (30) which is

$$\begin{bmatrix} \hat{w}_1 \\ \hat{w}_2 \end{bmatrix} = \frac{1}{|\theta|} \begin{bmatrix} \theta_{22} & -\theta_{21} \\ -\theta_{12} & \theta_{11} \end{bmatrix} \begin{bmatrix} \hat{p}_1 \\ \hat{p}_2 \end{bmatrix}, \tag{33}$$

where $|\theta| = \theta_{11}\theta_{22} - \theta_{12}\theta_{21} = |A| w_1^0 w_2^0 / p_1^0 p_2^0$. Since θ is semi-positive the elements of θ^{-1} have signs which depend upon the sign of $|\theta|$, which is the same as the sign of $|A|$. Since $|A| = a_{11} a_{12}(k_2 - k_1)$ when $a_{11}, a_{12} \neq 0$, it is evident that the relative factor intensities determine the signs of the elements of θ^{-1} just as they determined the signs of the elements of λ^{-1} in the previous section. The difference between $\hat{w}_2$ and $\hat{w}_1$ is

$$\hat{w}_2 - \hat{w}_1 = (\hat{p}_2 - \hat{p}_1)/|\theta|, \tag{34}$$

which is obtained from (33) using the fact that $\theta_{1j} + \theta_{2j} = 1$ for $j = 1,2$. This shows that if p_2/p_1 increases, then w_2/w_1 will increase by a greater percentage since $|\theta| < 1$. Finally, (33) may be used to prove the Stolper–Samuelson theorem which is:

Stolper–Samuelson theorem. If $\hat{p}_2 > \hat{p}_1$, $\theta > 0$ and $|\theta| > 0$,
then $\hat{w}_2 > \hat{p}_2 > \hat{p}_1 > \hat{w}_1$.   (35)

To prove this, write the solutions in (33) explicitly as

$$\hat{w}_1 = (\theta_{22} \hat{p}_1 - \theta_{21} \hat{p}_2)/|\theta| = \hat{p}_1 - \theta_{21}(\hat{p}_2 - \hat{p}_1)/|\theta|,$$
$$\hat{w}_2 = (\theta_{11} \hat{p}_2 - \theta_{12} \hat{p}_1)/|\theta| = \hat{p}_2 + \theta_{12}(\hat{p}_2 - \hat{p}_1)/|\theta|, \tag{33'}$$

where $|\theta| = \theta_{11}\theta_{22} - \theta_{12}\theta_{21} = \theta_{22} - \theta_{21} = \theta_{11} - \theta_{12}$ (prove as an exercise). If $\hat{p}_2 > \hat{p}_1$, $\theta_{21} > 0$, $\theta_{12} > 0$, and $|\theta| > 0$, it follows directly from (33') that

$\hat{w}_1 < \hat{p}_1$ and $\hat{w}_2 > \hat{p}_2$, thus proving (35).

In other words, the Stolper–Samuelson theorem states that if there is an increase in the relative price of a good, then the factor used intensively in the production of that good will experience an increase in real income, while the other factor will suffer a loss in real income. The remarkable feature of this result is that the "magnification effect" in (35) makes the effects upon the welfare of the factors unambiguous. This is because the real income of one factor in terms of both products increases, moving its budget constraint outwards and making it better off and the real income of the other factor in terms of both products declines moving its budget constraint inwards thus decreasing its welfare. If the result had been $\hat{p}_2 > \hat{w}_2 > \hat{p}_1$, then it would be necessary to know the utility function for the owner of factor 2 in order to determine whether he is better or worse off as a result of the price change.

The preceding analysis is based upon differential comparative statics involving small changes in product prices. However, the Stolper–Samuelson result can be proved quite simply for large changes in prices using the factor price diagram in fig. 4.8. Here p_2 increases while p_1 remains unchanged and the solution for w changes from w^0 to w^1. Clearly, w_2 has risen while w_1 has fallen. If p_2 increases by $\alpha\%$, then w_i^* is $\alpha\%$ higher than w_i^0 because the cost functions are linearly homogeneous in factor prices. However, $w_2^1 > w_2^*$ so that w_2 must have increased more than $\alpha\%$. In addition, w_1 has fallen. This proves (35) diagrammatically for the case where $\hat{p}_1 = 0$; when $\hat{p}_1 \neq 0$, a similar proof can be constructed.

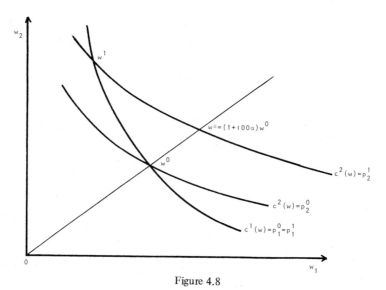

Figure 4.8

A verbal description of the logic behind the Stolper–Samuelson theorem is as follows. If the price of product 2 increases, industry 2 becomes more profitable at the initial factor prices. Industry 2 tries to expand production. However, if industry 2 uses a greater ratio of factor 2 to factor 1 than does industry 1, this attempted expansion of industry 2 will cause a greater excess demand for factor 2 than for factor 1 so the relative price of factor 2 increases.

One way to generalize the Stolper–Samuelson result to $M^* = N > 2$ dimensions is to look for conditions on θ such that θ^{-1} has diagonal elements all greater than unity. This would mean that factor i would gain in real income if product i experienced an increase in its price. This is the "weak Stolper–Samuelson" result. A strengthened version might require, in addition, that the off-diagonal elements of θ all be negative, in which case *every* other factor would lose when a product price increased. While such conditions can be found they are not easily interpreted, so this approach is not pursued further.

4.5.3. Reciprocity conditions

It is interesting to note the similarity between eqs. (16) and (28) due to the occurrence of matrix A in both. Together they imply the Samuelson (1953–54) *reciprocity conditions*:

$$\frac{\partial w_i(p,v)}{\partial p_j} = \frac{\partial y_j(p,v)}{\partial v_i}, \qquad i = 1, ..., N; \qquad j = 1, ..., M^* = N. \tag{36}$$

That is to say, a change in w_i due to a unit increase in p_j is equal to the increase in y_j due to a one unit increase in v_i. Thus, if we observe the effect upon the price of factor i of a change in the price of product j, we can infer the effect of a change in the endowment of factor i upon the output of product j. There is a duality between the price and endowment effects.

The Rybczynski and Stolper–Samuelson theorems are, however, expressed in terms of percentage effects. From (36) it follows that

$$\frac{\partial w_i}{\partial p_j} \frac{p_j}{w_i} = \frac{\partial y_j}{\partial v_i} \frac{v_i}{y_j} \frac{p_j y_j}{w_i v_i}. \tag{37}$$

Because of the term $p_j y_j / w_i v_i$ on the right-hand side of (37), it is *not* necessarily true that if the elasticity of w_i with respect to p_j is greater than one then the elasticity of output j with respect to endowment i is also greater than one.[12] Ethier

---

[12] When $M^* = N = 2$ both elasticities will exceed unity if one does.

(1974) has investigated conditions on the technology such that one does imply the other, i.e. such that λ^{-1} and θ^{-1} both have diagonal elements greater than unity. This provides a stronger one-to-one connection between factors and products than provided by either the Stolper–Samuelson or Rybczynski theorems taken separately.

4.6. Effect of a change in product prices upon outputs

In this section we examine the response of industry outputs around the production possibility frontier to changes in product prices. Some general conditions are obtained by recalling from Chapter 3 that the equilibrium output vector maximizes GNP on the production possibility set. Thus, if y^0 and y^1 are solutions when p^0 and p^1 are the respective product price vectors, then $p^0 y^0 \geqslant p^0 y^1$ and $p^1 y^1 \geqslant p^1 y^0$, since both y^0 and y^1 are feasible for both problems. Subtracting these inequalities yields:

$$(y^1 - y^0)(p^1 - p^0) \geqslant 0, \quad \text{i.e.} \quad \Delta y \, \Delta p \geqslant 0, \tag{38}$$

which indicates general conditions on the response of outputs to prices. Clearly, when p^1 and p^0 differ only in the ith element, (38) implies that $\Delta y_i \, \Delta p_i \geqslant 0$ or that an increase in the price of good i cannot cause its output to fall. Condition (38) is very general and does not take into account the special structure of our final-good model.

If $M^* > N$, then a small change in the prices of produced goods will generally cause $M^* - N$ industries to cease production, leaving N goods produced. Because such a response means that the output supply functions are discontinuous, we restrict attention to cases where $M^* \leqslant N$. The case where $M^* < N$ is more difficult than the $M^* = N$ case so it will be left to a later section.

When $M^* = N$, the solution for dw and $\hat{w}$ in terms of dp_* and $\hat{p}_*$, respectively, are given by (28) and (30), respectively. This change in factor prices in response to the change in product prices alters the optimal input vectors so the output levels for produced goods must alter to restore equilibrium in the factor markets. Assuming that the factors are all fully employed before and after the product price change, the factor market equilibrium conditions are:

$$\sum_{j=1}^{M^*} c_w^j(w) y_j = v. \tag{39}$$

Totally differentiating (39) with respect to w and $y^* = (y_1, ..., y_{M^*})$ yields:

$$\sum_{j=1}^{M^*} c_w^j(w^0)\,\mathrm{d}y_j + \left[\sum_{j=1}^{M^*} c_{ww}^j(w^0)\,y_j^0\right]\mathrm{d}w = 0, \tag{40}$$

where (w^0, y^0) is the initial equilibrium and $c_{ww}^j(w)$ is the $N \times N$ matrix of second derivatives of $c^j(w)$ with respect to the elements of w. Because of Shephard's lemma, $c_{ww}^j(w) = \partial c_w^j(w)/\partial w$ is the matrix of derivatives of input–output coefficients $c_{ij}(w)$ with respect to w. Define

$$S \equiv \sum_{j=1}^{M^*} c_{ww}^j(w^0)\,y_j^0. \tag{41}$$

The ik element of S is the change in demand for factor i by the whole production sector due to a one unit increase in the price of factor k if the vector of industry outputs were to remain constant. Because $c^j(w)$ is a concave and linearly homogeneous function, $c_{ww}^j(w)$ is a negative semi-definite matrix such that $w^{\mathrm{T}} c_{ww}^j(w) = 0$. Furthermore, since the y_j are positive the matrix S is also a negative semi-definite matrix such that $w^{\mathrm{T}} S = 0$.

Equation (40) may be rewritten as

$$A\,\mathrm{d}y_* + S\,\mathrm{d}w = 0, \tag{42}$$

where $A = [c_w^1(w^0), \ldots, c_w^{M^*}(w^0)]$ is the $N \times M^*$ matrix of input–output coefficients. Alternatively, (42) may be expressed in percentage changes in y_* and w as

$$\lambda \hat{y}_* + \epsilon \hat{w} = 0, \tag{43}$$

where ϵ is an $N \times N$ matrix with element $\epsilon_{ik} = s_{ik} w_k^0/v_i$, which is the elasticity of demand for factor i with respect to the price of factor k (see the problem set).[13] The solutions for $\mathrm{d}w$ and $\hat{w}$ have already been calculated as (28) and (30). Substituting these solutions into (42) and (43), respectively, and solving yields:

$$\mathrm{d}y_* = -A^{-1}S(A^{-1})^{\mathrm{T}}\,\mathrm{d}p_* \tag{44}$$

or, in percentage terms:

$$\hat{y}_* = -\lambda^{-1}\epsilon\theta^{-1}\hat{p}_*. \tag{45}$$

[13] The matrices ϵ, θ and λ are obviously closely related to A and S. If $\bar{x}$ is defined as a diagonal matrix with the elements of vector x along the diagonal for any vector x, then the matrix relations between λ, θ and ϵ, and A and S, are as follows: $\lambda \equiv \bar{v}^{-1}A\bar{y}_*$, $\theta \equiv \bar{p}_*^{-1}A^{\mathrm{T}}\bar{w}$, $\epsilon \equiv \bar{v}^{-1}S\bar{w}$.

The matrix $A^{-1}S(A^{-1})^T$ can be shown to be a negative semi-definite matrix.[14] Hence, $-A^{-1}S(A^{-1})^T$ is positive semi-definite. This indicates the nature of the response of outputs to product prices. One implication is that, when p_j increases, then y_j must not fall and will generally increase since the diagonal elements of a positive semi-definite matrix are non-negative (with at least one element positive). Moreover, the fact that the matrix has rank less than N implies that if y_j increases then some other output must fall (due to fixed resource endowment). Which industries expand (other than j) and which contract depends upon the sign structure of $-A^{-1}S(A^{-1})^T$.

The preceding proof that $\partial y_*/\partial p_* = -A^{-1}S(A^{-1})^T$ is a positive semi-definite matrix makes use of the industrial structure of the production sector. An alternative proof for a much more general economy is presented in Chapter 5. This proof uses the assumption that GNP is maximized to show that the GNP function is convex in product prices, which in turn implies the semi-definiteness of $\partial y_*/\partial p_*$. The proof is simpler and more elegant. The advantage of the current proof, however, is that it shows how $\partial y_*/\partial p_*$ is related to matrices A and S which describe the structure of the production sector.

4.7. A general treatment of the comparative statics

The purpose of this section is to indicate the nature of the response of outputs and factor prices to changes in product prices and factor endowments for the general case where $M^* \leqslant N$. In doing so the results obtained in the previous sections will be summarized in a compact way and the importance of the relationship of M^* to N will be highlighted.

If M^* goods are produced and all N factors are fully employed in equilibrium, then the equilibrium satisfies:

$$c^j(w) = p_j, \qquad j = 1, ..., M^*, \tag{46}$$

and

$$\sum_{j=1}^{M^*} c_w^j(w) y_j = v. \tag{47}$$

---

[14] To prove this note that $z^T A^{-1} S(A^{-1})^T z = t^T St \leqslant 0$, for all t, where $t^T \equiv z^T A^{-1}$ or $z \equiv A^T t$. Since A has full rank, N, any z can be constructed as $A^T t$ for some vector t. Thus, the quadratic form in z is non-positive for all z. Also, pre- and post-multiplication by a matrix of full rank, N, does not alter the rank of S, which is less than N since each $c_{ww}^j(w)$ has rank less than N. (Prove this as an exercise.) Thus, $A^{-1}S(A^{-1})^T$ is negative semi-definite. See problem 13 also.

When $M^* > N$, the solution for y_* is not unique and an arbitrary small change in p_* will cause $M^* - N$ industries to cease production, as previously explained. Furthermore, it is known that only N products need be produced when $M^* > N$ products can be profitably produced.[15] Thus, we assume in what follows that $M^* \leqslant N$ and that the solution (y_*^0, w^0) is unique.

Total differentiation of (46) and (47) yields:

$$A^T dw = dp_* \quad \text{or} \quad \theta \hat{w} = \hat{p}_* \tag{48}$$

and

$$A dy_* + S dw = dv \quad \text{or} \quad \lambda \hat{y}_* + \epsilon \hat{w} = \hat{v}, \tag{49}$$

where $A \equiv [c_w^1 (w^0), ..., c_w^{M^*} (w^0)]$, $S \equiv \Sigma_{j=1}^{M^*} y_j^0 c_{ww}^j (w^0)$, θ is the matrix of factor cost shares, λ is the matrix of industry shares in the amounts of the factors, and ϵ is the matrix of factor demand elasticities, all evaluated at the initial equilibrium. Eqs. (48) and (49) assume that the changes v are small enough to ensure that the same M^* goods are produced and the N factors remain fully employed. They may be written together as:

$$\begin{bmatrix} 0 & A^T \\ A & S \end{bmatrix} \begin{bmatrix} dy_* \\ dw \end{bmatrix} = \begin{bmatrix} dp_* \\ dv \end{bmatrix} \quad \text{or} \quad \begin{bmatrix} 0 & \theta \\ \lambda & \epsilon \end{bmatrix} \begin{bmatrix} \hat{y}_* \\ \hat{w} \end{bmatrix} = \begin{bmatrix} \hat{p}_* \\ \hat{v} \end{bmatrix}, \tag{50}$$

and solved as

$$\begin{bmatrix} dy_* \\ dw \end{bmatrix} = \begin{bmatrix} 0 & A^T \\ A & S \end{bmatrix}^{-1} \begin{bmatrix} dp_* \\ dv \end{bmatrix} \quad \text{or} \quad \begin{bmatrix} \hat{y}_* \\ \hat{w} \end{bmatrix} = \begin{bmatrix} 0 & \theta \\ \lambda & \epsilon \end{bmatrix}^{-1} \begin{bmatrix} \hat{p}_* \\ \hat{v} \end{bmatrix}, \tag{51}$$

if the inverses exist.

When $M^* = N$ and A have full rank, the inverses in (51) have a very special structure such that

$$\begin{bmatrix} dy_* \\ dw \end{bmatrix} = \begin{bmatrix} -A^{-1} S (A^{-1})^T & A^{-1} \\ (A^T)^{-1} & 0 \end{bmatrix} \begin{bmatrix} dp_* \\ dv \end{bmatrix} \quad \text{or} \quad \begin{bmatrix} \hat{y}_* \\ \hat{w} \end{bmatrix} =$$

[15] Recall the discussion of this at the end of section 3.3 in Chapter 3.

$$\begin{bmatrix} -\lambda^{-1}\epsilon\theta^{-1} & \lambda^{-1} \\ \theta^{-1} & 0 \end{bmatrix} \begin{bmatrix} \hat{p}_* \\ \hat{v} \end{bmatrix}. \tag{52}$$

This can be checked by using the formula for the inverse of a partitioned matrix, as in Johnston (1972, p. 93) and Hadley (1961, pp. 107–111). Alternatively, it is easier to notice that the recursive structure of (50), whereby dy_* does not enter the profit-maximization conditions, allows a sequential solution. First solve for $dw = (A^{\mathrm{T}})^{-1}dp_*$ and then substitute this solution into the factor market conditions and solve for dy_*. This, of course, is precisely the procedure followed in the previous sections. Thus, the solution (52) provides a compact summary of the formal results of sections 4.3–4.6.

When $M^* < N$, however, A is not a square matrix and has rank $M^* < N$. Thus, A^{-1} does not exist and the above sequential procedure cannot be used to solve (50). The profit-maximization equations have N variables in dw while there are only M^* equations. Thus, the factor market conditions are needed to help solve for dw, implying that, in general, dw will depend upon dv as well as dp. The solution for dw and dy_* depends, then, upon the complete structure of the inverse matrix in (51). The properties of this matrix have been derived by Diewert and Woodland (1977, appendix). Rather than consider these in detail, the essential features of the $M^* < N$ case is illustrated with two simple examples.

Example 1. Consider the very simple production sector which produces $M^* = 1$ good using $N = 2$ factors. The equilibrium conditions are

$$c^1(w_1, w_2) = p_1,$$
$$c_{11}(w_1, w_2)y_1 = v_1, \tag{53}$$
$$c_{21}(w_1, w_2)y_2 = v_2.$$

The single cost equation cannot determine both w_1 and w_2 without the remaining equations. In this model it is clear that the factor price ratio w_2/w_1 is determined by the factor endowments, and the cost equation then determines the absolute values of the prices. To see this take the ratio of the previous two equations to get:

$$v_2/v_1 = c_{21}(w_1, w_2)/c_{11}(w_1, w_2) =$$
$$= c_{21}(1, w_2/w_1)/c_{11}(1, w_2/w_1) \equiv \Phi(w_2/w_1),$$

the last equality occurring because the input–output coefficient functions are homogeneous of degree zero in prices. By the inverse function theorem, w_2/w_1 $= \Phi^{-1}(v_2/v_1)$, so that it is clear that the endowment ratio completely determines the factor price ratio. By the linear homogeneity of the cost function we obtain $w_1 c^1(1, w_2/w_1) = p_1$ which can then be used to solve for w_1. The solution for w_2 can then be found from $c^1(w_1, w_2) = p_1$. This example therefore differs significantly from the $M^* = N$ case where endowments do not affect factor prices which are completely determined by product prices.

To further illustrate the $M^* = 1, N = 2$ case the inverse matrix in (51) becomes:

$$
\begin{bmatrix} 0 & A^T \\ A & S \end{bmatrix}^{-1} = \begin{bmatrix} 0 & a_{11} & a_{21} \\ a_{11} & s_{11} & s_{12} \\ a_{21} & s_{21} & s_{22} \end{bmatrix}^{-1}
$$

$$
= \frac{1}{\delta} \begin{bmatrix} 0 & a_{21}s_{12} - a_{11}s_{22} & a_{11}s_{21} - a_{21}s_{11} \\ a_{21}s_{12} - a_{11}s_{22} & -a_{21}^2 & a_{11}a_{21} \\ a_{11}s_{12} - a_{21}s_{11} & a_{11}a_{21} & -a_{11}^2 \end{bmatrix}, \tag{54}
$$

where $\delta = -s_{22}a_{11}^2 + 2s_{12}a_{11}a_{21} - s_{11}a_{21}^2 > 0$ and $s_{ij} \equiv (\partial^2 c^1(w_1, w_2)/\partial w_i \partial w_j)y_1$. The matrix $S = [s_{ij}]$ is symmetric negative semi-definite such that $w^T S = 0$. This implies that $s_{ii} < 0$, $s_{12} = s_{21} > 0$ and $s_{11}s_{22} - s_{12}s_{21} = 0$ (see problem 13). Substituting (54) into (51) it is clear that an increase in p_1 will not affect output but will increase both factor prices since $s_{ii} < 0$ and $0 < s_{12}$. However, an increase in v_1 will cause output to rise, the price of factor 1 to fall, and the price of factor 2 to rise.

Example 2. Let $M^* = 2$ and $N = 3$, and furthermore let each industry use just two factors. The first industry uses factor 1 which is specific to it and a mobile factor 3, while industry 2 uses factor 2 and factor 3. The equilibrium conditions, assuming that all factors are fully employed and that both products are produced, are

$$c^1(w_1, w_3) = p_1,$$

$$c^2(w_2, w_3) = p_2,$$

$$c_{11}(w_1, w_3)y_1 = v_1, \tag{55}$$

$$c_{22}(w_2, w_3)y_2 = v_2,$$

$$c_{31}(w_1, w_3)y_1 + c_{32}(w_2, w_3)y_2 = v_3,$$

where the w arguments are explicitly omitted for factors not used. The third and fourth equations may be used to eliminate y_1 and y_2 from the fifth, so the complete model may be written as

$$c^1(w_1, w_3) = p_1,$$
$$c^2(w_2, w_3) = p_2, \qquad\qquad (56)$$
$$\frac{c_{31}(w_1, w_2)}{c_{11}(w_1, w_3)} v_1 + \frac{c_{32}(w_2, w_3)}{c_{22}(w_2, w_3)} v_2 = v_3.$$

System (56) may be totally differentiated with respect to (w_1, w_2, w_3) yielding a set of three linear equations which may be solved for (dw_1, dw_2, dw_3), or $(\hat{w}_1, \hat{w}_2, \hat{w}_3)$ if percentage changes are desired. Let $\ell_1(w_1/w_3) \equiv c_{31}(w_1, w_3)/c_{11}(w_1, w_3)$ and $\ell_2(w_2/w_3) \equiv c_{32}(w_2, w_3)/c_{22}(w_2, w_3)$ be the factor ratios in the two industries. Then $\hat{\ell}_1 = \sigma_1(\hat{w}_1 - \hat{w}_3)$ and $\hat{\ell}_2 = \sigma_2(\hat{w}_2 - \hat{w}_3)$, where σ_j is the Allen–Uzawa elasticity of substitution around the isoquant in industry j. Totally differentiating (56) and converting to percentage changes yields:

$$
\begin{bmatrix}
\theta_{11} & 0 & \theta_{31} \\
0 & \theta_{22} & \theta_{32} \\
\lambda_{31}\sigma_1 & \lambda_{32}\sigma_2 & -(\lambda_{31}\sigma_1 + \lambda_{32}\sigma_2)
\end{bmatrix}
\begin{bmatrix}
\hat{w}_1 \\
\hat{w}_2 \\
\hat{w}_3
\end{bmatrix}
=
\begin{bmatrix}
\hat{p}_1 \\
\hat{p}_2 \\
\hat{v}_3 - \lambda_{31}\hat{v}_1 - \lambda_{32}\hat{v}_2
\end{bmatrix}, \qquad (57)
$$

where θ_{ij} is the share of factor i in the unit cost for industry j, and λ_{ij} is the share of industry j in the total use of factor i. The derivation of (57) is left as an exercise. System (57) may be solved to yield:

$$
\begin{bmatrix}
\hat{w}_1 \\
\hat{w}_2 \\
\hat{w}_3
\end{bmatrix}
= \frac{1}{\delta}
\begin{bmatrix}
\theta_{22}\lambda_{31}\sigma_1 + \lambda_{32}\sigma_2 & -\theta_{31}\lambda_{32}\sigma_2 & \theta_{31}\theta_{22} \\
-\theta_{32}\lambda_{31}\sigma_1 & \theta_{11}\lambda_{32}\sigma_2 + \lambda_{31}\sigma_1 & \theta_{11}\theta_{32} \\
\theta_{22}\lambda_{31}\sigma_1 & \theta_{11}\lambda_{32}\sigma_2 & -\theta_{11}\theta_{22}
\end{bmatrix}
$$

$$
\times
\begin{bmatrix}
\hat{p}_1 \\
\hat{p}_2 \\
\hat{v}_3 - \lambda_{31}\hat{v}_1 - \lambda_{32}\hat{v}_2
\end{bmatrix}, \qquad (58)
$$

where $\delta \equiv \theta_{22} \lambda_{31} \sigma_1 + \theta_{11} \lambda_{32} \sigma_2 > 0$. Consider the effects of an increase in the price of product 1, the price of product 2 and the endowments remaining fixed. From (58) the effect upon the price of factor 1, the factor specific to industry 1, is $\hat{w}_1/\hat{p}_1 = (\theta_{22} \lambda_{31} \sigma_1 + \lambda_{32} \sigma_2)/(\theta_{22} \lambda_{31} \sigma_1 + \theta_{11} \lambda_{32} \sigma_2) > 1$ because $\theta_{11} < 1$. The effect on the price of factor 2, which is not used by industry 1, is $\hat{w}_2/\hat{p}_2 = -\theta_{32} \lambda_{31} \sigma_1/\delta < 0$. The effect upon the price of the mobile factor is $\hat{w}_3/\hat{p}_1 = \theta_{22} \lambda_{31} \sigma_1/(\theta_{22} \lambda_{31} \sigma_1 + \theta_{11} \lambda_{32} \sigma_2) < 1$. These results show that factor 1 gains in welfare since its real income in terms of each good has increased, while factor 2 loses welfare since its real income in terms of each good falls. However, it is not clear, without knowledge of its utility function, whether factor 3 gains or loses since its real income in terms of good 1 has fallen, but has risen in terms of good 2.

This model is precisely the one formulated by Jones (1971), Mussa (1974) and Mayer (1974) if factor 3 is a mobile factor (labour) and factors 1 and 2 are fixed capital installed in industries 1 and 2, respectively. According to their models, in the short run capital is not mobile so its rental rate will be different in the two industries. The above calculations show that an increase in the price of good 1 will raise the real income of capital in industry 1 and reduce the real income of capital in industry 2, while the effect upon the real income of labour is ambiguous. This contrasts with the Stolper–Samuelson result for the model where capital is perfectly mobile, which is the $M^* = N = 2$ case. In the $M^* = N = 2$ case the effect upon factor prices of a change in a product price depended only upon the structure of the matrix of cost shares, θ, and not upon the response of inputs to changes in factor prices which are reflected in the elasticities of substitution. This difference in results highlights the importance of the relative size of M^* and N. In the context of the Jones–Mussa–Mayer model the difference in results suggest that short-run responses may be quite different to long-run responses, where in the long run capital is perfectly mobile.

4.8. Notes on the literature

The topics discussed in this chapter have received considerable attention over the past thirty years, so the papers mentioned here represent only a tiny percentage of the literature. The factor price equalization theorem had its origins in the paper by Heckscher (1919) but was made rigorous for a two-product two-factor model by Samuelson (1948, 1949) who showed that for the cost equations to have a unique solution it was required that there be no factor intensity reversals. This condition has become known as the "Samuelson intensity condition". The relationship between product and factor prices and endowments for a general final-good production sector was treated by Samuelson (1953–54). A classic paper by McKenzie (1955) provided a rigorous treatment of the FPE problem for a very general production sector using activity analysis. The discussion of the question of the global invertibility (unique solution) of the cost equations culminated in a series of papers by Pearce, McKenzie and Samuelson published as a symposium by the *International Economic Review* in 1967. Samuelson's (1967) review of the debate is particularly useful.

The original statements on the Stolper–Samuelson and Rybczynski theorems are in Stolper and Samuelson (1941) and Rybczynski (1955). Further developments attempting to generalize these results to higher dimensions, particularly relating to the Stolper–Samuelson theorem, include Chipman (1969), Uekawa (1971), Kemp and Wegge (1969), Wegge and Kemp (1969), Ethier (1974) and Egawa (1978).

Jones (1971), Mayer (1974) and Mussa (1974) have examined the Stolper–Samuelson proposition for a two-product, two-factor model when one of the factors (capital) is immobile in the short run. Neary (1978) analyses this model further, while Batra and Casas (1976) work out the comparative statics for a two-product, three-factor model containing both the specific factor and two-dimensional models as special cases. For a more general treatment of the Stolper–Samuelson theorem see Ruffin and Jones (1977). The comparative statics for the two-dimensional model have been presented in a comprehensive manner by Jones (1965). The comparative statics for very general production sectors have been rigorously derived by Diewert and Woodland (1977), Jones and Scheinkman (1977) and Chang (1979).

Problems

1. Let there be $M^* = N$ goods produced and let good i use factor i and no other factor for $i = 1, ..., N$. That is, each factor is specific to one industry.
   (a) What happens to y_* when v_i increases?
   (b) What happens to w when p_i increases?
2. What shape does the production possibility frontier (PPF) take when the production functions are Leontief (fixed coefficients) and hence the cost functions are linear in factor prices?
   (a) Consider the case where $M = N = 2$.
   (b) Then consider the case where $N > 2 = M$.
   (c) Are factors fully employed at all points on the PPF?
3. Under what circumstances, if any, can the endowment vector v be in two cones of diversification $K(w^0, p)$ and $K(w^1, p)$ at once, where w^0 and w^1 are distinct solutions to the cost equations?

4. If $v \in K(w^0, p)$, defined by (7), will all M^* goods be produced? If all M^* goods are produced, is $v \in K(w^0, p)$?

5. If $M^* = 2$, $N = 1$ show that the production possibility frontier (PPF) is a straight line.

6. At the beginning of section 4.4 it was stated that if $M^* > N$, there exists a set of solutions for the output vector y_*.
   (a) Using the Lerner diagram for the case of $M^* = 3$ and $N = 2$, verify this statement by illustrating at least two solutions for y_*.
   (b) Hence, show that the production possibility frontier is a ruled surface, i.e. it consists of an infinity of straight lines (not necessarily parallel).

7. Consider a $M^* = 3$ product, $N = 3$ factor model where products 1 and 2 each use factors 1 and 3 and product 3 uses factors 2 and 3.
   (a) Set up the matrix of industry shares of factors, λ.
   (b) By examining the equation system $\lambda \hat{y}_* = \hat{v}$, deduce what happens to the output vector y_* when the endowment of factor 1 increases.
   (c) Set up the matrix of cost shares, θ.
   (d) By examining the equation system $\theta \hat{w} = \hat{p}_*$, deduce what happens to the factor price vector w when the price of product 1 increases.
   (e) If ambiguities arise, resolve them in terms of relative intensities with which factors are used.

8. If $M^* = N = 2$, show that industry 2 is factor 2 intensive when the share of factor 2 in the cost of production is greatest in industry 2. Note that this share definition of intensity is more general than the factor ratio definition in that the latter is only possible when both factors are used in both industries.

9. (a) Why is the locus of solutions for outputs in fig. 4.6 a straight line?
   (b) Derive the formula for this line.

10. Prove that $(y_2/y_1) \equiv d(y_2/y_1)/(y_2/y_1) = \hat{y}_2 - \hat{y}_1$.

11. Derive eq. (43) from (40).

12. (a) Derive eq. (57) by totally differentiating (56).
    (b) Calculate the solution (58) to equation system (57).

13. (a) Prove that $w^T c^j_{ww}(w) = 0$ and hence that $c^j_{ww}(w)$ has rank less than N.
    (b) Hence show that $w^T S = 0$ so S has rank less than N.
    (c) When $N = 2$ show that $s_{11}, s_{22} < 0, 0 < s_{12} = s_{21}$ because $w^T S = 0$ and S is negative semi-definite.

14. Let $M^* = 2$, $N = 3$ and let

$$A = \begin{bmatrix} 1 & 1 \\ 1 & 2 \\ 1 & 3 \end{bmatrix}$$

at a factor price vector w which solves the cost equations.

(a) If $v = (3 \quad 4 \quad 5)$, calculate the solution for the output levels y_1, y_2.

(b) Find another endowment vector v^0, not a multiple λv of v, where $\lambda > 0$, such that a non-negative solution can be found for y_1, y_2. Note that the factor prices will not be altered as a result of a change in endowments from v to v^0.

(c) Characterize the complete cone of diversification.

References

Apostol, T.M. (1957) *Mathematical Analysis* (Reading, Mass.: Addison-Wesley).

Batra, R.N. and F.R. Casas (1976) "A synthesis of the Heckscher–Ohlin and the neo-classical models of international trade", *Journal of International Economics* 6, 21–38.

Chang, W.W. (1979) "Some theorems of trade and general equilibrium with many goods and factors", *Econometrica* 47-3, May, 709–726.

Chiang, A. (1967) *Fundamental Methods of Mathematical Economics* (New York: McGraw-Hill).

Chipman, J.S. (1969) "Factor price equalization and the Stolper–Samuelson theorem", *International Economic Review* 10, October, 399–406.

Diewert, W.E. and A.D. Woodland (1977) "Frank Knight's theorem in linear programming revisited", *Econometrica* 45-2, March, 375–398.

Dixit, A.K. and V. Norman (1980) *Theory of International Trade* (J. Nisbet/Cambridge University Press).

Egawa, I. (1978) "Some remarks on the Stolper–Samuelson and Rybczynski theorems", *Journal of International Economics* 8, 525–536.

Ethier, W. (1974) "Some of the theorems of international trade with many goods and factors", *Journal of International Economics* 4, May, 199–206.

Gale, D. and H. Nikaido (1965) "The Jacobian matrix and global univalence of mappings" *Mathematische Annalen* 159, 81–93.

Hadley, G. (1961) *Linear Algebra* (Reading, Mass.: Addison-Wesley).

Heckscher, E. (1919) "The effect of foreign trade on the distribution of income", *Ekonomisk Tidskrift* 21, 497–512.

International Economic Review (1967) "Symposium on factor price equalization", 8-3, October, 255–306.

Johnston, J. (1972) *Econometric Methods*, 2nd edition (New York: McGraw-Hill).

Jones, R.W. (1965) "The structure of simple general equilibrium models", *Journal of Political Economy* 73, December, 557–572.

Jones, R.W. (1971) "A three factor model in theory, trade and history", in: J. Bhagwati, R.W. Jones, R. Mundell and J. Vanek (eds.), *Trade, Balance of Payments, and Growth* (Amsterdam: North-Holland).

Jones, R.W. and J. Scheinkman (1977) "The relevance of the two-sector production model in trade theory", *Journal of Political Economy* 85, 909–936.

Kemp, M.C. and L. Wegge (1969) "On the relation between commodity prices and factor rewards", *International Economic Review* 10, October, 407–413.

Mayer, W. (1974) "Short-run and long-run equilibrium for a small open economy", *Journal of Political Economy* 82, 955–968.

McKenzie, L.W. (1955) "Equality of factor prices in world trade", *Econometrica* 22-3, July, 239–257.

Mussa, A. (1974) "Tariffs and the distribution of income: The importance of factor specificity, substitutability, and intensity in the short and long run", *Journal of Political Economy* 82, 1191–1204.

Neary, J.P. (1978) "Short-run capital specificity and the pure theory of international trade", *Economic Journal* 88, September, 488–510.

Ruffin, R. and R.W. Jones (1977) "Protection and real wages: The neoclassical ambiguity", *Journal of Economic Theory* 14, 337–348.

Rybczynski, T. (1955) "Factor endowment and relative commodity prices", *Economica* 22-84, November, 336–341.

Samuelson, P.A. (1948) "International trade and the equalization of factor prices", *Economic Journal* 58, June, 163–184.

Samuelson, P.A. (1949) "International factor-price equalization once again", *Economic Journal* 59, June, 181–197.

Samuelson, P.A. (1953–54) "Prices of factors and goods in general equilibrium", *Review of Economic Studies* 21, 1–20.

Samuelson, P.A. (1967) "Summary on factor price equalization", *International Economic Review* 8-3, October, 286–295.

Stolper, W. and P.A. Samuelson (1941) "Protection and real wages", *The Review of Economic Studies* 9, November, 58–73.

Uekawa, Y. (1971) "Generalization of the Stolper–Samuelson theorem", *Econometrica* 39, March, 197–218.

Wegge, L. and M.C. Kemp (1969) "Generalizations of the Stolper–Samuelson and Samuelson-Rybczynski theorems in terms of conditional input–output coefficients", *International Economic Review* 10, October, 414–425.

CHAPTER 5

INTERMEDIATE INPUTS AND JOINT OUTPUTS

5.1. Introduction

While the final-good model dealt with in the previous chapter is the basic model used in the international trade literature, various extensions of the model are of considerable interest. The present chapter examines some of these extensions. The first extension is to allow for the existence of intermediate inputs. The second is to generalize the model further to include the possibility of joint production. The main aim in these discussions is to show how to model intermediate inputs and joint outputs, and to see to what extent the results obtained for the final good model are valid in these more general settings. Sections 5.2 and 5.4 carry out these extensions in models which explicitly deal with separate industries. Section 5.3 develops a very general model of the production sector and derives correspondingly general formulae for the response of outputs and factor prices to changes in product prices and factor endowments. This model does not explicitly deal with the industrial structure of the economy and may therefore be referred to as an aggregate model. This is the most general model since it contains all others as special cases, and will be used extensively in subsequent chapters.

5.2. Intermediate inputs

It is a central feature of the production processes of modern economies that many goods produced by one industry are used as inputs in other industries. For example, steel is a produced good which is used as an input in the production of many other goods such as automobiles. Such inputs are called intermediate inputs. Some of them may be pure intermediates in that they are never purchased by consumers, while others such as gasoline may be used as an input in another industry and may be purchased by the consumption sector. For many nations intermediates constitute a large proportion of the total volume of their international trade. Accordingly, it is important that due consideration is given to intermediate inputs in our model of the production sector.[1]

The production sector is assumed to consist of M industries each producing just one product, as with the final-good model. However, it is now assumed that the production function is

$$g_j = f^j(x_j, q_j),$$

where g_j is the gross output of good j, x_j is an N-dimensional vector of inputs of primary inputs or resources and q_j is an M-dimensional vector of inputs of intermediates. This is a very general formulation of the production function since it allows for the possibility that each good might be used as inputs in some industry. Of course, there may be some pure final goods which are never used as an input in any industry. The output g_j is called the gross output since it is possible that some of product j (e.g. wheat) may be used as an input in the production of j. In the final-goods model there was no distinction between the gross and net output of an industry, and no distinction between these and the net output of the production sector. Here, however, these concepts have to be distinguished from each other. The notation y_j will be reserved for the net output of product j by the production sector, which is the gross output g_j minus the inputs of j into all industries. For an open economy the net output of the production sector may be positive, in which case it is available for consumption or for export, or negative in which case it must be imported.

It is assumed that each industry minimizes the cost of production. The unit cost function is defined as

$$c^j(w, p) \equiv \min_{x_j, q_j} \{wx_j + pq_j : f^j(x_j, q_j) \geqslant 1, (x_j, q_j) \geqslant 0\} \tag{1}$$

and denotes the minimum cost of all inputs required to produce one unit of gross output. If the production function satisfies conditions (2.3') then the unit cost function will also satisfy conditions (2.3'). In particular it is a positive, linearly homogeneous, concave function of (w, p). Furthermore, Shephard's lemma indicates that $c_{ij}(w, p) \equiv \partial c^j(w, p)/\partial w_i$ is the optimal input of factor i and

[1] Capital is also an input which is produced. The distinction between capital and intermediate inputs is somewhat arbitrary, but is essentially that intermediates are non-durable and are used within the period, whereas capital is durable. Moreover, it is the service provided by capital which is an input while for intermediates the input is the good itself. In an intertemporal model of the Arrow–Debreu kind with commodities distinguished by date, there is no formal difference.

$c_{N+k,j}(w,p) \equiv \partial c^j(w,p)/\partial p_k$ is the optimal input of product k per unit of gross output of product j. Both depend upon w and p indicating possible substitutability between factors and intermediates (e.g. manual labour, machines and electricity). If an input is never used in industry j, then the derivative of the cost function with respect to its price is identically zero.

The net output of j by the industry is $g_j - c_{N+j,j}(w,p) g_j$. Another variable of interest is the net output of product j by the sector as a whole. The vector of (sector) net outputs is denoted as $y = (y_1, ..., y_M)$. Net output of j is gross output minus the sum of the inputs of j into all the industries. Since the input of j into industry k is $g_k \partial c^k(w,p)/\partial p_j$, the net output of j is

$$y_j = g_j - \sum_{k=1}^{M} g_k \, \partial c^k(w,p)/\partial p_j, \quad j = 1, ..., M. \tag{2}$$

The equilibrium conditions for the production sector may be written in terms of the unit cost functions as

$$c^j(w,p) - p_j \geqslant 0 \leqslant g_j, \qquad j = 1, ..., M, \tag{3}$$

$$\sum_{j=1}^{M} c_{ij}(w,p) g_j - v_i \leqslant 0 \leqslant w_i, \quad i = 1, ..., N. \tag{4}$$

These conditions have exactly the same interpretation as eqs. (3.2) and (3.4) which are the equilibrium conditions for the final-goods model of Chapter 3. Eq. (3) is the profit-maximization condition while (4) is the factor market equilibrium condition. The only differences between (3) and (4) and (3.2) and (3.4) are that the activity level is gross output whereas before it was both net and gross output, and that the cost function depends upon p as well as w. Given p and v the equilibrium conditions (3) and (4) may be solved for the equilibrium gross output vector g and the equilibrium factor price vector w. Having determined w and g, eq. (2) may then be used to calculate the equilibrium net output levels for the sector as a whole.

What is the effect of the introduction of intermediate inputs upon the results obtained in Chapter 4 for the final-good economy? Fortunately, a complete comparative static analysis is not required since it is easily shown that this extended model can be made to look very much like the final-good model. Hence, the results for the final-good model can be applied here, with appropriate reinterpretation.

First, consider the factor price equalization theorem. If (say, the first) M^* goods can be produced profitably then the equations $c^j(w,p) = p_j$ hold for $j = 1$, ..., M^*. For each solution $w > 0$ to these equations the optimal factor input—

output vectors $c_w^j(w, p)$, $j = 1, ..., M*$, form a cone $K(w, p)$. If the endowment vectors for two nations, who have the same cost functions and face the same prices, are in the interior of the same cone of diversification, then there exist output levels $y_1, ..., y_{M*} > 0$ such that the factor markets clear in each nation. In this case the two nations will have the same factor price vector. If the endowment vectors are not in the same cone, then they will have different factor prices. This is precisely the same argument as developed in Chapter 4 for the final-good model. The introduction of intermediates does not, therefore, affect the factor price equalization theorem.

5.2.1. Comparative statics

We now proceed to examine the comparative statics equations for a production sector which has an equilibrium (g^0, w^0) such that $w^0 > 0$ and g^0 has $M* = N$ positive elements. That is, it is assumed that there is full employment of all N factors and that $M* = N$ products are produced. Thus, the following relationships hold:

$$c^j(w^0, p) = p_j, \qquad j = 1, ..., M*, \tag{5}$$

$$\sum_{j=1}^{M*} c_{ij}(w^0, p) g_j^0 = v_i, \quad i = 1, ..., N. \tag{6}$$

As in the analysis of the final-good model in Chapter 4, it is assumed that the product price vector p and the endowment vector v change by small amounts such that full employment is maintained and the same $M*$ products are produced. This assumption permits the analysis of the effects of changes in p and v upon the equilibrium by differentiating (5) and (6) and solving the resulting equations for the changes in outputs and factor prices.

Before proceeding to carry out the comparative static analysis of (5) and (6) several complications that arise in the intermediate product model need to be discussed. The first complication is that there is no unique "output" concept. It has already been pointed out that we need to distinguish between the gross output of a product by the industry and the net output for the production sector. Both variables are of interest: the former as a measure of the scale of operation of the industry and the latter as the net amount produced by the production sector and hence available for final demand (or imported, if negative). In this regard it should also be noted that gross output is not the only measure of the scale of operation by an industry. Another measure, of perhaps more interest, is the value added by the industry, that is the excess of revenue minus the cost of intermediate inputs. In section 5.4 below the model will be reformulated to deal explicitly with industry values added. In the final-good model of the previous chapter there was no distinction between gross output and net output, while value added is simply price times gross (or net) output.

The second complication is that attention has to be given to changes in the prices of the goods which are not produced by any industry. This is because these goods may be used as inputs in a producing industry, and hence changes in their prices will influence the equilibrium. Similarly, attention has to be given to the effects of changes in product prices and factor endowments upon the net outputs of goods which are not produced. Again, this complication did not arise in the final-good model.

Having pointed out some complications arising from the intermediate good model, we now proceed with the comparative static analysis. Eqs. (5) and (6) may be totally differentiated to yield:

$$c_w^j(w^0,p)\,\mathrm{d}w = \mathrm{d}p_j - c_p^j(w^0,p)\,\mathrm{d}p, \quad j = 1, ..., M^*, \tag{7}$$

$$\sum_{j=1}^{M^*} c_w^j(w^0,p)\,\mathrm{d}g_j + \left[\sum_{j=1}^{M^*} c_{ww}^j(w^0,p)\,g_j^0\right]\mathrm{d}w$$

$$+ \left[\sum_{j=1}^{M^*} c_{wp}^j(w^0,p)\,g_j^0\right]\mathrm{d}p = \mathrm{d}v, \tag{8}$$

where $c_w^j(w^0,p)$ and $c_p^j(w^0,p)$ are the vectors of inputs of factors and intermediates, respectively, per unit of gross output of product j, and $c_{ww}^j(w^0,p)$ and $c_{wp}^j(w^0,p)$ are matrices of second derivatives of the unit cost function for industry j.

The first term in square brackets in (8) is a matrix whose ik element is the change in the production sector's demand for factor i due to a unit change in the price of factor k, given the industry outputs. In other words, it is the slope of the aggregate or production sector demand function for factor i with respect to the price of factor k. Similarly, the second bracketed term is a matrix whose ik element is the slope of the aggregate demand function for factor i with respect to the price of the kth intermediate input. The linear equations (7) and (8) may be solved for the changes in factor prices and industry outputs resulting from changes in product prices and factor endowments. To obtain the effect upon net outputs, these solutions may be substituted into the following equation, obtained by totally differentiating eq. (2) in vector form:

$$dy = dg - \left[\sum_{k=1}^{M^*} c_p^k(w^0, p) \, dg_k \right] - \left[\sum_{k=1}^{M^*} c_{pw}^k(w^0, p) \, g_k^0 \right] dw$$

$$- \left[\sum_{k=1}^{M^*} c_{pp}^k(w^0, p) \, g_k^0 \right] dp. \tag{9}$$

The first two terms take account of the changes in gross outputs, both directly and indirectly. The third term is the effect of changes in factor prices upon the inputs of intermediates into all the industries, while the last term is the analogous effect of changes in the prices of intermediate inputs. Specifically, the second pair of square brackets contain a matrix whose ik element is the change in sector demand for good i as an input due to a unit increase in the price of factor k, assuming that gross outputs are given. Similarly, the last pair of square brackets contain a matrix whose ik element is the change in sector demand for good i due to a unit increase in the price of good k, again assuming that gross outputs remain fixed.

It should be noted that in (8) and (9) the summations run over the M^* industries that produce, but they could just as well run over all M industries. Also note that p is the full vector of prices and is at least as long as p_*, which refers to the produced goods only.

Equations (7)–(9) provide the starting point for a general treatment of the comparative statics for the model. To simplify the exposition let us initially consider product price changes only for those products actually produced, and let us ignore any effects upon the net outputs of goods not produced. In doing this we are by-passing the second complication discussed above. In terms of eqs. (7)–(9), M can be replaced by M^*. First, we consider the effect of changes in factor endowments upon gross and net outputs and, secondly, we consider the effect of changes in product prices upon factor prices. In each case it is assumed that $M^* = N$.

5.2.2. Factor endowment changes

Let the endowment vector v change while the product price vector p remains fixed. If v changes within the cone of diversification, the factor prices will not alter and the same $M^* = N$ products will continue to be produced. Since neither w nor p change, eqs. (8) and (9) may be written as

$$A \, dg_* = dv \quad \text{and} \quad dy_* = (I - B) \, dg_*, \tag{10}$$

where $A = [c_w^1(w^0, p), ..., c_w^{M^*}(w^0, p)]$ is an N x M^* matrix of factor input–output coefficients, $B = [c_{p_*}^1(w^0, p), ..., c_{p_*}^{M^*}(w^0, p)]$ is an M^* x M^* matrix of intermediate input–output coefficients, and g_* and y_* are vectors whose elements correspond to those M^* industries which produce. If A and $I - B$ have inverses, the solutions for dg_* and dy_* are

$$dg_* = A^{-1} dv \quad \text{and} \quad dy_* = D^{-1} dv, \tag{11}$$

where $D \equiv A(I - B)^{-1}$ is an N x M^* matrix.

Now A is the matrix of factor input–output coefficients so it is clear from (11) that the effect of a change in endowments upon gross outputs is exactly the same as in a final-good economy – given by (4.16). Since this result has been discussed in detail in Chapter 4, it is unnecessary to pursue it further. What happens to net outputs? The formula here is similar to that for gross outputs except that D replaces A. What is D? The ijth element of D, d_{ij}, is the *total* amount of product i needed by the production sector to produce a net output of one unit of product j at the going prices (w^0, p). This is greater (actually, no less) than the *direct* amount of i used by industry j to produce one unit (gross) of product j since it may be necessary to use factor i in other industries which need to produce the inputs required by j. It is now shown that $D \equiv A(I - B)^{-1}$ is indeed the matrix of total factor requirements for one unit of net production of each good. If y_* is the required net output vector, the gross output vector must be $g_* = (I - B)^{-1} y_*$ and hence the vector of inputs of factors must be $Ag_* = A(I - B)^{-1} y_* = Dy_*$. Thus, to produce one unit of product j (net) requires d_{ij} units of factor i.

The matrix B corresponds to the Leontief input–output matrix, while $I - B$ is called the technology matrix. The Leontief model assumes that B is constant, whereas in the present model B depends upon the product and factor prices. Given these prices, as in the local comparative statics analysis, B is fixed so all of the results for the Leontief model apply here.[2] An important property of B is that $(I - B)^{-1}$ exists and is non-negative. To obtain this property, observe that the cost equations (5) may be rewritten as

$$A^T w^0 = [I - B^T] p, \tag{12}$$

with the aid of Shephard's lemma, where A and B are evaluated at (w^0, p). Let it be assumed that A is a *semi-positive matrix*, i.e. it contains at least one positive

[2] Leontief (1951) introduced the concept of an input–output table. For further exposition and results see, for example, Dorfman, Samuelson and Solow (1958, chs. 9, 10), Lancaster (1968, ch. 6) and Gale (1960, ch. 9).

element in every row and every column. This means that every factor is used by at least one industry and every industry uses at least one factor. If this is the case then the assumption that $w^0 > 0$ implies that $A^T w^0$ is a positive vector, i.e. that each industry has a positive factor cost. Since $p \geqslant 0$ satisfies (12) where the left-hand side is a positive vector, it follows that $(I - B^T) p > 0$. We can use the results of Gale (1960, pp. 296–297) to show that this is equivalent to saying that $(I - B)^{-1}$ exists and is non-negative, which was to be proved. In other words, the fact that $M^* = N$ industries produce in equilibrium, each with positive factor costs, implies (and is implied by) that $(I - B)^{-1}$ exists and is non-negative. This is equivalent to Gale's concept of a productive economy.

To illustrate the concepts of a productive economy, profitability and the non-negativity of $(I - B)^{-1}$, consider the following example for the case where $M^* = N = 2$. Let the matrix B of intermediate input–output coefficients and its inverse be

$$B = \begin{bmatrix} 0 & 2 \\ 1 & 0 \end{bmatrix} \quad ; \quad (I - B)^{-1} = \begin{bmatrix} -1 & -2 \\ -1 & -1 \end{bmatrix} .$$

In this example it takes 1 unit of product 2 to produce 1 unit of product 1, and 2 units of product 1 to produce 1 unit of product 2. Thus, it is not possible to produce a positive net output of product 1. In this case we say the economy is unproductive. An alternative way of looking at this example is to note that it contradicts the assumption that both industries are producing profitably. The vector of revenue minus the intermediate input costs is $(I - B^T) p = r$. For industry 1 this is $r_1 = p_1 - p_2$ and for industry 2 it is $r_2 = p_2 - 2p_1$. A little reflection will show that it is not possible to find product prices, not all zero, such that the net revenues, r_1 and r_2, are non-negative. The net revenues must be non-negative if both industries are producing since the primary factors have to be paid. Thus, the example matrix B contradicts the assumption that both industries produce.

Figure 5.1 illustrates the $M^* = N = 2$ cases from a geometric viewpoint. The technology matrix $\beta = (I - B) = (\beta_1, \beta_2)$ is described by the two vectors β_1 and β_2. They form a cone which contains the non-negative orthant, meaning the non-negative gross outputs g_1 and g_2 can always be found to obtain any point $y \geqslant 0$ as $y = \beta_1 g_1 + \beta_2 g_2 = (I - B) g$. This means that the economy is productive. The solid lines are normal (at right angles) to β_1 and β_2 and form the shaded cone P in the non-negative orthant. Any point $p \in$ int P must, by definition of P, satisfy $p^T \beta_i > 0$ so that each industry i earns a positive net revenue. The reader may verify that if β_1 is replaced by β_1^*, then a net output vector $y \geqslant 0$ cannot be pro-

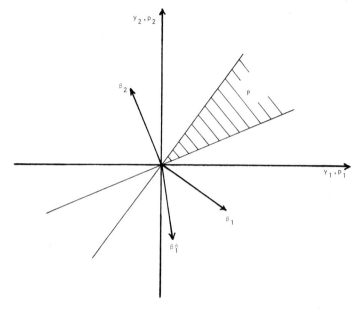

Figure 5.1

duced and the corresponding cone P does not overlap with the non-negative or-thant. Thus, "profitability" at non-negative prices and the productivity of the economy are equivalent.

The only property that matrix A has is that it is semi-positive. Since it has been shown that $(I - B)^{-1} \geqslant 0$, it follows that $D = A(I - B)^{-1} \geqslant 0$. Thus, A and D have the same non-negativity property and, since $D \geqslant A$, D will be semi-positive if A has this property.[3] In addition, they are both matrices of factor input–output coefficients. In view of this it is clear that the solutions for dy_* and dg_* in (11) may be interpreted in the same way. The effect of a change in v upon gross outputs depends upon the nature of A, the matrix of direct factor input–output coefficients, while the effect upon net outputs depends upon the nature of D, the matrix of total (direct plus indirect) factor input–output co-efficients.

Consider, for example, the standard case of $M^* = N = 2$. It is known that in a

---

[3] $D \geqslant A$ since the total factor requirements must be at least as great as the direct fac-tor requirements for the production of one unit of a good. For a proof see Lancaster (1968, ch. 6).

final-good model an increase in v_2 will increase gross (= net) output of the good which is relatively intensive in its use of factor 2, and decrease the output of the other good. Since the solutions in (11) have the same formal structure as for the final-good model, similar results apply. An increase in v_2 will increase the gross output of the good which is relatively intensive in its *direct* use of factor 2 and decrease the gross output of the other good. And an increase in v_2 will increase the net output of the good which is relatively intensive in its *total* use of factor 2 and decrease the net output of the other. This raises the question of whether the gross output of, say, good 2 could increase while its net output decreased, i.e. whether the ranking of the industries by their factor intensities depends upon whether the intensities refer to the direct or total factor input–output coefficients. When $M^* = N = 2$ this conflict is not possible. Product 2 is factor 2 intensive relative to product 1 when the determinant of the input–output matrix is positive. From the definition of D it follows that $|D| = |A|/|I - B|$, while it can be shown that $|I - B| > 0$, hence $|D|$ and $|A|$ have the same sign.[4] This shows that there is no conflict in the intensity rankings based upon A and D when $M^* = N = 2$.

When $M^* = N > 2$, it can be shown, using the same argument as used in Chapter 4, that if v_i increases, then at least one gross output will increase and at least one will fall and, moreover, the gross output that increases must do so by a greater percentage than the increase in v_i. Similarly, at least one net output will increase by a greater percentage than the increase in v_i, while at least one net output will fall. However, it is interesting to note that it is not necessary that a good whose gross output increases will also experience an increase in net output. If this were the case, then the corresponding elements of A^{-1} and D^{-1} would have the same sign. The following example shows that this need not be the case. Suppose A and B are given as

$$A = \begin{bmatrix} 1 & 1 & 1 \\ 1 & 2 & 0 \\ 0 & 0 & 1 \end{bmatrix} \quad ; \quad B = \begin{bmatrix} 0 & 0 & 0 \\ 0 & 0 & 2 \\ 0 & 0 & 0 \end{bmatrix} .$$

---

[4]   The inverse of $I - B$ is

$$(I - B)^{-1} = \frac{1}{|I - B|} \begin{bmatrix} 1 - b_{22} & b_{12} \\ b_{21} & 1 - b_{11} \end{bmatrix} ,$$

where $|I - B| = (1 - b_{11})(1 - b_{22}) - b_{12} b_{21}$. Since $(I - B)^{-1} \geq 0$ if the economy is productive, and $B \geq 0$, it follows that $|I - B| > 0$.

Then A^{-1} and $D^{-1} = (I - B) A^{-1}$ are:

$$A^{-1} = \begin{bmatrix} 2 & -1 & -2 \\ -1 & 1 & 1 \\ 0 & 0 & 1 \end{bmatrix} \;;\quad D^{-1} = \begin{bmatrix} 2 & -1 & -2 \\ -1 & 1 & -1 \\ 0 & 0 & 1 \end{bmatrix} .$$

The only difference between A^{-1} and D^{-1} is in the second element of the last column which is 1 in A^{-1} and -1 in D^{-1}. Thus, from (11) it follows that a 1 unit increase in the endowment of factor 3 will cause an increase in the gross output of product 2 of 1 unit, but a fall in its net output of 1 unit. The reason is that the gross output of product 3 increases by 1 unit, requiring the use of 2 units of good 2 as an input. Thus, the change in net output of good 2 is -1, equal to the additional gross output of 1 minus the additional intermediate input of 2.

In summary, it has been shown that the effects of changes in factor endowments upon industry gross outputs and upon product net outputs depend upon the structure of A and D, respectively. In each case the analysis provided in Chapter 4 for the final-good model may be applied in the present context, thus obviating the need for another detailed analysis.

5.2.3. Product price changes

Attention is now directed to the relationship between factor and product prices in an intermediate-good economy. If the prices of *produced* goods change such that the same M^* products remain in production, eq. (7) may be written as

$$A^T dw = (I - B) dp_* \quad \text{or} \quad D^T dw = dp_*. \tag{13}$$

This set of linear equations may be solved as

$$dw = (D^T)^{-1} dp_* = (D^{-1})^T dp_* \tag{14}$$

if the matrix D has an inverse. This result reduces to $dw = (A^{-1})^T dp_*$ when $B = 0$, which is the result obtained for a final-good model in Chapter 4. Since the matrix of total factor requirements, D, has the same non-negativity property as A, the results of Chapter 4 may be applied here. The only difference is that the effect of a change in p_* upon w depends on the structure of the matrix D of total factor input—output coefficients rather than the matrix A of direct input—output coefficients.

Consider, for example, the standard case where $M^* = N = 2$. It is known from the final-good model that an increase in the relative price of product 2 will raise the real income of the factor used intensively in the production of good 2, and will lower the real income of the other factor. Here this same conclusion holds if intensity is defined in terms of total factor input—output coefficients. Actually, as pointed out above, when $M^* = N = 2$ there is no conflict in the rankings of industries by intensities calculated using D and A. In the case where $M^* = N > 2$ it can be shown, using the same arguments as used in Chapter 4, that if p_j increases, then at least one factor price will rise by a greater percentage, and hence its real income will unambiguously increase, and at least one factor price will fall, implying that this factor is unambiguously worse off.

Now consider changes in prices for those intermediate inputs not produced by the economy. If no other prices change (7) may be written in matrix form as

$$A^T dw = -E \, dp_{**}, \tag{15}$$

where $dp_{**} = (dp_{M^*+1}, ..., dp_M)$ is the vector of changes in prices of non-produced intermediate inputs and $E = [c_{p_*}^{M^*+1}(w, p), ..., c_{p_*}^{M}(w, p)]$ is a matrix of input—output coefficients. The solution for dw is

$$dw = -(A^T)^{-1} E \, dp_*, \tag{16}$$

which depends upon both A^{-1} and E. The vector $E \, dp_{**}$ is the vector of changes in unit costs due to the changes in the prices of intermediate inputs and acts like a change in the product price vector.

5.2.4. Examples

Rather than continue to examine (16), it is more instructive to consider a simple example when $M = 3$ and $M^* = N = 2$.

Example 1. The full model for this example is

$$c^1(w_1, w_2, p_3) = p_1,$$
$$c^2(w_1, w_2, p_3) = p_2,$$
$$c_{11}(w_1, w_2, p_3) g_1 + c_{12}(w_1, w_2, p_3) g_2 = v_1, \tag{17}$$
$$c_{21}(w_1, w_2, p_3) g_1 + c_{22}(w_1, w_2, p_3) g_2 = v_2,$$

where it is assumed that products 1 and 2 are produced using the two primary factors and an intermediate good, 3, which is not produced and is therefore imported. Note that goods 1 and 2 are pure final goods since neither is used as an input. Totally differentiating the cost equations in (17) and converting to percentage changes yields:

$$\theta_{11}\,\hat{w}_1 + \theta_{21}\,\hat{w}_2 = \hat{p}_1 - \theta_{31}\,\hat{p}_3,$$
$$\theta_{12}\,\hat{w}_1 + \theta_{22}\,\hat{w}_2 = \hat{p}_2 - \theta_{32}\,\hat{p}_3,$$

$$(18)$$

where θ_{ij} is the share of input i in the cost of production. These two equations may be solved as

$$
\begin{bmatrix} \hat{w}_1 \\ \hat{w}_2 \end{bmatrix} = \frac{1}{\theta_{11}\theta_{22} - \theta_{12}\theta_{21}} \begin{bmatrix} \theta_{22} & -\theta_{21} \\ -\theta_{12} & \theta_{11} \end{bmatrix} \begin{bmatrix} \hat{p}_1 - \theta_{31}\,\hat{p}_3 \\ \hat{p}_2 - \theta_{32}\,\hat{p}_3 \end{bmatrix}.
$$

$$(19)$$

If $\hat{p}_1 = \hat{p}_2 = 0$, then

$$\frac{\hat{w}_1}{\hat{p}_3} = -\frac{\theta_{22}\theta_{31} - \theta_{21}\theta_{32}}{(\theta_{11}\theta_{22} - \theta_{12}\theta_{21})},$$

$$\frac{\hat{w}_2}{\hat{p}_3} = \frac{\theta_{12}\theta_{31} - \theta_{11}\theta_{32}}{(\theta_{11}\theta_{22} - \theta_{12}\theta_{21})},$$

$$(20)$$

$$\frac{\hat{w}_2 - \hat{w}_1}{\hat{p}_3} = \frac{\theta_{31} - \theta_{32}}{(\theta_{11}\theta_{22} - \theta_{12}\theta_{21})}.$$

The denominator, $\theta_{11}\theta_{22} - \theta_{12}\theta_{21}$, is positive if industry 2 is factor 2 intensive and negative if industry 2 is factor 1 intensive. If it is assumed that industry 2 is factor 2 intensive then the above result indicates that an increase in the price of the imported intermediate input will raise the price of factor 2 relative to factor 1 if $\theta_{31} > \theta_{32}$, i.e. if the intermediate input is less important in industry 2 than in industry 1. The effect upon the factor prices themselves is less clear cut. However, if industry 2 does not use the intermediate input ($\theta_{32} = 0$) then w_2 will rise and w_1 will fall.

If the price changes are due to a change in the tariff structure, the terms on the right-hand side of (18) are called "effective rates of protection". These effective rates of protection play the same role as percentage changes in product prices in a final-goods model in their effect upon factor prices. This topic will be taken up in more detail in our discussion of tariff protection in a later chapter.

Example 2. As a second example, consider the case where $M = N = 2$ and $M* = 1$. In this example the number of products produced is less than the number of factors, so arbitrary (small) changes in endowments will alter factor prices. As a consequence the effect of changes in product prices upon factor prices and the effect of changes in endowments upon industry and product outputs will depend not only upon the input–output coefficient matrices, but will also depend upon the response of these coefficients to changes in prices. The model is a special case of the previous example where product 2 is not produced, and is

$$c^1(w_1, w_2, p_3) = p_1,$$

$$c_{11}(w_1, w_2, p_3)g_1 = v_1, \tag{21}$$

$$c_{21}(w_1, w_2, p_3)g_1 = v_2.$$

The comparative static equations in terms of percentage differences are

$$\theta_{11}\,\hat{w}_1 + \theta_{21}\,\hat{w}_2 + \theta_{31}\,\hat{p}_3 = \hat{p}_1,$$

$$\hat{g}_1 + \epsilon_{11}\,\hat{w}_1 + \epsilon_{12}\,\hat{w}_2 + \epsilon_{13}\,\hat{p}_3 = \hat{v}_1, \tag{22}$$

$$\hat{g}_1 + \epsilon_{21}\,\hat{w}_1 + \epsilon_{22}\,\hat{w}_2 + \epsilon_{23}\,\hat{p}_3 = \hat{v}_2,$$

where ϵ_{ij} is the elasticity of demand for factor i with respect to the price of the input j. The solution is

$$
\begin{bmatrix} \hat{g}_1 \\[2mm] \hat{w}_1 \\[2mm] \hat{w}_2 \end{bmatrix}
= \frac{1}{\Delta}
\begin{bmatrix}
\theta_{11}\,\theta_{21}\,(\sigma_{11}\,\sigma_{22} - \sigma_{12}\,\sigma_{21}) & \theta_{11}\,\theta_{21}\,(\sigma_{21} - \sigma_{22}) & \theta_{11}\,\theta_{21}\,(\sigma_{12} - \sigma_{11}) \\[2mm]
\theta_{21}\,(\sigma_{12} - \sigma_{22}) & -\theta_{21} & \theta_{21} \\[2mm]
\theta_{11}\,(\sigma_{21} - \sigma_{11}) & \theta_{11} & -\theta_{11}
\end{bmatrix}
$$

$$
\times
\begin{bmatrix}
\hat{p}_1 - \theta_{31}\,\hat{p}_3 \\[2mm]
\hat{v}_1 - \epsilon_{13}\,\hat{p}_3 \\[2mm]
\hat{v}_2 - \epsilon_{23}\,\hat{p}_3
\end{bmatrix},
\tag{23}
$$

where $\Delta = \theta_{11}\,(\epsilon_{12} - \epsilon_{22}) + \theta_{21}\,(\epsilon_{21} - \epsilon_{11}) = \theta_{11}\,\theta_{21}\,[-\sigma_{11} - \sigma_{22} + 2\sigma_{12}]$, and where $\sigma_{ij} = \epsilon_{ij}\,\theta_{j1}^{-1}$ is the Allen–Uzawa elasticity of substitution between inputs i and j in industry 1. While the 3×3 matrix of σ's is negative semi-definite, let us suppose that the principal submatrix formed by deleting the third row and column is negative definite. This implies that $\Delta > 0$ if $\theta_{11}, \theta_{21} > 0$, and that $(\sigma_{11}\sigma_{22} - \sigma_{12}\sigma_{21}) > 0$ (see problem set).

With these sign restrictions in mind, let us consider the solution (23) in more detail. Let p_3 increase with $\hat{p}_1 = \hat{v}_1 = \hat{v}_2 = 0$. Then (23) can be used to show that $\hat{g}_1 < 0$, so output of good 1 falls (see problem set). The signs of $\hat{w}_1$ and $\hat{w}_2$, however, are not able to be signed without special assumptions regarding the relationships between the various Allen–Uzawa substitution elasticities. Depending on these elasticities both factor prices might fall, or either might rise. Clearly, both factor prices cannot rise since this would mean that all input prices have risen and so unit cost would exceed the price for product 1. In general, which factor price rises most (or falls least)? From (23) it follows that $\hat{w}_2 - \hat{w}_1 = -[(\theta_{11}(\sigma_{11} - \sigma_{21} - \sigma_{13} + \sigma_{23}) + \theta_{21}(\sigma_{12} - \sigma_{22} - \sigma_{13} + \sigma_{23})]\theta_{31}\hat{p}_3/\Delta$. Now it is a property of Allen–Uzawa substitution elasticities that $\sigma_{i1}\theta_{11} + \sigma_{i2}\theta_{21} + \sigma_{i3}\theta_{31} = 0$, $i = 1, 2, 3$. Using this property the following expression is obtained:

$$(\hat{w}_2 - \hat{w}_1)/\hat{p}_3 = (\sigma_{23} - \sigma_{13})\theta_{31}/\Delta. \tag{24}$$

This shows that the effect of a change in p_3 upon w_2/w_1 depends upon the relative magnitudes of the Allen–Uzawa elasticities of substitution between the intermediate input on the one hand, and the two primary factors. If the intermediate is more substitutable with factor 2 than factor 1, then $\sigma_{23} > \sigma_{13}$ and the price of factor 2 will rise relative to the price of factor 1. This is because as p_3 rises less of the intermediate input is used and so the demand for its closest substitute, factor 2, is increased, thus raising w_2.

If the endowment of factor 2 increases, while $\hat{p}_1 = \hat{p}_3 = \hat{v}_1 = 0$, then (23) shows that the price of factor 2 will fall and the price of factor 1 will rise. The effect upon output of good 1 is ambiguous in general. Output will rise if factors 1 and 2 are substitutes ($\sigma_{12} > 0$), but may fall if the primary factors are complements ($\sigma_{12} < 0$) in production.

This example serves to emphasize the importance of the dimension of the model in obtaining comparative statics results. Here, with one product produced using two factors and an imported intermediate input, the factor prices are affected by endowments. Furthermore, the effect of endowments upon output and the effect of product prices upon factor prices depend upon substitution elasticities rather than input–output coefficients. This is in contrast with the results obtained when the number of products produced equals the number of factors of production.

5.3. A general model of the production sector

In this section a very general model of the production sector is formulated and analysed. The model permits a very general technology but does not explicitly deal with the division of the production sector into industries. It is an aggregate model of production which contains the final-good model of Chapter 4 and the intermediate-good model of the previous section as special cases. Moreover, the existence of joint outputs as well as intermediate inputs will be permitted. In the following section the model will be disaggregated into industries.

This aggregate model is important in that it indicates the most general restrictions on the behaviour of a production sector. Behaviour of a final-good model or of an intermediate-good model will be more restrictive since they are more restrictive models. By examining the general results we are better able to put the results for a special economy into perspective.

The production sector takes as given the vector $p = (p_1, ..., p_M)$ of prices of producible goods and the vector $v = (v_1, ..., v_N)$ of endowments of the primary factors of production. Given these and the technology of production, the production sector chooses the vector of net outputs $y = (y_1, ..., y_M)$ for goods and the vector of factor prices $w = (w_1, ..., w_N)$. The technology is described by the production possibility set $Y(v)$, which is the set of net outputs y that can be produced with endowment vector v. The production sector is assumed to choose $y \in Y(v)$ to maximize gross national product (GNP) which is py. The factor prices are assumed to be equal to the marginal value products of the factors. The objective of this section is to formulate this model and indicate how y and w respond to changes in p and v.

5.3.1. The production possibility set and the GNP function

One choice for $Y(v)$ is to define it in terms of individual production functions as in eq. (3.12). In Chapter 3 it was shown that the decentralized production sector behaved in such a way that the equilibrium output vector maximized GNP on the set $Y(v)$. A similar result could have been shown for the intermediate-good model of the previous section. Thus, the assumption that y is chosen to maximize GNP is not unreasonable.[5]

---

[5] This statement needs to be qualified. For the models we are considering the statement is true. However, it is well known that a competitive solution of the production sector and the (centralized) maximum GNP solution do not coincide when (a) there exist externalities which are not internalized through the formation of an appropriate market, or (b) some agents are not price-takers, or (c) distortions occur in the factor market.

The maximization of GNP subject to the technology constraint yields the GNP function:

$$G(p, v) \equiv \max_{y} \{py: y \in Y(v)\}. \tag{25}$$

This states that the maximum GNP depends upon the product price vector p and the endowment vector v. In what follows the properties of this function are discussed. They depend upon the structure of the problem in (25) and upon the properties of the production possibility set $Y(v)$. The properties of this set and the resulting properties of the GNP function have been rigorously discussed in detail by Diewert (1973, 1974).

If v is treated as a variable vector, the technology set may be defined as $T \equiv \{(y, -v): y \in Y(v)\}$. This is a set in $(M + N)$-dimensional space and indicates the set of feasible net outputs of all commodities, which include products and factors. The assumptions regarding the technology may be expressed in terms of either T or $Y(v)$.

Assumptions on the technology. (a) T is a closed, non-empty subset of $(M + N)$-dimensional space; (b) if $(y, -v) \in T$, then $v \geqslant 0$; (c) T is a convex set; (d) T is a cone; (e) if $z^0 \in T$ and $z^1 \leqslant z^0$, then $z^1 \in T$; (f) $Y(v)$ is bounded from above for every $v \geqslant 0$; and (g) if $v > 0$, then there exists a $y^0 \gtrsim 0$ such that $y^0 \in Y(v)$. (26)

The interpretation of these rather formal conditions is as follows. Assumption (a) simply means that the set T contains its boundary and contains at least one point, while (b) indicates that primary factors cannot be produced. Assumption (c) means that the line joining any two points in T is also in T. For given v this means that the production possibility set $Y(v)$ is convex, i.e. the rate at which one product has to be given up as more of a second good is produced increases with the production of the second good. Also, if $X(y) \equiv \{v: (y, -v) \in T\}$ is the set of factor inputs which can produce vector y, then this set is also convex. Its boundary is, of course, the isoquant. The assumption (d) that T is a cone means that if $(y, -v) \in T$ and $\lambda \geqslant 0$, then $(\lambda y, -\lambda v) \in T$ or, equivalently, $\lambda y \in Y(\lambda v)$. This is the constant returns to scale (CRS) assumption. Assumption (e) indicates that there is free disposal, i.e. more input cannot yield less output. On the other hand (f) says that a fixed factor endowment cannot yield unlimited outputs of all goods, so there is some point $b = (b_1, ..., b_M)$, depending upon v, such that $b \geqslant y$ for all $y \in Y(v)$. This means that factors are needed by the production sector, but it does not rule out the possibility that *some* products may be produced without the input of a primary factor. The final assumption (g) is not used by

Diewert (1974), but is imposed to ensure that the production sector is capable of producing at least one positive output when it has a positive amount of all factors available. This means that the production sector is weakly productive. A stronger condition would be to assume that it is capable of producing a positive amount of every good, given positive factor endowments.

An illustration of the production possibility set $Y(v)$ is provided in fig. 5.2 for the case where $M = 2$. Notice that the technology is productive since a positive production of both goods is possible. For a price vector $p^0 > 0$ there is a

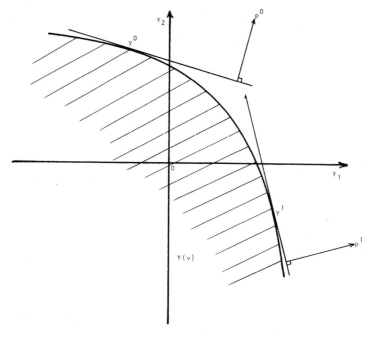

Figure 5.2

family of iso-GNP lines and the highest one attainable is shown supporting $Y(v)$ at the point y^0. Thus, y^0 solves problem (25). The net output of product 2 is positive while the net output of product 1 is negative, so that $-y_1^0$ must be imported. It is not possible to tell from this solution whether product 1 is produced by some firms, nor whether y_2^0 represents gross output as well as net output. To obtain such information a decomposition of the technology set into separate industry technology sets is required.

5.3.2. Properties of the GNP function

The GNP function can be shown to have the following properties:

> **Properties of** $G(p,v)$. (a) $G(p,v)$ is defined and is non-negative
> for all $p > 0$ and $v \geq 0$; (b) $G(p,v)$ is a continuous, linearly ho-
> mogeneous, convex function of p for all v; and (c) $G(p,v)$ is a
> continuous, linearly homogeneous, non-decreasing concave func-
> tion of v for all p, and is positive if $v > 0$.   (27)

The GNP function is non-negative because T is a cone and so producing $y = 0$
is always an option. The function will be well defined for $p > 0$ since the production possibility set is bounded from above by assumption. However, if $p_1 = 0$
say, then it is possible that product 1 could be imported in greater and greater
amounts and used as an input to produce greater and greater amounts of the other
products. In this case GNP could always be increased. Of course, there is a limiting value to it, namely the supremum. Thus, if $G(p, v)$ were to be redefined as a
supremum over $Y(v)$, then it would be well defined for all $p \geq 0$.

Property (b) concerns the effect of p upon GNP. From fig. 5.2 it is clear that
if all product prices are multiplied by $\lambda > 0$, the solution for y will be unchanged
and GNP will now be $G(\lambda p, v) = \lambda G(p, v)$. Thus, $G(p, v)$ is linearly homogeneous
in p. Convexity is explained as follows. Consider two price vectors, p^0 and p^1,
and the convex combination $p^\lambda \equiv \lambda p^0 + (1 - \lambda)p^1$, where $0 \leq \lambda \leq 1$. Let the
solutions for net output be y^0, y^1 and y^λ, respectively. It follows from the act
of maximization that $p^i y^i \geq p^i y$ for all $y \in Y(v)$. Hence,

$$G(p^\lambda, v) = p^\lambda y^\lambda = [\lambda p^0 + (1 - \lambda)p^1]y^\lambda$$
$$= \lambda p^0 y^\lambda + (1 - \lambda)p^1 y^\lambda \leq \lambda p^0 y^0 + (1 - \lambda)p^1 y^1$$
$$= \lambda G(p^0, v) + (1 - \lambda)G(p^1, v).$$

Since this inequality holds for all p^0 and p^1, the function is therefore convex
in p. Fig. 5.3 illustrates an iso-GNP curve in product price space for the case
where $M = 2$. Only one such curve need be shown since the linear homogeneity
property implies that all iso-GNP curves are "radial blow-ups" of one another.
The convexity property means that prices such as p^λ on the line joining p^0 and
p^1 yield GNP lower (strictly, no greater) than at p^0 (or p^1).

Property (c) concerns the effect of v upon GNP. In effect it says that, as a
function of v, GNP has all of the properties (2.3′) of a constant-returns-to-scale

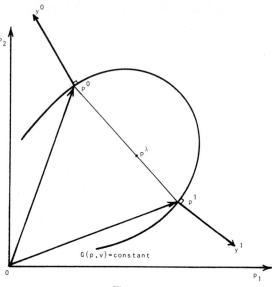

Figure 5.3

production function.[6] It is linearly homogeneous since if v is multiplied by $\lambda > 0$, then the production possibility set $Y(\lambda v) = \lambda Y(v)$ grows proportionately larger, due to constant returns to scale, and so the output level λy^0 is both possible and optimal. GNP is non-decreasing in v since (26, e) indicates that more of a factor cannot reduce the production possibility set (and will usually enlarge it). Thus, more of a factor cannot reduce GNP, and will usually increase it. Concavity in v occurs because of the convexity of the technology set T, as is now demonstrated. Let y^i be the solution when v^i is the endowment vector for $i = 0, 1$ and define $y^\lambda \equiv \lambda y^0 + (1 - \lambda)y^1$ and $v^\lambda \equiv \lambda v^0 + (1 - \lambda)v^1$, where $0 \leqslant \lambda \leqslant 1$. By convexity of T the production y^λ is possible when the endowment vector is v^λ, so

$$G(p, v^\lambda) \geqslant py^\lambda = p[\lambda y^0 + (1 - \lambda)y^1]$$
$$= \lambda py^0 + (1 - \lambda)py^1 = \lambda G(p, v^0) + (1 - \lambda)G(p, v^1).$$

[6]   The reader may find it instructive to see how the iso-GNP curve in factor quantity space is derived when there are several industries in the economy, by referring back to fig. 3.1 in Chapter 3. In that figure three unit value isoquants are drawn. The "convex hull" of these three curves is the curve *GCDEFH* which indicates the set of input vectors which can produce $\$1$ of GNP. If only one good is produced, then GNP will equal $\$1$ if we are on that good's unit-value isoquant. However, endowments on the line segments *CD* and *EF* can produce $\$1$ worth of GNP by producing goods 1 and 2 and goods 2 and 3, respectively. See also fig. 5.5 below.

Thus, $G(p, v)$ is concave in v. Finally, assumption (26,g) ensures that GNP will be positive if $v > 0$ and $p > 0$.

The preceding discussion of the properties of the GNP function is non-rigorous and is intended to show the nature of the proofs and to indicate the role played by the assumptions on the technology. The rigorous proofs are left to the reader and are dealt with in problems at the end of the chapter. Not all the assumptions in (26) are required to establish that $G(p, v)$ satisfies (27). However, they are all needed to prove that the technology set T and the GNP function $G(p, v)$ are dual or contain the same information. Diewert (1973, 1974), has proved that a function which satisfies (27) can be used to construct a set $\hat{T}$ which satisfies (26) and that the GNP function for set $\hat{T}$ is precisely the initial function. Also, it is true that the GNP function $G(p, v)$ contains sufficient information to reconstruct the technology set T. Thus, the GNP function and the technology sets are dual representations of the technology. This duality property allows us to make extensive use of the GNP function in theoretical and empirical work. Given a GNP function which satisfies (27), we know that there exists a technology set which gives rise to the GNP function even though it may not be possible to calculate it in practice. However, whether it can be calculated is of no real consequence since the GNP function contains all the information we need.

It is instructive to consider another characterization of the convexity of $G(p, v)$ in p, especially as it provides a simple intuitive proof for Hotelling's lemma which is discussed below. This characterization of convexity is that the function $G(p, v)$ is never below any support or tangent plane in the price space. Let y^0 be a solution to problem (25) when the price vector is p^0. If the price vector now changes to p^1 with solution y^1 it follows that $p^1 y^1 \geqslant p^1 y^0$. If the solution for y remained at y^0 for all p^1, then the GNP function would be $G(p, v) = py^0$ which is linear in p since y^0 is constant. However, the solution may change, in which case the inequality $G(p^1, v) = p^1 y^1 \geqslant p^1 y^0$ indicates that GNP never falls below $p^1 y^0$. Since this holds for all p^1 it follows that the GNP function $G(p, v)$ never falls below the linear function py^0. Evidently this linear function supports the GNP function at the point p^0 since $G(p, v) \geqslant py^0$ for all p with equality holding at $p = p^0$. Since this is true for all p^0, it follows that the GNP function never falls below any support or tangent plane and hence it is convex in p.

This demonstration of convexity shows, as a by-product, that the support plane to $G(p, v)$ at p^0 is described by py^0, where y^0 is the solution to (26) when $p = p^0$. If the solution y^0 is unique, the support plane is unique. In this case the slope of the linear function, which is y^0, equals the slope of the function $G(p, v)$ at p^0. Thus, $\partial G(p^0, v)/\partial p = y^0$, which is known as Hotelling's lemma. It indicates that the solution for y can be obtained by partially differentiating $G(p, v)$

with respect to p, a result analogous to Shephard's lemma for the cost function. If the solution is not unique, the support plane is not unique and so the derivative of $G(p, v)$ at p^0 does not exist. However, left- and right-hand derivatives will exist and the set of vectors between the left- and right-hand vectors of derivatives, called the subgradient, coincides with the set of solution vectors for y. These results are illustrated in fig. 5.4 for the case of $M = 2$. In fig. 5.4 (a) the GNP function is depicted as a function of p_1, given p_2^0 and v. One support plane

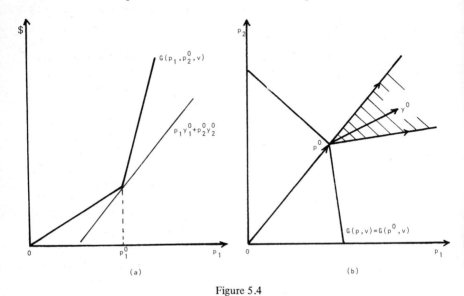

Figure 5.4

is drawn in, with slope y_1^0, although it is evident that there is a whole set of such planes corresponding to other solutions for y_1 at p^0. In fig. 5.4 (b) the set of gradients to $G(p, v)$ at p^0 form the shaded cone which contains the point y^0.

In summary, we have:

> **Hotelling's lemma.** The solution set for y to problem (25) is the set of subgradients $G_p(p, v)$. If $G(p, v)$ is differentiable at p, then the solution is unique and given by $G_p(p, v) = \partial G(p, v)/\partial p$. (28)

This is a very important result since it indicates how to obtain the output supply functions $y(p, v) = G_p(p, v)$ from the GNP function simply by partial differentiation.

Other important derivatives are $\partial G(p, v)/\partial v_i$, $i = 1, ..., N$, which indicate the increase in GNP due to an increase in v_i. These marginal value products can be interpreted as shadow prices which, in a competitive economy, will be equal to market prices for the factors of production. Of course, these derivatives may not exist. However, the left- and right-hand derivatives exist and the set of vectors between the vectors of left- and right-hand derivatives is called the supergradient of $G(p, v)$ with respect to v. It is left to the reader to draw diagrams analogous to those in fig. 5.4 to illustrate the relationship between GNP and the endowment vector.[7] In summary,

The equilibrium (shadow) factor prices are given by the set of supergradients $G_v(p, v)$. If $G(p, v)$ is differentiable at v, then the factor price vector is unique and given by $G_v(p, v) = \partial G(p, v)/\partial v$. (29)

The above discussion has concentrated on the properties of the GNP function, properties which derive from the assumptions about the technology and from the assumption of maximizing behaviour. The model is very general in that it contains as special cases the final-good model of Chapter 3 and 4 and the intermediate-good model of the previous section. Also, care was taken to consider the situations where $G(p, v)$ is not differentiable with respect to p and v since these correspond to situations where output levels and factor prices are non-unique. These situations can easily arise as we have already seen in Chapter 4.

5.3.3. Comparative statics

Attention is now focused on the response of the solution y and of w to changes in p and v. These responses are determined by the properties of $G(p, v)$, and are more easily characterized if it is assumed that the GNP function is twice continuously differentiable. Below, this differentiability assumption will be relaxed. If $G(p, v)$ is continuously differentiable with respect to p and v, then the output supplies and factor prices are unique for any given p and v due to (28) and (29). Thus, the output supply functions are

$$y(p, v) = G_p(p, v),$$ (30)

[7] The counterpart to fig. 5.4(b) can be obtained from fig. 5.5 below by choosing a point v^0 on the iso-GNP curve and depicting the gradient vector $G_v(p, v^0)$ which is interpreted as the factor price vector w^0. If the iso-GNP curve is drawn with a kink at v^0, then there will be a set of gradients.

and the factor price functions are

$$w(p, v) = G_v(p, v). \tag{31}$$

Hence, the assumption that $G(p, v)$ is twice continuously differentiable means that the output supply and factor price functions are once continuously differentiable. This is the minimal assumption for a local differential comparative statics analysis.

The GNP function is linearly homogeneous in p. This means that the output supply functions are homogeneous of degree zero in p, and are linearly homogeneous in v.[8] Since the GNP function is also linearly homogeneous in v, the same argument indicates that the factor price functions are homogeneous of degree zero in v, and are linearly homogeneous in p. These results are summarized as

$$y(\lambda p, v) = y(p, v),$$
$$w(\lambda p, v) = \lambda w(p, v), \tag{32}$$

and

$$y(p, \lambda v) = \lambda y(p, v),$$
$$w(p, \lambda v) = w(p, v), \tag{33}$$

where $\lambda > 0$. These imply that outputs depend upon relative not absolute product prices, while factor prices depend upon relative not absolute endowments. The former result is due to price-taking behaviour, while the latter is due to the CRS assumption.

Application of Euler's theorem to the output supply and factor price functions yields the following relations among their derivatives. Derivatives with respect to p obey

$$\text{(a)} \quad \sum_{k=1}^{M} \frac{\partial y_j(p, v)}{\partial p_k} \cdot p_k = 0, \qquad j = 1, ..., M, \quad \text{i.e. } G_{pp}(p, v)p = 0,$$

$$\text{(b)} \quad \sum_{k=1}^{M} \frac{\partial w_i(p, v)}{\partial p_k} \cdot p_k = w_i, \qquad i = 1, ..., N, \quad \text{i.e. } G_{vp}(p, v)p = G_v(p, v), \tag{34}$$

---

[8] If a function $f(x, y)$ is homogeneous of degree r in vector x, and homogeneous of degree s in vector y, then $\partial f(x, y)/\partial x_i$ is homogeneous of degree $r - 1$ in x, and is homogeneous of degree s in y. That is, differentiation reduces the degree of homogeneity by one. See Allen (1938, pp. 317–320) and Lancaster (1968, pp. 334–336) for further details on homogeneous functions.

while derivatives with respect to v obey

(a) $\displaystyle\sum_{k=1}^{N} \frac{\partial y_j(p, v)}{\partial v_k} \cdot v_k = y_j,$ $j = 1, ..., M,$ i.e. $G_{pv}(p, v)\, v = G_p(p, v),$

(35)

(b) $\displaystyle\sum_{k=1}^{N} \frac{\partial w_i(p, v)}{\partial v_k} \cdot v_k = 0,$ $i = 1, ..., N,$ i.e. $G_{vv}(p, v)\, v = 0.$

Since it is assumed that $G(p, v)$ is twice continuously differentiable, Young's theorem implies that the second derivative matrix is symmetric. In particular, this implies that

$$\left[\frac{\partial w_i(p, v)}{\partial p_j} \right] = \left[\frac{\partial^2 G(p, v)}{\partial p_j \partial v_i} \right] \equiv G_{pv}(p, v)$$

$$= G_{vp}(p, v) \equiv \left[\frac{\partial^2 G(p, v)}{\partial v_i \partial p_j} \right] = \left[\frac{\partial y_j(p, v)}{\partial v_i} \right]. \qquad (36)$$

This constitutes some of Samuelson's (1953) *reciprocity conditions* and means that the increase in w_i due to a one unit increase in p_j is equal to the increase in y_j due to an increase in v_i. Thus, there is a fundamental duality or equivalence between the effects of product prices upon factor prices on the one hand, and the effects of factor endowments on the output levels on the other. This duality has already been pointed out in the discussion of the final-good model in Chapter 4.

The GNP function is convex in p. This means that the $M \times M$ matrix of second derivatives (hessian) with respect to p is symmetric and positive semi-definite. Similarly, since the GNP function is concave in v, the hessian with respect to v is a symmetric negative semi-definite matrix. In view of (28) and (29) we therefore have

(a) $\quad G_{pp}(p, v) \equiv \left[\dfrac{\partial^2 G(p, v)}{\partial p_k \partial p_j} \right] = \left[\dfrac{\partial y_j(p, v)}{\partial p_k} \right]$

is positive semi-definite and symmetric,

(37)

(b) $\quad G_{vv}(p, v) \equiv \left[\dfrac{\partial^2 G(p, v)}{\partial v_k \partial v_i} \right] = \left[\dfrac{\partial w_i(p, v)}{\partial v_k} \right]$

is negative semi-definite and symmetric.

The symmetry properties of the matrices in (37) constitute the rest of the reciprocity conditions. They mean that the change in the output of j due to a unit increase in the price of product k is equal to the change in the output of k due to a unit increase in the price of j. Similarly, the change in the price of factor i due to a unit increase in the endowment of factor k is equal to the change in the price of factor k due to a unit increase in the endowment of i. The matrices in (37) are of rank less than M and N, respectively, because of conditions (34,a) and (35,b). The fact that the matrix in (37,a) is positive semi-definite and the matrix in (37,b) is negative semi-definite implies that special conditions must hold. In particular, it means that the diagonal elements satisfy

$$\text{(a)} \quad \frac{\partial^2 G(p,v)}{\partial p_j^2} = \frac{\partial y_j(p,v)}{\partial p_j} \geq 0, \quad j = 1, \ldots, M,$$

$$\text{(b)} \quad \frac{\partial^2 G^2(p,v)}{\partial v_i^2} = \frac{\partial w_i(p,v)}{\partial v_i} \leq 0, \quad i = 1, \ldots, N. \tag{38}$$

That is to say, the output of good i will never decrease and will generally increase when the price of i is raised, while the price of factor i will never rise and will generally decrease when the endowment of i increases.

The symmetry conditions allow (34) and (35) to be rewritten as

$$\text{(a)} \quad \sum_{k=1}^{M} \frac{\partial y_k(p,v)}{\partial p_j} \cdot p_k = 0, \quad j = 1, \ldots, M, \quad \text{i.e.} \quad pG_{pp}(p,v) = 0,$$

$$\text{(b)} \quad \sum_{k=1}^{M} \frac{\partial y_k(p,v)}{\partial v_i} \cdot p_k = w_i, \quad i = 1, \ldots, N, \quad \text{i.e.} \quad pG_{pv}(p,v) = G_v(p,v), \tag{39}$$

and

$$\text{(a)} \quad \sum_{k=1}^{N} \frac{\partial w_k(p,v)}{\partial p_j} \cdot v_k = y_j, \quad j = 1, \ldots, M, \quad \text{i.e.} \quad pG_{pv}(p,v) = G_p(p,v),$$

$$\text{(b)} \quad \sum_{k=1}^{N} \frac{\partial w_k(p,v)}{\partial v_i} \cdot v_k = 0, \quad i = 1, \ldots, N, \quad \text{i.e.} \quad vG_{vv}(p,v) = 0, \tag{40}$$

respectively. Eq. (39,a) indicates the relationships between the effects on all outputs of an increase in the price of product j. If the output of j rises ((38,a) is a strict inequality), then (39,a) indicates that some output must fall. Similarly, (40,b) indicates that if v_i increases and w_i falls ((38,b) is a strict inequality), then some factor price must rise. If $w_i > 0$ then (39,b) indicates that at least one output must rise when v_i is increased. Hence, because of the reciprocity relations (36), the price of factor i must rise if the price of that commodity increases. Similarly, if $y_j > 0$, then (40, a) shows that at least one factor price must rise when p_j is increased, while if $y_j < 0$, at least one factor price must fall. By the reciprocity conditions (36) this implies that if the endowment of that factor increases, then the output of j will increase if $y_j > 0$ and the input of $j(-y_j)$ will increase if $y_j < 0$.

5.3.4. Special cases

The above restrictions on the derivatives of the GNP function are derived from its properties and are restrictions on the response of outputs and factor prices to changes in product prices and factor endowments, under the differentiability assumption. Since the technology underlying the GNP function is very general, these restrictions are very weak. Stronger restrictions (results) can be obtained only by imposing stronger assumptions on the technology. For example, if the technology consists of a set of M final-good production functions, stronger results are obtained. These have been derived in Chapter 4 and, of course, they satisfy restrictions (30) and (40). For example, in the $M^* = M = N$ case, eq. (4.52) is the solution for the derivatives of y_* and w with respect to p_* and v. Part of this solution is that the $N \times N$ matrix $G_{vv}(p, v) = w_v(p, v) = 0$, meaning that factor prices are not responsive to small changes in v. This is the factor price equalization result which means that the matrix of second derivatives of $G(p, v)$ with respect to v is a zero matrix. That is, $G(p, v)$ is locally linear in v. Fig. 5.5 illustrates this situation for the case of $M^* = M = 2$ in the Lerner diagram. The convex hull of the two unit value isoquants is the solid curve which consists of part of the unit value isoquants and the line segment AB. It is the set of endowments v for which $G(p, v) = 1$. Iso-GNP curves for other GNP levels could be drawn in, but in view of the linear homogeneity of $G(p, v)$ in v they all have the same shape and are therefore not depicted. The normal w^0 to AB is the equilibrium factor price vector *for any* v in the diversification cone AOB. Thus, within the diversification cone the GNP function is linear.

Other specific results contained in (4.52) relate to the effects of endowments on outputs leading to the Rybczynski theorem, the effects of product prices on factor prices leading to the Stolper–Samuelson theorem, and the effects of product prices on outputs. In each case the resulting formulae relate specifically to the industrial structure imposed by the model. The result in Chapter 4 that $\partial y / \partial p$ is a positive semi-definite matrix was tedious to obtain, and it is noteworthy that it is easily derived from the GNP function simply by recognizing that $G_{pp} = \partial y / \partial p$

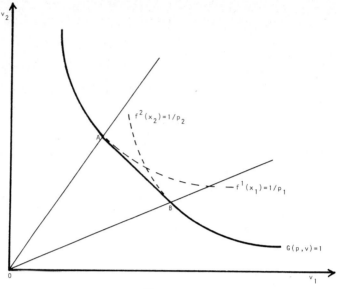

Figure 5.5

is positive semi-definite because $G(p, v)$ is concave and linearly homogeneous in p. Of course, (4.52) gives a formula for this matrix in terms of more basic variables and is therefore more informative. Further aspects of the relationship between (4.52) and $G(p, v)$ are left to the reader.

5.3.5. *General results on effects of product price and factor endowment changes*

Some of the implications of changes in product prices have been discussed. We now consider whether the essence of the Stolper–Samuelson theorem holds in this general model. From (34,b) we obtain:

$$\sum_{k=1}^{M} \frac{\partial w_i(p, v)}{\partial p_k} \frac{p_k}{w_i} = 1, \quad i = 1, ..., N. \tag{41}$$

Each term in the sum is an elasticity of a factor price with respect to a product price. For the sum to be unity it is not necessary for any term to be greater than one or for any term to be negative. This means that when the price of a good increases no factor price need increase by a greater percentage and no factor price need fall.[9] Thus, in contrast with the intermediate-good model of the previous section and the final-good model of Chapter 4, no factor need gain in real income and hence welfare and no factor need lose money income as a result of a price change. Of course, (41) indicates that if there is a product whose price increase causes i to gain in real income in terms of that good (the elasticity is greater than one), then there must exist at least one other good such that an increase in its price will cause w_i to fall.

A similar argument applies to the Rybczynski theorem. From (35,a) we obtain:

$$\sum_{k=1}^{N} \frac{\partial y_j(p,v)}{\partial v_k} \frac{v_k}{y_j} = 1, \quad j = 1, ..., M. \tag{42}$$

Again it is not necessary that any elasticity of output j with respect to the endowment of any factor should be greater than unity or less than zero. In contrast to the intermediate-good and final-good models, it is possible that when the endowment of a factor increases, the outputs of all goods increase less than proportionately than the increase in endowment. Of course, if one output does increase more than proportionately, some other output must fall.

These observations emphasize that a general model like we have here may yield weak results. As more structure is imposed on the model the results strengthen. A comparison of the present results with those of the previous section for the intermediate good model shows that the essential features of the Stolper–Samuelson and Rybczynski theorems are lost in moving to our general model.

The above restrictions on the response of y and w to changes in p and v were based upon the differentiability assumption. Without this assumption some general restrictions can be imposed as a direct consequence of the maximization behaviour of the production sector. If y^i is a solution to the maximum GNP problem when the price vector is p^i, $i = 0, 1$, then $p^0 y^0 \geqslant p^0 y^1$ and $p^1 y^1 \geqslant p^1 y^0$ since y^0 and y^1 are feasible for both problems. These inequalities yield:

$$(p^1 - p^0)(y^1 - y^0) \geqslant 0 \quad \text{or} \quad \Delta p \Delta y \geqslant 0. \tag{43}$$

This is the restriction on the response of p to y, when $G(p,v)$ is not known but it is known that it satisfies (27). If p^0 and p^1 differ only in the ith term, (43) indicates that an increase in p_i will not decrease y_i (and will generally increase it).

---

[9] The reader may verify that condition (40, a) converted to elasticity form does not imply that some elasticity must be greater than one or less than zero. (34,b) and (40,a) are the only restrictions on the price derivatives.

The fact that $G(p, v)$ is concave in v means that $G(p, v^1) \leqslant G(p, v^0) + w^0(v^1 - v^0)$, where w^0 is a gradient or subdifferential of g with respect to v at v^0 and is therefore, by (29), the equilibrium factor price vector. Similarly, $G(p, v^0) \leqslant G(p, v^1) + w^1(v^0 - v^1)$. Also, the homogeneity property implies that $w^i v^i = G(p, v^i)$, $i = 0, 1$. Hence, the above inequalities may be added yielding, after some rearrangement:

$$(w^1 - w^0)(v^1 - v^0) \leqslant 0 \quad \text{or} \quad \Delta w \Delta v \leqslant 0. \tag{44}$$

This is a general restriction on the response of w to changes in v. As a special case when only the ith term in Δv is positive, it implies that $\Delta w_i \leqslant 0$.

5.4. Joint outputs [10]

The purpose of this section is to formulate a model of the production sector consisting of K industries each of which is permitted to produce more than one product and to use intermediate inputs. In effect, we are simply taking the aggregate model of the previous section and are making the additional assumption that the technology can be described by K separate transformation functions, which shall be referred to as industries. Thus, we are disaggregating the model and focusing attention upon industries. The model is more general than that of section 5.2, however, since joint production is permitted and the number of industries does not have to equal the number of goods.

By joint production is meant the situation where the technology facing the industry cannot be described by separate production functions for each of the produced goods. If separate production functions exist, then the model of the production sector is precisely as formulated in section 5.2. If, however, the technology for the production of a good is influenced by the amount of another good being produced, then the goods are said to be joint. The technology for industry j may be described by a technology set T_j. The boundary of this set is the transformation frontier written implicitly as $t^j(u_j, -x_j) = 0$, where u_j is the M-dimensional vector of net outputs of goods and x_j is the N-dimensional vector of inputs of primary factors. If the kth element of u_j is positive, then product k is produced by industry j; if the kth element is negative, then it is used as an intermediate input; and if the kth element is zero product, k is neither an input nor an output. While it is possible that certain commodities only enter as outputs, and others do not enter the production process for a particular industry,

---

[10] This section is of a specialized nature and may be omitted without loss of continuity.

the model does not require such a classification a priori. In general, unless T_j actually prevents it, a commodity may enter as an output or an input or not at all, depending upon relative prices.

Let there be K industries, each of which may jointly produce up to M products using as inputs up to N primary and up to M intermediate inputs. It is evident that the concept of an industry coincides with the concept of a production process or technology. What is being assumed is that there are a finite number, K, production processes which may be described by a transformation frontier. This transformation frontier cannot be described by two or more frontiers, each involving fewer products. Thus, K is the minimal number of "minimal" frontiers which describe the technology of the production sector. As a special case, there may be no joint production, in which case each industry can produce but one product and so $K = M$. This is then the intermediate product model dealt with in section 5.2. If, furthermore, intermediate inputs are not permitted, the model reduces to the final-goods model of Chapter 4.

5.4.1. Value added and unit value added cost functions

Each industry j is assumed to maximize profit $pu_j - wx_j$ subject to the condition that $(u_j, -x_j) \in T_j$, where the product and factor price vector are given. It will be convenient to assume a two-stage maximization process. In the first stage u_j is chosen to maximize value added pu_j subject to the technology. This yields the *value added function*

$$\pi^j(p, x_j) \equiv \max_{u_j} \{pu_j : (u_j, -x_j) \in T_j\}, \quad j = 1, ..., K, \tag{45}$$

which depends upon the product price vector p and the factor input vector x_j. It should be recognized that if T_j satisfies conditions (26) which were specified for the aggregate technology set, then $\pi^j(p, x_j)$ is formally the same as the GNP function $G(p, v)$ and therefore satisfies conditions (27). Here, however, it is called a value added function.[11]

Of particular interest is property (27,c) which states, in terms of the value added function, that $\pi^j(p, x_j)$ satisfies all of the usual conditions for a CRS production function with respect to x_j. That is, for a given p, the value added is a non-decreasing, linearly homogeneous, concave function of x_j. Treating it as such,

---

[11] Diewert (1973) calls it a "variable profit function", while Lau (1978) refers to it as a "restricted profit function".

we can think of choosing x_j to minimize the factor cost subject to producing a given amount of value added. Thus, we define

$$c^j(w, p) \equiv \min_{x_j} \{wx_j : \pi^j(p, x_j) \geqslant 1\}, \quad j = 1, ..., K, \tag{46}$$

as the *unit value added* (factor) *cost function*.

Each industry must choose a vector of net outputs u_j and a vector of factor inputs x_j to maximize profits, given the product and input prices. Using the concepts of a value added function, and a unit value added (factor) cost function, we can think of the industry as choosing a "quantity" of value added (i.e. number of dollars of value added) to maximize profits, which are value added minus factor cost. If r_j denotes the value added, profit is $r_j - c^j(w, p)r_j = r_j[1 - c^j(w, p)]$ because of CRS. Maximizing profit with respect to $r_j \geqslant 0$ yields an unbounded solution when $c^j(w, p) < 1$, i.e. when it costs less than \$1 to produce \$1 of value added. This unbounded solution is inconsistent with competitive equilibrium so it is ruled out. Thus, $c^j(w, p) \geqslant 1$ and the solution for r_j must satisfy the Kuhn –Tucker conditions

$$c^j(w, p) - 1 \geqslant 0 \leqslant r_j, \quad j = 1, ..., K. \tag{47}$$

If $c^j(w, p) > 1$, then (47) indicates that $r_j = 0$, whereas if $c^j(w, p) = 1$, then any $r_j \geqslant 0$ maximizes profits.

Because the unit value added cost function for given p is really an ordinary unit cost function, Shephard's lemma applies and hence the factor market equilibrium conditions may be written as

$$\sum_{j=1}^{K} c_{ij}(w, p) r_j - v_i \leqslant 0 \leqslant w_i, \quad i = 1, ..., N, \tag{48}$$

where $c_{ij}(w, p) \equiv \partial c^j(w, p)/\partial w_i$ is the demand for factor i per unit of value added in industry j. Equilibrium in the production sector is therefore described by the $K + N$ conditions, (47) and (48), in terms of the vector $w = (w_1, ..., w_N)$ of factor prices and the vector $r = (r_1, ..., r_K)$ of industry value added. It will be recognized that these conditions are a generalization of (3.6) and (3.7) of Chapter 3 to deal with intermediate inputs and joint outputs. The only formal difference between these two sets of equations is that in (47) and (48) the cost functions depend upon the full vector of product prices and consequently changes in p will affect (possibly) all cost equations and in non-proportional ways.

The unit value added cost function has some important properties. The first is proved and discussed in detail in Diewert (1978a), and is

The unit value added cost function $c^j(w,p)$ is (a) a positive, continuous from above, real valued function for $w > 0, p > 0$; (b) quasi-concave in (w,p); (c) homogeneous of degree -1 in p; and (d) non-decreasing and linearly homogeneous in w. (49)

The second, which is proved in Woodland (1977, p. 531), is extremely useful in that it enables the optimal net outputs to be obtained by simple differentiation of the unit value added cost function.

If $c^k(w,p)$ is differentiable with respect to p, and $c^k(w,p) = 1$, then $b_{jk}(w,p) \equiv -\partial c^k(w,p)/\partial p_j$ is the optimal net output of product j in industry k. (50)

In view of this result, the net output vector for the whole economy is

$$y = \left[\sum_{k=1}^{K} b_{jk}(w,p)\, r_k \right] = - \sum_{k=1}^{K} c_p^k(w,p)\, r_k, \tag{51}$$

where each term in the sum is the net output of good j in industry k. Once (47) and (48) are solved for w and r, their solutions can be substituted into (51) to yield the economy net outputs.

5.4.2. Equilibrium and comparative statics

Consider an equilibrium with full employment of all N factors at a positive factor price vector w and with K^* industries producing. Let it be supposed, without loss of generality, that the first K^* are producing and define $r^* = (r_1, ..., r_{K^*}) > 0$. Without knowing more about the technology it is not possible to infer how many goods are produced from knowledge of K^*. The equilibrium conditions may now be written as

$$c^j(w,p) = 1, \quad j = 1, ..., K^*, \tag{52}$$

$$\sum_{j=1}^{K^*} c_w^j(w,p)\, r_j = v. \tag{53}$$

Total differentiation of these conditions yields:

$$A^T dw = B^T dp, \tag{54}$$

$$A\,dr + S\,dw + R\,dp = dv, \tag{55}$$

where $A = [c_w^1(w,p), ..., c_w^{K^*}(w,p)]$ is an $N \times K^*$ matrix of factor inputs per unit of value added, $B = -[c_p^1(w,p), ..., c_p^{K^*}(w,p)]$ is an $M \times K^*$ matrix of net outputs of goods per unit of value added, $S \equiv \Sigma_{j=1}^{K^*} r_j\, c_{ww}^j(w,p)$ is an $N \times N$ matrix of slopes of the aggregate factor demand functions with respect to the factor prices, and $R = \Sigma_{j=1}^{K^*} r_j\, c_{wp}^j(w,p)$ is an $N \times M$ matrix of the slopes of the aggregate factor demand functions with respect to the product prices. Finally, total differentiation of (51), ignoring the industries which do not produce any value added, yields:

$$dy = B\,dr - R^T dw - U\,dp, \tag{56}$$

where $U \equiv \Sigma_{j=1}^{K^*} r_j\, c_{pp}^j(w,p)$ is an $N \times M$ matrix of slopes of the (negative of the) aggregate net output functions with respect to the product prices.

If p and v change by dp and dv such that full employment is maintained with the same K^* industries operating, then (54) and (55) may be solved for dw and dr. Then (56) will yield dy. The nature of the solutions depend crucially upon the number of industries K^* relative to the number of factors N, just as in . the intermediate-good model of section 5.2 and the final-good model of Chapter 4.

If $K^* = N$, matrix A is square and, if of full rank, has an inverse. Hence, the solution takes the form:

$$dw = (A^{-1})^T B^T dp, \tag{57}$$

$$dr = A^{-1}dv - [A^{-1}S(A^{-1})^T B^T + A^{-1}R]dp, \tag{58}$$

$$dy = BA^{-1}dv - [U + BA^{-1}S(A^{-1})^T B^T + BA^{-1}R + (BA^{-1}R)^T]dp. \tag{59}$$

When $K^* \neq N, A$ is not square and (54) and (55) must be jointly solved as

$$\begin{bmatrix} dw \\ dr \end{bmatrix} = \begin{bmatrix} S & A \\ A^T & 0 \end{bmatrix}^{-1} \begin{bmatrix} -R & I \\ B^T & 0 \end{bmatrix} \begin{bmatrix} dp \\ dv \end{bmatrix}. \tag{60}$$

The details of the solution (60) are provided in the appendix to Diewert and Woodland (1977), but we do not pursue these here.

Consider the special case where $K^* = N = M$, i.e. the number of industries producing is equal to the number of factors and also the number of products. In this case both A and B are square matrices, which we assume possess inverses.

Then $D \equiv AB^{-1}$ may be interpreted as the matrix of total factor inputs of i needed to produce exactly one unit of net output of good j, with zero outputs of all other goods. The verification of this statement is left as an exercise. If there is no joint production the matrix B will be of the form $B = I - B^*$, where $B^* \geqslant 0$, in which case $B^{-1} \geqslant 0$. Thus, $D = AB^{-1} \geqslant 0$ also. This allows us to interpret the effect of product price changes upon factor prices, and the effect of endowment changes on product net outputs in the same way as for the final-good economy. Eqs. (57) and (59) indicate that $\partial w/\partial p = (D^{-1})^{T}$ and $\partial y/\partial v = D^{-1}$. This argument was dealt with above in section 5.2 and so will not be repeated.[12]

What is of interest here is what happens when there is joint production. In this case B^{-1} may have negative elements so that $D = AB^{-1}$ may have negative elements. Hence, the arguments used in the derivations of results for the final-good model cannot be directly applied in the present context. To illustrate, suppose that $K^* = N = M = 2$. Let

$$A = \frac{1}{4} \begin{bmatrix} 3 & 1 \\ 1 & 3 \end{bmatrix} \quad \text{and} \quad B = \frac{1}{12} \begin{bmatrix} 7 & 5 \\ 5 & 7 \end{bmatrix}. \tag{61}$$

Then

$$D = \begin{bmatrix} 2 & -1 \\ -1 & 2 \end{bmatrix} \quad \text{and} \quad D^{-1} = \frac{1}{3} \begin{bmatrix} 2 & 1 \\ 1 & 2 \end{bmatrix}. \tag{62}$$

In this example an increase in the endowment of any one factor will increase the output of both goods since $\partial y/\partial v = D^{-1}$. Similarly, an increase in the price of any one good will raise the reward of both factor prices since $\partial w/\partial p = (D^{-1})^{T} > 0$. This contrasts with the results for a non-joint product model which require that one output must fall when an endowment is increased, and one factor reward must fall when a product price is increased.

The above example does not say anything about percentage changes. If the equations in (54) are converted to percentage form they may be written as

$$\alpha \hat{w} = \beta \hat{p}, \tag{63}$$

where α is a matrix of shares of factors in the value added, and β is a matrix of shares of products in value added. Then

---

[12] It should be noted that the matrix B in the present section corresponds to $I - B$ of section 5.2, if the analyses of section 5.2 and 5.4 are being compared.

$$\delta\,\hat{w} = \hat{p} \quad \text{and} \quad \hat{w} = \delta^{-1}\hat{p}, \tag{64}$$

where $\delta \equiv \beta^{-1}\alpha$. If α and β were given by the matrices specified for A and B in (61), then δ and δ^{-1} would be those given for D and D^{-1} in (62). Thus, it is clear from δ^{-1} and (64) that an increase in either price will raise the nominal reward to both factors but not sufficient to raise real reward of either factor. Thus, the Stolper–Samuelson result does not occur.

Similarly, if only v changes, eqs. (55) and (56) may be converted to percentage changes as

$$\lambda\hat{r} = \hat{v} \quad \text{and} \quad \hat{y} = \mu\hat{r}, \tag{65}$$

where λ is a matrix of industry shares in the factor endowments and μ is a matrix of industry shares in the net outputs of goods. If $\epsilon \equiv \lambda\mu^{-1}$, we have that

$$\epsilon\hat{y} = \hat{v} \quad \text{and} \quad \hat{y} = \epsilon^{-1}\hat{v}. \tag{66}$$

Again, if λ and μ are given by the matrices in (61), then ϵ and ϵ^{-1} are given by the matrices in (62). Hence (66) shows that the Rybczynski theorem does not hold. If either factor endowment increases, both outputs will increase such that neither one increases by a greater percentage than the increase in the factor endowment.

These examples illustrate that the Rybczynski and Stolper–Samuelson theorems do not necessarily apply when joint production is permitted.[13] The reason for this is that B^{-1} is not necessarily non-negative, hence $D = AB^{-1}$ is not necessarily non-negative and D^{-1} does not have the required structure. Of course, there will exist instances where B^{-1} is non-negative and the Rybczynski and Stolper–Samuelson theorems hold. Chang, Ethier and Kemp (1980) have investigated the possibilities, and conclude that these theorems continue to hold in a significant proportion of cases.

Before concluding this chapter, it should be noted that the factor price equalization theorem continues to hold under joint production. If the first K^* industries can produce profitably, then the equations $c^j(w, p) = 1$ hold for $j = 1, ..., K^*$. For each solution $w > 0$ to these equations the optimal (factor) input–output vectors $c_w^j(w, p)$, $j = 1, ..., K^*$, form a cone $K(w, p)$. If the endowment vectors for two nations, who have the same cost functions and face the same prices, are in the interior of the same cone of diversification, then the two nations will have the same vector of factor prices. If the endowments are not in

---

[13]   This illustrates the conclusion reached in section 5.3 for the aggregate model.

the same cones, they will have different factor prices. This is precisely the same argument used in Chapter 4 for the final-goods model and in section 5.2 for the intermediate-input model. Of course, the cone of diversification will be degenerate unless $K^* \geqslant N$, i.e. unless the number of industries actually producing is at least as great as the number of factors.

5.5. Concluding comments

In this chapter three different approaches have been taken in order to generalize the final-goods model of Chapter 4 to allow for intermediate inputs and joint outputs. In section 5.2 the model of Chapter 4 was extended in a straightforward manner simply by including the prices of products in the unit cost function in recognition of intermediate inputs. The activity levels for the industries were gross outputs. To deal with both intermediate inputs and joint outputs, it was found convenient to treat the value added by an industry as the activity level and so, in section 5.4, the model was formulated in terms of unit value added factor cost functions. For the case of intermediate inputs, these two approaches are just alternative ways of formulating exactly the same model. The value added approach has the advantage that it also handles joint outputs.

Section 5.3 was devoted to an aggregate model in which separate industries were not explicitly considered. This approach is most general since it allows for a very general technology and industrial structure. The GNP function was defined and its properties used to obtain comparative statics results. These results are most general and contain the results obtained from the final-good and intermediate-input models as special cases.

Which approach should be taken depends upon what questions are being asked and upon how much structure is being imposed on the model of the production sector. If we are interested in the response of net outputs and factor prices to an exogenous increase in the price of a traded good (such as oil), then the aggregate approach would be sufficient. If detail on how the price increase will affect separate industries is desired, then the approach of sections 5.2 or 5.4 is necessary. If joint production is unimportant for the economy in question, then the approach of section 5.2 will suffice.

The main conclusions reached in this chapter are as follows. First, the essence of the factor price equalization theorem continues to hold when intermediate inputs and joint outputs are permitted. Secondly, the distinction between industry activity levels and production sector net outputs is important and requires special attention. However, thirdly, when intermediate inputs are permitted the Stolper–Samuelson and Rybczynski propositions continue to hold with appropriate reinterpretation. Fourthly, these theorems do not necessarily hold when joint production is permitted, although there are many instances where they continue to hold.

5.6. Notes on the literature

One of the earliest papers introducing intermediate inputs into the theory of trade was McKenzie (1953). In this paper intermediate inputs were incorporated into McKenzie's analysis of Graham's (1948) classical model of world trade. It was pointed out that the introduction of trade in intermediate inputs enlarges the world production possibility set and opens up the possibility of a reversal in the pattern of specialization, and the structure of efficient production and trade was analysed. See also Chipman (1965). Other papers on the role of intermediates are McKinnon (1966), who was primarily concerned with tariffs, Melvin (1969), on the gains from trade, and Chang (1977), on the gross and net output–price relationships.

The analysis of the two-dimensional model with intermediates seems to have begun with Vanek (1963) who assumed fixed coefficients of production. A comprehensive treatment of the variable coefficients version of this model by Chang and Mayer (1973) deals with the Rybczynski and Stolper–Samuelson theorems, the net and gross transformation functions and the import demand function building on the work of Kemp (1969). Batra and Casas (1973) analyse a model where a pure intermediate input (not consumed) is used to produce two final goods, their results reflecting the unequal numbers of goods and factors. Many other papers dealing with intermediates in the two-dimensional model are concerned with the nature and role of the effective rate of protection. This topic will be dealt with in detail in a later chapter.

Recently, several papers have provided detailed formulations and comparative static analyses of general production models involving multiple and unequal numbers of products, factors and industries. These are Chang (1979), Diewert and Woodland (1977), Jones and Scheinkman (1977), and Woodland (1977). Each of these deals with joint outputs as well as intermediate inputs. Conditions for the existence of flat segments of the production possibility frontier and the factor requirements isoquant have been provided by Kemp, Manning, Nishimura and Tawada (1980), using a primal (production function) approach.[14] A close

---

[14] The factor requirements isoquant is the lower boundary of the factor requirements set $X(y) \equiv \{x : y \in Y(x)\}$.

examination of the two-sector model with joint outputs has been undertaken by Chang, Ethier and Kemp (1980).

The classic paper by McKenzie (1955) on factor price equalization dealt with a very general model of production which incorpoates intermediate inputs and joint outputs. Other papers dealing with factor price equalization are Suzumura (1971), Kuga (1972) and Samuelson (1953).

Samuelson (1953) also introduced the concept of the gross national product function whose properties were utilized by Diewert (1974) to provide very general comparative static results for the aggregate production model. The GNP function has been studied in detail for the two-product, two-factor, final-good model by Chipman (1972), and has been used extensively by Wegge (1974, 1979) and Dixit and Norman (1980). The duality between the Rybczynski and Stolper –Samuelson theorems in the aggregate model is dealt with by Kemp and Ethier (1975). For further details on the value added function (formally equivalent to the variable profit and GNP functions) see Diewert (1978b) for a formal treatment and Khang (1971) for its use in international trade theory.

Problems

1. (a) If matrix $\Sigma = [\sigma_{ij}]$ is negative semi-definite, prove that $\Delta \equiv \sigma_{11} + \sigma_{22} - 2\sigma_{12} \leqslant 0$. (*Hint:* $\Delta = x \Sigma x$, where x is very special.)
   (b) If Σ is negative definite prove that $\Delta < 0$.
   (c) If Σ is negative definite prove that $\sigma_{11}\sigma_{22} - \sigma_{12}\sigma_{21} > 0$.
2. Consider example 2 of section 5.2.
   (a) Prove that $\hat{g}_1/\hat{p}_3 = -\delta/\Delta < 0$, where $\delta \equiv \epsilon_{11}\epsilon_{22} - \epsilon_{12}\epsilon_{21} = \theta_{11}\theta_{21} (\sigma_{11}\sigma_{22} - \sigma_{12}\sigma_{21}) > 0$ and $\Delta \equiv \theta_{11}\theta_{21}[-\sigma_{11} - \sigma_{22} + 2\sigma_{12}] > 0$.
   (b) What happens to imports of product 3?
   (c) If v_2 increases what happens to imports of product 3?
3. In the two-product, two-factor case with intermediate inputs but no joint production, show that the relationship between prices and gross outputs are "normal" ($\partial g_j/\partial p_j > 0$, $\partial g_i/\partial p_j < 0$, $j \neq i$) if the intermediate input–output coefficients are fixed. Are there weaker sufficient conditions?
4. Prove that the GNP function $G(p, v)$ satisfies condition (27) if the technology satisfies (26).
5. If constant returns to scale is not assumed, which properties of $G(p, v)$ are affected, and how?
6. Suppose that, in a final-good model, there are some factors which are industry-specific and others that are perfectly mobile.
   (a) Show that the GNP function is of the form:

$$G(p, v_m, v_1, ..., v_M)$$

$$= \max_{\{x^j\}} \left\{ \sum_{j=1}^{M} p_j f^j(v_j, x^j): \sum_{j=1}^{M} x^j \leqslant v_m, (x^1, ..., x^M) \geqslant 0 \right\},$$

where v_m is the vector of mobile factors and v_j is the jth industry-specific vector of factors.

(b) Characterize the solution to this maximization problem.

(c) Write down the output supply functions and the factor market equilibrium conditions.

7. Consider the industry-specific factor model of problem 6 in the special case where there are $M + 1$ factors, one mobile and the remaining M factors each specific to one industry.

(a) Prove that an increase in the price of good j will (i) raise the real return to j's specific factor; (ii) reduce the price of all other specific factors; (iii) raise the production of good j; and (iv) reduce production of all other goods.

(b) Prove that an increase in the endowment of specific factor i will (v) raise output of good i; (vi) reduce output of all other goods; (vii) reduce the price of all specific factors; and (viii) raise the price of the mobile factor.

8. Define the joint cost function as $C(w, y) \equiv \min_x \{wx: (y, -x) \in T\}$, which is an alternative to $G(p, v)$ as a characterization of the technology. The equilibrium conditions may be expressed as

$$p = C_y(w, y) \quad \text{and} \quad v = C_w(w, y).$$

(a) Explain why the equilibrium conditions can be written in this way.

(b) Assuming existence of second derivatives and relevant inverses, derive a formula for the relationships between the second derivatives of C and those of G.

(c) If there are no joint outputs or intermediate inputs, show that $C(w, y) = \sum_{j=1}^{M} c^j(w) y_j$.

(d) Does $G(p, v)$ factor in this way?

9. For the intermediate-good model of section 5.2 define the joint cost function in terms of gross outputs as $C(w, p, g) \equiv \sum_{j=1}^{M} c^j(w, p) g_j$. Suppose that all goods are produced for simplicity.

(a) Derive expressions for all first and second derivatives of $C(w, p, g)$ and interpret them.

(b) Rewrite the equilibrium conditions in terms of C's derivatives.

(c) Derive a full set of comparative statics equations for the effects of p and v upon w, g and y.

(d) Using this result show that $\partial y/\partial p$ is positive semi-definite.

(e) This is the hard way of obtaining this result which follows because $G(p, v)$ is concave in p (much easier!). What is the advantage, if any, of your expression for $\partial y/\partial p$?

References

Allen, R.G.D. (1938) *Mathematical Analysis for Economists* (London: Macmillan).

Batra, R.N. and F.R. Casas (1973) "Intermediate products and the pure theory of international trade: A neo-Heckscher–Ohlin framework", *American Economic Review* 63-3, June, 297–311.

Chang, W.W. (1977) "Tariff structure and output adjustment in the presence of interindustry flows", *Journal of International Economics* 7, 329–342.

Chang, W.W. (1979) "Some theorems of trade and general equilibrium with many goods and factors", *Econometrica* 47-3, May, 709–726.

Chang, W.W. and W. Mayer (1973) "Intermediate goods in a general equilibrium trade model", *International Economic Review* 14-2, June, 447–459.

Chang, W.W., W. Ethier and M.C. Kemp (1980) "The theorems of international trade with joint production", *Journal of International Economics* 10, 377–394.

Chipman, J.S. (1965) "A survey of the theory of international trade: Part 1, The classical theory", *Econometrica* 33-3, July, 477–519.

Chipman, J.S. (1972) "The theory of exploitative trade and investment policies: A reformulation and synthesis", in: *International Economies and Development* (New York: Academic Press), pp. 209–244.

Diewert, W.E. (1973) "Functional forms for profit and transformation functions", *Journal of Economic Theory* 6, 284–316.

Diewert, W.E. (1974) "Applications of duality theory", in: M.D. Intriligator and D.A. Kendrick (eds.), *Frontiers of Quantitative Economics*, vol. 2 (Amsterdam: North-Holland Publishing Co.).

Diewert, W.E. (1978a) "Duality approaches to microeconomic theory", in: K.J. Arrow and M.D. Intriligator (eds.), *Handbook of Mathematical Economics* (Amsterdam: North-Holland Publishing Co.).

Diewert, W.E. (1978b) "Hicks' aggregation theorem and the existence of a real value-added function", in: M. Fuss and D. McFadden (eds.), *Production Economics: A Dual Approach to Theory and Applications*, (Amsterdam: North-Holland Publishing Co.).

Diewert, W.E. and A.D. Woodland (1977) "Frank Knight's theorem in linear programming revisted", *Econometrica* 45-2, March, 375–398.

Dixit, A.K. and V. Norman (1980) *Theory of International Trade* (J. Nisbet/Cambridge University Press).

Dorfman, R., P.A. Samuelson and R.M. Solow (1958) *Linear Programming and Economic Analysis* (New York: McGraw-Hill).

Gale, D. (1960) *The Theory of Linear Economic Models* (New York: McGraw-Hill).

Graham, F.D. (1948) *The Theory of International Values* (Princeton: Princeton University Press).

Jones, R.W. and J. Scheinkman (1977) "The relevance of the two-sector production model in trade theory", *Journal of Political Economy* 85, 909–936.

Kemp, M.C. (1969) *The Pure Theory of International Trade and Investment* (Englewood Cliffs, N.J.: Prentice-Hall).

Kemp, M.C. and W. Ethier (1975) "A note on joint production and the theory of international trade", in: M.C. Kemp (ed.), *Topics in the Theory of International Trade*, ch. 7.

Kemp, M.C., R. Manning, K. Nishimura and M. Tawada (1980) "On the slope of the single-country and world commodity-substitution and factor-substitution surfaces under conditions of joint production", *Journal of International Economics* 10, 395–404.

Khang, C. (1971) "An iso-value locus involving intermediate goods and its application to the pure theory of international trade", *Journal of International Economics* 1-3, August, 315–326.

Kuga, K. (1972) "The factor price equalization theorem", *Econometrica* 40-4, July, 723–736.

Lancaster, K. (1968) *Mathematical Economics* (New York: Macmillan).

Lau, L. (1978) "Some applications of profit functions", in: M. Fuss and D. McFadden (eds.), *Production Economics: A Dual Approach to Theory and Applications* (Amsterdam: North-Holland Publishing Co.).

Leontief, W.W. (1951) *The Structure of the American Economy, 1919–1939*, 2nd edition (New York: Oxford University Press).

McKenzie, L.W. (1953) "Specialization and efficiency in world production", *Review of Economic Studies* 21, 165–180.

McKenzie, L.W. (1955) "Equality of factor prices in world trade", *Econometrica* 23-3, 239–257.

McKinnon, R.I. (1966) "Intermediate products and differential tariffs: Generalization of Lerner's symmetry theorem", *Quarterly Journal of Economics* 80, November, 584–615.

Melvin, J. (1969) "Intermediate goods, the production possibility curve, and gains from trade", *Quarterly Journal of Economics* 83, February, 141–151.

Samuelson, P.A. (1953) "Prices of factors and goods in general equilibrium", *Review of Economic Studies* 21–1, 1–20.

Suzumura, K. (1971) "International equalization of factor prices in Leontief model with variable coefficients", *Metroeconomica* 23-1, 1–15.

Vanek, J. (1963) "Variable factor proportions and inter-industry flows in the theory of international trade", *Quarterly Journal of Economics* 77, February, 129–142.

Wegge, L.L. (1974) "Notes on the regional product function", *Tijdschrift voor Economie* 19-2.

Wegge, L.L. (1979) "Conjugate small country production equilibrium concepts", *Journal of International Economics* 9, 173–196.

Woodland, A.D. (1977) "Joint outputs, intermediate inputs and international trade theory", *International Economic Review* 18-3, October, 517–533.

CHAPTER 6

CONSUMER DEMAND, INCOME DISTRIBUTION AND GENERAL EQUILIBRIUM

6.1. Introduction

The previous three chapters have dealt in considerable detail with the production sector of the economy. In the present chapter the consumption side of the economy is modelled and attention is then focused on the nature of the system of export supply and import demand functions which describe a nation's trading plans. Thus, the model of the whole economy will have been completed. This model is of direct interest since it provides the framework within which we can investigate the effects of exogenous changes, such as in the prices of traded goods and in the endowments of fixed factors, upon production, consumption and the volume and pattern of the international trade of an economy. While attention is confined to a single economy for which the prices of traded goods are exogenous, later chapters will use the present formulation as part of a model of world trade involving many nations.

In the following section the net export functions are defined for an economy with many individual consumers, whose incomes are determined endogenously, and with many producers. Section 6.3 is devoted to the question of whether the consumption sector can be treated as if it behaved like an individual consumer, as is possible for the production sector. This is a crucial question given the important role the concept of an aggregate consumer has played in the literature. In section 6.4 a diagrammatic representation of the complete model of the small open economy is provided for the two-dimensional case. Section 6.5 examines in some detail the concept of the trade utility function, its dual, the indirect trade utility function, the net revenue function and the relationship of these to the net export functions. Finally, the effect upon the model of the existence of non-traded goods and variable factor supplies is briefly examined.

6.2. Consumer demand and the net export functions

6.2.1. The consumption sector

Consumption decisions in an economy are made by individual consumers (or households) who are assumed to maximize their welfare or utility subject to the constraint imposed by their limited incomes. It is assumed that there are L consumers who take as given their income m^{ℓ} and the product price vector $p = (p_1, ..., p_M)$. Each consumer ℓ chooses the consumption vector $z^{\ell} \geqslant 0$ to maximize his utility function $u^{\ell}(z^{\ell})$ subject to the budget constraint $pz^{\ell} \leqslant m^{\ell}$. As discussed in Chapter 2, this yields the indirect utility function:

$$V^{\ell}(p, m^{\ell}) \equiv \max_{z^{\ell}} \{u^{\ell}(z^{\ell}): pz^{\ell} \leqslant m^{\ell}, z^{\ell} \geqslant 0\}, \quad \ell = 1, ..., L, \tag{1}$$

which indicates the maximum utility consumer ℓ can attain with income ℓ when prices are p. Conditions (2.3) are assumed for the utility function and these ensure that all income is spent. In this case the indirect utility function can be obtained as $V^{\ell}(p, m^{\ell}) = \{\mu^{\ell}: E^{\ell}(p, \mu^{\ell}) = m^{\ell}\}$ in terms of the expenditure function $E^{\ell}(p, \mu^{\ell})$. The ordinary (Marshallian) demand functions are given in vector form as

$$z^{\ell} = \phi^{\ell}(p, m^{\ell}) = E_p^{\ell}(p, V^{\ell}(p, m^{\ell})), \quad \ell = 1, ..., L. \tag{2}$$

Consumers obtain income from the sale of factor services to the production sector. In the absence of taxes, total factor income is also equal to the revenue received by the production sector and is denoted in the following alternative ways:

$$m = G(p, v) = vw(p, v) = py(p, v), \tag{3}$$

where the $w(p, v) = G_v(p, v)$ is the vector of factor price functions and $y(p, v) = G_p(p, v)$ is the vector of (net) output supply functions. The income of individual ℓ is determined endogenously according to the distribution function $m^{\ell}(p, v; \alpha)$, where α is a vector of parameters. These functions must satisfy the adding-up identity

$$\sum_{\ell=1}^{L} m^{\ell}(p, v; \alpha) \equiv G(p, v), \tag{4}$$

implying that all income gets distributed to consumers, and they are assumed to be homogeneous of degree zero in prices. While modelling the income distribution functions is not a primary concern for our purposes, it is worth noting that the above formulation is very general. As an important example, we might define a consumer as the sole owner of a specific factor in which case there are $L = N$ consumers with incomes $m^i(p, v; \alpha) \equiv w_i(p, v)v_i$, $i = 1, ..., N$. In this example it is the "functional" distribution of income which is important. Alternatively, it could be assumed that consumer ℓ has a fixed endowment of factors given by the vector v^ℓ so his income is $m^\ell(p, v; \alpha) \equiv w(p, v)v^\ell$. In this second example the parameter vector $\alpha = (v^1, ..., v^L)$. As another possibility, it may be that consumer ℓ's endowment vector is some proportion α^ℓ of total endowment, in which case $m^\ell(p, v; \alpha) = \alpha^\ell w(p, v)v$. For present purposes, however, we need simply assume that income gets distributed according to some set of distribution functions satisfying (4).

Given α, the demands for goods by consumers ultimately are determined by the product price vector and the vector of factor endowments. Specifically, for each (p, v) the production sector yields an equilibrium income or GNP. This income is allocated to individuals who consume according to their demand functions. The vector of aggregate demand functions, obtained by summing the individual demand functions, is

$$z(p, v; \alpha) \equiv \Phi(p, m^1, ..., m^L) \equiv \sum_{\ell=1}^{L} \phi^\ell(p, m^\ell), \tag{5}$$

where $m^\ell = m^\ell(p, v; \alpha)$. This expression for the aggregate demand vector emphasizes the importance of the income distribution and the dependence of the latter upon product prices and factor endowments.

It will be useful to define the aggregate expenditure function

$$E(p, \mu) \equiv \sum_{\ell=1}^{L} E^\ell(p, \mu^\ell), \tag{6}$$

where $\mu = (\mu^1, ..., \mu^L)$ is a vector of utility levels. In view of Shephard's lemma it follows that

$$z(p, v; \alpha) = E_p(p, \mu) = \sum_{\ell=1}^{L} E_p^\ell(p, \mu^\ell), \tag{7}$$

where $\mu^\ell = V^\ell(p, m^\ell(p, v; \alpha))$. Thus, $E_p(p, \mu)$ is the vector of aggregate Hicksian demand functions.

6.2.2. Net export functions

The vector of *excess supply* or *net export* functions may now be defined as

$$x(p, v; \alpha) \equiv y(p, v) - z(p, v; \alpha) \equiv G_p(p, v) - \Phi(p, m^1, ..., m^L), \qquad (8)$$

which is the excess of planned (net) production over planned consumption, given the product price vector p, the endowment vector v, and α. Previous chapters have devoted considerable attention to the properties of the net supply functions. The logical extension of this work is to examine the properties of the demand functions, and hence determine the properties of the net export functions.

The effect on the net export vector of an exogenous change in the price vector is obtained by differentiating (8) and making use of the Slutsky decomposition of a price change.[1] Thus,

$$x_p(p, v; \alpha) = (G_{pp} - E_{pp}) - \sum_{\ell=1}^{L} \phi_m^\ell (m_p^\ell - \phi^\ell), \qquad (9)$$

where it is noted that x_p is an $M \times M$ matrix and hence each term in the summation is the outer product between vector ϕ_m^ℓ ($= \partial\phi^\ell/\partial m^\ell$) and $m_p^\ell - \phi^\ell$. The first term, $G_{pp} - E_{pp}$, is a positive semi-definite matrix (since G is concave and E is convex in p) of pure substitution terms — substitution around the production possibility frontier, and substitution by all consumers around their indifference curves. The total of the latter effect is $E_{pp} = \sum_{\ell=1}^{L} E_{pp}^\ell$. The last term in (9) gives the weighted income effects. The term $-\phi_m^\ell \phi^\ell$ is the income effect of a pure price change upon demand, which of course is negative for price increases. However, a change in p will cause GNP to change and individual ℓ shares in this change to the extent of m_p^ℓ. Thus, $\phi_m^\ell m_p^\ell$ is the change in the demand vector due to this change in income. If the income effects were absent, we would have the result that x_p is a positive semi-definite matrix which would imply, among other things, that $\partial x_i/\partial p_i \geq 0$. However, the income effects are not absent and so, without imposing further conditions, the response of exports to the increase in p_j cannot be further characterized.[2]

What general restrictions do the net export functions have with respect to price changes? First, they satisfy the Walras law:

$$\sum_{i=1}^{M} p_i x_i(p, v; \alpha) \equiv px(p, v; \alpha) \equiv 0, \quad \text{for all } p \geq 0, v \geq 0, \qquad (10)$$

[1] See eq. (2.34) of Chapter 2 for the Slutsky decomposition of the price effect on consumer demand.
[2] Sonnenschein (1972) and Debreu (1973) have shown that, in general, if the number of individuals is at least as great as the number of goods, the only property satisfied by the excess supply functions is Walras' law (eq. (10) below). If the number of goods exceeds the number of individuals, then further Slutsky-like restrictions are possible, as demonstrated by Diewert (1977).

which means that there is a balance of trade. This follows because all GNP is distributed to consumers who then spend it all on consumption, hence the value of consumption equals the value of production. An imbalance of trade would only be possible if we had permitted a leakage from or injection into the flow of income, such as lending and borrowing from abroad. Secondly, in addition to the Walras law, the net export functions are homogeneous of degree zero in p, i.e.

$$x(\lambda p, v; \alpha) \equiv x(p, v; \alpha), \quad \lambda > 0. \tag{11}$$

This is because the supply functions $G_p(p, v)$ are homogeneous of degree zero in p, the demand functions are homogeneous of degree zero in (p, m^ϱ), and the income distribution functions are assumed to be homogeneous of degree zero in p. In view of (11) Euler's theorem implies that

$$\sum_{j=1}^{M} p_j \frac{\partial x_i(p, v; \alpha)}{\partial p_j} \equiv 0, \quad i = 1, ..., M, \quad \text{i.e. } x_p(p, v; \alpha)p \equiv 0. \tag{12}$$

This implies that each row of x_p has at least one negative element and at least one positive element, if some element is not zero. Hence, each good's net exports will increase in response to an increase in the price of some good and will decrease in response to an increase in the price of some other good.

Thirdly, the balance of trade condition (10) may be differentiated to obtain:

$$\sum_{i=1}^{M} p_i \frac{\partial x_i(p, v; \alpha)}{\partial p_j} + x_j(p, v; \alpha) \equiv 0, \quad j = 1, ..., M,$$

$$\text{i.e. } px_p(p, v; \alpha) + x(p, v; \alpha) \equiv 0. \tag{13}$$

The effect upon net exports of a change in endowments is obtained by differentiation of (8) as

$$x_v(p, v; \alpha) = G_{pv} - \sum_{\varrho=1}^{L} \phi_m^\varrho m_v^\varrho, \tag{14}$$

where, again, the term $\phi_m^\varrho m_v^\varrho$ is the outer product. The production effect is $G_{pv} = y_v(p, v)$, which has been extensively discussed in Chapters 4 and 5, where it was shown that, under reasonable conditions, some outputs will increase and some will fall as a result of an increase in the endowment of any one factor of production. Again, however, the consumption effects are more difficult to characterize since they are summations over individuals with different preferences and different income effects, some of which may be negative.

Are there general restrictions which apply even when consumption aggregation is not possible? Differentiation of the balance of trade condition (10) yields:

$$\sum_{i=1}^{M} p_i \frac{\partial x_i(p, v; \alpha)}{\partial v_j} \equiv 0, \quad j = 1, ..., M, \quad \text{i.e. } px_v(p, v; \alpha) \equiv 0. \qquad (15)$$

This imposes a general restriction on the response of exports to endowment changes, and implies that not all net exports can rise and not all net exports can fall. If the jth column of x_v is non-zero, then some net exports will rise while others will fall if the endowment of j increases.

Under what conditions are the net export functions homogeneous of degree one in v? This is an interesting question since homogeneity means that the size of endowments only determines the scale of trade, not its composition, a property which is important to the Heckscher–Ohlin theory of trade to be discussed in Chapter 7. It is known from the previous chapters that the supply functions are linearly homogeneous in v due to constant returns to scale, as is the aggregate income or GNP function $G(p, v)$. If, when the scale of v is increased, the endowments of all individuals are increased proportionately, then all incomes will increase by the same percentage. Consumption of all goods will increase by this percentage only in the special case where all income elasticities of demand are unity, i.e. when all utility functions are homothetic. If they are, then net exports of all goods will have increased by the same percentage. In summary:

> If all utility functions are homothetic and individual incomes are
> linearly homogeneous in v, then $x(p, \lambda v; \alpha) = \lambda x(p, v; \alpha)$, for all
> p, v and $\lambda > 0$. $\qquad (16)$

It is evident that the properties of the aggregate demand, and hence net export, functions depend upon the individual income distribution functions and upon the individual utility functions so that, in general, their analysis will be very complex. This suggests that in order to obtain useful restrictions on our results, some additional structure has to be imposed on the income distribution functions and/or the utility functions. Because of this, much of the literature on international trade theory is based upon the assumption that the consumption sector behaves as if it were a single consumer with well-behaved preferences.

6.2.3. *The case of one consumer*

We now consider the properties of the net export functions when it is assumed that the consumption sector behaves as if it were a single consumer maximizing a utility function subject to the aggregate budget constraint $pz \leqslant G(p, v)$. In this case net exports may be written as

$$x(p, v) = G_p(p, v) - \phi(p, G(p, v)), \tag{17}$$

where $\phi(p, m) \equiv E_p^0(p, V(p, m))$, $V^0(p, m)$ is the (scalar) solution for μ^0 to $E^0(p, \mu^0) = m$, and μ^0 is the level of utility for the fictional, single consumer denoted by superscript zero.

Equation (9), describing the effect of a change in prices upon net exports, now becomes

$$x_p(p, v) = (G_{pp} - E_{pp}^0) - \phi_m x. \tag{18}$$

If $x = 0$, meaning that the initial equilibrium involves no trade, then x_p is a positive semi-definite matrix. This constrains the response of x to changes in p and, in particular, indicates that $\partial x_i / \partial p_i \geqslant 0$, i.e. an increase in p_i would cause good i to be exported, if it were to be traded. However, when initially there is trade the last term on the right-hand side of (18) does not vanish. If all goods are "normal", meaning that $\phi_m > 0$, the sign structure of the last term depends upon the sign structure of x. If good j is exported, the jth column of the last term is negative, and is positive if j is imported. Moreover, the matrix $\phi_m x$ is asymmetric and not necessarily semi-definite (either positive or negative). Hence, the last term precludes any neat result concerning the sign structure of x_p.

However, let us consider the effect of an increase in the price of good j upon the net exports of the same good j. In this case (18) implies that

$$\partial x_j / \partial p_j = \partial y_j / \partial p_j - \partial E_j^0 / \partial p_j - x_j \phi_{jm}. \tag{19}$$

Since the first two terms sum to a non-negative number, it follows that

$$\partial x_j / \partial p_j \geqslant 0, \quad \text{if } x_j < 0. \tag{20}$$

That is to say, if good j is imported, an increase in its price will cause net exports to increase (strictly not decrease) which means that net imports decrease. If, however, good j is exported, it is possible for the third term in (19) to dominate, especially if exports of j are large, so that exports might decrease as a result of an increase in the price. The reason is the income effect. As p_j increases, money income increases and dominates the Slutsky real income decrease, so the total income effect is to raise consumption of good j. This increased consumption could outweigh the increase in production and the reduced consumption due to the pure substitution (Hicksian) effect of the price change. While this somewhat counter-intuitive result is possible, it is less likely to occur if exports and/or ϕ_{jm} are small.

If aggregation of the consumption sector is possible, the effects of a change in endowments upon net exports can be obtained by differentiating (17) with respect to v. This yields:

$$x_v(p, v) = G_{pv} - \phi_m G_v. \tag{21}$$

Since $G_{pv} = y_v$ and $G_v = w$, the factor price vector, (21) may be rewritten in component form as

$$\partial x_i / \partial v_j = \partial y_i / \partial v_j - \phi_{im} w_j. \tag{22}$$

Since $\phi_{im} w_j > 0$ if good i is normal and factor j is not free, it follows that $\partial x_i / \partial v_j$ will be negative if $\partial y_i / \partial v_j < 0$ (for example, if product i is intensive in its use of the *other* factor in a two-product, two-factor, non-joint production model) and of uncertain sign otherwise.

The assumption that the consumption sector can be aggregated has added some structure to the model, but has not enabled us to be very much more specific about the signs of the derivatives of the net export functions. Nevertheless, there is added structure and an enormous simplification of the model which are valuable in the analysis of various trade problems. This is the main reason why the assumption is made in much of the literature, and in the present book. The following section is devoted to a discussion of the conditions under which this assumption is valid in a many consumer economy.

6.3. Aggregate demand functions and preferences

It would be extremely convenient if the aggregate demand quantities responded to prices and aggregate income in the same manner that an individual's demand quantities respond to prices and the individual's income. If this were the case we could ignore individual differences in tastes and income in the calculation of aggregate demand quantities and, moreover, the latter could be obtained as the solution to a constrained aggregate utility function maximization problem. While this is often assumed in the literature, the conditions under which such aggregation is possible are quite stringent. Alternative sufficient conditions for aggregation are now discussed.

6.3.1. *Restrictions on demand functions – the Gorman polar form*

Consider the situation where there are L consumers who individually maximize
their utility functions $u^\ell(z^\ell) \leqslant m^\ell$ and $z^\ell \geqslant 0$. Each consumer faces the same
price vector p, and we treat individual incomes parametrically. Two questions
are asked. First, under what circumstances can we write the solutions for the ag-
gregate demand vector $z \equiv \Sigma_{\ell=1}^L z^\ell$ as a function of p and aggregate income $m \equiv
\Sigma_{\ell=1}^L m^\ell$ alone? Secondly, if there are such circumstances, will these aggregate
demand functions have the same properties as individual demand functions, i.e.
are they derivable from an aggregate or community utility function?

The first question may be rephrased to ask for conditions under which a
change in the distribution of a given aggregate income does not affect aggregate
demand. If the individual demand functions are differentiable we may obtain
the change in the aggregate demand vector due to a change in incomes as

$$\mathrm{d}z = \sum_{\ell=1}^L \phi_m^\ell(p, m^\ell)\mathrm{d}m^\ell = 0, \tag{23}$$

which is set equal to zero. The permissible changes in income must satisfy

$$\sum_{\ell=1}^L \mathrm{d}m^\ell = 0 \tag{24}$$

if aggregate income is fixed and individual incomes must remain non-negative,
but otherwise they are unconstrained. For (23) to hold for all choices of $\mathrm{d}m^1$,
..., $\mathrm{d}m^L$ which satisfy (24), it is clearly necessary for vector $\phi_m^\ell \equiv \partial\phi^\ell/\partial m^\ell$ to
be the same for all individuals $\ell = 1, ..., L$. This means that everyone must change
their consumption of good j by the same amount in response to a unit increase
in income, irrespective of their incomes. This condition must hold for all possible income configurations and for all $p \geqslant 0$ if the aggregate demand functions
are to be independent of the income distribution. Accordingly, the individual
demand functions must be linear in incomes, with the same slope with respect
to incomes. That is, they may be written as

$$\phi^\ell(p, m^\ell) = \alpha^\ell(p) + \beta(p)m^\ell, \quad \ell = 1, ..., L, \tag{25}$$

where the slope with respect to income, $\beta(p)$, is common to all individuals. The
corresponding aggregate demand functions are

$$\phi(p, m) \equiv \sum_{\ell=1}^L \phi^\ell(p, m^\ell) = \alpha(p) + \beta(p)m, \tag{26}$$

where $\alpha(p) \equiv \Sigma_{\ell=1}^{L} \alpha^{\ell}(p)$ and $m \equiv \Sigma_{\ell=1}^{L} m^{\ell}$. Clearly, changes in the income distribution, which do not affect aggregate income, do not affect aggregate demand. The individual expenditure and corresponding indirect utility functions which generate the demand functions (25) can be shown to be

(a) $\quad E^{\ell}(p, \mu^{\ell}) = A^{\ell}(p) + B(p)\mu^{\ell},$

(b) $\quad V^{\ell}(p, m^{\ell}) = [m^{\ell} - A^{\ell}(p)]/B(p),$

$$(27)$$

where $A^{\ell}(p)$ and $B(p)$ are functions which satisfy all of the usual properties of a unit cost function. These are sometimes referred to as the *Gorman polar form* for preferences.[3]

The second question posed above relates to the preferences underlying the aggregate demand functions (26). Since the aggregate demand functions are also linear in income, they are also obtainable from a community utility function problem in which the community utility function has a Gorman polar form. Let

$$V^{0}(p, m) \equiv \max_{z} \{u^{0}(z): pz \leqslant m, z \geqslant 0\} \qquad (28)$$

be the community indirect utility function, where $u^{0}(z)$ is the community direct utility function. Also, let $E^{0}(p, \mu^{0})$ be the corresponding expenditure function. Then, just as (27) yields (25), the community indirect utility and expenditure functions which yield (26) are of the Gorman polar form given by

(a) $\quad E^{0}(p, \mu^{0}) = A(p) + B(p)\mu^{0},$

(b) $\quad V^{0}(p, m) = [m - A(p)]/B(p),$

$$(29)$$

where $A(p) \equiv \Sigma_{\ell=1}^{L} A^{\ell}(p)$ and $\mu^{0} = \Sigma_{\ell=1}^{L} \mu^{\ell}$.

This result may be explained as follows. The aggregate expenditure function is the sum of individual expenditure functions of the form (27, a) and can be written as

$$E(p, \mu) \equiv \sum_{\ell=1}^{L} E^{\ell}(p, \mu^{\ell}) = \sum_{\ell=1}^{L} A^{\ell}(p) + B(p) \sum_{\ell=1}^{L} \mu^{\ell}$$

$$= A(p) + B(p)\mu^{0} = E^{0}(p, \mu^{0}). \qquad (30)$$

---

[3] This result, as well as the necessary and sufficient conditions for aggregation, was derived by Gorman (1953). For a discussion and empirical estimation of the Gorman polar form, see Blackorby, Boyce and Russell (1978).

That is, the aggregate expenditure function is separable in a function $W(\mu) = \sum_{\ell=1}^{\ell} \mu^\ell = \mu^0$ of the utility vector. There exists, therefore, an aggregator function (simple sum) which allows us to ignore the distribution of utilities. The expenditure function written in terms of μ^0, the sum of utilities, may be called a community expenditure function. It is a perfectly valid expenditure function with corresponding community direct and indirect utility functions $u^0(z)$ and $V^0(p, m)$ (as in (29, b)), respectively.

Gorman's results, outlined above, are based upon a very important assumption, namely that all individuals consume a positive amount of every good. If this is the case, the Gorman result is that a necessary and sufficient condition for there to exist a community utility function generating the aggregate demands is that the individual demand functions have the form (25) or, equivalently, that the individual expenditure and indirect utility functions have the form (27). The community expenditure, indirect utility, and demand functions are then given by (29, a), (29, b) and (26), respectively.

Gorman's result shows that there can exist a community utility function without requiring everyone to have the same preferences. Differences in preferences are reflected in the fact that the functions $A^\ell(p)$ may be arbitrarily different among individuals. Also, these preferences will be non-homothetic unless $A^\ell(p) \equiv 0$. However, if we do not restrict ourselves to situations where each individual consumes a positive vector of goods, then further structure is forced upon individual preferences, as is now demonstrated.

Figure 6.1 illustrates the expansion paths corresponding to two different price vectors in quantity space for a consumer with Gorman polar form preferences. Two indifference curves are also drawn. Aggregation is possible if all consumers have expansion paths which are parallel to this consumer's for each price vector. It is evident from fig. 6.1 that, for any given price vector, there is an income below which consumption of one good will become zero. For example, when $p = p^2$ the locus of solutions for z as m falls to zero is TSO, which coincides with $E_p^\ell(p^2, \mu^\ell) = \alpha^\ell(p^2) + B(p^2)\mu^\ell$ only when $z > 0$. Evidently, two people with the *same* preferences depicted in fig. 6.1 will have the same response to a change in income only if both are on the same linear segment, OS or ST. If one consumer is on ST and the other is on OS their responses to an income change will be different. Hence, aggregate demand will depend on the income distribution. The Gorman result, therefore, assumes that all individuals consume positive amounts of every good, and under these circumstances there can be differences in preferences characterized by differences in the $A^\ell(p)$ functions. Thus, the Gorman result is valid for those income variations which maintain positive demands.

When zero consumptions and arbitrary income distributions are permitted, then fig. 6.1 suggests the requirement that all expansion paths $E_p^\ell(p, \mu)$ should

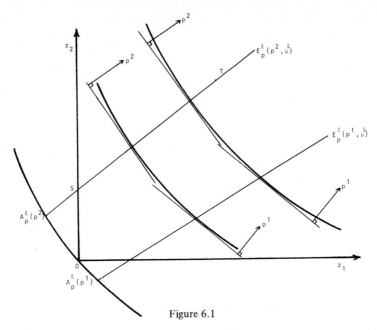

Figure 6.1

pass through the origin, which requires that $A^{\ell}(p) \equiv 0$. In such a case all consumers will have the same expenditure function $E^{\ell}(p, \mu^{\ell}) = B(p)\mu^{\ell}$ and hence the *same preferences*, which are *homothetic*. That is to say, the indirect utility function is $V^{\ell}(p, m^{\ell}) = m^{\ell}/B(p)$, while demands are proportional to income. In fact, it can be formally proved that a necessary and sufficient condition for there to exist a community utility function generating aggregate demands, when consumption vectors are simply constrained to be non-negative and all possible price and income distributions are feasible, is that individual preferences be identical and homothetic. This intuitively plausible result has been formally proved by Chipman and Moore (1973) under quite general conditions.

While it has been shown that, under certain conditions, aggregate demands can be obtained as a solution to an aggregate utility function maximizing problem, it should be stressed that the latter is a purely fictional problem without any welfare significance. That is, the consumption sector behaves *as if* it were a single consumer even though it is made up of many individuals with different incomes and (possibly) different utility functions. Moreover, no welfare significance can be attached to the amount of aggregate utility. If aggregate utility increases, it is not necessarily true that consumers are better off than they were. In a later chapter we return to this question of welfare and income distribution in some detail.

6.3.2. *Restrictions on income distributions – Samuelson's social utility function*

While the preceding discussion focused upon restrictions on the ordinary demand (hence preference) functions allowing the income distribution to be arbitrary, the following discussion is concerned with restrictions on the income distribution functions and allows individual utility functions to be arbitrarily different. Samuelson (1956) established a rather remarkable result that, despite arbitrarily different individual preferences, we can construct a community or social utility function $u^0(z)$ yielding the aggregate demand functions, provided that aggregate income is always optimally distributed so as to maximize a social welfare function. Although the practical validity for this approach to the aggregation of preferences is doubtful, it is nevertheless of some interest to examine it in more detail.

Suppose that there exists a *social welfare function*

$$W = W(u^1(z^1), ..., u^L(z^L)), \tag{31}$$

which indicates society's evaluation of its citizens. In addition, suppose that society is able to allocate a given total income m among the L individuals without affecting m, and that it chooses the allocation to maximize the social welfare function. That is, society maximizes W subject to the aggregate budget constraint $p \sum_{\ell=1}^{L} z^\ell = m$, obtaining a solution for $z^1, ..., z^L$, and then allocates income $m^\ell \equiv pz^\ell$ to individual $\ell = 1, ..., L$. Each individual will then choose the same solution z^ℓ (assuming uniqueness) for his consumption vector. Thus, society manipulates individual incomes so as to obtain the highest level of social welfare.

To show that such an income distribution scheme leads to the possibility of aggregation of preferences, Samuelson made ingenious use of the famous aggregation theorem of Hicks (1946). Hicks' result is that if two or more goods have the same price, they may be aggregated and the consumer's utility maximization problem may be reformulated in terms of the aggregate or composite good.[4] To illustrate this result consider the case where there are three goods, the utility function is $u(x_1, x_2, x_3)$, the budget constraint is $p_1 x_1 + p_2 x_2 + p_3 x_3 = m$, and it is always true that $p_1 = p_2$. Define the quantity of the composite good as $x_0 \equiv x_1 + x_2$ and its price as $p_0 = p_1 = p_2$. The problem of maximizing $\{u(x_1, x_2, x_3): \sum_i p_i x_i = m, (x_1, x_2, x_3) \geqslant 0\}$ can be solved sequentially, first by maximizing with respect to x_1 and x_2 for a given x_3, and then by maximizing with respect

---

[4] Actually, all that is needed is that the prices of the goods in question always bear a fixed ratio to each other. In the present application the prices are equal so the more general case is not needed. For further details and formal proofs of Hicks' composite good theorem see Diewert (1978).

to x_3. For a given x_3 the income left over for expenditure on goods 1 and 2 is $m_0 \equiv m - p_3 x_3$, so the expenditure constraint for the first maximization problem in the sequence is $p_1 x_1 + p_2 x_2 = p_0(x_1 + x_2) = m_0$. Solving this problem we get:

$$u^0(x_0, x_3) \equiv \max \{u(x_1, x_2, x_3): p_0(x_1 + x_2) = m_0, \tag{32}$$

$$(x_1, x_2) \geq 0\},$$

which is the maximum utility attainable for a given consumption x_3 of good 3. This maximum utility also depends upon m_0/p_0 which, in view of the expenditure constraint, may be identified as x_0. Since $u^0(x_0, x_3)$ incorporates the maximization with respect to x_1 and x_2, it remains to maximize $u^0(x_0, x_3)$ with respect to x_0 and x_3 subject to the budget constraint. This problem is

$$\max_{x_0, x_3} \{u^0(x_0, x_3): p_0 x_0 + p_3 x_3 = m, (x_0, x_3) \geq 0\}, \tag{33}$$

since $p_0 x_0 = m_0$. It turns out that the function $u^0(x_0, x_3)$ has all of the usual properties of a utility function, so (33) is a standard consumer utility maximization problem. Thus, since $p_1 = p_2 = p_0$, it has been possible to aggregate goods 1 and 2 into a composite good 0 and solve the original utility maximization problem by solving problem (33). This result is extremely useful when interest is centred on good 3 and the composite good 0 rather than on goods 1 and 2 separately.[5]

Now consider the application of Hicks' composite good theorem to the problem of maximizing the social welfare function subject to the aggregate budget constraint $p \sum_{\ell=1}^{L} z^\ell = m$. Treating this is an ordinary consumer problem, it is noted that there are LM quantities to choose, namely the quantities of the M goods for each of L consumers. However, it is of note that each consumer faces the same price p_i for good i so that, by Hicks' composite good theorem, the quantities of good i for all the individuals may be aggregated and the maximization problem rewritten in terms of the aggregate or composite good quantity $z_i \equiv \sum_{\ell=1}^{L} z_i^\ell$. Since this can be done for all goods $i = 1, ..., M$, it follows that

---

[5]   This result is often used in microeconomics textbooks, where a many-good problem is reduced to a two-good problem by aggregating all but one good into a composite called "all other goods". In the analysis of labour supply, the composite good comprises all consumption goods other than leisure, and if its price p_0 is set equal to unity then $x_0 = m_0$ is total consumption expenditure.

$$\max\left\{W(u^1(z^1), ..., u^L(z^L)): p \sum_{\ell=1}^{L} z^\ell = m, (z^1, ..., z^L) \geqslant 0\right\}$$

$$= \max\left\{u^0(z_1, ..., z_M): \sum_{i=1}^{M} p_i z_i = m, (z_1, ..., z_M) \geqslant 0\right\}$$

$$= V^0(p, m), \tag{34}$$

where $u^0(z)$ is the social utility function and $V^0(p, m)$ is the corresponding indirect social utility function. Had the original welfare maximization problem been solved for $z^1, ..., z^L$, then $z = \Sigma_{\ell=1}^L z^\ell$ would coincide with the solution for z to the aggregate utility maximization problem in (34). Since $u^0(z)$ has all of the usual properties of a utility function, its maximization subject to the aggregate budget constraint constitutes a standard utility maximization problem and consequently yields aggregate demand functions with the standard properties. Thus, a policy of choosing individual incomes $m^\ell = pz^\ell$ to maximize a social welfare function leads individuals to choices for consumptions whose aggregate can be interpreted as having come from an aggregate or social utility function maximization problem. In this case the social utility function does have welfare significance.

While such an optimal income distribution policy does allow the aggregation of consumption decisions in the manner indicated, it should be reiterated that its practical relevance must be judged as very small.[6]

[6]   An alternative sufficient condition for aggregation based upon both the utility functions and the distribution of income was developed by Eisenberg (1961). Eisenberg's condition is that each consumer's utility function be homothetic, but not necessarily identical, and that income is distributed in fixed proportions. Actually, Eisenberg's result can be generalized somewhat in the following manner. Let the demand functions be $\phi^\ell(p, m^\ell) = \alpha^\ell(p) + \beta^\ell(p)m^\ell$ for $\ell = 1, ..., L$. These imply that preferences belong to the Gorman polar form family, but do *not* require that $\beta^\ell(p)$ be the same for all ℓ. If $m^\ell = k^\ell m$, where k^ℓ is the proportion of income m allocated to individual ℓ, the aggregate demands may be written as

$$z = \sum_{\ell=1}^{L} \phi^\ell(p, k^\ell m) = \alpha(p) + \beta(p, k)m \equiv \phi(p, m; k),$$

where

$$\alpha(p) \equiv \sum_{\ell=1}^{L} \alpha^\ell(p) \quad \text{and} \quad \beta(p, k) \equiv \sum_{\ell=1}^{L} \beta^\ell(p)k^\ell.$$

For a given vector $k = (k^1, ..., k^L)$, the aggregate demand functions $\phi(p, m; k)$ belong to the class of Gorman polar form demand functions. While the proof is left as a problem, it is noted that the properties of the $\alpha^\ell(p)$ and $\beta^\ell(p)$ functions (positive, non-decreasing, linearly homogeneous, concave) carry over to $\alpha(p)$ and $\beta(p, k)$. Thus, there exists a utility function whose indirect is a Gorman polar form, which yields $\phi(p, m; k)$ as the demand functions. Thus, aggregation is possible. Of course, the aggregate utility function has no welfare significance. Moreover, the practical significance of this aggregation result is limited by the strict requirement on income distribution.

6.3.3. *The Scitovsky indifference map*

A useful approach enabling the interpretation of the aggregate consumption vector obtained by aggregating the consumptions of the L individuals as the solution
to an aggregate problem, is provided by the concept of a Scitovsky indifference
map (Scitovsky, 1942). This approach imposes no special restrictions on individual preferences or upon income distribution and, accordingly, yields a weaker
and different result than those just discussed.

Let $\mu = (\mu^1, ..., \mu^L)$ be the vector of utility levels for the L individuals in the
economy. Then

$$Z^{\ell}(\mu^{\ell}) \equiv \{z^{\ell}: u^{\ell}(z^{\ell}) \geqslant \mu^{\ell}, z^{\ell} \geqslant 0\} \tag{35}$$

is the set of consumption vectors which yield at least utility level μ^{ℓ} to individual ℓ.
This is often referred to as the "level set" whose lower boundary is the indifference curve. The aggregate level set, or Scitovsky set, is defined as the sum of the
individual sets and is

$$Z(\mu^1, ..., \mu^L) \equiv \sum_{\ell=1}^{L} Z^{\ell}(\mu^{\ell}). \tag{36}$$

Since $Z^{\ell}(\mu^{\ell})$ is the set of consumptions which give individual ℓ at least utility
level μ^{ℓ}, $Z(\mu^1, ..., \mu^L)$ is the set of aggregate consumptions such that each individual is able to achieve at least utility level μ^{ℓ} $\ell = 1, ..., L$. Its boundary is called
a Scitovsky indifference curve. Fig. 6.2 illustrates these sets for the case $L = 2$
individuals and $M = 2$ goods. Any vector in $Z^1(\mu^1)$ and any vector in $Z^2(\mu^2)$
when summed yield a vector in $Z(\mu^1, \mu^2)$.

Let it be supposed that individual 1 has income $\bar{m}^1$, faces a price vector $\bar{p}$,
and that his maximum utility level is $\bar{\mu}^1 = u^1(\bar{z}^1)$ attained at consumption vector $\bar{z}^1$. The situation is illustrated in fig. 6.2, where the individual budget lines
are drawn tangent to the level sets at the optimal consumption points. The aggregate budget line must also be tangent to the aggregate level set, or Scitovsky
set, at the point $\bar{z} = \bar{z}^1 + \bar{z}^2$.[7] This fact allows us to interpret $\bar{z}$ as the solution
to an aggregate optimization problem. We cannot view it as the solution to an
aggregate utility maximization problem since we have merely established the
existence of one aggregate indifference curve, *not* a utility function. However, it
is evident that we can view $\bar{z}$ as the solution to the minimum aggregate expenditure problem

---

[7]   The proof of this is left as an exercise.

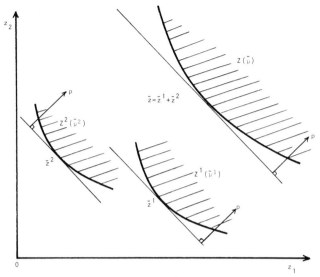

Figure 6.2

$$\overline{p}\overline{z} = E(\overline{p}, \overline{\mu}) \equiv \min_{z} \ \{\overline{p}z: z \in Z(\overline{\mu}^{1}, ..., \overline{\mu}^{L}), z \geqslant 0\}. \tag{37}$$

That is, $\overline{z}$ is the minimum cost aggregate consumption vector which enables the individuals to obtain the utility vector $\overline{\mu} = (\overline{\mu}^{1}, ..., \overline{\mu}^{L})$. To obtain a higher level of utility for some individual, it would be necessary to have a higher aggregate income. It is noted that $E(p, \mu)$, defined by (37), is identical to the previous definition of it as the sum of individual expenditure functions, (6), and hence no new notation is introduced. This is because $Z(\mu)$ is the sum of individual level sets. If we were to allow for interdependent preferences, then this additivity property of Z and E would disappear.

The above interpretation of the aggregate consumption vector $\overline{z}$ is only valid when individuals maximize utility given their individual incomes and a common price vector. Hence, it is of limited usefulness since it is required that the individual consumption vectors and utility functions be known before $Z(\overline{\mu})$ can be known. Nevertheless, the concept of a Scitovsky set will prove useful as a theoretical device.

To understand why a community utility function cannot exist in general under the present assumptions, it is important to recognize that there are an infinite number of Scitovsky indifference curves passing through each point in the goods space. If the fixed aggregate $\overline{z}$ were to be allocated amongst L individuals there would exist an infinity of Pareto optimal allocations, corresponding to points on the contract curve in the Edgeworth–Bowley box diagram. Each such (positive) allocation is characterized by a tangency of all indifferent curves. Thus, there is an infinity of utility vectors $\mu = (\mu^1, ..., \mu^L)$ attainable when the aggregate consumption bundle is $\bar{z}$. To each such vector there is a Scitovsky set $Z(\mu)$ whose boundary, the Scitovsky indifference curve, passes through $\bar{z}$. The details of this argument are left to the reader as an exercise.

6.3.4. Summary

This section now concludes with a brief summary. It has been shown that aggregate demands can be obtained from aggregate demand functions, which depend upon prices and aggregate income, and which have all of the usual properties of individual demand functions under two separate sets of restrictions. Restrictions on individual utility functions require them to belong to the family of Gorman polar forms. If the price–income configurations are restricted to those for which all persons consume some of each good, then differences in individual preferences are compatible with the existence of a community utility function. If not, then the Gorman polar forms for preferences are such that all individuals have the same homothetic preferences. On the other hand, if incomes are optimally distributed to maximize a social welfare function, then aggregation is possible without any restrictions on the individual utility functions. Neither result provides a very convincing argument in favour of the existence of an aggregate utility function and aggregate demand functions in practice. Finally, without special restrictions on income distribution or individual utility functions, it was shown that the aggregate budget line is tangent to the Scitovsky indifference curve (supports the Scitovsky set), but of course this does not imply the existence of aggregate demand functions.

6.4. Diagrammatic description of equilibrium in an open economy

It is instructive at this point to consider a diagrammatic description of the competitive equilibrium for a simple open economy. For this purpose suppose that there are two goods produced using two primary factors of production, the product price and endowment vectors being given. The aim is to illustrate the determination of the equilibrium outputs, resource allocation, consumptions and trades.

Figure 6.3 illustrates the determination of the equilibrium production levels using the production possibility set and the procedures developed in Chapters

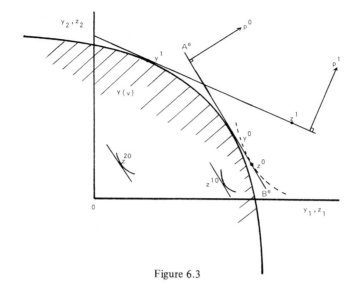

Figure 6.3

3–5. The highest iso-GNP line attainable is tangent to the production possibility set at y^0. This highest iso-GNP line, $A^0 B^0$, defines the aggregate budget line for the consumption sector. If the consumption sector consisted of one individual, or all individuals have Gorman polar form preferences, or income is distributed optimally to maximize a social welfare function, it is known from the previous section that we can think of the aggregate consumption vector z^0 as being obtained by maximizing an aggregate or community utility function subject to the aggregate budget constraint. In such cases z^0 is a point of tangency between the budget line $A^0 B^0$ and an indifference curve which is drawn as the dashed curve in fig. 6.3. Of course, if aggregation is not possible, then z^0 cannot be derived in this way. The use of the dashed curve is meant to emphasize this point. While z^0 cannot be *derived* from a single utility maximizing problem in general, the previous section shows that there will always exist a Scitovsky indifference curve, such as the dashed one in fig. 6.3, which is tangent to the aggregate budget line at z^0. As emphasized in the previous section, it can only be drawn once z^0 is known.

How is z^0 determined in general, i.e. when aggregation is not possible? Suppose there are two individuals whose incomes are determined as the market (rental) value of their ownership of the primary resources. Chapters 3–5 dealt with how factor prices were determined by commodity prices and factor endowments. Fig. 6.4 illustrates this for the case where there are two industries, the curves being

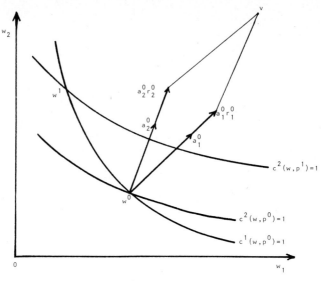

Figure 6.4

the sets of factor prices for which the industries make zero profits.[8] The inter-section determines the equilibrium factor price vector w^0 when both industries produce at levels r_1^0 and r_2^0, using up all of the factor endowment. The optimal vectors per unit of value added are a_1^0 and a_2^0 drawn perpendicular to the iso-cost curves at w^0 in accordance with Shephard's lemma.

Knowing w^0 and the endowments of the two individuals, the income distri-bution is determined. Fig. 6.3 illustrates the budget lines for each individual as well as the aggregate budget line. Each individual's consumption vector is a point of tangency between the budget line and the highest attainable indifference curve. The aggregate consumption vector z^0 lies on the aggregate budget line.

Thus, we have illustrated the internal equilibrium for an open economy using a series of diagrams. The equilibrium trade vector is obtained as the difference $x^0 = y^0 - z^0$ between the production and consumption vectors. This implicitly assumes that domestic production always satisfies (as far as is possible) the do-mestic market first, and then the foreign market if there is a surplus. The net export functions are illustrated in fig. 6.5, where net exports are plotted versus the price of product 2. The price axis may be reinterpreted as the price ratio

---

[8] If there is no joint production or intermediate inputs, then they are described by $c^j(w) = p_j^0$, $j = 1, 2$, where $c^j(w)$ is the unit (output) cost function. In general they are de-scribed by $c^j(w, p^0) = 1, j = 1, 2$, where $c^j(w, p)$ is the unit value added cost function.

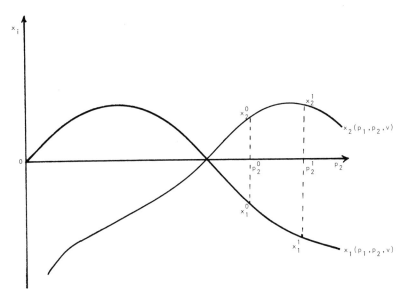

Figure 6.5

p_2/p_1 rather than the price of product 2, since the net export functions are homogeneous of degree zero in prices.

An alternative representation of the equilibrium trading plans of the economy is provided by the concept of an *offer curve*, which has received bountiful attention in the case of $M = 2$. This case is illustrated in fig. 6.6 in which the axes measure the net exports of the two goods. The vector $x^0 = y^0 - z^0$ obtained from fig. 6.3 is drawn in fig. 6.6 at right angles to the price vector p^0. The line drawn through the origin and on which x^0 lies is interpreted as the trade budget line since it indicates all trade vectors for which the balance of trade (excess of the value of exports over the value of imports) is zero. If the price vector changes, then production will change, incomes will change, and so will consumptions. Hence, the trade vector changes. The offer curve is the locus of all equilibrium trades corresponding to all possible price vectors, and is depicted in fig. 6.6. The direct association between trades and prices (price ratio) is given, of course, by fig. 6.5.

It is important to realize and understand the consequences for an economy of change in the product price vector. The consequences for the economy's trade are illustrated via the offer curve which is a summary of a host of events within the production and consumption sectors. The point is best made by Edgeworth (1894, pp. 424–426) who wrote that:

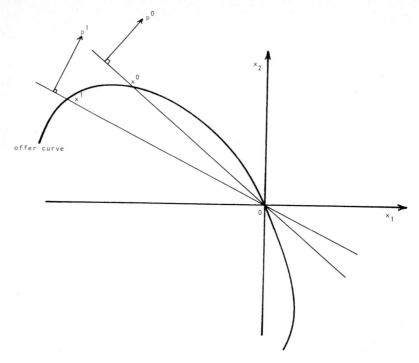

Figure 6.6

the movement along a supply-and-demand curve of international trade should be considered as attended with rearrangements of internal trade; as the movement of the hand of a clock corresponds to considerable unseen movements of the machinery.

To illustrate this point, consider the case where there is an increase in the price of good 2. Since industry 2 is now more profitable, resources will move from the production of good 1 to the production of good 2. This movement around the production possibility curve is illustrated in fig. 6.3. To obtain the effect upon factor prices we can invoke the Stolper–Samuelson theorem if it is supposed that joint production does not exist. Hence, we know that w_2 will rise by a greater percentage than p_2, and w_1 will fall. This is illustrated in fig. 6.4, where w^1 is the new factor price vector.[9] Each firm will now use a greater ratio of factor 1

---

[9]   In the general case such precise conclusions are not possible, as discussed in Chapter 5.

to factor 2 since factor 1 is now relatively cheap. Once new incomes for consumers are determined, new consumption bundles are chosen and hence the new aggregate consumption vector z^1 is obtained (as illustrated in fig. 6.3). The new trades are illustrated in fig. 6.5 and 6.6. Notice that it is possible for exports of good 2 actually to fall as the price of good 2 increases so that the offer curve can be backward bending. This is due to a strong income effect outweighing the substitution effect on demand for the exported good.

This description has been rather brief; the reader will find it useful to fill in the details. Also, while this analysis illustrates the way in which the economy responds to a change in product price, it is not very precise in obtaining the quantitative effects. Clearly, one source of vagueness is in the income distribution effects. The reader may find it instructive to relate the diagrammatic treatment of this section to the effects of changes in prices carried out in section 6.2.

6.5. Direct and indirect trade utility functions

It is often very convenient to focus attention on the trade vector without having to derive it explicitly as the difference between production and consumption. Consequently, the trade utility function developed geometrically by Meade (1952) and its corresponding indirect utility function are now briefly discussed. Also discussed is the net revenue function, which is the difference between the GNP and expenditure functions.

The (direct) trade utility function is defined as

$$U(x,v) \equiv \max_{z} \{u(z): z \in Y(v) - x, z \geqslant 0\}, \tag{38}$$

where $u(z)$ is a community utility function and the net export vector x is given.[10] If x is taken as exogenous, the set of possible consumption points is $Y(v) - x$. The trade utility function gives the maximum level of utility that can be obtained by consuming on this consumption set. It can be shown that $U(x,v)$ is quasi-concave in (x, v), non-decreasing in v and non-increasing in x.[11] If U had been expressed in terms of net imports, $-x$, it would have the exact properties of an ordinary utility function. However, we find it convenient to work with net exports.

The set of net exports which yields utility level μ when the endowment vector is v is

---

[10] Previously we have used a superscript zero to denote the fictional single consumer. We now omit this superscript and treat μ as a scalar.
[11] The proofs of this and other propositions of this section can be found in Woodland (1980). See also the problem set.

$$X(\mu, v) \equiv \{\mu : U(x, v) \geqslant \mu\} \equiv Y(v) - Z(\mu), \tag{39}$$

where $Z(\mu) \equiv \{z : u(z) \geqslant \mu\}$ is the level set for consumption. The maximum net revenue (balance of trade) function is

$$S(p, \mu, v) \equiv \max_{x} \{px : x \in X(\mu, v)\} \equiv G(p, v) - E(p, \mu), \tag{40}$$

which is the difference between the GNP and expenditure functions. It is worth noting that $X(\mu, v)$ and $S(p, \mu, v)$ can be defined for a many-consumer economy without aggregation by defining $Z(\mu)$ as the Scitovsky set and μ as a vector of utilities. However, the trade utility functions require the aggregation assumption.

The indirect trade utility function may be defined in alternative ways as

$$H(p, b, v) \equiv \max_{x} \{U(x, v): px + b \geqslant 0\}$$

$$\equiv V(p, G(p, v) + b) \equiv \{\mu : S(p, \mu, v) + b = 0\}, \tag{41}$$

where b is "borrowing", or income available from sources other than production.[12] Expressed in terms of G and E the budget constraint (assumed binding) is $E(p, \mu) = G(p, v) + b \equiv m$ from which utility is solved as $V(p, G(p, v) + b)$, which we can identify as $H(p, b, v)$.

6.5.1. Properties of S

In view of the derivative properties of G and E, it follows immediately that

$$x = S_p(p, \mu, v) = G_p(p, v) - E_p(p, \mu), \tag{42}$$

which is the vector of "compensated" (Hicksian) net export functions. The ordinary net export functions are obtained by substituting the indirect utility function for μ in (42). Hence, we have the following identities:

$$x(p, b, v) \equiv S_p(p, \mu, v) \equiv x(p, -S(p, \mu, v), v) \tag{43}$$

$$\equiv G_p(p, v) - \phi(p, G(p, v) + b),$$

---

[12]   The introduction of b is for future reference. If $b = 0$, then expenditure equals income and the following developments are entirely compatible with previous sections. Also, since we are dealing with a single-consumer model, the argument α of the net export functions is dropped. In short, the current net export function $x(p, b, v)$ introduced below is in fact the old $x(p, v; \alpha)$ if $b = 0$.

where $\mu = H(p, b, v)$. Hence, differentiation of the centre identities yields:

$$S_{pp} = x_p - x_b S_p = x_p + \phi_m S_p, \qquad (44)$$

which is the Slutsky-type pure substitution effect of a change in p. Note also that $S_{pp} = G_{pp} - E_{pp}$. In addition,

$$x_b = -\phi_m = S_{p\mu}/S_\mu = E_{p\mu}/E_\mu \qquad (45)$$

in the income effect upon net exports.

The function S is convex in prices, since G is convex and E is concave in prices. It is concave and non-decreasing in v since G is concave and non-decreasing in v. Also, $S_v = G_v$ is the factor price vector. Finally, it is decreasing in μ since E is increasing in μ. These properties, especially those with respect to prices, will be used extensively in later chapters.

6.5.2. *Properties of H*

The derivatives of H may be obtained by differentiating the budget constraint expressed in terms of S. Thus, we find that

$$\begin{aligned}
H_b &= -1/S_\mu, \\
H_p &= S_p H_b, \\
H_v &= S_v H_b,
\end{aligned} \qquad (46)$$

whence

$$x(p, b, v) = H_p(p, b, v)/H_b(p, b, v), \qquad (47)$$

which is an open economy version of Roy's identity. Alternatively, (47) may be obtained by differentiating $H = V(p, G(p, v) + b)$ with respect to p and using Roy's identity and Hotelling's lemma.

For future reference we write down the general properties of the indirect trade utility function in the form of a theorem:

Theorem. Under our maintained assumptions regarding the technology and preferences, the indirect trade utility function is (a) a continuous and real valued function for $p > 0$, $v \geqslant 0$ and finite $b \geqslant -G(p, v)$; (b) quasi-convex in p; (c) homogeneous of degree zero in (p, b); (d) non-decreasing in b; and (e) non-decreasing and quasi-concave in v. (48)

A full proof of this result is not given here.[13] Proofs of most properties are very straightforward and these are contained in the problem set. The quasi-convexity of H in prices is not immediate, although quasi-convexity is a property of the ordinary indirect utility function, and so it will be useful to provide the proof of this property. To derive this property we rewrite H as

$$H(p, b, v) \equiv \max_{z} \{u(z): pz \leqslant G(p, v) + b, z \geqslant 0\} \qquad (49)$$

using the definition of the indirect utility function $V(p, m)$. Consider three price vectors p^0, p^1 and $p^\lambda \equiv \lambda p^0 + (1-\lambda)p^1$, for $0 \leqslant \lambda \leqslant 1$. By definition $H(p, b, v)$ is quasi-convex on $p \geqslant 0$ if for any $p^0, p^1 \geqslant 0, H(p^\lambda, b, v) \leqslant \max \{H(p^0, b, v), H(p^1, b, v)\}$. Let $Z^i \equiv \{z: p^i z \leqslant G(p^i, v) + b, z \geqslant 0\}$ be the constraint set for (49) when the price vector is p^i, $i = 0, 1, \lambda$. Then $Z^\lambda \subset Z^0 \cup Z^1$. To prove this suppose, on the contrary, that $z^* \in Z^\lambda$, but $z^* \notin Z^0 \cup Z^1$. The latter implies that $p^0 z^* > G(p^0, v) + b$ and $p^1 z^* > G(p^1, v) + b$, which imply that $\lambda p^0 z^* + (1-\lambda)p^1 z^* = p^\lambda z^*$ [using the definition of p^λ] $> \lambda(G(p^0, v) + b) + (1-\lambda)(G(p^1, v) + b) = \lambda G(p^0, v) + (1-\lambda)G(p^1, v) + b \geqslant G(p^\lambda, v) + b$ [due to the fact that $G(p, v)$ is convex in p]. This implication, that $p^\lambda z^* > G(p^\lambda, v) + b$, contradicts the assumption that $z^* \in Z^\lambda$. Hence, if $z^* \in Z^\lambda$, then $z^* \in Z^0 \cup Z^1$. This implies that the maximum utility obtained on Z^λ cannot be greater than the maximum of the maximum utilities obtained on either Z^0 or Z^1. That is, $H(p^\lambda, b, v) \leqslant \max \{H(p^0, b, v), H(p^1, b, v)\}$, which was to be proved.

In summary, the functions $U(x, v), H(p, b, v)$ and $S(p, \mu, v)$ have been introduced as valuable tools for later analyses. The value of duality theory is that it enables us to use functions which economize on the number of variables explicitly considered and allows concentration of attention on those of primary interest. When the focus of interest is on the trade vector and product prices, the concepts introduced here are therefore useful.

6.6. Non-traded goods and endogenous factor supplies

Throughout the above discussion of the nature of net export functions, the presence of non-traded goods and endogenous factor supplies has been implicitly ignored. While these phenomena will be dealt with in more detail in a later chapter, it may be useful briefly to indicate how they can be accommodated in the model.

Non-traded goods cannot be assumed to have exogenous prices since their market is completely domestic. One way to model non-traded goods is to re-

---

[13]   See Woodland (1980, pp. 911–912) for a full proof of this theorem.

define the indirect trade utility function as

$$\hat{H}(p_t, b, v) \equiv \max_{x_t} \{U(x_t, x_n, v): p_t x_t + b \geqslant 0, x_n = 0\}, \tag{50}$$

where the subscripts t and n refer to traded and non-traded goods, respectively. In this problem the net exports for all non-traded goods are set equal to zero and only the price vector for traded goods is exogenous. This new indirect trade utility function, expressed in terms of the prices of traded goods, has all of the properties of H as given in (48). The net revenue function can be similarly redefined as

$$\hat{S}(p_t, \mu, v) \equiv \max_{x_t} \{p_t x_t: x = (x_t, 0) \in X(\mu, v)\} \tag{51}$$

and it will also have the same properties as S. Thus, non-traded goods can be 'netted out" of the model, and the resulting net export functions for traded goods $\hat{x}_t(p_t, b, v)$ will have the same properties as in a model with no non-traded goods. This is an important observation since for many problems we do not have to explicitly consider non-traded goods. However, if attention is turned from exports to production, consumption, and the prices of non-traded goods, then they will have to be considered explicitly.

If the market equilibrium conditions for non-traded goods, $x_n(p_t, p_n, b, v) = 0$, is solved for p_n as $p_n = p_n(p_t, b, v)$, then the relationship between the net export functions for traded goods with and without non-traded goods' prices eliminated is

$$\hat{x}_t(p_t, b, v) = x_t(p_t, p_n(p_t, b, v), v). \tag{52}$$

Factor supplies which depend upon decisions by consumers may be treated in a similar manner, since they also have the feature that their market is purely domestic. The most obvious endogenous factor supply is labour, of course. Consumers will choose the endogenous factor supplies as part of their utility maximizing problem, given prices of goods and the endogenous factors and their (to them) exogenous income. This supply of the endogenous factors will have to equal the demand by the production sector. For given prices of goods and the endowment of the exogenous factors, there will be an equilibrium supply of the endogenous factors to the production sector. For present purposes the simplest way of handling endogenous factor supplies is to treat them just like non-traded goods. Thus, any factor with an endogenous supply may be classified as a good with negative net supply by the production sector and negative demand by the consumption sector. Then the above treatment of non-traded goods applies to endogenous factor supplies.

6.7. Notes on the literature

In this chapter attention has been focused on the consumption sector, and upon the nature and properties of net export functions. Unlike the production sector, the conditions for treating the consumption section as if it were a single utility maximizing consumer are quite stringent. Consequently, the reader should remain aware of these conditions when the analysis makes use of the aggregation assumption.

The basic references on the conditions for aggregation based upon restrictions on preferences are Gorman (1953) and Chipman and Moore (1973), the latter being quite technical. The derivation of a social utility function based upon the assumption that the income distribution is chosen to maximize a social welfare function is presented in Samuelson (1956), which must be regarded as essential reading. The requirement that the social welfare function be quasi-concave in the ML-dimensional vector of consumptions of every individual $(z^1, ..., z^L)$ has been discussed by Gorman (1959) and Negishi (1963). Eisenberg (1961) has the result that aggregation is possible if income shares are constant. His work is extended by Chipman and Moore (1973) and Diewert (1980). Finally, Chipman (1974) deals with the question of aggregation under the maintained hypothesis of homothetic preferences.

The question of what restrictions are satisfied by the economy's net supply functions, without special assumptions or preferences or the income distribution, has been addressed by Sonnenschein (1972), Debreu (1973), Diewert (1977) and others. In particular, if the number of consumers exceeds the number of goods then no Slutsky symmetry restrictions need apply, but if the number of consumers is less than the number of goods, then Slutsky-like restrictions do apply to the excess supply functions.

The diagrammatic illustration of equilibrium culminating in the offer curve is well established in the literature. For a treatment of the offer curve when income distribution is important see Johnson (1959). For more formal treatments of the two-product case see Jones (1972) and Woodland (1974).

The concept of a trade indifference map is due to Meade (1952) who makes extensive use of its geometry. Chipman (1970) discusses the trade utility function, its associated expenditure function (the negative of our net revenue function $S = G\text{-}E$, i.e. $E\text{-}G$) and the resulting net import functions. The relationship between the trade utility function and the indirect trade utility function, and applications of the latter may be found in Woodland (1980); see also Chipman (1979). The trade utility function is used extensively by Dixit and Norman (1980), who call it the Meade utility function.

Problems

1. A nation produces a single consumer good and a pure intermediate good (not demanded by consumers), using capital and labour.
   (a) Write down the net export functions for the two goods. Does the income distribution affect these functions?
   (b) Derive the effect of a change in the terms of trade upon net exports, and hence draw the offer curves. Is the added structure of this model apparent in your answer?
   (c) Describe in words the effects upon the economy of an increase in the world price of the intermediate input.

2. Let $u(z) = -\sum_{j=1}^{M} a_j \exp\{(b_j - z_j)/a_j\}$.
   (a) Is this a valid utility function? If so, are there any restrictions on the parameters and/or z?
   (b) Show that the expenditure function is $E(p, \mu) = \Sigma(b_j - a_j \ln p_j)p_j + [\ln(\Sigma a_j p_j) - \ln \mu] \Sigma a_j p_j$.
   (c) Hence, derive the indirect utility function and the ordinary demand functions.
   (d) Check that the demand functions satisfy the budget constraint.
   (e) Is this a Gorman polar form?

3. Consider the problem of maximizing the social welfare function $W(\mu^1, ..., \mu^L)$, where $\mu^\ell = V^\ell(p, m^\ell)$ and total income is fixed at m.
   (a) Derive the first-order conditions for a solution for $m^1, ..., m^L$. Interpret these conditions.
   (b) What are the second-order conditions, and what do they imply?
   (c) Find sufficient conditions on W and the V^ℓ for W to be quasi-concave in incomes.

4. Prove that the direct trade utility function $U(x, v)$ is
   (a) quasi-concave in (x, v) and
   (b) non-decreasing in v.

5. Prove that the indirect trade utility function $H(p, b, v)$ is
   (a) homogeneous of degree zero in (p, b);
   (b) quasi-concave in v; and
   (c) non-decreasing in v.

6. Let $\hat{S}(p_t, x_n, \mu, v) \equiv \max\{p_t x_t : (x_t, x_n) \in X(\mu, v)\}$, where x_n is given and explicitly incorporated in $\hat{S}$.
   (a) Interpret $\hat{S}_n \equiv \partial \hat{S}/\partial x_n$ at $x_n = 0$.
   (b) If $\hat{H}(p_t, b, x_n, v)$ is the solution for μ to $\hat{S}(p_t, x_n, \mu, v) + b = 0$, derive $\hat{H}_n \equiv \partial H/\partial x_n$ in terms of the derivatives of $\hat{S}$.

(c) Hence, obtain expressions for the non-traded-good price function $p_n(p_t, b, v)$.
(d) Notice that x_n appears in $\hat{S}$ and $\hat{H}$ just like v. Comment on this.
7. (a) Construct a diagram to illustrate the derivation of the trade indifference map from the production possibility set and the ordinary (consumption) indifference map.
   (b) Use the resulting trade indifference map to construct the offer curve.
   (c) Is aggregation of the consumption section necessary for the existence of an offer curve?
8. Provide the proofs of the argument of footnote 6 regarding the existence of a community utility function when income shares are fixed.
9. Suppose that there are two consumers, a capitalist who owns all the capital and a labourer who owns all the labour. Only two goods are produced.
   (a) Specialize eq. (9) for this case.
   (b) If the consumers specialize in consumption (in different goods) examine the effects on net exports of a change in the price of the exported good. Can you obtain some meaningful propositions?
10. Let the expenditure function be $E(p, \mu) = e(p)\mu$.
    (a) Show that $\phi_{im}(p, m) = \phi_{jm}(p, m)$.
    (b) Hence, show that $\phi_p(p, m) \equiv \partial\phi(p, m)/\partial p$ is a symmetric, negative semi-definite matrix.
    (c) Does this imply that $x_p(p, v)$, where $x(p, v) \equiv G_p(p, v) - \phi(p, G(p, v))$, is a symmetric, positive semi-definite matrix? Explain.

References

Blackorby, C., R. Boyce and R.R. Russell (1978) "Estimation of demand systems generated by the Gorman polar form; A generalization of the S-branch utility tree", *Econometrica* 46-2, March, 345–363.
Chipman, J.S. (1965) "A survey of the theory of international trade: Part 2, The neoclassical theory", *Econometrica* 33-4, October, 685–760.
Chipman, J.S. (1970) "Lectures on the mathematical foundations of international trade theory", Institute of Advanced Studies, Vienna, mimeo.
Chipman, J.S. (1974) "Homothetic preferences and aggregation", *Journal of Economic Theory* 8, 26–38.
Chipman, J.S. (1979) in: J. Green and J. Scheinkman *General Equilibrium, Growth, and Trade: Essays in Honor of Lionel McKenzie* (New York: Harcourt Brace and Jovanovich/ Academic Press).
Chipman, J.S. and J.C. Moore (1973) "Aggregate demand, real national income, and the compensation principle", *International Economic Review* 14-1, February, 153–181.
Debreu, G. (1973) "Excess demand functions", Working Paper IP-177, University of California at Berkeley.
Diewert, W.E. (1977) "Generalized Slutsky conditions for aggregate consumer demand functions", *Journal of Economic Theory* 15, 353–362.

Diewert, W.E. (1978) "Hicks' aggregation theorem and the existence of a real value-added function", in: M. Fuss and D. McFadden (eds.), *Production Economics: A Dual Approach to Theory and Applications*, vol. 2 (Amsterdam: North-Holland), pp. 17–52.

Diewert, W.E. (1980) "Symmetry conditions for market demand functions", *Review of Economic Studies* 47, 595–601.

Dixit, A.K. and V. Norman (1980) *Theory of International Trade* (J. Nisbet/Cambridge University Press).

Edgeworth, F.Y. (1894) "Theory of international values", *Economic Journal* 4, 424–443.

Eisenberg, E. (1961) "Aggregation of utility functions", *Management Science* 7, July, 337–350.

Gorman, W.M. (1953) "Community preference fields", *Econometrica* 21, January, 63–80.

Gorman, W.M. (1959) "Are social indifference curves convex?", *Quarterly Journal of Economics* 73, 485–496.

Hicks, J.R. (1946) *Value and Capital*, 2nd edition (Oxford: Clarendon Press).

Johnson, H.G. (1959) "International trade, income distribution and the offer curve", *Manchester School of Economic and Social Studies* 27, 241–260.

Jones, R.W. (1972) "Activity analysis and real incomes: Analogies with production models", *Journal of International Economics* 2, 277–302.

Meade, J.E. (1952) *A Geometry of International Trade* (London: Allen and Unwin).

Negishi, T. (1963) "On social welfare function", *Quarterly Journal of Economics* 77-1, February, 156–158.

Samuelson, P.A. (1956) "Social indifference curves", *Quarterly Journal of Economics* 70, February, 1–22.

Scitovsky, T. (1942) "A reconsideration of the theory of tariffs", *Review of Economic Studies* 9, 89–110.

Sonnenschein, H. (1972) "Market excess demand functions", *Econometrica* 40, 549–563.

Woodland, A.D. (1974) "Demand conditions in international trade theory", *Australian Economic Papers* 13-33, December, 209–224.

Woodland, A.D. (1980) "Direct and indirect trade utility functions", *Review of Economic Studies* 47, 907–926.

CHAPTER 7

FREE TRADE EQUILIBRIUM AND TRADE THEORIES

7.1. Introduction

This chapter is concerned with the nature of free competitive trade between economies. In particular, attention is focused on several "theories of international trade" that have played an important role in the historical development of modern international trade theory. As will become clear, the competitive framework yields the result that international trade occurs if the autarky or pre-trade prices (ratios) are different from one country to another, since it is a price differential which, in the absence of transportation costs, encourages a potential trade. Accordingly, the various "theories of international trade" are really different explanations of why pre-trade prices are not the same for all economies. The classical theory of comparative advantage emphasizes differences in technology as the source of pre-trade price differentials, while the Heckscher—Ohlin—Samuelson theory emphasizes differences in relative factor endowments between countries and differences in input ratios between products. Of course, there are other possible reasons for pre-trade price differentials, such as differences in tastes, income distribution, and the structure of taxation. They have not received as much attention in the literature as technology and endowments, however.

In the following section the equilibrium conditions for a closed or autarky equilibrium and a full trading equilibrium are presented and discussed. The famous offer curve diagram is used to provide a convenient geometric description. Sections 7.3 and 7.4 are devoted to the classical and Heckscher—Ohlin—Samuelson theories of trade, while section 7.5 contains a mathematical treatment of equilibrium in a closed economy and its relationship to the full trading equilibrium. The relationship between factor endowments and commodity trade in a general Heckscher—Ohlin—Samuelson model is considered in section 7.6. Section 7.7 examines some problems in extending comparative advantage theory to many dimensions, and section 7.8 concludes the chapter with notes on the literature.

7.2. General equilibrium for a trading world

For most purposes it suffices to consider a trading world consisting of the home nation and a single foreign nation, which may be thought of as the "rest of the world". Where this simplified view of the world is inappropriate for our purposes, a multi-nation model will be used.

Let it be supposed that the net export or excess supply functions for tradeable goods are $x_i(p, v)$, $i = 1, ..., M$, for the home nation.[1] Variables and functions for the foreign nation will be denoted by attaching an asterisk (∗) to the home nation variable or function. Hence, the net export functions for the foreign nation are $x_i^*(p^*, v^*)$, $i = 1, ..., M$. If neither nation trades internationally, the competitive autarky equilibrium price vectors for the two nations are obtained as solutions to

$$x_i(p, v) \geqslant 0 \leqslant p_i, \quad i = 1, ..., M, \tag{1}$$

and

$$x_i^*(p^*, v^*) \geqslant 0 \leqslant p_i^*, \quad i = 1, ..., M, \tag{2}$$

respectively. These conditions say that if the equilibrium price for good i is positive, then excess supply for i must be zero (the market clears), and if equilibrium is characterized by an excess supply for good i, then it must be a free good. If attention is restricted to goods which have a positive cost of production, then a positive excess supply at a zero price is not possible, and hence equilibrium will be characterized by zero excess supplies at positive prices.

If the two nations have free trade with each other, and if it is assumed that there are no transportation or other costs of trade, there is no longer any reason why prices should be different internationally.[2] If traders see a price differential they will buy where the good is cheap and sell it where it is more expensive, thus making a profit. This they will continue to do so long as a price differential exists. However, the effect of many traders operating in this way is to raise the price in the cheaper source nation and lower it in the expensive source nation. Eventually, the price differential will disappear entirely if there is free trade for it is only then that any additional such trade does not yield positive profits. Accordingly, the equilibrium trading price vector is obtained as the solution to

---

[1]   In the previous chapter two other arguments of the net export functions were introduced, namely a vector of parameters of the income distribution functions (α) and "borrowing" (b). It is assumed here that each nation spends its entire income so $b = 0$ always, and α is fixed. Since both are fixed they are omitted as arguments for simplicity.

[2]   In later chapters tariffs will be considered in detail.

$$X_i(p, v, v^*) \equiv x_i(p, v) + x_i^*(p, v^*) \geqslant 0 \leqslant p_i, \qquad i = 1, ..., M, \tag{3}$$

where $X_i(p, v, v^*)$ is the world excess supply function for good i. As with (1) and (2), generally we are concerned with equilibria for which all prices are positive, in which case world excess supplies are zero.

Since the national excess supply functions are homogeneous of degree zero in prices and satisfy Walras' law (zero trade balance), it follows that the world excess supply functions also satisfy these two properties. Thus, in (1)–(3) only M-1 excess supply functions are needed to establish an equilibrium price vector which, however, is only determined up to a factor of proportionality. Since only price ratios are determined by the equilibrium conditions, it is evident that differences in national currencies and exchange rates play no essential role in the model. One might normalize prices in both nations in the same way and suppose that the exchange rate remains fixed at unity. Alternatively, one might suppose that the prices in terms of local currencies get normalized in some arbitrary and perhaps random manner, and that the exchange rate adjusts to ensure the equality of prices under free trade expressed in one of the two currencies. The former approach is simplest since it effectively means that there is just one currency. However, it does not matter which approach is used.

The most popular way of depicting a trading equilibrium is by the use of offer curves for the case where there are $M = 2$ goods. Fig. 7.1 shows the offer curves for both the home (H) and foreign (F) nations. While the axes refer to excess supplies for the home nation, as was the case when offer curves were introduced in Chapter 6, for the foreign nation they refer to *excess demands*. Thus, the point x^0, where the curves cross, will be a point of trading equilibrium since at the price vector p^0 both nations wish to trade at x^0. The home nation wishes to import $-x_1^0$ units of good 1 in exchange for x_2^0 units of good 2, while the foreign nation wishes to export $-x_1^0$ units of good 1 in exchange for x_2^0 units of good 2.

Several points should be noted about the trading equilibrium. First, while it is given by the point of intersection, x^0, of the offer curves H and F, there is a second point of intersection at the origin. However, this cannot be an equilibrium trade since the two nations only want to be there if they face their own *pre-trade* equilibrium prices. The pre-trade equilibrium price vectors are normal to the respective offer curve at the origin. This is the geometric consequence of the fact that along the offer curve $px \equiv 0$ and hence $p\,dx + x\,dp = 0$. At the autarky equilibrium $x = 0$ and so $p\,dx = 0$, where p is the autarky price vector and dx is the slope of the offer curve at the autarky trade, $x = 0$. Thus, p is normal or at right angles to the offer curve at the autarky point. Accordingly, the intersection of the two offer curves at the origin is of no interest except if they are tan-

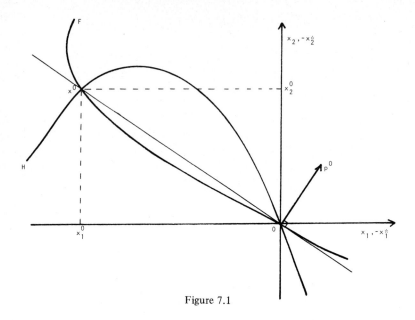

Figure 7.1

gent to each other there, in which case the free trade equilibrium involves no trade and coincides with the common autarky equilibria.

Secondly, there may exist multiple solutions to (3) or, in terms of fig. 7.1, the offer curves may cross each other several times. Multiple solutions complicate the analysis of equilibrium, although stability conditions may be used to reduce the number of equilibria which are of interest. More will be said on the question of stability in a later chapter. The possibility of multiple solutions will be ruled out for the remainder of this chapter.

Thirdly, while the offer curves have been drawn smoothly in fig. 7.1, they may contain linear segments and have abrupt changes in slope. This is because the solutions for outputs and consumptions for a given price vector may not be unique but comprise a convex set. An example of such an offer curve is provided below in section 7.3.

Fourthly, while we have subsumed the role of the income distribution in the excess supply functions, it should be recognized that its role is important. The interested reader should refer to Johnson (1959) for a treatment of income distribution and the offer curve. For simple models of trade with two classes of consumers see Jones (1972), Woodland (1974) and Ruffin (1977).

7.3. The classical theory of comparative advantage

The classical theory of comparative advantage was developed primarily by Ricardo and Torrens in the early 1800s. The principal aim of the economists was to prove that free trade was better than no trade or protection-limited trade, a fact which should always be kept in mind when evaluating their work. As such the theory is strictly in the area of welfare economics, to which detailed attention will be given in a later chapter on the gains from trade. A secondary aim, which is our main concern here, was the development of a theory which explains the pattern of trade flows. This is the positive, as opposed to normative, aspect of their work although the two aspects were seldom separated.

In what follows the classical model of trade is developed as a special case of our general equilibrium model. This special case is obtained by assuming that each nation can produce at most $M = 2$ goods (the same two goods in each nation) using a single factor of production, say labour. Moreover, joint production and intermediate inputs are excluded. All the usual assumptions, such as competitive behaviour and constant returns to scale (CRS) in production, are made. Since there is just one factor of production, the CRS assumption implies that the input coefficients are fixed.[3] The equilibrium conditions for the production sector may be written as

$$a_1 y_1 + a_2 y_2 - v \leqslant 0 \leqslant w,$$
$$p_1 - a_1 w \leqslant 0 \leqslant y_1, \tag{4}$$
$$p_2 - a_2 w \leqslant 0 \leqslant y_2,$$

where v is the endowment of the single factor (labour), w is the wage rate, y_i is the output of good i, p_i is the price of good i, and $a_i > 0$ is the constant input of labour per unit of output of good i.

Before trade let it be assumed that both goods are produced, implying that the profit conditions in (4) hold with strict equality. Positive product prices imply that the wage rate is positive, hence the pre-trade price ratio is $p_2/p_1 = a_2/a_1$. Thus, the price ratio is equal to the ratio of input–output coefficients or the comparative labour costs. A similar set of equilibrium conditions is assumed to hold for the foreign nation, so the two pre-trade price ratios are

$$p_2/p_1 = a_2/a_1 \quad \text{and} \quad p_2^*/p_1^* = a_2^*/a_1^*. \tag{5}$$

---

[3] The proof is left to the reader as an exercise.

There will be a difference in autarky or pre-trade price ratios if, and only if, the input–output ratios are different. Thus, in this model the necessary and sufficient condition for trade is that there is a difference in the comparative labour costs in the two nations. Moreover, since there are only two goods, we can predict the pattern of trade from knowledge of the autarky equilibrium prices. If

$$p_2/p_1 < p_2^*/p_1^*, \quad \text{or equivalently} \quad a_2/a_1 < a_2^*/a_1^*, \tag{6}$$

then the home nation will export good 2 and import good 1, while the foreign nation will import good 2 and export good 1. If (6) holds, the home nation is said to have a *comparative advantage* in the production of good 2, and hence a comparative disadvantage in the production of good 1. Conversely, the foreign nation must have a comparative disadvantage in the production of good 2, and a comparative advantage in the production of good 1. Thus, we obtain the

> **Comparative cost theory.** A nation will export the good in which it has a comparative advantage, and import the other good in which it has a comparative disadvantage.

The importance of this theory is that it establishes that trade will occur if there is a difference in comparative costs, and that the pattern of trade can be predicted from knowledge of these comparative costs. At the time it was developed it was especially important because it showed that trade did not depend upon a nation having an *absolute* advantage in the production of some good, a belief held by Adam Smith. The home nation is said to have an absolute disadvantage in the production of both goods if $a_1 > a_1^*$ and $a_2 > a_2^*$, meaning that more labour is required to produce each good at home than in the foreign nation. Clearly, it is possible for the a's to be such that $a_2/a_1 < a_2^*/a_1^*$ so that the home nation has a comparative advantage in the production of good 2 even though it has an absolute disadvantage in both goods. The implication of the comparative cost doctrine is that technologically less developed nations can carry out trade with advanced nations.

If trade is permitted, the equilibrium world price ratio will be between the two autarky price ratios. Since the latter are equal to the comparative labour cost ratios under diversification in autarky, the world equilibrium price ratio must satisfy

$$a_2/a_1 \leqslant p_2/p_1 \leqslant a_2^*/a_1^*, \tag{7}$$

if $a_2/a_1 < a_2^*/a_1^*$. Ricardo did not explain how the equilibrium price ratio would be determined, except that it would depend upon demand conditions in the two countries. It was left to Mill, Marshall and Edgeworth formally to introduce demand through the concept of offer curves based upon the existence of a single consumer or a community utility function. Of course, offer curves exist without these restrictive assumptions and can be used to illustrate the trading equilibrium for the classical model. Fig. 7.2 illustrates the net export functions for the classical model, while fig. 7.3 provides an alternative illustration using offer curves. At the autarky price ratio $\rho^0 \equiv p_2^0/p_1^0$ in the home nation, the equilibrium supplies are not unique and can be any point on the production possibility frontier in fig. 7.4. Thus, the net export function is set valued for this price ratio, as illustrated in fig. 7.2. Accordingly, the offer curve consists of a line segment, as illustrated in fig. 7.3. If $\rho > \rho^0$, then the home nation will specialize in the production of good 2 and the net export becomes unique since the production is unique. Similarly, if $\rho < \rho^0$ only good 1 is produced and once again the net export (import) of good 2, is unique. The net export and offer curves for the foreign nation have a similar shape except that the line segments occur at the foreign nation's autarky price ratio $\rho*^0$. The equilibrium price ratio ρ^e is established where the home nation's desired trade coincides with that of the foreign nation.

It is clearly possible for the equilibrium price ratio to be at one of the limits

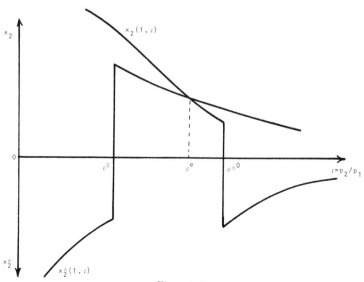

Figure 7.2

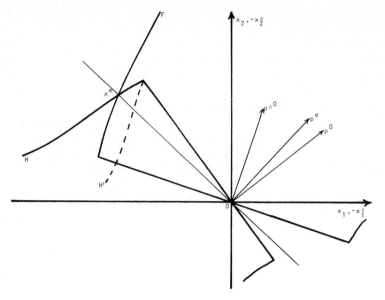

Figure 7.3

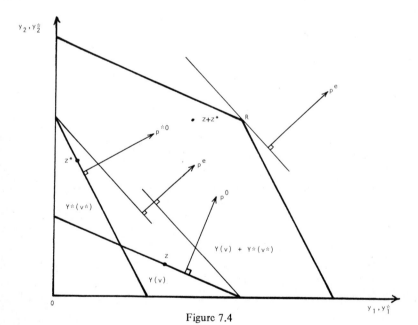

Figure 7.4

of (7). This is illustrated in fig. 7.3 by the home offer curve H' which cuts F along its linear segment. In this case, despite the fact that $\rho^e = \rho^{0*}$, the foreign nation imports good 2 in return for exports of good 1. Consumption in the foreign nation will be unchanged compared with autarky, but production will have moved along the production possibility frontier to accommodate the trading desires of the producers and consumers in the home nation. The more likely situation is, however, described by offer curve H with the equilibrium price ratio strictly between the autarky price ratios. In this case it is evident from fig. 7.4 that each nation will *specialize* in the production of the good in which it has a comparative advantage, relying entirely upon imports for its consumption of the other good.

While the welfare gains from international trade are discussed in detail in a later chapter, it seems appropriate, given the emphasis of the classical economists on the gains from trade, briefly to consider this topic now. If the equilibrium price vector is strictly between the autarky price ratios, specialization in production takes place and the aggregate budget constraint (income line) for the consumption sector lies above the production possibility set, except at the point of specialization. This is illustrated in fig. 7.4, where the aggregate budget lines are drawn at right angles to p^e. There are gains from trade in the sense that the consumption possibilities under trade (area within the trade aggregate budget line) are greater than under autarky (area under the production possibility frontier). This is basically the argument used by the classical economists. An alternative demonstration of the efficiency of free trade is to show that the world production, hence consumption, possibility set contains the world autarky consumption point in its interior. The world production possibility set is obtained as the sum $Y(v) + Y^*(v^*)$ of the individual production possibility sets. Its boundary is obtained only if at least one nation specializes in production, the point R being obtained only if both nations specialize according to their comparative advantage. Since the autarky production (consumption) points are not generally ones of specialization, they sum to a point in the interior of the world production (consumption) possibility set as illustrated in fig. 7.4. In this sense, from a world viewpoint, free trade is superior to no trade.

7.3.1. Generalization

The preceding account of the classical theory was based upon the assumption that only two goods can be produced and that there is just one factor of production. Moreover, intermediate goods were ignored despite the fact that most of the numerical examples used by the classical economists involved such goods.

Any attempt to generalize the Ricardian model of comparative advantage must raise the crucial question: What is the essence of the Ricardian model? Is it the labour theory of value, fixed production coefficients, or differences in efficiency in a technical sense? The labour theory of value follows from having labour as the only factor of production. Fixed production coefficients are a direct consequence of having one factor of production and assuming constant returns to scale. Thus, these features of the Ricardian model result from the dimensionality of the model. Therefore it appears that the essence of the Ricardian model must lie in the assumption that there are *differences in technical efficiency in production* between nations. If so, then the Ricardian theory may be interpreted as a special case of a more general theory which states that trade occurs because of differences in relative efficiencies in production between nations.

To illustrate this essential feature of the Ricardian model, in what follows it is reformulated to eliminate the assumptions that labour is the only factor and that there are fixed coefficients in production. Suppose, for example, that there are two factors of production which are used to produce two goods. Suppose, in addition, that two nations have the same factor endowment vector v, the same aggregate demand functions $\phi_j(p, m) = \beta_j(p)m$ derived from a homothetic community utility function, but have different production functions. If they had the same production functions they would be identical with the same autarky price vectors, implying that no trade would occur even if it were permitted. Let the production functions be

$$y_j = \gamma_j f^j(q_j), \quad j = 1, 2, \tag{8}$$

where q_j is a vector of inputs and γ_j is an efficiency parameter. The function f^j applies to both nations, but the efficiency parameters are possibly different. For simplicity set $\gamma_1 = \gamma_1^*$ and suppose that $\gamma_2 > \gamma_2^*$. This means that both nations are equally efficient in the production of good 1, but that the home nation is more efficient in the production of good 2 since it can obtain more output with the same input than the foreign nation. The relation $\gamma_2/\gamma_1 > \gamma_2^*/\gamma_1^*$ is interpreted as meaning that the home nation has a comparative advantage in the production of good 2. For the comparative cost theory to be valid under this definition of comparative advantage it is necessary to show that, under our demand assumptions, good 2 will be exported by the home nation. To show this, we need only prove that the home nation production possibility frontier is steeper than the foreign nation's along any ray through the origin, as in fig. 7.5. If a is a point of autarky equilibrium for the home nation, then b cannot be a point of autarky equilibrium for the foreign nation since the indifference curve through b has the same slope as that through a because of homothetic preferences, while the slope

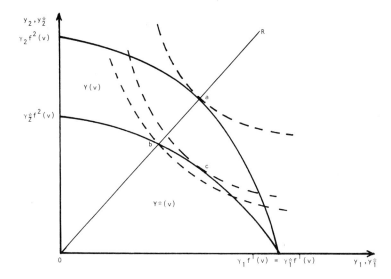

Figure 7.5

of the production possibility frontier at b is less. The autarky equilibrium has to be at point c where the slopes of the production possibility frontier and the indifference curve are the same and equal to the autarky price ratio. Thus, the autarky price ratios are related by

$$\rho^0 < \rho^{*0}, \quad \text{if } \gamma_2/\gamma_1 > \gamma_2^*/\gamma_1^*, \tag{9}$$

with product 2 being relatively cheap at home. Hence, if trade is permitted the home nation will export good 2, in which it has a comparative advantage, and import good 1, in which it has a comparative disadvantage.

The "steepness assertion" is now proved. To do this we first note that the model of the production sector may be written in terms of output in "efficiency units". These "efficiency units" are y_j/γ_j whose production functions are $f^j(q_j)$, $j = 1, 2$. The cost function is

$$C^j(w, y_j/\gamma_j) = \min_{q_j} \{wq_j : f^j(q_j) \geqslant y_j/\gamma_j, q_j \geqslant 0\} = c^j(w)y_j/\gamma_j, \tag{10}$$

where $c^j(w) \equiv C^j(w, 1)$ is the cost of producing 1 unit of j when $\gamma_j = 1$, or one efficiency unit of j. Clearly, the larger is γ_j the smaller the cost of producing a given amount of j in natural units. The equilibrium conditions for the production sector, assuming that y and w are positive, are

$$c^j(w) = \gamma_j p_j, \quad j = 1, 2,$$

$$\sum_{j=1}^{2} c_{ij}(w) (y_j/\gamma_j) = v_i, \quad i = 1, 2. \tag{11}$$

The term $\gamma_j p_j$ may be interpreted as the price of an "efficiency unit" of j. It is known from Chapter 4 that an increase in the relative price of a good will increase that good's output and reduce the output of the other good. In the present context, if γ_2 increases relative to γ_1 then the price ratio $\gamma_2 p_2/\gamma_1 p_1$ rises and consequently the production of good 2 rises in "efficiency units" while the "efficiency unit" production of good 1 falls. Thus, $(y_2/\gamma_2)/(y_1/\gamma_1) = (y_2/y_1)/(\gamma_2/\gamma_1)$ rises and since γ_2/γ_1 has risen, y_2/y_1 must rise. We can imagine that the increase in γ_2/γ_1 corresponds to a shift from the foreign nation's γ's to those of the home nation. Since the price ratio in natural units, p_2/p_1, has not changed this means that an increase in γ_2/γ_1 implies that y_2/y_1 has risen and hence that the home nation's production possibility frontier is steeper than that of the foreign nation along any ray through the origin. For example, in fig. 7.5 the slope of the home frontier at a is greater (in absolute terms) than the slope of the foreign frontier at b since the point of equal slope is to the north-west of a by the above demonstration. Thus, the "steepness assertion" is indeed true, and hence our generalization of the Ricardian comparative cost theory is valid.

7.3.2. Concluding comments

This model is a generalization of the simple Ricardian model in the sense that it emphasizes the essential feature of the Ricardian model which falls out as a special case. If there is just one factor of production, then the production functions may be written as $y_j = \gamma_j q_j$, where q_j is the input of labour and units have been chosen so that the input–output coefficient is unity when γ_j is unity. This shows that γ_j can be identified with the inverse of the input–output coefficient $(1/a_j)$. Hence (9) and (6) are equivalent, and so the simple Ricardian model is indeed a special case.

If it is agreed that the essence of the Ricardian theory of comparative advantage is international differences in technology, the Ricardian model can be generalized in many ways depending upon how these differences are characterized. The above generalization is based upon differences in indices of product-augmenting efficiency. One might also model differences in indices of factor-augmenting efficiency. Such a model turns out to be formally the same as the factor endowments model dealt with in the following section. Alternatively, one can assume international differences in a matrix $[\gamma_{ij}]$ of indices of efficiency of factor i in industry j. Such a model is much more complicated and yields few additional insights. The Ricardian model and its generalization dealt with in this section serve to provide simple illustrations of the general proposition that international differences in technology are a cause of trade.

7.4. The factor endowments theory of trade

An unusually large proportion of the international trade literature has been concerned with the factor endowments or factor proportions theory initiated by Heckscher (1919), developed and extended by his student Ohlin (1933), and crystalized by Stolper and Samuelson (1941) and Samuelson (1948, 1949). In its modern version it is cast in terms of a two-product, two-factor model in which the only difference that exists between nations is their relative factor endowments. The only source for differences in autarky prices for goods is the difference in relative factor endowments, which consequently is the only cause of trade.

From a historical viewpoint, the theory was important for at least two reasons.[4] First, it provided an explanation for differences in comparative advantage (interpreted as autarky prices) which was not based upon differences in technology, and which explicitly incorporated the factor market and so allowed an investigation of the connection between international trade and the distribution of income. This the classical theory was not able to do. Secondly, it represented the first attempt to show a minimal or sufficient condition for the existence of international trade. In particular, it shows that, even if knowledge is spread from the innovative nations to the less innovative nations and the demonstration effect causes tastes to coincide in all nations, there would still exist a sufficient reason for profitable international trade. The reason is a difference in relative factor endowments between nations, together with a technology in which different goods require different factor input proportions. Thus, in establishing a sufficient reason for trade, the simplicity of the model is its virtue.

While the theory concentrates entirely upon a difference in factor endowments as *a* sufficient cause for trade, it should be recognized that there are other sufficient conditions. Presumably, the considerable attention given to the theory is motivated to a large extent by the belief that differences in endowments con-

---

[4] See Lancaster (1957).

stitute the most important reason for trade. When the model is viewed as a description of reality, its simplicity loses some of its virtue and consequently we should be careful in applying its predictions to the real world.

7.4.1. The Heckscher–Ohlin–Samuelson model

The model of trade underlying the factor proportions theory of trade is now developed in detail. The production sectors of the home and foreign nation consist of two industries producing two products using two factors of production. The models of the production sector are therefore a special case of that in Chapter 3 where $M = 2$ and $N = 2$. Thus, constant returns to scale (CRS) and competitive behaviour are assumed. It is also assumed that consumer demands may be obtained by maximizing a community utility function subject to the aggregate budget constraint, and that this utility function is homothetic. An important assumption, to be discussed in detail below, is that the Samuelson intensity condition (SIC) holds. This assumption requires that the factor ratios or intensities in the two products are different and do not reverse themselves for all factor price ratios. Finally, it is assumed that the technology and the community utility functions are the same in the two nations. Hence, the two nations are identical in all respects, except in their endowments of the primary factors.

It is an important feature of the model that scale is of no importance because of the assumptions that there are constant returns to scale in production and that community preferences are homothetic. Thus, doubling the endowment of both factors, with fixed product prices, will cause outputs of both goods to double because of CRS, and since GNP will double, consumption of both goods will double due to homothetic preferences. If the initial situation is one of autarky, the final situation is also an autarky equilibrium. Thus, it is a difference in *relative* not absolute factor endowments which is the cause of a difference in autarky prices. We say that the home nation has a relative abundance of factor 2 if

$$v_2/v_1 > v_2^*/v_1^*, \tag{12}$$

where, as usual, the asterisk denotes the foreign nation.

Out task is to show that if (12) holds then the home nation will export good 2 and import good 1, while the foreign nation will import good 2 and export good 1 if free trade is permitted. To show this result it is sufficient to show that the autarky price ratio p_2/p_1 in the home nation is less than in the foreign nation. Since the nations differ only in their relative factor endowments, we accomplish our task by seeing how the autarky price ratio changes as the endowment ratio

v_2/v_1 is increased from the foreign nation's endowment ratio to that of the home nation.

The model for either nation may be expressed as

$$c^j(w_1, w_2) - p_j \leqslant 0 \leqslant y_j, \quad j = 1, 2,$$

$$\sum_{j=1}^{2} c_{ij}(w_1, w_2)y_j - v_i \leqslant 0 \leqslant w_i, \quad i = 1, 2, \tag{13}$$

$$G(p, v) \equiv \sum_{j=1}^{2} p_j y_j \equiv \sum_{i=1}^{2} w_i v_i, \tag{14}$$

$$z_j = \beta_j(p)G(p, v), \quad j = 1, 2, \tag{15}$$

$$y_j - z_j \geqslant 0 \leqslant p_j, \quad j = 1, 2. \tag{16}$$

Conditions (13) are the equilibrium conditions for the production sector, (14) is the definition of GNP, (15) gives the demand functions when the utility function is homothetic, and (16) constitutes the market equilibrium conditions for goods under autarky. Assume that $w > 0$, $p > 0$, so factor and goods markets clear at positive prices.

7.4.2. The factor endowments theory

Suppose that an equilibrium is established and consider the effect upon that equilibrium of an increase in v_2/v_1. It was established in Chapter 4 than an increase in v_2/v_1 would, if p remained fixed, cause an increase in y_2/y_1 if and only if industry 2 was factor 2 intensive relative to industry 1. Let us suppose that this is the case for all possible factor price vectors. That is, we assume

Samuelson intensity condition (SIC). Industry 2 is factor 2 intensive relative to industry 1. That is, $|A(w)|, |\theta|, |\lambda| > 0$, for all $w > 0$.[5] (17)

---

[5]   Recall that $A(w)$ is the matrix of input–output coefficients $c_{ij}(w)$, θ is the matrix of cost shares, and λ is the matrix of factor input shares. Also, recall that the condition $|A(w)| > 0$ is equivalent to the condition $c_{22}(w)/c_{12}(w) > c_{21}(w)/c_{11}(w)$, if $c_{12}(w)$ and $c_{11}(w)$ are positive, which is the usual interpretation of the statement that industry 2 is factor 2 intensive relative to industry 1.

For fixed p, GNP will change as a result of the increase in v_2/v_1 and so consumption demands will change. However, it is evident from (15) that the ratio z_2/z_1 will not change for fixed p. Thus, for fixed p, there will be an excess supply of good 2 and an excess demand for good 1 since z_2/z_1 has not altered and y_2/y_1 has increased. This cannot be an autarky equilibrium. To achieve an autarky equilibrium p_2/p_1 must fall to reduce y_2/y_1 and increase z_2/z_1 until they become equal. Thus, we have proved that an increase in v_2/v_1 will cause a fall in p_2/p_1 if industry 2 is always factor 2 intensive relative to industry 1. The preceding argument is illustrated in fig. 7.6, where the superscript 0 denotes the initial situation, the superscript 1 denotes the final situation, and the superscript 2 denotes the situation when endowments have changed but p has not.

The argument of the previous paragraph may be directly applied to show that if $v_2/v_1 > v_2^*/v_1^*$ (that is, the home nation is relatively abundant in factor 2) and if industry 2 is always factor 2 intensive, then the autarky price ratios satisfy $p_2/p_1 < p_2^*/p_1^*$. Hence, if trade is permitted, the home nation will export good 2 and import good 1, which is what we set out to prove. Notice that if it had been assumed that the foreign nation was relatively abundant in factor 2 *or* that product 2 was always factor 1 intensive, then the same argument would have shown that $p_2/p_1 > p_2^*/p_1^*$ in which case the home nation would export good 1 and import good 2. In summary, we have

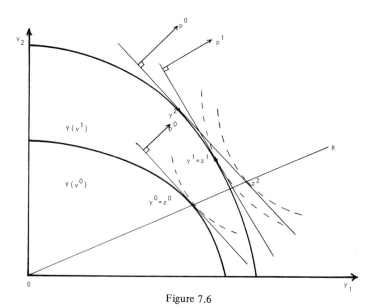

Figure 7.6

Heckscher–Ohlin–Samuelson (HOS) theorem. If two nations have autarky equilibrium conditions of the form (13)–(16), with the same technology and the same community preferences, and if relative factor intensities do not reverse then, under free trade each nation will export that good which uses relatively intensively the factor in which it has a relative abundance, and import that good which uses relatively intensively the relatively scarce factor.   (18)

This theorem establishes that if $v_2/v_1 \neq v_2^*/v_1^*$, then trade will take place and predicts the pattern of trade from knowledge of relative factor endowments and the relative factor intensities of the technology. The theorem is plausible in that each nation economizes on the scarce factor by importing the good which is intensive in its use of that factor.

There are other implications of the model, arising from the adjustments to the free trade equilibrium. Consider once again the case where (12) and (17) hold. Then the free trade price ratio p_2^e/p_1^e will clearly lie between the autarky price ratios. Thus, in the home nation free trade implies an increase in p_2/p_1 which causes resources to move from industry 1 to 2 resulting in an increase in y_2 and a decrease in y_1. In other words, the home nation produces more of the good in which it has a comparative advantage arising from its relative abundance of factor 2, and produces less of the good which is intensive in its use of the scarce factor. Conversely, in the foreign nation y_2^* falls and y_1^* increases. Thus, free trade pushes each nation towards, but not necessarily to, specialization in the goods they export. On the demand side, since p_2/p_1 has increased at home consumers substitute good 1 for good 2 and so reduce z_2/z_1. In the foreign nation, consumers increase z_2^*/z_1^* as a result of a fall in the relative price of good 2. Since they face the same prices under free trade and since the consumption ratios depend only upon prices due to the common homothetic preferences, the consumption ratios in the two nations become equal. Thus, free trade causes consumption ratios to converge while it causes production ratios to diverge towards specialization in the HOS model.

7.4.3. *Role of the assumptions*

Attention is now turned to the role played by the assumptions underlying the HOS theory of trade. Consider, first, the Samuelson intensity condition. Fig. 7.7 traces out the locus of autarky price ratios $\rho \equiv p_2/p_1$ corresponding to all possible factor endowment ratios $\nu \equiv v_2/v_1$ for the model given by (13)–(16). Our previous argument stated that if ν increased, and if product 2 was factor 2 inten-

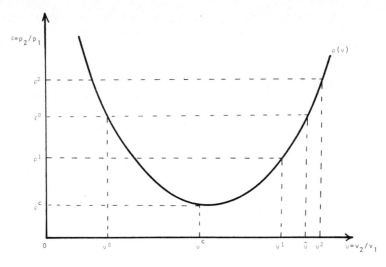

Figure 7.7

sive, then ρ would fall. Thus, the curve in fig. 7.7 in the neighbourhood of v^0 is downward-sloping. As ρ falls so does the factor price ratio $\omega \equiv w_2/w_1$ due to the Stolper–Samuelson theorem discussed in Chapter 4. Hence, both industries substitute factor 2 for factor 1 and become more intensive in their use of factor 1. We know from the analysis of Chapter 4 that it is possible that the relative intensities can reverse themselves, in which case industry 1 will become factor 2 intensive relative to industry 2. This occurs if industry 2's ratio of factor 2 to factor 1 falls sufficiently faster than industry 1's as a result of the fall in ω. If a reversal occurs, say when $v = v^c$ and $\rho = \rho^c$, then for $v > v^c$ ρ will now *increase* as a result of further increases in v, at least until the next intensity reversal occurs, if indeed it does occur. Thus, factor intensity reversals cause the $\rho(v)$ curve to be non-monotonic. Consequently, knowing that $v > v^0$ is not sufficient to determine the pattern of free trade between nations having these endowment ratios. If v^0 is the foreign endowment ratio and the home nation's ratio is between v^0 and $\bar{v}$, say at v^1, then the home nation will export good 2 and import good 1. In this case the HOS prediction is true for the foreign nation which exports good 1 which is relatively intensive in factor 1 in the foreign nation, but is no longer true for the home nation since it exports good 2 which is now relatively intensive in factor 1 which is its scarce factor. On the other hand, if the home nation's ratio is higher than $\bar{v}$, say at v^2, then $\rho^2 > \rho^0$, in which case the home nation will export good 1 and import good 2. In this case the HOS prediction is true for the home nation but not for the foreign nation. The difficulty is, of course, that each good is no longer unambiguously associated with a particular factor. The conclusion to be drawn from this discussion is that the SIC is crucial to the proof of the HOS theorem.

A second assumption which deserves special attention is that aggregate demands come from a community utility function, which is homothetic and identical in the two nations. The role of the homotheticity assumption is, in conjunction with CRS in production, to ensure that scale does not matter. Clearly, if the homotheticity assumption were dropped the conclusion of the HOS theorem may not hold if the two economies are sufficiently different in size. Even more obvious is the result that international differences in community preferences, even if homothetic, may upset the HOS conclusions. In either case, the HOS conclusions may not hold if preferences are sufficiently biased in favour of the good that uses the abundant factor that this good becomes relatively expensive. Verification of these statements is left to the reader in the problem set.

A third assumption is that the technology is identical in the two nations. Relaxation of this assumption allows differences in technology to outweigh differences in endowments since the position and shape of the production frontiers depends upon both endowments and technology. While differences in technology may upset the HOS conclusions, if the differences are not sufficiently strong the HOS conclusions will continue to hold.

While we could continue to show that the conclusions of the HOS theorem may not hold if various assumptions are relaxed, such an exercise is not very profitable. Since the assumptions are sufficient, but not necessary, for the theorem to be valid, their relaxation leads to the possibility but not necessity that the conclusions of the HOS theorem do not hold. Moreover, all except the SIC are made to make the point that, even if the only difference between nations is their relative factor endowment, trade will take place and in accordance with the HOS theorem.

7.5. A mathematical treatment of the HOS model

In this section a formal comparative statics analysis of the HOS model given by (13)–(16) is presented, drawing upon the earlier material in Chapter 4. Following this analysis a general treatment of the case where there are more than two goods and factors is considered, and the question of whether the HOS theory can be generalized is addressed.

Consider the model given by (13)–(16) and suppose there is an equilibrium for given v with y, w, and p all positive. The task is to obtain the response of these vectors to a small change in v. Since interest in the previous section centred on endowment, output and price ratios the analysis will be conducted in terms of these ratios. Differentiation of the profit-maximization conditions in (13) yields:

$$\hat{w}_2 - \hat{w}_1 = (\hat{p}_2 - \hat{p}_1)/|\theta|, \tag{19}$$

where θ is the matrix of cost shares. This result was obtained in Chapter 4 as eq. (4.34). Differentiation of the factor market equilibrium conditions in (13) yields:

$$\hat{y}_2 - \hat{y}_1 = (\hat{v}_2 - \hat{v}_1)/|\lambda| + (\hat{w}_2 - \hat{w}_1)(\epsilon_{12} + \epsilon_{21})/|\lambda|, \tag{20}$$

where λ is the matrix of industry shares of the factors, and ϵ is the matrix of market price elasticities of demand for the factors given the output vector.[6] This result, obtained from (4.23) and (4.43), indicates the effect on the output ratio y_2/y_1 of changes in v_2/v_1 and w_2/w_1. Substitution of (19) into (20) yields the effect of the product price and endowment ratios upon the output ratio as

$$\hat{y}_2 - \hat{y}_1 = (\hat{v}_2 - \hat{v}_1)/|\lambda| + o_s(\hat{p}_2 \quad \hat{p}_1), \tag{21}$$

where $o_s \equiv (\epsilon_{12} + \epsilon_{21})/|\lambda| \cdot |\theta| \geqslant 0$ is the elasticity of transformation around the production possibility frontier. This elasticity is non-negative because $|\lambda|$ and $|\theta|$ always have the same sign, and because $\epsilon_{12}, \epsilon_{21} \geqslant 0$ since they are cross-price elasticities of factor demands in a two-factor model.[7] Eq. (21) summarizes the comparative statics of the production sector when the number of products and factors is two.

On the consumption side we note that (15) yields $z_2/z_1 = \beta_2(p)/\beta_1(p)$, where the $\beta_i(p)$ functions are homogeneous of degree zero and hence functions of p_2/p_1 alone. Hence,

$$\hat{z}_2 - \hat{z}_1 = -o_D(\hat{p}_2 - \hat{p}_1), \tag{22}$$

where

$$o_D \equiv \partial\ln(\beta_2/\beta_1)/\partial\ln(p_1/p_2) = -\partial\ln(\beta_2/\beta_1)/\partial\ln(p_2/p_1) > 0$$

[6] The details of the derivation of (19) and (20) from (13) are left to the problem set.
[7] The proof is left to the problem set.

may be interpreted as the elasticity of substitution around the indifference curve.[8] Since z_2/z_1 is independent of m the latter plays no role in the comparative statics.

The goods market equilibrium conditions (16) require, with $p > 0$, that supply equals demand before and after the change in endowments. Hence, $\hat{z}_2 - \hat{z}_1 = \hat{y}_2 - \hat{y}_1$ is required. Using this condition the right-hand sides of (21) and (22) may be equated and the resulting equation solved for $\hat{p}_2 - \hat{p}_1$ as

$$\hat{p}_2 - \hat{p}_1 = -(\hat{v}_2 - \hat{v}_1)/(\sigma_D + \sigma_s). \, |\lambda|, \tag{23}$$

which indicates the response of p_2/p_1 to a change in v_2/v_1. This solution may be substituted into either (21) or (22) to obtain the effect upon $y_2/y_1 = z_2/z_1$ as

$$\hat{y}_2 - \hat{y}_1 = \hat{z}_2 - \hat{z}_1 = (\hat{v}_2 - \hat{v}_1)\,\sigma_D/(\sigma_D + \sigma_s) \, |\lambda|. \tag{24}$$

Finally, (23) may be substituted into (19) to obtain the effect upon w_2/w_1 as

$$\hat{w}_2 - \hat{w}_1 = -(\hat{v}_2 - \hat{v}_1)/(\sigma_D + \sigma_s) \, |\lambda| \cdot |\theta|. \tag{25}$$

Clearly, the solutions (23)–(25) are only valid if $\sigma_D + \sigma_s > 0$, which is required for the equilibrium price ratio to be unique. We therefore assume that $\sigma_D + \sigma_s > 0$.

The terms σ_D and σ_s are non-negative and $\sigma_D + \sigma_s > 0$, while the common sign of $|\lambda|$ and $|\theta|$ depends upon the relative factor intensities of the two goods. If industry 2 is relatively factor 2 intensive, then $|\lambda|, |\theta| > 0$. In this case an increase in v_2/v_1 will cause a fall in p_2/p_1 (from (23)), a rise in y_2/y_1 if $\sigma_D > 0$ (from (24)), and a fall in w_2/w_1 (from (25)). If $|\lambda|, |\theta| < 0$, then w_2/w_1 still falls but now the effects upon p_2/p_1 and y_2/y_1 are reversed. Eq. (23) makes it clear that if $|\lambda|$ does not change sign then any increase in v_2/v_1 will have a monotonic (increasing if $|\lambda| < 0$, decreasing if $|\lambda| > 0$) effect upon p_2/p_1 and hence the HOS theorem is valid. If, however, $|\lambda|$ changes sign, then this monotonic relationship is destroyed and the HOS prediction may not hold true.

The preceding analysis has provided explicit formulae for the various comparative statics effects, which were rigorously demonstrated from a *qualitative*

---

[8] The Hicksian demand functions are $z_i = \mu \, \partial e(p)/\partial p_i \equiv \mu \, e_i(p)$, where μ is the utility level and $e(p)$ is the unit utility expenditure function. The utility level is determined by setting expenditure equal to income as $\mu = m/e(p)$. Hence, the ordinary demand functions are $z_i = m \, e_i(p)/e(p)$ so $\beta_i(p) \equiv e_i(p)/e(p)$. Taking ratios of the Hicksian and ordinary demand functions we obtain that $z_2/z_1 = e_2(p)/e_1(p) = \beta_2(p)/\beta_1(p)$. Thus, σ_D represents the percentage change in z_2/z_1 due to a 1% change in p_1/p_2 when utility μ is constant or income m is constant. Hence, σ_D is indeed the elasticity of substitution around the isoquant.

viewpoint in the discussion of the HOS theorem in the preceding section. The advantage of the formal analysis is that it crystalizes the arguments and allows us to calculate the *quantitative* effects given information on σ_D, σ_s, $|\lambda|$ and $|\theta|$. It is not unreasonable to suppose that statistical estimates of these variables are available for most modern economies.

7.6. Factor endowments and commodity trade in a general HOS model

Consider now a more general model of trade between two nations in which there are M commodities and N factors of production. The net output or supply functions are given in vector form by

$$y(p, v) = G_p(p, v), \tag{26}$$

which are derived from the GNP function $G(p, v)$ by differentiation with respect to p. The technology is very general allowing for intermediate inputs and joint outputs, as described in Chapter 5, section 5.3. The demand functions are derived from a homothetic utility function and are

$$z(p, v) = \beta(p) \, G(p, v). \tag{27}$$

Hence, the net export or excess supply functions are

$$x(p, v) \equiv y(p, v) - z(p, v). \tag{28}$$

Since there are more than two commodities which may be traded, it is not obvious that we need simply calculate the effect of a change in endowment vector v upon the closed equilibrium price vector to obtain the effect of v upon the nation's equilibrium trading pattern, as was done for the two-commodity model. The reason is that, in general, it is not necessarily true that a nation will export a good for which the autarky price (or some normalization thereof) is less than in the foreign nation. This result is due to Drabicki and Takayama (1979) who refer to it as an "antinomy in the theory of comparative advantage". The reasons for this result are, first, that the trading pattern depends upon the equilibrium price *vector* which is established and, secondly, that this price vector need not lie between the autarky price vectors.[9] In view of these observations, an analysis of

---

[9]   This latter observation is the second "antinomy in the theory of comparative advantage" discussed by Drabicki and Takayama (1979). Both antinomies are discussed further in section 7.7 below.

the pattern of commodity trade must deal explicitly with the equilibrium conditions for a trading world.

The following approach is taken. Assume that two nations have the same technology and the same homothetic preferences, as with the HOS model of the previous sections. Assume, in addition, that both have the same relative factor endowments, i.e. the endowment vectors are on the same ray through the origin. Clearly, they will have the same autarky equilibrium price vector, assumed to be unique up to a factor of proportionality. If free trade were now possible, no trade need occur and so the free trade and autarky equilibria are identical. The plan is to let the endowment vector of the home nation change by a small amount and to calculate the effect of this change upon the free trade equilibrium price vector. In this way the relationship between factor endowments and commodity trade will be highlighted.

The equilibrium conditions for free trade, under the above assumptions, are

$$x(p, v) + x^*(p, v^*) = 0 \tag{29}$$

if the equilibrium price vector is strictly positive. Condition (29) says that the world excess supply of each good j, which is the sum of the home nation's excess supply and the foreign nation's excess supply, is zero. While a distinction between the home and foreign nation is made, it should be remembered that $v = v^*$ and $x(p, v) \equiv x^*(p, v)$ since they are identical by assumption.

The effect of a change in v upon p may be obtained by assuming differentiability of the excess supply functions and totally differentiating (29). This yields:

$$x_p dp + x_v dv + x_p^* dp = 2x_p dp + x_v dv = 0, \tag{30}$$

where $x_p \equiv \partial x(p, v)/\partial p$ as usual, and it is recognized that $x_p = x_p^*$ at the initial equilibrium. Eq. (30) may be used to obtain an explicit solution for dp provided that it is normalized.[10] However, this solution is not needed for present purposes.

---

[10]   Since the excess supply functions are homogeneous of degree zero in prices, it follows that $x(p, v) = x(1, \rho, v)$, where $\rho \equiv (\rho_2, ..., \rho_M)$ and $\rho_j \equiv p_j/p_1$ with a similar expression for the foreign nation. This means that only the vector of price ratios matters. Also, since each nation's excess supply functions satisfy Walras' law, it is only necessary to use M-1 of the conditions in (29) to determine the equilibrium vector of price ratios, ρ. If $x_2 \equiv (x_2, ..., x_M)$ is the vector of M-1 excess supplies with x_2^* similarly defined, the solutions for $d\rho$ may be written as

$$d\rho = -\tfrac{1}{2} [x_{2\rho}]^{-1} x_{2v} dv$$

if $[x_{2\rho}]^{-1}$ exists. Clearly, other normalizations may be used.

The resulting effect upon the free trade vector is therefore

$$\mathrm{d}x = x_p \mathrm{d}p + x_v \mathrm{d}v$$

$$= -(\tfrac{1}{2})x_v \mathrm{d}v + x_v \mathrm{d}v$$

$$= (\tfrac{1}{2})x_v \mathrm{d}v \equiv (\tfrac{1}{2})\mathrm{d}x^s, \tag{31}$$

where $\mathrm{d}x^s = x_v \mathrm{d}v$ is the change in x due to v alone.

Since x is initially a zero vector, the vector $\mathrm{d}x$ is the new trade vector for the home nation. Eq. (31) shows that the total effect of a change in v upon x_2, taking into account the adjustment of world prices, is exactly one-half of the direct effect which assumes that prices are constant. Hence, the pattern of free trade, indicated by the sign structure of x, is determined by the sign pattern of $\mathrm{d}x^s = x_v \mathrm{d}v$. That is, if at given prices a change in the endowment vector causes good j to be in excess supply, then it will end up being exported once the free trade price vector is re-established. The relationship between endowments and the pattern of commodity trade is therefore determined by the matrix x_v.

A typical element of $x_v(p, v)$ may be expressed in terms of the GNP function as

$$x_v(p, v) = G_{pv}(p, v) - \beta\, G_v(p, v). \tag{32}$$

Recognizing that $w = G_v(p, v)$ is the factor price vector, $y = G_p(p, v)$ is the net supply vector, and that $y = \beta\, G(p, v)$ initially, we obtain:

$$\frac{\partial x_j}{\partial v_i} \cdot \frac{v_i}{y_j} = \frac{\partial y_j}{\partial v_i}\frac{v_i}{y_j} - u_i \equiv \gamma_{ji} - u_i, \tag{33}$$

where $u_i \equiv w_i v_i / G(p, v)$ is the share of factor i in national income and $\gamma_{ji} \equiv \partial \ln y_j / \partial \ln v_i \equiv (\partial y_j / \partial v_i)(v_i / y_j)$ is the percentage increase in the output of j due to a 1% increase in the endowment of factor i. It will be realized that γ_{ji} is the "Rybczynski elasticity of output of j with respect to the endowment of i". The second term on the right-hand side of (33), u_i, is the percentage increase in GNP caused by a 1% increase in the endowment of i and, in view of homothetic preferences, is also the percentage increase in demand for each good.[11]

What (33) indicates is that the effect of a change in the endowment of factor

---

[11] The elasticity of income with respect to v_i is $[\partial G(p, v)/\partial v_i]v_i/G(p, v) = w_i(p, v)v_i/G(p, v) \equiv u_i$ since the wage rate for factor i is the marginal value product of i, $w_i(p, v) = \partial G(p, v)/\partial v_i$.

i upon the trade of commodity j depends upon the relative sizes of γ_{ji} and u_j. Much of the literature has concentrated upon generalizations of the Rybczynski theorem to many dimensions and is essentially concerned with the sign structure of $\Gamma = [\gamma_{ji}]$. Clearly, what is important for the effect of endowments upon trade is the relationship of the γ_{ji} to u_j.

To clarify the relationship between (33) and the previous literature on the generalization of the Rybczynski and HOS theorems, consider the case where the numbers of commodities and factors are the same, $M = N$, and where there are no joint outputs.[12] In this case the $M \times N$ matrix $\Gamma = [\gamma_{ji}] = \lambda^{-1}$, where $\lambda \equiv [\lambda_{ij}]$ is the $M \times N$ matrix of shares of each industry j in the total endowment of factor i. The *weak Rybczynski property* (WRP) is that there is an ordering of factors and products such that $\Gamma = \lambda^{-1}$ has diagonal elements which are greater than unity. The *strong Rybczynski property* (SRP) requires that the diagonal elements exceed unity and, in addition, that the off-diagonal elements be non-positive. The relationship between these properties and the trade pattern is provided in the following theorem:

> **Theorem.** If Γ satisfies the weak Rybczynski property, then an increase in the endowment of factor i will cause commodity i to be exported. If Γ satisfies the strong Rybczynski property, then, in addition, *all* other goods will be imported. (34)

The proof follows directly from the definitions of the two Rybczynski properties and the fact that the factor income shares lie between zero and unity.

It is tempting to define the *weak HOS property* (local) to mean that there is an ordering of commodities and factors such that, in the neighbourhood of the autarky equilibrium, an increase in the endowment of factor i will cause commodity i to be exported for each i. Corresponding to this the *strong HOS property* (local) may be defined to require an increase in the endowment of factor i to cause commodity i to be exported and, in addition, all other goods to be imported. Clearly, (34) says that the WRP is sufficient for the weak HOS property to hold, while the SRP is sufficient for the strong HOS property to hold. On the other hand, the Rybczynski properties are not necessary for the corresponding HOS properties to hold. Indeed, the Rybczynski effects given by the γ_{ji} need only bear an appropriate relationship to the u_j, not to zero and/or unity.

It was established in Chapter 4 that when $M = N = 2$ it is always possible to

---

[12] The case of intermediate inputs poses no special problems since we need only interpret λ below as the matrix of total (direct plus indirect) industry demands for the factors of production. See Chapter 5.

renumber commodities so that λ^{-1} has the SRP. Hence, the strong HOS property also holds. In this case theorem (34) or eq. (33) indicate that an increase in v_2 will cause commodity 2 to be exported and commodity 1 to be imported. Moreover, when $M = N = 2$ the relative factor intensities enable us to identify the required numbering of commodities and hence the trade pattern.

It is interesting to note that (33) may be rewritten in terms of Diewert's (1974) elasticities of intensities which are

$$\gamma'_{ji} \equiv \frac{G \, \partial^2 G/\partial p_j \partial v_i}{\partial G/\partial p_j \, \partial G/\partial v_i} = \frac{G \, \partial y_j/\partial v_i}{y_j w_i}. \tag{35}$$

It is easily shown that $\gamma_{ji} = \gamma'_{ji} u_i$ or $\gamma'_{ji} = \gamma_{ji}/u_i$, so that γ'_{ji} can be interpreted as a normalization of γ_{ji} which makes it symmetric, i.e. $\gamma'_{ji} = \gamma'_{ij}$. Using the intensity elasticities (33) becomes

$$\frac{\partial x_j}{\partial v_i} \frac{v_i}{y_j} = (\gamma'_{ji} - 1)u_i. \tag{36}$$

Thus, an increase in factor i will cause commodity j to be exported if and only if the elasticity of intensity γ'_{ji} exceeds unity. These elasticities of intensity provide a direct relationship between factors and commodity trade.

An alternative expression to (33) may be obtained using the reciprocity conditions as

$$\frac{\partial x_j}{\partial v_i} \frac{p_j}{w_i} = (\theta^{ij} - s_j), \tag{37}$$

where $\theta^{ij} \equiv \partial \ln w_i/\partial \ln p_j = (\partial w_i/\partial p_j) p_j/w_i$ is the "Stolper–Samuelson elasticity" of w_i with respect to p_j and $s_j \equiv p_j y_j/G$ is the share of product j in national income. Thus, $\partial x_j/\partial v_i > 0$ if the Stolper–Samuelson elasticity θ^{ij} exceeds s_j. Jones and Scheinkman (1977) suggest that λ_{ij}/s_j be compared to unity as an indication of the effect of v_i upon x_j. The above expressions show that the relevant comparison is between λ^{ij}/u_i or θ^{ij}/s_j or γ_{ji} and unity, not between λ_{ij}/s_j and unity.

Some general inequalities

Some general restrictions relating factor endowments, product prices, and commodity trade are implied by the model. These are given in the following theorems.

Theorem. (Effect of factor endowments on commodity trade).
The bilinear form dx $x_v(p, v)$d$v \geqslant 0$ for all d$v \neq 0$. (38)

Proof. From (31) it follows that dx $x_v(p, v)$ dv = $\frac{1}{2}$ dv $[x_v(p, v)]$ $[x_v(p, v)]$ dv which is a quadratic form in dv. This quadratic form is positive semi-definite and hence is non-negative for all dv.[13]

This theorem provides a general restriction on dx which must hold irrespective of the nature of the transformation elasticities in production or the substitution elasticities in consumption. Of course, except when $M = N$, these elasticities play a role in determining $x_v(p, v)$.

The effect of endowments upon the free trade prices is given by

Theorem. (Effect of factor endowments on free trade commodity prices).
The bilinear form dp $x_v(p, v)$ d$v \leqslant 0$ for all d$v \neq 0$. (39)

Proof. From (30) it follows that dp $x_v(p, v)$dv = -2dp x_p dp which is a quadratic form in dp. It can be shown using the results of Chapter 6 (see problem set) that, at the initial equilibrium in which $x = 0$, $x_p = S_{pp}$, where $S = S(p, \mu, v)$ = $G(p, v) - E(p, \mu)$. Thus, x_p is a positive semi-definite matrix, and so dp $x_v(p, v)$dv = -2 dp x_p d$p \leqslant 0$ for all dp (hence dv) which was to be proved.

In summary, it has been shown that in a general model with many products and factors, the relationship between factor endowments and commodity trade, in the neighbourhood of autarky, depends upon the nature of the matrix $x_v(p, v)$. Theorem (38) gives a bilinear inequality or "generalized correlation" between endowments and trade. Eqs. (33), (36) and (37) provide more detail in terms of various elasticities. Evidently, the simple relationship between endowments and trade which exists for the two-factor, two-product case becomes weaker in the many-factor, many-product context.

7.7. Problems of dimensionality

The Ricardian and HOS theories are cast in terms of models involving small dimensions. In this section various problems which arise in attempting to generalize these theories to many dimensions are reviewed.

---

[13] See, for example, Hadley (1961, pp. 254–255).

7.7.1. Antinomies in the theory of comparative advantage

First, consider the proposition that, when there are just two tradeable goods, knowledge of the pre-trade price ratios in the home and foreign nation is sufficient to predict the pattern of free trade. Since the excess supply function for good 2, $x_2(p_1, p_2, v)$, is homogeneous of degree zero in prices, it may be rewritten in terms of some normalization of prices, such as the price ratio $\rho \equiv p_2/p_1$, as $x_2(p_1, p_2, v) = x_2(1, \rho, v)$. If the same normalization is applied to the foreign nation we can compare prices by comparing ρ with ρ^*, the foreign price ratio. Suppose that the excess supply functions are continuous and that the equations $x_2(1, \rho, v) = 0$ and $x_2^*(1, \rho^*, v) = 0$ have unique solutions, ρ^0 and ρ^{*0} respectively, with $\partial x_2(1, \rho^0, v)/\partial\rho > 0$ and $\partial x_2^*(1, \rho^{*0}, v^*)/\partial\rho^* > 0$, as in fig. 7.2. Then it follows that the solution to $x_2(1, \rho^e, v) + x_2^*(1, \rho^e, v^*) = 0$ for the free trade equilibrium price ratio, ρ^e, must be between the autarky price ratios, ρ^0 and ρ^{*0}, although it may not be unique. Hence, if $\rho^0 < \rho^{*0}$, then $\rho^0 < \rho^e < \rho^{*0}$, ignoring the possibility that the free trade price ratio coincides with one of the autarky price ratios, and so the home nation will export good 2 and import good 1 under free trade. Thus, a comparison of autarky price ratios is sufficient to establish the free trade pattern, under the above-mentioned assumptions.

Suppose now that there are many, say M, goods. In this case there are M-1 price ratios $\rho_j \equiv p_j/p_1, j = 2, ..., M$. Is it still true that if the autarky prices are such that $\rho_j < \rho_j^*$, then the home nation will export good j? Drabicki and Takayama (1979) have shown that the answer is "not necessarily", and provide an example. However, it is easy to demonstrate that such a pairwise comparison of price ratios is in general fruitless by considering an alternative normalization. Let prices now be divided by p_2 rather than p_1. Then for good j the price ratios are $p_j/p_2 = \rho_j/\rho_2$ and $p_j^*/p_2^* = \rho_j^*/\rho_2^*$. The condition that $\rho_j < \rho_j^*$ is not sufficient to make any statement about the relative magnitudes of p_j/p_2 and p_j^*/p_2^*. If a pairwise comparison were sufficient to determine the trade pattern, then the normalization should not matter. Since it obviously does matter, pairwise comparisons of price ratios (or any other normalization of prices) are not sufficient to determine the trade pattern.

This result can be further illustrated for the M product HOS model of section 7.6. It is easily shown that the effect upon the vector of autarky price ratios, $\rho = (\rho_2, ..., \rho_M)$, of a change in factor endowment is given by (see problem set)

$$\mathrm{d}\rho_A = -[x_{2\rho}]^{-1}[x_{2v}]\mathrm{d}v = 2\mathrm{d}\rho_F. \tag{40}$$

Here $\mathrm{d}\rho_A$ is the difference between autarky price ratios while $\mathrm{d}\rho_F$ is the vector of differences between the free trade price ratios and those in the foreign nation.

Using (40) we obtain that

$$dx_2 = -\tfrac{1}{2} x_{2\rho} \, d\rho_A, \tag{41}$$

which indicates the relationship between the home nation's free trade vector and the difference in autarky price ratios, $d\rho_A$. Now $x_{2\rho}$ is a negative definite matrix. However, this does not provide sufficient structure to ensure that sign $dx_2 = -$sign $d\rho_A$. It is easy to construct examples where goods which are more expensive at home than abroad (in terms of price ratios) before trade, end up being exported (see problems). However, while such examples are possible this model provides an overall negative correlation between differences in autarky price ratios and the pattern of free trade. This negative correlation is obtained from (41) as

$$dx_2^T \, d\rho_A = \tfrac{1}{2} \, d\rho_A^T \, x_{2\rho} \, d\rho_A < 0, \quad \text{for all } d\rho_A \neq 0, \tag{42}$$

where the inequality follows because $-x_{2\rho}$ is negative definite. Condition (42) indicates that dx_2 and $d\rho_A$ are at an obtuse angle to each other and are therefore negatively correlated.[14] In an "aggregate" sense goods with higher prices at home will be imported, and those with lower prices will be exported. While these results are for the HOS model, which is a highly structured model, they are contained as special cases of more general results obtained in the following subsections.

There are two related issues raised above. The first is that the free trade price ratios may not all be between the autarky price ratios. In our HOS example with small differences in endowments this difficulty does not arise since (40) implies that $d\rho_F = \tfrac{1}{2} d\rho_A$. The second issue is that a nation may not export a good just because the free trade price exceeds the autarky price. Both points together imply that a nation may not export a good even though the home autarky price is less than the autarky price abroad. We now consider these issues in more detail under general conditions.

7.7.2. A general relationship between free trade and autarky prices

A general relationship between free trade and autarky prices may be established. Let p^0 and p^{*0} be the autarky price vectors, p^f be the free trade price vector,

---

[14] For this interpretation of the sign of the inner product of two vectors see Hadley (1961, pp. 32–33).

and x^f and x^{*f} be the free trade net export vectors. In Chapter 6 it was shown that the net export vector x maximizes the trade utility function $U(x, v)$ subject to the balance of trade condition $px \geqslant 0$. Since $x = 0$ is feasible for any p it follows that $\mu^f = U(x^f, v) \geqslant U(0, v) = \mu^0$ (trade cannot reduce welfare). From the definition of $S(p, \mu, v)$ as the maximum of px on the set $X(\mu, v)$ of trades yielding at least utility level μ, and since S is non-increasing in μ, it follows that

$$0 = S(p^0, \mu^0, v) \geqslant S(p^0, \mu^f, v) \geqslant p^0 x^f$$
$$0 = S^*(p^{*0}, \mu^{*0}, v^*) \geqslant S^*(p^{*0}, \mu^{*f}, v^*) \geqslant p^{*0} x^{*f}. \tag{43}$$

The market equilibrium condition is that $x^f + x^{*f} = 0$, while the balance of trade conditions are that $p^f x^f = 0$ and $p^f x^{*f} = 0$. Hence, subtraction of the inequalities in (43) yields the inequalities

$$(p^0 - p^f)x^f = p^0 x^f \leqslant 0 \quad \text{and} \quad (p^{*0} - p^f)x^f = p^{*0} x^f \geqslant 0. \tag{44}$$

These inequalities show that p^0 and p^{*0} are on opposite sides of a hyperplane whose normal is the free trade net export vector, x^f, since $p^0 x^f \leqslant 0$ indicates that p^0 is at an obtuse angle to x^f, while $p^{*0} x^f \geqslant 0$ indicates that p^{*0} is at an acute angle to x^f. Since $p^f x^f = 0$, it follows that p^f is on this hyperplane separating p^0 and p^{*0}. It is in this sense that p^f is between p^0 and p^{*0}. That is,

$$p^0 x^f \leqslant 0 = p^f x^f \leqslant p^{*0} x^f. \tag{45}$$

When there are just two goods, it follows that the free trade price ratio is between the autarky price ratios. However, when there are many goods the most general statement that can be made is (45), since we can always choose technologies and tastes to come arbitrarily close to violating (45). It becomes clear, therefore, that the free trade price vector does not have to be between the autarky price vectors in the Eudidean sense (under a common normalization). Thus, the existence of examples of "antinomies" developed by Drabicki and Takayama (1979) for the case of three goods, in which the free trade price ratios are not all between the autarky price ratios, is not surprising. The consequence of these observations is that a comparison of autarky prices is not sufficient to establish the pattern of trade.

7.7.3. The relationship between prices and net exports

However, the above inequalities contain an important result concerning the connection between prices and the free trade net export vector. The inequality $p^0 x^f \leq 0$ in (43) shows that there is a *negative correlation* between the autarky price vector and the free trade net export vector. Since $p^f x^f = 0$ under a balance of trade we have that

$$\Delta p \Delta x = (p^f - p^0)(x^f - x^0) = (p^f - p^0)x^f \geq 0, \tag{46}$$

where $x^0 = 0$ is the autarky net export vector. This shows that the difference between free trade and autarky prices are positively correlated with the free trade net export vector. There is a tendency to export those goods with higher world prices than autarky prices.

Of course the role of world prices in (46) is trivial, since (46) can be written without p^f. An alternative result in terms of both autarky price vectors is

$$(p^0 - p^{*0})x^f \leq 0 \tag{47}$$

obtained by subtracting the right-hand from the left-hand side of (45). This establishes a negative correlation between the trade vector and the difference in autarky price vectors. Thus, a nation tends to export those goods whose autarky price at home is less than abroad (under some normalization of prices). This is established by Dixit and Norman (1980) and Deardorff (1980) who describes (47) as a generalization of the notion of trade being determined by comparative advantage. Again, since we can always choose technologies and preferences to come arbitrarily close to violating (47), it is the strongest statement that can be made concerning the relationship between autarky prices and free trade net exports without special restrictions on the model.

7.7.4. Use of ratios

The second point of this section is that comparison of ratios also becomes meaningless in attempts to generalize the Ricardian or HOS theories. For example, in the HOS theory the concepts of relative abundance of factors and relative intensities of goods play an important role. When there are two factors of production such concepts are meaningful the way they are defined and used. However, if the number of factors is $N > 2$ it is fruitless to try to generalize the notion of, say, relative abundance by pairwise comparisons of ratios. As with price ratios discussed above, to say that the home nation is relatively abundant in factor i if $v_i/v_1 > v_i^*/v_1^*$ is not useful since by changing the normalization we cannot rank v_i/v_2 and v_i^*/v_2^* without additional information. Any useful definition of relative factor abundance must be based upon the complete endowment vectors. The same comment applies to the notions of intensities.

7.7.5. Many-nation models and aggregation

The third point to be raised in this section concerns the number of trading nations. Can all of the foreign nations be grouped together as the "rest of the world" and treated as if the group behaved as a single nation? The answer to this question depends upon the purpose. In terms of obtaining the offer curve describing all possible trades that can be made, there is no difficulty as long as there is a single price at which each good can be traded with each of the foreign nations. The situation where transport costs or tariffs create different prices will be dealt with in a later chapter.

The assumptions underlying the HOS model (general version) are sufficient to allow aggregation over nations. On the supply side this is because each nation has the same CRS technology implying that $Y(v^*) = \Sigma_{k=1}^{K} Y_k(v_k^*)$, where v_k^* is the endowment vector for nation k (to be proved in the problem set) and $v^* \equiv \Sigma_{k=1}^{K} v_k^*$. K foreign nations collectively choose an output vector in their aggregate production possibility set which depends upon their aggregate endowment vector, v^*. On the demand side the assumption of identical homothetic preferences means that the distribution of foreign income amongst the foreign nation does not affect the aggregate demand functions. Hence, all foreign nations can be aggregated without loss of generality in the HOS model.

Consider now the Ricardian model. Since the technology is presumably different in each nation, aggregation of the foreign production possibility sets leads to an aggregate foreign production possibility set which does not have the same properties as the individual ones. For example, in fig. 7.4 the two sets sum to a set with two line segments of different slopes. The autarky price ratio for this aggregate foreign nation is between the individual comparative cost ratios and depends upon demand conditions. Clearly, this is a case where aggregation is not useful. Hence, a treatment of the Ricardian model in a many-nation world requires explicit treatment of all nations. We do not pursue this problem here, however.

7.8. Notes on the literature

International trade arises because of differences in autarky prices for traded goods. Different theories of trade that have been developed emphasize different causes for autarky price differentials. In this chapter attention has been concentrated upon the classical theory based upon technology and the Heckscher–Ohlin–Samuelson theory based upon differences in factor endowments coupled with different input requirements of products. These are the theories which are central to the literature on trade theory. Of course, other causes of autarky price differentials exist; for example, differences in preferences, income distribution, scale economies, the degree of monopolistic behaviour, and the taxation structure. While these are recognized in the literature they have not received the same attention as technology and endowments. Amano (1964) provides an excellent summary of the effects of endowments, technology, scale economies, and preferences upon autarky prices in a simple two-product, two-factor model. See also the problem set. For a discussion of taxation as a cause of trade see Melvin (1970).

There is a vast literature on the Ricardian and HOS theories of trade, which will only be touched upon in these brief notes. The surveys by Chipman (1965), which includes an interesting discussion of the origins of the classical theory, Chipman (1966) and Bhagwati (1964) cover both theories. In addition there is Viner's (1937) account of the classical theory.

The classical theory of Ricardo (1951) has received considerable attention by Graham (1923) and more recently by McKenzie (1954a, 1954b, 1955) and Whiten (1953) who applied linear programming and activity analysis techniques to multi-product and multi-factor versions of the Ricardian model. See also Jones (1961) and, for a survey, Takayama (1972). All of these papers assume fixed coefficients of production which contrasts with the view expressed in section 7.3 concerning the essence of the Ricardian model.

In addition to the works of Heckscher, Ohlin and Samuelson already mentioned, important papers on the two-dimensional model include Jones (1956, 1965) and Lancaster (1957). Inada (1967) has pointed out the importance of the assumption that the autarky equilibria are unique. The role of income distribution leading to a relaxed version of the HOS theorem was provided by Ruffin (1977) and Woodland (1974).

Attempts to extend the HOS theorem to the case of many products and factors include Vanek (1968) and Horiba (1974) in terms of net factoral trade flows. The many-product, two-factor case is considered by Melvin (1968) and Jones (1956) who argued that the trade pattern is based upon a ranking of industries by their factor intensities. Further discussion can be found in Bhagwati (1972) and Deardorff (1979). The treatment in section 7.6 is based upon Dixit and Woodland (1981).

The demonstration of difficulties in extending the usual two-dimensional analysis of the relationships between autarky and free trade prices, and autarky prices and the pattern of free trade was undertaken by Drabicki and Takayama (1979). General treatments of these relationships are given by Deardorff (1980) and Dixit and Norman (1980).

Problems

1. Consider a Ricardian model of trade with three nations. Suppose that each nation has the same homothetic aggregate utility function.
    (a) Show that the world production possibility frontier consists of (at most) three linear segments with slopes given by the three nations' comparative cost ratios.
    (b) Show that, depending upon preferences, the equilibrium free trade price ratio may be equal to one of the autarky price ratios or may be between a pair of autarky price ratios. (Note that equilibrium in this model can be attained by maximizing the (common) utility function subject to being in the world production possibility set.)
    (c) For each possible solution considered in part (b), determine each nation's production and consumption choices.
    (d) Draw the offer curves of each nation.
    (e) By aggregating nations 2 and 3 derive the "rest of the world" offer curve and determine the equilibrium.
2. Two economies have a similar structure. They produce two products using two factors with fixed coefficients of production. The community utility function is Leontief, i.e. products are always consumed in fixed proportion, independent of product prices. The two nations have the same technology, same tastes but different factor endowments.
    (a) Write down the equilibrium conditions for such a closed economy. Carefully identify all the endogenous variables in your formulation.
    (b) Show that if $v \equiv v_2/v_1$ and $v^* \equiv v_2^*/v_1^*$ are both greater than or both less than a critical value v^c, then $\rho \equiv p_2/p_1 = p_2^*/p_1^* \equiv \rho^*$ in autarky.
    (c) Identify the common price ratio and v^c in (b) in terms of exogenous variables.
    (d) Comment upon the result obtained in (b) in terms of the Heckscher–Ohlin theorem.
    (e) What is the role, if any, of the assumption of Leontief preferences in obtaining the result in (b)?

3. Consider the two-dimensional HOS model of trade extended to allow for two classes of consumers: capitalists who own all the capital and labourers who own all the labour. Capitalists in both nations have the same homothetic preferences. Similarly, all labourers in both nations have the same homothetic preferences which may, however, be different from those of capitalists.
   (a) Write down the autarky equilibrium conditions for one of the nations.
   (b) Derive the effect of a change in $\nu \equiv v_2/v_1$ upon the autarky equilibrium price ratio $\rho \equiv p_2/p_1$.
   (c) Hence, evaluate the validity of the HOS theorem under these relaxed assumptions.

4. Consider an economy with two factors, two products and homothetic aggregate preferences such as discussed in section 7.5.
   (a) Derive (19) and (20) from (13).
   (b) Prove that $\sigma_S \geqslant 0$. When will it be positive? Zero?
   (c) If $\sigma_D > 0$ and $\sigma_S = 0$, show that $\partial x_2/\partial \rho > 0$ for all $\rho \equiv p_2/p_1$, i.e. the offer curve does not "bend downwards".
   (d) Draw the locus of solutions for z_2 (demand) as a function of ρ. Note that the locus is not downward-sloping everywhere. Why?
   (e) If the production possibility frontier becomes linear ($\sigma_S \to \infty$) show that $\partial x_2/\partial \rho < 0$ when production is specialized in product 2, and $\partial x_2/\partial \rho > 0$ when production is specialized in product 1. That is, the offer curve must "bend downwards" in the non-linear part.
   (f) Parts (c) and (e) suggest that if σ_S is positive and finite then x_2 may rise or fall as ρ increases. Show that (i) x_2 first rises and then falls as ρ increases from the autarky price ratio, and (ii) x_2 never falls back to 0. This shows that there is a unique solution to the autarky equilibrium condition for the autarky price ratio ρ^0. [Rather, ρ^0 is unique if we rule out interval solutions.]

5. Prove that, for the general HOS model of section 7.6, $\partial x/\partial p \equiv x_p$ is a positive semi-definite matrix when evaluated at the autarky equilibrium. [The Slutsky decomposition of a price effect in consumption will be useful.] If evaluated away from the autarky equilibrium, is this property maintained?

6. In the analysis of the general HOS model of section 7.6 the expression $x_v dv$ occurs frequently.
   (a) Show that CRS implies $x (1, \rho, v) = v_1 x (1, \rho, 1, v)$, where $v = (v_2, ..., v_N)$ is the vector of endowment ratios $v_i \equiv v_i/v_1$.
   (b) Hence, write the expression for the change in x due to a change in v in elasticity form involving v and v_1.

7. (a) Derive (40).
   (b) Provide an example of a positive definite matrix $[\partial x_2/\partial \rho]$ and vector

$d\rho_A$ such that goods with higher prices at home under autarky (appropriate element of $d\rho_A$ positive) are not necessarily imported under free trade. (See (41).)

8. (a) If there is free trade in a HOS model, will factor prices equalize across nations?

   (b) Suppose that instead of free trade in goods there was free mobility of factors but no trade in goods. How would the equilibrium be affected, if at all?

9. Suppose that the strong assumptions regarding demand in the HOS model are eliminated such that the excess supply functions are continuous and obey Walras' law.

   (a) When $N = M = 2$, depict the excess supply function $x_2(1, \rho, v)$ with possibly many autarky equilibria.

   (b) Include an excess supply function for the foreign nation and illustrate free trade equilibria which are (i) consistent with the HOS trade pattern and (ii) are inconsistent with this pattern.

10. Consider a two-product, two-factor economy with cost functions $c^j(w; \gamma^j) = p_j$, and unit expenditure function $e(p, \delta)$, where γ^1, γ^2 and δ are vectors of shift parameters.

    (a) Write down the conditions for a closed equilibrium.

    (b) Extend the mathematical analysis of section 7.6 to deal with changes in technology via γ^j, and tastes via δ. (This parallels Amano, 1964.)

    (c) Specialize the results for the (augmentation) cases where $e(p, \delta) = \bar{e}(p_1/\delta_1, p_2/\delta_2)$ and (i) $c^j(w, \gamma^j) = \bar{c}^j(w)/\gamma^j$ (γ^j is scalar) (product augmentation); (ii) $c^j(w, \gamma^j) = \bar{c}^j(w_1/\gamma_1, w_2/\gamma_2)$ (factor augmentation).

    (d) Hence, obtain the separate effects of differences in endowments, tastes and technology upon the autarky price ratio and hence free trade. Comment on the results for technological differences of the type (i) and (ii).

11. Let $y_j = f^j(q_1^j \gamma_1^j, ..., q_N^j \gamma_N^j)$ be the production function in industry j, where γ_i^j is the index of efficiency of factor i in industry j. (The normal case of equal and given efficiencies is where $\gamma_i^j = 1$ for all i, j.)

    (a) Show that the unit cost function is of the form $c^j(w_1/\gamma_1^j, ..., w_N/\gamma_N^j)$.

    (b) Write down the equilibrium conditions for the production sector in terms of the variables $w_i^j \equiv w_i/\gamma_i^j$ and $y_i^j = y_j/\gamma_i^j$.

    (c) If $\gamma_i^j = \gamma^j$ for all i show that the model can be expressed in terms of $w, v, (p_j\gamma^j)$ and (y_j/γ^j). Interpret.

    (d) If $\gamma_i^j = \gamma_i$ for all j show that the model can be expressed in terms of $p, y, (w_i/\gamma_i)$ and $(v_i\gamma_i)$. Interpret.

References

Amano, A. (1964) "Determinants of comparative costs: A theoretical approach", *Oxford Economic Papers* 16-3, November, 389–400.

Bhagwati, J. (1964) "A survey of the theory of international trade", *Economic Journal*, March, 1-84.

Bhagwati, J. (1972) "The Heckscher–Ohlin theorem in the multi-commodity case", *Journal of Political Economy* 80-5, September/October, 1052–1055.

Chipman, J.S. (1965) "A survey of the theory of international trade: Part 1, The classical theory ', *Econometrica* 33-1, July, 447–519.

Chipman, J.S. (1966) "A survey of the theory of international trade: Part 3, The modern theory", *Econometrica* 34-1, January, 18–76.

Deardorff, A.V. (1979) "Weak links in the chain of comparative advantage", *Journal of International Economics* 9, 197–209.

Deardorff, A.V. (1980) "The general validity of the law of comparative advantage", *Journal of Political Economy* 88-5, October, 941–957.

Diewert, W.E. (1974) "Applications of duality theory", in: M.D. Intriligator and D.A. Kendricks (eds.), *Frontiers of Quantitative Economics*, vol. 2 (Amsterdam: North-Holland Publishing Company).

Dixit, A.K. and V. Norman (1980) *Theory of International Trade* (J. Nisbet/Cambridge University Press).

Dixit, A.K. and A.D. Woodland (1981) "The relationship between factor endowments and commodity trade", forthcoming in *Journal of International Economics*.

Drabicki, J.Z. and A. Takayama (1979) "An antinomy in the theory of comparative advantage", *Journal of International Economics* 9, 211–223.

Graham, F.D. (1923) "The theory of international values re-examined", *Quarterly Journal of Economics* 28, November.

Hadley, G. (1961) *Linear Algebra* (Reading Mass.: Addison-Wesley).

Heckscher, E. (1919) "The effect of foreign trade on the distribution of income", *Ekonomisk Tidskrift* 21, 497–512.

Horiba, Y. (1974) "General equilibrium and the Heckscher–Ohlin theory of trade: The multi-country case", *International Economic Review* 15-2, June, 440–449.

Inada, K. (1967) "A note on the Heckscher–Ohlin theorem", *Economic Record* 43, March, 88–96.

Johnson, H.G. (1959) "International trade, income distribution and the offer curve", *Manchester School of Economic and Social Studies* 27, 241–260.

Jones, R.W. (1956) "Factor proportions and the Heckscher–Ohlin theorem", *Review of Economics Studies* 24, 1–10.

Jones, R.W. (1961) "Comparative advantage and the theory of tariffs: A multi-country multi-commodity model", *Review of Economic Studies* 28, June, 161–175.

Jones, R.W. (1965) "The structure of simple general equilibrium models", *Journal of Political Economy* 73, December, 557–572.

Jones, R.W. (1972) "Activity analysis and real incomes: Analogies with production models", *Journal of International Economics* 2, 277–302.

Jones, R.W. (1980) "Comparative and absolute advantage", unpublished paper.

Jones, R.W. and J. Scheinkman (1977) "The relevance of the two-sector production model in trade theory", *Journal of Political Economy* 85, 909–936.

Lancaster, K. (1957) "The Heckscher–Ohlin trade model: A geometric treatment", *Economica* 24, 19–39.

McKenzie, L.W. (1954a) "On equilibrium in Graham's model of world trade and other competitive systems", *Econometrica* 22, April, 147–161.

McKenzie, L.W. (1954b) "Specialization and efficiency in world production", *Review of Economic Studies* 21, June, 165–180.

McKenzie, L.W. (1955) "Specialization in production and the production possibility locus", *Review of Economic Studies* 23, 56–64.

Melvin, J.R. (1968) "Production and trade with two factors and three goods", *American Economic Review* 58, December, 1249–1268.

Melvin, J.R. (1970) "Commodity taxation as a determinant of trade", *Canadian Journal of Economics* 3-1, February, 62–78.

Ohlin, B. (1933) *Interregional and International Trade* (Cambridge, Mass.: Harvard University Press).

Ricardo, D. (1951) "On the principles of political economy and taxation", in: P. Sraffa (ed.), *The Works and Correspondence of David Ricardo*, vol. 1, ch. 7.

Ruffin, R. (1977) "A note on the Heckscher–Ohlin theorem", *Journal of International Economics* 7, November, 403–405.

Samuelson, P.A. (1948) "International trade and the equalization of factor prices", *Economic Journal*, June, 163–184.

Samuelson, P.A. (1949) "International factor-price equalization once again", *Economic Journal*, June, 181–197.

Stolper, W.F. and P.A. Samuelson (1941) "Protection and real wages", *Review of Economic Studies* 9, November, 58–73.

Takayama, A. (1972) *International Trade* (New York: Holt Rinehart and Winston).

Vanek, J. (1968) "The factor proportions theory: The N-factor case", *Kyklos* 21-4, 749–756.

Viner, J. (1937) *Studies in the Theory of International Trade* (Harper).

Whiten, T.M. (1953) "Classical theory, Graham's theory and linear programming in international trade", *Quarterly Journal of Economics* 67, November.

Woodland, A.D. (1974) "Demand conditions in international trade theory", *Australian Economic Papers* 13, December, 209–224.

CHAPTER 8

NON-TRADED GOODS AND ENDOGENOUS FACTOR SUPPLIES[1]

8.1. Introduction

Previous chapters have been concerned with a model in which all goods are tradeable at zero cost, and in which factor endowments are exogenously given. The purpose of the present chapter is to extend the model to include the existence of non-traded goods and factors of production for which the supplies are endogenously determined.

The extension of the model to include non-traded goods and endogenous factor supplies is warranted by their importance in the real world. Goods may be non-traded for several reasons.

(a) Some cannot be transported from one nation to another, and residents of one nation cannot consume these goods by travelling to the producing nation. In other words, these goods have some intrinsic feature which prevents their trade internationally.

(b) Some goods may be tradeable but the costs of transportation are such that trade is not profitable. While it is possible to develop a model of international trade and transportation in which the transport costs and the list of non-traded goods is endogenously determined, for the present this list will be taken as given.

(c) There may be legal barriers to trade in some goods.

The most obvious factors of production that have endogenous supplies are the various types of labour services. The classical theory of labour supply has the supply of labour determined in the same way as the demand for consumer goods and depending upon commodity prices, non-labour income and the wage rate. Moreover, the participation of individuals, especially married women, in the labour force also depends upon these variables and is consequently endogenous.

---

[1] This chapter may be omitted without loss of continuity.

The phenomena of non-traded goods and endogenous factor supplies are dealt with in a single chapter because they are *formally* identical in the way they affect the model. The demands for non-traded goods and the supplies of endogenous factors are derived from the utility-maximizing behaviour of consumers. The supplies of non-traded goods and the demands for factors of production are derived from the profit-maximizing behaviour of producers. Assuming that the factor services are not traded internationally, it is evident that factors with endogenous supplies are formally non-traded goods with negative net demands and negative net outputs. While they could be treated together in a common framework, separate treatments will be given for ease of interpretation of the results.

The inclusion of non-traded goods and endogenous factor supplies in the model involves a significant departure from the models of the previous chapters. There the production sector for an open economy could be treated independently of the consumption sector since all prices for goods and endowments of factors were exogenous. Now, however, the prices of non-treated goods and the supplies of endogenous factors will alter as a result of changes in the prices of tradeable goods and the endowments of fixed factors. The extent of the alterations in the prices of non-traded goods and in endogenous factor supplies depends upon the preferences of consumers as well as the technology. Accordingly, the separation of production and consumption decisions is no longer tenable.

8.2. Non-traded goods

8.2.1. Alternative model formulations

In what follows alternative but equivalent formulations of a model of trade with non-traded goods are developed under the strong simplifying assumption that aggregate demands are determined by maximizing a community utility function subject to the aggregate budget constraint. It is assumed that there are M goods of which the first M_t are traded and the remaining $M_n \equiv M - M_t$ are non-traded. The price vector is partitioned as $p = (p_t, p_n)$. As usual there are N factors of production and the technology is as described in Chapter 5, section 5.3, until otherwise noted.

The minimum expenditure function for the consumption sector is $E(p_t, p_n, \mu)$, where μ is the level of utility. The maximum utility obtained when income is m is obtained by solving $E(p_t, p_n, \mu) = m$ for $\mu = V(p_t, p_n, m)$ which is the indirect utility function. Shephard's lemma indicates that the demand vector $z = (z_t, z_n)$ is obtained by differentiating the expenditure function with respect to p. The production sector chooses the net output vector $y = (y_t, y_n)$ to obtain maximum GNP which is denoted as $G(p_t, p_n, v)$. If the GNP function is differentiable, then the optimal net output vector is obtained by differentiating the GNP function with respect to p. In general, when $M > N$ the GNP function may not be differentiable but the set of subgradients $G_p(p, v)$ exists and is the set of optimal net output vectors.

Equilibrium for an economy which trades freely at prices p_t given endowment vector v requires that the prices of non-traded goods adjust to clear the market for these goods. Assuming that $p_n > 0$ the conditions may be written as

$$E(p_t, p_n, \mu) = G(p_t, p_n, v), \tag{1}$$

$$E_n(p_t, p_n, \mu) \in G_n(p_t, p_n, v), \tag{2}$$

where the subscript n denotes differentiation with respect to p_n.[2] These two conditions may be solved for p_n and μ. If G is differentiable with respect to p_n then $G_n(p_t, p_n, v) = \partial G(p_t, p_n, v)/\partial p_n$ is unique and the "$\in$" in (2) may be replaced by "$=$".

The function $E_n(p_t, p_n, \mu)$ is the Hicksian or compensated demand function for non-traded goods. If eq. (1) is solved for μ as $\mu = V(p_t, p_n, G(p_t, p_n, v))$ and this is substituted into the compensated demand functions, then the ordinary demand functions $z_n = \phi_n(p_t, p_n, G(p_t, p_n, v)) \equiv E_n(p_t, p_n, V(p_t, p_n, G(p_t, p_n, v)))$ are obtained. Thus, an alternative formulation of the model is

$$\phi_n(p_t, p_n, G(p_t, p_n, v)) \in G_n(p_t, p_n, v), \tag{3}$$

which may be solved for p_n.

In either formulation p_n is endogenously determined as a function $p_n = p_n(p_t, v)$ of the prices of tradeable goods and the endowment vector. The net export vector for tradeable goods may be obtained as

$$x_t \in G_t(p_t, p_n, v) - E_t(p_t, p_n, \mu) \tag{4}$$

or

[2] To allow for zero prices condition (2) may be rewritten as

$$E_n(p_t, p_n, \mu) - y_n \leqslant 0 \leqslant p_n$$

and

$$y_n \in G_n(p_t, p_n, v).$$

$$x_t \in G_t(p_t, p_n, v) - \phi_t(p_t, p_n, G(p_t, p_n, v)), \tag{5}$$

where $\phi_t(p_t, p_n, G) \equiv E_t(p_t, p_n, V(p_t, p_n, G))$. Again, if the GNP function is differentiable with respect to p_t, then $G_t(p_t, p_n, v) = \partial G(p_t, p_n, v)/\partial p_t$ is unique and the "$\in$" in (4) and (5) may be replaced by "$=$".

The role played by non-traded goods is evident from (4) or (5) when it is recognized that (1) and (2), or (3), determine p_n endogenously. In general p_n depends upon production and consumption decisions precluding the treatment of the production sector separately from the consumption sector.

8.2.2. Net export functions

To illustrate the role played by non-traded goods, the equations describing the effects of changes in the prices of traded goods and of factor endowments are now derived for the case where differentiability may be assumed. Let the excess supply functions be

$$x_i(p_t, p_n, v) \equiv G_i(p_t, p_n, v) - \phi_i(p_t, p_n, G(p_t, p_n, v)), \quad i = t, n, \tag{6}$$

where p_n is determined by

$$x_n(p_t, p_n, v) = 0. \tag{7}$$

If p_t and v change, then p_n changes by

$$dp_n = -x_{nn}^{-1}[x_{nt}\,dp_t + x_{nv}dv], \tag{8}$$

and the net export vector for traded goods changes by

$$\begin{aligned} dx_t &= x_{tt}\,dp_t + x_{tn}\,dp_n + x_{tv}\,dv \\ &= [x_{tt} - x_{tn}\,x_{nn}^{-1}\,x_{nt}]\,dp_t + [x_{tv} - x_{tn}\,x_{nn}^{-1}\,x_{nv}]\,dv, \end{aligned} \tag{9}$$

where $x_{tn} \equiv \partial x_t(p_t, p_n, v)/\partial p_n$, etc. Eq. (9) implicitly gives the derivatives of the "reduced form" net export functions $\hat{x}_t(p_t, v) \equiv x_t(p_t, p_n(p_t, v), v)$ in terms of those of the "structural" net export functions $x_i(p_t, p_n, v)$. This emphasizes that there is a direct effect of a change in p_t (or v) upon x_t and an indirect effect through the resulting change in the prices of non-traded goods.

The various derivatives in (9) may be expressed in terms of the demand and supply functions by noting that the model may be written in terms of $S(p,\mu,v)$ $= G(p,v) - E(p,\mu)$ as

$$S(p_t, p_n, \mu, v) = 0, \tag{1'}$$

$$S_n(p_t, p_n, \mu, v) = 0, \tag{2'}$$

$$x_t = S_t(p_t, p_n, \mu, v). \tag{4'}$$

Thus, we obtain that

$$x_{ij} = \partial x_i(p_t, p_n, v)/\partial p_j = S_{ij} - \phi_{im} S_j, \quad i,j = t,n, \tag{10}$$

and

$$x_{iv} \equiv \partial x_i(p_t, p_n, v)/\partial v = S_{iv} - \phi_{im} S_v = G_{iv} - \phi_{im} G_v, \quad i = t,n, \tag{11}$$

where $S_{ij} = G_{ij} - E_{ij}$, $\phi_{im} = S_{i\mu}/S_\mu = E_{i\mu}/E_\mu$, $S_v = G_v$ and $S_{iv} = G_{iv}$. Eq. (10) is the Slutsky decomposition of the effects of a price change, extended to the open economy. Notice that $S_n = 0$ so that the last term in (10) drops out when $j = n$. That is, the total effect equals the pure substitution effect when p_n changes.

Equations (10) and (11) may be used to rewrite (8) and (9) in terms of the more basic derivatives of S (or of G and E). A more effective approach is to define

$$\hat{S}(p_t, \mu, v) \equiv S(p_t, P_n(p_t, \mu, v), v), \tag{12}$$

where $p_n = P_n(p_t, \mu, v)$ is the solution for p_n from (2'), and to relate the derivatives of this function to those of S and the reduced form net export functions $\hat{x}_t(p_t, v)$. It will be recalled from Chapter 6 that $\hat{S}(p_t, \mu, v)$ is the net revenue function for the indirect trade utility function in which $x_n = 0$ has been set, and therefore has the same properties as S. Using (12) we find that $x_t = \hat{S}_t = S_t$ and that

(a) $\quad \hat{x}_{tt} \equiv \partial \hat{x}_t(p_t, v)/\partial p_t = x_{tt} - x_{tn} x_{nn}^{-1} x_{nt} = \hat{S}_{tt} - \hat{\phi}_{tm} S_t,$

$$\tag{13}$$

(b) $\quad \hat{x}_{tv} \equiv \partial \hat{x}_t(p_t, v)/\partial v = x_{tv} - x_{tn} x_{nn}^{-1} x_{nv} = \hat{S}_{tv} - \hat{\phi}_{tm} S_v,$

where

$$\hat{S}_{tt} = S_{tt} - S_{tn} S_{nn}^{-1} S_{nt},$$
$$\hat{S}_{tv} = S_{tv} - S_{tn} S_{nn}^{-1} S_{nv}, \qquad\qquad (14)$$
$$\hat{S}_{t\mu} = S_{t\mu} - S_{tn} S_{nn}^{-1} S_{n\mu},$$

and

$$\hat{\phi}_{tm} = \hat{S}_{t\mu}/\hat{S}_{\mu} = \phi_{tm} - S_{tn} S_{nn}^{-1} \phi_{nm}. \qquad\qquad (15)$$

Thus, there is a Slutsky-type effect of a price change — a pure substitution effect and an income effect. The income effect given by $\hat{\phi}_{tm}$ is not necessarily non-negative even if all goods are normal, since it also takes account of the effects of changes in p_n upon net exports of t. It is this fact which leads to the possibility of results different from the standard model with no non-traded goods; for example, the possibility that imports of good i rise when its price increases. On the other hand, it is noted that $\hat{S}_{tt}$ is a positive semi-definite matrix.

In Chapter 6 it was observed that non-traded goods could be "netted out" and reduced form net export functions for traded goods could be obtained in the same way as in a model without non-traded goods. The above calculations show explicitly how the reduced form functions are derived, and how their derivatives relate to the structural net export functions.

In the previous chapter it was shown that there is a negative correlation between the autarky price vector and the free trade price vector. In view of the above comments regarding the fact that non-traded goods may be netted out of the problem, it should be no surprise that this negative correlation carries over a model with non-traded goods. That is,

$$(p_t^1 - p_t^0)(x_t^1 - x_t^0) = (p_t^1 - p_t^0) x_t^1 = -p_t^0 x_t^1 \geqslant 0, \qquad\qquad (16)$$

where p_t^0 is the autarky price vector, $x_t^0 = 0$, and p_t^1 and x_t^1 are the free trade price and net export vectors. The proof follows that for the corresponding proposition in Chapter 7 and is relegated to the problem set.

Condition (16) relates to the effect of the opening up of trade upon the net export vector. It does not indicate what will happen if the price vector p_t increases, i.e. it does not refer to a comparison of post-trade price and net export vectors. For this comparison (local) reference is made to (13, a) from which the correlation between dx_t and dp_t is

$$dp_t \, dx_t = dp_t \, \hat{S}_{tt} \, dp_t - dp_t \, \hat{\phi}_{tm} \, S_t \, dp_t. \qquad\qquad (17)$$

The first term in (17) is a positive semi-definite quadratic form in dp_t. The second term is not necessarily positive definite and consists of all the "income effects" of a price change, and so prevents the demonstration of a positive correlation between dp_t and dx_t. The first point to note about this result is that it is not due to the presence of non-traded goods, since a similar expression occurs without non-traded goods. A second point is that this result holds up even if the utility function is homothetic, again as in the case of no non-traded goods.[3]

8.2.3. The effect of external on internal prices

A change in the price vector of traded goods will cause the prices of non-traded goods to change, as indicated in (8). The relationship between p_n and p_t may be described in terms of the bilinear form:

$$dp_n^T x_{nt} dp_t = dp_t^T x_{nt}^T x_{nn}^{-1} x_{nt} dp_t \geq 0, \quad \text{for all } dp_t \neq 0, \tag{18}$$

where the transpose notation is explicitly used. The proof of this statement arises from the fact that $x_{nn} = S_{nn}$ (from (10) using $S_n = 0$) is a positive semi-definite matrix, a property maintained after pre- and post-multiplication by another matrix. Indeed, it seems reasonable to assume that x_{nt} and x_{nn} are of full rank, in which case x_{nn} is positive definite implying the strict inequality in (17).

Condition (17) establishes a "generalized correlation" between dp_t and dp_n. For example, if the price of one traded good (j) increases and all non-traded goods are gross substitutes ($\partial x_n / \partial p_j < 0$) with the traded good, then $x_{nt} dp_t < 0$ and so the price of at least one non-traded good will fall. Possibly all traded goods may suffer falling prices, but not all can have rising prices. Conversely, if all non-traded are gross complements with good j, then the price of at least one non-traded good must rise.

8.2.4. The effects on production and consumption

Finally, the effects upon demands, z_i, and outputs, y_i, are

$$dz_i = [E_{it} + \phi_{im} x_t] dp_t + E_{in} dp_n + \phi_{im} G_v dv, \quad i = t, n, \tag{19}$$

---

[3] This was to be demonstrated for the case of no non-traded goods in the problem set of Chapter 6.

$$dy_t = G_{tt}\,dp_t + G_{tn}\,dp_n + G_{tv}\,dv, \tag{20}$$

and, of course, $dy_n = dz_n$. Again (16) and (17) emphasize the direct and indirect effects of a change in p_t and v. More will be said about these effects below.

8.2.5. *The case of one non-traded good*

To further illustrate the role played by non-traded goods consider the special case when there is just one non-traded good. Given the prices for traded goods and the endowment vector, the supply function (or correspondence) for the non-traded good may be derived and illustrated in fig. 8.1 as G_n. At p_n^0 the supply quantity is non-unique but for all other p_n it is unique. By varying p_n and taking into account the price and income effects the demand curve for the non-traded good is obtained and drawn in fig. 8.1 as ϕ_n. Is it necessary that this curve be downward-sloping? It is relatively easy to show that ϕ_n must be downward-sloping (strictly speaking, non-increasing) everywhere except, possibly, when $y_n > z_n$, as long as it is assumed that the non-traded good is normal, i.e. its consumption increases when income increases. Indeed, irrespective of whether the non-traded good is normal the demand function ϕ_n is shown to be downward-

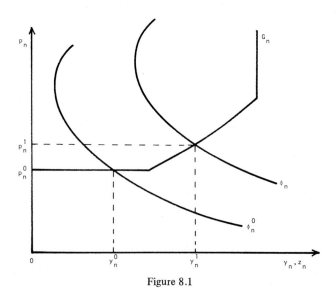

Figure 8.1

sloping in the neighbourhood of the equilibrium price. The total effect upon z_n of a change in p_n, if G is differentiable, is

$$\frac{\mathrm{d}z_n}{\mathrm{d}p_n} = E_{nn}(p_t, p_n, \mu) + \phi_{nm}(p_t, p_n, m)[G_n(p_t, p_n, v)$$

$$- \phi_n(p_t, p_n, m)], \tag{21}$$

where $\mu = V(p_t, p_n, m)$ and $m = G(p_t, p_n, v)$. Since the expenditure function is concave in prices, $E_{nn} \leqslant 0$, meaning that the compensated demand curve is non-increasing. If $E_{nn} < 0$, then E_n is downward-sloping. Hence (21) indicates that the total response of z_n to a change in p_n when the market for the non-traded good clears, $G_n = \phi_n$, is equal to the response along the compensated demand function E_n. Thus, the demand curve, ϕ_n, drawn in fig. 8.1 is downward-sloping in the neighbourhood of the equilibrium price. If $\phi_{nm} > 0$, then $\mathrm{d}z_n/\mathrm{d}p_n < 0$ when $G_n < \phi_n$, and $\mathrm{d}z_n/\mathrm{d}p_n$ can only occur if G_n is sufficiently greater than ϕ_n so that the income effect outweighs the substitution effect, E_{nn}.[4]

The equilibrium price for the non-traded good is p_n^1 and the corresponding quantity demanded and supplied is y_n^1. A shift of preferences resulting in a shift in the position and shape of ϕ_n would clearly alter the equilibrium price and quantity. However, if ϕ_n^0 is the demand curve, then there exist preference shifts which would alter the shape and position of ϕ_n^0 but which would not alter the equilibrium price, which in this case is p_n^0. In this case, at least for these limited shifts in preference, it is evident that the price is determined by supply considerations and is independent of demand conditions. This example points out the crucial requirement for the independence of production from consumption decisions, namely that the (inverse) supply curve be flat in the neighbourhood of equilibrium. For this to occur the GNP function has to have a special structure. As will be seen below, many of the papers on non-traded goods contain assumptions about the production sector which ensure that G_n is flat and hence ensure the separation of production from consumption decisions.

Two qualifications are required. First, it should be emphasized that the separation is not global unless G_n is flat throughout. Secondly, the separation simply means that p_n is determined by supply considerations. Actually, the consumption sector does play a role since it determines the *quantity* of the non-traded good produced and consumed in this case. Moreover, once y_n is so determined,

[4] The demonstration is for all $p_n \neq p_n^0$ in fig. 8.1. If $p_n = p_n^0$ initially, one has to distinguish between an increase in p_n, in which case it is the right-hand derivative of G with respect to p_n that is used in the above demonstration, and a decrease in p_n, in which case the left-hand derivative (here zero) is used.

the set of equilibrium productions for other goods will be reduced in size, possibly to a single point. Hence, the separation of production from consumption decisions occurs only in a limited sense.

As an illustration of a case where G_n is flat consider the model used by Komiya (1967) in which there are $M = 3$ goods, one of which is non-traded, and $N = 2$ factors of production. Let all goods be pure final goods and suppose that production is non-joint. If all three goods are produced and the factors are fully used, then the production possibility frontier is a ruled surface and the output quantities are not uniquely given, as explained in Chapter 3. The equilibrium conditions for the production sector are

$$c^j(w_1, w_2) = p_j, \qquad j = 1, 2, 3, \tag{22}$$

$$\sum_{j=1}^{3} c_{ij}(w_1, w_2) y_j = v_i, \quad i = 1, 2, \tag{23}$$

where c^j denotes the unit cost function and c_{ij} denotes its derivative with respect to w_i. Let good 1 be non-traded. Evidently (22) involves three equations in three unknowns — w_1, w_2 and p_1. Barring singular situations these unknowns are uniquely determined by (22) without consideration to (23), or to the demand for the non-traded good. Once w is known, (23) is a set of two linear equations in the three unknown outputs. The market clearing condition for non-traded goods

$$\phi_1(p_1, p_2, p_3, G(p_1, p_2, p_3, v)) \in G_1(p_1, p_2, p_3, v), \tag{24}$$

described in fig. 8.1, determines p_1 and y_1. Knowing y_1, (23) involves only two unknown outputs which may be obtained uniquely.

8.2.6. The general case

In the general case where there are M_t^* traded goods and M_n^* non-traded goods produced non-jointly using N factors of production, what is the condition for determining p_n by supply considerations alone? In this case the equilibrium conditions are

$$c^j(w) = p_j, \qquad j = 1, ..., M^*, \tag{25}$$

$$\sum_{j=1}^{M^*} c_{ij}(w) y_j = v_i, \qquad i = 1, ..., N, \tag{26}$$

and

$$\phi_i(p, G(p, v)) = y_i, \quad i \text{ non-traded}, \tag{27}$$

where $G(p, v) = wv = py$ is the GNP function.[5] There are $M^* = M_t^* + M_n^*$ equations in (25) involving $N + M_n^*$ unknowns. Accordingly, if $M_t^* \geqslant N$ then, barring singularities of course, the $N + M_n^*$ unknowns in w and p_n are determined by (25) alone. Of course, for these solutions to be equilibria solutions the factor markets and the non-traded goods' markets have to clear with M^* goods being produced. That is, v has to be in the cone of diversification formed by (w, p), and $\phi_n(p, G(p, v))$ has to be in the set of productions $G_n(p, v)$ for non-traded goods.[6] In short,

> If the number of traded goods actually produced, M_t^*, is at least as great as the number of fully used factors, N, then the price vector for the M_n^* non-traded goods produced, p_n, is determined by supply considerations (25) alone. (28)

If $M_t^* < N$, then the cost equations (25) are not sufficient to determine the prices of all factors and non-traded goods. Even (25) and (26) are not sufficient since they involve $M^* + N$ equations in $M^* + N + M_n^*$ unknowns. Accordingly, the equilibrium solution for p_n depends upon the factor endowments and the demand functions for non-traded goods.

The following sections are concerned with the effect upon the equilibrium prices for factors and non-traded goods, outputs, and net exports of changes in endowments and the price of traded goods. If these changes are small and do not alter the pattern of production or cause unemployment of any factor, then the effects may be obtained by applying a differential comparative statics analysis to eqs. (25)–(27). The resulting equations are

$$
\begin{bmatrix}
0 & 0 & A_t^{\mathrm{T}} & 0 \\
0 & 0 & A_n^{\mathrm{T}} & -I \\
A_t & A_n & S & 0 \\
0 & -I & 0 & E_{nn}
\end{bmatrix}
\begin{bmatrix}
dy_t \\
dy_n \\
dw \\
dp_n
\end{bmatrix}
=
\begin{bmatrix}
I & & 0 \\
0 & & 0 \\
0 & & I \\
-(E_{nt} + \phi_{nm} x_t^{\mathrm{T}}) & -\phi_{nm} w^{\mathrm{T}}
\end{bmatrix}
\begin{bmatrix}
dp_t \\
dv
\end{bmatrix}, \tag{29}
$$

---

[5] This formulation assumes that all goods are pure final goods. The model is easily extended to the case where goods may be used as intermediate inputs. See Chapter 5.

[6] See Chapters 4 and 5 for a discussion of cones of diversification.

where $A \equiv [c_w^1(w), \ldots, c_w^{M^*}(w)] = [A_t, A_n]$ is the matrix of factor input–output coefficients partitioned according to traded and non-traded goods, $S \equiv \Sigma_{j=1}^{M^*} y_j c_{ww}^j(w)$ is an $N \times N$ negative semi-definite matrix, E_{pp} is an $M^* \times M^*$ negative semi-definite matrix (Slutsky substitution matrix) partitioned according to traded and non-traded goods, ϕ_m is an $M^* \times 1$ vector of derivatives of the demand functions with respect to income (partitioned), x_t is an $M_t^* \times 1$ vector of net exports of traded goods and explicit transpose notation has been used. Derivation of (29) is the subject of one of the problem sets. Clearly, if non-traded goods are ommitted (29) corresponds to (4.50) in Chapter 4. Alternatively, if traded goods are ommitted (29) is applicable to a closed economy. In terms of percentage changes (29) may be written as

$$
\begin{bmatrix}
0 & 0 & \theta_t & 0 \\
0 & 0 & \theta_n & -I \\
\lambda_t & \lambda_n & \epsilon & 0 \\
0 & -I & 0 & \sigma_{nn}
\end{bmatrix}
\begin{bmatrix}
\hat{y}_t \\
\hat{y}_n \\
\hat{w} \\
\hat{p}_n
\end{bmatrix}
\begin{bmatrix}
I & 0 \\
0 & 0 \\
0 & I \\
-[\sigma_{nt} + \gamma_n \xi_t] & -\gamma_n \alpha \hat{v}
\end{bmatrix}
\begin{bmatrix}
\hat{p}_t \\
\hat{v}
\end{bmatrix}, \quad (30)
$$

where θ is a matrix of factor shares in the industries costs, λ is a matrix of industry shares in the factors of production, ϵ is a matrix of price elasticities of factor demands, σ is a matrix of price elasticities of the Hicksian demand functions for goods, γ is a column vector of income elasticities of demand for goods, ξ_t is a column vector of shares of net exports in GNP, and α is a column vector of shares of factors in GNP. The derivation of (30) is also relegated to the problem set.

8.3. The effects of factor endowments

Attention is now directed to the effects upon factor prices, the prices of non-traded goods, commodity net outputs and the pattern of trade of a change in the endowments of a small trading economy in which the prices of traded goods are given. In obtaining these effects it will be assumed that the changes in endowments are small enough not to alter the pattern of specialization in production. The model is that described by eqs. (25), (26) and (27) (or, equivalently, (3)), or in differential form by (29).

8.3.1. The prices of factors and non-traded goods

The focus of attention here is the extension of the factor price equalization theorem. That is, under what conditions will two nations trading at the same world prices p_t have the same prices for factors and non-traded goods? The way to proceed to answer this question is suggested by the discussion in the previous section, and in Chapters 4 and 5 on the factor price equalization theorem.

Clearly, the same technology is required, so let that be assumed. Also, the number of traded goods produced, M_t^*, needs to be at least as great as the number of fully used factors, N, in view of the discussion in section 8.2. Then, barring singularities, eq. (25) may be solved for w and p_n as a function of p_t. The solutions are not necessarily unique. Let w^i, p_n^i denote the ith solution.[7] For one of these to constitute an equilibrium solution it is necessary that it be consistent with the market equilibrium conditions for factors *and* non-traded goods.

Let $K_t^i = K_t(w^i, p_t, p_n^i)$ denote the cone of diversification, defined as the set of endowments for which non-negative outputs for the M_t^* traded goods are possible:

$$K_t^i = K_t(w^i, p_t, p_n^i) \equiv \left\{ u: \sum_{j=1}^{M_t^*} c_w^j(w^i) y_j = u; \ (y_1, ..., y_{M^*}) \geqslant 0 \right\}, \qquad (31)$$

where $c_w^j(w^i)$ is the factor input–output vector in industry j. Also, define

$$J^i = J(p_t, p_n^i) \equiv \{ u: \phi_n(p_t, p_n^i, G(p_t, p_n^i, u)) \in G_n(p_t, p_n^i, u) \}, \qquad (32)$$

which is the set of endowments for which the demand vector for non-traded goods is also an optimal production vector for non-traded goods. If the endowment vector is in the interior of $G_t^i \equiv J^i \cap K_t^i$, then (w^i, p_n^i) is an equilibrium price vector for factors and non-traded goods. Indeed, since it can be shown that $G_t^i \cap G_t^j$ is empty, it is not possible for an endowment vector to be in the interior of two such sets simultaneously, and hence (w^i, p_n^i) will be the unique equilibrium internal price vector.

If two nations produce the same M_t^* traded goods at the world price vector p_t, have the same technology and the same demand functions for non-traded goods, then the sets J^i and K_t^i are applicable to both nations. As long as their endowment vectors are in the same set $G_t^i \equiv J^i \cap K_t^i$, then both nations will have (w^i, p_n^i) as the equilibrium price vector for factors and non-traded goods. This result is formalized as:

---

[7]   It is assumed that there are a finite number of distinct solutions.

Theorem. Let two or more nations have the same technology (same cost or GNP functions), face the same prices for traded goods, produce the same M_t^* traded goods, and have the same demand functions for non-traded goods. Let $G_t^i \equiv J^i \cap K_t^i$. If these nations' endowment vectors are in the interior of the same set G_t^i, then they will have the same prices for factors and for non-traded goods, namely (w^i, p_n^i). $\hspace{1cm}$ (33)

While this theorem establishes sufficient conditions for the equalization of the prices of factors and non-traded goods amongst nations, several points should be noted. First, theorem (33) does not specify whether G_t^i has an interior, or even whether it exists. To have a meaningful result conditions for a non-empty interior are needed, for it is only then that small arbitrary differences in endowments between nations do not cause differences in prices. Evidently, if $M_t^* \geqslant N$ and the factor input–output vectors $c_w^j(w^i)$, $j = 1, ..., M_t^*$, have rank N, then the cone K_t^i has a non-empty interior. If $M_t^* < N$, then (25) cannot be solved for (w_i, p_n^i), and the M_t^* input–output vectors have rank at most $M_t^* < N$ and so the diversification cone is degenerate.[8]

What can be said about J^i? Let ϕ_n be continuous and increasing in income and let G be continuous and increasing in v (meaning that factor prices are posi-. tive). Then ϕ_n is continuous and increasing in v with a unique ϕ_n for each v. If also $G_n(p_t, p_n^i, v)$ is unique (G is differentiable) and continuous in v, then there will, barring singularities, be only a finite number of distinct v in the set J^i. If, however, $G_n(p_t, p_n^i, v)$ is a convex set of optimal output vectors for non-traded goods with a non-empty interior, then it is possible to change v by a small amount, have G_n shift by a small amount and have a slightly altered demand vector in it. In fig. 8.1, if an endowment increases by a small amount, ϕ_n^0 will shift to the right slightly as will the supply correspondence G_n. Clearly, they will still intersect at price p_n^0. Thus, J^i can have a non-empty interior and hence it is possible for $J^i \cap K_t^i$ to have a non-empty interior.

For the case where $M^* = 3$, $M_n^* = 1$ and $N = 2$, Ethier (1972) has obtained a sufficient condition for $J^i \cap K_t^i$ to have a non-empty interior. To illustrate this case consider fig. 8.2, which depicts the demand and supply of the non-traded good in relation to the endowment of factor 2, v_2, given v_1. For the prices vector (w^i, p_n^i) which constitutes an equilibrium, $\overline{v}_2/v_1$ and $\overline{\overline{v}}_2/v_1$ are the optimal factor ratios for the two traded goods, while for the non-traded good the optimal ratio is v_2^n/v_1. Any $v_2 \in (\overline{v}_2, \overline{\overline{v}}_2)$ corresponds to $v \in K_t^i$. One of the problem sets

---

[8]   Note the similarity of this argument with that used in the context of the discussion of the factor price equalization theorem in Chapter 4.

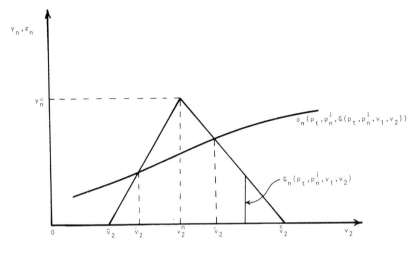

Figure 8.2

asks for a demonstration that the greatest production, y_n^*, of the non-traded good occurs when the endowment of factor 2 is v_2^n, and that the maximal values of y_n vary linearly with v_2, as indicated in fig. 8.2. Note that any y_2 below the upper boundary of the triangle is optimal so that the line segment from the upper boundary to the v_2-axis corresponds to $G_n(p_t, p_n^i, v)$. If $\phi_n(p_t, p_n^i, G(p_t, p_n^i, v))$ is strictly increasing and continuous in v_2, as previously assumed, and $\phi_n(p_t, p_n^i, G(p_t, p_n^i, v_1, v_2^n)) < y_n^*$, then it is clear that the demand function for the non-traded good must intersect the interior of the triangle. Thus, the set $[\tilde{v}_2, \bar{\bar{v}}_2]$ is the set of endowments of v_2 such that the factor markets clear with all goods produced ($v_2 \in (\overline{v}_2, \overline{\overline{v}}_2)$) and such that the market for the non-traded good clears. This has a non-empty interior.[9]

The second point to note about theorem (33) is that $G_t^i = J^i \cap K_t^i$ is not necessarily a cone, so that the size of the economies in question matters. This is evident from the discussion in the previous paragraph which took v_1 to be given. If the utility function is homothetic, then the demand functions for non-traded goods, $\phi_n(p_t, p_n^i, G(p_t, p_n^i, v))$ are homogeneous of degree one in income G, which in turn is homogeneous of degree one in v. In this case ϕ_n is homogeneous of degree one in v as is the supply correspondence $G_n(p_t, p_n^i, v)$ so that G^i is homogeneous of degree one in v and, hence, is a cone. Hence, the scale of the economies does not matter in this special case.

---

[9] See Ethier (1972, p. 138) for a proof that the set G_t^i has a non-empty interior.

The third point to note about theorem (33) concerns the assumption that the demand functions for non-traded goods are the same in each nation. This was a convenient assumption enabling G_t^i to be applicable to all nations. However, if the demand functions are different, J^i and hence $G_t^i = J^i \cap K_t^i$ will be different for each nation. Nevertheless, by construction if each nation's endowment vector is inside its own G_t^i set, then each nation will have (w^i, p_n^i) as the price vector for factors and non-traded goods. Thus, the assumption of identical demand functions is not necessary for factor and non-traded goods price equalization. This is evident from fig. 8.2 where another demand function could be drawn to pass through the interior of the production triangle yielding another G_t^i set consistent with (w_i, p_n^i).

Finally, it is noted that theorem (33) is based upon the definition of K_t^i as the diversification cone for producible *traded* goods. Suppose we define K^i as the diversification cone formed by the optimal input vectors for all producible goods, both traded and non-traded. Then $K_t^i \subset K^i$, but $K_t^i = K^i$ only if the input vectors for non-traded goods are contained in K_t^i, i.e. only if they are spanned by the input vectors for traded goods. If this is not the case then K^i is larger than K_t^i and, moreover, it is quite possible that int $(K^i \cap K^j) \neq \emptyset$, i.e. not empty. This is illustrated by Ethier (1972, p. 135). The implication is that int $(G^i \cap G^j) \neq \emptyset$ is possible, where $G^i \equiv J^i \cap K^i$. Thus, if $v \in$ int $(G^i \cap G^j)$ both (w^i, p_n^i) and (w^j, p_n^j) are possible equilibrium domestic price vectors, and so we cannot say that $v \in$ int G^i implies that $(w, p_n) = (w^i, p_n^i)$. Hence, theorem (33) cannot be stated in terms of G^i and K^i. However, by writing it in terms of G_t^i and K_t^i we can be sure that int $(K_t^i \cap K_t^j) = \emptyset$ and hence that int $(G_t^i \cap G_t^j) = \emptyset$, so that $v \in$ int G_t^i implies $(w, p_n) = (w^i, p_n^i)$.[10]

8.3.2. Commodity outputs

If endowments change, what will be the effect upon the outputs of the traded and non-traded goods? To answer this, consider the case where the change in endowments does not alter the prices of the factors and non-traded goods, sufficient conditions for which having been provided by the discussion surrounding (33).

Since $M^* > N$ is assumed and all prices are fixed, conditions (26) are not sufficient to determine all output levels. However, condition (27) provides an extra

[10] The proof that $K_t^i \cap K_t^j$ has an empty interior is the subject of one of the problems. McKenzie (1955, p. 245) provides a proof for the case of no non-traded goods, which also applies here.

M_n^* conditions so that, in total, there are $M_n^* + N$ conditions in $M^* = M_t^* + M_n^*$ unknowns. To enable a unique solution for $(y_1, ..., y_{M*})$ it is required that $N \geqslant M_t^*$. But since $M^* = M_t^* + M_n^* > N$ is assumed, $M_t^* = N$ is required. In this case the demand functions $\phi_n(p, G(p, v))$ determine the production of non-traded goods, y_n, which allows (26) to be solved for the production levels for the remaining traded goods, y_t. On the other hand, if $M_t^* > N$, then y_t cannot be uniquely determined given $y_n = \phi_n(p, G(p, v))$.

The effect upon y_n of a change in v is determined by the demand conditions alone, as

$$dy_n = \phi_{nm} G_v dv. \tag{34}$$

Since G_v is the price vector for factors and ϕ_{nm} is the response of demands to income, assumed to be positive for (normal goods), (34) shows that an increase in the endowment of any one factor will increase the demand, hence production, of all non-traded goods.

If $M_t^* = N$, then the effect upon y_t can be obtained from (26), or directly from (29), as

$$dy_t = A_t^{-1}[dv - A_n dy_n] = A_t^{-1}[I - A_n \phi_{nm} G_v]dv = A_t^{-1}(I - D)dv, \tag{35}$$

where $A = [A_t\, A_n]$ is the matrix of input–output coefficients partitioned between traded and non-traded goods industries, and $D \equiv A_n \phi_{nm} G_v$.[11]

Equation (35) shows that the effects upon y_t of a change in v depend upon the demand functions and the technology matrix for non-traded goods, as expected. When can we use A_t and dv alone to predict the direction of a change in y_t? Clearly, what is required is that the vector of factors remaining after the inputs into the non-traded goods sector have been deducted from the total endowment vector, must move in the same direction as the total endowment vector.

This is precisely what does occur, as is now demonstrated. It will be convenient to work in terms of percentage changes so we rewrite (34) as

$$\hat{y}_n = \gamma_n \alpha \hat{v}, \tag{36}$$

where γ_n is a vector of income elasticities of demand for non-traded goods and $\alpha = (\alpha_1, ..., \alpha_N)$ is a vector of distributive factor shares, $\alpha_i \equiv w_i v_i/m$. Also, we have

[11] It is implicitly assumed here that all traded goods are produced to eliminate the need for additional notation to distinguish between produced and non-produced traded goods.

$$\lambda_t \, \hat{y}_t = \hat{v} - \lambda_n \, \hat{y}_n = [I - \lambda_n \gamma_n \alpha] \, \hat{v} \equiv \delta \, \hat{v}, \tag{37}$$

where $\lambda = (\lambda_t \lambda_n)$ is the partitioned matrix of industrial shares of the inputs, $\lambda_{ij} \equiv a_{ij} y_j / v_i$. By defining $d = \text{diag} (1 - \lambda_n \, 1)$ as the diagonal matrix of shares of the factors available for traded goods, (37) may be rewritten as

$$\lambda_t^0 \, \hat{y}_t \equiv d^{-1} \lambda_t \, \hat{y}_t = d^{-1} \delta \, \hat{v} \equiv \delta^0 \, \hat{v} \equiv \hat{v}_t, \tag{38}$$

where $\lambda_t^0 \equiv d^{-1} \lambda_t$ is the matrix of industrial shares of the factors in the traded goods sector only and $\hat{v}_t$ is the percentage change in the vector v_t, of factors available to the traded goods sector. The matrix λ_t^0 is non-negative and each row sums to unity, hence (38) looks precisely like the Rybczynski equations for a model with no non-traded goods, except that the right-hand side is $\hat{v}_t$, not $\hat{v}$. However, these are related through $\delta^0 \equiv d^{-1} \delta$ whose diagonal elements have the sign of the diagonal elements of δ which are

$$\delta_{ii} = 1 - \left(\sum_j \lambda_{ij} \gamma_j \right) \alpha_i = 1 - \sum_j \theta_{ij} c_j, \tag{39}$$

where $\theta_{ij} \equiv w_i a_{ij} / p_j$, $c_j \equiv p_j \phi_{jm}$ is the marginal propensity to consume j, and the sums are over non-traded goods only. The second equality is to be demonstrated in the problem set, as are the properties

$$\delta_{ij} \begin{cases} \geqslant 0, & j = i, \\ \leqslant 0, & j \neq i. \end{cases} \tag{40}$$

This result, together with (38), implies that if the endowment of factor j increases, then the amount remaining for use by the traded goods sector increases for factor j and decreases for all other factors. Hence, from the results of Chapter 4, at least one traded good's supply will expand (at a greater rate than v_j) and the supply of at least one traded good will fall. In the case where there are $N = 2$ factors and $M_t^* = 2$ traded goods produced, one industry will expand and the other contract, and the expanding industry is the one which uses factor j more intensively.[12] Of course, it is also possible to derive the subset of endowment changes for which the standard results still hold, but this task is left as an exercise.

The special case where non-traded goods have income elasticities of demand equal to unity is of interest, since it leads to a simplification of the output ef-

---

[12]   See Ethier (1972) for a treatment of this case.

fects of an endowment change allowing a full generalization of the standard Rybczynski results to the case of non-traded goods. If all income elasticities of demand are unity, then $\gamma_n = 1$ and $\delta 1 = [I - \lambda_n 1 \alpha] 1 = 1 - \lambda_n 1$, since $\alpha 1 = 1$. Hence, $\delta^0 1 = d^{-1} \delta 1 = d^{-1}(1 - \lambda_n 1) = 1$. Pre-multiplying (38) by the inverse of δ^0 we have that

$$\lambda_t^* \hat{y}_t = (\delta^0)^{-1} \lambda_t^0 \hat{y}_t = \delta^{-1} \lambda_t \hat{y}_t = \hat{v}, \tag{41}$$

where $\lambda_t^* \equiv (\delta^0)^{-1} \lambda_t^0 = \delta^{-1} \lambda_t$. If $\delta 1 > 0$, meaning that all factors are used by the traded goods sector, it can be shown that δ^{-1} exists and is non-negative, whence $\lambda_t^* \geqslant 0$.[13] Also, $\lambda_t^* 1 = (\delta^0)^{-1} \lambda_t^0 1 = (\delta^0)^{-1} 1 = 1$, since $\lambda_t^* 1 = 1$ and $\delta^0 1 = 1$, as shown above. Hence (41) is precisely the same as for a model with no non-traded goods, with share matrix λ_t^*. All of the Rybczynski-type results discussed in Chapter 4 apply here.

The question of interpretation of these results arises, however, since the matrix λ_t^* depends upon λ_n and α as well as λ_t. However, it is noted that $|\lambda_t^*| = |\lambda_t|/|\delta|$ and that $|\delta| > 0$.[14] In the case of two produced traded goods and two factors of production, the sign of the determinant indicates the relative intensities in production. Thus, industry 2 is factor 2 intensive in terms of the "net distribution matrix" λ_t^* if and only if it is factor 2 intensive in terms of the original distribution matrix λ_t. Specifically, the two equations in (37) or (41) may be subtracted to obtain:

$$\hat{y}_2 - \hat{y}_1 = (\hat{v}_2 - \hat{v}_1)/|\lambda_t|/|\delta|, \tag{42}$$

where $-1 < |\lambda_t^*| = |\lambda_t|/|\delta| < 1$. Thus, an increase in the ratio v_2/v_1 causes y_2/y_1 to rise if product i is factor i intensive. Moreover, the standard magnification effect, $\hat{y}_2 > \hat{v}_2 > \hat{v}_1 > \hat{y}_1$, also occurs. It should be noted that the full magnification effect cannot be derived as a general result without a condition such as $\gamma_n = 1$.

It has been shown that the assumption of unitary elasticities of demand for non-traded goods allows the model to be written in a form precisely the same as for a model without non-traded goods. And, at least in the two-dimensional case, the "net" and original intensities of products correspond exactly in sign. An implication of this result is that, in the two-dimensional case, the Heckscher—Ohlin

---

[13] See, for example, Takayama (1974, p. 383). The basic theorem is that if a matrix B has non-positive off-diagonal elements and there exists an x such that $Bx > 0$, then B is non-singular and $B^{-1} \geqslant 0$.

[14] See Takayama (1974, p. 383). Since δ has positive row sums and non-positive off-diagonals its principal minors are all positive.

theorem will also hold in the presence of non-traded goods provided they have unitary income elasticities of demand. But this follows from the assumption of homothetic preference, which is made for the Heckscher–Ohlin model anyway.

8.3.3. Net exports

The net export vector for traded goods is $x_t = y_t - z_t$, which changes by

$$dx_t = [A_t^{-1} [I - A_n \phi_{nm} w] - \phi_{tm} w] \, dv \tag{43}$$

in response to a change in endowments when $M_t^* \geqslant N$. Let the endowment of factor j increase. Since the output of at least one traded good increases proportionately more than v_j, and since one output contracts, it follows that a sufficient condition for the first product's net export to increase and the second product's net export to decrease is that they be normal goods.

8.4. The effects of prices of traded goods

This section is concerned with the effects of changes in the prices of traded goods upon the prices of factors and non-traded goods, and upon industry outputs and net exports.

8.4.1. Prices of factors and non-traded goods

Consider the case where $M_t^* \geqslant N$, enabling the profit-maximization conditions (25) to be solved for the equilibrium (w, p_n) vector. In terms of (29) it is noted that the first two of the four sets of equations involve dw and dp_n only and, moreover, may be solved as

$$dw = (A_t^T)^{-1} dp_t, \tag{44}$$

$$dp_n = A_n^T dw = A_n^T (A_t^T)^{-1} dp_t, \tag{45}$$

if $M_t^* = N$ and A_t has full rank. In this case p_t determines w which then determines p_n. The effect of foreign prices on the rewards to factors is exactly the same as when all goods are traded. Of course, if $M_t^* > N$, then the M_t^* profit-maximization conditions for traded goods are over-determined, and in general a change in p_t will cause the production of some goods to cease.

In terms of percentage changes (45) is

$$\hat{p}_n = \theta_n \hat{w} = \theta_n \theta_t^{-1} \hat{p}_t, \tag{46}$$

where θ_n and θ_t are matrices of cost shares in the traded and non-traded goods industries. It is well known (see Chapter 4) that if one traded good's price increases, the magnification effect requires some factor prices to increase by a greater percentage and some factor prices to fall. On the other hand, (46) requires $\hat{p}_n$ to be a weighted average of the changes in factor prices, so that its elements can be no greater than the maximum percentage increase in a factor price nor less than the minimum. Clearly, there can be no definite relationship between the values of the elements of $\hat{p}_n$ and $\hat{p}_t$. Consider, for example, the case where there are two traded goods and one non-traded good produced using two factors. The solution in (46) becomes

$$\hat{p}_n = \frac{\theta_{2n} - \theta_{21}}{\theta_{22} - \theta_{21}} (\hat{p}_2 - \hat{p}_1) + \hat{p}_1, \tag{47}$$

where θ_{ij} is the share of factor i in the cost of producing j, and $j = n$ denotes the non-traded good. This shows that whether p_n rises or falls when p_2 rises depends upon relative intensities. If industries 2 and n are both more or both less intensive than industry 1 in the use of factor 2, then $\hat{p}_n > 0$ when $\hat{p}_2 > 0 = \hat{p}_1$. If θ_{21} is between θ_{22} and θ_{2n}, then $\hat{p}_n < 0$. Moreover, the coefficient of $(\hat{p}_2 - \hat{p}_1)$ in (47) has range minus infinity to plus infinity, although extreme values will cause the pattern of production to change.

8.4.2. *Commodity outputs*

In the case where $M_t^* = N$ (44) and (45) may be substituted into the third and fourth equation sets of (29) which may then be solved as

$$dy_n = E_{nn} \, dp_n + [E_{nt} + \phi_{nm} \, x_t^T] \, dp_t$$
$$= [E_{nn} A_n^T (A_t^T)^{-1} + E_{nt} + \phi_{nm} \, x_t^T] \, dp_t \tag{48}$$

and

$$dy_t = -A_t^{-1} [A_n \, dy_n + S \, dw] = [A_t^{-1} A_n E_{nn} A_n^T (A_t^{-1})^T$$
$$+ A_t^{-1} A_n E_{nt} + A_t^{-1} A_n \phi_{nm} \, x_t^T + A_t^{-1} S(A_t^{-1})^T] \, dp_t. \tag{49}$$

When there are no non-traded goods the second and third terms in (49) do not appear. The remaining two matrices are negative semi-definite since E_{nn} and S are both negative semi-definite. Thus, dy_t/dp_t is a positive semi-definite matrix describing the response of outputs to their prices. However, when non-traded goods are included, as in (49), the second and third matrices destroy this property. This means that it is possible to construct examples in which an increase in the price of good j causes a fall in its output due to the effect on the prices of the non-traded goods. A price change causes the demand for non-traded goods to change because of the substitution effects (E_{nt} and E_{nn}) and income effects arising directly from the change in the traded good's price ($\phi_{nm}\, x_t^T$). This, in turn, alters the quantities of factors available for the traded goods sector. Thus, the total effect upon y_t is a combined effect of a direct price change for the traded good, an indirect effect through the prices of non-traded goods, and another indirect effect through an alteration in the factor endowment available to the traded goods sector. Hence, it is little surprise that "perverse" output responses are possible.

To illustrate the possibility of "perverse" output responses consider the case of $M_t^* = 2$ traded goods, $M_n^* = 1$ non-traded good, and $N = 2$ factors. The eqs. (48) and (49) may be rewritten in terms of percentage changes as

$$\hat{y}_n = \sigma_{nn}\,\hat{p}_n + [\sigma_{nt} + \gamma_n\,\xi_t]\,\hat{p}_t, \tag{50}$$

$$\hat{y}_t = -\lambda_t^{-1}\,[\lambda_n\,\hat{y}_n + \epsilon\,\hat{w}], \tag{51}$$

where $\hat{w}$ and $\hat{p}_n$ are given by (46). For the special case under consideration,

$$\hat{y}_n = \sigma_{nn}(\hat{p}_n - \hat{p}_1) + (\sigma_{n2} + \gamma_n\,\xi_2)\,(\hat{p}_2 - \hat{p}_1)$$

$$= \left[\sigma_{nn}\frac{(\theta_{2n} - \theta_{21})}{(\theta_{22} - \theta_{21})} + \sigma_{n2} + \gamma_n\,\xi_2\right](\hat{p}_2 - \hat{p}_1), \tag{52}$$

obtained using (50) and (47), and observing that $\xi_1 + \xi_2 = 0$ and $\Sigma_j\,\sigma_{nj} = 0$. If good 2 is exported, then $\xi_2 > 0$ and the third term is positive indicating an increase in the demand for the non-traded good due to an increase in real income. If good n and 2 are substitutes in consumption, $\sigma_{n2} > 0$, there will be a further increase in the demand for the non-traded good. Finally, if θ_{2n} is between θ_{22} and θ_{21}, then p_n will fall, causing another increase in demand for the non-traded good. Thus, these assumptions imply that y_n increases in response to an increase in p_2. Alternatively, if good 2 is imported, goods 2 and n are complements, and θ_{2n} is not spanned by θ_{22} and θ_{21}, then y_n will fall in response to an increase in p_2.

Specializing (51) to the case of two-traded goods, one non-traded good and two factors yields:

$$
\begin{bmatrix} \hat{y}_1 - \hat{y}_n \\ \hat{y}_2 - \hat{y}_n \end{bmatrix} = \frac{1}{|\lambda_t|} \begin{bmatrix} \lambda_{12} - \lambda_{22} \\ \lambda_{21} - \lambda_{11} \end{bmatrix} \hat{y}_n + \frac{1}{|\lambda_t|}
$$

$$
\begin{bmatrix} -(\lambda_{22}\,\epsilon_{12} + \lambda_{12}\,\epsilon_{21}) \\ \\ \lambda_{21}\,\epsilon_{12} + \lambda_{11}\,\epsilon_{21} \end{bmatrix} (\hat{w}_2 - \hat{w}_1), \tag{53}
$$

where $\hat{y}_n$ is given by (52), $\hat{w}_2 - \hat{w}_1 = (\hat{p}_2 - \hat{p}_1)/(\theta_{22} - \theta_{21})$, and $|\lambda_t| \equiv \lambda_{11} \lambda_{22} - \lambda_{12} \lambda_{21}$. The ratio y_2/y_1 changes according to

$$
\hat{y}_2 - \hat{y}_1 = \frac{\lambda_{1n} - \lambda_{2n}}{|\lambda_t|} \hat{y}_n + \frac{[\epsilon_{12}(1 - \lambda_{2n}) + \epsilon_{21}(1 - \lambda_{1n})]}{|\lambda_t|(\theta_{22} - \theta_{21})} (\hat{p}_2 - \hat{p}_1). \tag{54}
$$

The coefficient of $(\hat{p}_2 - \hat{p}_1)$ is positive since $\epsilon_{12}, \epsilon_{21} > 0$ and $|\lambda_t|$ and $(\theta_{22} - \theta_{21})$ have the same sign (see problem set). It is the elasticity of transformation around the production possibility frontier for traded goods for a given production of the non-traded good. The first term represents the effect, via (52), on the production of the non-traded good resulting in a shift in the production possibility frontier for traded goods. Clearly, this shift can result in a bias towards the production of either good. If, as in the four sentences following (52), $\hat{y}_n > 0$, then $\hat{y}_2 - \hat{y}_1 > 0$ if $(\lambda_{1n} - \lambda_{2n})/|\lambda_t| > 0$. Now $|\lambda_t|$ is positive if and only if industry 2 is factor 2 intensive relative to industry 1, while $\lambda_{1n} - \lambda_{2n} > 0$ means that the non-traded good uses a greater percentage of factor 1 than factor 2. Thus, as y_n increases it raises the ratio of factor 2 to factor 1 available for the traded goods industries causing output of good 2 (intensive in factor 2) to rise in accordance with Rybczynski's theorem.

8.5. Endogenous factor supplies

There are several ways of handling endogenous factor supplies when the source of endogeneity is through the utility-maximizing decisions of consumers. The first is to treat them formally the same as non-traded goods. In this case the "GNP function" would be expressed as $G(p, w_e, v_f)$, where w_e is the price vector for endogenous factors and v_f is the endowment of fixed factors. Then, by Hotelling's lemma the derivative of G with respect to w_e would yield the negative of the production sector's demand function for endogenous factors. On the consumption side the demands for goods and the supplies of endogenous factors would be written as functions of p, w_e and G. The vector w_e would then be determined by the market-clearing condition for the endogenous factors. This is similar to the treatment of non-traded goods, and emphasizes the formal equivalence between these commodity types. The disadvantage of this approach is that G no longer represents GNP but the return to fixed factors, and it makes the interpretation of many results awkward. Conversely, non-traded goods could be treated using the concepts of conditional demand and reservation price functions, as is done below for endogenously supplied factors.

An alternative formulation which minimizes the deviation from previous models is to maintain the GNP function $G(p, v)$, where $v = (v_e, v_f)$, and to have the consumption sector maximize a utility function $u(z, v_e)$ subject to $pz - w_e v_e \leqslant w_f v_f \equiv m_f$ and $z \geqslant 0$, $0 \leqslant v_e \leqslant \overline{v}_e$. Here utility depends upon the supply of endogenous factors, v_e, which can be no greater than some fixed vector $\overline{v}_e$, and m_f is fixed income (income of fixed factors). If w_e is treated as given, the supply function for v_e is generated. The consumption sector solves its utility-maximization problem by first minimizing $pz - w_e v_e$ for a given utility level μ and then finding the utility level for which this minimum expenditure equals fixed income, m_f, since the utility function is assumed to be weakly increasing in z and $-v_e$. Consider the minimization of $pz - w_e v_e$ sequentially, minimizing with respect to z first, for a given v_e as well as μ. This yields the *conditional* expenditure function:

$$E(p, \mu, v_e) \equiv \min_{z} \{pz: u(z, v_e) \geqslant \mu, \ z \geqslant 0\}. \tag{55}$$

The maximum level of utility attainable, given v_e, is derived by setting $E(p, \mu, v_e) = w_e v_e + w_f v_f = m$ and solving for μ. This yields the conditional indirect utility function $V(p, m, v_e)$. It is noted that the conditional expenditure function has all the usual properties of an expenditure function with respect to μ (increasing) and p (non-decreasing, linearly homogenous and concave), and that it is non-decreasing and convex in v_e.[15] Hence, we have that $E_e(p, \mu, v_e) \geqslant 0$ and $E_{ee}(p, \mu, v_e)$ is positive semi-definite.

The second stage of the utility maximization problem is to choose v_e. It is evident that $V(p, m; v_e)$ will be maximized if and only if $E(p, \mu, v_e) - w_e v_e$ is minimized with respect to v_e. The Kuhn–Tucker condition for the minimization of $E(p, \mu; v_e) - w_e v_e$ subject to $v_e \geqslant 0$, assuming differentiability, is

$$E_e(p, \mu, v_e) - w_e \geqslant 0 \leqslant v_e, \tag{56}$$

it being assumed that the constraint $v_e \leqslant \bar{v}_e$ is never binding. The vector of derivatives $w_e^* \equiv E_e(p, \mu, v_e) \equiv \partial E(p, \mu, v_e)/\partial v_e$ may be interpreted as the *reservation wage* vector.[16] If, for some factor, the reservation wage exceeds the market wage, then (56) indicates that the supply of that factor will be zero. If the supply of a factor is positive, then the market and reservation wages are equal.

The reservation wage may be expressed in terms of (p, m, v_e) by substituting $\mu = V(p, m; v_e)$ into $E_e(p, \mu, v_e)$ to get

$$\phi_e(p, m, v_e) \equiv E_e(p, V(p, m, v_e), v_e). \tag{57}$$

Since $m = G(p, v_e, v_f)$, an alternative expression is

$$h_e(p, v_e, v_f) \equiv \phi_e(p, G(p, v), v_e) \equiv E_e(p, V(p, G(p, v), v_e), v_e), \tag{58}$$

where only the exogenous variables appear as arguments. The conditional demand functions for goods are $\phi_p(p, m, v_e) \equiv E_p(p, V(p, m, v_e), v_e)$.

The model is completed by noting that the production sector chooses $v_e \geqslant 0$ to maximize $G(p, v_e, v_f) - w_f v_f$, yielding the Kuhn–Tucker condition

$$G_e(p, v_e, v_f) - w_e \leqslant 0 \leqslant v_e, \tag{59}$$

where $G_e \equiv \partial G(p, v_e, v_f)/\partial v_e$ is interpreted as the shadow price vector. It is easy to show that (56) and (59) imply

$$S_e(p, \mu, v_e, v_f) \equiv G_e(p, v_e, v_f) - E_e(p, \mu, v_e) \leqslant 0 \leqslant v_e, \tag{60}$$

---

[15] The proof of the convexity of $E(p, \mu, v_e)$ in v_e is as follows. Let z^i be the solution for z in the problem

$$E(p, \mu, v_e^i) \equiv \min_z \{pz: u(z, v_e^i) \geqslant \mu\}, \quad \text{for } i = 0, 1,$$

and define $v_e^\lambda \equiv \lambda v_e^{0'} + (1 - \lambda) v_e^1$ and $z^\lambda \equiv \lambda z^0 + (1 - \lambda) z^1$. Then $u(z^\lambda, v_e^\lambda) \geqslant \mu$ due to the quasi-concavity of the utility function. Hence, z^λ is feasible when v_e^λ is the endowment vector. Thus,

$$E(p, \mu, v_e^\lambda) \leqslant pz^\lambda = \lambda pz^0 + (1 - \lambda) pz^1$$
$$= \lambda E(p, \mu, v_e^0) + (1 - \lambda) E(p, \mu, v_e^1),$$

which shows that $E(p, \mu, v_e)$ is convex in v_e.

[16] According to this definition w_e^* is the vector of factor prices which would induce the consumer to supply v_e of the endogenous factors. Sometimes in the labour supply literature the term "reservation wage" refers to the minimum wage which would induce an individual to supply a positive amount of labour. See, for example, Heckman (1974). The present definition includes this as a special case.

where $S(p, \mu, v_e, v_f) \equiv G(p, v_e, v_f) - E(p, \mu; v_e)$ and in which w_e has been eliminated. Condition (60) represents the market equilibrium condition for endogenous factor supplies in terms of reservation and shadow price functions.[17] The equilibrium factor price vector is any vector w_e satisfying $G_e \leqslant w_e \leqslant E_e$.

8.5.1. *Illustration*

The preceding model is illustrated in fig. 8.3 for the case of one endogenous factor. The downward-sloping curve is the shadow wage rate $G_e(p, v_e, v_f)$ expressed as a function of v_e. It is downward-sloping or constant since G is concave in en-

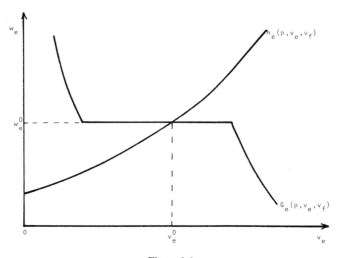

Figure 8.3

dowments. The upward-sloping curve is the reservation wage rate $h_e(p, v_e, v_f)$ $\equiv E_e(p, V(p, m, v_e), v_e) \equiv \phi_e(p, m, v_e)$, where $m = G(p, v_e, v_f)$. Equilibrium is established at (w_e^0, v_e^0), where the shadow and reservation wages are equal.

The reservation wage function has a slope given by

$$dw_e = h_{ee} dv_e = [E_{e\mu}(V_e + V_m G_e) + E_{ee}] dv_e = E_{ee} dv_e, \qquad (61)$$

---

[17] See the problem set for a derivation of (60) obtained by directly maximizing $V(p, m, v_e)$, where $m = G(p, v_e, v_f)$.

since $V_e + V_m G_e = 0$. This result is obtained by differentiating the equation $E(p, \mu, v_e) = G(p, v_e, v_f)$ with respect to μ and v_e and observing that (60) holds with equality when $v_e > 0$. Eq. (61) indicates that the reservation wage is an upward-sloping function of v_e if and only if $E_{ee} > 0$. E_{ee} is the matrix of second derivatives of the expenditure function with respect to v_e and is positive semi-definite since E is convex in v. Hence, in the case of one endogenous factor $E_{ee} \geq 0$, so that h_e is a non-decreasing function of v_e in the neighbourhood of the equilibrium.

8.5.2. Alternative formulation in terms of S

The model may be conveniently rewritten in terms of the function $S(p, \mu, v_e, v_f)$ as

(a) $\quad S(p, \mu, v_e, v_f) = 0$,

(b) $\quad S_e(p, \mu, v_e, v_f) = 0$. $\hfill$ (62)

Condition (62,b) may be solved for $v_e = v(p, \mu, v_f)$ which can then be substituted into (62,a) to obtain:

$$\tilde{S}(p, \mu, v_e) \equiv S(p, \mu, v(p, \mu, v_f), v_f) \hfill (63)$$

as a reduced form net revenue function, analogous to the function $\acute{S}$ obtained in the case of non-traded goods. The equilibrium condition reduces to $\tilde{S}(p, \mu, v_f) = 0$, which yields the solution for utility as a function of (p, v_f), namely the indirect trade utility function.

8.6. Analysis of the endogenous factor supply model

In this section the endogenous supply model is briefly analysed. The discussion will be fairly brief since, as pointed out above, the endogenous factor supplies can be treated formally the same as non-traded goods, which have been discussed in detail above. The general structure is emphasized but a detailed treatment is left to the interested reader.

8.6.1. Factor price equalization

First, consider the question of factor price equalization. If there are at least N goods produced then the cost equations (25) determine all factor prices. This determines a diversification cone $K(p, w)$ of endowments for which the factor market can clear. Also determined is the supply of endogenous factors, and this resulting supply vector for all factors must be in the cone $K(p, w)$ if w is to be an equilibrium price vector. If two nations have the same technology and produce the same $M \geqslant N$ goods in equilibrium, then they will have the same cone $K(p, w)$. If, in addition, their endowment vectors are in the same cone, the two nations will have the same w vector. For this to occur they will require "similar" supply functions for the endogenous factors. For example, in fig. 8.3 the diversification cone corresponds to the flat portion of G_e. If two nations have the same technology, G_e applies to each and they will have the same price for the endogenous factors if their supply curves cross G_e on its flat portion.

8.6.2. Commodity outputs and prices

Secondly, consider the response of outputs to product prices. The output functions are $y = G_p(p, v_e, v_f)$, hence

$$dy = G_{pp} \, dp + G_{pe} \, dv_e. \tag{64}$$

Thus, there is the usual effect given by G_{pp}, and the indirect effect caused by a change in v_e due to a change in p. The latter effect is obtained by differentiating the market equilibrium condition $E_e(p, V(p, m, v_e), v_e) = G_e(p, v_e, v_f)$ with respect to v_e and p and solving for

$$dv_e = (G_{ee} - E_{ee})^{-1} \left[(E_{ep} - G_{ep}) + \phi_{em} \, x \right] dp, \tag{65}$$

where $\phi_{em} \equiv \partial \phi_e / \partial m = E_{e\mu}/E_\mu$ is the response of the reservation wage to an increase in m. Substitution of (65) into (64) yields:

$$dy = \left[G_{pp} - G_{pe} \, S_{ee}^{-1} \, G_{ep} + G_{pe} \, S_{ee}^{-1} \, (E_{ep} + \phi_{em} \, x) \right] dp. \tag{66}$$

The first term, G_{pp}, is a positive semi-definite matrix. The second term is also positive semi-definite since $-S_{ee}$ is positive definite. The third term is not positive semi-definite and may cause perverse output responses.

To illustrate this possibility let there be two products and two factors, one of which has an endogenous supply, and let p_2 increase. Then (64) indicates that the normal response, with v_e fixed, is for y_2 to rise and y_1 to fall. The vector G_{pe} indicates the effect of a change in v_e upon the output vector G_p. Thus, if product 2 is intensive in its use of v_e then the second element of G_{pe} is positive and the first is negative. If $dv_e > 0$, then clearly y_2 rises because p_2 has risen and because v_e has increased. On the other hand, if $dv_e < 0$, then the two effects are of opposite sign and y_2 could fall in response to an increase in p_2. Fig. 8.4 illustrates this case. Initially, the equilibrium is at $(y_1^0, y_2^0, v_e^0) = a^0$. If p_2 increases and v_2 were to be fixed at v_e^0, production would move along the conditional production frontier from a^0 to a^2. If v_e falls to v_e^1, then production moves to the new conditional production frontier at a^1, where the shift is sufficiently strong to make $y_2^1 < y_2^0$.

When will v_e actually fall in response to an increase in p_2? Since $G_{ee} - E_{ee} < 0$, a sufficient condition for v_e to fall is that the second element of each of the vectors in the sum in square brackets in (65) be positive. If $E_{ep_2} > 0$, then an increase in the (compensated) supply of the endogenous factor would cause the demand for good 2 to increase (e.g. an increase in labour supply results in an increased demand for beer). If $G_{ep_2} < 0$, then good 2 is not intensive in its use of the endogenous factor (e.g. beer is capital intensive). Finally, the last term is posi-

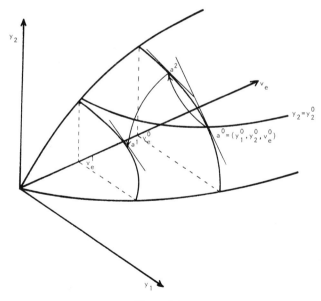

Figure 8.4

tive if $x_2 > 0$ (good 2 is exported) and $\phi_{em} > 0$ meaning that an increase in non-labour income raises the reservation wage. In these circumstances an increase in p_2 causes the shadow wage to fall and the reservation wage to rise, requiring a reduction in v_e to re-establish equality.

The effect of a product price change upon net exports is obtained by differentiating $x = \tilde{S}_p(p, \mu, v_f)$ and the balance of trade condition $\tilde{S}(p, \mu, v_f) = 0$ with respect to p to obtain:

$$dx = (\tilde{S}_{pp} - \tilde{\phi}_m x)\, dp, \tag{67}$$

where

(a) $\quad \tilde{S}_{pp} = S_{pp} - S_{pe} S_{ee}^{-1} S_{ep}$,

(b) $\quad \tilde{\phi}_m \equiv \tilde{S}_{p\mu}/\tilde{S}_\mu = \phi_{pm} - S_{pe} S_{ee}^{-1} \phi_{em}$. $\qquad (68)$

It is easy to prove that $\tilde{S}_{pp}$ is positive semi-definite since S_{pp} and $-S_{ee} = E_{ee} - G_{ee}$ are positive semi-definite. The "reduced form" income effect, $\tilde{\phi}_m$, which takes account of changes in the supply of endogenous factors, is a combination of the conditional income effect on demand, ϕ_{pm}, and the income effect on the reservation wage, ϕ_{em}. These will be positive for normal goods and factors, but there is no presumption that $\tilde{\phi}_m$ will be positive. Accordingly, some "perverse" outcomes (i.e. outcomes that do not occur in a model with only fixed factors) are possible. For example, if the price of an imported good i increases, the level of imports of i will decline in a model without endogenous factors, as shown in Chapter 6. A necessary (but not sufficient) condition for imports of i to rise $(dx_i/dp_i = \tilde{S}_{ii} - \tilde{\phi}_{im} x_i < 0)$ in the present model is that $\tilde{\phi}_{im}$ be negative. If there is just one endogenous factor $S_{ee} > 0$, and so a necessary condition for $\tilde{\phi}_{im} < 0$ is $S_{ie} = G_{ie} - E_{ie} > 0$. In general S_{ie} can be of either sign.

More precise results may be obtained by assuming just one endogenous factor and by assuming that the utility function takes the separable form $u(z, v_e) \equiv \bar{u}(\hat{u}(z), v_e)$. In this case the expenditure function has the structure $E(p, \mu, v_e) \equiv \epsilon(p, \sigma(v_e, \mu))$, where $\sigma(v_e, \mu) \equiv \max_\xi \{\xi: \bar{u}(\xi, v_e) \geq \mu\}$, the proof of which is the subject of one of the problems. The demand functions for goods may be expressed as

$$\phi_p(p, m) \equiv \epsilon_p(p, v(p, m)), \tag{69}$$

where $v(p, m)$ is the solution to $\epsilon(p, \sigma) = m$ for σ, and is the indirect utility function corresponding to $\hat{u}(z)$. It is easy to verify that $E_{pe} = \epsilon_{p\sigma} \sigma_e = \sigma_e \epsilon_\sigma(\epsilon_{p\sigma}/\epsilon_\sigma)$

$= E_e \, \phi_{pm}$. This relationship may be used to rewrite the second term, $S_{pe} = G_{pe} - E_{pe}$, in a more structured form.

For example, when there is just one endogenous factor the ith element of S_{pe} is

$$S_{ie} = G_{ie} - E_{ie} = \frac{E_e}{p_i} \left[\frac{G_{ie} \, p_i}{G_e} - \phi_{im} \, p_i \right] = \frac{E_e}{p_i} \left[\theta^{ie} - c_i \right], \tag{70}$$

where $c_i \equiv \phi_{im} \, p_i$ is the marginal propensity to consume good i out of income m, the equality between G_e and E_e has been used, and where $\theta^{ie} \equiv G_{ie} \, p_i / g_e = \partial \ln w_e / \partial \ln p_i$ is the elasticity of the shadow price of factor e with respect to the price of product i. The latter is related to the concept of relative factor intensities, as explained in Chapters 4 and 5.

Consider the special case where there are two products and two factors, one of which is endogenous, and all goods are normal. Then either $\theta^{ie} \geqslant 1$ or $\theta^{ie} \leqslant 0$, while $0 \leqslant c_i \leqslant 1$. The necessary condition for a perverse effect of a change in p_i upon imports of i is therefore that $\theta^{ie} > c_i$. If industry i is intensive in its use of the endogenous factor ($\theta^{ie} > 1$), then this condition is satisfied. If, on the other hand, industry i is not intensive in its use of the endogenous factor, then $\theta^{ie} \leqslant 0 \leqslant c_i$ and the perverse case cannot possibly occur.

An alternative way of looking at the question of perversity is to rewrite (67), using (65), as

$$\begin{aligned} dx &= [S_{pp} - \phi_{pm} \, x] \, dp + S_{pe} \, dv_e \\ &= [S_{pp} - \phi_{pm} \, x] \, dp - S_{pe} \, S_{ee}^{-1} \, [S_{ep} - \phi_{em} \, x] \, dp. \end{aligned} \tag{71}$$

If p_i increases, the direct effect given by the first bracketed term is for imports of i to fall. Thus, to get a perverse effect it is necessary that $S_{ie} \, dv_e < 0$. Using the special case of the previous paragraph, if i is e intensive, then $S_{ie} > 0$ and it is necessary for the supply of the endogenous factor to fall for a perverse effect on imports. Conversely, if industry i is intensive in the other factor, $S_{ie} < 0$ and it is necessary for the supply of the endogenous factor to rise.

8.6.3. Factor and product prices

Now, consider the effect of a change in product prices upon factor prices. Since $w = G_v(p, v_e, v_f)$ it follows that

$$dw = G_{vp} \, dp + G_{ve} \, dv_e, \tag{72}$$

where dv_e is given by (65). Again, the first term represents the usual response discussed in detail in Chapters 4 and 5. The second term is the effect of the consequent change in the supply of endogenous factors. Suppose factor e is intensively used in industry i. Then the usual response is for w_e to rise when p_i rises. The second term will be $G_{ee} \, dv_e$ and, since $G_{ee} \leqslant 0$, it is necessary that $dv_e > 0$ for w_e to fall when p_i rises. In this case the increase in p_i causes w_e to rise (usual effect) but also causes v_e to rise which reduces the shadow price of the endogenous factor. Possibly the second (indirect) effect might outweigh the direct effect causing w_e to fall.

If v is in the interior of the diversification cone, then $G_{ve} = 0$ and so the usual effect of a change in p occurs. In this case the effect on w can be obtained from the profit-maximization (cost = price) conditions alone.

8.6.4. Symmetry

Finally, consider the symmetry between the effects of changes in endowments upon commodity outputs and of changes in commodity prices upon factor rewards. The reduced form solutions for v_e, w_e and y may be written as

$$
\begin{aligned}
v_e &= v_e(p, v_f), \\
w_e &= w_e(p, v_f) \equiv G_e(p, v_e(p, v_f), v_f), \\
w_f &= w_f(p, v_f) \equiv G_f(p, v_e(p, v_f), v_f), \\
y &= y(p, v_f) \equiv G_p(p, v_e(p, v_f), v_f).
\end{aligned}
\tag{73}
$$

The first equation is the solution to the equilibrium condition

$$
E_e(p, V(p, G(p, v_e, v_f), v_e), v_e) = G_e(p, v_e, v_f) \quad \text{for } v_e.
$$

The remaining equations follow from the properties of the GNP function $G(p, v_e, v_f)$. Differentiation of (73) yields:

$$
\begin{aligned}
w_{ep} &= G_{ep} + G_{ee} \, v_{ep}, \\
w_{fp} &= G_{fp} + G_{fe} \, v_{ep}, \\
y_p &= G_{pp} + G_{pe} \, v_{ep},
\end{aligned}
\tag{74}
$$

and

$$w_{ef} = G_{ef} + G_{ee} \, v_{ef},$$

$$w_{ff} = G_{ff} + G_{fe} \, v_{ef}, \qquad (75)$$

$$y_f = G_{pf} + G_{pe} \, v_{ef},$$

where v_{ep} is given by (65) and v_{ef} (to be calculated in the problem set) has a similar structure. Both v_{ep} and v_{ef} depend upon preferences and contain income effects which are asymmetric.

The symmetry between the effects of factor endowments on commodity outputs and of commodity prices on factor prices in the standard model with no endogenous factors was a direct consequence of the symmetry of the matrix of second-order partial derivatives of the GNP function. In the present notation these symmetry conditions are $G_{pe} = G_{ep}$ and $G_{pf} = G_{fp}$. In addition, G_{pp}, G_{ee} and G_{ff} are symmetric matrices. In the context of the present model, does symmetry in the sense of $w_{fp} = y_f$ hold? The difference between these matrices is

$$w_{fp} - y_f = G_{fe} \, v_{ep} - G_{pe} \, v_{ef} \neq 0, \qquad (76)$$

which is non-zero in general, indicating that symmetry does not hold.

Moreover, the equality of the effect of a unit change in the endowment of factor i upon the price of factor k, and the effect of a unit change in the endowment of factor k upon the price of factor i in the standard model no longer holds when endogenous factors exist. This is because the expression for w_{ff} in (75) contains the matrix v_{ef} which is not symmetric.

8.7. Concluding comments

In this chapter attention has focused on the way by which non-traded goods and endogenous factor supplies may be modelled, and upon the effect of their inclusion in some comparative static results obtained in previous chapters. The important feature of their inclusion is that the convenient separation of production sector decisions from those of the consumption sector no longer occurs because the prices of non-traded goods and endogenous factors are endogenously determined. Not unexpectedly, therefore, the results of previous chapters concerning the effect of exogenous prices and endowments upon commodity outputs and factor prices need serious modification. Many results which were unambiguous now become ambiguous, with the possibility of "perverse" results.

In subsequent chapters the role of non-traded goods and endogenous factors will be further discussed.

8.8. Notes on the literature

Non-traded goods have only recently begun to receive the attention that they deserve, given their importance in most economies. Komiya (1967) provides a detailed treatment of a model containing two traded goods, one non-traded good and two primary factors. Further analysis, especially of the basic theorems arising from the Heckscher–Ohlin model, was carried out by Ethier (1971, 1972), the latter work forming the basis of the current treatment. McKenzie (1955) dealt with non-traded goods in his seminal paper on factor price equalization. Ethier's work on the Rybczynski theorem was further developed by Flam (1979) who gave conditions for the full magnification effect to hold. Jones (1974) constructs a simple model in which there is one non-traded good, the exported good is not consumed and the imported good is not produced at home. The model's simplicity permits the interconnectedness of the domestic and foreign markets to be high-lighted, and is considered in the problem set. A survey of the pre-1970 literature is provided by McDougall (1970).

The effect of endogenous factor supplies upon international trade has received less attention. The primary treatment is Kemp and Jones (1962). The present treatment uses the conditional expenditure function and the concepts of reservation and shadow wages. The conditional demand functions and reservation wage functions have properties similar to ordinary demand functions, including Slutsky-type decompositions of price and quantity effects, which have been used in this chapter. For formal treatments of conditional expenditure and demand functions see, for example, Pollak (1969) and Neary and Roberts (1980). Some empirical evidence has been used by Martin and Neary (1980) to suggest that perverse output effects are unlikely in practice.

Problems

1. Consider a model with two traded and one non-traded good, and two factors of production. Suppose that the optimal factor ratio for non-traded goods exceeds those for traded goods, and that the latter exhibit a factor intensity reversal.
   (a) Redraw fig. 8.2 for this situation.
   (b) Indicate the sets $K^i, J^i, G^i, K_t^i, G_t^i, \ i = 1, 2$.
   (c) Is int $(G^1 \cap G^2) = \varnothing$ in your figure? If not, depict a case where this is so. If so, depict a case where it is not so.
   (d) In each figure indicate the possibilities for equalization of domestic prices.

2. Prove that $K_t^i \cap K_t^j$ has an empty interior for $j \neq i$.

3. (a) Demonstrate that $\lambda_{ij}\alpha_i = \theta_{ij}\beta_j$, where α_i is the income share of factor i and β_j is the income share of product j.

   (b) Hence, show that $\delta_{ii} = 1 - (\Sigma_j \lambda_{ij}\gamma_j)\alpha_i = 1 - \Sigma_j \theta_{ij}c_j$, where the sums are over non-traded goods only (i.e. prove (39)).

   (c) Show that $\beta_j = c_j/\gamma_j \geqslant c_j$ for non-traded goods and hence that $\delta_{ii} \geqslant 0$ (strict inequality if i is used by the traded goods sector).

   (d) Show that $|\lambda_t|$ and $(\theta_{22} - \theta_{21})$ have the same sign if there are two traded goods, one non-traded good and two factors.

4. Consider the effect of endowment changes on outputs in a model with two traded goods, one non-traded good and two factors.

   (a) Derive the subset of percentage changes in $(\hat{v}_1, \hat{v}_2)$ such that $\hat{y}_2 - \hat{y}_1$ has the sign of $\hat{v}_2 - \hat{v}_1$, when industry 2 is factor 2 intensive relative to industry 1.

   (b) Show that if $\hat{v}_2 > \hat{y}_n > \hat{v}_1$, then $\hat{y}_2 > \hat{v}_2 > \hat{v}_1 > \hat{y}_1$ when industry 2 is factor 2 intensive relative to industry 1.

5. Consider a model in which there are two factors, one non-traded good, an export good which is not consumed and an import good which is not produced at home.

   (a) Derive an expression for the effect of a change in the terms of trade (normalize the import price) upon the price of non-traded goods. What can be said about the relative price of non-traded goods to import and export prices?

   (b) If the price of the export good increases, what happens to exports and imports.

   (c) What effect will an increase in the price of imports have upon the factor prices?

   (d) Upon the output of the exported good?

6. Suppose that only non-traded goods are consumed (this is reasonable if it is believed that all goods must pass through the distribution sector — part of the production sector — to get to consumers).

   (a) Write down the equilibrium conditions in terms of the expenditure, $E(p_n, \mu)$, and GNP functions, $G(p_t, p_n, v)$.

   (b) Show that $\hat{\phi}_{im}$ is positive if $G_{in} > 0$ when there is just one non-traded good.

   (c) Show that the balance of trade condition can be written as $p_t G_t = 0$ or, equivalently, as $p_n G_n = G$.

   (d) For the case of one non-traded good draw G and G_n as functions of p_n and depict the condition $p_n G_n = G$.

   (e) In this case show that a balance of trade implies equilibrium for the non-traded good, and vice versa.

7. Derive condition (56) by maximizing $V(p, G(p, v_e, v_f), f_e)$ with respect to v_e and using the relationship between V and E.
8. (a) Use the equilibrium condition $E_{e'}(p, V(p, G(p, v_e, v_f), v_e), v_e) = G_e(p, v_e, v_f)$ to obtain the effect of a change in v_f upon v_e, as $-S_{ee}^{-1}[G_{ef} - \phi_{em}G_f]$. (This is v_{ef} in (75) and (76).)
   (b) Hence, obtain the effect upon the output vector.
   (c) Describe your result.
   (d) Can you obtain some definite results for the case of two products and two factors, one being endogenous?
9. Let the utility function take the separable form $u(z, v_e) = \bar{u}(\hat{u}(z), v_e)$.
   (a) Show that the conditional expenditure function has the form $E(p, \mu, v_e) = \epsilon(p, \sigma(v_e \mu))$, where $\sigma(v_e, \mu) \equiv \max_\xi \{\xi: \bar{u}(\xi, v_e) \geqslant \mu\}$.
   (b) Derive the demand functions for goods as in (69).
   (c) Why do they have this structure?
10. Let $E(p, \mu, v_e)$ be the conditional expenditure function with corresponding conditional indirect utility function $V(p, m, v_e)$, and conditional demand and reservation price functions $\phi_p(p, m, v_e) \equiv E_p(p, V(p, m, v_e), v_e)$ and $\phi_e(p, m, v_e) \equiv E_e(p, V(p, m, v_e), v_e)$.
    (a) Show that $\phi_{pp} = E_{pp} - \phi_{pm}\phi_p$, $\phi_{pe} = E_{pe} - \phi_{pm}\phi_e$, $\phi_{ep} = E_{ep} - \phi_{em}\phi_p$ and $\phi_{ee} = E_{ee} - \phi_{em}\phi_e$.
    (b) The expressions in (a) are Slutsky-type relationships. Interpret them.
11. If the prices of all traded goods move in strict proportion (say fixed, for simplicity) all traded goods can be aggregated into a Hicksian composite good. Show that the open economy equilibrium is formally the same as a closed economy equilibrium, and depict it on a diagram.

References

Ethier, W. (1971) "The two sector neoclassical production model: A geometic note and an extension to nontraded goods", *Australian Economic Papers* 10-17, December, 188–195.
Ethier, W. (1972) "Nontraded goods and the Heckscher–Ohlin model", *International Economic Review* 13-1, February, 132–147.
Flam, H. (1979) "The Rybczynski theorem in a model with non-traded goods and indecomposable inter-industry flows", *International Economic Review* 20-3, October, 661–670.
Heckman, J.J. (1974) "Shadow prices, market wages and labor supply", *Econometrica* 42, July, 679–694.
Jones, R.W. (1974) "Trade with non-traded goods: The anatomy of interconnected markets", *Economica* 41-162, May, 121–138.
Kemp, M.C. and R.W. Jones (1962) "Variable labour supply and the theory of international trade", *Journal of Political Economy* 70-1, February, 30–36.
Komiya, R. (1967) "Nontraded goods and the pure theory of international trade", *International Economic Review* 8-2, June, 132–152.

Martin, J.P. and J.P. Neary (1980) "Variable labour supply and the pure theory of international trade", *Journal of International Economics* 10, 549–559.

McDougall, I.A. (1970) "Nontraded commodities and the pure theory of international trade", in: I.A. McDougall and R.H. Snape (eds.), *Studies in International Economics* (Amsterdam: North-Holland Publishing Company), ch. 10.

McKenzie, L.W. (1955) "Equality of factor prices in world trade", *Econometrica* 23-3, July, 239–257.

Neary, J.P. and K.S.W. Roberts (1980) "The theory of household behaviour under rationing", *European Economic Review* 13, 25–42.

Pollak, R.A. (1969) "Conditional demand functions and consumption theory", *Quarterly Journal of Economics* 83, 60–78.

Takayama, A. (1974) *Mathematical Economics* (New York: Holt Rinehart and Winston).

CHAPTER 9

THE WELFARE EFFECTS OF INTERNATIONAL TRADE

9.1. Introduction

The previous chapters have demonstrated the conditions under which nations will trade with each other and, therefore, have been concerned with the positive aspects of international trade. Attention is now turned to some normative questions regarding international trade. In particular, we wish to discuss whether, and if so, in what sense, it is possible to state (a) that free trade is better than no trade, and (b) that some trade (restricted by quotas or tariffs) is better than no trade.

These are very interesting and important questions from both theoretical and policy points of view. From a theoretical point of view, the answers must deal with the problem of interpersonal comparisons of individual welfare since it is almost always the case that any policy change, such as a move from no trade to free trade, causes some individuals to benefit and others to lose in terms of individual welfare. Unless there exist policy instruments which are used to redistribute real incomes such that some individuals benefit and no individual loses as a consequence of the policy change, it is not possible to state that the policy represents a gain without the explicit use of a social welfare function.

These questions are also of vital importance for practical economic policy-making. The existence of international organizations such as the General Agreement on Tariffs and Trade (GATT), whose primary aim is to obtain, through a series of multilateral negotiations, a world-wide reduction in tariffs and other impediments to free international trade, is based upon the belief that free trade is optimal and that a movement towards free trade is welfare improving.

Additional questions are also asked. One is the question of whether free trade is optimal for a nation. It will be shown that free trade is sub-optimal if the nation's trade is large enough to influence world prices. This is true whether the concept of optimality is Pareto optimality or that of maximizing a social welfare function. Another question addressed is whether a greater price divergence from autarky prices will raise welfare.

Before proceeding with the analysis of the welfare aspects of international trade, the model developed in the previous chapters and used here is briefly reviewed. The world consists of two nations, the home nation and the foreign nation which is also to be interpreted as "the rest of the world". Production in the home nation occurs in the production possibility set $Y(v)$ which satisfies conditions (5.26) in Chapter 5. The production vector is chosen to maximize the value of net output thus yielding the GNP function $G(p, v)$ which is dual to $Y(v)$ and satisfies conditions (5.27) of Chapter 5. The production sector is very general allowing for joint production and intermediate products. The GNP is allocated to L individual consumers according to the functions $m^{\ell}(p, v, \alpha)$. Consumption vectors are chosen by each individual to maximize his utility function $u^{\ell}(z^{\ell})$ $\geqslant 0$ subject to the budget constraint $pz^{\ell} \leqslant m^{\ell}(p, v, \alpha)$ and $z^{\ell} \geqslant 0$.[1] This yields the indirect utility function $V^{\ell}(p, m^{\ell})$ which may be obtained by solving for utility in the equation $E^{\ell}(p, \mu^{\ell}) = m^{\ell}$, where $E^{\ell}(p, \mu^{\ell})$ is the expenditure function. The utility functions are assumed to satisfy conditions (2.3) of Chapter 2. The dual expenditure functions therefore satisfy conditions (2.7) of Chapter 2 while the indirect utility functions satisfy conditions (2.39). The aggregate expenditure function is $E(p, \mu)$, where $\mu = (\mu^{1}, ..., \mu^{L})$ and may be defined as the sum of individual expenditure functions or, equivalently, as the minimum expenditure on the Scitovsky set $Z(\mu)$. The preceding account defines the maintained assumptions of the model.[2]

9.2. The gains from free trade

In evaluating two different situations, such as autarky and free trade, a basis of comparison must be chosen. There are generally two options. The first is to avoid interpersonal comparisons of utility in which case an unambiguous (Pareto) improvement in welfare occurs only when no individual becomes worse off and at least one has an increase in utility. The second is to assume the existence of a social welfare function which allows a direct comparison of different situations in terms of social welfare. This social welfare function can, in general, have as arguments all sorts of economic variables such as the consumption vectors for

---

[1] For the convenience of the discussion below it is assumed that utility functions have been normalized to be non-negative for all non-negative consumption vectors.

[2] The following analysis treats all goods as tradeable and all factors as fixed, but can be modified without much diffculty if these assumptions are relaxed.

individuals, production vectors, price vectors and so forth. A special type of social welfare function which has received considerable attention is the "individual-istic" function where the arguments of the social welfare function are the utility levels for the individuals that make up the society.

In this section the concept of an improvement in welfare of society in the sense of Pareto is used to analyse the gains from trade as viewed by the con-sumers within a single nation. It is shown that if lump-sum transfers of income are possible, then free international trade, together with appropriate transfers, allows every individual to be no worse off, and some to possibly gain, compared with autarky.

The concepts of an allocation, a Pareto improvement in welfare, and Pareto optimality, are now introduced formally.

An *allocation relative to C* is a matrix of individual consumption vectors $Z \equiv (z^1, ..., z^L)$ such that $Z1 = \Sigma_{\ell=1}^{L} z^{\ell} \in C$.[3] (1)

Pareto improvement in welfare. Consider two allocations relative to C, namely $\hat{Z}$ and $\overline{Z}$. The allocation $\hat{Z}$ is a Pareto improvement in welfare over $\overline{Z}$ if $u^{\ell}(\hat{z}^{\ell}) \geqslant u^{\ell}(\overline{z}^{\ell})$ for all ℓ with strict inequali-ty for at least one ℓ. $\hat{Z}$ is said to be Pareto superior to $\overline{Z}$. If the weak inequality holds, $\hat{Z}$ is preferred (superior) or indifferent to $\overline{Z}$. (2)

Pareto optimality. If $\hat{Z}$ is an allocation relative to C and there does not exist another allocation superior to $\hat{Z}$, then $\hat{Z}$ is said to be Pareto optimal. (3)

These definitions are expressed in the consumption space on which individu-al utility functions are defined. Often we will deal directly in the utility space. Then a Pareto improvement in welfare is expressed as $\hat{\mu} \gtrless \overline{\mu}$ (where $\gtrless$ means $\geqslant$ but $\neq$) and $\hat{\mu}$ is Pareto optimal if there is no $\mu \in UP^*(C)$, the utility possibility set for C (to be defined below), such that $\mu \gtrsim \hat{\mu}$.

9.2.1. *Trade gains and the compensation principle*

Under autarky the nation chooses a production point $y^0 \in Y(v)$ which , if the autarky price vector p^0 is positive, is also the comsumption vector, $z^0 = y^0$.

---

[3] Here 1 is a column vector of ones.

The vector of utility levels obtained under autarky is $\mu^0 = (\mu^{10}, ..., \mu^{L0})$. Suppose that the price vector established as a result of trade is $p^1 \neq p^0$ and that the production vector is now y^1, the consumption vector is z^1, and the utility vector is μ^1. Our competitive model implies that

$$p^1 z^1 = G(p^1, v) \geqslant p^1 z^0. \tag{4}$$

The inequality in (4) occurs because $z^0 \in Y(v)$, and is therefore a feasible production when prices are p^1, and because $G(p^1, v)$ is the maximum revenue earned by the production sector. The equality in (4) occurs because all net revenue, $G(p^1, v)$, earned by the production sector is available for spending by the consumption sector. It will all be spent since it has been assumed that each individual's utility function is weakly increasing.

Inequality (4) is of vital importance to the demonstration of the gains from trade. It indicates that under trade at price vector p^1 the autarky consumption vector is contained in the aggregate budget set. If the economy consisted of just one individual it would be evident that he would be no worse off under trade than under autarky. Indeed, if a strict inequality held in (4) so that $p^1 z^1 > p^1 z^0$, then the individual must now be better off than under autarky. This follows since the individual can increase his consumption of all goods compared to z^0 and hence increase his level of utility.

However, when there are many individuals the problem is more difficult, since some may experience an increase in utility as a result of trade while others may experience a decrease. That this is possible is made evident by considering a simple two-product, two-factor model with two individuals, for example a capitalist who owns all the capital and a labourer. In the case of no joint production the Stolper–Samuelson theorem of Chapter 4 indicates that if the price ratio changes (due to trade) one of the factors gains and one loses in terms of real incomes and hence utility levels. The question naturally arises as to whether it is possible for the individual who gains to transfer income to the one who loses, such that both end up better off than under autarky.

Since inequality (4), as a strict inequality, shows that $p^1 z^1 = G(p^1, v) > p^1 z^0$, it is possible to redistribute $G(p^1, v)$ amongst the consumers such that each one can attain his autarky consumption vector, if p^1 is maintained. If $z^{\ell 0}$ and $z^{\ell 1}$ denote the autarky and post-trade consumption vectors for individual ℓ, then he can be allocated income $\bar{m}^\ell \equiv p^1 z^{\ell 0} + \epsilon^\ell$, where the $\epsilon^\ell > 0$ are chosen so that $\Sigma_{\ell=1}^L \epsilon^\ell = p^1 z^1 - p^1 z^0 > 0$. Since $\epsilon^\ell > 0$, $z^{\ell 0}$ is in the interior of his budget set corresponding to income $\bar{m}^\ell$ and hence his maximum attainable utility level exceeds the autarky level $\mu^{\ell 0}$. Hence, there exists a lump-sum redistribution of income accompanying free trade which will make every individual better off than under autarky. This argument showing the gains from trade is sometimes referred to as the "compensation principle".

A simple geometric demonstration of the gains from trade accompanied by a lump-sum income redistribution is provided in figure 9.1. The boundary of the Scitovsky set $Z(\mu^0)$ corresponding to the autarky utility vector μ^0 is drawn tangent to the production possibility set at y^0. Under trade the price vector p^1 is established and the aggregate budget line is tangent to the production possibility set at y^1. The important point to note is that this budget line passes through the interior of the Scitovsky set $Z(\mu^0)$. Thus, in this case there exist available aggregate consumption vectors, between A and B along the budget line, which in principle can be distributed among the individual consumers to make them all better off than under autarky. Of course, if this redistribution takes place via a redistribution of income rather than goods, it has to be shown that there is an income transfer which will increase the welfare of all individuals. The argument of the previous paragraph showed the existence of such a transfer. Several comments concerning the above argument are required.

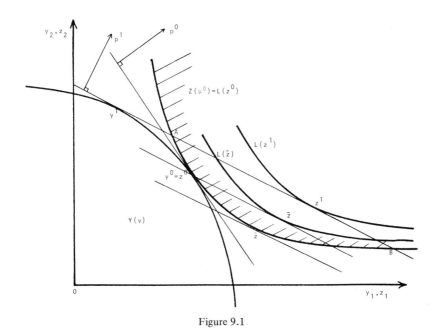

Figure 9.1

9.2.2. A necessary and sufficient condition for gains from trade

First, it has been shown that the condition $G(p^1 v) > p^1 z^0$ is sufficient for the demonstration that free trade accompanied by a lump-sum redistribution of income is Pareto superior to autarky. This condition is not necessary. The necessary and sufficient condition for trade with lump-sum redistributions to be Pareto superior to autarky is that $G(p^1, v) > E(p^1, \mu^0) \equiv \min_z \{p^1 z : z \in Z(\mu^0)\}$. That is, the revenue produced by the production sector must be greater than the minimum income necessary to attain the autarky utility vector. If this condition holds, then it is possible to redistribute $G(p^1, v)$ to enable each person to attain greater utility than under autarky. If $G(p^1, v) = E(p^1, \mu^0)$, then $G(p^1, v) - E(p^1, \mu^0) = \Sigma_{\ell=1}^L [m^\ell - E(p^1, \mu^{\ell 0})] = 0$, where $\Sigma_{\ell=1}^L m^\ell = G(p^1, v)$, so that if some individuals get incomes in excess of the minimum necessary to maintain their autarky utility levels then others must get less and hence become worse off as a result of trade. Since z^0 is an element of both $Y(v)$ and $Z(\mu^0)$ it is not possible that $G(p^1, v) < E(p^1, \mu^0)$. Thus, we have

> **Theorem.** Under the maintained assumptions of the model, a necessary and sufficient condition for trade at price vector p^1 accompanied by a lump-sum redistribution of income to be Pareto superior to autarky is that $G(p^1, v) > E(p^1, \mu^0)$.[4]   (5)

An illustration of this result in terms of utility possibility sets is provided in figure 9.2. Let

$$UP(p, v) \equiv \{\mu : E(p, \mu) \leqslant G(p, v)\} \tag{6}$$

be the utility possibility set for (p, v), which is the set of all utilities that can be obtained by redistributing income $G(p, v)$ to the utility-maximizing individuals. The set $UP(p^1, v)$ is illustrated in figure 9.2 with boundary AB which is called the utility possibility frontier. It is downward-sloping since, when all income is spent, any reallocation causes someone to suffer a reduction in his level of utility. Since $E(p, \mu^0) \leqslant G(p, v)$ for all p, it follows that $\mu^0 \in UP(p^1, v)$, where p^1 is the equilibrium free trade price vector. Indeed, if $E(p^1, \mu^0) < G(p^1, v)$, then $\mu^0 \in \text{int } UP(p^1, v)$, by the argument of the previous paragraph. Thus, it is always possible to find an income distribution to move the utility vector from μ^1 established under free trade to a point such as $\mu^3 > \mu^0$.

---

[4] Of course, this result and indeed the whole discussion ignores the possibility that there are (real input) costs associated with carrying out the redistribution of income.

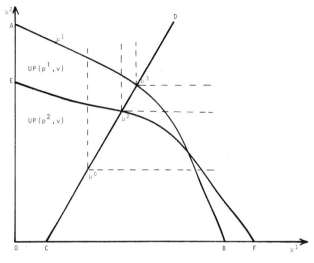

Figure 9.2

9.2.3. The case of a large nation

The second comment concerns the implicit assumption that the redistribution of income does not influence the price at which trade takes place. This assumption is not tenable unless the nation is infinitesimal relative to the rest of the world or aggregate demand is not affected by an income redistribution.[5] If this assumption is relaxed by assuming that the home nation can affect world prices, the demonstration of the superiority of free trade over autarky must take into account the price effects of the income redistribution. Let $x^*(p, v^*, \alpha^*)$ be the vector of foreign excess supply functions, where α^* is a vector of parameters determining its income distribution.[6] Then the aggregate demand vector available to the home nation is

$$\varsigma(p, v, v^*, \alpha^*) \equiv G_p(p, v) + x^*(p, v^*, \alpha^*). \tag{7}$$

The set of demand vectors available for some $p \geqslant 0$ is

$$\hat{\varsigma}(v, v^*, \alpha^*) \equiv \{z: z = \varsigma(p, v, v^*, \alpha^*), p \geqslant 0\}, \tag{8}$$

---

[5] Recall the discussion in Chapter 6 concerning the conditions for aggregate demand to be independent of the income distribution.
[6] The foreign nation may be redistributing income so as to achieve a Pareto improvement from trade.

which is Baldwin's (1952) free trade consumption frontier. Note that the set $\hat{\zeta}(v, v^*, \alpha^*)$ is never in the interior of $Y(v)$, and lies outside $Y(v)$ except when $x^*(p, v^*, \alpha^*) = 0$. To prove this, suppose on the contrary that $\hat{\zeta}(p, v, v^*, \alpha^*)$ is in the interior of $Y(v)$. Then $G(p, v) > p\hat{\zeta}(p, v, v^*, \alpha^*) = G(p, v) + px^*(p, v^*, \alpha^*) = G(p, v)$, which is a contradiction.

Figure 9.3 illustrates its relationship to $Y(v)$. As drawn, $\hat{\zeta}$ intersects the interior of $Z(\mu^0)$ between C and D, indicating that there exist prices for which the aggregate consumption vector, consistent with producer and foreign equilibrium, could be distributed to make everyone better off than under autarky. Of course, this is a necessary condition for the existence of an income redistribution which is welfare improving in the sense of Pareto. For price vector p^2 in figure 9.3 to be an equilibrium price vector, there must exist an income distribution for which z^2 is the equilibrium aggregate demand vector. For each price vector we can construct the set of aggregate demands corresponding to arbitrary distributions of the total income $G(p, v)$. This set is

$$\Phi(p, G(p, v)) \equiv \{z: z = E_p(p, \mu), E(p, \mu) = G(p, v)\}. \tag{9}$$

For p^2 it is the interval EF in figure 9.3, where the dashed lines through E and F are the envelopes of the income expansion paths of consumers, forming the

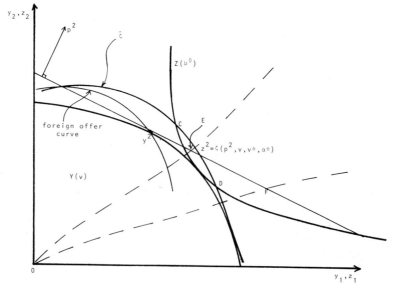

Figure 9.3

set of feasible aggregate demands when the price vector is p^2.[7] In this case p^2 is indeed an equilibrium price vector for some income distribution since EF and CD have a common point which is z^2.

Chipman and Moore (1972) have presented a formal proof of the following theorem, under certain regularity conditions.

> **Theorem**. Let there exist a closed equilibrium represented by (Z^0, p^0, y^0), where p^0 is the autarky price vector, y^0 is the production vector and $Z^0 = [z^{10}, ..., z^{L0}]$ is the allocation matrix. Then there exists a free trade equilibrium (Z^1, p^1, y^1) such that
> $$\mu^{\ell 1} \equiv u^\ell(z^{\ell 1}) \geqslant u^\ell(z^{\ell 0}) \equiv \mu^{\ell 0} \text{ for all } \ell = 1, ..., L. \tag{10}$$

This theorem establishes that, whatever the autarky distribution of income is, there is a free trade equilibrium with an accompanying income distribution under which no individual is worse off than under autarky. An outline of the argument of the proof is now presented. The proof proceeds by examining the consequences of optimally redistributing income to maximize a social welfare function $W(\mu)$ and then choosing a special welfare function to establish the conclusion of (10). For any p and total income m the social welfare maximization problem is

$$V(p, m) \equiv \max_{\ell} \left\{ W(\mu) : \mu^\ell = V^\ell(p, m^\ell), \sum_{\ell=1}^{L} m^\ell \leqslant m, (m^1, ..., m^L) \geqslant 0 \right\}, \tag{11}$$

where $V^\ell(p, m^\ell)$ is the indirect utility function for individual ℓ, and m^ℓ is the income allocated to individual ℓ. The function $V(p, m)$ is the indirect social utility function which is assumed to have all of the properties of an individual indirect utility function.[8] Consequently, there is a direct (Samuelson) social utility function $u(z)$ which is dual to $V(p, m)$ such that

---

[7] The set enclosed by the dashed lines and defined by (9) is the consumption counterpart to the diversification cone in production. If all consumers have homothetic preferences (not necessarily the same) the income expansion paths are rays through the origin and so the set of feasible aggregate demands will be a convex cone.

[8] Recall the discussion of this problem in Chapter 6. Also, recall that the indirect utility function is $V(p, m) = V(p/m, 1) \equiv V^*(p^*)$, where $p^* \equiv p/m$ for $m > 0$. The function V^* is continuous, quasi-convex and non-increasing in p^*. Clearly, the social welfare function and the individual indirect utility functions require sufficient structure to ensure that $V(p, m)$ has these properties. For example, Chipman and Moore (1972), following Samuelson (1956), Gorman (1959) and Negishi (1963), assume that the individual direct utility functions, $u^\ell(z^\ell)$, and the social welfare function, $W(\mu)$, are continuous, monotonic and concave and prove that $v(z)$ is monotonic and concave. In this case $u(z)$ is a "well behaved" utility function with a "well behaved" dual or indirect representation, $V(p, m)$.

In Chapter 6 the social utility functions were denoted by a superscript 0 (a fictional consumer), but this superscript is dropped here.

$$V(p, m) = \max\{u(z): pz \leqslant m, z \geqslant 0\} \tag{12}$$

for all $p > 0$ and $m \geqslant 0$. As explained in Chapter 6, this means that the consumption sector behaves as if it were a single consumer with utility function $u(z)$ and budget m. For any p and m the solution to (11) yields the optimal income distribution which yields individual demands $z^\ell = \phi^\ell(p, m^\ell)$ adding up to the aggregate demand vector which solves (12). Thus, if $V(p, m)$ satisfies the properties of an individual indirect utility function, a free trade equilibrium based upon (12) can be obtained by an appropriate (optimal) distribution of income.

Now let the social welfare function take the special form

$$W(\mu) \equiv \min \left\{ \frac{\mu^\ell - \mu^{\ell 0}}{c^\ell}, \ell = 1, ..., L \right\}, \tag{13}$$

where $c = (c^1, ..., c^L) > 0$. Clearly, the solution to (11) requires that $\mu^\ell = \max\{0, \mu^{\ell 0} + c^\ell W(\mu)\}$. Suppose that there is a competitive equilibrium based upon aggregate demand functions generated from (12), with optimal utility vector μ^2. Since μ^0 is a feasible utility vector for any free trade price vector, it follows that $W(\mu^2) \geqslant W(\mu^0)$. This implies that $\mu^{\ell 2} = \max\{0, \mu^{\ell 0} + c^\ell W(\mu^2)\} \geqslant \max\{0, \mu^{\ell 0} + c^\ell W(\mu^0)\} = \mu^{\ell 0}$, since $W(\mu^0) = 0$ and $\mu^0 \geqslant 0$. That is to say, the distribution of income, which is optimal for W defined by (13) and for which there is a free trade equilibrium, yields a level of utility for everyone which is at least as high as they obtained under autarky. This establishes that a nation can always redistribute income such that free trade does not harm any individual irrespective of the autarky distribution of income.

Figure 9.2 illustrates the L-shaped indifference surfaces for the social welfare function defined by (13) as the dashed lines, and the locus of solutions for μ as the path OCD. In this case the optimal income distribution accompanying free trade is assumed to yield a price vector p^2 such that μ^0 is in the interior of $UP(p^2, v)$ and hence $\mu^2 > \mu^0$ is possible.

The autarky utility vector is μ^0, while the equilibrium price vector under free trade with no optimal income redistribution is p^1 yielding utility vector μ^1. If income could be optimally redistributed without affecting the price vector, then a point such as μ^3 is attainable, as previously explained. However, the redistribution may cause the price to alter in general. The Chipman–Moore argument demonstrates that $\mu^2 > \mu^0$ can be attained by maximizing (13).

9.2.4. Potential or actual gains?

The preceding argument has shown that free trade accompanied by appropriate lump-sum income redistributions is Pareto superior to autarky in the sense that no consumer is worse off under free trade and some can be made better off (in the case of a strict inequality as in theorem (5)). While the Paretian criterion is only one of several criteria that could be used to evaluate the desirability of a change in situations, it has wide acceptance among economists. Consequently, the demonstration of the gains from free trade using the Paretian criterion provides a powerful argument for free trade. There are some qualifications which must be discussed, however.

The first qualification arises in the case where the required income redistributions (compensation) are not actually made. In such a case some individuals will suffer a reduction in welfare and others will gain as a result of the introduction of free trade. All one can say in such a case is that free trade is *potentially* superior to no trade in the sense that it would be Pareto superior *if* appropriate compensation were to be paid. This is, of course, much weaker than the statement that free trade *is* Pareto superior to no trade. If compensation is not paid. then it is difficult to argue in favour of free trade, unless one is prepared to base the argument upon a demonstration that the nation has a social welfare function which has actually increased in value. In this case the value judgement is made that the gains to the gainers outweigh the losses to the losers. The difficulty with this social welfare function approach is that it may not exist; different people may have different ideas on the weights to be given to each individual.

There are various reasons why the compensation may not be paid. One such reason is that lump-sum redistributions may not be politically feasible. This raises the question of whether it is possible to restructure the argument to deal with "compensation" indirectly using a pre-specified set of tax instruments. In this vein Dixit and Norman (1980) have demonstrated that for an open economy free trade accompanied by an appropriate system of domestic taxes on commodities and factors is Pareto superior to no trade. The domestic taxes are chosen so that consumer and factor prices are the same as under autarky, whence consumers attain their autarky utility levels, and it is shown that such taxes are consistent with the aggregate budget constraints. A complete demonstration is left to the problem set. This is an important contribution to the literature since it alleviates the need to rely upon lump-sum redistributions.

9.3. The sources of the gains from trade

The previous section has demonstrated the existence of a Pareto improvement
in welfare due to free international trade accompanied by lump-sum income
distributions. In this section the sources of such gains in welfare are identified
and briefly discussed.

As theorem (5) indicates, gains from trade will occur if the gross national
product under trade is greater than the minimum expenditure needed to maintain the autarky utility vector, $G(p^1, v) > E(p^1, \mu^0)$. Since these are equal under autarky, $G(p^0, v) = E(p^0, \mu^0)$, it follows that there are two sources of gains
from trade: an increase in GNP due to the new (world) price vector and a reduction in the minimum expenditure required to maintain the autarky utility vector
due to the new price vector.

Suppose that the production possibility frontier has a kink at the autarky production point such that production does not respond to the change in product
prices due to the opening up of trade. Then $G(p^1, v) = p^1 y^0 = p^1 z^0$ so that the
autarky consumption vector remains feasible. There will be a gain from trade if
and only if the new price vector p^1 results in a lower cost of living (maintenance
of μ^0). Thus, there will be a gain if at least one individual is able to substitute
relatively cheaper goods for more expensive goods thus lowering the cost of living.
An obvious exception to this possibility is where each individual has "Leontief
preferences" characterized by L-chaped indifference curves implying that the
Scitovsky indifference curve is L-chaped. If gains from trade occur, then it is
clear that they are due to substitution possibilities in consumption. These may
be referred to as the "gains from trade due to consumption substitution" or the
gains from pure exchange.

Alternatively, suppose that there are no gains from trade due to consumption
substitution. Then there will be gains due to production substitution if the production sector alters the net output vector in response to the price change. If this
is the case then $G(p^1, v) = p^1 y^1 > p^1 y^0 = p^1 z^0 = E(p^0, \mu^0)$ if y^1 is not also
a possible solution under autarky. Thus, there are gains from becoming more
specialized in goods (on average) whose prices have increased as a result of trade
and producing less (on average) of those goods whose prices have fallen.

These two components of the gains from trade may be depicted in figure 9.1
by drawing two additional budget lines with normal p^1. The first is drawn passing
through y^0 and it represents the budget line for the case where production does
not respond to prices. The second is drawn tangent to the boundary of $Z(\mu^0)$,
say at a point $\hat{z}$, and it represents the minimum expenditure necessary to maintain the autarky living standards. The welfare gains obtained by moving from z^0
to the three successively higher budget lines corresponding to price vector p^1

may be illustrated by superimposing indifference curves of the social utility function on the figure. Let $L(z^0) \equiv \{z: u(z) \geqslant u(z^0)\}$ be the set of consumption
vectors that yield at least as much social utility as under autarky, where $u(z)$ is
the social utility function corresponding to the social welfare function $W(\mu)$ defined by (13). Under these circumstances $L(z^0) = Z(\mu^0)$, since they have the
same definition, implying that the Scitovsky indifference curve coinincides exactly with the indifference curve for the social utility function.[9] Other social indifference curves may be drawn tangent to the upper two budget lines yielding optimal consumption vectors $\bar{z}$ and z^1. These are well-behaved indifference curves
so social utility increases as consumption moves from z^0 or $\hat{z}$ (these are equally
preferred) to $\bar{z}$ to z^1. The increase in utility from z^0 or $\hat{z}$ to $\bar{z}$ is the gain due to
consumption substitution, while the increase obtained in the move from $\bar{z}$ to z^1
is due to substitution in production.

9.4. Utility possibility sets

The discussion in section 9.2 introduced the concept of a utility possibility set
whose upper boundary is called the utility possibility frontier. A brief discussion
of various sorts of utility possibility sets is now given. Let

$$UP^*(C) \equiv \left\{\mu: \mu^\ell = u^\ell(z^\ell), \ell = 1, ..., L; \sum_{\ell=1}^{L} z^\ell \in C\right\} \tag{14}$$

be defined as the set of utility vectors which are feasible given that the vector
of quantities available for redistribution amongst the L individuals is any element of some set C. Figure 9.4 illustrates the set $UP^*(z^0)$, where z^0 is the
autarky consumption vector from figure 9.3. Also illustrated is $UP^*(Y(v))$ which
is the set of all μ feasible under autarky. Finally, let

$$B(p^2, Y(v)) \equiv \{z: p^2 z \leqslant G(p^2, v)\} \tag{15}$$

be the set of consumptions possible when the price vector is p^2 and income is
maximized over $Y(v)$. Its upper boundary is the budget line tangent to $Y(v)$ at
y^2 in figure 9.3. The set of utilities feasible when consumers in aggregate face

---

[9] Chipman and Moore (1972, p. 163) show that the set $L(z^0)$ defined for *any* social
welfare function which "rationalizes" an equilibrium (here, the closed equilibrium), i.e. for
which $L(z^0)$ supports $Y(v)$ at z^0, contains $Z(\mu^0)$ as a subset. That is, $Z(\mu^0) \subset L(z^0)$. For
the particular social welfare function (13) used here it can also be shown that $L(z^0) \subset Z(\mu^0)$
so that they coincide.

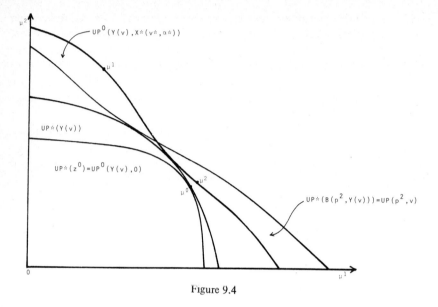

Figure 9.4

this budget set is $UP^*(B(p^2, Y(v))$, which is also illustrated in figure 9.4. Since $z^0 \in Y(v) \subset B(p^2, Y(v))$ it follows that $UP^*(z^0) \subset UP^*(Y(v)) \subset UP^*(B(p^2, Y(v)))$. Also, the first two UP^* sets have some boundary points in common since z^0 is a boundary point of $Y(v)$. Similarly, for the second two UP* sets.

The utility possibility set $UP^*(C)$ is defined in terms of all feasible allocations of aggregate consumption vectors in all C. The utility possibility set $UP(p, v)$ defined by (6) is expressed in terms of prices and the expenditure function which assumes optimal behaviour of consumers. It indicates the utility possibilities for all feasible *income allocations*. Nevertheless, it should be evident that $UP(p, v) = UP^*(B(p, Y(v)))$.

Samuelson's (1962) argument in favour of free trade over autarky is that $UP^*(Y(v))$ is a subset of $UP^*(B(p^2, Y(v)))$. Any utility vector which is feasible under autarky is also feasible under free trade, and there will generally be utility vectors which are available under free trade but not under autarky. This is a general result which does not deal with the nature of redistribution required to achieve a Pareto improvement in welfare. Note that the allocation of goods required to achieve a Pareto improvement in welfare might well be inconsistent with a competitive equilibrium.

It is useful to define the set of utilities which are possible under a competitive equilibrium and an income redistribution scheme. The boundary of the consumption possibility set under free trade is $\hat{\xi}(v, v^*, \alpha^*)$ defined by (8). Consequently, the utility possibility set under free trade equilibrium is $UP^*(\hat{\xi}(v, v^*, \alpha^*))$. Alternatively, we may define the set of utilities possible for a free trade competitive equilibrium in terms of the aggregate expenditure function as

$$UP^0 (Y(v), X^*(v^*, \alpha^*)) \equiv \{\mu: E_p(p, \mu) \leqslant G_p(p, v) +$$
$$+ x^*(p, v^*, \alpha^*), p \geqslant 0\}, \tag{16}$$

where $X^*(v^*, \alpha^*) \equiv \{x^*(p, v^*, \alpha^*): p \geqslant 0\}$ is the set of foreign offers. This utility possibility set differs from (6) in that it requires the consumption vector to be feasible, given the amounts available from production and the foreign nation. The boundary of $UP^0(\cdot)$ is obtained by setting $E_p(p, \mu) = G_p(p, v) + x^*(p, v^*, \alpha^*)$, which means that the commodity markets clear and that $E(p, \mu) = G(p, v)$. In this case p is an equilibrium price vector consistent with the vector of utilities, μ. Once p is known, the appropriate income for individual ℓ is determined as $m^\ell = E^\ell(p, \mu^\ell)$. Thus (16) defines the set of utilities possible for a competitive economy under free trade.

If the economy is a small open economy trading at a fixed price vector p^2, then we can think of X^* as a plane with normal p^2 passing through the origin. In this case $UP^0(Y(v), X^*) = UP(p^2, v)$. Finally, the set of utilities possible for a competitive equilibrium under autarky is obtained by setting $X^* = 0$ in (16) and is therefore $UP^0(Y(v), 0)$.

These utility possibility sets are depicted in figure 9.4. Clearly, $UP^0(Y(v), 0)$, the autarky set, is a subset of each of the free trade utility possibility sets. This is because $0 \in X^*$ whether X^* corresponds to the small or to the large economy assumption. The frontiers of the two trade utility possibility sets cross each other if p^2 is an equilibrium free trade price vector for some income distribution.

The superiority (or rather, non-inferiority) of free trade over autarky is represented by the fact that the closed economy's utility possibility set is contained within the free trade set. If the autarky utility vector μ^0 is in the interior of $UP^0(Y(v), X^*(v^*, \alpha^*))$, as it is in figure 9.4, then $\mu^2 > \mu^0$ can be attained by an appropriate redistribution of income. Thus, if μ^1 was established by free trade without redistribution of incomes, income redistribution can be used to attain a Pareto improvement in welfare.

9.5. Is some trade better than no trade?

This section is concerned with the question of whether it is possible to demonstrate that non-free trade accompanied by lump-sum redistributions of income is a Pareto improvement in welfare over autarky. This question is more important from a practical viewpoint than that concerning free trade in view of the prevalence of tariffs and other impediments to trade which exist in the real world.

Let it be assumed that trade is not free but is subject to a structure of taxes. Let $p*$ and p denote the vectors of world (foreign) and domestic prices, respectively. They are assumed to be related by $p = p* + t$, where t is a vector of per unit taxes on trade. If $t_j > 0$ and good j is being imported, then t_j is an import tax, whereas if j is being exported t_j is an export subsidy. If $t_j < 0$ and good j is being imported, then t_j is an import subsidy, whereas if j is being exported t_j is an export tax. It is assumed that $-p* \leqslant t \leqslant p$ thus ruling out the possibility of negative prices. Competitive behaviour by traders ensures that $p = p* + t$. As before, let the superscripts 0 and 1 denote autarky and post-trade vectors.

Since (4) continues to hold in the present context the revenue earned by the production sector is sufficient to allow the autarky consumption vector to be purchased. However, the trade taxes yield a net tax revenue of

$$r \equiv t(z^1 - y^1), \tag{17}$$

which may be positive, zero or negative. Total revenue available for spending by the consumption sector is $G(p^1, v) + r$. Since all such revenue will be spent (4) implies that

$$p^1 z^1 = G(p^1, v) + r \geqslant p^1 z^0 + r \geqslant p^1 z^0, \quad \text{if } r \geqslant 0. \tag{18}$$

Thus, if the net revenue obtained by the government is non-negative, then the total income available for consumption is sufficient to ensure that the autarky consumption vector z^0 is in the aggregate budget set. Hence, this income can be redistributed to allow all individuals to consume their autarky consumption vectors at price vector p^1.

Of course, the condition that $r \geqslant 0$ is sufficient to demonstrate the gains from tax-ridden trade. The necessary and sufficient condition is that $G(p^1, v) + r \geqslant E(p^1, \mu^0)$ using the same reasoning as that surrounding theorem (5). Since it is likely that $G(p^1, v) > E(p^1, \mu^0)$, the net revenue earned may be negative when there are gains from trade.

Theorem. Under the maintained assumptions of the model, a necessary and sufficient condition for tax-ridden trade at price vector p^1 accompanied by a lump-sum redistribution of income to be Pareto superior to autarky is that $G(p^1, v) + r > E(p^1, \mu^0)$. (19)

Evidently theorem (5) is the special case of theorem (19) where there are no taxes and hence $r = 0$. Now consider other special cases. First, if there are only trade taxes (either import taxes or export taxes), then $r > 0$ and, since $G(p, v) \geqslant E(p, \mu^0)$ for all p, there will be a gain from such trade. Secondly, if there are only trade subsidies, then $r < 0$ and there is the possibility that there is insufficient income available to attain the autarky utility vector μ^0. It is easy to demonstrate that this is possible and it suffices to consider an economy with just one consumer. This demonstration is left to the reader as an exercise and is the subject of one of the problems at the end of the chapter.

To deal with the possibility that the income redistribution may influence world prices, the same type of argument that was used in the discussion of theorem (10) may be invoked. For any social welfare function there corresponds a social utility function. Suppose that it is used to generate aggregate demands and that there is a competitive equilibrium when the trade tax vector is t. If this welfare function is given by (13), then social welfare will have increased, implying a Pareto improvement, if μ^0 is feasible. Evidently, μ^0 is feasible if and only if $G(p^1, v) + r \geqslant E(p^1, \mu^0)$, where p^1 is the equilibrium domestic price vector. This is not guaranteed to hold.

The utility possibility set under competitive trade with taxes is defined analogously to (16) as

$$UP^0 (Y(v), X^*(v^*, \alpha^*), t) \equiv \{\mu: E_p(p, \mu) \leqslant G_p(p, v) +$$
$$+ x^*(p^*, v^*, \alpha^*), p = p^* + t, p \geqslant 0, p^* \geqslant 0\}, \tag{20}$$

where tx^* is the net tax revenue. If p^* is an equilibrium price vector, then $p^*E_p(p, \mu) = p^*G_p(p, v) + p^*x^*(p^*, v^*, \alpha^*)$, whence $E(p, \mu) = G(p, v) + tx^*(p^*, v^*, \alpha^*)$, which is the aggregate budget constraint. The set of μ for which there is an equilibrium defines the frontier of the utility possibility set under a trade tax structure t. Unlike the free trade situation where $t = 0$, μ^0 is not necessarily an element of this set if $tx^* < 0$. Thus, the gains from trade cannot be established without the condition on r in (19).

The preceding results concerning the gains from trade arise from the observation that for $\mu^1 \gtrsim \mu^0$ it is necessary and sufficient that $m^1 > E(p^1, \mu^0)$, where p^1 is the price vector facing consumers and m^1 is their *disposable income* in situation 1, and lump-sum income redistributions are possible. Situations other than those considered above may be dealt with in the same way. For example, suppose that there exist production and consumption taxes as well as trade taxes. Disposable income will consist of GNP evaluated at producer prices plus net tax revenue which includes trade, production and consumption taxes. It can be shown (see problem set) that a sufficient condition for international trade under trade, production and consumption taxes to be potentially superior to autarky under production and consumption taxes is that net trade taxes plus the change in net domestic taxes evaluated at the tax rates in the trade situation be non-negative. This general result is due to Ohyama (1972).

The essential message which the above discussion yields is that we can isolate situations where trade is potentially Pareto superior to no trade, but there are other situations for which the superiority of trade cannot be established. Thus, it is not always the case that any trade is better than no trade.

9.6. Is free trade optimal for a nation?

It has been demonstrated that free trade is better than no trade and that some trade is better than no trade if the net tax revenue is not "too negative", under the assumption of optimal lump-sum transfers of income. It is now demonstrated that the tempting proposition that free trade is better than some (tax-ridden) trade is false unless the world price vector is fixed. It generally is possible to restrict trade by a set of taxes thereby altering world prices in a monopolistic manner and enabling welfare of all individuals to increase. If social welfare is maximized by this procedure, the resulting tariff vector is called the optimal tariff structure.

Let the economy have a social welfare function which is maximized by optimally distributing disposable income among the individual consumers. This yields the social utility function and its dual, the indirect social utility function $V(p, m)$. The net tax revenue is $r = (p - p^*)x^*(p^*, v^*, \alpha^*)$, where it is assumed that $p^* > 0$ and hence world markets clear so that the foreign net export vector x^* is equal to the home nation's net import vector. The level of social utility or welfare obtained is

$$H(p, v, p^*, v^*, \alpha^*) \equiv V(p, m), \tag{21}$$

where

$$m = G(p, v) + (p - p^*)x^*(p^*, v^*, \alpha^*) = G(p, v) +$$
$$+ px^*(p^*, v^*, \alpha^*), \tag{22}$$

since $p^*x^*(p^*, v^*, \alpha^*) = 0$ for all p^* (i.e. balance of trade assumed).

The optimal tariff problem is to maximize social utility by choosing p and p^*.

If $p = p^*$, then the tax vector is $t = p - p^* = 0$ and the level of social welfare attained is $V(p^*, G(p^*, v))$, where p^* is the equilibrium free trade price vector. If $p \neq p^*$, then $t \neq 0$ and these optimal tariffs yield a higher level of social welfare than under free trade. Maximization of (21) subject to $p \geqslant 0$ and $p^* \geqslant 0$ yields the Kuhn–Tucker conditions.[10]

(a) $V_p + V_m [G_p(p, v) + x^*(p^*, v^*, \alpha^*)] \leqslant 0 \leqslant p,$

(23)

(b) $V_m [px_p^*(p^*, v^*, \alpha^*)] \leqslant 0 \leqslant p^*.$

Since $V_m > 0$ almost everywhere it is assumed to be positive at the solution to (23) and so (23) is equivalent to

(a) $G_p(p, v) + x^*(p^*, v^*, \alpha^*) - (-V_p/V_m) \leqslant 0 \leqslant p,$

(24)

(b) $px_p^*(p^*, v^*, \alpha^*) \leqslant 0 \leqslant p^*.$

The first set of conditions simply state that world markets must be in equilibrium since $-V_p/V_m \equiv \phi(p, m)$ is the demand vector by Roy's identity. The second set of conditions states that if $p^* > 0$, then

$$px_p^*(p^*, v^*, \alpha^*) = [p \, \partial x^*(p^*, v^*, \alpha^*)/\partial p_j^*] = 0. \tag{25}$$

That is, p is orthogonal to each vector $\partial x^*/\partial p_j^*, j = 1, \ldots, M$. The latter measure the response of x^* to a change in an element of the price vector along the foreign excess supply function, or the slope of the foreign offer curve $X^*(v^*, \alpha^*)$. Thus (25) implies that the domestic price vector is orthogonal to the foreign offer curve at the solution to the welfare-maximization problem.

The solution to the optimal tariff problem is illustrated in figure 9.5. The foreign offer curve is labelled F. At the point $x = -x^*$, p is orthogonal to F. The home nation offer curve under no trade taxes is H, and under the optimal trade taxes it is H^1. The dashed curve drawn tangent to F and, of course, its tangent plane with normal p, is the highest trade indifference curve attainable on F. The trade utility function expresses utility in the x space and is dual to the indirect trade utility function $H(p, v) \equiv V(p, G(p, v))$.

If the foreign offer curve is $X^* \equiv \{x^*: p^*x^* = 0\}$ for some given p^*, the above analysis based upon differentiability needs to be modified since the ex-

---

[10] See, for example, Mangasarian (1969, p. 156) for a statement of the necessity of the Kuhn–Tucker conditions.

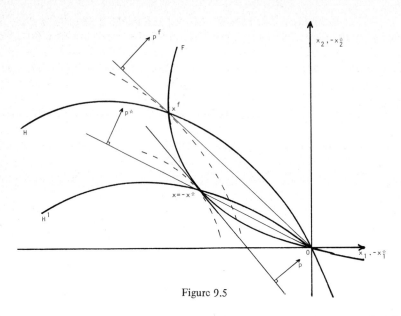

Figure 9.5

cess supply is a correspondence rather than a function. Indeed, in general $x^*(p^*, v^*, \alpha^*)$ may be a correspondence. To allow for this possibility we write the optimal trade tax problem as

$$\max_{p, \, x^*}\{V(p, G(p,v) + px^*): x^* \in X^*(v^*, \alpha^*), p \geqslant 0\}. \tag{26}$$

The difference is that x^* replaces p^* as a choice variable. The conditions for a solution $(\bar{p}, \bar{x}^*)$ are

(a) $\quad [G_p(\bar{p},v) + V_p/V_m - \bar{x}^*] \leqslant 0 \leqslant \bar{p},$

(b) $\quad \bar{p}\bar{x}^* = \max_{x^*}\{\bar{p}x^*: x^* \in X^*(v^*, \alpha^*)\}.$

$$\tag{27}$$

The simultaneous solution of the equations in (27) yields $(\bar{p}, \bar{x}^*)$ from which $\bar{p}^*$ and hence the optimal taxes $\bar{t} \equiv \bar{p} - \bar{p}^*$ are obtained. The first condition is obtained similarly to (24, a) by assuming that $V_m > 0$. Since x^* enters the objective function as the net tax revenue component, $\bar{p}x^*$, of disposable income, it clearly must be chosen to maximize net tax revenue. Thus, $\bar{p}$ is orthogonal to the set X^* at the point x^*, as (25) indicates for the case where X^* is described by differentiable excess supply functions. If $X^* = \{\dot{x}^*: p^*x^* = 0\}$, where p^* is given, then $\bar{p}$ must be equal to $\bar{p}^*$ up to a positive factor of proportionality. Hence, the optimal tariff is zero in this case.

If the social welfare function chosen for the purposes of optimization is $W(\mu)$ defined by (13), where μ^0 is now taken to be the free trade utility vector, possibly that attained under optimal redistribution to attain a Pareto improvement over autarky but not necessarily, it can be shown that the optimal trade taxes together with optimal income redistributions are Pareto superior to free trade. The argument is precisely the same as that following (13). Since the free solution is available the maximum level of social welfare is at least as great as under free trade. Hence, from the structure of (13) no individual suffers a loss in utility. Indeed, if the optimal trade tax vector is not zero, then social welfare and hence individual utility levels must have increased.[11] In summary,

> **Theorem.** A policy of optimal trade taxes and income redistributions, based upon $W(\mu)$ defined by (13), where μ^0 is the free trade utility vector, is Pareto superior to free trade if the optimal taxes are not all zero. (28)

Properties of the optimal tax structure

The optimal tax vector $\bar{t} \equiv \bar{p} - \bar{p}^*$ is not unique since both $\bar{p}$ and $\bar{p}^*$ may be increased or decreasing proportionately without affecting the solution to (27), a fact which the reader is asked to prove in the problem set. For example, the domestic and foreign price vectors may be normalized to be in the unit simplex $S \equiv \{p: 1^T p = \Sigma_{j=1}^{M} p_j = 1, p \geqslant 0\}$ in which case $1^T \bar{t} = 0$. In this case, some of the taxes are negative and some are positive. If $\bar{t}_j > 0$, then the domestic price is higher than the foreign price, hence $\bar{t}_j$ is the unit import duty if j is imported while it is the unit export subsidy if j is exported. If $\bar{t}_j < 0$, then it is a per unit import subsidy or a per unit export tax. Of course, the normalization of the price vectors, and hence the tax vector, is not unique. Suppose that $\bar{t}_k = \min \{t_i\}$. Then p^* can be normalized, say to be in S, and $\bar{t}$ can be normalized, say by setting $\bar{t}_k = 0$. Thus, $\bar{p}_k = \bar{p}_k^*$ and $\bar{t}_i \geqslant 0$ for all $i \neq k$.[12]

---

[11] Chipman and Moore (1972) point out that this argument is a straightforward application of their argument concerning the Pareto superiority of free trade over no trade.

[12] Those who prefer to express tariffs in ad valorem form and deal with price ratios will recognize that

$$\frac{\bar{p}_j}{\bar{p}_i} = \frac{(1 + \tau_j)}{(1 + \tau_i)} \frac{\bar{p}_j^*}{\bar{p}_i^*},$$

where p_i and $p_i^* > 0$ and $\tau_j \equiv \bar{t}_j/\bar{p}_j^*$ is the ad valorem rate of tax. If, for example, good j is exported and $\tau_j > 0$, then exports of j are being subsidized. The rate of subsidy based upon the domestic price is $\sigma_j \equiv -\tau_j/(1 + \tau_j)$. Thus, $\bar{p}_j^* = (1 - \sigma_j)\bar{p}_j = \bar{p}_j/(1 + \tau_j)$, which is equivalent to the relationship $\bar{p}_j^*(1 + \tau_j) = \bar{p}_j$.

Horwell and Pearce (1970), following Graaf (1949), have investigated the question of whether the optimal tax structure can be normalized such that all imports and exports are taxed (rather than subsidized). If one good is exported they show that, under certain conditions imposed on the supply and demand functions, a positive tariff structure for imports is always possible. In general, their sufficiency conditions do not enable them to establish that $\bar{t}$ can be normalized to exhibit only taxes, although they speculate that taxes are "more likely" than subsidies. When there are just $M = 2$ goods then, without any special conditions, it is always possible for $\bar{t}$ to be normalized so that trade (either exports or imports or both) are taxed. (See the problem set.)

The concept of an optimal tax structure as dicussed above is based upon the assumption that society maximizes a social welfare function and undertakes appropriate redistributions. If we ignore such centralized planning and consider a decentralized economy in which incomes are allocated according to factor ownership, does there still exist a tariff structure which is optimal in some sense? Certainly, if the economy is not infinitesimal, then it has market power which can be exploited by the government imposing a set of trade taxes. What is not immediately obvious is how they should be set and what is the objective function, if there is one.

The concept of optimality that will be used to characterize an optimal trade tax structure in an economy without a social welfare function and lump-sum redistributions is that of Pareto optimality within the nation in question. Thus, the trade tax vector is said to be Pareto optimal for a nation if it is impossible to change it and thereby raise the utilities of any group of individuals without reducing the utility levels of others within the nation.

The set of utility vectors which are feasible when international markets clear and the trade tax vector $t = p - p^*$ is arbitrarily given is

$$UP^*(Y(v) + X^*(v^*, \alpha^*)) = \{\mu: S_p(p, \mu, v) +$$

$$+ x^*(p^*, v^*, \alpha^*) \geq 0, p \geq 0, p^* \geq 0\}, \tag{29}$$

where $S(p, \mu, v) \equiv G(p, v) - E(p, \mu)$ and S_p is the net export vector.[13] When $t = p - p^* = 0$ the set of utilities defined by (29) corresponds to the free trade

---

[13]   Under an optimal tax situation domestic and foreign prices can be independently chosen so the consumption possibility set becomes $Y(v) + X^*(v^*, \alpha^*)$. The utility possibility set is therefore $UP^*(Y(v) + X^*(v^*, \alpha^*))$. Equivalently, the boundary of the consumption possibility set is defined by $G_p(p, v) + x^*(p^*, v^*, \alpha^*)$. Feasible utility vectors are those for which $E_p(p, \mu) \leq G_p(p, v) + x^*(p^*, v^*, \alpha^*)$, that is $S_p(p, \mu, v) + x^*(p^*, v^*, \alpha^*) \geq 0$.

utility frontier. If some given tax structure is imposed, either in per unit or ad valorem form, another utility possibility frontier is defined.

Let p, p^* and μ be consistent with a competitive equilibrium. Then $0 = p^*S_p + p^*x^* = p^*S_p = pS_p - tS_p = S + tx^*$ which is the budget constraint. Differentiating the budget constraint we get that

$$-S_\mu d\mu = (S_p + x^*)dp + px_p^* dp^* = px_p^* dp^* \tag{30}$$

since the markets are assumed to clear. If $px^* = 0$, then the right-hand side of (30) is zero, implying that $d\mu \geq 0$ is not possible if $-S_\mu = E_\mu > 0$. That is, a small change in p^* cannot increase the utility of some individuals and lower the utility of no one. However, if $px_p^* \neq 0$, then it is possible to choose dp^* such that the right-hand side of (30) is positive. In this case $d\mu > 0$ can be achieved by changing p^* in the correct direction, showing that the initial situation is not Pareto optimal for the nation. Clearly, Pareto optimality can be attained by choosing p^* such that in equilibrium the condition $p\,x_p^*(p^*,v^*,\alpha^*) = 0$ holds. This is precisely the same characterization of the optimal tax obtained by maximizing a social utility function. The difference between the two optimal tax structures is that the social utility optimal tax structure is Pareto superior to any other tax structure including free trade (zero taxes) if the social welfare function is of the form of (13), whereas under the Pareto optimal tax structure no such comparison is possible. This is because it yields a Pareto optimal situation which may involve some people becoming worse off than under free trade, depending upon how income is distributed.

It should be noted that the condition $p\,x_p^*(p^*,v^*,\alpha^*) = 0$ is only part of the complete characterization of the Pareto optimal tax vector, which includes the market equilibrium condition for goods and distribution of income and net tax revenue to consumers. A complete characterization is left to the reader.

Finally, it is important to note that from the world point of view free trade is Pareto optimal since all consumers and producers face the same prices for traded goods. Clearly, if a nation imposes a tariff structure which is Pareto optimal from its viewpoint, the resulting equilibrium is Pareto suboptimal from the world viewpoint.

9.7. Welfare and world prices

Since trade at a price vector which differs from the autarky price vector increases welfare, it is tempting to venture the proposition that the gain in welfare will be greater the greater is the divergence between the autarky and free price vectors.

This proposition is indeed true for the case of two goods, as is easy to verify. When there are more than two goods, however, the truth of the proposition depends upon the definition of "greater divergence".

9.7.1. The indirect trade utility function

A small open economy trading freely at a price vector p obtains a level of social utility equal to

$$H(p, b, v) \equiv V(p, G(p, v) + b) \equiv \max_{z} \{u(z):$$
$$pz \leqslant G(p, v) + b, z \geqslant 0\}, \tag{31}$$

where V is the indirect social utility function corresponding to a social welfare function defined by (13), $G(p, v)$ is the GNP function and the scalar b, introduced for use later, is set equal to zero. The function H is called the *indirect trade utility function* discussed in Chapter 6. Clearly, the effect upon social utility of a change in p depends upon the properties of H with respect to p. The general properties of this function are indicated in theorem (6.48) and in (6.47). The properties of particular interest here are that $H(p, b, v)$ is quasi-convex in p and the net export vector is obtained by differentiation as

$$x(p, b, v) = H_p(p, b, v)/H_b(p, b, v) =$$
$$= G_p(p, v) - \phi(p, G(p, v) + b). \tag{32}$$

A final property of $H(p, r, v)$, which is important for present purposes, is contained in

> **Theorem.** Let $V(p, m)$ and $G(p, v)$ be sufficiently differentiable for $H(p, b, v)$ to be differentiable with respect to p and b at $p^0 \geqslant 0$ and $b^0 = 0$ such that $H_b(p^0, b^0, v) > 0$. Then the price vector p^0 is a closed equilibrium price vector if and only if $H(p^0, b^0, v) \leqslant H(p, b^0, v)$ for all $p \geqslant 0$. (33)

Proof. Let $H(p^0, b^0, v) \leqslant H(p, b^0, v)$ for all $p \geqslant 0$. The necessary Kuhn–Tucker conditions for this are that $H_p(p^0, r^0, v) \geqslant 0 \leqslant p^0$.[14] Since $H_b(p^0, b^0, v) > 0$ by assumption, it follows that these conditions may be rewritten as $x(p^0,$

---

[14]   See Mangasarian (1969, p. 156).

$b^0, v) \geqslant 0 \leqslant p^0$, which are the closed market equilibrium conditions. Thus, p^0 is a closed equilibrium price vector.

Now let p^0 be a closed equilibrium price vector. Then, by.definition, there exists a production vector y^0 such that $p^0 y^0 = G(p^0, v)$, and a consumption vector z^0 which solves (31) for $p = p^0$, and these satisfy the market equilibrium condition $y^0 - z^0 \geqslant 0 \leqslant p^0$. For any $p \geqslant 0$ it follows that $pz^0 \leqslant py^0$ [since $y^0 \geqslant z^0] \leqslant G(p, v)$ [due to the definition of G as a maximum of py over $Y(v)$ which contains y^0]. Hence, z^0 is feasible for problem (31) for any $p \geqslant 0$. Hence, $H(p, b^0, v) \geqslant u(z^0) = H(p^0, b^0, v)$ for all $p \geqslant 0$. This completes the proof of the theorem.[15]

9.7.2. Effects of changes in world prices

With these properties of the indirect trade utility function in hand, the effect of a change in p upon the level of utility can easily be established. Theorem (33) states that any $p \geqslant 0$ will yield a utility level at least as great as that yielded by the closed equilibrium price vector p^0, which is another way of characterizing the gains from trade. Because of this, the quasi-convexity property implies:

Theorem. For any free trade price vector $p \geqslant 0, H(p, b^0, v) \geqslant H(p^\lambda, b^0, v) \geqslant H(p^0, b^0, v)$, where $p^\lambda \equiv \lambda p^0 + (1 - \lambda)p, p^0$ is the closed equilibrium price vector and $b^0 = 0$. (34)

Thus, as the price vector p moves out along a ray passing through p^0 the level of utility increases. It is according to this definition of greater divergence (being further out along the ray) that Kemp (1969) argues the truth of the proposition that the greater the divergence of the free trade price vector from the autarky price vector the greater are the gains from trade. Figure 9.6 illustrates the contours of the function $H(p, b^0, v)$ on the unit simplex for the case where there are $M = 3$ goods. Utility increases in any direction from p^0.

The difficulty with the Kemp definition of greater divergence is that it only allows a comparison of price vectors along a single ray. However, a comprehensive definition of distance with which to measure the divergence between *any* two price vectors and which will ensure the validity of the proposition can only

[15] The differentiability conditions in theorem (33) can be dispensed with, and the first part of the proof altered accordingly as in Woodland (1980). Differentiability with respect to p at p^0 implies that the excess supply vector at p^0 is unique. In general this may be too strong an assumption as consideration of the Ricardian model shows.

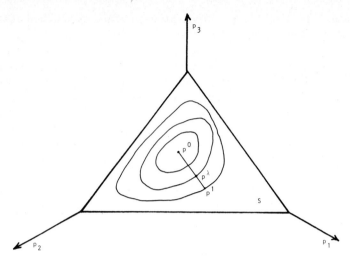

Figure 9.6

be given in terms of the indirect trade utility function. But such a definition would make the proposition a tautology. Without imposing special conditions upon $H(p, b, v)$, the proposition contained in (34) appears to be the most general statement that can be made using prior information only.

If, however, ex post information may be used, then (32) allows welfare comparisons in terms of Laspeyre's import and export price indices. The Laspeyre's export price index is defined as the current value of base period exports divided by the base period value of the base period exports. Similarly, the Laspeyre's import price index is the current evaluation of base period imports divided by the base period valuation of the base period imports. Let the net export vector be written as $x = (x_e, -x_m)$, where $x_e > 0$ is the vector of exports and $x_m > 0$ is the vector of imports and $p = (p_e, p_m)$ is defined conformably. Then the Laspeyre's export and import price indices are

$$P_e^t \equiv \frac{p_e^t x_e^0}{p_e^0 x_e^0} \quad ; \quad P_m^t \equiv \frac{p_m^t x_m^0}{p_m^0 x_m^0} \, , \tag{35}$$

where the superscript 0 refers to the base and the superscript t refers to any other period. These formulae are the standard ones used by most nations to measure export and import prices. We say that the "terms of trade" improve when P_e^t / P_m^t increases, by analogy with the two-product model.

If $b = 0$, there is a balance of trade and hence the denominators in (35) are equal. Thus, $P_e^t/P_m^t = p_e^t x_e^0/p_m^t x_m^0$ has increased from period 0 to period t if $p_e^t x_e^0 > p_m^t x_m^0$ or, alternatively, $p^t x^0 = (p^t - p^0)x^0 > 0$, that is if the current (t) value of the base period net exports increases. It is now shown that if p changes from p^0 to p^t such that $p^t x^0 > 0$, then utility will increase. For *small* changes, $dp = p^t - p^0$, this result follows from (32) which states that

$$d\mu/H_b = dp H_p(p^0, b, v)/H_b(p^0, b, v) = dp\, x(p^0, b, v) = (p^t - p^0)x^0.$$

In view of this it is clearly the case that utility increases if and only if $(p^t - p^0)x^0$ is positive, meaning that the terms of trade measured by P_e^t/P_m^t have increased. For large price changes the same result holds. If $p^t x^0 \geqslant p^0 x^0$, then $G(p^t, v) - p^t z^0 \geqslant p^t y^0 - p^t z^0$ [due to the definition of G as a maximum] $= p^t x^0 \geqslant p^0 x^0 = 0$. Thus, z^0 is feasible for problem (31) defining $H(p^t, b, v)$ and hence $H(p^0, b, v) \leqslant H(p^t, b, v)$. If $p^t x^0 > p^0 x^0$, then $G(p^t, v) - p^t z^0 > 0$ and hence $H(p^0, b, v) < H(p^t, b, v)$ since $u(z)$ is weakly increasing. If $p^t x^0 < p^0 x^0$, then z^0 is not feasible under p^t so that $H(p^t, b, v)$ and $H(p^0, b, v)$ cannot be ranked. In summary, the following has been proved:

> **Theorem.** Social utility increases (under a balance of trade) as a result of a change in product prices from p^0 to p^t if the terms of trade measured by P_e^t/P_m^t increase. That is, $H(p^t, 0, v) > H(p^0, 0, v)$ if $p^t x^0 > p^0 x^0 = 0$. Social utility is increasing for *small* price changes, dp, from p^0 if and only if $dp x^0 > 0$. (36)

This result is a strengthened version of the result in Krueger and Sonnenschein (1967) and Kemp (1964) who only prove the "if" part of (36). If the social utility function is based upon the social welfare function defined by (13), then (36) indicates that an improvement in the terms of trade is welfare improving in the sense of Pareto if they are accompanied by optimal income redistributions. As Krueger and Sonnenschein demonstrate, the fact that $P_e^2/P_m^2 > P_e^1/P_m^1 > 1$ does not imply that welfare is greater under p^2 than p^1. In other words, welfare does not necessarily increase when the Laspeyre's export price index increases at a faster rate than the Laspeyre's import price index. However, if the weights are continually revised and set equal to the last period's export and import vector, then increases in the resulting weight-revised terms of trade do result in increases in welfare. That is,

$$\frac{p_e^2 x_e^1}{p_m^2 x_m^1} > \frac{p_e^1 x_e^0}{p_m^1 x_m^0} > 1 \quad \text{implies } H(p^2, 0, v) > H(p^1, 0, v) >$$

$$> H(p^0, 0, v). \tag{37}$$

Finally, we note that if there is not a balance of trade then the preceding results need to be appropriately modified.

9.7.3. The case when there are trade taxes

The preceding discussion has assumed that the nation in question is trading freely with the rest of the world. If this assumption is relaxed such that the nation imposes a vector of trade taxes and subsidies, what can be said about the effect of changes in world prices upon the level of social utility? Let the domestic price vector p and the foreign price vector p^* be related by $p = p^* + t$, where t is the trade tax vector.

The tax revenue is $b \equiv (p^* - p)x = -tx$, where $x = H_p/H_b$. The social utility is $H(p, b, v) = V(p, G(p, v) - tx)$. By differentiating with respect to p^* and recognizing that $p = p^* + t$, the effect of a change in p^* upon social utility is

$$dH = H_p\,dp + H_b(-t\,dx - x\,dt), \qquad dt = dp - dp^*,$$

whence

$$dH/H_b = (H_p/H_b - x)\,dp - t\,dx + x\,dp^*.$$

The term in brackets is zero since $x(p, b, v) = H_p/H_b$. Hence

$$dH/H_b = x\,dp^* - t\,dx. \tag{38}$$

The free trade case previously dealt with occurs when $t = 0$. If $t \neq 0$, then a new term appears. This term is the additional net tax revenue that would be generated *if* the new trade vector were to be taxed at the initial rate per unit of trade, t. If, for example, the price change were to cause net tax revenue (when evaluated at the initial rate) to increase and the terms of trade improved, then utility would increase. However, if tax revenue falls then it is possible for utility to fall even though the terms of trade improve.

To be more specific about the effects of a change in p^* upon utility when trade taxes and subsidies occur, it is necessary to evaluate dx/dp^*, or to calculate dH more directly. Following the latter approach the balance of trade for the small nation may be written as

$$p^*x = p^*S_p(p, \mu, v) = 0, \tag{39}$$

where $p = p* + t$. If the tax rates are fixed in ad valorem terms, then $t = Tp*$, where T is a diagonal matrix of ad valorem rates based upon foreign prices. Eq. (39) expresses the balance of trade condition, and determines the level of utility μ as a function of t, $p*$ and v. Total differentiation of (39) when $t = Tp*$ yields

$$\mathrm{d}\mu = [S_p(p, \mu, v) + p*S_{pp}(p, \mu, v)(I + T)]\,\mathrm{d}p*/[-p*S_{p\mu}(p,\mu,v)] \qquad (40)$$

where the denominator is positive if no good is inferior. This implicitly defines the set of price changes, $\mathrm{d}p*$, which will yield greater utility, a set which can be calculated if the initial solution and the second derivatives of S are known.

9.8. Notes on the literature

The basic propositions on the gains from free trade using the compensation prin-ciple were developed by Samuelson (1938, 1962) and Kemp (1962). These authors showed that trade enlarges the consumption possibility set for a nation and that the utility possibility set is therefore larger under free trade. The dem-onstration of the gain from free or restricted trade for an infinitesimally small open economy proceeds by showing that the autarky comsumption point is at-tainable under trade and therefore lump-sum income transfers exist which will result in trade being Pareto superior to autarky. Ohyama (1972) provides a very useful synthesis of various propositions regarding welfare and trade which are special cases of his theorem 1. In particular he demonstrates that tax-ridden trade is better than no trade if the net tax revenue is non-negative.

When the transfers affect the equilibrium price vector it has to be shown that there exist transfers which yield an equilibrium which is Pareto superior to autar-ky. The paper by Chipman and Moore (1972) shows that the maximization of a special welfare function will yield the required Pareto improving lump-sum in-come transfers. For other proofs of the gains from trade within a general equilib-rium context see Grandmont and MacFadden (1972) and Otani (1972).

The general nature of the propositions of welfare economics has been survey-ed by Chipman and Moore (1978) who deal with the case of trade gains and the question of whether compensation need be paid. Dixit and Norman (1980a) demonstrate the superiority of free trade over autarky using indirect taxation rather than lump sum taxes to redistribute incomes. In Dixit and Norman (1980b) they show that, choosing indirect taxation rates, only the terms of trade effects can prevent free trade from being superior to restricted trade.

Throughout this chapter it has been assumed that the production sector al-ways maximizes GNP, i.e. that there are no distortions in the production sector.

If there exist externalities or other distortions such as monopoly behaviour and taxes, it is not inevitable that GNP will be maximized. Consequently, the theorems on trade gains have to be modified and, in general, one cannot demonstrate that trade is beneficial. For a treatment of some of these issues see Wan (1972) (on externalities) and Kemp (1969).

The relationship between the terms of trade and welfare was addressed by Krueger and Sonnenschein (1967) and Kemp (1969) and generalized by Ohyama (1972).

Problems

1. (a) Draw the offer curves for the home and foreign nations and the home nation's autarky trade indifference curve on a diagram. (Consumption decisions are based upon a social utility function.)
   (b) The offer curve of the home nation is contained on one side of the autarky trade indifference curve. Why?
   (c) Show that restricted trade (towards the origin along the foreign offer curve) is better than no trade, but may be better than free trade.
   (d) Show that expanded trade (away from the origin along the foreign offer curve) may be worse than no trade.

2. (a) Draw the consumption possibility sets for an economy in (i) autarky $[Y(v)]$; (ii) free trade at a fixed world price vector $[B(p, Y(v))]$; (iii) free trade within a foreign nation with net supply functions $x^*(p^*, v^*, \alpha^*)$ $[\hat{\xi}(v, v^*, \alpha^*)]$; and (iv) able to impose optimal trade taxes without retaliation $[Y(v) + X^*(v^*, \alpha^*)]$. Be precise in your derivations.
   (b) Depict the corresponding utility possibility sets $UP^*(\cdot)$ for a two-person economy.

3. In fig. 9.3, when p^2 is the price vector, only aggregate demands along EF will be observed for any possible income distribution. For the case where the dashed lines through E and F form a cone (homothetic preferences) show
   (a) that the frontier of $UP^*(B(p^2, Y(v)))$ corresponds to the allocations of consumptions along EF to the two consumers along OE and OF, and
   (b) that aggregate consumptions along the budget line to the left of E and the right of F yield utility vectors inside the frontier of $UP^*(B(p^2, Y(v)))$.

4. In fig. 9.1 we can draw in the Scitovsky set $Z(\mu^1)$, where μ^1 is the utility vector under free trade with optimal income redistributions, using the social welfare function (13). It will (a) be tangent to AB and (b) its boundary will not cross that of $Z(\mu^0)$. Explain both (a) and (b).

5. Let there be domestic production and consumption taxes denoted, t_s and t_d, as well as trade taxes t. Let superscripts 0 and 1 denote autarky and trading situations and allow taxes to be different in the two situations. Show that a sufficient condition for disposable income m^1 to allow the purchase of the autarky consumption vector $(m^1 \geqslant p_d^1 z^0 \geqslant E(p_d^1, \mu^0))$, where p_d^1 denotes the consumer price vector, is that $t(z^1 - y^1) + t_d^1(z^1 - z^0) + t_s^1(y^1 - y^0) \geqslant 0$.

6. Consider a situation of autarky with no taxes, and free trade with no lump-sum income redistributions but with taxes on consumption and the use of factors.
   (a) Show that a consumption vector equal to $p^0 - p^1$ and a tax on the use of factors in production of $w^0 - w^1$, where superscripts 0 and 1 denote autarky and free trade prices, respectively, will leave all consumers at their autarky utility levels.
   (b) Show that these taxes are feasible in the sense that net tax revenue is non-negative.
   (c) Discuss these results.

7. (a) Explain why the optimal tax vector $t = p - p^*$ is homogeneous of degree zero.
   (b) Are the corresponding ad valorem rates also homogeneous of degree zero?

8. The optimal trade tax structure is (partially) characterized by $px_p^* = 0$.
   (a) Use the relationship $x_p^* = S_{pp}^* - \phi_m^* x^*$ (see (6.44)) and the properties of S^* to show that $px_p^* = t S_{pp}^* - \iota^* x^*$, where $\iota^* = p\phi_m^*$.
   (b) Delete the first equation and set $t_1 = 0$ to get $t_2 S_{22}^* - \iota_2^* x_2^* = 0$. Hence, show that if $x_2^* > 0$ (good 1 is exported by the home country) and if S_{22}^* has positive diagonal and non-positive off-diagonal elements, then $t_2 > 0$. Interpret these conditions on S_{22}^*.
   (c) Similarly, show that if $x_2^* < 0$, then $t_2 < 0$ under the same conditions on S_{22}^*. Interpret your result.
   (d) In what sense can it be suggested that taxes are "more likely" than subsidies in the optimal tax structure?

9. (a) Show that the foreign balance of trade condition implies that $p^* x_p^* + x^* = 0$ and hence that $px_p^* = tx_p^* - x^* = 0$ is a characterization of the optimal trade tax.
   (b) Hence, for the case of two goods with $t_1 = 0$, show that $\tau_2 = 1/\xi_{22}^*$ is the optimal ad valorem rate of tax for good 2, where $\xi_{22}^* \equiv x_{22}^* p_2 / x_2^*$ is the foreign price elasticity of import demand or export supply.
   (c) Use the characterization $px_p^* = tS_{pp}^* - \iota^* x^* = 0$ obtained in the previous problem to show, again for two goods and $t_1 = 0$, that $\tau_2 = \iota_2^* / \bar{\xi}_{22}^*$, where

$\bar{\xi}^*_{22} \equiv S^*_{22} p^*_2 / x^*_2$ is the pure substitution price elasticity of import demand or export supply.

10. There are many ways of deriving the optimal trade tax characterization. Obtain characterizations from the following problem formulations and compare them with that of the text.
   (a) $\max\{u(G_p(p, v) - x^*(p^*, v^*, \alpha^*))\}$ (note that $\rho G_{pp}(p, v) = 0$ has solution $\rho = p$ up to a factor of proportionality, a result used extensively in Chapter 11).
   (b) $\max\{U(-x^*(p^*, v^*, \alpha^*), v)\}$.
   (c) $\max\{\mu: S_p(p, \mu, v) + x^*(p^*, v^*, \alpha^*) = 0\}$ (use the same hint as in (a)).
   (d) $\max\{\mu: S(p, \mu, v) + px^*(p^*, v^*, \alpha^*) = 0\}$ (note that the market equilibrium condition is one of the optimality conditions).

11. Using the offer-curve diagram (x space) or the production possibility set diagram (y and z space) show for a one-person economy that:
   (a) $H(p, 0, v)$ is minimized at the autarky price vector;
   (b) H increases as p_j increases if $x_j > 0$; and
   (c) H decreases as p_j increases if $x_j < 0$.

References

Baldwin, R.E. (1952) "The new welfare economics and gains in international trade", *Quarterly Journal of Economics* 66-1, February, 91–101.

Chipman, J.S. and J.C. Moore (1972) "Social utility and the gains from trade", *Journal of International Economics* 2, 157–172.

Chipman, J.S. and J.C. Moore (1978) "The new welfare economics 1939-1974", *International Economic Review* 19-3, October, 547–584.

Dixit, A.K. and V. Norman (1980a) *Theory of International Trade* (J. Nisbet/Cambridge University Press).

Dixit, A.K. and V. Norman (1980b) "The gains from free trade", *Warwick Economic Research Paper* 173, July.

Gorman, W.M. (1959) "Are social indifference curves convex?", *Quarterly Journal of Economics* 73, 485–496.

Graaf, J. de V. (1949) "On optimal tariff structures", *Review of Economic Studies* 17, 47–59.

Grandmont, J.M. and D. McFadden (1972) "A technical note on classical gains from trade", *Journal of International Economics* 2, 109–125.

Horwell, D.J. and I.F. Pearce (1970) "A look at the structure of optimal tariffs rates", *International Economic Review* 11-1, February, 147–161.

Kemp, M.C. (1962) "The gain from international trade", *Economic Journal*, December, 803–819.

Kemp, M.C. (1964) *The Pure Theory of International Trade* (Englewood Cliffs, N.J.: Prentice-Hall).

Kemp, M.C. (1969) *The Pure Theory of International Trade and Investment* (Englewood Cliffs, N.J.: Prentice-Hall).

Krueger, A.O. and H. Sonnenschein (1967) "The terms of trade, the gains from trade and price divergence", *International Economic Review* 8-1, February, 121–127.

Mangasarian, D.L. (1969) *Nonlinear Programming*, (New York: McGraw-Hill).

Negishi, T. (1963) "On social welfare function", *Quarterly Journal of Economics* 77-1, February, 156–158.

Ohyama, M. (1972) "Trade and welfare in general equilibrium", *Keio Economic Studies* 9-2, 37–73.

Otani, Y. (1972) "Gains from trade revisited", *Journal of International Economics* 2, 127–156.

Samuelson, P.A. (1939) "Welfare economics and international trade", *American Economic Review*, June, 261–266.

Samuelson, P.A. (1956) "Social indifference curves", *Quarterly Journal of Economics*, February, 1–22.

Samuelson, P.A. (1962) "The gains from international trade once again", *Economic Journal*, December, 820–829.

Scitovsky, T. (1942) "A reconsideration of the theory of tariffs", *Review of Economic Studies* 9, 89–110.

Wan, H. (1972) "A note on trading gains and externalities", *Journal of International Economics* 2, 173–180.

Woodland, A.D. (1980) "Direct and indirect trade utility functions", *Review of Economic Studies* 47, 907–926.

CHAPTER 10

TRANSFERS, TARIFFS AND TAXES

10.1. Introduction

An obvious feature of the international trading scene is the prevalence of tariffs, quotas and other impediments to trade. Originally imposed to provide an easily collected source of government revenue, tariffs on the imports of goods have now become important instruments of the economic policies of most nations. It is therefore important to have a clear idea of the effects of changes in tariff rates upon the prices of goods and services, both at home and abroad, upon the distribution of income, the output mix, the pattern of consumption and trade, as well as upon the tariff revenue earned by the government.

While most attention is usually given to the effect of tariffs upon the internal structure of the economy, it is also true that taxes not directly imposed upon trade, for example production and consumption taxes, will have an effect upon the pattern and volume of trade and hence product prices. In addition, policies which affect the distribution of disposable incomes between nations will also have an effect upon product prices, trade and the internal structure of nations. An example of such a policy is the transfer of income between nations due to reparations payments or foreign aid. Accordingly, the present chapter is devoted to an analysis of the effects of these types of policies in addition to tariffs.

We will assume the existence of a community utility function yielding aggregate demand functions with all the properties of individual demand functions. This simplifies the analysis substantially and the results obtained require appropriate qualifications. The tastes of the consumption sector are described by the expenditure function $E(p, \mu)$ or by the indirect utility function $V(p, m) \equiv \max \mu \{\mu: E(p, \mu) \leqslant m\}$, where m is income. Income is made up of two parts: that generated by the production sector as factor income, $G(p, v)$, and other income, r, which may be positive or negative. Other income might be, for example, reparation payments received, tariff revenue, or production tax revenue depending up-

290 International trade and resource allocation

on the policy being analysed. Alternatively, the tastes and technology may be described by the indirect trade utility function $H(p, r, v) \equiv V(p, G(p, v) + r)$.

The vector of excess supply functions is

$$x(p, r, v) \equiv G_p(p, v) - \phi(p, m), \tag{1}$$

where $\phi(p, m) \equiv E_p(p, V(p, m))$ is the vector of consumer demand functions, $G_p(p, v)$ is the vector of supply (net) functions and $m \equiv G(p, v) + r$. The excess supply functions can also be obtained from the indirect trade utility function as $x(p, r, v) \equiv H_p(p, r, v)/H_r(p, r, v)$ in accordance with an extension of Roy's identity. It is noted that the excess supply functions (a) are homogeneous of degree zero in p, and (b) satisfy the identity $px(p, r, v) \equiv r$, which is Walras' law when $r = 0$.

A similar structure holds for the foreign nation whose functions and variables are distinguished by an asterix ($*$). The world excess supply functions are

$$X \equiv x(p, r, v) + x^*(p^*, r^*, v^*). \tag{2}$$

No arguments have been given to X, since they will vary from model to model. In general $X = X(p, \alpha)$, where α is a vector of parameters and p is the price vector under consideration. Then p^0 is said to be an equilibrium price vector when $X(p^0, \alpha) \geqslant 0 \leqslant p^0$ which, when $p^0 > 0$, requires that all markets clear, i.e. $X(p^0, \alpha) = 0$. In what follows it will be assumed that $p^0 > 0$.

In the models to be considered below the excess supply functions (a) will be homogeneous of degree zero in prices and (b) will satisfy Walras' law, namely $p\,X(p, \alpha) \equiv 0$. Accordingly, the price vector may be normalized and one market may be ignored. There will be economy of notation, at the slight risk of confusion, if $p = (p_1, p_2)$, where $p_2 = (p_2, ..., p_M)$ is the vector of all prices except the first. In the special case where $M = 2$, then vector p_2 is a scalar and is the price of good 2. Similarly, let $X_2 = (X_2, ..., X_M)$. It is also noted that if $p_1 > 0$, then $X_i(p, \alpha) = X_i(p_1, p_2, \alpha) = X_i(1, p_2/p_1, \alpha)$ due to the homogeneity property. Alternatively, setting $p_1 = 1$, $X_i(p, \alpha) = X_i(1, p_2, \alpha)$. Thus, p_2 may be interpreted as p_2 when $p_1 = 1$ or as p_2/p_1.

It should be noted that the above model allows p to differ from p^* due to the existence of trade taxes. The vector p^* will be termed the world price or foreign price vector, thus ignoring the possibility that the foreign nation also imposes trade taxes. If it does then p^* is the world price vector. Another point is that alternative normalizations of prices could be used, such as restricting p to the unit simplex, but our choice of fixing p_1 is convenient.

10.2. Stability of world markets[1]

Before proceeding to analyse various policies using the comparative statics technique, it is necessary that some space be devoted to the question of stability of
equilibrium. If the equilibria being compared in the comparative statics analyses
are not stable, then such analyses are of little interest. In addition, the stability
condition may be useful in establishing the comparative statics results if it is
forced upon the model.

10.2.1. Walrasian price adjustment mechanism

One approach to the stability question is to assume that all internal markets adjust instantaneously, but that world markets do not. The price vector adjusts
over time according to some "price adjustment mechanism", but there is no actual trading out of equilibrium. If the price vector converges to an equilibrium
price vector from any initial point, the system is said to be *globally stable*. If it
converges to an equilibrium price vector from any point in its neighbourhood,
then this equilibrium is said to be *locally stable*. Formally, the adjustment mechanism usually specified is

$$\dot{p}_2 \equiv \mathrm{d}p_2(t)/\mathrm{d}t = -K\, X_2(p,\alpha), \tag{3}$$

where K is a matrix of adjustment coefficients and $p_2(t)$ is the time path of p_2.[2]
If K is diagonal with positive diagonal elements (3) states that the price of each
good increases if there is an excess demand and decreases in the case of an excess
supply. The M-1 equations in (3) form a set of non-linear first-order differential
equations. In the neighbourhood of an equilibrium $p^0 = (p_1^0, p_2^0) > 0$, where p_1^0
is the normalized value of p_1, they may be linearized and written as

$$\dot{p}_2 = \mathrm{d}(p_2 - p_2^0)/\mathrm{d}t = -K\, X_{22}(p^0,\alpha)\,(p_2 - p_2^0), \tag{4}$$

where $X_{22} \equiv \partial X_2/\partial p_2$, which is a system of linear first-order differential equations in $p_2 - p_2^0$. The local stability of p_2^0 coincides with the stability of (4). The

---

[1] A convenient reference on the concepts and conditions for stability is Takayama (1974,
ch. 3). See also Arrow and Hahn (1971) and the survey by Negishi (1962).
[2] More generally, one might specify that $\dot{p}_2 = -k(X_2(p_2,\alpha))$, where k is an $(M-1) \times 1$
vector of functions of $X_2(p_2,\alpha)$. Then in (4) below K would be the matrix of derivatives of
k with respect to X_2 evaluated at $X_2(p^0,\alpha)$.

necessary and sufficient condition for the stability of (4) is that the real parts of the eigenvalues of the matrix $-K\, X_{22}(p^0, \alpha)$ be negative.[3]

In the case of $M = 2$, (4) is a single linear differential equation and is easily solved as

$$p_2(t) = p_2^0 + [p_2(o) - p_2^0] \exp\{-K\, X_{22}(p^0, \alpha)t\}. \qquad (5)$$

Evidently, $p_2(t) \to p_2^0$ as $t \to \infty$ if and only if $K\, X_{22}(p^0, \alpha) > 0$. Since $K > 0$ by assumption, this is equivalent to the condition

$$X_{22}(p^0, \alpha) \equiv \partial X_2(p^0, \alpha)/\partial p > 0. \qquad (6)$$

That is, local stability is equivalent to the condition that the world excess supply function slopes upward at the equilibrium price. If p_2 is slightly above p_2^0, there is an excess supply and, according to (4), the price will fall towards p_2^0; conversely, if p_2 is slightly below p_2^0 there is an excess demand and the price will rise towards p_2^0.

The stability condition (6) may be expressed in terms of the derivatives of the national excess supply functions. It can be shown (see problem set) that $X_{22} = -\Delta x_2/p_2$, where $\Delta \equiv (\xi_{22}^* + \xi_{11} + 1) = -(\xi_{22} + \xi_{11}^* + 1)$, and $\xi_{ij} \equiv x_{ij} p_j/x_i$ is the elasticity of supply of good i with respect to the price of good j (similarly for ξ_{ij}^*). If good 1 is imported by the home nation, then $x_2 > 0$ and the condition that $X_{22} > 0$ is equivalent to $\Delta < 0$. This is the famous *Marshall–Lerner condition*. It is expressed in terms of the own price elasticities of import demand in the home ($\xi_{11} = x_{11}p_1/x_1 = \partial\ln(-x_1)/\partial\ln p_1$) and the foreign ($\xi_{22}^* = x_{22}^*p_2/x_2^* = \partial\ln x_2^*/\partial\ln p_2$) nations. The second expression for Δ above is in terms of export supply elasticities.

Evidently, the stability condition may be expressed in terms of all sorts of elasticities: in terms of export supply elasticities rather than import demand elasticities as in the Marshall–Lerner condition; in terms of elasticities of the offer curves; or in terms of the demand and supply elasticities of each nation, as in Jones (1961). However, we have no need for such expressions and so use (6) as the stability condition.

In view of the homogeneity of excess supply functions in prices it follows from Euler's theorem that condition (6) may be rewritten as

$$\frac{\partial X_2}{\partial p_1} = -\frac{\partial X_2}{\partial p_2}\frac{p_1}{p_2} < 0, \qquad (7)$$

---

[3] See, for example, Takayama (1974, p. 310).

which is the characterization of the concept of gross substitutability. In general, *gross substitutability* occurs when

$$\frac{\partial X_i(p, \alpha)}{\partial p_j} < 0, \quad \text{for all} \quad i, j = 1, ..., M, \quad \text{with} \quad j \neq i \tag{8}$$

for all p. That is, an increase in the price of good j *reduces* the excess supply of *all* other goods. Arrow, Block and Hurwicz (1959) have shown that the assumption of gross substitutability, together with the assumptions that the excess supply functions satisfy Walras' law and are homogeneous of degree zero in prices, is sufficient to establish the global stability of a competitive equilibrium model (such as the present model). The assumption of gross substitutability is quite restrictive. When $M = 2$ (7) shows that it requires $\partial X_2/\partial p_2 > 0$ for all p, i.e. excess supply functions slope upwards throughout, which rules out many plausible functions. Moreover, this assumption also implies the uniqueness of equilibrium (as is evident in the $M = 2$ case). Thus, while the gross substitutability assumption simplifies the analysis, it is very restrictive.

Returning to the linearized system (4), it is noted that the necessary and sufficient conditions for its stability have been developed and are known as the Routh–Hurwitz conditions. Unfortunately, they are too cumbersome to be of much use in theoretical analysis, unless $M \leqslant 4$.

10.2.2. Quantity adjustment mechanisms

The preceding discussion of the stability of world markets is based upon a price adjustment mechanism formulated by Samuelson (1947). Alternatively, a quantity adjustment mechanism may be postulated and the stability conditions derived. For example, Amano (1968) has rehabilitated Marshall's quantity adjustment mechanism and related the resulting stability conditions to those obtained from a price adjustment mechanism.

Amano considers the stability of both temporary and a long-run equilibria. A temporary equilibrium is established for a given production vector for goods. In this equilibrium producers may not be maximizing profits at the market prices. Over time producers adjust their production decisions to improve their profits and a long-run equilibrium occurs when they achieve profit maximization.

Formally, the temporary equilibrium is described as follows. Since outputs are given, the incomes of each nation are

$$m \equiv py \leqslant G(p, v) \quad \text{and} \quad m^* \equiv p y^* \leqslant G^*(p, v^*). \tag{9}$$

Hence, the product demand vectors are $\phi(p, m)$ and $\phi^*(p, m^*)$, respectively, assuming aggregation of the consumption sector. The temporary equilibrium conditions determining the price vector p are, therefore,

$$y - \phi(p, m) + y^* - \phi^*(p, m^*) = 0, \tag{10}$$

where m and m^* are defined by (9). It is noted that Walras' law holds so that only $(M\text{-}1)$ of the equations in (10) are needed to obtain p up to a factor of proportionality.

For given y and v the solution p to (10) yields a solution for the factor price vector. For example, when there are just final goods the factor market equilibrium conditions

$$\sum_{j=1}^{M} c^j_w(w)y_j = v \tag{11}$$

yield a solution for w which may be written as $w = w(y, v)$. Amano postulated that outputs would respond positively to an excess of price over long-run cost. That is,

$$\dot{y}_j = h_j(p_j - c^j(w(y, v))), \qquad j = 1, ..., M, \tag{12}$$

where $h_j > 0$ is the speed of adjustment in industry j. Eq. (12) is a set of nonlinear first-order differential equations in y.[4] A similar set of equations may be obtained for the foreign nation:

$$\dot{y}^*_j = h^*_j(p_j - c^{*j}(w^*(y^*, v^*))), \qquad j = 1, ..., M. \tag{13}$$

The movement of the economies through time is described by the differential equations (12) and (13), which reflect the adjustment of producers to prices, and the temporary market equilibrium condition (10).

Amano obtained the local stability conditions for this model for the case where $M = 2$, and related his conditions to those obtained by others for similar

---

[4]   Amano did not express his differential equation using cost functions. The expression in (12) makes it clear that producers are responding to current profits measured by the difference between price and current costs. However, it is evident that the vector $c(y, w)$ of costs coincides with the price vector $\bar{p}$ that would bring forth output vector y under profit maximization, where $\bar{p}$ is normal to the production possibility frontier at y. Thus, Amano let $\dot{y}_j = h_j(p_j - \bar{p}_j)$, where $\bar{p} = t_y(y, -v)$ and where $t(y, -v) = 0$ is the transformation or production possibility frontier.

models. When $M = 2$, the model consists of a differential equation for y_2 and another for y_2^* plus one temporary equilibrium condition, since the transformation functions $t(y, -v) = 0$ and $t^*(y^*, -v^*) = 0$ determine y_1 and y_1^* and the system is homogeneous of degree zero in prices. Let $p_2 = \Pi(y_2, y_2^*)$ be the solution for p_2 from (10). Then, the Routh–Hurwitz conditions for the local stability of the two linearized differential equations in y_2 and y_2^* are

(a) $h_2 h_2^* [t_{22} t_{22}^* - \Pi_{y_2^*} t_{22} - \Pi_{y_2} t_{22}^*] > 0,$

(b) $h_2(\Pi_{y_2} - t_{22}) + h_2^*(\Pi_{y_2^*} - t_{22}^*) < 0,$

$$(14)$$

where Π_{y_2} and $\Pi_{y_2^*}$ are the derivatives of Π with respect to y_2 and y_2^*, respectively, t_{22} and t_{22}^* are the derivatives of $t_2(y, -v)$ and $t_2^*(y^*, -v)$ with respect to y_2 and y_2^*, and t_2 and t_2^* are the (normalized) derivatives of the transformation functions representing the costs of production for good 2 in the two countries (see footnote 4).

In this model the temporary equilibrium always holds. If a simple Samuelsonian price adjustment mechanism is postulated, the local stability condition for the temporary equilibria implies that Π_{y_2}, $\Pi_{y_2^*} < 0$ if good 2 is normal in both nations (see problem set). This simply means that a higher output level in either nation will reduce the price of good 2. It is also true that $t_{22}, t_{22}^* > 0$ since, for example, an increase in y_2 requires an increase in the price of good 2 to sustain it as a profit-maximization solution. Finally, $h, h^* > 0$ by assumption. These sign conditions imply that condition (14, a) holds. Thus, it has been demonstrated that the stability of the temporary equilibria price mechanism, together with normality of good 2 in consumption, is sufficient for Amano's long-run quantity adjustment model to be stable.[5]

10.2.3. Comment

There are, of course, as many stability conditions for a model as there are adjustment mechanisms. Above we have considered just two such mechanisms. The first assumes that all internal adjustments are instantaneous, so that the nation is always on its offer curve, and that world prices for traded goods adjust sluggishly to the state of disequilibrium in world markets. The second mechanism assumes that world prices adjust instantaneously to clear markets, while producers adjust

---

[5]   Amano allows the transformation frontier to be non-convex in which case t_{22} and t_{22}^* are not necessarily positive. In this case long-run stability requires more than the stability of the temporary equilibria.

sluggishly to the state of profitability. It is not difficult to construct alternative models of adjustment and obtain their stability conditions, but we shall not do so. In the ensuing analysis the Walrasian stability condition will be extensively used to obtain comparative statics results.[6]

10.3. The transfer problem

If one nation transfers income to another nation, what will be the effect upon world prices and upon the real incomes of both nations? Examples of such transfers are reparation payments, which provided the source of the problem, and foreign aid programs.

Let r denote the amount of income transferred from the home to the foreign nation. Their incomes are therefore $m \equiv G(p, v) + r$ and $m^* \equiv G^*(p, v^*) - r$. The world excess supply functions, for all goods except the first, are

$$X_2(p, r) \equiv G_2(p, v) - \phi_2(p, G(p, v) + r) + G_2^*(p, v^*) - \\ - \phi_2^*(p, G^*(p, v^*) - r) = 0, \tag{15}$$

where p is the equilibrium price vector. The effect of a small change in r upon p_2 is obtained from (15) as

$$dp_2 = -X_{22}^{-1}(p, r) X_{2r}(p, r) dr, \tag{16}$$

where $X_{2r}(p, r) \equiv \partial X_2(p, r)/\partial r = \phi_{2m}^* - \phi_{2m}$.

In the case where $M = 2$, $X_{22}(p, r) > 0$ if the model is locally stable. If this condition is imposed then the effect of a change in r depends upon $X_{2r}(p, r)$ alone. This is the difference in the two nations' responses in consumption to changes in income. If $\phi_{2m}^* > \phi_{2m}$, then the increase in income of the home nation raises demand for good 2 by a lesser amount than demand falls in the foreign nation. Hence, at the initial price p there will exist an excess supply of good 2 on the world market. The stability condition ensures that this excess supply will result in a reduction in the price of good 2. Thus, in the case of $M = 2$ there is a clear answer to the question of how a transfer of income will affect world prices.

This solution to the question of how an international transfer of income affects the price vector is hardly surprising in view of the discussion in Chapter 6

[6] It should also be noted that the adjustment models dealt with above are somewhat ad hoc in that they do not allow for trading out of equilibrium. Consequently they are not intended to be models of disequilibrium.

of conditions under which income redistributions would not affect aggregate demands. Here the answer is the same. A transfer of income from one nation to another will not affect world prices only if both nations have the same marginal propensities to consume all goods. Otherwise aggregate demands will change as a result of the income transfer and world prices will alter.

What can be said when $M > 2$? If gross substitutability holds at (p, r), then it can be shown that $X_{22}^{-1}(p, r) \geqslant 0$.[7] But this only allows the result that $\mathrm{d}p_2 < 0$ if $\phi_{2m}^* - \phi_{2m}^* > 0$. That is to say, if the propensity to consume goods 2, ..., M in the home nation is less than in the foreign nation there will be a world excess supply for all these goods and hence their prices will fall relative to that of good 1.

Also of interest to both nations is the effect of the transfer upon their real incomes. Assuming that the consumption sector maximizes a community utility function subject to the aggregate budget constraint, the effect of a transfer upon the utility levels may be calculated using the indirect trade utility function. For the home nation it is $H(p, r, v) \equiv V(p, G(p, v) + r)$. The (normalized) change in utility is

$$\frac{\mathrm{d}H}{H_r} = \frac{H_p}{H_r}\,\mathrm{d}p + \mathrm{d}r = x\,\mathrm{d}p + \mathrm{d}r = x_2\,\mathrm{d}p_2 + \mathrm{d}r,$$

since $x = H_p/H_r$ as explained in Chapter 9, and since $\mathrm{d}p_1 = 0$ by assumption. Substituting expression (16) for $\mathrm{d}p_2$ yields:

$$\frac{\mathrm{d}H}{\mathrm{d}r}\frac{1}{H_r} = [1 - x_2\,X_{22}^{-1}\,X_{2r}] = [1 - x_2\,X_{22}^{-1}(\phi_{2m}^* - \phi_{2m})]. \tag{17}$$

Direct calculation establishes that

$$X_{22} = s + (\phi_{2m}^* - \phi_{2m})x_2, \tag{18}$$

where $s \equiv [G_{22} + G_{22}^* - E_{22} - E_{22}^*]$ is the matrix of pure substitution price effects upon world excess supply.

When $M = 2$ all the terms in (17) and (18) are scalars allowing (17) to be written as

$$\frac{\mathrm{d}H}{\mathrm{d}r}\frac{1}{H_r} = \frac{s}{X_{22}}. \tag{19}$$

[7] See Takayama (1974, p. 392).

Since $s > 0$ (strictly, $s \geqslant 0$) it is clear from (19) that the level of utility increases if the market is stable, i.e. $X_{22} > 0$. Thus, under stability, the nation which receives a transfer of income from another nation will gain in welfare. The giving nation evidently loses since the competitive equilibrium is a Pareto optimum.

When $M > 2$, no such clear-cut result is apparent. Is it possible, therefore, that a nation could suffer a reduction in real income as a consequence of a transfer of income to it? Or will the assumption that the world markets are stable rule out such a possibility? Intuitively, it seems unreasonable that the number of goods should matter, and hence the utility of the receiving nation should increase if the markets are stable. The stability conditions are sufficiently complex, however, that a proof has not been obtained. When $M = 3$ the stability conditions are sufficiently simple to work with, and it turns out that they can be used to prove that the receiving nation gains. The Routh–Hurwicz necessary and sufficient conditions for stability are that (i) $\text{tr}(X_{22}) > 0$ and (ii) $|X_{22}| > 0$.[8] Direct calculation of the determinant of X_{22} expressed as (18) yields the relationship:

$$| X_{22} | = | s | \, \{ 1 + (\phi^{*}_{2m} - \phi_{2m})^{\mathrm{T}} \, s^{-1} \, x_2 \}. \tag{20}$$

A direct calculation of X_{22}^{-1} allows (17) to be written as

$$\frac{\mathrm{d}H}{\mathrm{d}r} \frac{1}{H_r} = \frac{| s |}{| X_{22} |}. \tag{21}$$

Since s is a positive definite matrix its determinant is positive.[9] Thus, part (ii) of the stability conditions, which requires $|X_{22}| > 0$, may be used to establish that the nation receiving a transfer of income gains utility.

The preceding analysis shows how world prices and real incomes are affected by a transfer of income from one nation to another. The real income of the recipient will rise if the markets are stable, at least in the case of $M \leqslant 3$ goods. The reader may wish to derive an alternative expression for the change in real incomes of the recipient nation, and to rework the analysis when the transfer is in the form of goods rather than income.

---

[8] The trace of a square matrix, denoted tr, is the sum of the diagonal elements.

[9] Strictly, s is positive semi-definite. However, it is assumed that it is of full rank and hence positive definite.

10.4. Taxes on international trade

The most common form of government intervention in international trade is the imposition of import duties or tariffs. On the export side subsidies and taxes are not uncommon. In this section trade taxes are modelled and comparative statics analyses are performed to obtain the effects upon an economy of a change in trade taxes.

10.4.1. The model with trade taxes

The competitive nature of the model ensures that domestic and world prices will differ by exactly the amount of taxation or subsidy as long as each good continues to be traded. If this were not the case then some trader could buy where the good was cheapest and sell in the more expensive market making a profit. In a competitive economy this profit opportunity will be taken and the resulting trading activity will persist until profits are reduced to zero.

The relationship between domestic and foreign prices (denoted, as usual, by an asterisk (∗)) is

$$p_i = (1 + t_i)p_i^*, \tag{22}$$

where t_i is the ad valorem (percentage of world price) rate of tax. If good i is imported by the home nation, then t_i is the rate of import duty if $t_i > 0$, or the rate of import subsidy if $t_i < 0$. The actual tax revenue per unit is $t_i p_i^*$. If good i is exported, then a tax or subsidy rate might be expressed as a percentage of the domestic price. Then $p_i^* = (1 + s_i)p_i$, where s_i is the rate of export tax (negative if exports are subsidized), which may be written in the form (22) by setting $t_i = -s_i/(1 + s_i)$. Thus, (22) is applicable for all types of trade taxes.[10] Evidently, the restriction $\infty > t_i > -1$ is required to ensure finite positive prices.

---

[10] In reality taxes are often imposed on trade in one direction. For example, the relationship

$$t_i = \begin{array}{l} 0.5, \ \ x_i < 0, \\ 0, \ \ \ x_i \geqslant 0, \end{array}$$

indicates that a 50% tax is imposed on imports but there are no taxes or subsidies on exports of good i. We shall ignore this and treat t_i as fixed, thus assuming that we know the pattern of trade.

The tariff revenue (net) is

$$R = -\sum_{i=1}^{M} t_i p_i^* x_i, \qquad (23)$$

where x_i is the net export of good i (hence $-x_i$ is the net import). The way in which this revenue is spent is an important determinant of the effects of trade taxes. In the present model it is assumed that the revenue is raised and fully distributed to consumers without the use of any factor inputs. To avoid problems concerned with the tax distribution the assumption of aggregation of the consumption sector is maintained. Thus, the consumption sector has income

$$m = G(p, v) + R, \qquad (24)$$

where $G(p, v)$ is the GNP function. The consumption sector therefore consumes according to the demand vector $\phi(p, m)$. The production sector produces according to the supply vector $G_p(p, v)$. The net export vector for the home nation is therefore

$$x = G_p(p, v) - \phi(p, m). \qquad (25)$$

The model is completed by imposing the world market clearing conditions

$$X \equiv x + x^*(p^*, v^*) = 0, \qquad (26)$$

where $x^*(p^*, v^*)$ is the net export function for the foreign nation and p^* is the world price vector. As usual, one of the equations in (26) is redundant and the price vectors are only determined up to a factor of proportionality.

10.4.2. *Symmetry of trade taxes*

Since the model is homogeneous of degree zero in prices, it is also homogeneous of degree zero in the $1 + t_i$ terms. This can be seen by taking good 1 as a numeraire and dividing (22) by $p_1 > 0$ to obtain:

$$\frac{p_j}{p_1} = \frac{1 + t_j}{1 + t_1} \frac{p_j^*}{p_1^*} = (1 + \tau_j) \frac{p_j^*}{p_1^*}, \qquad j = 2, ..., M, \qquad (27)$$

where $1 + \tau_j \equiv (1 + t_j)/(1 + t_1)$. The relationship (27) together with the homogeneity of the model in prices is important and leads directly to the demonstration of the symmetry of import and export taxes. Let good 1 be imported subject to an import duty of rate t_1 and let good j be freely exported. Then $1 + \tau_j = 1/(1 + t_1)$. Secondly, let good j be subject to an export tax of rate s_j based upon the domestic price while good 1 is freely imported. Then $p_j^* = (1 + s_j)p_j$, which may be rewritten as $p_j = p_j^*/(1 + s_j) = (1 + \tau_j)p_j^*$, where now $1 + \tau_j = 1/(1 + s_j)$. Evidently, if the rate of export tax s_j is equal to the rate of import duty t_1, then the value of $1 + \tau_j$ is the same in each case. The wedge between foreign and domestic price *ratios* is the same in each case and hence the equilibrium solution is the same.[11] Thus, under the assumptions of the model there is a symmetry or equivalence between import and export taxes.

Several points need to be noted concerning the symmetry result. First, if more than one good is imported then a uniform tariff rate on all imports is equivalent to a uniform export tax rate on all exports. Secondly, the tax rate on any good can be set at zero with no effect upon the equilibrium solution if the other tax rates are appropriately modified. If, for example, the tax rate t_1 is to be made zero, then (27) indicates that the price ratios are unaffected if $(1 + t_j)$ is replaced by $1 + \tau_j = (1 + t_j)/(1 + t_1)$. That is, the rate of tax expressed in terms of foreign prices becomes

$$\tau_j = (t_j - t_1)/(1 + t_1), \qquad (28)$$

which in general is not a uniform change in rates. Actually, this formula for τ_j emphasizes that it is the *difference* in rates $t_j - t_1$ that is important, not the levels. Thirdly, the assumptions of the model are crucial. For example, the unimportance of the income distribution in the model is clearly very crucial. Finally, while the argument has been expressed in terms of taxes, it is evident that it accomodates subsidies which are, of course, simply negative taxes.

10.4.3. Model reformulation

Since it has been shown that a tax structure can always be normalized to have one of the tax rates equal to zero, the ensuing analysis makes use of the normalized tax rates τ_j defined by (28) in which $\tau_1 = 0$. This is convenient since $\tau_j = t_j$ if it is true that $t_1 = 0$, and since $\partial \tau_j/\partial t_j = 1/(1 + t_1) > 0$ and $\partial \tau_j/\partial t_1 = -(1 + t_j)/(1 + t_1)^2 < 0$. In addition, one price can be normalized so $p_1 = 1$ is assumed. Thus, in the model the price vectors $p_2 = (p_2, ..., p_M)$ and $p_2^* = (p_2^*, ..., p_M^*)$ are

---

[11] To complete the proof the reader might check that only price ratios matter by checking that the tax revenue is the same in each case.

determined. These prices are related by $p_i = (1 + \tau_i)p_i^*$ or, alternatively, as $p_i^* = (1 + \sigma_i)p_i$, where $\sigma_i = -\tau_i/(1 + \tau_i)$ is the rate of tax based upon domestic prices. The tax revenue may be written as

$$R = -\sum_{i=1}^{M} \tau_i p_i^* x_i = -\sum_{i=2}^{M} \tau_i p_i^* x_i = \sum_{i=2}^{M} \sigma_i p_i x_i. \tag{29}$$

The model determining p_2 and p_2^* is given by (29), (24) and

$$X_2 = x_2 + x_2^*(p^*, v^*) = 0, \tag{30}$$

$$x_2 = G_2(p, v) - \phi_2(p, m), \tag{31}$$

and

$$p_i = (1 + \tau_i)p_i^* \quad \text{or} \quad p_i^* = (1 + \sigma_i)p_i, \qquad i = 2, ..., M, \tag{32}$$

where the subscript 2 means a vector formed by deleting the first element.[12]

The model determines foreign and domestic prices given a tax structure. In what follows interest centres upon the effects of a change in the tax structure upon both foreign and domestic prices. Once this is done the effects upon production, consumption, income, tax revenue, factor prices and the allocation of resources may easily be calculated.

10.5. Trade taxes in the two-commodity model

The main points regarding trade taxes can be obtained fairly easily using a two-commodity model of world trade. A consideration of other complications such as the existence of non-traded goods and many traded goods will be provided in a later section.

10.5.1. Effects of trade taxes

The basic effects of trade taxes may be explained by supposing that there are initially no taxes and then considering the consequences of imposing import

---

[12] Notice that p and p^* have been maintained as arguments of the various functions even though the first price in each vector is normalized at unity. This is done to avoid defining new functions. The alternative is to rewrite the model using price ratios p_j/p_1. For example, the demand functions are then $\phi_2(p, m) = \phi_2(1, \rho, \tilde{m}) \equiv \tilde{\phi}_2(\rho, \tilde{m})$, where $\rho_i \equiv p_i/p_1$ and $\tilde{m} \equiv m/p_1$. The interested reader may wish to complete this formulation in terms of ρ and ρ^*.

duties. If world prices are unaffected, as they would be for a small open economy, (22) indicates that the domestic prices would rise by the amount of the per unit equivalent $(t_i p_i^*)$ of the tariff for all imported goods (for goods not imported $t_i = 0$ by assumption). Thus, domestically there is a rise in the price of importable goods relative to exportable goods. This is the *direct price effect* of a tariff. As a consequence there will be a *production effect*. The outputs of importable goods will rise by drawing resources away from the exportable goods industries. This yields a change in GNP described by $G(p, v)$ and this may be termed the *GNP effect*. The income and consumption effects are more difficult to calculate. The reason is that the level of tariff revenue R is required to determine the total income and hence the consumption vector of goods, but R depends upon the level of imports, which depend upon the consumption vector and hence R. There is, therefore, a simultaneity between these variables making the analysis more difficult than on the production side. The *revenue* and *consumption* effects can nevertheless be calculated as will be shown below.

The preceding formulation of the model with trade taxes assumes that they are imposed in ad valorem form. Alternatively, they could have been expressed in per unit form. While in many ways it is simpler to deal with per unit taxes, the following sections concentrate upon ad valorem tax rates because most of the literature does so and most trade taxes in the real world are expressed in ad valorem form. However, in section 10.7 below per unit taxes are used and the reader may wish to relate the results obtained there (specialized to the two-commodity case) to those obtained in this section.

Figure 10.1 illustrates the effects of a tariff imposed on the imports of good 1 for the case where there are $M = 2$ goods. The initial domestic and world price vector is p^0 generating the output vector y^0 and consumption vector z^0. The import tariff on good 1 changes the domestic price vector p^1 leaving the world price vector at p^0. The production effect is the movement around the transformation frontier from y^0 to y^1 resulting in a greater output of good 1 at the expense of good 2. The new GNP line is G^1. Of course the budget line for the consumption sector will be further from the origin than G^1 owing to the tariff revenue earned, but will be parallel to G^1 since consumers also face the tariff-distorted price vector p^1. How far out will the budget line be? It will not be beyond the initial indifference curve μ^0 since this would imply a welfare gain as a result of the tariff, and this is not possible for a small open economy, as explained in Chapter 9. There are two conditions which allow z^1 to be found. First, the net export vector $x^1 = y^1 - z^1$ must satisfy the condition $p^0 x^1 = 0$, which says that the balance of trade is zero. This means that z^1 must be along the line labelled A. Secondly, since the consumption sector faces p^1 this price vector must be normal to the highest attainable indifference curve at z^1 for utility maximization.

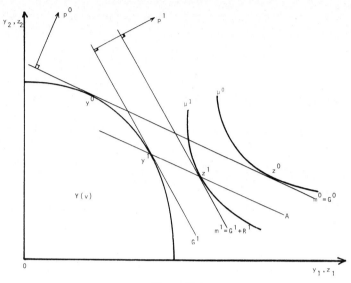

Figure 10.1

These two conditions thus ensure a solution such as z^1 in fig. 10.1. The difference between the lines G^1 and m^1 is due, of course, to the tariff revenue R^1.

The preceding discussion is based upon the assumption that the world price
vector is not affected by the imposition of the tariff. If the nation is not small,
then the resulting adjustment in its trade with the rest of the world will require
an alteration in the world price vector to re-establish market equilibrium. This
change in the world price vector is called the *terms of trade effect*, which is illustrated in fig. 10.2 using offer curves. The home offer curve under free trade is
H, while the tariff-distorted offer curve is H^1 obtained by tracing out the locus
of net export vectors corresponding to different foreign price vectors but all
with the same tariff rate. The point x^1, obtained as $y^1 - z^1$ from fig. 10.1, is a
point on H^1. The equilibrium point is at x^2 where H^1 intersects the foreign offer curve F. The tariff revenue expressed in terms of good 2 (that is, R/p_2) is AC,
of which AB is spent on good 2 and BC is spent on good 1. The domestic price
vector is p^2. Point D would be the net export vector for the economy if the tariff
revenue were ignored, whereas A is the equilibrium net export vector once account is taken of how the tariff revenue is spent.

Having examined the effects of the tariff diagrammatically for the case of
$M = 2$ goods, attention is now turned to a mathematical analysis. If foreign prices
are not affected by a change in the tax structure, the foreign offers will be un-

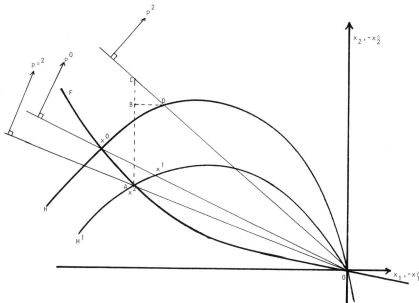

Figure 10.2

affected and domestic variables may be treated as functions of the tax rates primarily through their effects on domestic prices. To aid the discussion let the home nation import good 1 and export good 2 and let the tariff rate on good 1 be increased. In view of the normalization (28) of the tariff structure it follows that $\tau_2 \equiv -t_1/(1 + t_1)$ and hence $\sigma_2 \equiv -\tau_2/(1 + \tau_2) \equiv t_1$.

An increase in t_1 will cause τ_2 to fall and hence p_2 will fall by $dp_2 = p_2^* \, d\tau_2$. This will cause a production effect of $dy_2 = G_{22} \, dp_2$, where $G_{22} \equiv \partial G_2/\partial p_2$, and obviously there will be an increase in the output of good 1. Since $R = -\tau_2 p_2^* x_2$ the increase in tax revenue is $dR = -p_2^* x_2 \, d\tau_2 - \tau_2 p_2^* dx_2$. The change in GNP is $dG = G_2 dp_2$. Hence, the change in disposable income is $dm = dG + dR = \phi_2 \, d\tau_2 - \tau_2 p_2^* \, dx_2$. The change in the consumption of good 2 is $dz_2 = \phi_{22} dp_2 - \phi_{2m} dm$. Substituting for dm and dp_2 using the Slutsky relation $\phi_{22} \equiv E_{22} - \phi_2 \, \phi_{2m}$, where E_{22} is the income compensated effect of an increase in p_2 upon z_2, the change in z_2 is

$$dz_2 = E_{22} \, p_2^* \, d\tau_2 - \phi_{2m} \, \tau_2 p_2^* dx_2,$$

consisting of a pure substitution and an income effect. Having obtained dy_2 and dz_2 the explicit solution for dx_2 is

$$dx_2 = \frac{(G_{22} - E_{22})p_2^*}{1 + c_2 t_1} d\tau_2,$$ (33)

where $c_2 \equiv p_2 \phi_{2m}$ is the marginal propensity to consume good 2 and the relationship $\tau_2 p_2^* / p_2 = \tau_2 / (1 + \tau_2) = -t_1$, has been used.

The denominator in (33) is positive when good 2 is normal ($c_2 > 0$) and $t_1 > 0$. The numerator is positive since $G_{22} > 0$ and $E_{22} < 0$. Hence, an increase in t_1 causing a *fall* in τ_2 will cause the home nation's exports of good 2 to decline when world prices are fixed. Clearly, imports of good 1 will also fall. One can easily verify that the effects upon tax revenue, disposable income and hence consumption are ambiguous.

10.5.2. Effect upon foreign prices

It has just been shown that an increase in the tariff on good 1 will reduce the exports of good 2 when the foreign prices are fixed. Since foreign trade offers are unchanged, the increase in the tariff rate has created a world excess demand for good 2. Assuming stability of the world markets this will require an increase in p_2^* to clear the markets. Thus, the higher tariff improves the terms of trade of the home nation since good 2 is its export good, and worsens the terms of trade of the other nation.

Formally, equilibrium in the world market requires that $X_2(p^*, \tau) = 0$. Thus, $X_{22} dp_2^* + X_{2\tau} d\tau_2 = 0$, whence

$$dp_2^* = -X_{22}^{-1} X_{2\tau} d\tau_2,$$ (34)

where $X_{22} \equiv \partial X_2 / \partial p_2^*$ and $X_{2\tau} \equiv \partial X_2 / \partial \tau_2$. Stability requires that $X_{22} > 0$. The term $X_{2\tau}$ is the coefficient of $d\tau_2$ in (33) which was shown to be positive. Hence, $dp_2^* / d\tau_2 = -X_{22}^{-1} X_{2\tau} < 0$.

The assumption that the tax revenue is redistributed to consumers and is spent according to their preferences is rather crucial to this result. If the government spends the tax revenue, then it may be the case that the terms of trade will deteriorate as a result of the tariff. This occurs if the government's marginal propensity to consume good 1 is sufficiently high that a world excess demand for it rather than good 2 is created by the tariff. This is referred to as *Lerner's paradox*, precise conditions for which are left for the problem set.

10.5.3. Effects upon domestic prices

Having obtained the effect of trade taxes upon the foreign price p_2^* it is possible to obtain the effect upon p_2 via the relation $p_2 = (1 + \tau_2)p_2^*$. However, it will be simpler and instructive to derive the effect upon p_2 directly. For this purpose let the world excess supply for good 2 be a function of p_2 and σ_2, rather than p_2^* and τ_2, and hence write the equilibrium condition as $X_2(p, \sigma) = 0$. Total differentiation of this expression yields:

$$dp_2 = -X_{22}^{-1} X_{2\sigma} \, d\sigma_2, \tag{35}$$

where $X_{22} \equiv \partial X_2/\partial p_2$ and $X_{2\sigma} \equiv \partial X_2/\partial \sigma_2$. The term $X_{2\sigma}d\sigma_2$ indicates the effect on world excess supplies of a change in our tariff structure, while X_{22}^{-1} converts this excess supply vector into the required price change.

In the case of $M = 2$ goods currently under consideration X_{22} is a scalar and is positive if the market is stable. Therefore the effect of a change in σ_2 depends in sign only upon the sign of $X_{2\sigma}$. The expression for $X_{2\sigma}$ is obtained as follows. The change in x_2 when p_2 remains fixed is given in implicit form by

$$dx_2 = -\phi_{2m}[\sigma_2 p_2 dx_2 + p_2 x_2 d\sigma_2]$$

obtained by differentiating (31), (24) and (29). The explicit solution is

$$dx_2 = -\phi_{2m}p_2 x_2 d\sigma_2/[1 + \phi_{2m}p_2\sigma_2]. \tag{36}$$

The change in the foreign excess supply of good 2 is

$$dx_2^* = x_{22}^* \, p_2 \, d\sigma_2. \tag{37}$$

Putting these results together it follows that

$$X_{2\sigma} = x_{22}^* p_2 - \phi_{2m}p_2 x_2/[1 + \phi_{2m}p_2\sigma_2] \tag{38}$$

or

$$X_{2\sigma} = x_2^*\{\xi_{22}^*(1 + \tau_2) + c_2/[1 + c_2\sigma_2]\}, \tag{39}$$

where $\xi_{22}^* \equiv x_{22}^* \, p_2^*/x_2^*$ is the foreign nation's own price elasticity of net exports of good 2 and $c_2 \equiv \phi_{2m}p_2$ is the home nation's marginal propensity to consume good 2 out of income.

For the concrete example under consideration it was supposed that the home nation imports good 1 and exports good 2 and that the tariff rate on good 1 is increased. In view of normalization (28) of the tariff structure $\tau_2 = -t_1/(1 + t_1)$ implying that $\sigma_2 = -\tau_2/(1 + \tau_2) = t_1$. If foreign prices remained constant after increasing t_1 (that is, σ_2) the domestic price p_2 would have fallen indicating a reduction in the relative price of exportables or a rise in the relative price of importables. Since $X_{22} > 0$ under stability, a reduction in p_2 when foreign prices adjust requires $X_{2\sigma} < 0$. Under what circumstances will this result hold?

If good 2 is not inferior in consumption at home, $\phi_{2m} > 0$, while $x_2 > 0$ since good 2 is exported. Thus, the second term in (38) is positive, meaning that an increase in the tariff rate will reduce exports of good 2 due to the additional consumption arising from the extra tax revenue. This reduces the world excess supply of good 2 (i.e. creates an excess demand) given domestic prices. On the other hand, it was proved in Chapter 6 that $x_{22}^* > 0$ whenever $x_2^* < 0$, i.e. an increase in the price of imports p_2^* will always cause imports to fall and hence net exports x_2^* to rise, so that the first term in (38) is positive. Thus, $X_{2\sigma}$, being the difference between positive terms, can apparently be of either sign.

To simplify further consider the case where $t_1 = 0$ so, initially, there is free trade. Then $\tau_2 = \sigma_2 = 0$ and the domestic price of good 2 responds according to

$$dp_2 \gtreqless 0, \quad \text{if and only if} \quad \xi_{22}^* + c_2 \gtreqless 0. \tag{40}$$

The foreign elasticity of import demand ξ_{22}^* is negative, while $0 < c_2 < 1$ if good 2 is normal (neither inferior nor superior).[13] Thus, if the foreign import demand is elastic, $\xi_{22}^* < -1$, then it follows from (40) that $dp_2 < 0$ and the expected effect of a tariff is obtained. To obtain the unexpected or perverse result that $dp_2 > 0$, i.e. a tariff will reduce the relative price of the importable good, it is necessary that $\xi_{22}^* > -1$, meaning an inelastic import demand function for the foreign nation. Of course, this condition is not sufficient unless $c_2 \geqslant 1$. Sufficiency requires that the absolute value of this elasticity be less than c_2, that is $|\xi_{22}^*| < c_2$. Thus, the foreign import demand function has to be "sufficiently" inelastic. In this case a tariff with domestic price constant will raise the relative price of good 2 to the foreign nation which reduces its import demand for that good by less than the home nation's demand increases due to the income effect of the tariff revenue. Accordingly, the price of good 2 (domestic and foreign) must rise to re-establish equilibrium in the world markets.

This condition was first obtained by Metzler (1949) who argued that the per-

---

[13] It is easily verified that ξ_{22}^*, defined above as the own-price elasticity of net exports, may be interpreted as the own-price elasticity of import demand when $x_2^* < 0$.

verse result might not be simply an academic curiosity, but relevant to certain nations. As examples, he considered the case of tariff policy in Australia, Latin America and the United States in the 1800s. In the case of Australia his argument has been challenged by McDougall (1962) who shows that the empirical evidence is against the likelihood that the condition for perversity is satisfied.

If initially there exists a tariff, the condition on ξ_{22}^* for a perverse result is less stringent. To see this note that a perverse result requires

$$\xi_{22}^* + c_2/\omega > 0, \tag{41}$$

where $\omega \equiv (1 + c_2 \sigma_2)/(1 + \sigma_2)$. Since $\omega < 1$ when $c_2 < 1$, it follows that ξ_{22}^* can now be greater than c_2 in absolute value under perversity. As σ_2 rises, ω falls towards c_2 so that in the limit the condition becomes $\xi_{22}^* > -1$.

10.5.4. *Income distribution*

Once the effect of a change in trade taxes upon the domestic prices is obtained, the effects upon factor prices, production levels, consumption and individual incomes can be calculated. For the case of a two-factor, two-final good model, most of these effects may be obtained by recalling the results of Chapter 4.

Suppose that a tariff on the imports of good 1 causes the domestic price of good 1 to rise relative to total of good 2. According to the Stolper–Samuelson theorem this will lead to a rise in the real income of the factor used intensively in the production of good 1, and a reduction in the real income of the other factor. This statement, of course, refers to the factors' real incomes derived from the production sector and ignores the redistribution of the tax revenue.[14]

10.6. Production and consumption taxes

In this section the effects of taxes on production and consumption are investigated, and their relationship to trade taxes established.

---

[14] The role of the redistribution of the tax revenue has been discussed thoroughly by Bhagwati and Johnson (1961).

10.6.1. Production taxes

While trade taxes imply a difference between domestic and foreign prices, pro-duction taxes cause domestic producers to use different prices than the rest of the world which comprises the foreign country and domestic consumers. Let p^* now be the demand price vector, and let p be the domestic supply price vector. Then σ_j represents the rate of the production tax for good j based upon domes-tic prices and so $p_j^* = (1 + \sigma_j)p_j$. This relationship may be rewritten as $p_j = (1 + \tau_j)p_j^*$. Now the net tax revenue is

$$R = \sum_{j=2}^{M} \sigma_j p_j G_j = -\sum_{j=2}^{M} \tau_j p_j^* G_j, \tag{42}$$

since $\sigma_1 = \tau_1 = 0$ by an appropriate normalization of the tax structure. The mod-el is defined by

$$X_2 = x_2 + x_2^*(p^*, v^*) = 0, \tag{43}$$

where

$$x_2 = G_2(p, v) - \phi_2(p^*, m), \tag{44}$$

$$m = G(p, v) + R, \tag{45}$$

and R is defined by (42).

For the case of $M = 2$ the effect of a change in the production tax rate upon domestic and foreign prices is obtained as follows. Writing $X_2 = X_2(p^*, \tau) = 0$ and differentiating yields $dp_2^* = -X_{22}^{-1} X_{2\tau} \, d\tau_2$. Stability ensures that $X_{22} > 0$ so it remains to sign $X_{2\tau} \equiv \partial X_2/\partial \tau_2$. Differentiation of (44), (45) and (42) with re-spect to τ_2 yields:

$$X_{2\tau} = x_{2\tau} = G_{22} \, p_2^* \, [1 + c_2 \tau_2] = G_{22} p_2^* \left[\frac{1 + \sigma_2 c_1}{1 + \sigma_2} \right] > 0, \tag{46}$$

where $c_1 \equiv 1 - c_2$ is the marginal propensity to consume good 1. Thus, $dp_2^*/d\tau_2 < 0$ and hence $dp_2^*/d\sigma_2 > 0$. It has therefore been established that an increase in the rate of production tax on good 2 will raise the world (and consumer) price of that good. If good 2 is exported by the home nation, a higher production tax will improve its terms of trade and worsen the terms of trade of the foreign country.

Is it necessary that the supply price p_2 falls? The expression for the change in p_2 is

$$\frac{dp_2}{d\tau_2} = \frac{p_2^* x_{22}^* - p_2^* E_{22} - c_2 x_2}{X_{22}}, \tag{47}$$

where E_{22} is the Slutsky pure substitution effect on the demand for good 2 as a result of an increase in its price. The reader may verify that the numerator has an ambiguous sign. The expectation would be that $dp_2/d\tau_2 > 0$, i.e. an increase in the production tax rate (fall in τ_2) would reduce the supply price. If good 2 is exported, then $x_{22}^* > 0$ and since $E_{22} < 0$ the first two terms in the numerator are positive. Hence, to get a negative numerator the third term would have to be sufficiently large. In other words, p_2 could increase if the substitution effects by domestic consumers and foreigners away from good 2 (whose demand price has risen) are smaller than the income effect on domestic consumption created by the tax increase.

The above discussion is concerned with an increase in the tax on good 2. From the earlier discussion of symmetry it is clear that this analysis applies to subsidies as well as taxes, imposed on either good. It is also to be noted that the analysis applies irrespective of whether the net output of the good in question is positive (output) or negative (input).

10.6.2. Consumption taxes

Now let p_j refer to demand prices and p_j^* to producer and foreign prices. Then since $p_j = (1 + \tau_j)p_j^*$, the consumption tax based upon producer prices is τ_j. The model becomes (43) and (45) together with

$$x_2 = G_2(p^*, v) - \phi_2(p, m) \tag{48}$$

and

$$R = -\sum_{j=2}^{M} \sigma_j p_j \phi_j = \sum_{j=2}^{M} \tau_j p_j^* \phi_j, \tag{49}$$

where $\sigma_1 = \tau_1 = 0$ by an appropriate normalization of the tax structure.

Write $X_2 = X_2(p^*, \tau) = 0$ and consider the two-good case. Again the effect of a change in τ_2 upon p_2^* depends upon the sign of $X_{2\tau} \equiv \partial X_2/\partial \tau_2$ under stability. Differentiation yields

$$X_{2\tau} = \frac{-E_{22} p_2^*}{1 - \sigma_2 c_2} = -E_{22} p_2^* \left[\frac{1 + \tau_2}{1 + \tau_2 c_1} \right] > 0. \tag{50}$$

Thus, $dp_2^*/d\tau_2 = -X_{22}^{-1} X_{2\tau} < 0$, meaning that an increase in the consumption tax rate on good 2 will reduce the world (supply) price of that good. If good 2 is exported, then the terms of trade of the home nation worsen while those of the foreign nation improve. The expression for the change in the demand price is

$$\frac{dp_2}{d\tau_2} = \frac{p_2^* x_{22}^* + p_2^* G_{22} - x_2 c_2/(1 + \tau_2 c_1)}{X_{22}}. \tag{51}$$

In general this expression has an ambiguous sign. Normal expectation is for the demand price to rise. However, if the domestic producers and the foreigners respond very little to the reduction in the supply price (x_{22}^* and G_{22} are small) then it is possible for the income effect on consumption given by the last term in the numerator of (51) to dominate if $x_2 > 0$, thus causing a drop in p_2^* sufficiently large to allow p_2 to fall.

10.6.3. Relationship with trade taxes

Production taxes create a wedge between prices facing producers and those facing consumers and foreigners. Consumption taxes create a wedge between prices facing consumers and those facing producers and foreigners. Trade taxes create a wedge between foreign and domestic prices. This suggests that a system of production and consumption taxes could be made equivalent to a set of trade taxes.

Let p_j denote consumer prices, p_j^* foreign prices, and p_j^s producer prices. A consumption tax of rate t_j will mean that the consumption price is $p_j = (1 + t_j)p_j^*$, while the production price is $p_j^s = p_j^*$. If, in addition, the producer is given a subsidy of rate t_j, then the producer price will be $p_j^s = (1 + t_j)p_j^*$ and the consumer price will be $p_j = (1 + t_j)p_j^*$ as before. Thus, $p_j = p_j^s = (1 + t_j)p_j^*$, so domestic prices are the same. Moreover, this relationship between domestic and foreign prices is exactly that which arises from a tariff of rate t_j (or subsidy rate if good j is exported), as given in (17). Thus, a trade tax of rate t_j is equivalent to a combined consumption tax of rate t_j and a production subsidy of rate t_j.

The importance of this result is that any set of trade taxes can be eliminated without affecting the equilibrium by replacing them with an appropriate set of production and consumption taxes. The reader may wish to speculate on the implications for attempts by organizations of nations to increase the volume of trade by reducing tariffs.

10.7. Trade taxes with many goods

The analysis of the previous two sections was devoted primarily to the consideration of the effects of trade, production and consumption taxes in a model with
just two traded goods. In this case the condition for stability is very simple and
can be effectively used in order to obtain qualitative comparative statics results.
By expressing the equilibrium condition in terms of the price vector of interest
at the time, the comparative static equations contain the term X_{22} (the derivative of world excess supply of good 2 with respect to the price of good 2 of interest at the time) which is positive by stability. Hence, we were able to minimize the amount of differentiation, since X_{22} never had to be explicitly calculated and the stability condition was directly used.

When there are many goods the necessary and sufficient stability conditions
are fairly complex and do not provide much help in the comparative statics. A
sufficient stability condition is that all goods are gross substitutes. In this case
X_{22} has positive diagonal and negative off-diagonal elements and $X_{22}^{-1} \geqslant 0$, which
is a little more help.

In what follows attention is confined to several remarks concerning the general effects of trade taxes. To simplify expressions let t now be the per unit
trade tax vector so tax revenue is $-tx$.[15] Then writing the equilibrium condition
as $X(p^*, t) = 0$ we obtain that $\mathrm{d}p_2^* = -X_{22}^{-1} X_{2t} \mathrm{d}t_2$, where $X_{22} \equiv \partial X_2/\partial p_2^*$ and
$X_{2t} \equiv \partial X/\partial t_2 = \partial x_2/\partial t_2$. The latter is obtained analogously to (33) as

$$x_{2t} \equiv \partial x_2(p^*, t)/\partial t_2 = (I - \phi_{2m} t_2)^{-1} S_{22}, \tag{52}$$

where $S_{22} = G_{22} - E_{22}$. When taxes are initially zero this becomes $x_{2t} = S_{22}$
which is a positive definite matrix (definiteness assumed). Since its diagonal elements are positive an increase in the trade tax on good i alone will cause an excess
supply of good i if world prices remain fixed. However, even if gross substitutability is assumed so that $X_{22}^{-1} \geqslant 0$, it does not appear that the world price of good
i will necessarily fall. This is in contrast with the two commodity case where a
trade tax reduces the world price of the taxed good.

To obtain the effect of trade taxes upon domestic prices we could use the
relation $\mathrm{d}p = \mathrm{d}p^* + \mathrm{d}t$. Alternatively, we can write the equilibrium condition as
$X(p, t) = 0$ and obtain $\mathrm{d}p = -X_{22}^{-1} X_{2t} \mathrm{d}t_2$, where $X_{22} \equiv \partial X_2/\partial p_2$ and $X_{2t} \equiv$
$\partial X_2/\partial t_2$. The latter is obtained by first differentiating $x_2 = G_2(p, v) - \phi_2(p, G(p, v)$
$- t_2 x_2)$ with respect to t_2 to obtain:

---

[15]   The reader may wish to rework this section using ad valorem trade tax rates.

$$\mathrm{d}x_2 = (I - \phi_{2m} t_2)^{-1} x_2 \mathrm{d}t_2,$$

whence

$$X_{2t} \equiv \partial X_2(p, t)/\partial t_2 = (I - \phi_{2m} t_2)^{-1} \phi_{2m} x_2 - x_{22}^*. \tag{53}$$

When taxes are initially zero $X_{2t} = \phi_{2m} x_2 - x_{22}^*$, a matrix whose elements can be either sign in general. The matrix X_{2t} (with $t = 0$) may be expressed in element form as $X_{2t} = [\phi_{im} x_j - x_{ij}^*] = [(p_i \phi_{im} + x_{ij}^* p_i/x_j^*) x_j/p_i]$, the diagonal elements being $(p_i \phi_{im} + x_{ii}^* p_i/x_i^*) x_i/p_i = (c_i + \xi_{ii}^*) x_i/p_i$, where c_i is the marginal propensity to consume i at home and ξ_{ii}^* is the own price elasticity of export supply of good i abroad. Clearly, the diagonal elements can be of either sign since $\xi_{ii}^* < 0$ is possible, just as in the two-commodity model as explained previously. In addition to the ambiguity of the signs of the elements of X_{2t}, further ambiguity arises in X_{22}. Even if gross substitutability is assured little can be said about the specific effects of a trade tax upon domestic prices.

The effects of trade taxes upon utility levels can be found by differentiating the indirect trade utility functions $\mu = H(p, -tx, v)$ and $\mu^* = H^*(p^*, 0, v)$. Thus,

$$\mathrm{d}\mu = H_p \mathrm{d}p + H_b(-t\mathrm{d}x - x\,\mathrm{d}t)$$

and, since $x = H_p/H_b$ and $p = p^* + t$,

$$\mathrm{d}\mu/H_b = x\mathrm{d}p^* - t\,\mathrm{d}x. \tag{54}$$

If $t = 0$ initially, welfare improves if and only if the Laspeyre's terms of trade index improves. For the foreign nation

$$\mathrm{d}\mu^*/H_b^* = x^*\mathrm{d}p^* = -x\mathrm{d}p^* \tag{55}$$

so that

$$\mathrm{d}\mu/H_b + \mathrm{d}\mu^*/H_b^* = -t\,\mathrm{d}x. \tag{56}$$

If $t = 0$ initially one nation can only gain at the expense of the other.

The expressions for X_{22} have not been obtained as yet. If $X(p^*, t) = 0$ defines the world excess supply functions in terms of world prices the expression for X_{pp}, which contains X_{22} as a submatrix, is

$$X_{pp} = (S_{pp} + S_{pp}^*) - (\phi_m - \phi_m^*)x \tag{57}$$

when $t = 0$. If $\phi_m = \phi_m^*$, as would be the case if preferences were identical and homothetic in the two countries, for example, then $X_{pp} = S_{pp} + S_{pp}^*$ which is positive semi-definite. In this case it turns out that stability is assured.[16] Moreover,

$$dp_2^* = -X_{22}^{-1} X_{2t} dt_2 = -sS_{22} dt_2, \tag{58}$$

where $s \equiv S_{22} + S_{22}^*$, and hence $dp_2^* dt_2 = -dt_2 sS_{22} dt_2 < 0$ for all dt_2. Thus, there is a *negative correlation* between world prices and the trade tax vector. In general, preferences will be different so that this correlation may not occur. Nevertheless one might argue that if preferences are sufficiently similar then the negative correlation will occur.

Non-traded goods

If there exist non-traded goods, will the analysis of the effects of trade taxes be altered? It turns out that non-traded goods cause little difficulty, as is now briefly explained.

It will be recalled from Chapters 6 and 8 that non-traded goods can be "netted out" of the net export functions, which may be written as $x_t = \hat{x}_t(p_t, v)$, where t denotes traded goods. These functions are homogeneous of degree zero in p_t and satisfy the balance of trade condition $p_t \hat{x}_t(p_t, v) \equiv 0$. The only difference between these reduced form net export functions and those obtained without non-traded goods is that the income effect component of the price effects may not be non-negative even if all goods are normal (see $(8.13) - (8.15)$). With this qualification the results in the present chapter can be applied to a model with non-traded goods in a formal sense.

For example, the question of the symmetry of a uniform tax on imports and a uniform tax of exports is readily answered. There is a symmetry because of the homogeneity of $\hat{x}_t(p_t, v)$ in p_t and the fact that domestic prices are homogeneous of degree one in p_t.

If $(p_1^*(1 + \tau), p_2^*, p_n^0)$ is the equilibrium price vector when goods in group 1 (imports, say) are taxed at the common rate τ, then it is clear that $p_t = (p_1^*, p_2^*(1 + \tau)^{-1})$ is also an equilibrium price vector for traded goods and that all domestic prices will be raised by the factor $(1 + \tau)^{-1}$. Thus, $p_n = p_n^0(1 + \tau)^{-1}$ is the new equilibrium price vector for non-traded goods. This outline of a proof of

---

[16]   The necessary and sufficient condition for stability is that the real parts of the eigenvalues of X_{22} be positive. If X_{22} is positive definite its eigenvalues are positive and hence stability is assured. See Takayama (1974, pp. 310, 316).

symmetry avoids McDougall's (1970, p. 182) concern with McKinnon's (1966) proof and emphasizes the crucial element, namely homogeneity in prices.

It is also true that a uniform tax of rate τ on imports (or a uniform tax of the same rate on exports since these are equivalent, as shown above) is equivalent to (a) a uniform production subsidy and a uniform consumption tax of rate τ on importables, and (b) a uniform production tax and a uniform consumption subsidy of rate $\tau/(1 + \tau)$ on exportables. This is just as in the model without non-traded goods. Details are left to the problem set.

As another example, the conditions for the Metzler paradox require no modification, except in the interpretation of the derivatives of the reduced form functions. The same applies to the transfer problem.

When the analysis has to go behind the net export functions, then explicit consideration of the role of non-traded goods is required, however. This applies, for example, to the effects of trade taxes upon factor prices or, quite obviously, upon the prices of non-traded goods.

10.8. Effective rates of protection

10.8.1. The problem

Considerable literature has been devoted in the last decade to the theoretical and empirical analysis of the concept of "effective rates of protection" following the formal development of the concept by Corden (1966). The concept arose in order to provide a measure of protection afforded by the complete trade tax structure to each industry in the context of a model involving imported intermediate inputs. Nominal tax rates apply to *commodities*, whereas effective tax rates apply to *industries* and take into account the fact that the tax structure may raise the domestic prices of inputs into an industry as well as its outputs. Clearly, in such cases the level of nominal trade taxes on only the outputs of an industry may provide little information on the total protection afforded an industry by the complete trade tax structure. In the words of Corden (1966, p. 222):

> ...ordinary *nominal* tariffs apply to commodities, but resources move between economic activities. Therefore, to discover the resource–location effects of a tariff structure one must calculate the protective rate for each activity, that is, the *effective* protective rate. This is the main message of the new theory of tariffs.

There has been considerable confusion in the literature concerning the role that effective rates of protection are expected to play. Presumably, they are expected to play a role analogous to the role played by nominal trade tax rates in a final-good model, that is one in which there are no intermediate inputs or joint outputs. In the final-good model there is no distinction between the vector of net outputs, y, and the vector of gross industry outputs, g. A change in the vector of nominal per unit trade taxes, t, under fixed world prices will cause domestic prices to change by $dp = dt$. The effect on y and g is $dy = dg = G_{pp}\,dp = G_{pp}\,dt$, where G_{pp} is a positive semi-definite matrix. Moreover, nominal value added in industry j is $V_j = p_j g_j$ which is a product of a price and quantity, so g_j may be interpreted as real value added. Thus, real value added, gross output and net output are equal and are related to changes in nominal taxes via the positive semi-definite matrix G_{pp}.

If intermediate inputs and/or joint outputs are introduced into the model there is a distinction between net output, gross output and "real value added" (for which a consistent index may not exist) and this is the source of the effective protection problem. It is still true, of course, that $dy = G_{pp}\,dp = G_{pp}\,dt$, where G_{pp} is positive semi-definite so nominal tax rates are relevant to the prediction of net outputs. The question arises, however, of whether gross outputs or "real value added" (or some other measure of the activity level) are related to some measure of effective rates of protection via a positive semi-definite matrix. If so, then the analogy with the relationship between nominal tax rates and net outputs is complete.

Whether attention should be focused upon gross outputs, or a measure of "real value added", or some other measure of the activity level is not clear a priori but depends upon the aim of the researcher. The gross output level is a convenient choice, but if there is joint production there are several outputs to choose from. Similarly, there is a choice of factor input to act as the activity level of interest. For these reasons value added has been accorded special interest since value added is the amount of revenue available as payment to all factors or the value of net output of the industry and thus aggregates over factors, or goods.

10.8.2. Separability and real value added

If the effective rate of protection is to play a role analogous to the nominal rate of trade tax in a final-good model, it must be interpreted as the change in the price of some variable which is to be explained. Given the Corden (1966) definition, a natural choice is real value added. Accordingly, this approach is now pursued by supposing that nominal value added by each industry is the product of a price index called the price of real value added, and a quantity index called the quantity of real value added.

Consider a very general model of the economy in which K industries produce M products using N factors of production. Production may be joint and products may be used as intermediate inputs. This is the model dealt with in detail in Chapter 5, section 5.4. Each industry has a transformation function which we suppose to be of the separable form

$$t^j(u_j, -x_j) = \bar{t}^j(u_j, -f^j(x_j)) = 0, \quad j = 1, ..., K, \tag{59}$$

where u_j is the vector of net outputs of goods and x_j is the input vector for factors. The interpretation of (59) is that factors combine to produce a fictional intermediate product, which is called real value added, in amount $f^j(x_j)$. This is then used along with other (non-fictional) intermediate inputs to produce one or more outputs. The assumption of constant returns to scale implies that $f^j(x_j)$ is linearly homogeneous in x_j while $t^j(u_j, -f^j)$ is homogeneous of degree zero in $(u_j, -f^j)$. It will be assumed that f^j is also non-decreasing and concave, so that it is a valid constant returns to scale production function.

The maximum (nominal) value added obtained by industry j when the price vector is p and x_j is the factor input vector can be shown to factor as (see problem set)

$$V^j(p, x_j) \equiv \max_{u_j} \{pu_j: \bar{t}^j(u_j, -f^j(x_j) = 0\} = \pi^j(p)f^j(x_j), \tag{60}$$

where

$$\pi^j(p) \equiv \max_{u_j} \{pu_j: \bar{t}^j(u_j, -1) = 0\} \tag{61}$$

is the unit value added function, which has all the properties of a GNP function. Thus, the combination of the separability and constant returns to scale assumptions yields a nominal value added function with a very special structure. Nominal value added becomes the product of a price index $\pi^j(p)$, the price of real value added, and a quantity index $f^j(x_j)$, the quantity of real value added. Thus, we can unambiguously talk of the price and quantity of real value added. It is noteworthy that the nominal value added function has the structure of (60) if and only if the technology is separable between factors and products as in (59), although we have only demonstrated the if part above.[17]

The product form of the nominal value added function gives a very special structure to the GNP function. The latter is

$$G(p,v) \equiv \max_{y} \{py: y \in Y(v)\}$$

$$\equiv \max \left\{ p \sum_{j=1}^{K} u_j: \overline{t}^j(u_j, -f^j(x_j)) = 0, x_j \geqslant 0 \, j = 1, ..., K; \right.$$

$$\left. \sum_{j=1}^{K} x_j \leqslant v \right\}$$

$$\equiv \max \left\{ \sum_{j=1}^{K} \pi^j(p) f^j(x_j): \sum_{j=1}^{K} x_j \leqslant v, (x_1, ..., x_K) \geqslant 0 \right\}$$

$$= G^*(\pi^1(p), ..., \pi^K(p), v). \tag{62}$$

The function $G^*(\pi^1, ..., \pi^K, v) = G^*(\pi, v)$ is a GNP function for a fictional economy producing K final goods, via the production functions $f^j(x_j)$, and facing the price vector $\pi = (\pi^1, ..., \pi^K)$. Each industry has a price index $\pi^j(p)$ for real value added (the fictional final good). Treating the value of this index as a price variable and defining $r_j \equiv f^j(x_j)$ as the quantity of real value added, it is clear that $r = G^*_\pi(\pi, v)$ is the vector of supply functions for real value added. Moreover,

$$\partial r(\pi, v)/\partial \pi = G^*_{\pi\pi}(\pi, v) \tag{63}$$

indicates how r responds to a change in π.

Since $G^*(\pi, v)$ is a GNP function it is convex and linearly homogeneous in π. Thus, $G^*_{\pi\pi}$ is a positive semi-definite matrix such that $\pi G^*_{\pi\pi} = 0$. This shows that the relationship between π and r in this model involving intermediate inputs and joint outputs is precisely analogous to the relationship between price vector p and the net output vector y (which, in a final-good model, is also gross output and real value added). The appropriate definition of an effective rate of protection in the present context is therefore

$$e_j \equiv [\pi^j(p + t) - \pi^j(p)]/\pi^j(p), \quad j = 1, ..., K, \tag{64}$$

which is the percentage increase in the price index for real value added due to the trade tax vector t.

The structure of the model under separability can be further highlighted by writing down the equilibrium conditions in terms of price and quantity indices of real value added as

(a) $\quad \gamma^j(w) - \pi^j(p) \geqslant 0 \leqslant r_j, \quad j = 1, ..., K,$

(b) $\quad \sum_{j=1}^{K} \gamma_w^j(w) r_j - v \leqslant 0 \leqslant w,$

(65)

where $\gamma^j(w) \equiv \min \{wx_j : f^j(x_j) \geqslant 1, x_j \geqslant 0\}$ is the minimum factor cost of producing one unit of real value added, and r_j is the quantity of real value added produced. These conditions correspond exactly to those specified for a final-good economy as in (3.6) and (3.7).

The price indices $\pi^j(p)$ are linearly homogeneous and convex in p and they depend upon the nature of the technology. The special case

$$\pi^j(p) = \sum_{i=1}^{M} b_{ij}^* p_i, \quad j = 1, ..., K, \tag{66}$$

where the b_{ij}^* are constant input–output coefficients (per unit of real value added) is of particular interest. In this case

$$e_j = \sum_{i=1}^{M} b_{ij}^* t_i \Big/ \sum_{i=1}^{M} b_{ij}^* p_i = \sum_{i=1}^{M} \beta_{ij}^* \tau_i, \quad j = 1, ..., K, \tag{67}$$

where $\tau_i \equiv t_i/p_i$ is the ad valorem rate of tax on good i, and $\beta_{ij}^* \equiv p_i b_{ij}^* / \sum_{k=1}^{M} p_k b_{kj}^*$ is the share of good i in the value added in industry j. Formula (67) shows that e_j is a weighted average of ad valorem tax rates, with weights equal to the contribution of each good to value added. It is in this form that Corden (1966) defined the effective rate of protection, except that his model did not allow for joint production and therefore $K = M$. The specification in (66) and (67) is particularly convenient for empirical work since the matrix $\beta^* = [\beta_{ij}^*]$ is readily observable and most countries publish it, usually as $\beta^* = 1 - \alpha$, where α is the Leontief input–output matrix in share form for an intermediate-input model excluding joint production. Thus calculation of effective rates of protection of the form (67) is a relatively easy task.

In general the price indices for real value added will not be of the simple linear form (66). In this case the calculation of effective rates of protection will differ depending on whether the tax rates are large or small. If they are large then calculation of the effective rates via (64) requires knowledge of the price indices $\pi^j(p)$. These can be estimated using econometric techniques, as explained by Woodland (1977, pp. 529–530). If the tax rates are small the effective rates may be approximated linearly as

$$e_j \doteqdot \hat{\pi}^j(p) = \mathrm{d}\pi^j(p)/\pi^j(p) = \sum_{i=1}^{M} [p_i \pi_i^j(p)/\pi^j(p)] \hat{p}_i = \sum_{i=1}^{M} \beta_{ij}^*(p) \tau_i, \tag{68}$$

where $\pi_i^j(p) \equiv \partial \pi^j (p)/\partial p_i$ is the net output of good i per unit of real value added in industry j, $\beta_{ij}^*(p) \equiv p_i \pi_i^j(p)/\pi^j(p)$ is the share of good i in the value added in industry j, and $\tau_i \equiv t_i/p_i = \mathrm{d}p_i/p_i \equiv \hat{p}_i$ is the percentage change in the price of good i (assuming world prices fixed).

This formula is exactly the same as that given by (67) for the case of fixed coefficients, which is hardly surprising since (66) is obtained by linearizing $\pi^j(p)$. Thus, the original Corden (1966) formula is valid even though the input—output coefficients are not fixed as long as attention is restricted to small tax rates (or changes therein). Of course, this considerably reduces the usefulness of the formula, since most applications are to situations where taxes are sufficiently large for (68) to be invalid as an approximation.

Three final remarks can be made. First, since the conditions in (65) are precisely the equilibrium conditions for a final-good economy, the various theorems established for that model apply here. For example, in the present context the Stolper—Samuelson theorem concerns the relationship between π and w. Thus, if there are just two industries and two factors, an increase in π^2 relative to π^1 (that is, industry 2 has a higher rate of effective protection) and industry 2 is factor 2 intensive, then w_2/w_1 will rise. In fact, $\hat{w}_2 > \hat{\pi}^2 = e_2 > \hat{\pi}^1 = e_1 > \hat{w}_1$, which is Jones' magnification effect. Also, Rybczynski's theorem can be re-expressed in terms of v and r.

Secondly, the effective rate of protection has some desirable properties. If we write $e_j(\tau)$, then

(a) $e_j(\lambda 1) = \lambda, \quad \lambda \geqslant 0,$

(69)

(b) $\partial e_j/\partial \tau_i = \beta_{ij}^*.$

The first property indicates that a uniform tax rate (λ) will give equal effective rates of protection to all industries (λ). The second indicates that a higher nominal rate for good i will raise the effective rate if i is an output and reduce it if i is an input in industry j.

Finally, it must be emphasized that there are limitations to the role that effective rates of protection can play in predicting the quantity of real value added. We know that in a many-product model there is a non-negative correlation between p and y of the form $\mathrm{d}p\mathrm{d}y = \mathrm{d}pG_{pp}\mathrm{d}p \geqslant 0$. Similarly, in the present model $\mathrm{d}\pi\mathrm{d}r = \mathrm{d}\pi G_{pp}^* \, \mathrm{d}\pi \geqslant 0$ indicates a non-negative correlation between π and r. Without knowing $G_{\pi\pi}^*$ it is not possible to be more precise about the relationship between π and r. There is a tendency for industries with high effective rates of protection to produce more real value added than those with low rates, but we cannot say that they will do so on an individual industry basis.

10.8.3. Gross outputs

If the separability assumption does not hold then consistent indices of the price and quantity of real value added do not exist. Alternative measures of activity levels are required. If joint production is ruled out, each industry, j, produces just one good, j, and so a natural choice for the activity level is the gross output, g_j. Another is own value added defined as $V^j(p, x_j)/p_j$. In what follows attention is focused on gross outputs in a model with no joint production.

For such a model the equilibrium conditions may be written as

(a) $c^j(w, p) - p_j \geq 0 \leq g_j \quad j = 1, ..., M,$

(b) $\sum\limits_{j=1}^{M} c_w^j(w, p)g_j - v \leq 0 \leq w$

$$(70)$$

where $c^j(w, p)$ is the unit cost (gross output) function for product (industry) j. This is precisely the model of Chapter 5, section 5.2. If p changes by a small amount due to the imposition of a trade tax, or due to a change in an existing trade tax, the comparative static equations are

(a) $A^T dw = (I - B^T)dp,$

(b) $A dg + C_{ww} dw + C_{wp} dp = dv = 0,$

$$(71)$$

where $C(p, w, g) \equiv \sum_{j=1}^{M} g_j c^j(w, p)$ is the aggregate cost function, and therefore

$$C_{ww} = \sum\limits_{j=1}^{M} g_j c_{ww}^j(w, p) \quad \text{and} \quad C_{wp} = \sum\limits_{j=1}^{M} g_j c_{wp}^j(w, p)$$

are the matrices of effects upon aggregate demands for factors of changes in w and p, respectively, and $A = [c_w^1, ..., c_w^M] = C_{gw}$ and $B = [c_p^1, ..., c_p^M] = C_{gp}$ are input–output matrices. The solution to (71) for dg when $M = N$ and A has full rank, is

$$dg = -[A^{-1}C_{ww}(A^{-1})^T + A^{-1}C_{wp}(I - B^T)^{-1}] (I - B^T)dp. \qquad (72)$$

The term $(I - B^T)dp$ is the change in the vector of values added ignoring any changes that might take place in B as a result of the changes in p and w. It is the impact or initial effect upon values added that forms the numerator in the Corden formula for the effective rate of protection which, in the present model, is

$$e_j = \left[dp_j - \sum_{i=1}^{M} b_{ij}dp_i \right] \Big/ \left(p_j - \sum_{i=1}^{M} b_{ij}p_i \right) = \sum_{i=1}^{M} \beta_{ij}\tau_i, \tag{73}$$

where β_{ij} is the share of i in value added of j.

The matrix premultiplying $(I - B^T)dp$ in (72) is not positive semi-definite in general and consequently gross outputs are not related to the Corden effective rates of protection in a manner analogous to the relationship between p and y. However, a sufficient condition for this matrix to be positive semi-definite is for $C_{wp} = 0$, since $A^{-1}C_{ww}(A^{-1})^T$ is negative semi-definite. For C_{wp} to be identically zero it is sufficient that $c^j_{wp} = 0$ for all j, which means that factor inputs per unit of gross outputs are not affected by product prices or, equivalently, that intermediate inputs per unit of gross output are not affected by factor prices. This means that the cost function takes the additive form $c^j(w,p) = \gamma^j(w) + \delta^j(p)$, whence $\pi^j(p) \equiv p_j - \delta^j(p)$ is the value added price index (per unit of gross output). Nominal value added is $\pi^j(p)g_j$, which is the product of a price and quantity. This is analogous to the separability case developed above, except that the quantity index of real value added is replaced by the gross output of j.[18] The equilibrium conditions can be written as (65) with g_j replacing r_j and with $K = M$. The GNP function can be written as $G^*(\pi, v)$, where $g = G^*_\pi(\pi, v)$ and $\partial g/\partial \pi = G^*_{\pi\pi}$. Thus, g and π are related in a manner analogous to that between y and p, for small or large changes. If $C_{wp} = 0$ locally only, then $\partial g/\partial \pi$ is given by the matrix preceding $(I - B^T)dp$ in (72) and is positive semi-definite so the desired relationship holds only for small changes in p and hence π.

It is noted that for $c^j_{wp} = 0$ it is not necessary that $c^j_{ww} = 0$ or $c^j_{pp} = 0$ so that there can be substitution amongst intermediate inputs and amongst factors but not between factors and intermediates. Clearly, the case where B is fixed is a special case since then $c^j_{pw} = 0$ and so $C_{wp} = 0$. Another special case is where A is fixed, for then $c^j_{wp} = 0$ and again $C_{wp} = 0$.

While the effective protection literature does not concern itself with factor prices, it is worth noting that for small changes in trade taxes the effective rates of protection are related to factor prices in exactly the same way that nominal trade taxes are related to factor prices in a model without intermediate inputs. This follows from (71,a).

---

[18] The additive unit (gross output) cost function implies more than the existence of an index of real value added. The existence of an index of real value added means that the production function is of the form $g_j = F^j(q_j, f^j(x_j))$, where q_j is the input vector for intermediates, whence the unit cost function is of the form $c^j(w, p) = \bar{c}^j(\gamma^j(w), p)$. The special case where $c^j(w, p) = \gamma^j(w) + \delta^j(p)$ is dual to the production function $g_j = \min \{h^j(q_j), f^j(x_j)\}$, in which intermediates as well as factors aggregate with the aggregates being used in fixed proportion to produce gross output.

10.8.4. Concluding remarks

It has been shown that if commodities and factors are separable groups in the transformation function then nominal value added is the product of a price and quantity index for what is called real value added, and the price and the quantity indices are related analogously to the relationship between prices and net outputs. The effective rate of protection, analogous to nominal taxes, is then the percentage change in the price index for real value added. When input–output coefficients for intermediates (per unit of real value added) are fixed, or taxes are small, the effective rates can be calculated easily using these input–output coefficients using Corden's (1966) formula.

When there is just one output per industry, gross output can be taken as the activity level and separability of commodities and factors in the production function, which makes the cost function additive, again ensures the existence of a real value added function and corresponding price index. Again constancy of the input–output matrix for intermediates (per unit of gross output) is not required, but makes the Corden formula valid.

For small taxes the Corden formula is valid if $C_{wp} - 0$, which means that, locally, the factor input–output coefficients are not responsive to changes in product prices. If this condition does not hold, then $\mathrm{d}g$ and $(I - B^{\mathrm{T}})\mathrm{d}p$ are not related by a positive semi-definite matrix (except by accident), and hence the effective tariff formula does not play an analogous role to nominal taxes. In other words, effective rates of protection and gross outputs may not be non-negatively correlated.

The reader may wonder why so much attention has been given in the literature to effective rates of protection. Why not proceed directly to a formula, such as (72), and calculate the exact effect upon g of a change in tax rates? Or for large tax rates or changes therein, why not calculate the new equilibrium directly? These procedures are beginning to be used, but they require much more information (such as on substitution elasticities) than the simple effective tax formula which only requires knowledge of the input–output matrix for intermediates. Unfortunately, as the preceding analysis shows, they are appropriate only under severe restrictions on the technology.

10.9. Notes on the literature

The use of stability conditions to help sign comparative statics results is well established in the literature and is known as Samuelson's correspondence principle. Except for small dimensions, stability conditions unfortunately provide little structure. For two-dimensional applications the reader is referred to Jones (1961) and Amano (1968). The relevant theory of stability is to be found in Takayama (1974).

For a lengthy treatment of the transfer problem see Samuelson (1952). See also Chipman (1974).

The effects of tariffs upon the terms of trade and domestic prices in a two-commodity model has been extensively dealt with by Bhagwati and Johnson (1961) who consider two classes of consumers, variable labour supply and government spending of the tariff revenue. The classic article is Metzler (1949). McDougall (1970) surveys the effects of tariffs in a model with a non-traded good, but many of his results can be obtained more simply using the "netting out" result and reduced form net export functions. McKinnon (1966) considers a three-commodity model, one being a pure intermediate product. Suzuki (1976) considers a more general three-commodity model and establishes conditions for a tariff to worsen the terms of trade (defined rather restrictively). The effects of trade taxes upon domestic prices is established and the effects upon factor prices and resource allocation are obtained by reference to the analysis of Chapters 4 and 5. Thus, the references there on the Stolper—Samuelson theorem are relevant here.

There is a vast literature on the concept of effective rates of protection. The initial formal development is in Corden (1966) with further discussion in Corden (1969, 1971), where the existence of a real value added function is assumed.

The importance of deciding what role effective rates of protection are expected to play has been emphasized by Ethier (1971, 1972, 1977). True effective rates define a support plane for the frontier for whatever measure of activity level is chosen. These true rates may differ according to the choice of activity level, and may involve aspects of the technology in addition to input—output coefficients. Ethier (1977) appears to de-emphasize the role of separability. The role of separability is emphasized by Bruno (1973), Jones (1971, appendix 2), Bhagwati and Srinivason (1973), Khang (1973), Woodland (1977) and Jones (1975) who uses a multi-commodity version of the specific factor model.

The case where separability does not occur has been dealt with by many of the above authors including Bhagwati and Srinivason (1973) who write value added as the product of a Divisia quantity and price index which are, however, inconsistent indices unless separability holds. They establish conditions for an increase in the price index to cause the quantity index to increase for that industry, assuming that the percentage increase in the price index exceeds a common rate of increase in all other industries. This is a very special situation. This approach has, however, been taken up by many authors. Uekawa (1979) establishes necessary and sufficient conditions for the Bhagwati—Srinivason requirement to work. Sufficient conditions for gross output to respond positively to the Bhagwati–Srinivason tariff change are provided by Ohyama and Suzuki (1980) and Yabuuchi and Tanaka (1981) for the case where there are non-traded intermediate inputs.

Problems

1. Consider the equilibrium described by $X_1(p_1, p_2) = 0$ and $X_2(p_1, p_2) = 0$, where the subscripts denote subvectors of $p = (p_1, p_2)$ and $X = (X_1, X_2)$. Consider three different adjustment mechanisms: (i) $\dot{p}_1 = X_1(p_1, p_2)$ and $\dot{p}_2 = X_2(p_1, p_2)$; (ii) $\dot{p}_1 = X_1(p_1, p_2)$, where p_2 is given; and (iii) $\dot{p}_1 = X_1^*$ $(p_1) \equiv X_1(p_1, p_2(p_1))$, where $p_2(p_1) \equiv \{p_2 : X_2(p_1, p_2) = 0\}$.
   (a) Describe the nature of the adjustment mechanisms.
   (b) Show that $X_{11}^* \equiv \partial X_1^* / \partial p_1 = X_{11} - X_{12} X_{22}^{-1} X_{21} = X^{11}$ (the first block of the inverse matrix of $X_{pp} \equiv \partial X / \partial p$).
   (c) When p_1 and p_2 (and X_1, X_2) are scalars, derive the Routh–Hurwitz conditions for stability in each case,
   (d) Compare the results in (c).
2. Let $w = w(y, v)$ be the solution for w in (11). Also, let $C(w)$ be the vector of cost functions, $C = (c^1, ..., c^M)$.
   (a) Show that $C(w\ (y, v))$ is orthogonal to the transformation function $t(y, -v) = 0$, i.e. proportional to $t_y(y, -v) = 0$.
   (b) Now permit intermediate inputs so that the unit cost function is $c^j(w, p)$ and (11) now reads as $\sum_{j=1}^{M} c_w^j(w, p) g_j = v$, where g_j is gross output. Is it the case that $C(w(g, v), p)$ is orthogonal to the transformation function?
3. Consider Amano's model of adjustment.
   (a) Obtain the conditions for the local stability of the temporary equilibrium.
   (b) Show that local stability implies that Π_{y_2}, $\Pi_{y_2}^* < 0$ if good 2 is normal in both nations.
4. (a) In an M-commodity model of trade show that $X_{ij} = (\xi_{ij} - \xi_{ij}^*) x_i / p_j$, where $X = x(p, v) + x^*(p, v)$, $\xi_{ij} \equiv x_{ij} p_j / x_i$ and $\xi_{ij}^* \equiv x_{ij}^* p_j / x_i^*$.
   (b) Show that $\sum_j \xi_{ij} = 0$ and $\sum_i \xi_{ij} (p_i x_i / p_j x_j) + 1 = 0$ for all i, j, respectively. What properties of $x(p, v)$ do these rely upon?
   (c) For the case of $M = 2$ commodities show that $X_{22} = -\Delta x_2 / p_2$, where $\Delta = \xi_{22}^* - \xi_{22} = \xi_{11} + \xi_{22}^* + 1 = -(\xi_{22} + \xi_{11}^* + 1)$.
   (d) When $M = 3$ express the Routh–Hurwitz conditions in terms of the ξ elasticities. Try to interpret them.
5. In the text, the stability condition in a two-commodity model of trade was expressed as $X_{22} > 0$. It was also expressed in terms of elasticities of the net

export function, in the form of the "Marshall–Lerner condition".

(a) By using the decomposition of net exports as supply minus demand, re-write the stability condition in terms of supply and demand elasticities.

(b) Derive Jones' (1961, pp. 200–201) condition for stability. Interpret his "supply" and "demand" elasticities.

(c) Can you write the stability condition in terms of production substitution elasticities?

(d) Is it useful to decompose the stability condition in these ways?

6. Let the model of income transfer be written as

$$S(p, \mu, v) + r = 0,$$

$$S^*(p, \mu^*, v^*) - r = 0,$$

$$S_p(p, \mu, v) + S_p^*(p, \mu^*, v^*) = 0,$$

where $S(p, \mu, v) \equiv G(p, v) - E(p, \mu)$.

(a) Differentiate this system with respect to μ, μ^* and $p_2 = (p_2, ..., p_M)$ and write the resulting equations in matrix form. One can now solve the system directly or by using a formulae for the inverse of a partitioned matrix, which is equivalent to eliminating a subset of variables and solving directly the resulting reduced set of equations. The expression obtained depends upon your choice of which variables to eliminate.

(b) Eliminate dp_2 and obtain a reduced set of equations in $(d\mu, d\mu^*)$. Solve these to get $-S_\mu d\mu = D^{-1} dr$, where $D = 1 - x_2 s^{-1} (\phi_{2m} - \phi_{2m}^*)$ is a scalar, and $-S_\mu^* d\mu^* = -D^{-1} dr$.

(c) Alternatively, eliminate $(d\mu, d\mu^*)$ first, solve the resulting reduced set of equations for dp_2, and hence obtain $-S_\mu d\mu$.

(d) Compare your results in (b) and (c) with (16) and (17).

7. Consider a two-commodity model of world trade.

(a) Rewrite the Marshall–Lerner condition as $\Delta = \sigma_{22} + \sigma_{22}^* - (c_1 + c_2^* - 1)$
$= \sigma_{22} + \sigma_{22}^* - (1 - c_2 - c_1^*) < 0$ (the home nation imports good 1), where $\sigma_{ij} = S_{ij} p_j / S_i$ is a pure substitution elasticity.

(b) Show that a sufficient condition for stability is that $c_2 + c_1^* < 1$.

(c) If initially trade taxes are zero show that the relation $[\xi_{22}^* + c_2] > 0$, the condition for a trade tax on imports of good 1 to *reduce* the domestic price of good 1 (Metzler paradox), is consistent with the stability condition, namely $\Delta < 0$.

8. Suppose that, instead of tax revenue being redistributed to consumers, the government spends the tax revenue in a fixed ratio on the two goods.

(a) Obtain an expression for the effect upon the terms of trade of a trade tax (import duty) on good 1.

(b) Show that the terms of trade may deteriorate as a result of the tariff, and indicate the conditions for this result.

(c) What is the effect upon the domestic price ratio?

9. Let there be two traded goods and one non-traded good and consider the imposition of a small import tax on good 1. Write the equilibrium condition as $X_2(p_t, \sigma) = 0$, where p_t is the domestic price vector for traded goods and σ is the vector of tax rates.

(a) Interpret the adjustment mechanism behind the stability condition $X_{22} \equiv \partial X_2/\partial p_2 > 0$.

(b) Show that $X_{2\sigma} \equiv \partial X_2/\partial \sigma_2 = x_{22}^* p_2 + \alpha p_2 x_2/(1 - \alpha p_2 \sigma_2)$, where $\sigma \equiv S_{nn}^{-1} S_{2n} \phi_{nm} - \phi_{2m}$ and $S \equiv G(p_t, p_n, v) - E(p_t, p_n, \mu)$.

(c) Show that $dp_n = G_{nn}^{-1} \phi_{nm} \, dR$ if p_t is fixed.

(d) Hence, show that $dp_n > 0$ under initial free trade.

(e) What does the existence of the non-traded good imply about the likelihood of obtaining the Metzler paradox? Do you think your answer would be different if the third good was traded rather than non-traded?

10. Let the technology for an industry producing a single output using intermediates (q) and factors (x) be of the separable form $g = F(q, f(x))$, where f and F are non-decreasing, linearly homogeneous and concave.

(a) Show that the unit (gross output) cost function is of the form $c(w, p) = \bar{c}(\gamma(w), p)$.

(b) Show that the Allen–Uzawa elasticity of substitution between factors i and intermediate input j is the same for all factors i.

(c) Show that the Allen–Uzawa elasticity of substitution between factors i and j is $\sigma_{ij} = \hat{\sigma}_{ij}/s_\gamma + \sigma_{\gamma\gamma}$, where $\hat{\sigma}_{ij}$ is the elasticity of substitution on the real value added function, and s_γ is the cost share of real value added.

(d) If $F(q, f(x)) = \min \{h(q), f(x)\}$ show that $c(w, p) = \gamma(w) + \delta(p)$.

11. Equilibrium in a model with traded goods (types 1 and 2) and non-traded goods (n) may be expressed by (i) $G_t(p_t^s, p_n^s, v) - E_t(p_t^d, p_n^d, \mu) + x^*(p_t^*) = 0$, (ii) $p_t^*(G_t(\cdot) - E_t(\cdot)) = 0$ and (iii) $G_n(\cdot) - E_n(\cdot) = 0$, where $p_t = (p_1, p_2)$, and superscripts s and d denote producer and consumer prices. Prove that a uniform tax of rate τ on imports (1) is equivalent to:

(a) a uniform tax of rate τ (based upon domestic prices) on exports (2);

(b) a uniform production subsidy and a uniform consumption tax on importables both at rate τ;

(c) a uniform consumption subsidy and a uniform production tax on exportables both at rate $\tau/(1 + \tau)$. (Consumption and production tax rates are based upon market prices.)

(d) Are these equivalent to a uniform production tax on exportables and a uniform consumption tax on importables? Explain.

12. Let the equilibrium conditions under trade taxes be written as $S(p, \mu, v) = 0$, $S^*(p^*, \mu^*, v^*) = 0$, $S_p + S_p^* = 0$ and $p = p^* + t$. Let t change from its initial value $t = 0$, fixing p_1 and t_1.
   (a) Derive the comparative statics equations, eliminate dp_2, and solve the resulting equations for $-S_\mu d_\mu$ and $-S_\mu^* d_\mu^*$.
   (b) Hence, prove that if a transfer to the home nation would raise its welfare (problem 6 and Dixit and Norman, 1980), then a change in t of $dt = \alpha S_2^*$, where α is a positive scalar, will raise welfare. (Use the result that if A and B are conformable positive definite matrices, then AB is positive definite.)
   (c) Interpret this result. Will any small tax vector raise welfare?

References

Amano, A. (1968) "Stability conditions in the pure theory of international trade: A rehabilitation of the Marshallian approach", *Quarterly Journal of Economics* 82-2, May, 326–339.

Arrow, K.J. and F. Hahn (1971) *General Competitive Analysis* (San Francisco: Holden-Day, Inc.).

Arrow, K.J., H.D. Block and L. Hurwicz (1959) "On the stability of the competitive equilibrium II", *Econometrica* 27, 82–109.

Bhagwati, J. and H.G. Johnson (1961) "A generalized theory of the effects of tariffs on the terms of trade", *Oxford Economic Papers* 13-3, October, 225–253.

Bhagwati, J.N. and T.N. Srinivason (1973) "The general equilibrium theory of effective protection and resource allocation", *Journal of International Economics* 3, 259–282.

Bruno, M. (1973) "Protection and tariff change under general equilibrium", *Journal of International Economics* 3, 205–226.

Chipman, J.S. (1974) "The transfer problem once again", in: G. Horwich and P.A. Samuelson (eds.), *Trade, Stability and Macroeconomics: Essays in Honor of Lloyd A. Metzler* (New York: Academic Press), pp. 19–78.

Corden, W.M. (1966) "The structure of a tariff system and the effective protection rate", *Journal of Political Economy* 74-3, June, 221–237.

Corden, W.M. (1969) "Effective protection rates in the general equilibrium model: A geometric note", *Oxford Economic Papers* 21-2, July, 135–141.

Corden, W.M. (1971) "The substitution problem in the theory of effective protection", *Journal of International Economics* 1, 35–57.

Dixit, A.K. and V. Norman (1980) *Theory of International Trade* (J. Nisbet/Cambridge University Press).

Ethier, W. (1971) "General equilibrium theory and the concept of the effective rate of protection", in. H.G. Grubel and H.G. Johnson (eds.), *Effective Tariff Protection* (Geneva: GATT and Graduate Institute of International Studies), ch. 2.

Ethier, W. (1972) "Input substitution and the concept of the effective rate of protection", *Journal of Political Economy* 80-1, January–February, 34–47.

Ethier, W. (1977) "The theory of effective protection in general equilibrium: Effective-rate analogues of nominal rates", *Canadian Journal of Economics* 10-2, May, 233–245.

Jones, R. (1961) "Stability conditions in international trade: A general equilibrium analysis", *International Economic Review* 2-2, May, 199–209.

Jones, R. (1975) "Income distribution and effective protection in a multi-commodity trade model", *Journal of Economic Theory* 11, 1–15.

Khang, C. (1973) "Factor substitution in the theory of effective protection: A general equilibrium analysis", *Journal of International Economics* 3, 227–244.

McDougall, I.A. (1962) "A note on 'tariffs, the terms of trade, and the distribution of the national income' ", *Journal of Political Economy* 70-4, August, 393–399.

McDougall, I.A. (1970) "Non-traded commodities and the pure theory of international trade", in: I.A. McDougall and R.H. Snape (eds.), *Studies in International Economics* (Amsterdam: North-Holland), ch. 10, pp. 157–192.

McKinnon, R.I. (1966) "Intermediate products and differential tariffs: a generalization of Lerner's symmetry theorem", *Quarterly Journal of Economics* 80, November, 584–615.

Metzler, L. (1949) "Tariffs, the terms of trade, and the distribution of the national income", *Journal of Political Economy* 57, 1–29.

Negishi, T. (1962) "The stability of a competitive economy: A survey article", *Econometrica* 30-4, October, 635–669.

Ohyama, M. and K. Suzuki (1980) "Interindustry flows, non-traded intermediate goods and the theory of effective protection: A general equilibrium analysis", *Journal of International Economics* 10, 567.

Samuelson, P.A. (1947) *Foundations of Economic Analysis* (Cambridge: Harvard University Press).

Samuelson, P.A. (1952) "The transfer problem and transport costs: The terms of trade when impediments are absent", *Economic Journal* 64, June, 278–304.

Suzuki, K. (1976) "The deterioration of the terms of trade by a tariff", *Journal of International Economics* 6, 173–182.

Takayama, A. (1974) *Mathematical Economics* (Hinsdale, Ill.: The Dryden Press).

Uekawa, Y. (1979) "The theory of effective protection, resource allocation and the Stolper–Samuelson theorem", *Journal of International Economics* 9, 151–171.

Woodland, A.D. (1977) "Joint outputs, intermediate inputs and international trade theory", *International Economic Review* 18-3, October, 517–533.

Yabuuchi, S. and K. Tanaka (1981) "Non-traded inputs, interindustry flows, resource allocation and the ERP theory", *Journal of International Economics* 11, 99–111.

CHAPTER 11

TRADE POLICY

11.1. Introduction

In this chapter various aspects of international trade policy are discussed. Most of the analysis concerns the use of tariffs as the main instrument of trade policy, although consideration is also given to import and export quotas as well as production and consumption taxes.

The first topic concerns the use of tariffs in attaining various non-economic objectives which a nation may have. Next is the question of how to slightly change the tariff structure to raise welfare when large changes, such as the complete elimination of tariffs, are infeasible. Then follows a discussion of customs unions and free trade areas from both normative and positive viewpoints.

11.2. Trade taxes and quotas

While trade taxes are the most obvious of the many forms of interference with international trade by governments, there are many non-tariff barriers. These take many forms, such as international differences in packaging regulations, health standards and moral suasion. The most important of these non-tariff barriers are quotas which limit the amount of imports (or exports) of goods in either quantity or value.

What are the effects of quotas? Are they different from the effects of trade taxes? Consider first the case where world prices are fixed, as for a small open economy. An effective quota on the imports of a good will create an excess demand for that good at home. Its price will therefore rise, under our competitive economy assumptions, until the excess demand vanishes, i.e. until the nation wishes to import precisely the amount allowable under the quota rule. Thus, the effect of an import quota is to raise the domestic price, just as for a tariff. In-

deed, the resulting difference between the domestic and world price is sometimes referred to as the *implicit tariff* for the quota.[1]

A major difference between the quota and the imposition of a tariff (at the
implicit tariff level) is in the income distribution effects. Under a tariff the government collects the tariff revenue, whereas under a quota it receives no revenue
unless it sells rights to import to firms and/or individuals. The allocation of the
quota to firms and/or individuals is an important part of the quota scheme. The
quota allocation may be established by some specific set of rules (for example,
each firm's quota is proportionate to its imports during the last five years), by
auction or tender. The individual quotas may or may not be transferable. In either
case the equilibrium (market or shadow) value of a one unit quota is the implicit
tariff. Under a quota, the implicit tariff revenue accrues to the holders of individual
quotas. In the model used in the previous chapter it was assumed that the income
distribution was irrelevant to the equilibrium solution. If that assumption is maintained, then it is evident that a quota will have exactly the same effects as the
imposition of a tariff at the implicit tariff rate.

11.2.1. Quantity quotas on trade

The preceding discussion can be put more formally as follows. Let p and $p*$ be
the domestic and foreign price vectors. Consider a partition of goods into two
classes, and let q_2 be the vector of required net exports of those goods in the
second class. In equilibrium, $p_1 = p_1^*$ holds for the freely traded class. If the quota
system is effective then

$$x_2 = q_2, \tag{1}$$

meaning that net exports will equal the quota. Note that the quotas could be
maximum or minimum requirements on imports or exports. Total income in the
home nation is

$$m = G(p, v) - (p - p*)x, \tag{2}$$

consisting of income from normal production activities plus the profit derived
by importers and exporters. The latter would be zero without quotas. Under
quotas $-(p - p*)x = -(p_2 - p_2^*)x_2 = -(p_2 - p_2^*)q_2$, since $p_1 = p_1^*$. Assuming
aggregation of the consumption sector, the net export vector is

---

[1]   See Corden (1971, p. 213).

$$x = G_p(p, v) - \phi(p, m), \tag{3}$$

where $G_p(p, v)$ is the supply function, ϕ is the demand function, and income m is defined by (2). The model is completed by adding the world market equilibrium conditions:

$$X = x + x^*(p^*, v^*) = 0, \quad p_1 = p_1^*. \tag{4}$$

If the world price vector is fixed, as for a small open economy, then the model need not be closed and (4) may be ignored.

It should be evident that the equilibrium solution to (1)–(4) yields an implicit tariff vector $t \equiv p - p^*$ which, if imposed instead of the quota, would yield precisely the same solution. Under the quota, q_2 is given and determines t; under the tariff, t is given and determines x such that $x_2 = q_2$. Thus, under our assumptions of competition and aggregation of the consumption sector, there is an equivalence between quotas and tariffs. An equilibrium solution obtained under either one may be reproduced using the other form of trade intervention.

11.2.2. Value quotas

The preceding discussion is concerned with separate quotas for each good. An alternative scheme is to impose a value quota for a subset of goods, for example textiles or agricultural products. It seems natural to choose the foreign prices in order to value the goods. Then the value quota may be written as

$$p_2^* x_2 = r_2, \tag{5}$$

where the subscript 2 denotes the subset of goods included in the quota. To model import–export behaviour under this constraint, imagine a competitive trading sector of the economy. The trading sector maximizes its profit subject to the value constraint. Its profit function is

$$\pi(p^*, p, r_2) \equiv \max_{x} \{(p^* - p) x : p_2^* x_2 = r_2\}. \tag{6}$$

If $p_1 \neq p_1^*$, profit is unbounded since the trader can buy low and sell high and there is no constraint on the volume of trade. Of course, this solution is inconsistent with a full competitive equilibrium in which $p_1 = p_1^*$ must therefore hold. If $p_1 = p_1^*$, the solution for x_1 in (6) is indeterminate. Of course, x_1 is made determinate (except in singular cases) by the market equilibrium conditions. All this underlies the previous formulation of equilibrium.

What has to be the relationship between p_2 and p_2^*? For a finite solution for x_2 to exist, it must be the case that

(a) $p_2^* - p_2 + \lambda p_2^* = 0,$

$$(7)$$

(b) $p_2^* x_2 = r_2,$

where λ is the Lagrange multiplier associated with the quota and is interpreted as the marginal profit due to a unit decrease in r_2. Evidently (7,a) may be re-written as

$$\frac{p_j - p_j^*}{p_j^*} = \lambda \tag{8}$$

for each good j in the subset of goods involved in the quota. Since a reduction in r_2 is a relaxation of the quota, $\lambda \geqslant 0$. If $\lambda > 0$, then (8) indicates that a finite solution for x_2 requires that the domestic prices of all constrained goods be higher than the foreign prices by a common factor, namely λ. The solution for x_2 is indeterminate unless only one good is constrained. Again, the market equilib-rium conditions are needed to obtain a determinate solution. The complete model is given by (2)–(5) and (7).

Evidently, the equilibrium solution determines λ for any given r_2. This λ may be interpreted as the shadow price of a $\$1$ trade quota and if the quotas are trade-able λ will be the equilibrium market price. It may also be interpreted as an im-plicit (ad valorem) tariff rate which, if imposed instead of the value quota, would yield precisely the same equilibrium. Under the quota, r_2 determines λ; under the tariff, λ determines x_2 such that $p_2^* x_2 = r_2$.[2] Thus, a value quota is equiva-lent to a *uniform* ad valorem tariff on all of the constrained goods.

11.2.3. General restrictions

The quantity and value quotas have been treated separately for expositional pur-poses. They are special cases of the restriction

$$R x_2 = r, \tag{9}$$

---

[2]   This assumes that there is a strictly monotonic relationship between λ and r_2. Other-wise the same λ may be associated with more than one r_2.

where R is a matrix and r is a vector. The quantity quota occurs when $R = I$, the identity matrix, and $r = q_2$, the vector of quantities required. The value quota occurs when $R = p_2^*$ and $r = r_2$ is the value required. It is easy to show that a finite solution to the trader's problem of maximizing $(p^* - p)\, x$ subject to $Rx_2 = r$ requires that

$$p_2 - p_2^* = \lambda R, \tag{10}$$

where λ is a vector of Lagrange multipliers. It is left to the reader to complete this more general analysis.

Finally, brief attention is given to quotas on production and consumption. If the production quota is specified as $Ry_2 = r$, where the subscript 2 once again refers to the subset of goods included in the quota, producers will maximize GNP subject to this restriction. However, it is useful to imagine a marketing sector which acts as an intermediary between producers at home on the one hand and consumers and the foreign nation on the other. The marketing sector maximizes its profits obtaining:

$$\pi(p, p^*, R, r) \equiv \max_{y} \{(p^* - p)\, y : Ry_2 = r\}. \tag{11}$$

A finite solution for y requires that

(a) $p_1 = p_1^*$,

(b) $p_2^* - p_2 = \lambda R$, \hfill (12)

(c) $Ry_2 = r$,

where λ is a vector of Lagrange multipliers associated with the quota.

If separate quantity quotas are specified for each good, then $R = I$ and r is the vector representing the values of the individual quotas. It may be interpreted as the vector of implicit (unit) tax rates on production. If there is a single value (unit) quota in which the producer prices are used, then $R = p_2$ and r is the dollar value required. In this case λ may be interpreted as the ad valorem of production tax applied to all goods in the subset which are included in the quota. Thus, a uniform production tax structure is equivalent to a value of production quota.

A similar analysis applies for consumption quotas, but the details are left for the problem set.

11.3. Optimal tax policies for achieving quota solutions

In the previous section it was demonstrated that quotas of various sorts could be attained by the price system by a judicious choice of taxes. In the case of trade quotas, a system of trade taxes can be used instead. Also, a system of production taxes can be found to attain production quotas, and a system of consumption taxes can achieve consumption quotas. But are these choices optimal? This question arises because, for example, it may be argued that the attainment of a given level of production of a good above its competitive level requires a price increase. This could be obtained by a tariff on the imports of this good as well as by a production subsidy or a consumption subsidy. Since each may be used to attain this production objective, the question of which is the best way to attain it is important.

To obtain the optimal tax policies which can achieve quota solutions, it is convenient to rewrite the model slightly. To allow for production, consumption and trade taxes a distinction is made between foreign prices, p^*, consumer prices, p, and producer prices, p^s. Market equilibrium is defined by

$$G_p(p^s, v) - E_p(p, \mu) + x^*(p^*, v^*) = 0, \tag{13}$$

where $G(p^s, v)$ is the GNP function and $E(p, \mu)$ is the expenditure function. If the economy is small, then p^* may be taken as exogenous and the balance of trade condition replaces (13) as the appropriate constraint;

$$p^*[G_p(p^s, v) - E_p(p, \mu)] = 0. \tag{14}$$

The advantage of this formulation is that it avoids a detailed account of how disposable income is affected by net tax revenue.[3]

---

[3]   The balance of trade condition (14) may be written in a more familiar form:

$$E(p, \mu) = G(p^s, v) + (p^* - p^s) G_p(p^s, v) + (p - p^*) E_p(p, \mu)$$

$$= G(p^s, v) + (p^0 - p^*) [E_p(p, \mu) - G_p(p^s, v)] + (p^0 - p^s) G_p(p^s, v) + (p - p^0)E_p(p, \mu)$$

by using the relationships $E(p, \mu) = pE_p(p, \mu)$ and $G(p^s, v) = p^s G_p(p^s, v)$. This states that consumer expenditure equals income from production plus net tax revenue consisting of net trade taxes ($p^0 - p^*$ is the import tax vector), net production taxes ($p^0 - p^s$ is the production tax vector) and net consumption taxes ($p - p^0$ is the consumption tax vector), where p^0 is interpreted as the domestic market price vector. Clearly, p^0 need not appear, as shown in the first expression.

11.3.1.   Optimality without quotas

Without quota constraints, the optimal tax problem is to choose prices to maximize the level of utility, μ, subject to either (13) or (14) for a small open economy. The differences between the price vectors p, p^s and p^* can, of course, be used to calculate the implied tax structure. The first-order conditions for a solution with positive prices are

(a) $1 - \lambda p^* E_{p\mu}(p, \mu) = 0$ (μ),

(b) $\lambda p^* G_{pp}(p^s, v) = 0$ (p^s),   (15)

(c) $-\lambda p^* E_{pp}(p, \mu) = 0$ (p),

and (14) for the case of a small open economy. Here λ is the Lagrange multiplier associated with constraints (14) while G_{pp}, E_{pp} and $E_{p\mu}$ are matrices of second partial derivatives.

It is now demonstrated that, when $\lambda \neq 0$, (15,b) and (15,c) imply that producer and consumption prices are equal to foreign prices and hence no taxes are optimal. Now $G_{pp}(p^s, v)$ is a positive semi-definite matrix such that $p^s G_{pp}(p^s, v) = 0$, a condition which follows by recognizing that G_p is homogeneous of degree zero and applying Euler's theorem. If $G_{pp}(p^s, v)$ has rank $M - 1$, which is assumed, then the equation $\rho G_{pp}(p^s, v) = 0$, where ρ is a vector, has a non-trivial solution for ρ which is unique up to a factor of proportionality.[4,5] Thus (15,b) implies that $p^s = p^*$, choosing λ as the factor of proportionality. That is, producer and foreign prices are equal. A similar argument shows that $p = p^*$ as a result of (15,c). Hence, it has been shown that it is optimal to have no taxes when p^* is given.

The result obtained in the preceding paragraph will be used extensively in this chapter and is sufficiently important that it is formally recorded as:

Theorem. Let the $M \times M$ matrix function $A(x)$ be such that $xA(x) = 0$ for all $x = (x_1, \dots, x_M)$. If $A(x)$ has rank $M - 1$ for given x, then the vector equation $yA(x) = 0$ has the solution $y = \alpha x$, where α is any finite scalar.   (16)

[4]   See, for example, Hadley (1961, pp. 174–176) for a statement and proof of this result.
[5]   It is interesting to note that the assumption that G_{pp} has rank $M - 1$ is equivalent to the assumption that there is local controllability of supply by means of prices as used by Weymark (1979). If G_{pp} has rank equal to $M - 1$, then any feasible small change in the output vector can be achieved by a suitable small change in the price vector.

If the relevant constraint is (13), then the first-order conditions are

(a) $1 - \rho E_{p\mu}(p, \mu) = 0$ (μ),

(b) $\rho G_{pp}(p^s, v) = 0$ (p^s),   (17)

(c) $-\rho E_{pp}(p, \mu) = 0$ (p),

and

$$\rho x_p^*(p^*, v^*) = 0 \qquad (p^*). \tag{18}$$

Because of (16) conditions (17, b and c) imply that consumer and producer prices are equal and proportional to ρ. Condition (18) is the usual characterization of the optimal tariff encountered in Chapter 9, and implies that ρ is orthogonal to the foreign offer curve. Thus, when p^* is not fixed the optimal tax policy will include a set of trade taxes. Recognizing this result, the ensuing analysis assumes p^* is constant leaving it implicit, and for the reader to check, that if p^* is not constant a set of trade taxes will be required.

11.3.2. Optimality under quotas

Now consider the optimal price or tax policy when a quota on trade in a subset of goods is required. The problem is to maximize μ subject to the balance of trade condition (14) and the quota written as

$$R[G_p(p^s, v) - E_p(p, \mu)] = r, \tag{19}$$

where $R = [0 \ I]$ and $r = (0 \ r_2)$ is a vector if separate quotas are required, or $R = (0 \ p_2^*)$ and r is a scalar if an overall value quota is required. The first-order conditions for a solution with positive prices are

(a) $1 - (\lambda p^* + \kappa R) E_{p\mu}(p, \mu) = 0$ (μ),

(b) $(\lambda p^* + \kappa R) G_{pp}(p^s, v) = 0$ (p^s),   (20)

(c) $-(\lambda p^* + \kappa R) E_{pp}(p, \mu) = 0$ (p),

and (14) and (19), where κ is a vector of Lagrange multipliers associated with

(19). Conditions (20,b and c) imply that producer and consumer prices are equal and differ from foreign prices if $\kappa \neq 0$. That is,

$$p = p^s = p^* + \frac{\kappa}{\lambda} R, \qquad \lambda > 0. \tag{21}$$

In the case where separate quotas are specified for all goods in subset 2, (21) becomes

$$
\begin{aligned}
p_1 &= p_1^s = p_1^*, \\
p_2 &= p_2^s = p_2^* + \kappa_2/\lambda.
\end{aligned}
\tag{22}
$$

Thus, the optimal policy is the imposition of a set of trade taxes, κ_2/λ. In the case where an overall value constraint is imposed it reduces to

$$
\begin{aligned}
p_1 &= p_1^s = p_1^*, \\
p_2 &= p_2^s = p_2^* (1 + \kappa/\lambda), \qquad \lambda > 0,
\end{aligned}
\tag{23}
$$

where κ/λ is a scalar. Thus, the optimal policy is the imposition of a uniform ad valorem rate of trade tax, κ/λ, on the goods in subset 2.

A production quota may be dealt with in a similar way. The constraint becomes

$$R\, G_p(p^s, v) = r, \tag{24}$$

and the first-order conditions are

(a) $1 - \lambda p^* E_{p\mu}(p, \mu) = 0$ $\qquad$ (μ),

(b) $(\lambda p^* + \kappa R)\, G_{pp}(p^s, v) = 0$ $\qquad$ (p^s), $\qquad\qquad$ (25)

(c) $-\lambda p^* E_{pp}(p, \mu) = 0$ $\qquad$ (p),

and (14) and (24). Thus, by an appropriate normalization

$$
\begin{aligned}
p &= p^*, \\
p^s &= p^* + \frac{\kappa}{\lambda} R,
\end{aligned}
\tag{26}
$$

so the optimal policy is to impose a set of production taxes. Under separate quotas for each good in subset 2, different rates of tax are optimal in general, whereas under a value quota a uniform ad valorem tax rate is required.

Similarly, it is readily demonstrated that a set of consumption taxes is optimal for attaining a consumption quota.

The superiority of production taxes over trade taxes when a quota on production is desired is illustrated in fig. 11.1. Initially the price vector is p^* yielding utility level μ^0 with production y^0 and consumption z^0. If $y_2 = \bar{y}_2$ is the required level of production of good 2, the producer price vector must change to p^1. Under a production subsidy to good 2, consumer prices will remain equal to foreign

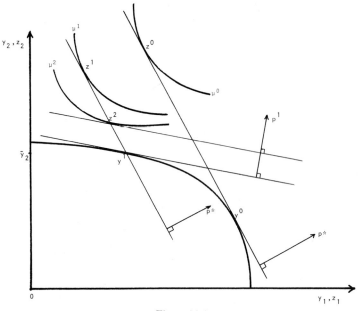

Figure 11.1

prices (p^*) and hence consumption will be along the budget constraint $p^* z = p^* y^1$ at z^1 yielding a maximum utility level $\mu^1 < \mu^0$. However, a tariff on the imports of good 2 would cause consumers to face p^1. Consequently, the consumption point must be along the balance of trade constraint $p^* z = p^* y^1$ as before, but must also be at a point of tangency between an indifference curve and the budget line which has normal $p^1 \neq p^*$. Accordingly, the consumption point must be at z^2, which is between z^1 and y^1, yielding a level of utility $\mu^2 < \mu^1$. Thus, while a tariff could be used to attain $\bar{y}_2$ output of good 2, it is inferior to a production subsidy.

11.3.3. *Value quotas and variable foreign prices*

It has been assumed so far that value quotas use foreign prices to evaluate goods, and that foreign prices are fixed. If they are variable then the optimal policy must take account of the effect of foreign prices upon the foreign trade offers and also upon the value of the quota. Consider first the case of the production value quota (24). The first-order conditions for the optimal policy when $p*$ is to be chosen are (17,a) and (17,c) together with

(a) $(\rho + \kappa p^* R) G_{pp} = 0$ (p^s),

(27)

(b) $\rho x_p^* + \kappa R G_p = 0$ (p^*),

and (13) and (24). Here $p = \rho$ is the consumer price vector and $p^s = \rho + \kappa p^* R$ is the producer price vector. The difference between p and $p*$ denotes the vector of trade taxes. In this case it is generally true that the tax rates will not be the same within a value-constrained group of goods, and that all goods require taxes. The reason for this is that not only can the quantities of the goods be selected to satisfy a value constraint, but the prices to be used to evaluate the goods can also be chosen. The effect on these prices of a set of taxes has to be taken into account, and these effects will depend upon the slopes of all demand and supply functions.

We conclude this section with a general proposition regarding the use of tax policies to attain specific quantitative solutions. The general proposition, due to Bhagwati (1971) and quoted in Vandendorpe (1974), is that

> when distortions have to be introduced into the economy, because the values of certain variables (i.e., production or employment of a factor in an activity) have to be constrained, the optimal (or least-cost) method of doing this is to choose that policy intervention that creates the distortion affecting directly the constrained variable.

Thus, when production is to be constrained the optimal policy instrument is a production tax, when consumption is to be constrained it is a consumption tax, and when trade is to be constrained a trade tax is optimal. In this way the distortion avoids being imposed on variables whose values are not to be constrained.

11.4. Piecemeal trade tax policies

While it is possible to develop optimal tax formulae to take advantage of power in world markets or to attain certain quantitative objectives, it is often the case that governments cannot put these into practice. If the optimal policies require large tax changes governments may be reluctant to proceed for political reasons. Also, the information about the technology and preferences required for the implementation of the formulae may not be very reliable, or even available, some distance away from the present position of the economy. Thus, in recent years there has been growing interest in developing piecemeal tax policies which are designed to increase welfare by the use of small changes in tax rates on a subset of tax instruments.

Needless to say, another reason why optimal tax formulae may not be very useful in practical policy deliberations is that they usually are based upon the optimization of a community utility function. It is known that the validity of such an exercise depends upon the existence of optimal income redistributions. If these are not available then any optimal tax formulae must take into account individual utility functions. This can be done by optimizing a Bergson–Samuelson social welfare function. Alternatively, one can search for Pareto improving tax formulae, i.e. those which will raise the utility of some individuals and lower the utility of none. The present analysis will, however, maintain the existence of a community utility function.

Suppose that a small open economy with a community utility function has no internal tax distortions but does have taxes imposed upon its trade with the rest of the world. It is well known that the optimal tax policy is to reduce all trade taxes to zero and hence have free trade. If this (supposedly) large change in tax rates is not possible, can a piecemeal policy be found to raise welfare? It might be conjectured that any reduction in taxes on trade would raise welfare. That this is not necessarily true is a simple illustration of the theory of second best.[6] In the present context a reduction in one distortion may reduce welfare, given the existence of other distortions. Hence, the question arises as to whether the set of tax changes which improve welfare can be conveniently characterized. It will be shown below that proportional reductions in all tax rates will improve welfare under certain conditions. Also, the reduction of the highest tax rate to the next highest will also improve welfare, again under certain conditions.[7]

Let the utility level be given by the indirect trade utility function $\mu = H(p, r, v)$, where p is the vector of domestic prices, v is the endowment vector and r is the net tax revenue. Let $p = p^* + t$, where p^* is the foreign price vector and t is the (per unit) tax vector. The tax revenue is $r = -tx$, where the net export vec-

---

[6] The theory of second best was developed by Meade (1955a) and Lipsey and Lancaster (1956).
[7] The following relies heavily upon the work of Lloyd (1974), Hatta (1977a), Fukushima (1979), and also Bertrand and Vanek (1971).

tor $x = H_p/H_r$.[8] The change in utility due to a small change in t is proportional to

$$d\mu/H_r = (H_p/H_r)\,dp + dr$$
$$= x\,dp + dr \tag{28}$$
$$= x\,dp^* - t\,dx,$$

since $dr = -t\,dx - x\,dt$ and $dp = dp^* + dt$. Here $H_r = 1/E_\mu(p,\mu) > 0$ is the marginal utility of income, hence $d\mu/H_r = d\mu\,E_\mu(p,\mu)$ may be interpreted as the change in utility expressed in terms of income. If foreign prices are fixed, then the utility change is proportional to $-t\,dx$. In view of the balance of trade condition $p^*x = 0$, the change in utility when p^* is fixed is proportional to

$$d\mu/H_r = -t\,dx = -\sum_j \tau_j\,p_j^*\,dx_j = \sum_{j\neq k}(\tau_k - \tau_j)\,p_j^*\,dx_j, \tag{29}$$

where $\tau_j \equiv t_j/p_j^*$ is the ad valorem rate of tax for good j based upon the foreign price.

Equation (29) gives the effect on welfare of a tax change expressed in terms of the response of net exports. If $\tau_k > \tau_j$ for all $j \neq k$, *and* a small change in tax rates caused the net exports of all other goods ($j \neq k$) to rise, then welfare improves since the right-hand side of (29) is then positive. For example, if good k is imported and τ_k is the highest tariff rate, then a sufficient condition for welfare to improve is for *all* exports to increase and *all other* imports to fall. This result, which is due to Bertrand and Vanek (1971), requires the knowledge of the effect of the change in the tax vector upon net exports. To be of use in policy formation these effects have to be predicted, which requires knowledge of the nature of preferences and technology at the initial equilibrium.

It is convenient to express the net export vector as

$$x = S_p(p,\mu,v) = G_p(p,v) - E_p(p,\mu), \tag{30}$$

where $S(p,\mu,v) \equiv G(p,v) - E(p,\mu)$. Of course, the solution of the equation $S(p,\mu,v) + r = 0$ for μ yields the indirect trade utility function $\mu = H(p,r,v)$ and, indeed, eq. (28) may be obtained using S rather than H. Differentiation of (30) yields $dx = S_{pp}\,dp + S_{p\mu}\,d\mu$. Since $H_r = -1/S_\mu$ and $\phi_m = S_{p\mu}/S_\mu = E_{p\mu}/E_\mu$ is the vector of responses of demands to income, the change in x may be rewritten as $dx = S_{pp}\,dp + \phi_m\,t\,dx$ in view of (28) with $dp^* = 0$. The explicit solution is

---

[8] See eq. (6.47).

$$dx = [I - \phi_m t]^{-1} S_{pp} \, dt, \tag{31}$$

where $dp = dt$. This formula permits the calculation of dx in response to a change in t using information on $S_{pp} = G_{pp} - E_{pp}$, the matrix of net substitution elasticities, and ϕ_m, the income effects on the demands for goods.

If (31) is substituted into (29) the change in utility becomes proportional to

$$d\mu/H_r = -t \, [I - \phi_m t]^{-1} S_{pp} \, dt, \tag{32}$$

which could be used to calculate utility improving changes in t. However, a more useful expression, yielding a simple piecemeal rule, is obtained below.

An alternative piecemeal rule has been developed by Lloyd (1974) and extended by Hatta (1977a) to deal with non-traded goods. To obtain this rule the model is expressed by the balance of trade condition:

$$p^* \, S_p \, (p, \mu, v) = 0, \tag{33}$$

where $p = p^* + t$. For any given p^* this equation determines the level of utility as a function of t. The effect of t upon μ is obtained by differentiation which yields

$$p^* [S_{pp} \, dt + S_{p\mu} \, d\mu] = 0,$$

and

$$d\mu = - p^* \, S_{pp} \, dt/p^* \, S_{p\mu}.$$

Since $\phi_m = E_{p\mu}/E_\mu = S_{p\mu}/S_\mu$ is the income effect in demand, and $H_r = -1/S_\mu$, $pS_{pp} = 0$ and $p^* = p - t$, the change in utility is proportional to

$$d\mu/H_r = p^* S_{pp} \, dt/\iota = -tS_{pp} \, dt/\iota, \tag{34}$$

where $\iota \equiv p^* \phi_m = (p - t)\phi_m = 1 - t\phi_m$. If no good is inferior, $\phi_m > 0$ and hence the denominator in (34) is positive so the effect upon utility depends upon the sign of the numerator.[9] Suppose just one tax rate is changed, say t_k. Then the numerator of (34) may be expressed as

---

[9] Non-inferiority of all goods is sufficient but not necessary for $\iota \equiv p^* \phi_m$ to be positive. Moreover, in the context of a closed economy with commodity taxes, Hatta (1977a) has shown that a necessary condition for Walrasian stability is that ι be non-negative, where p^* is the producer price vector.

$$-tS_{pk}\,dt_k = -\sum_j \sigma_j p_j S_{jk}\,dt_k$$

$$= \sum_{j \neq k} (\sigma_k - \sigma_j) p_j S_{jk}\,dt_k$$

$$= \sum_{j \neq k} (\tau_k - \tau_j)(1 + \tau_k)^{-1}(1 + \tau_j)^{-1} p_j S_{jk}\,dt_k, \tag{35}$$

where the relationship $\sum_j p_j S_{jk} = 0$, $k = 1, \ldots, M$, has been used, $\tau_j \equiv t_j / p_j^*$ is the ad valorem rate of tax based on foreign prices and $\sigma_j \equiv \tau_j (1 + \tau_j)^{-1} = t_j / p_j$ is the ad valorem rate based on domestic prices.

A condition for expression (35) to be positive can now be obtained. Since $(1 + \tau_j) = p_j / p_j^* > 0$ for all j, the sign of (35) depends upon the relationship of the tax rate on good k to those on other goods $(\tau_k - \tau_j)$, the signs of the S_{jk} and whether the tax rate on k is raised or lowered. Consider the case where the tax rate on good k is reduced. Clearly, a sufficient condition for (35) to be positive when $dt_k = p_k^* d\tau_k < 0$ is that $\tau_k \geq \tau_j$ and $S_{jk} \leq 0$ for all $j \neq k$ with strict inequalities holding for at least one $j \neq k$. In this case (34) and (35) imply that utility is raised by reducing the highest tax rate. Conversely, if $\tau_k \leq \tau_j$, then an increase in the tax rate will raise welfare under the same condition on the S_{jk} terms. What is the interpretation of this condition? The term S_{jk} is the pure substitution effect on net exports of good j (k) of a change in the price of good k (j). If $S_{jk} > 0$, goods j and k are called net complements, and if $S_{jk} < 0$, they are called net substitutes. If all goods are net substitutes, then an increase in p_k (with utility constant) will raise exports of good k $(S_{kk} > 0)$ and reduce exports of all other goods $(S_{jk} < 0)$.

Formally, the result obtained is as follows

> **Theorem.** If (a) $\iota \equiv p^* \phi_m > 0$ and (b) all goods are net substitutes for k $(S_{jk} < 0$ for all $j)$, and (c) the ad valorem trade tax on good k is greatest $(\tau_k > \tau_j$ for all $j)$ (lowest), then utility will increase if the tax rate on good k is reduced (increased). (36)

The change in utility is given by

$$H_r^{-1}\,d\mu/dt_k = \sum_{j \neq k} (\tau_k - \tau_j)(1 + \tau_k)^{-1}(1 + \tau_j)^{-1} p_j S_{jk}/\iota. \tag{37}$$

The conditions on S_{jk} and $\tau_k - \tau_j$ in theorem (36) can be weakened, as is clear from the preceding paragraph, but at the expense of more cumbersome wording.

This theorem gives sufficient conditions for raising welfare. It is noteworthy that the intuitively reasonable policy of reducing the highest tax to the next highest requires rather special conditions on S_{pp} for utility to increase. Moreover, if these conditions hold it is also true that raising the lowest tax rate will increase welfare. If all the off-diagonal elements of S_{pp} are negative, then the piecemeal policy of reducing the highest tax rates and raising the lowest will eventually result in a uniform ad valorem tax rate structure. If this rate is positive, imports are taxed and exports subsidized at the same rate (based upon foreign prices). Then relative prices at home are equal to those abroad and hence there is no protection afforded any industry relative to free trade and, indeed, net tax revenue is zero. This is, of course, equivalent to free trade which is optimal for a price-taking economy.

Proportional tax changes

Another piecemeal policy which will raise welfare irrespective of the nature of S_{pp} is to reduce tax distortions proportionally. The changes in t which will raise utility are those for which the numerator in (34) is positive, assuming that no good is inferior.

Thus, the condition for a change in t to raise welfare if $\iota > 0$ is that

$$t \, S_{pp} \, \mathrm{d}t < 0. \tag{38}$$

Given S_{pp} and t, the set of welfare improving tax changes, $\mathrm{d}t$, can be calculated. If $\mathrm{d}t = \alpha t$, where α is a scalar, then (38) may be written as

$$\alpha t \, S_{pp} \, t < 0. \tag{39}$$

Since S_{pp} is a positive semi-definite matrix $t \, S_{pp} \, t \geqslant 0$ and it is assumed that $t \, S_{pp} \, t > 0$ for $t \neq 0$ and $t \neq p$.[10] Thus, it has been shown that utility is increased if

$$\mathrm{d}t = \alpha t, \quad \alpha < 0, \tag{40}$$

a result obtained by Lloyd (1974) and Fukushima (1979).

This condition means that $\mathrm{d}t_j = \alpha t_j$ for all j and hence all taxes, expressed as per unit taxes, are reduced in proportion to the initial tax levels. Since the ad valorem rates are $\tau_j \equiv t_j / p_j^*$, the condition that $\mathrm{d}t_j / t_j = \alpha$ requires that $\mathrm{d}\tau_j / \tau_j = \alpha$. Thus, proportional reductions in all tax rates, measured in either per unit or ad

---

[10] If $t = p$, then $p^* = 0$ which is obviously an irrelevant case, as is the case where $t = 0$.

valorem terms, will raise utility assuming only that $\iota > 0$ a sufficient condition for which is that no good is inferior.

Actually, this result is a special case of a more general result due to Fukushima (1979). The above result is that proportional reductions in tax rates which point to zero will raise welfare. But of course, uniform ad valorem rates are just as good as zero rates of tax, suggesting that some changes in taxes in the direction of uniform ad valorem rates will raise welfare. This is, indeed, true. For example, let $dp = dt = \alpha t - \alpha\beta p^* = \alpha(t - \beta p^*)$. This implies that $d(\tau_j - \beta) = d\tau_j = dt_j/p_j^* = \alpha(\tau_j - \beta)$, an equiproportional change α in the difference between all ad valorem tax rates and the uniform rate β. The change in utility is positive for such a change in t if

$$t\,S_{pp}\,dt = t\,S_{pp}\,[\alpha t - \alpha\beta p^*] = \alpha(1 + \beta)\,t\,S_{pp}\,t < 0. \tag{41}$$

This reduces to (39) when the uniform rate is $\beta = 0$. Since $t\,S_{pp}\,t > 0$, and $1 + \beta > 0$ (to ensure that $p^* > 0$ if β were imposed) (41) indicates that $\alpha < 0$ ensures that $dt = \alpha t - \alpha\beta p^*$ will raise utility. Formally,

> **Theorem.** If $\iota \equiv p^*\phi_m > 0$, a change of $d\tau_j = \alpha(\tau_j - \beta)$ in ad valorem rates towards the uniform rate $\beta > -1$ will raise welfare. (42)

It is important to recognize that this result applies when *all* rates not currently equal to β are changed and in such a way that the deviations from β are proportionately reduced. This is a fairly specific policy recommendation, and unlike theorem (36) does not rely upon special conditions on S_{pp}.

If S_{pp} is known in the neighbourhood of the initial equilibrium, it may be used in conjunction with (38) to obtain the complete set of small tax changes which will raise welfare. Evidently, the signs of the elements of $\gamma \equiv -t\,S_{pp}$ indicate whether to raise or lower taxes on specific goods. If $\gamma_k > 0$, then any $dt_k < 0$ may be chosen, for example. This raises the question of how to choose the level of dt_k. If, for example, the policy constraint is $dt^T dt = k > 0$, meaning that tax changes are restricted to a circle with radius $k^{1/2}$, then the dt which maximizes the increase in utility is

$$dt = \gamma/\lambda \tag{43}$$

where $\lambda \equiv (\gamma^T\gamma/k)^{1/2} > 0$. Thus, tax reductions are chosen proportional to $\gamma = -t\,S_{pp}$ in this example, requiring differences amongst percentage changes in tax rates. This is in contrast with the piecemeal policy suggestion of Fukushima, and illustrates the value of information in selecting the appropriate tax policy.

11.5. Discriminatory trade policies: Normative theory of trading clubs

The present section is concerned with the situation in which a group of nations form a club or association with the aim of reducing the barriers to trade within the club but possibly maintaining barriers to trade between the club members and the rest of the world. If external barriers are maintained, then the trade policies of the club members are discriminatory since the treatment given trade differs depending upon whether the trade flow is between club members or not. Kemp (1969, pp. 20–21) defines various types of possible arrangements. A free trade association is one in which trade between club members is free. A customs union is a free trade area which imposes a common set of taxes on trade with the rest of the world. A trading club exists when the club members exchange *small* reductions in trade taxes. Each type will be simply called a club, unless reference is specifically being made to one of these.

11.5.1. Optimal club policy

Consider a world of many countries whose tastes and technologies are described by $S^k(p^k, \mu^k) \equiv G^k(p^k, v^k) - E^k(p^k, \mu^k)$, where the argument v^k has been subsumed into the function S^k, μ^k is the level of utility and p^k is the domestic price vector. Equilibrium in the world market for goods is given by the market-clearing condition:

$$\sum_k S_p^k(p^k, \mu^k) = 0, \tag{44}$$

where the sum is over all nations k and where $S_p^k(p^k, \mu^k) \equiv \partial S^k(p^k, \mu^k)/\partial p^k$. Let p denote the "world price" vector, the difference $t^k \equiv p^k - p$ being the vector of per unit trade taxes imposed by nation k.[11] If trade taxes are imposed as ad valorem rates based upon the world price, then

$$p^k = R^k p, \tag{45}$$

where $R^k = \text{diag}(1 + \tau_j^k)$ and $\tau_j^k \equiv t_j^k/p_j$ is the ad valorem rate of tax. The balance of trade condition for nation k is

$$p S_p^k(p^k, \mu^k) = 0. \tag{46}$$

[11] One can think of the existence of a mythical trading post external to each nation and through which all trade takes place. Then p is the price vector in operation at the trading post.

Given R^k for each nation the equilibrium solution for the world and domestic price vectors and the levels of welfare can be obtained from (44)–(46). Of course, one of the equations in (44) is redundant because of Walras' law and p (and hence p^k) is determined only up to a factor of proportionality.

Now consider a club consisting of nations $1, ..., K$. The club takes as given the ad valorem trade tax rates in the remaining nations. This allows the aggregation of all other nations into one "dummy nation" called the rest of the world. To do this observe that (45) and (46) may be solved for μ^k as $\mu^k = H^k(p)$ which is homogeneous of degree zero in p. Thus, the net export vector for the rest of the world is

$$x^*(p) \equiv \sum_{k>K} S_p^k(R^k p, H^k(p)). \qquad (47)$$

This function is homogeneous of degree zero in p and satisfies the balance of trade condition $px^*(p) = 0$.[12]

Suppose that the club wishes to maximize a social welfare function $W(\mu)$, where $\mu = (\mu^1, ..., \mu^K)$ by choosing an appropriate tax policy. It is bound by the requirement of product market equilibrium, now expressed as

$$\sum_{k=1}^{K} S_p^k(p^k, \mu^k) + x^*(p) = 0. \qquad (48)$$

It ignores the balance of trade condition for the individual club members and hence allows income transfers within the club. However, the club's balance of trade is necessarily zero since that of the rest of the world is zero. The optimal policy is obtained by maximizing $W(\mu)$ subject to (48) with respect to $\mu, p^1, ..., p^K$ and p. The first-order conditions for a solution include

(a) $W^k + \lambda S_{pu}^k(p^k, \mu^k) = 0, \qquad k = 1, ..., K,$

(b) $\lambda S_{pp}^k(p^k, \mu^k) = 0, \qquad k = 1, ..., K,$ (49)

(c) $\lambda x_p^*(p) = 0,$

where λ is the vector of Lagrange multipliers associated with (48) and $W^k \equiv \partial W(\mu)/\partial \mu^k$. Applying theorem (16), condition (b), implies that λ and p^k differ only by a factor of proportionality which, without loss of generality, can be taken to be unity. Thus, $p^k = \lambda$ for all k, meaning that all club members have the same domestic prices, and hence there must be free trade within the club. Moreover, they

---

[12]   The proofs of these statements are left for the problem set.

must all have the same external trade tax structure. The external tax in per unit form is $t = \lambda - p$ and is given by the familiar optimal tax characterization in (49,c).

In summary, it has been demonstrated that the club will maximize its social welfare if it forms a customs union with no internal trade taxes and with a common optimal tax structure for trade with the rest of the world. If the club is very small in the sense that the world price can be taken as given, then, as with a single nation, the club's optimal trade tax vector is $t = 0$ and hence completely free trade by the club members is optimal. This is true despite the existence of trade taxes in the rest of the world.

The optimal tax rates, the equilibrium world price vector and the optimal utility vector depend crucially upon the social welfare function $W(\mu)$. It would be fortitous indeed if at this solution each nation in the club had a zero trade balance. Thus, transfers of income within the club are generally required to support the optimal policy. What possibilities exist if such transfers are not feasible and each nation is required to balance its trade? Assuming that the club forms a customs union with free internal trade and with a common external trade tax vector, equilibrium is described by the market-clearing condition (48), and the K balance of trade conditions (46) where $p^k = p^1$ for all $k = 1, ..., K$. The choice of the external tax rates now has to be considered. Let them be determined by

$$p^k \, x_p^*(p) = 0, \qquad k = 1, ..., K, \tag{50}$$

which is the usual characterization of the optimal tax structure.

But in what sense is it now optimal? The equilibrium described by (46), (48) and (50) can be viewed as the solution to the problem of optimizing a social welfare function subject to (48) if the social welfare function is carefully chosen. This choice is the basis of Negishi's (1969) proof of the existence of equilibrium and requires that W^k be equal to the inverse of the equilibrium marginal utility of income in nation k. Since the latter is readily shown to be $-1/p^k \, S_{p\mu}^k \, (p^k, \mu^k)$, the solution to (46), (48) and (50) satisfies the necessary conditions for an optimal solution when $W^k = -p^k \, S_{p\mu}^k \, (p^k, \mu^k)$. It is in this sense that the club's policy is optimal.

Since the domestic price vector of each club member is orthogonal to $x_p^*(p)$, the solution is Pareto optimal from the point of view of the club. That is to say, no other policy on the club's part can increase the welfare of one member without reducing the welfare of another. Pareto optimality here requires that maximum advantage be taken of the curvature of the foreign excess supply functions (i.e. of the club's monopoly power), and that the allocation of the resulting trade vector between club members be optimal. If the external tax vector does not satisfy

(50), then it is not optimal in the sense described in the previous paragraph. While internal free trade ensures that the trade vector with the rest of the world is optimally allocated between the club members, they could do better by altering the external tariff appropriately. For a proof of the Pareto optimality of (50) from the viewpoint of the club, the reader is referred back to Chapter 9, section 9.6, where the Pareto optimal trade tax structure for a nation of many consumers and no lump-sum transfers was characterized. Exactly the same proof applies here.

11.5.2. Second-best club policy

What is the optimal club policy if for some reason the common external tax vector is regarded as fixed in ad valorem terms and is not optimal? If the club can redistribute income using lump-sum taxes and subsidies, and if all goods are traded, then it can achieve the optimum solution by a system of consumption and production taxes. This is because any set of trade taxes can be replaced, without affecting the competitive equilibrium, by a set of production and consumption taxes. If this policy is not feasible it may be possible to improve social welfare by imposing taxes on internal club trade. Negishi (1969) has shown for a $K = 2$, two-product model that it may be Pareto optimal to have a set of consumption and trade taxes within the club. By such a policy the club can, say, reduce the amount of internal trade and expand the amount of external trade. By creating internal distortions club welfare is reduced. However, if the external tariff on imports is greater than is optimal, the expansion of external trade will move towards its "optimal" amount and welfare will increase. Negishi essentially shows that there is a net gain in welfare, i.e. that this policy leads to Pareto optimality.

Negishi's result may be obtained as follows (the method is quite different from his). Let the club consist of nations 1 and 2 and suppose that all external trade is undertaken by nation 1. The constraint which makes the policy problem one of "second best" is that the external trade tax vector is not a choice vector and production taxes are not permitted. Let p be the world price vector, p^k be the producer price vector in nation k and q^k be the consumer price vector in nation k. Also, let $p^1 = (I + T^1) p$, where $T^1 = \text{diag}(\tau_j^1)$ and τ_j^1 is the ad valorem rate of tax on net imports into nation 1 from outside the club. These ad valorem rates are fixed. The market equilibrium condition is

$$G_p^1(p^1, v^1) - E_q^1(q^1, \mu^1) + G_p^2(p^2, v^2) - E_q^2(q^2, \mu^2) + x^*(p) = 0. \quad (51)$$

If $W(\mu^1, \mu^2)$ is maximized subject to (51) and the relation $p^1 = (I + T^1) p$, the necessary conditions for a solution are

(a) $\quad W^k - \lambda E^k_{q\mu}(q^k, \mu^k) = 0 \qquad (\mu^k),$

(b) $\quad \lambda x^*_p(p) + (I + T^1) \theta = 0 \qquad (p),$

(c) $\quad \lambda G^1_{pp}(p^1, v^1) - \theta = 0 \qquad (p^1),$ $\qquad\qquad\qquad\qquad (52)$

(d) $\quad \lambda G^2_{pp}(p^2, v^2) = 0 \qquad\qquad (p^2),$

(e) $\quad \lambda E^k_{qq}(q^k, \mu^k) = 0 \qquad\qquad (q^k),$

where λ and θ are vectors of Lagrange multipliers.

Conditions (d) and (e) imply that $p^2 = q^1 = q^2 = \lambda$, meaning that there are no consumption taxes in nation 2 and the consumer prices in nation 1 are identical to domestic prices for nation 2. Condition (c) implies that $p^1 \neq \lambda$ if $\theta \neq 0$, and hence that there are consumption taxes in nation 1 and trade taxes between nations 1 and 2. Thus, the optimal club policy involves internal distortions when the external trade tax vector is not a policy instrument and has been set at a non-optimal level. Of course, if $\theta = 0$, then T^1 is optimal and the solution requires free trade.

If consumption taxes are not permitted it is easy to show that the optimal policy requires a vector of taxes on internal club trade. This means that consumers (and producers) face different prices in the two nations.

11.5.3. Optimal club policy under individual balance of trade restrictions

The previous analysis has assumed the possibility of transfers of income between club members to support the optimal solutions for a pre-specified welfare function $W(\mu)$. If such transfers are ruled out then each nation must balance its trade. In order to do this it may be necessary to have different tariffs in each nation, in which case a customs union is not optimal.

Let x^{k0} and x^{k*} be the vectors of net trade between nation k and the other club members (0) and the rest of the world (*), respectively. Let p^0 and p be the club and world price vectors. Then the constraints are

(a) $S_p^k(p^k, \mu^k) = x^{k0} + x^{k*}$,

(b) $p^0 x^{k0} + p x^{k*} = 0$,

$$\text{(c)} \quad \sum_{k-1}^{K} x^{k0} = 0, \tag{53}$$

(d) $\sum_{k=1}^{K} S_p^k(p^k, \mu^k) + x^*(p) = 0$.

The first is that net exports are allocated to other club members or to the rest of the world. The second is the balance of trade condition which has two terms corresponding to the two directions of trade. The third condition says that the club markets must clear, while the last says that the world markets must clear. The club is assumed to maximize $W(\mu)$ subject to (53) yielding the following necessary conditions:

(a) $W^k + (\lambda^k + \lambda) S_{p\mu}^k(p^k, \mu^k) = 0$,

(b) $(\lambda^k + \lambda) S_{pp}^k(p^k, \mu^k) = 0$,

$$\text{(c)} \quad \lambda x_p^*(p) + \sum_{k=1}^{K} \theta^k x^{k*} = 0,$$

$$\text{(d)} \quad \sum_{k=1}^{K} \theta^k x^{k0} = 0, \tag{54}$$

(e) $-\lambda^k + \theta^k p^0 + \rho = 0$,

(f) $-\lambda^k + \theta^k p = 0$,

where λ^k, θ^k, ρ and λ are the Lagrange multipliers for the respective constraints in (53).

Condition (b) implies that $p^k = \lambda^k + \lambda$, while (f) says that $\lambda^k = \theta^k p$. Thus, $p^k = \lambda + \theta^k p$, where λ is the club price vector inclusive of the external trade tax vector. Thus, the trade tax vector for nation k is $p^k - p = (\lambda - p) + \theta^k p$ and consists of a common part, $(\lambda - p)$, and a term, $\theta^k p$, specific to nation k. The ad valorem rate of tax on the external trade of good j is

$$\tau_j^k \equiv (p_j^k - p_j)/p_j = (\lambda_j - p_j)/p_j + \theta^k = \tau_j + \theta^k. \tag{53}$$

Here τ_j is the rate of tax common to all club members, while θ^k, which is independent of j, is the "premium" added to nation k's tax schedule to ensure that there is a balance of trade. Note that while the tariff rates are different (possibly) in each nation, they differ only by a constant and hence the ranking of goods by the sizes of the tax rates is the same for all club members.

Using (54,e) it follows that $p^k - p^0 = (\rho + \lambda - p^0) + \theta^k p^0$. Hence, the ad valorem rate of tax on the club trade of good j is

$$\sigma_j^k \equiv (p_j^k - p_j^0)/p_j^0 = (\rho_j + \lambda_j - p_j^0)/p_j^0 + \theta^k = \sigma_j + \theta^k. \tag{54}$$

Again the tax rates differ between club members by the additive term θ^k.

These results show that a customs union may not be the best way of maximizing a club social welfare function. They allow for different rates of trade taxes on external trade. Also, they allow for trade taxes on internal club trade. The two rates of taxes, τ_j^k and σ_j^h, may be different so that the club is discriminatory in its trade policy.

If the balance of trade constraints are ineffective then $\theta^k = 0$ for all k, and hence $\lambda^k = 0$ and $\rho = 0$.[13] Thus, $p^k = \lambda \neq p$ for all k and so a customs union is optimal.

11.5.4.   The Ohyama–Kemp–Wan proposition

Ohyama (1972) and Kemp and Wan (1976) show that a customs union which maintains the same external trade vector as occurred before the formation of the customs union can be a Pareto improvement for the world as a whole, provided suitable transfers of income within the union are made.

Consider an initial equilibrium with prices $\bar p^1, ..., \bar p^K$, and $\bar p$ and utility levels $\bar \mu^1, ..., \bar u^K$, and $\bar u^*$. The net trade vector for nations 1, ..., K is $\bar x = - x^*(\bar p)$. Now treat $\bar x$ as fixed and find the set of $\mu = (\mu^1, ..., \mu^K)$ for which

$$\sum_{k=1}^{K} S_p^k(p, \mu^k) = \bar x \tag{55}$$

for some $p > 0$. This is the utility possibility set for the club given the net export vector $\bar x$. If the preunion utility vector $\bar \mu$ is on the boundary of this set then no Pareto improvement can be made, given $\bar x$. If $\bar \mu$ is not on the boundary, then there is a point $\bar{\bar \mu} \gtrsim \bar \mu$ on the boundary which is supported by price $\bar{\bar p}$. The club can attain $\bar{\bar \mu}$ by making $\bar{\bar p}$ the club price if incomes can be redistributed appropriately.

---

[13]   At least one of the θ^k is zero since, by Walras' law, one of the balance of trade conditions is automatically satisfied if the remainder are satisfied and the markets are in equilibrium.

The external tariff is $\bar{\bar{p}} - \bar{p}$ and internal club trade is free, making it a customs union. In general the utility of at least one nation in the club will increase if the preclub prices are not equal. Since the price vector in the rest of the world is as before, utility levels there will be unaltered.

This simple and elegant argument shows that a customs union so formed will generally be a Pareto improvement from a world point of view, and can never reduce the welfare of any nation. As Kemp and Wan emphasize, the argument applies to any number of nations in a club, and to any preclub situation. Given the existence of a customs union, the argument applies to the extension of the union to include new members. The limiting case is where all nations are included in the club, in which case no further Pareto improvements are possible. Such a sequence of events provides a Pareto improving way of attaining Pareto optimality.

The preceding argument may be amended to deal with the case where lump-sum international transfers are not permitted by allowing the imposition of commodity taxes. In this case the customs union can set external trade taxes and internal commodity taxes (on goods and factors) so as to ensure an equilibrium that is Pareto superior to a restricted trade equilibrium in the absence of a customs union. This important amendment is due to Dixit and Norman (1980, 192–194).

11.6. Discriminatory trade policies: Positive theory of clubs

The preceding analysis has concentrated on the normative theory of clubs, developing optimal policies. In practice it may not be possible to execute optimal policies, and yet free trade or preferential trading arrangements are often negotiated. Much of the literature on customs unions is concerned with the question of whether a particular agreement will raise the welfare of the individual member nations when there are no international transfers of income. Also, although less often asked, there is the question of how the trading arrangement will affect such variables as the terms of trade, consumption and production levels, and the volume and pattern of trade.

In what follows a general model of trade with discriminatory tariffs is outlined, and then specialized to indicate the effect of a change in the trade tax structure upon the welfare of individual nations.

Let $t_{jk}^{\ell k}$ be the ad valorem rate of tax on the trade flow of product j between ℓ and k as imposed by k. The trade of j between ℓ and k is $e_j^{\ell k} \geq 0$. Traders will choose trades to maximize their profits. The zero profit condition requires that

$$p_j^k - (1 + t_{jk}^{\ell k})(1 + t_{j\ell}^{\ell k}) p_j^\ell \leq 0 \leq e_j^{\ell k}. \tag{55}$$

Thus, the profit obtained from buying one unit of j in ℓ, paying the taxes at ℓ's border and k's border, and selling in k is zero if the trade is positive, but if this profit is negative then the trade is zero. As Kemp (1969, pp. 17, 20) points out, certain restrictions on the tax rates must be imposed to prevent circular trades. For example (55) implies that

$$(1 + t_{jk}^{\ell k})(1 + t_{j\ell}^{k\ell})(1 + t_{jk}^{k\ell})(1 + t_{j\ell}^{k\ell}) \geqslant 1, \tag{56}$$

with a strict equality if both $e_j^{\ell k}$ and $e_j^{k\ell}$ are positive. Condition (56) means that it is not profitable to buy \$1 worth of good j in $\ell(k)$ take it to $k(\ell)$ and bring it back to $\ell(k)$. That is, for example, a subsidy on imports into $\ell(k)$ should not outweigh the tariff on imports into $k(\ell)$. Conditions such as (56) can be derived for any circular trade from k to ℓ, to ..., to k. It is assumed that all such conditions are satisfied so that circular trade is not profitable. Also, note that if (56) holds with strict inequality, then there cannot be simultaneous trades of j from ℓ to k and from k to ℓ.

The total net export of j by k is

$$x_j^k = \sum_{\ell \neq k} (e_j^{k\ell} - e_j^{\ell k}) = \sum_{\ell \neq k} x_j^{k\ell}, \tag{57}$$

where $x_j^{k\ell} \equiv e_j^{k\ell} - e_j^{\ell k}$ is the net trade between ℓ and k. The net tax revenue is

$$r^k = \sum_{\ell \neq k} t_{jk}^{\ell k}(1 + t_{j\ell}^{\ell k}) p_j^\ell e_j^{\ell k} + \sum_{\ell \neq k} t_{jk}^{k\ell} p_j^k e_j^{k\ell}. \tag{58}$$

The net export vector is given by

$$x^k = S_p^k(p^k, \mu^k) \tag{59}$$

and μ^k is determined by the budget constraint

$$S^k(p^k, \mu^k) + r^k = 0. \tag{60}$$

Alternatively, and equivalently,

$$x^k = H_p^k(p^k, r^k)/H_r^k(p^k, r^k), \tag{61}$$

where $\mu^k = H^k(p^k, r^k) \equiv V^k(p^k, G^k(p^k, v^k) + r^k)$ is the indirect trade utility function. Finally, the market clearing conditions are that

$$\sum_{k=1}^{K} x^k = 0. \tag{62}$$

Equilibrium is described by (55), (57), (58), (62) and either (59) and (60) or (61). The model is more complicated than under non-discriminatory trade since specific attention has to be given to trades between each pair of nations. Also, it is general in the sense that trade taxes are distinguished by the direction of trade. If no export taxes or subsidies are levied, then $t_{j\ell}^{\ell k} = 0$ simplifying (55) and (56). If there is no distinction between imports and exports in the sense that the trade tax causes a wedge between domestic and world prices then $1 + t_{jk}^{\ell k} = 1/(1 + t_{jk}^{k\ell})$. In this case it can be shown that the profit on the trade of j from ℓ to k is minus that on the trade of j from k to ℓ. Thus, if positive profits are ruled out then the left-hand side of (55) must be zero. Hence, the model can be expressed in terms of *net* trades and the taxes on net trades, denoted $t_j^{\ell k} \equiv t_{jk}^{\ell k}$ denoting the tax rate imposed by k on trade between ℓ and k. Conditions (55) and (58) become

$$p_j^k = (1 + t_j^{\ell k}) p_j^{\ell k} \text{ and } p_j^\ell = (1 + t_j^{\ell k}) p_j^{\ell k} \tag{55'}$$

where $p_j^{\ell k} = p_j^{k\ell}$ is the "world price" for trade between ℓ and k, and

$$r^k = \sum_j \sum_{\ell \neq k} t_j^{\ell k} p_j^{\ell k} x_j^{\ell k}. \tag{58'}$$

All studies of preferential trading clubs assume a particular pattern of trade between several (usually three) nations. Most assume that the changes in the world tax structure do not affect the trading pattern, and then proceed to analyse the effects of the tax changes, usually on the welfare of each nation. A useful survey and synthesis of these attempts is provided by Lloyd (1980). The present treatment will simply outline the methodology used.

The utility level attained by nation k depends upon the domestic price vector p^k and net revenue r^k, as can be seen from (59) and (60) or via the indirect trade utility function $\mu^k = H^k(p^k, r^k)$. In what follows the change in r^k will be expressed in several forms which can then be interpreted. For small changes in tax rates, $d\mu^k$ is proportional to

$$- S_\mu^k \, d\mu^k = x^k \, dp^k + dr^k, \tag{63}$$

where $- S_\mu^k > 0$. Thus, an increase in tax revenue with fixed domestic prices raises welfare, while domestic price increases raise welfare if the goods in question are exported and reduce welfare if they are imported. The change in the domestic price vector is

$$dp^k = (I + T^{\ell k}) \, dp^{\ell k} + P^{\ell k} \, dt^{\ell k}, \tag{64}$$

where $T^{\ell k}$ and $P^{\ell k}$ are diagonal matrices. The change in tax revenue is

$$\mathrm{d}r^k = \sum_{\ell \neq k} [x^{\ell k} (\mathrm{d}p^k - \mathrm{d}p^{\ell k}) + (p^k - p^{\ell k}) \, \mathrm{d}x^{\ell k}]. \tag{65}$$

Thus

$$-S_\mu^k \, \mathrm{d}\mu^k = \sum_{\ell \neq k} x^{k\ell} \, \mathrm{d}p^{\ell k} + \sum_{\ell \neq k} p^{\ell k} \, T^{\ell k} \, \mathrm{d}x^{\ell k}. \tag{66}$$

The first term in (66) is the *terms of trade effect* of the tax change. Indeed, it is the Laspeyre's terms of trade index in which account is taken of the pattern of trade. It consists of terms of both signs. If the price of an export good increases on the world market, then welfare increases, whereas it falls if the price of an imported good increases. This second term in (66) is the *tax revenue effect* and is the change in revenue that would occur at the *initial* tax rates as a consequence of the change in the trade vector. If the tax rate on j is positive, an increase in imports $(\mathrm{d}x_j^{\ell k} > 0)$ from ℓ as a consequence of the tax change will raise utility.

Of course, expression (66) is of limited usefulness. If one were to observe the responses then the right-hand side of (66) may be calculated and the welfare effects are thus determined, but after the event. The problem is that $\mathrm{d}p^{\ell k}$ and $\mathrm{d}x^{\ell k}$ are *endogenous* variables. To obtain an expression in terms of exogenous variables a complete comparative statics solution is required. As expected, this does not yield very fruitful expressions, hence the concentration on expressions such as (66).

Another such expression is obtained as follows. Define $\alpha_j^{\ell k} \equiv \mathrm{d}x_j^{k\ell}/\mathrm{d}x_j^k$ as the percentage of the change in net export of j by k which go to ℓ, and rewrite the second term in (66) as $-\bar{t}^k \, \mathrm{d}x^k$, where

$$\bar{t}_j^k \equiv \sum_{\ell \neq k} p_j^{\ell k} \, t_j^{\ell k} \, \alpha_j^{\ell k}. \tag{68}$$

Then differentiate (59) to obtain $\mathrm{d}x^k = S_{pp}^k \, \mathrm{d}p^k + S_{p\mu}^k \, \mathrm{d}\mu^k$, and substitute into (66) to obtain:

$$a^k \, \mathrm{d}\mu^k = \sum_{\ell \neq k} x^{k\ell} \, \mathrm{d}p^{\ell k} - \bar{t} \, S_{pp}^k \, \mathrm{d}p^k, \tag{69}$$

where

$$a^k \equiv -S_\mu^k \, [1 - \bar{t}^k \, \phi_m^k] \tag{70}$$

and $\phi_m^k \equiv S_{p\mu}^k/S_\mu^k$ is the response of demands to income. Expression (69) is in terms of $\mathrm{d}p^{\ell k}$ and $\mathrm{d}p^k$, but this is deceiving since a^k depends upon $\alpha_j^{\ell k} \equiv \mathrm{d}x_j^{k\ell}/$

dx_j^k. If k's tax rates are non-discriminatory, $t_j^{\varrho k} = t_j^k$, then $p_j^{\varrho k} = p_j$ is the world price of j and $\overline{\tau}_j^k = p_j^k - p_j = t_j^k p_j$. In this case (69) reduces to a familiar expression for the utility effects of a tariff change (eq. (34)).

Expressions (63), (66) and (69) provide alternative characterizations for the change in utility as a result of a change in the tax structure. As Lloyd (1980) notes, the positivity of each RHS term is sufficient, but, of course, not necessary, for the nation to gain. Authors differ in their choice of expression and arrangement of the RHS terms when discussing the welfare effects of customs unions and other preferential trading arrangements. To obtain expressions depending only upon exogenous data requires, however, a full comparative statics analysis of the model of the world economy. For small tax changes it may be appropriate to assume that the trading pattern does not alter. For large changes the pattern may change and there is no alternative but to compute the equilibrium solutions before and after the tax change and to then compare these solutions.

11.7. Notes on the literature

The equivalence between trade quotas and taxes under competitive conditions has been established by Bhagwati (1965). He also considered departures from competition which lead to the breakdown of this equivalence. See also Bhagwati (1968).

The derivation of optimal tax policies (assuming an aggregate utility function) to achieve non-economic objectives is due primarily to Bhagwati (1971) and Bhagwati and Srinivason (1969). A more general treatment, including valuation restrictions, was developed by Vandendorpe (1974). These papers employ a primal approach while the treatment in this chapter makes use of duality.

The theory of piecemeal tax policy in international trade has been influenced strongly by recent developments in the public finance literature. See, for example, the work by Dixit (1975), Hatta (1977b) and Diewert (1978). The analysis of gradual tax reform in open economies has its origins in the work by Meade (1955a) and Foster and Sonnenschein (1970). A useful synthesis of results using duality theory is provided by Smith (1980). The papers by Hatta (1977a) and Fukushima (1979) develop their results for a model with non-traded goods, whereas the development in the text and in Lloyd (1974) considers only traded goods. The conditions for a reduction in the highest to the next highest tax rate to be welfare improving when non-traded goods exist must include the assumption that non-traded and traded goods are net substitutes. Hatta and Fukushima (1979) have also shown that for a two-good model with many countries, a reduction in the highest tax rate to the next highest, or a proportional reduction in all tax rates, will be a Pareto improvement for the world, assuming that international transfers of income are feasible. Whether these results can be extended to include many goods, and the case where international transfers are not feasible is, at this point, an open question.

The theory of discriminatory trade policies involves an enormous literature. The major references includes the pioneering work by Viner (1950) and Meade (1955b), the survey by Lipsey (1960), and the more recent contributions by Vanek (1965) and Kemp (1969). Most of the literature has been concerned with the question of whether a particular trading agreement (e.g. a customs union) would raise the welfare of the member nations. Thus, attention focused on the sufficient conditions for a welfare improvement using the concepts of trade creation and trade diversion. A useful general treatment of the welfare effects of a customs union using revealed preference theory is provided in Ohyama (1972). More recent treatments of very special models have been carried out by Berglas (1979), Riezman (1979) and Corden (1976) and are synthesized by Lloyd (1980). The present treatment has concentrated upon optimal club policies, a topic taken up by Negishi (1969) and Kemp and Wan (1976). For a treatment of the optimality of customs union when no international transfers of income are possible, but where domestic consumption and production taxes are feasible, see Dixit and Norman (1980).

Problems

1. Consider a general quota on net exports of the form $Rx_2 = r$, where R is a matrix and r is a vector.
    (a) Write down and explain the trader's profit maximization problem, and derive the conditions for a finite solution.
    (b) Hence, write down the equilibrium conditions for this economy.
    (c) What tax policy would achieve the same equilibrium?
2. A consumption quota of the form $Rz_2 = r$ is imposed.
    (a) Write down the equilibrium conditions for this economy.
    (b) If the quota is a quantity restriction on each of the goods in question, what tax policy would yield the same equilibrium?
    (c) Repeat (b) for the case where the quota is in value terms (using fixed world prices).
3. Consider a consumption quota of the form $Rz_2 = r$.
    (a) Derive the optimal tax policy for attaining this quota in a small open economy and show that it involves free trade, no production taxes but a set of consumption taxes.

(b) Show that the consumption taxes apply only to z_2, that they are uniform if the quota is in value terms (in world prices) but not uniform in general if the quota is a quantity restriction on each good.

(c) Rework your analysis for the case of a large open economy, and compare results.

4. (a) Illustrate on the offer curve diagram the effects upon equilibrium of an import quota imposed by the home nation.

(b) Indicate the size of the implicit tariff.

(c) Illustrate the situation if the implicit tariff is imposed.

(d) What are the consequences of the imposition of an export quota?

5. Suppose there exist non-traded goods. Then the balance of trade condition under a vector of trade taxes t is $p_t^* \hat{S}_t(p_t, \mu) = 0$, where $p_t = p_t^* + t$, $\hat{S}(p_t, \mu_t) \equiv S(p_t, P_n(p_t, \mu_t), \mu)$, $P_n(p_t, \mu) \equiv \{p_n: S_n(p_t, p_n, \mu) = 0\}$, and subscripts t and n denote traded and non-traded goods. (The function $\hat{S}$ was discussed in detail in Chapter 8, section 8.2, which is important for answering this question.)

(a) If each non-traded good is a net substitute for all goods and no good is inferior, prove that $\hat{\phi}_{tm} \equiv \hat{S}_{t\mu}/\hat{S}_\mu > 0$. (*Hint*: Use the familiar result that if A has positive diagonal and negative off-diagonal elements then $A^{-1} \geq 0$.)

(b) Discuss the implication of this result for the properties of net export functions (reduced form) for traded goods compared to the case of no non-traded goods.

(c) Hence, show that the proof of theorem (36) applies directly to the case of non-traded goods, since $\hat{S}$ has the same properties as S under the assumptions of (a). That is to say, if no good is inferior, non-traded goods are net substitutes for all goods and the highest (lowest) trade tax rate is reduced (raised), then welfare increases.

(d) Show also that the proof in the text that a proportional reduction in all trade tax rates will raise welfare applies directly to the case where there are non-traded goods, since $\hat{S}$ has the same properties as S under the assumptions of (a).

6. Let the budget constraint for a nation be written as $S(p, \mu, v) + r = 0$, where $r = (p^* - p)S_p = -tS_p$ is net tax revenue.

(a) Show that the marginal utility of income is $-1/S_\mu = -1/pS_{p\mu}$.

(b) Derive from the budget constraint the expression $d\mu/H_r = x\,dp^* - t\,dx$ (eq. (28)) when the tax vector changes by dt.

7. Prove that $x^*(p)$, defined by (47), is (a) homogeneous of degree zero in p and (b) satisfies the balance of trade condition $px^*(p) \equiv 0$.

8. Let two nations form a trading club and agree to maximize $W(\mu^1, \mu^2)$ by

lump-sum income redistributions. There is a fixed, non-optimal trade tax vector on external club trade and all external trade occurs through nation 1. Characterize and discuss the optimal club policies when (a) no consumption taxes are permitted and when (b) no domestic (production, consumption) taxes are permitted.

9. The optimal trade tax policy requires the solution of

$$R(p, v^*) \equiv \max_{x^*} \{px^* : x^* \in X^*(v^*)\} = \max_{p^*} \{px^*(p^*, v^*)\}.$$

(a) Show that $R(p, v^*)$ is homogeneous of degree zero and convex in p, and that $R_p(p, v^*) = x^*(p^*, v^*)$. (That is, $R(p, v^*)$ is similar to a GNP function.)

(b) The utility possibilities for a trading club of K nations with internal free trade are defined by the budget constant $\Sigma_k S^k(p, \mu^k, v^k) + R(p, v^*) = 0$. Hence, show that $-\Sigma_k S^k_\mu \, d\mu^k = 0$ in equilibrium, proving that free internal club trade with an optimal tax structure is Pareto optimal from the point of view of the club.

References

Bhagwati, J. (1965) "On the equivalence of tariffs and quotas", in: R.E. Baldwin et al. (eds.), *Trade, Growth and the Balance of Payments – Essays in Honor of Gottfried Haberler* (Chicago).

Bhagwati, J. (1968) "More on the equivalence of tariffs and quotas", *American Economic Review* 58-1, March, 142–146.

Bhagwati, J. (1971) "The generalized theory of distortions and welfare", in: J. Bhagwati, R.W. Jones, R.A. Mundell and J. Vanek (eds.), *Trade, Balance of Payments and Growth: Papers in Honor of Charles P. Kindleberger* (Amsterdam: North-Holland Publishing Co.), 69–90.

Bhagwati, J.N. and T.N. Srinivason (1969) "Optimal intervention to achieve noneconomic objectives", *Review of Economic Studies* 36-1, January, 27–38.

Berglas, E. (1979) "Preferential trading theory: The *N* commodity case", *Journal of Political Economy* 87-2, 315–331.

Bertrand, T.J. and J. Vanek (1971) "The theory of tariffs, taxes and subsidies: Some aspects of the second best", *American Economic Review* 61-5, December, 925–931.

Corden, W.M. (1971) *The Theory of Protection* (Oxford: Clarendon Press).

Corden, W.M. (1976) "Customs union theory and the nonuniformity of tariffs", *Journal of International Economics* 6, 99–106.

Diewert, W.E. (1978) "Optimal tax perturbations", *Journal of Public Economics* 10, 139–177.

Dixit, A. (1975) "Welfare effects of tax and price changes", *Journal of Public Economics* 4, 103–124.

Dixit, A.K. and V. Norman (1980) *Theory of International Trade* (Cambridge University Press).

Foster, E. and H. Sonnenschein (1970) "Price distortion and economic welfare", *Econometrica* 38, 281–296.

Fukushima, T. (1979) "Tariff structure, nontraded goods and theory of piecemeal policy recommendations", *International Economic Review* 20-2, June, 427–435.

Hadley, G. (1961) *Linear Algebra* (Addison-Wesley Publishing Co.).

Hatta, T. (1977a) "A recommendation for a better tariff structure", *Econometrica* 45-8, November, 1859–1869.

Hatta, T. (1977b) "A theory of piecemeal policy recommendations", *Review of Economic Studies* 44, 1–22.

Hatta, T. and T. Fukushima (1979) "The welfare effects of tariff rate reductions in a many country world", *Journal of International Economics* 9, 503–511.

Kemp, M.C. (1969) *A Contribution to the General Equilibrium Theory of Preferential Trading* (Amsterdam: North-Holland Publishing Co.).

Kemp, M.C. and H.Y. Wan (1976) "An elementary proposition concerning the formation of customs unions", *Journal of International Economics* 6, 95–97.

Lipsey, R.G. (1960) "The theory of customs unions: A general survey", *Economic Journal*, September, 496–513.

Lipsey, R.G. and K. Lancaster (1956) "The general theory of second best", *Review of Economic Studies* 24, 11–32.

Lloyd, P.J. (1974) "A more general theory of price distortions in open economies", *Journal of International Economics* 4, 365–386.

Lloyd, P.J. (1980) "3 x 3 theory of customs unions", Seminar Paper 14, Institute for International Economic Studies, University of Stockholm, June; forthcoming in *Journal of International Economics*.

Meade, J.E. (1955a) *Trade and Welfare* (Oxford University Press).

Meade, J.E. (1955b) *The Theory of Customs Unions* (Amsterdam: North-Holland Publishing Co.).

Negishi, T. (1969) "The customs union and the theory of the second best", *International Economic Review* 10-3, October, 391–398.

Ohyama, M. (1972) "Trade and welfare in general equilibrium", *Keio Economic Studies* 9-2, 37–73.

Riezman, R. (1979) "A 3 x 3 model of customs unions", *Journal of International Economics* 9, 341–354.

Smith, A. (1980) "Optimal taxation in open economies", London School of Economics, February.

Vandendorpe, A.L. (1974) "On the theory of non-economic objectives in open economics", *Journal of International Economics* 4-1, April, 15–24.

Vanek, J. (1965) *General Equilibrium of International Discrimination* (Harvard University Press).

Viner, J. (1950) *The Customs Union Issue* (New York).

Weymark, J. (1979) "A reconciliation of recent results in optimal taxation theory", *Journal of Public Economics* 12, 171–189.

CHAPTER 12

EMPIRICAL STUDIES

12.1. Introduction

Although this book is primarily concerned with the theory of international trade, the theory only comes alive when used to provide an understanding of observations from the real world or when the theory is tested empirically. In the present chapter various empirical applications of the theory of international trade are surveyed.

The purpose here is not to provide a detailed compendium of all empirical work in the area of international trade, since that would require more space than a single chapter can accommodate. Moreover, such an account of empirical findings would be out of place in a book on international trade theory. Rather, the purpose is to give the reader the flavour of the main empirical studies that have been undertaken and which are strongly related to the theory that has been expounded in the preceding chapters of this book. The emphasis is not so much on the empirical results, although these may be important and interesting in their own right, but upon the relationship of the empirical study to the theory. Concern is with the extent of the simplification or the violation of the theory to obtain an empirically feasible model, the information needed, the objectives of the exercise and, of course, the conclusions obtained.

12.2. Estimation of import demand and export supply functions

12.2.1. Net export functions

The vector of net exports of a competitive economy in static equilibrium may be written as

$$x = G_p(p^s, v) - E_p(p^d, \mu), \tag{1}$$

where p^s is the supply price vector, p^d is the demand price vector, v is the endowment vector, and the state of technology and tastes are given. If μ is a vector of utilities for each consumer, the distribution of income among individuals has to be taken into account in order to eliminate μ. Let it be assumed that aggregation of the consumption sector is possible so that μ is a scalar. It can then be found by solving the budget constraint written in alternative ways as

(a) $p^* x = p^* [G_p(p^s, v) - E_p(p^d, \mu)] = B$

    or $\tag{2}$

(b) $E(p^d, \mu) = G(p^s, v) - t^x x + t^d E_p(p^d, \mu) + t^s G_p(p^s, v) - B \equiv m,$

where t^x, t^d and t^s are vectors of trade, consumption and production taxes, $p^d = p^* + t^x + t^d$, $p^s = p^* + t^x - t^s$ and B is the balance of trade. Using (2,b) net exports may be written as

$$x = G_p(p^s, v) - \phi(p^d, m) \tag{3}$$

where $\phi(p^d, m) = E_p(p^d, V(p^d, m))$ and $V(\cdot)$ denotes the solution for μ to (2,b).

In general, therefore, the export vector depends upon the world prices (p^*), the balance of trade (B), producer and consumer prices (p^s, p^d) or, equivalently, tax rates on trade, production and consumption (t^x, t^s, t^d), the endowments of factors of production (v), the state of technical knowledge and tastes. Reference has already been made to income distribution as a determinant of demand and hence net exports. There are other variables that can be made endogenous such as the prices of non-traded goods or the quantities of variable factor supplies which add some complexity to the model but which do not affect the analysis much. Also, dynamic considerations, such as saving and international borrowing which affects B, are ignored. Nevertheless, the above formulation is sufficient for the purposes of exposition.

Studies which attempt to obtain numerical estimates of the net export functions differ in the closeness of their empirical models to the underlying theoretical model, such as the above. They also differ as to which variables are treated as exogenous or explanatory variables. Finally, they differ considerably with regard to the level of aggregation. The following review is not intended to be comprehensive, but attempts to indicate ways in which empirical work can and does proceed.

Any attempt to estimate the net export functions using observations on the relevant variables must involve a considerable simplification. If there were no data or computer limitations the procedure would be to choose functional forms for G and E (or V), which then provide functional forms for net exports in terms of all the exogenous variables, and to estimate the parameters of these functional forms by statistical procedures. However, with many goods and factors this approach would require a large number of independent observations and a computational burden beyond the capacity of our available technology.

To reduce the estimation to a manageable size one can impose structure on the model by aggregating over goods, simplifying functional forms or by ignoring some variables. Aggregation involves an implicit assumption of separability, although this is usually not made explicit. The assumption includes the requirement that there exist quantity and price aggregators so that the researcher can concentrate on the role of these aggregates without having to consider their components. Simplification of functional forms occurs, for example, when non-linear relationships are linearized. Finally, some variables may be ignored on the ground that, while they may be required in the theoretical model, there is a presumption that they will not be important empirically.

12.2.2. Consistent aggregation

All empirical studies aggregate over goods and factors, usually to a very high level. Price and quantity indices are then used for these aggregate commodities. Here we briefly consider the assumptions underlying consistent aggregation, i.e. aggregation which loses no information.

There are three valid bases for aggregation. The first is Hicksian aggregation which can occur if the prices of a group of commodities always move in strict proportion. Then a Hicksian composite commodity can be defined with price and quantity indexes which behave as for a single good. The second is Leontief aggregation which can occur if the quantities of a group of commodities always move in strict proportion. Then a consistent quantity index can be constructed yielding a consistent price index also. Aggregation of the Hicksian and Leontief types is based upon fortuitous movements of prices or quantities and, unless the model is very special, such movements are unlikely.

A third basis relies upon functional structure. For example, suppose the GNP function $G(p, v)$ can be written as

$$G(p, v) = G'(P, V), \tag{4}$$

where $P = (P_1, ..., P_j, ...)$, $V = (V_1, ..., V_i, ...)$, $P_j = P_j(p_j)$ and $V_i = V_i(v_i)$, where p_j and v_i are subvectors of p and v, respectively. Then G is said to be weakly separable in the groups of goods and factors $j = 1, 2 ...$ and $i = 1, 2 ... .P_j(p_j)$ is interpreted as a price index for goods in group j, while $V_i(v_i)$ is a quantity index for factors in group i.

This GNP function can be obtained from the transformation function

$$T(y, v) = T'(Y, V) = 0, \tag{5}$$

where $Y = (Y_1, ..., Y_j, ...)$ and $Y_j = Y_j(y_j)$ is a quantity index of outputs in group j. The assumption which allows this is that the functions $Y_j(y_j)$ are linearly homogeneous. Then

$$\max_{y_j} \{p_j y_j: \ Y_j(y_j) = Y_j\}$$

$$= Y_j \max_{y_j/Y_j} \{p_j y_j/Y_j: \ Y_j(y_j/Y_j) = 1\} = Y_j P_j(p_j), \qquad Y_j \neq 0, \tag{6}$$

where $P_j(p_j)$ can be interpreted as a revenue, variable profit or "GNP" function. Thus,

$$G(p, v, \alpha) \equiv \max \left\{ \sum_j p_j y_j: \ T'(Y_1(y_1), ..., V) = 0 \right\}$$

$$= \max \left\{ \sum_j P_j(p_j) Y_j: \ T'(Y, V) = 0 \right\}$$

$$= G'(P, V). \tag{7}$$

Clearly, $G'(P, V)$ is a valid GNP function expressed in aggregates so all of the usual properties apply. Accordingly,

$$Y = G'_P(P, V); \qquad W = G'_V(P, V) \tag{8}$$

yields the net supply functions for aggregate goods, Y, and the factor price indices for aggregate factors, W.

A similar analysis applies to the consumption sector. If the utility function is $u(z) = u'(Z)$, where $Z = (Z_1, ...)$ and $Z_i = Z_i(z_i)$ is a linearly homogeneous aggregator over group i, then the expenditure function takes the form $E(p, u) = E'(P^d, u)$, where $P^d = (P_1^d, ...)$ and $P_i^d = P_i^d(p_i)$ is a consistent price index for group i. Note that this function is different from the corresponding one on the production side, and to emphasize this it is distinguished notationally by the d superscript. The indirect utility function is $V(p, m) = V'(P^d, m)$ and the demand functions for the aggregate quantities take the form:

$$Z = E_P'(P^d, V'(P^d, m)) = \phi'(P^d, m).$$ (9)

The essential aspect of the existence of the consistent quantity and price indices in the manner outlined above is that decentralized budgeting can occur. Price indices are used to decide upon aggregates. Once the aggregates are chosen the only remaining problem is to allocate the aggregate amongst its components. On the production side,

$$y_j = \partial G/\partial p_j = \partial G'/\partial P_j \cdot \partial P_j/\partial p_j,$$

$$w_i = \partial G/\partial v_i = \partial G'/\partial V_i \cdot \partial V_i/\partial v_i;$$ (10)

while on the consumption side,

$$z_j = \partial E/\partial p_j = \partial E'/\partial P_j^d \cdot \partial P_j^d/\partial p_j.$$ (11)

Further details concerning the relationship between decentralized budgeting, aggregation and functional structure can be found in the survey by Blackorby, Primont and Russell (1975). Berndt and Christensen (1973b) and Blackorby and Russell (1976) relate functional structure to the Allen–Uzawa elasticities of substitution.

The important point to note, however, is that whenever aggregates are used then either implicitly or explicitly assumptions are being made about the observed relationship between prices (Hicksian aggregation), quantities (Leontief aggregation) or functional structure. Typically, researchers use price and quantity indices of a simple form such as the Laspeyres or Paasche indices. For a survey of index number theory including a discussion of functional forms for indices, see Diewert (1976).

Below we consider various empirical studies which differ primarily in the way goods are grouped and aggregated and in the choice of functional forms.

Attention is now focused on some specific ways of proceeding in empirical studies.

12.2.3. *Production sector models*

One approach which has recently been taken by Burgess (1974a, 1974b) and Kohli (1978) is to treat traded goods exclusively as inputs to or outputs from the production sector. Thus, on the import side these authors treat imported goods as intermediate inputs which are used by the production sector but are not consumed by the consumption sector. There are two arguments used here. First, for many nations imports of semi-finished goods and investment goods constitute a very high proportion of total imports. Secondly, even those goods normally thought of as finished consumer goods pass through the production sector since it includes firms associated with transportation, distribution and retailing. On the export side, Kohli assumes that exported goods are different from domestic consumer and investment goods. In other words, imported and exported goods are defined such that there is no domestic demand by consumers for them.

Given that only the GNP function is relevant, aggregation can simplify the problem by giving it the structure:

$$G(p, v) = G'(P_N, P_X, P_M, V_K, V_L),\tag{12}$$

where $P_j \equiv P_j(p_j)$, $V_i = V_i(v_i)$ are linearly homogeneous functions of vectors p_j and v_i, where $j = N, X, M$ for non-traded, exported and imported goods and $i = K, L$ for capital and labour inputs. Structure (12) assumes homogeneous separability and allows the interpretation of $P_j(p_j)$ as the price index for category j. $G'(\cdot)$ is the GNP function expressed in terms of price indices for non-traded, exported, and imported goods and quantity indices for capital and labour.

The above is illustrative of how the model can be formulated using separability. Clearly, one need not aggregate all non-traded goods, or all exports, or all capital, for example. Kohli aggregates non-traded goods into two groups: investment and consumer goods. Capital and labour might be aggregated as in Clements' (1980) otherwise more general model.

To make the model operational, a functional form is needed. Following Kohli one can choose a translog functional form defined generally by

$$\ln f(x) = a_{00} + \sum_{i=1}^{n} a_{0i} \ln x_i + \frac{1}{2} \sum_{i=1}^{n} \sum_{j=1}^{n} a_{ij} \ln x_i \ln x_j,\tag{13}$$

where $a_{ij} = a_{ji}$ for $i, j \geqslant 1$, and where linear homogeneity in x (or a subvector of x) can be imposed via linear restrictions on the parameters (a's). This is a useful functional form since it yields simple share equations to estimate and it belongs to the general class of "flexible functional forms" in the sense that it can be used to provide a second-order approximation to any function of x.[1]

Now in general the revenue share of product j and the income share of factor i in GNP may be obtained by the logarithmic differentiation of the GNP function as follows:

---

[1]   See Diewert (1974) and Lau (1974) for further aspects and examples of flexible functional forms.

(a) $\partial \ln G(p, v)/\partial \ln p_j = p_j (\partial G/\partial p_j)/G,$

(14)

(b) $\partial \ln G(p, v)/\partial \ln v_i = v_i (\partial G/\partial v_i)/G.$

If the translog function is applied to (12), then

$$\ln G = a_{00} + \sum_j a_{0j} \ln P_j + \tfrac{1}{2} \sum_j \sum_k a_{kj} \ln P_j \ln P_k$$

$$+ \sum_i b_{0i} \ln V_i + \tfrac{1}{2} \sum_i \sum_k b_{ki} \ln V_i \ln V_k$$

$$+ \sum_i \sum_j c_{ij} \ln V_i \ln P_j + \sum_j d_j \ln P_j t + \sum_i e_i \ln V_i t,$$

(15)

in which time, t, has been included as a variable to represent exogenous technical change (though the quadratic term in t has been omitted). Using (14) the shares for goods and factors are

(a) $S_j \equiv \dfrac{P_j Y_j}{\sum P_k Y_k} = a_{0j} + \sum_k a_{jk} \ln P_k + \sum_i b_{ji} \ln V_i + d_j t,$

(16)

(b) $s_i \equiv \dfrac{W_i V_i}{\sum W_k V_k} = b_{0i} + \sum_j b_{ij} \ln P_j + \sum_k c_{ik} \ln V_k + e_i t,$

where $\sum_j a_{0j} = \sum_i b_{0i} = 1$, $\sum_j a_{ij} = 0$ and $\sum_j b_{ji} = 0$ and $\sum_i c_{ik} = 0$ for $i \geqslant 1$, $b_{ij} = b_{ji}$ and $c_{ij} = c_{ji}$ for $i, j \geqslant 1$, $\sum_j d_j = 0$ and $\sum_i e_i = 0$ are the conditions required for G' to be linearly homogeneous in product prices and linearly homogeneous in factor quantities.

Given sufficient time series observations for a nation on the GNP shares, product prices, factor quantities and time t, one can estimate the set of multivariate regression equations using standard techniques.[2] This provides estimates of all parameters of $\ln G'$ (hence G') with the exception of the constant (factor of proportionality, $\exp(a_{00})$, for G') a_{00}. Hence, one can obtain estimates of $\partial Y_j/\partial P_k$, $\partial Y_j/\partial V_i = \partial W_i/\partial P_j$, $\partial W_i/\partial V_j$, $\partial Y_j/\partial t$ and $\partial V_i/\partial t$, up to a factor of proportionality, and the corresponding elasticities. For example, the affects upon net outputs are, in elasticity form:

---

[2] Typically, one adds classical disturbances to the right-hand sides of (16). The disturbances in (16,a) sum identically to zero since the observed and predicted shares sum to unity. This implies that the disturbances are correlated, and that one equation is redundant and may therefore be ignored. Similarly for (16,b). Zellner's (1962) two-step estimator or the maximum likelihood estimator may be used. If not all prices and endowments are truly exogenous, simultaneous equation estimators may be required.

(a) $\quad \partial \ln Y_j / \partial \ln P_k = \partial \ln S_j / \partial \ln P_k + \partial \ln G / \partial \ln P_k - \delta_{jk} = a_{jk}/S_j + S_k - \delta_{jk},$

(b) $\quad \partial \ln Y_j / \partial \ln V_i = \partial \ln S_j / \partial \ln V_i + \partial \ln G / \partial \ln V_i = b_{ji}/S_j + s_i,$ (17)

(c) $\quad \partial \ln Y_j / \partial t = \partial \ln S_j / \partial t + \partial \ln G / \partial t = e_i/S_j + \partial \ln G / \partial t,$

where δ_{jk} is unity if $j = k$ and zero otherwise (Kronecker delta).

Kohli (1978) estimated a set of equations like (16) for the Canadian economy using aggregate time series data for the period 1949–1972. His goods were consumption, investment, exported and imported goods (the government sector being excluded) with capital and labour as inputs. The net output of imported goods is clearly negative since they are not produced but are used as inputs. The own-price elasticity of demand for imports is estimated to be approximately -1, while the own-price supply elasticity for exports varies between 1.5 and 2.2. The wage rate is shown to fall in response to an increase in the price of imports and to rise if export prices increase. The return to capital responds in the opposite manner. Also, an increase in the price of investment or export goods leads to an increase in the demand for imports, but an increase in the price of consumption goods has the opposite effect. Finally, an increase in the capital stock reduces both imports and exports. This is not a contradiction of the Rybczynski theorem since it does not necessarily hold under joint production, as shown in Chapter 5.

Studies along similar lines to, and predating, Kohli's were carried out by Burgess (1974a, 1974b). Each study concentrates upon the estimation of an import demand function. In the first study, Burgess (1974a) assumes that the transformation function can be written in a separable form as

$$T(y_0, Y_M, V_K, V_L, \alpha) = T'(y_0, F(-Y_M, V_K, V_L, \alpha)) = 0$$

or

$$Y_0 = F(V_M, V_K, V_L, \alpha),$$

where Y_0 is "output", and $V_M \equiv -Y_M (y_M)$, V_K and V_L are inputs of imports, capital and labour. He assumes a translog functional form for F, Hicks' neutral technical change, and cost minimization and obtains share equations of the form:

$$s_i \equiv \frac{W_i V_i}{\Sigma W_j V_j} = a_{0i} + \sum_j a_{ij} \ln V_j, \quad i = M, K, L,$$ (18)

where $\Sigma a_{0i} = 1$, $\Sigma_j a_{ij} = 0$, $a_{ij} = a_{ji}$ for $i, j \geqslant 1$, and W_i is the price index for input i. The effects of an increase in the price of imports upon imports, and the returns to capital and labour, if W_M, K and L are exogenous, are

$$\partial V_M/\partial W_M = F_{MM}^{-1}; \quad \partial W_i/\partial W_M = F_{iM} F_{MM}^{-1}, \quad i = K, L, \tag{19}$$

the derivatives being estimated from (18). Also, the share of capital in total factor income increases or decreases as the term $(F_L F_{MK} - F_K F_{ML}) \gtrless 0$.

Burgess uses U.S. data for the period 1947–1968 to estimate (18) and then calculates responses of interest. He finds that $0 < F_{ML} > F_{MK}$ throughout the period so that an increase in the price of imports will reduce the wage–rental ratio. Also he found $(F_L F_{MK} - F_K F_{ML}) > 0$, so that an increase in the price of imports raises the share of GNP accruing to capital. The estimates of the own-price elasticity of demand for imports varied from -1.6 to -2.04. This elasticity takes output level and other input prices as given and is therefore not directly comparable with Kohli's.

In the second study Burgess (1974b) considers investment and consumer goods, capital, labour and imported goods. He defines the joint cost function

$$C(Y, W) \equiv \min_{V} \{WV: T'(Y, V) = 0\}, \tag{20}$$

which is dual to the GNP function. Notice that product outputs (investment and consumer goods) and input (labour, capital and imports) prices are taken as given, whereas in the GNP function output prices and input quantities are given. Also, in the GNP function imports would be included with goods.

Using a translog functional form with Hicks' neutral technical change on annual U.S. data for the period 1929–1969 he obtained the results that imports are substitutable with labour and complementary to capital. Thus, an increase in the price of imports will raise the demand for labour and reduce the demand for capital. Also, Burgess finds that a shift in the composition of final output towards consumption goods will raise the demand for labour and reduce the demand for both capital and imports. The estimates of the own-price elasticity of demand for imports ranged from -0.51 to -0.66. This elasticity takes output composition and other input prices as given.

In another paper Burgess (1976) uses an alternative functional form for the joint cost function, defines two different outputs (durables and non-durables, non-governmental services and structures) and estimates the model on annual U.S. data for the period 1948–1969. In this study the elasticity of demand for imports varies from -0.19 to -1.6, the estimates for most years being greater than -1. Again, imports are found to be substitutable for labour and complementary to capital. Also, these elasticities take output composition and other input prices as given. Unfortunately, elasticities based upon given prices for outputs and imports and given factor quantities (which seem more plausible assumptions) were not calculated in either study. However, Burgess (1976) indicates that higher tariffs distribute income in favour of labour if separability or non-jointness are imposed, but that this result is very sensitive to other special restrictions that were tested.

The production sector approach described above has the advantage of explicitly connecting the demand for imports and the supply of exports to the industrial structure of the economy. It assumes that imports and exports are non-competitive in the sense that the imported good is not produced at home nor is the exported good consumed at home. The studies are highly aggregate in nature because of the systems approach to estimation required by the cross-equation parameter restrictions and the adding-up property of shares which makes the stochastic terms (usually appended to the share equations) correlated. However, the approach can be extended to a detailed breakdown of imports using separability. For example, one can specify a functional form for $P_M(p_M)$ in (4) and derive share equations for each import good. These may be estimated separately from the rest of the model. The negative of the demand functions for imported goods is

$$y_M = G_M = G_M' \ \partial P_M / \partial p_M, \tag{21}$$

made up of two parts — the imports per unit of "aggregate imports" times the demand for "aggregate imports".

12.2.4. Consumer demand models for imports

An alternative procedure (for imports) is to assume that imported goods are final goods which do not enter or leave the production sector. Then the demand for imports is the consumer demand for these goods which depends upon prices and income. If imported goods (M) and all other goods (o) form separable groups in the expenditure function, then the demand function for aggregate imports can be written as

$$-x_M = \phi_M' (P_M, P_o, m), \tag{22}$$

where P_M is the price index for imports and P_o is the price index for other goods. Typically a log-linear relationship is assumed but this is inconsistent with demand theory.[3] It also ignores the endogeneity of m. The advantage is that the equation is simple to estimate and the parameters are directly interpreted as price and income elasticities of demand. Houthakker and Magee (1969) have undertaken an extensive study of import and export demand functions for 15 developed countries using annual data for the period 1951–1966. They conclude that there are marked disparities in income elasticities of demand for imports among countries, and that price elasticities tend to be low.

Alternatively, Gregory (1971) assumed a CES utility function in which case the logarithm of the ratio of imports to domestic (other) demand is a linear function of the logarithms of the relative prices. Income drops out because of the assumption of homothetic preferences implied by the CES function. This formulation may be obtained as follows. Let $V(P, m) = m/e(P)$, where $e(P) \equiv (\Sigma\, a_i P_i^{-b})^{-1/b}$ is the CES unit expenditure function, dual to the CES utility function. Then Roy's identity yields:

$$\ln(Z_M/Z_o) = \ln(a_M/a_o) - \sigma \ln(P_M/P_o), \qquad (23)$$

where $\sigma \equiv (1 + b)$ is the elasticity of substitution between imports and domestic goods and Z_i denotes demand for good i.

An equation similar to (23) can be obtained from a producer model of demand for imports if all other inputs are aggregated, all outputs are aggregated and a CES cost or production function is assumed. Then (23) follows if Z_i is the demand for i by producers. This approach has been used by Alaouse, Marsden and Zeitsch (1977) to estimate the elasticity of substitution between imported and domestic inputs for various industries in Australia.

The CES function at the aggregate level imposes severe restrictions on the estimates. Not only are all other goods aggregated but there is also the constancy of the elasticity of substitution and the assumption of homothetic preferences.

12.2.5. *Models with producer and consumer demand*

Clements (1980) has estimated a general equilibrium model in which a demand function for imports and a supply function for exports are obtained. If we ignore the role played by money and saving in his model, his approach corresponds

---

[3]   The log-linear demand system $\ln \phi_i(p, m) = a_i + \Sigma_j\, b_{ij}\, \ln p_j + c_i\, \ln m$ is inconsistent with demand theory in that it cannot be derived from utility-maximizing behaviour except in the special case where $b_{ii} = -1$, $b_{ij} = 0$, $j \neq i$, and $c_i = 1$ for all i, j. In this special case the demand functions are $\phi_i(p, m) = \exp(a_i)\, m/p_i$ and the utility function (direct and indirect) is Cobb–Douglas. The inconsistency has long been well known, but see Basman, Battalio and Kagel (1973) for a formal proof. See also the problem set.

closely to (3). He distinguishes three goods: non-tradeables, exportables and importables. Importables and exportables are net outputs from the production sector, are consumed and are traded. That is, unlike Kohli and Burgess, Clements assumes that imports and exports are perfect substitutes for domestically produced goods. Thus (3) takes the form:

$$X_i = G_i' (P_N, P_X, P_M, V(v)) - \phi_i' (P_N, P_X, P_M, m), \quad i = N, X, M, \quad (24)$$

where $X_N = 0$ and $V(v)$ is an aggregate index of factor inputs.

The model was estimated using U.S. data for the period 1952–1971. A 10% tariff on imports was estimated to cause a 20% reduction in imports every year with imports being 32% lower in the long run.[4] Despite the relatively poor performance of the model, which was very ambitious, the approach is consistent with the theory and should be subjected to further confrontations with the data.

12.2.6. Import allocation models

The separability assumption may be used to aggregate commodities as indicated above. Here we consider several models of allocation of aggregate imports among various components.

The approaches taken differ as to the number of import aggregates defined and on the definitions of the components of each aggregate. The Armington (1969) model distinguishes imported goods by country of origin, and this convention has been followed by many others such as Berner (1976) and Hickman and Lau (1974). In these papers each nation has an import quantity index which is a CES function of import quantities from each country. The price index is also a CES function. Let it be written as

$$P(p) = [\sum_i a_i p_i^{1-\sigma}]^{1/(1-\sigma)}; \quad \sum_i a_i = 1, \quad (25)$$

where p_i is the price of imports from country i. The imports from i are then

$$M_i = P_i(p) M^* = M^* a_i p_i^{-\sigma} P^\sigma, \quad (26)$$

where $M^* = F(M_1, ...)$ is the quantity index of imports, which is not observed. Suppose that $M \equiv \sum_i M_i$ is observed and is determined elsewhere in a larger model.

---

[4] The model was based upon an intertemporal optimizing problem for the consumer, yielding a distinction between short- and long-run equilibrium.

The problem is to allocate M among nations according to the cost minimization principles implicit in $P(p)$. Summing (26) we obtain M in terms of M^* which can therefore be eliminated to obtain the allocation equations:

$$M_i = M \, a_i \, p_i^{-\sigma} \, [\Sigma a_j p_j^{-\sigma}]^{-1} \equiv M \, \Pi_i (p). \tag{27}$$

Given M, the least cost allocation is determined by (27) which is non-linear in parameters. Hickman and Lau (1974) choose to linearize $\Pi_i(p)$ around the point $p = 1$ to simplify the estimation. This yields:

$$M_i \doteq a_i M - \sigma a_i \, [p_i - \sum_j a_j p_j] M, \tag{28}$$

which can be used as a set of estimation equations for obtaining estimates of the a_i's and σ. However, Hickman and Lau observe that $M_i/M = a_i$ in the base period when $p = 1$, and use the base period observations on M_i/M to obtain a_i. Then $p^m \equiv \Sigma_j a_j p_j$ can be calculated as a price index for imports and so (28) can be rewritten and estimated as

$$M_i - a_i M = -\sigma \, a_i \, [p_i - p^m] M. \tag{29}$$

Hickman and Lau also consider other factors such as trends, expectations and adjustment lags. The model for one nation can be combined with those of other nations in a closed world trading system. They applied their model to 27 nations or groups of nations using 9 annual export trade matrices for the years 1961–1969. The elasticity of substitution was estimated for each nation. They judged that the model with expectations and trend was best, yielding estimates of the long-run elasticity of substitution ranging from 0 to 9 and averaging 2.5. The average short-run elasticity was 1.5.

For alternative applications and specifications of the destination import-allocation model see Armington (1969), Berner (1976), Barten (1971), and Barten and d'Alcantara (1977).

12.2.7. *The small country assumption*

The models considered above assume that each country is sufficiently small that it is a price-taker. From a theoretical viewpoint what matters is that all decision-makers act as price-takers so that the competitive assumption is valid. This is consistent with the existence of a large country made up of lots of decision-makers, even if the country's trade does affect world prices.

rom an estimation point of view this means that the world prices may not be truly exogenous and so may be correlated with disturbances in the net export functions giving rise to simultaneous equation bias in the estimates of the parameters. With this in mind some researchers estimate export demand functions for countries that are presumed to have some effect on world prices. An interesting test of the small country (fixed world price) assumption was undertaken by Appelbaum and Kohli (1979) for the Canadian economy. They could not reject the small country assumption for Canadian imports. However, the small country hypothesis was rejected in the case of Canadian exports.

12.3. Input–output studies

The production function studies referred to in the previous section are highly aggregated and were designed to obtain import demand and export supply functions, although they do yield estimates of elasticities of commodity net outputs and factor prices with respect to commodity prices and factor endowments. An alternative approach for studying the relationship between production and trade is to use detailed input–output tables. In this section two types of studies which use input–output tables are considered.

12.3.1. Leontief paradox

Leontief (1953) carried out some calculations and derived conclusions which created a prolonged flurry of activity among international trade theorists and applied researchers. He calculated the amounts of capital and labour required to produce exports worth $1 million, and the amounts required to produce imports worth $1 million for the U.S. economy for the year 1947. His results are provided in table 12.1. Thus,

Table 12.1

	Exports ($ million)	Import replacements ($ million)
Capital ($ million)	2,550,780	3,091,339
Labour (man years)	182.313	170.004

$$\left(\frac{K}{L}\right)_{\text{exports}} = \frac{2,550,780}{182.313} < \frac{3,091,339}{170.004} = \left(\frac{K}{L}\right)_{\text{imports}}, \tag{30}$$

i.e. the capital–labour intensity of exports is less than for import replacements.

Now if we believe that (a) the two-factor Heckscher–Ohlin–Samuelson (HOS) theorem is applicable, and (b) the U.S. has an abundance of capital relative to the rest of the world, then the U.S. should export goods which have a capital–labour ratio greater than those which are imported. However, (30) contradicts this prediction so that either (c) the calculations, or (a), or (b) are incorrect. The popular belief is that (b) is correct, and if the calculations are valid it must be that (a) is incorrect. This contradiction of (a) is called the *Leontief paradox*, which ceases to be a paradox, of course, if it is conceded that (a) or (b) or (c) are incorrect.

Leontief obtained the figures shown in table 12.1 as follows. Consider a production sector with many products which can be used as intermediate inputs. For given product and factor prices the relationships between net output (y), gross output (g) and factor requirements (r) are

$$y = (I - B) g; \quad Ag = r, \tag{31}$$

where $B = [b_{ij}]$ is the Leontief input–output table of elements b_{ij} equal to the input of product i used to produce one unit (gross) of j, and $A = [a_{ij}]$, where a_{ij} is the input of factor i used to produce one unit of j. Thus,

$$r = A (I - B)^{-1} y. \tag{32}$$

Leontief then sets y equal to the export vector for 1947, normalized to be worth $1 million, and calculates r. Since he considers only capital and labour as factors, r has only two elements and is given in the column labelled "Exports" in table 12.1. The exercise was repeated with y equal to the import vector for 1947, normalized to be worth $1 million, and the result appears in the last column of table 12.1.

How can the conflict between Leontief's results and (a) and (b) be resolved? Attempts to resolve the issue have generated an immense literature which is only skimmed here. Leontief's own resolution was to argue that (a) is indeed correct but that if factors are measured in efficiency units with one man-hour of U.S. labour equal to three man-hours of foreign labour, an assertion for which he gave no evidence, then the U.S. is really labour abundant and the results confirm the HOS hypothesis. This raises the question of whether it is ever possible to distinguish between differences in endowment quantities and differences in technology. It depends on how factors are defined.

Some criticisms of Leontief's study relate to the data used, 1947 being perhaps too close to the Second World War to be a normal year. Leontief (1956) repeated the calculations for 1951 as did Baldwin (1971) using the 1958 input—output table for the U.S., the paradox being confirmed. Similar calculations have been carried out for many other countries with mixed results. However, Baldwin (1979) studied 36 different countries using their trade data but input—output tables for the U.S., Japan and the E.E.C. and concluded that the Leontief paradox applied to quite a number of other countries commonly believed to be capital abundant.

Other criticisms relate to the applicability of the HOS theorem to U.S. trade. Some have pointed to the possibility of factor intensity reversals which can invalidate the HOS predictions. Others have indicated that differences in technology and tastes as well as the tax structure can also invalidate the HOS predictions and have argued that such differences exist. Also, there is the criticism that the HOS theorem is based upon a two-factor model which is obviously unrealistic. From the discussion of the relationship between factor endowments and commodity trade in a multi-dimensional framework in Chapter 7, it is evident that one cannot expect unambiguous trade predictions. All that can be hoped for is a correlation between endowments and trade. Accordingly, some such as Baldwin (1971, 1979), Hufbauer (1970) and Leamer (1974) have considered a more detailed breakdown of factors, with special concentration on the skill component of labour and research and development as inputs. The role of natural resources as a factor not dealt with by Leontief has also received attention, although the data limitations severely restrict the empirical work, which mainly consists of eliminating natural resource products from consideration.

These studies find that variables other than the capital—labour ratio are important explanatory variables for the trade pattern. Baldwin (1971) uses the 1958 input—output table for the U.S. economy together with a wide range of other data, for example on characteristics of the labour force, and carries out an extensive analysis of the determinants of net exports by regression techniques. He concludes that the elimination of natural resource products reduces, but does not reverse, the evidence in favour of the Leontief paradox. Also, the regressions show that research and development is an important factor in export industries and that the skilled labour (particularly in the form of engineers and scientists) is also more important in these industries than in import-competing industries.

Attempts to deal with other factors by combining them with labour or capital to maintain a two-factor framework raise the question of the appropriateness of aggregation. The conditions required for consistent aggregation have already been referred to in this chapter and are quite severe. Suppose that there are three factors — capital (K), skilled labour (L_s) and unskilled labour (L_u). Do we combine K and L_s, or L_s and L_u, or K and the human capital component of L_s? Consistent aggregation may be based upon Leontief or Hicks' aggregation or the existence of a separable functional structure in production. Similarly, there is the question of whether capital and natural resources can be aggregated. Detailed tests are required to establish whether such aggregation is justified. Those that are available tend to reject the aggregation hypothesis. See, for example, Berndt and Christensen (1973a, 1974), Denny and Fuss (1977), and Woodland (1978).

12.3.2. *Effective rates of tariff protection*

The input–output table produced by many countries following Leontief's pioneering work gave rise to numerous calculations of effective rates of tariff protection following the initial theoretical treatment by Corden (1966) and empirical study by Balassa (1965). The formula for the effective rates of protection in industry j in a non-joint production economy is

$$e_j = \left(\tau_j - \sum_{i=1}^{M} \beta_{ij} \tau_i \right) \bigg/ \left(1 - \sum_{i=1}^{M} \beta_{ij} \right), \quad j = 1, ..., M, \tag{33}$$

where τ_i is the nominal rate of tariff on good i, $\beta_{ij} \equiv b_{ij} p_i/p_j$ is the cost of input i per dollar output of good j, and b_{ij} is the input–output coefficient at pre-tariff prices p. Given an input–output table, usually published as β (in value form), it is a simple matter to calculate the effective protection rates e_j. The effective rates are supposed to give a better measure of the effect of the whole structure of tariffs upon the *industries* in question than nominal tariffs which apply to products, since effective rates take account of tariffs on intermediate inputs.[5]

Corden (1976) lists some of the difficulties encountered in the calculation of effective rates of protection. There is the problem of aggregation since "the" output of an industry may not be perfectly substitutable with the imported product, and input–output coefficients and tariff rates are averages over a group of more basic industries or products. There is also the question of how to deal with non-traded intermediate inputs, different procedures giving different answers. In general it has been found that effective rates of protection exceed nominal rates but that the rankings of industries by each rate are highly correlated. The former observation is to be expected from the definitions since nominal tariffs measure the percentage change in the value of gross output while effective tariffs measure the percentage change in value added, and since nominal rates tend to be higher for outputs than inputs.

It was shown in Chapter 10 that the effective rate formula (33) is based upon the assumption of a fixed B matrix except for small tariffs. Typically the formula

---

[5] See the discussion of effective rates of protection in Chapter 10.

has been applied for large tariffs using the input—output matrix for the post-tariff (existing) situation. This raises the question of whether the B matrix is indeed independent of prices in practice. If not then the appropriate effective rate formula is a non-linear function of tariff rates and prices whose parameters need to be estimated econometrically. The existence of such a consistent formula depends on the separability of the transformation function for each industry between factors and products (including traded intermediate inputs). The tests that have been undertaken have been highly aggregated and impose severe unwanted restrictions on the functional forms when separability is imposed and so are biased somewhat in favour of rejecting the hypothesis of separability. However, Burgess (1974a, 1974b) rejects the hypothesis of separability of capital and labour from imports in the production function for the U.S. Berndt and Wood (1975) reject the separability of capital and labour from energy and materials for the U.S. Denny and May (1977) formally reject the existence of a real value added function for Canadian manufacturing. Woodland (1977) provides estimates showing significant response of intermediate inputs to price changes in Canadian manufacturing. The evidence to date is, therefore, strongly against the hypotheses underlying zero substitution and the existence of a real value added function.

Corden (1976, p. 61) notes that in the area of effective protection there has been "a genuine interaction between theory and empirical work: empirical work has been stimulated by theory, theoretical problems have been raised by empirical work, and theoretical contributions have been made as a by-product of empirical work". The same comments can be applied to the literature on the Leontief paradox.

12.4. Production function studies

Reference has already been made to various studies of production functions. The production sector approach to the demand for imports involves the estimation of the aggregate technology, as do the empirical tests of the substitution and aggregation hypotheses relating to effective protection. Here attention is focused on studies relating to the possibility of factor intensity reversals, to international differences in technology, and to the jointness of the technology.

12.4.1. Factor intensity reversals

An early attempt to examine empirically the possibility and likelihood of factor intensity reversals, which can upset the factor price equalization and HOS theorems, was by Minhas (1962). Minhas' conclusion was that factor intensity reversals are an empirical reality. He obtained his conclusion from the results of estimating the parameters of a CES (constant elasticity of substitution) production function for 24 different products using cross-section data for 19 countries. Writing the CES production function as

$$y = f(x) = \gamma \left[\sum_i \delta_i x_i^{-\beta}\right]^{-1/\beta}, \quad \beta > -1, \ \sum \delta_i = 1, \tag{34}$$

where $\sigma = 1/(1 + \beta)$ is the elasticity of substitution and γ is an efficiency parameter, the unit cost function is

$$c(w) = \gamma^{-1} \left[\sum_i \delta_i^{-\sigma} w_i^{1-\sigma}\right]^{1/(1-\sigma)}. \tag{35}$$

By Shephard's lemma the optimal $x_i/y = c_i(w)$, so

$$\ln(x_i/y) = -\sigma \ln \epsilon_i + \sigma \ln(p/w_i), \tag{36}$$

where $\epsilon_i \equiv \delta_i \gamma^{-\beta}$ and the price of the output, p, is assumed to be equal to unit cost (profit maximization). In Minhas' application there are two inputs — capital and labour — but only the labour equation in (36) was estimated, by ordinary least squares regression.

The factor ratios are related to factor price ratios by

$$\ln(x_2/x_1) = \sigma \ln \epsilon_1/\epsilon_2 + \sigma \ln(w_1/w_2). \tag{37}$$

Since the parameters σ, ϵ_1 and ϵ_2 are permitted to be different in each industry, factor intensity reversals are possible if the σ's are different, as demonstrated in Chapter 4. Setting the factor ratios equal in two industries, (37) may be used to calculate the common factor price ratio which ensures that (37) is satisfied for both products. If this factor price ratio is in the empirically relevant range and the σ's are different, factor intensity reversals will have been shown to be a reality. Minhas presents results which show this to be the case. For example, his estimates include the figures shown in table 12.2, which can be used to show that

Table 12.2

	ϵ_1	ϵ_2	σ
Dairy products	0.874	0.262	0.721
Pulp and paper	0.649	0.320	0.965

the factor ratios are equal in the two industries if $w_1/w_2 = 2.136$, which Minhas claims to be in the empirically relevant range.

Leontief (1964) criticizes Minhas on the grounds that since only one equation in (36) was estimated ($i = 1 =$ labour), ϵ_2 was not obtained from (36), yet no explanation for the estimate of ϵ_2 was given. Leontief uses some of Minhas' data to obtain indirect estimates for ϵ_2 and concludes that the results are strongly in favour of no intensity reversals in the relevant range. Of course, the appropriate procedure is to estimate both equations in (36) taking account of the fact that σ enters both. Then the calculations of Minhas could be reworked.

More recently Yeung and Tsang (1972) have presented evidence in favour of factor intensity reversals. They use a generalization of the CES function to allow for homogeneity of degree other than unity and for the elasticity of substitution to depend on the input ratio. They apply the model to cross-section data on 17 U.S. manufacturing industries and calculate intensity reversal points and obtain a large number of them.

12.4.2. International differences in technology

Arrow, Chenery, Minhas and Solow (1961) (hereafter ACMS) estimated, and in fact derived, the CES production function and provide some evidence on international differences in technology. From (36) the factor ratios are

$$\ln (x_2/x_1) = \sigma \ln (\delta_1/\delta_2) + \sigma \ln (w_1/w_2), \tag{38}$$

since $\epsilon_2/\epsilon_1 = \delta_2/\delta_1$. If two nations, say the United States and Japan, have the same production function except possibly for the γ parameter, then

$$\ln (x_2/x_1)_{\text{U.S.}} - \ln (x_2/x_1)_J = \sigma [\ln (w_1/w_2)_{\text{U.S.}} - \ln (w_1/w_2)_J]. \tag{39}$$

Thus, σ may be obtained from observations on the ratios (x_2/x_1) and (w_1/w_2) for the United States (U.S.) and Japan (J). ACMS (1961) calculate σ in this way for 28 industries. Then δ_1 and $\delta_2 = 1 - \delta_1$ are calculated from (38). The results obtained show that factor intensity reversals occur in the empirically relevant range for many pairs of industries.

ACMS (1961) also compare parameter estimates between countries. They use data for 19 different countries to obtain estimates of σ for each of 24 industries (as in Minhas, 1962). Then, noting that

$$\ln (\delta_1/\delta_2) = \ln (x_2/x_1)/\sigma - \ln (w_1/w_2) \tag{40}$$

from (38), they calculate the "predictions" of δ_2/δ_1 and find that these vary little from industry to industry. The conclusion is that the variations in the production function estimates are primarily due to variations in the efficiency parameter γ rather than in the δ's or σ. Hence, the isoquant maps are similar for these countries, with just the labelling being different. This tends to support the generalization of the Ricardian model of Chapter 7 in which comparative advantage was formulated in terms of relative neutral efficiency differences between products.

The conclusions of ACMS (1961) must be viewed with caution, however, since they are based upon limited data and no formal tests were undertaken. For example, the estimates of σ obtained from (39) arise from just two observations so they are forcing a line to go through two points with σ as the slope. Statistically, there are zero degrees of freedom.

12.4.3. Jointness of the technology

The technology is said to be non-joint in factor inputs if the production possibility set can be defined, as in eq. (3.12), in terms of separate production functions for each product. That is, non-jointness is equivalent to our definition of a final-good model of the production sector. This model has considerably more structure than the general production model discussed in Chapter 5, section 5.3, and it is therefore of interest to see whether the data can be assumed to come from the simpler model.

It has been shown by Hall (1973) that a necessary and sufficient condition for the technology to be non-joint in factor inputs is that the joint cost function defined by (20) has the additive form:

$$C(Y, W) = \sum_j C^j(W) \, Y_j, \tag{41}$$

where j runs over all goods (here expressed as aggregates). If the joint cost function is chosen to be

$$C(Y, W) = \sum_i \sum_j \sum_k \sum_\ell a_{ijk\ell} \, (Y_i \, Y_j \, W_k \, W_\ell)^{1/2}, \tag{42}$$

then non-jointness can be imposed by enforcing the parameter restrictions

$$a_{ijk\ell} = 0, \quad \text{all } i, j, k, \ell; \quad i \neq j. \tag{43}$$

The cost function under (43) takes the form of (41) where the unit cost functions have the generalized Leontief functional form:

$$C^j(w) = \sum_k \sum_\varrho a_{jjk\varrho} (W_k W_\varrho)^{1/2}. \tag{44}$$

Both Burgess (1976) and Kohli (1981) have estimated the joint cost function (42) for the U.S. economy. Burgess distinguishes two types of outputs (durables and non-durables, non-governmental services and structures) and three inputs (imports, labour and capital) and uses annual data 1948–1969. Kohli uses annual data on two outputs (consumer goods and investment goods) and two inputs (labour and capital) for the period 1949–1973. They estimate the expenditure equations

(a) $\quad Y_j P_j = Y_j \, \partial C / \partial Y_j = \sum_i \sum_k \sum_\varrho a_{ijk\varrho} (Y_i Y_j W_k W_\varrho)^{1/2}$

and $\hfill (45)$

(b) $\quad W_k V_k = W_k \, \partial C / \partial W_k = \sum_i \sum_j \sum_\varrho a_{ijk\varrho} (Y_i Y_j W_k W_\varrho)^{1/2}$

jointly, taking into account the cross-equation parameter restrictions, the adding-up property $\Sigma P_j Y_j = \Sigma W_k V_k$, and technical change. Kohli is unable to reject the hypothesis of non-jointness (43), while Burgess rejects it at the 5% but not at the 1% level of significance. While the evidence is not strongly against non-jointness, more studies are needed to obtain a conclusion to this question.

12.5. International comparisons of consumer preferences

Differences in consumer preferences between nations have important implications for international trade. These differences can be the cause of trade, for example. Also, many comparative statics results contain terms involving differences in marginal propensities to consume. For example, in Chapter 10 it was shown that a transfer of income to a nation would improve its terms of trade if its marginal propensity to consume the imported good was lower than the foreign nation's. In this section some empirical studies of international differences in consumer preferences are examined.

Houthakker (1957) used approximately 40 household surveys from 30 countries in his investigation of Engel's law, namely that the proportion of income spent on food declines as income is increased. He regressed the log of consumption of food, clothing, housing and miscellaneous items on the log of total expenditure and the log of family size for each sample. Since no price variability was assumed within a particular survey, price effects cannot be estimated. Houthakker concludes that the expenditure elasticities (equal to income elasticities only if total expenditure is proportional to income) vary among countries but that the range of variation is not great and hence the elasticities can be regarded as "similar". However, no formal tests were undertaken. In a second study, Hout-hakker (1965) uses combined cross-section and time-series data on expenditure for five categories of consumption for the OECD countries, and concludes that there are significant differences in the demand elasticities. Again he used the double logarithmic functional form.

Several other studies have been undertaken using time-series data and a systems approach to estimation. These studies assume a particular utility function, and derive a set of expenditure equations which are then estimated jointly. Most of these studies employ the linear expenditure system (LES) which is a special case of the Gorman polar form. The latter may be written as

$$V(p, m) = [m - A(p)] /B(p), \tag{46}$$

from which the expenditure functions are derived as

$$p_i z_i = p_i A_i(p) + \beta_i(p) [m - A(p)], \tag{47}$$

where $\beta_i(p) \equiv p_i B_i(p)/B(p)$ is the marginal propensity to consume good i, and A_i and B_i are derivatives of A and B with respect to p_i. To make the model operational, functional forms for $A(p)$ and $B(p)$ are required. If

$$A(p) \equiv \sum_i p_i a_i \quad \text{and} \quad B(p) = \sum_i b_i p_i^{-\rho}, \tag{48}$$

then we get the generalized linear expenditure system (GLES) with $A_i(p) = a_i$ a constant, and $\beta_i(p) = b_i p_i^{-\rho}/[\sum_j b_j p_j^{-\rho}]$, depending upon prices. If, in addition, $\rho \to 0$, then $\beta_i(p) \to b_i/\sum_j b_j = b_i$, normalizing $\sum b_j = 1$. In this case both $A_i(p)$ and $\beta_i(p)$ are constants and (47) becomes the LES:

$$p_i z_i = p_i a_i + b_i [m - \sum_j p_j a_j]. \tag{49}$$

Using data on expenditures and income (usually taken to be total expenditure) the parameters can be estimated using multivariate regression techniques on the LES or GLES. This is the approach of Goldberger and Gamaletsos (1970), Gamaletsos (1973), Parks and Barten (1973) and Lluch and Powell (1975). In the first two studies the LES was applied to time-series data on prices and expenditures on five categories of consumption (food, clothing, rent, durables and other) for a number of OECD nations. In the Gamaletsos study the GLES and the indirect addilog expenditure system were also estimated. The results show considerable differences among countries in the estimates for the parameters and for the income and price elasticities.

Parks and Barten (1973) attempt to explain international differences in the parameter estimates by taking into account differences in population composition — specifically the age structure. They use the LES and data on 14 OECD countries for the years 1950–1967 and divide expenditure into the same five categories as in the previous studies. They regress the widely differing (over nations) estimates of the a_i and b_i parameters on the proportions of the population in each age category and also income. The conclusion is that these variables contribute significantly to the international differences in the a_i parameters but not for the b_i parameters.

In a similar manner Lluch and Powell (1975) attempt to explain international differences in the estimates of the price and income elasticities obtained from the LES by differences in GNP per capita. They use time-series data on expenditures for eight categories of goods for 19 countries, which differ markedly in their level of industrialization and of GNP per capita. Again large differences in the elasticities are obtained, and GNP per capita contributes significantly to some of these differences.

The conclusion to emerge from these studies is that there appears to be significant international differences in demand systems.

12.6. Programming and general equilibrium models of trade

Recently there have been a number of attempts to perform calculations of the effects of changing tariffs and other exogenous variables upon the equilibrium solution for trading economy by the use of "large scale" models involving many goods and actual data for specific economies. These attempts are briefly discussed here under the general heading of "programming and general equilibrium models", although not all of them use mathematical programming techniques for solution.

The concept of effective rates of protection was developed as a convenient way of taking account of intermediate inputs in determining the effect of the tariff structure upon the industrial structure. As emphasized in Chapter 10, just as nominal tariff rates indicate how domestic product prices are affected by tariffs so the effective rates are meant to indicate the effect of tariffs upon the "price" of the industry's activity level, say value added. By themselves they cannot be unambiguous predictors of activity levels, just as nominal tariffs cannot be unambiguous predictors of net outputs of goods (except when there are only two goods).[6] Hence, there is still an important role for explicit calculations of the effects of changes in tariffs, taking account of the full set of equilibrium conditions.

There are two ways of proceeding. First, a differential comparative statics calculation can be used in which case only the first-order effects of changes in the tariff structure are obtained. Secondly, the equilibrium solution can be calculated for two different tariff structures and the solutions compared. Evidently, the second approach requires more information about the nature of production and utility functions than the first, in which only their local properties are needed.

12.6.1. *Differential comparative statics approach*

The differential comparative static approach has been used by Taylor and Black (1974) to calculate the effects of alternative commercial policies upon the Chilean economy using a 35-sector model. Of the 35 industries, 10 produce non-traded goods, 6 produce export goods, and 19 produce importable goods. Apart from intermediate inputs, the model contains a non-competitive import good and a primary factor, labour; capital being assumed fixed in each industry. Import prices are fixed but export prices depend upon the level of exports.

A major problem in all empirical models which deal explicitly with individual industries concerns the choice of dimensions. It was emphasized in Chapters 4 and 5 that comparative statics results depend crucially on the number of activities relative to the number of fully employed factors in a constant-returns-to-scale competitive model. In the present instance if there are two factors, labour and capital, then for arbitrarily given product prices only two industries will produce in general. If all do produce at a particular price vector, in general a small change in the price vector will cause all but two industries to disappear. Of course, the prices of non-traded goods are not given arbitrarily, but there are many traded good prices that are.

How can the model yield "sensible" answers that have all industries continuing to produce? The "solution" of Taylor and Black is to assume that there are as many capital inputs as there are sectors so that (small) variations in prices can be accommodated by adjustments in the returns to capital as well as the common wage for labour.

The conditions for profit maximization under positive production of all goods with no joint production are

---

[6]   But recall that prices (nominal tariffs) and net outputs are positively correlated. This can easily be shown as a consequence of the maximization of GNP.

$$c^j(p, w, r_j) = p_j,$$ (50)

where the product prices are given for all traded goods. The factor market equilibrium conditions are

$$c_r^j g_j = K_j \quad \text{and} \quad \sum_j c_w^j g_j = L,$$ (51)

where $c_r^j \equiv \partial c^j / \partial r_j$, $c_w^j \equiv \partial c^j / \partial w$, g_j is gross production of j, and K_j is the fixed stock of capital and industry j. Thus, there are fewer goods (activities) than factors so that the GNP function is smooth, and the gross outputs are determinate. Implicit in (50) is the assumption that the endowments are in the diversification cone for any prices chosen. Thus, price variations cannot be "too large".

Various special assumptions were used by Taylor and Black to simplify the data requirements. First, it was assumed that capital and labour combined in Cobb–Douglas form so that the share of labour in value added was constant. Secondly, intermediate inputs entered the production function in fixed-coefficient form or Cobb–Douglas form (as a second experiment) requiring only data on the input–output table for the supply side. Thirdly, preferences were assumed to be additively separable so that all cross-price elasticities could be obtained from information on own-price and income elasticities. Finally, export prices for each good were assumed to depend on the exports of that good alone.

Assuming the wage rate to be fixed, the effects of various changes in tariffs were calculated and compared under several specifications of the technology. The usefulness of the effective rates of protection for predicting gross output effects was examined, the conclusion being that they are poor predictors when intermediate inputs enter the technology via a Cobb–Douglas production function, but are good predictors for the case of fixed coefficients.

12.6.2. Calculation of general equilibrium solutions

A general equilibrium model of the Canadian economy was solved by Boadway and Treddenick (1978) under a variety of assumptions about the tax structure. The basic approach may be explained as follows, choosing a model with no internal taxes for simplicity. The model consists of many products produced by themselves, capital, and labour with all products being traded internationally at prices depending upon the volume of trade. The production sector is characterized by (50) and (51), but where the rental rate is common to all industries and is normalized to unity. Boadway and Treddenick make the partial equilibrium assumption that the foreign demands for net exports are a function of own prices.

To make the system homogeneous in prices an "exchange rate", e, is introduced and the net export functions written as $x_i^*(p_i^*)$, where $ep_i^* + t_i = p_i$ is the domestic price. The balance of trade condition becomes

$$p^* x^*(p^*) = 0 \quad \text{or} \quad px^*((p-t)/e) = 0. \tag{52}$$

Assuming that all goods are produced (50) may be solved for $p = P(w)$ since r is fixed by the normalization. Eq. (52) can be solved for $e = e(w, t)$. Hence, $x = x(w, t)$ and income $m = wL + rK = tx = m(w, t)$. The demand vector is $z = \phi(p, m(w, t)) = z(w, t)$. Gross outputs are $g = [I - B(p, w)]^{-1} z(w, t) + x(w, t) = g(w, t)$, where $B = [\partial c^j / \partial p_k]$ is the matrix of input–output coefficients. Hence, the labour market equilibrium condition can be written as

$$\sum_j c_w^j(w, r) g_j(w, t) = L, \tag{53}$$

which may be solved for $w = w(t)$. The solution for all other variables can then be obtained by substituting this expression for w.

The algorithm depends upon the assumption that all goods are produced whence $p = P(w)$. The only difficult computations involve the solutions of (52) and (53) for e and w, respectively, but these can readily be dealt with by various algorithms for solving non-linear equations. The assumption that all goods are produced is accommodated by the net export functions and adjustments in e. This approach can be contrasted with that of Taylor and Black (1974).

The model can be generalized in various ways. For example, it is not difficult to take care of domestic taxes. Boadway and Treddenick also consider inter-industry wage differentials, the treatment of imports as imperfect substitutes for domestic inputs, and differentiate between imports and exports. In their application they assume fixed coefficients for intermediates while labour and capital combine in Cobb–Douglas or CES forms. The utility function is Cobb–Douglas so that expenditure shares are constants. The application is to a 16-industry and also a 56-industry model of the Canadian economy.

Some of their results are as follows. When trade taxes are reduced to zero, the level of utility falls (though by a relatively small amount) indicating that the tax structure exploits the monopoly power resulting from the import and export functions whose elasticities were fixed arbitrarily at three different levels. It was also found that the tariff appears to favour the tertiary industries and to hurt most manufacturing and primary industries, contrary to conventional beliefs about Canadian tariffs. The tariffs also raise the wage–rental ratio. For the 16-industry case the rank correlation between the effective tariff rates and logarithmic changes in industry outputs was very low (lower than for nominal tariffs), thus providing further evidence against the predictive power of effective rates of protection.

While Boadway and Treddenick (1978) use an algorithm which exploits the assumed structure of the model, there is a need for more general solution techniques. Shoven and Whalley (1974) have applied Scarf's algorithm to the calculation of a full competitive equilibrium in a model of international trade with trade taxes. The algorithm is based on fairly general assumptions about the production and demand response functions. They illustrate the algorithm on an example with two countries each producing two products with two factors and having two consumers, but do not consider an application to a real situation with many sectors. An alternative algorithm, which is based upon finding a fixed point in factor price space, has been developed by Helpman (1976), but again only example problems were solved.

These general equilibrium algorithms require much more information than the comparative statics procedure but, of course, can answer many more interesting questions.

12.6.3. Mathematical programming models

Another set of studies concerns the use of linear programming techniques. The application of linear programming to the production sector should be clear. Given product prices, factor endowments and a technology with fixed input–output coefficients for both factors and intermediates, the GNP function $G(p, v)$ is obtained by solving the linear programming problem of maximizing GNP subject to the endowment constraints. If the input–output vectors are not fixed but are contained in polyhedral sets, then linear programming can still be used by defining dummy activities for each extreme point of the polyhedral set. Less well known is the possibility of using linear programming to handle the case where input–output vectors belong to an arbitrary convex set, as in the neoclassical model in which case the boundary is smooth. One approach is to approximate the smooth set by a finite set of points, bringing us back to a polyhedral set. Another is to use the algorithm of Van Slyke, as indicated by Diewert and Woodland (1977) who exploit duality theory. The idea is to choose any feasible input–output vector and solve the linear programming problem which yields the shadow price vector for factors, w. Then using the cost function $c^j(w,p)$ the optimal input–output vector $(b_j, a_j) = (c_p^j, c_w^j)$ is obtained. This new vector is used in the next linear programming problem. Thus, the calculations iterate until convergence is achieved. While this algorithm has great potential for solving the maximum GNP problem for large neoclassical economies, it has not yet been applied to a real problem.[7]

If the utility function is of the Leontief fixed coefficient form, linear programming can be used to solve more general problems. In this vein Lage (1970) attempted to analyse the effects of tariffs on the Japanese economy. Under the Leontief assumption the expenditure function is $E(p, \mu) = (p\,\alpha)\mu$, where α is a fixed vector, so that the consumption vector is $z = E_p(p, \mu) = \alpha\mu$, which is independent of prices. The nation maximizes utility by solving

$$\max \{\mu: (I - B)g - x - \alpha\mu \geq 0,\ Ag \leq v, p^*x \geq 0\}, \tag{54}$$

where p^* is the world price vector such that $p_j^* = 0$ for non-traded goods. The Lagrange multipliers (shadow prices) for the constraints are, respectively, the domestic prices, p, the factor price vector, w, and the "exchange rate", e, which can be seen to be equal to the marginal utility of income. This is the free trade solution for a small open economy.

Under trade taxes one can solve (54) with p^* replaced by $(p^* + t)x \geq 0$. This is not quite the budget constraint that the nation faces. The only thing wrong is that these calculations assume that the consumer does not receive the tax revenue $(-tx)$ and must balance his trade. If *all* goods are traded, then the production vector is given by the solution to this problem, and the solution for the demand vector is augmented by an amount which uses the tariff revenue $(-tx)$, and so the true trade balance is restored. One can then calculate the cost of the tariff as the difference between μ under free trade and μ under the second programming problem augmented by the tariff revenue. If some goods are non-traded, their prices (dual variables) will have to adjust to accommodate the extra demand coming from the tariff revenue and so the production point may shift. Lage (1970) suggests keeping the output of non-traded goods fixed at the solution to the second programming problem and then resolving the problem allowing only the outputs of traded goods to vary. The difference between the resulting μ and the free trade μ is taken to be a measure of the production cost of protection.

The model was applied to a 33-sector model of the Japanese economy under upper and lower capacity constraints on the gross output vector. This is Lage's way of ensuring "sensible" answers given that only four sectors produce non-traded goods and there is only one factor, labour. Without the capacity constraints it is likely that only the non-traded goods sectors and two traded goods sectors would produce. Contrast this solution to the problem with those by Taylor and Black (1974) and Boadway and Treddenick (1978).

There have been other studies of trade taxes using programming models, such

---

[7] For further details on this algorithm see Chapter 3, appendix B.

as by Evans (1972) for Australia. This model was the prototype for a rather extensive model of the Australian economy described by Dixon, Parmenter, Ryland and Sutton (1977). This model is designed to assess the impact of various policy and exogenous changes upon the industrial structure of the economy and is based, like those discussed above, on microeconomic lines, although it is embedded in a more traditional macroeconomic model.

At a quite different level, Baldwin and Lage (1971) have developed a linear programming model of trade-balancing tariff reductions. This is an attempt to formally model the principles behind the Kennedy Round of the General Agreement on Tariffs and Trade (GATT) Negotiations. The principle was to make multilateral reductions in tariffs subject to each country's balance of trade being essentially unchanged. The programming model was formulated to find tariff reductions which would maximize world income subject to these constraints. The model was Keynesian in nature, concentrating on income and tariff effects in an aggregate framework.

12.7. Concluding comments and notes on the literature

Empirical research is important, not only for providing estimates of the various concepts used in the development of international trade theory but also for providing evidence on whether the assumptions made in theoretical models are realistic. The above survey indicates how many researchers have undertaken empirical studies relevant to trade theory, but it has only skimmed the surface. There are also many areas that were not surveyed, for example foreign investment and the dynamics of product development, the international transmission of technical knowledge, and learning by doing. For more extensive surveys see Stern (1976), Corden (1976) and Leamer and Stern (1970).

If the studies referred to are not representative of the totality of empirical work in trade theory it is primarily because of the selection criteria indicated at the outset. On the whole these studies are closely related to the theory. While there is a role for more ad hoc empirical studies in that they can sometimes bring to light important empirical regularities, they are limited in scope. Empirical work needs to be closely related to the theory if the empirical results are to be satisfactorily interpreted and evaluated.

Accordingly, it is my view that more empirical work should be undertaken on general equilibrium models, and on supply and demand systems, with the emphasis on systems. Recent advances in computer technology, the development of functional forms for multi-variable utility and production functions without severe restrictions on curvature, and hopefully improved data bases permit such work to take place. Specifically, there should be more work done on the estimation of import demand and export supply functions which are embedded in a general model of the economy. At this stage only Kohli and Burgess have estimated these functions as an integral part of the production sector. Further developments incorporating the demand side, as by Clements, are needed. At the same time a greater breakdown of commodities and factors is needed. The studies referred to in section 12.6 under the heading of "programming and general equilibrium models" represent an important step in this direction. However, the assumptions made regarding the technology and preferences have been rather restrictive (to enable implementation). This is where the estimation of large-scale production and consumption models comes in, since without such estimates the information needed for policy simulations is not available. It is also a feature of data sources and hence the programming and general equilibrium models that, while considerable detail and disaggregation occurs for goods, little emphasis is given to factors. Thus, the input—output tables have many rows and columns, but usually only two factors, labour and capital, are distinguished. Further disaggregation and data on other factors such as land and natural resources are needed.

Problems

1. Let $T(y_1, y_2, v_1, v_2) = 0$ be the transformation frontier with GNP function $G(p_1, p_2, v_1, v_2)$. Let $T(\cdot) \equiv T'(Y_1(y_1), y_2, V_1(v_1), v_2) = 0$, where $Y_1(y_1)$ and $V_1(v_1)$ are linearly homogeneous functions of vectors y_1, v_1.
   (a) Show that $G(\cdot) = G'(P_1, p_2, V_1, v_2)$, where $P_1 = P_1(p_1)$ is convex and linearly homogeneous.
   (b) Show that the elasticity of transformation τ_{ij} between good i in group 1 and good j in group 2 is independent of i, where $\tau_{ij} \equiv G_{ij}G/G_i G_j$ and subscripts denote derivatives with respect to product prices.
   (c) Show that $G_1' \equiv \partial G'/\partial V_1$ can be interpreted as the price of V_1.
2. Consider the joint cost function $C(Y_N, Y_X, W_M, W_L, W_K)$ and the GNP function $G(P_N, P_X, P_M, V_L, V_K)$ as alternative representations of the same technology under competitive behaviour. Burgess (1974b, 1976) presents price elasticities of demand for M, L, and K given $(Y_N, Y_X, W_M, W_L, W_K)$, whereas it may be more appropriate to treat $(P_N, P_X, P_M, V_L, V_K)$ as given.
   (a) Use the fact that $P_j = \partial C/\partial Y_j$, $V_i = \partial C/\partial W_i$, $Y_j = \partial G/\partial P_j$, and $W_i = \partial G/\partial V_i$ (where $P_M \equiv W_M$, $V_M \equiv -Y_M$) to provide a relationship between the second derivative matrices of C and G. That is, express the second derivatives of G in terms of those of C, and vice versa. (*Hint:* Define (Y_N, Y_X, W_L, W_K) and (P_N, P_X, V_L, V_K) as vectors, and use the formula for the inverse of a partitioned matrix.)

(b) Use this relationship to show how to calculate the elasticity of demand for imports, $(\partial^2 G/\partial P_M^2) P_M/(\partial G/\partial P_M) = -\partial \ln(-Y_M)/\partial \ln P_M$, in terms of the derivatives of the joint cost function C.

(c) Hence, explain what information you need to calculate this elasticity, given that you have an estimate of C not G.

(d) If there is just one output derive the condition on Allen–Uzawa substitution elasticities ($\sigma_{ij} \equiv C C_{ij}/C_i C_j$, where subscripts denote derivatives with respect to the W_i) for a tariff on imports to raise W_L/W_K and hence the share of factor income going to labour.

3. Let $\ln z_i = \ln a_i + \Sigma_j b_{ij} \ln p_j + c_i \ln m$, $i = 1, ..., M$, be a set of log-linear demand functions.

(a) Show that they are homogeneous of degree zero in (p, m) when $\Sigma_j b_{ij} + c_i = 0$ for all i.

(b) Form the sum $\Sigma_i p_i z_i$, and show that it equals m if $b_{ii} = -1$, $b_{ij} = 0$ for $j \neq i$, $c_i = 1$ and $\Sigma a_i = 1$. If these parameter restrictions do not hold, will expenditure equal income?

(c) What utility function is implied by the restrictions in (b)?

4. Taylor and Black assume additive preferences, i.e. $u(z) = \Sigma u^i(z_i)$, so that cross-price elasticities can be calculated from knowledge of direct price and income elasticities and budget shares.

(a) Derive the first-order conditions for a solution to the utility-maximization problem under additive preferences. These yield $z_i = \phi_i(p, m)$ and $\lambda = \lambda(p, m) \equiv V_m(p, m)$ – the Lagrange multiplier.

(b) By differentiation of these conditions show that $\lambda_j/\lambda_m = -(\phi_j + m\omega\phi_{jm})$ and $\phi_{ij} = \phi_{im}(\lambda_j/\lambda_m + \omega m p_j^{-1} \delta_{ij})$, where subscripts denote derivatives as usual, δ_{ij} is the Kronecker delta and $\omega \equiv (m \lambda_m/\lambda)^{-1}$ is Frisch's "flexibility of the marginal utility of money".

(c) Hence, show that the pure substitution effect is $E_{ij} \equiv \phi_{ij} + \phi_{im} z_j = -m\omega \phi_{im}(\phi_{jm} - p_j^{-1} \delta_{ij})$ which, when $j \neq i$, is $E_{ij} = -m\omega\phi_{im} \phi_{jm}$.

(d) Show that $\eta_{ij} \equiv \phi_{ij} p_j/\phi_i = \eta_{im} [\omega(\delta_{ij} - \eta_{jm} s_j) - s_j]$.

(e) Finally, show that $\omega = (\eta_{ii} + s_i \eta_{im})/(1 - s_i \eta_{im}) \eta_{im}$, and hence that the cross-price elasticities η_{ij} ($j \neq i$) can be calculated using information on $s_i, s_j, \eta_{ii}, \eta_{im}$ and η_{jm} alone.

5. A simple open economy produces one product using an imported material input, labour and capital. The produced good is consumed at home and exported. There is a tariff on imports. You are commissioned to estimate the import demand function.

(a) Formulate your model of the economy.

(b) Specify the empirical model whose parameters you would estimate. Be precise about the functional forms, the parameters, and the data that you need.

(c) Indicate how you will use the parameter estimates to calculate elasticities (or other concepts) of interest.

(d) Carry out your plan of action for a country of your choice and discuss your results.

References

Alaouze, C.M., J.S. Marsden and J. Zeitsch (1977) "Estimates of the elasticity of substitution between imported and domestically produced commodities at the four digit ASIC level", Working Paper 0-11, IMPACT Project, Industries Assistance Commission, Canberra, July.

Appelbaum, E. and U.R. Kohli (1979) "Canada–U.S. trade: Tests for the small-open-economy hypothesis", *Canadian Journal of Economics* 12, 1–14.

Armington, P.S. (1969) "A theory of demand for products distinguished by place of production", *International Monetary Fund Staff Papers* 16-1, March, 159–176.

Arrow, K.J., H.B. Chenery, B.S. Minhas and R.M. Solow (1961) "Capital labor substitution and economic efficiency", *Review of Economics and Statistics* 43-3, August, 225–250.

Balassa, B. (1965) "Tariff protection in industrial countries: An evaluation", *Journal of Political Economy* 73, 573–594.

Baldwin, R.E. (1971) "Determinants of the commodity structure of U.S. trade", *American Economic Review* 61, March, 126–146.

Baldwin, R.E. (1979) "Determinants of trade and foreign investment: Further evidence", *Review of Economics and Statistics* 61-1, February, 40–48.

Baldwin, R.E. and G.M. Lage (1971) "A multilateral model of trade-balancing tariff concessions", *Review of Economics and Statistics* 52, 237–245.

Barten, A.P. (1971) "An import allocation model for the common market", *Cahiers Economiques de Bruxelles* 50, 3–14.

Barten, A.P. and G. d'Alcantara (1977) "Models of bilateral trade flows", in: H. Albach et al. (eds.), *Quantitative Wirtschaftsforschung* (Wilhelm Krelle), pp. 43–77.

Basman, R.L., R.C. Battalio and J.H. Kagel (1973) "Comment on R.P. Byron's 'The restricted Aitken estimation of sets of demand relations' ", *Econometrica* 41-2, March, 365–370.

Berndt, E.R. and L.R. Christensen (1973a) "The translog function and the substitution of equipment, structures, and labor in U.S. manufacturing 1929–68", *Journal of Econometrics* 1, 81–114.

Berndt, E.R. and L.R. Christensen (1973b) "The internal structure of functional relationships: Separability, substitution, and aggregation", *Review of Economic Studies* 40, July, 403–410.

Berndt, E.R. and L.R. Christensen (1974) "Testing for the existence of a consistent aggregate index of labor inputs", *American Economic Review* 64, 391–404.

Berndt, E.R. and D.O. Wood (1975) "Technology, prices and the derived demand for energy", *Review of Economics and Statistics* 56, August, 259–268.

Berner, R. (1976) "Total import and gross output demands in the context of a multisector general equilibrium model", *International Finance Discussion Paper* 88, Federal Reserve System.

Blackorby, C. and R.R. Russell (1976) "Functional structure and the Allen partial elasticities of substitution: An application of duality theory", *Review of Economic Studies* 43-2, June, 285–291.

Blackorby, C., D. Primont and R.R. Russell (1975) "Budgeting, decentralization and aggregation", *Annals of Economic and Social Measurement* 4-1, 23–44.

Boadway, R. and J. Treddenick (1978) "A general equilibrium computation of the effects of the Canadian tariff structure", *Canadian Journal of Economics* 11-3, August, 424–446.

Burgess, D.R. (1974a) "Production theory and the derived demand for imports", *Journal of International Economics* 4, 103–117.

Burgess, D.R. (1974b) "A cost minimization approach to import demand equations", *Review of Economics and Statistics* 56-2, May, 225–234.

Burgess, D.F. (1976) "Tariffs and income distribution: Some empirical evidence for the United States", *Journal of Political Economy* 84-1, February, 17–45.

Clements, K.W. (1980) "A general equilibrium econometric model of the open economy", *International Economic Review* 21-2, June, 469–488.

Corden, W.M. (1966) "The structure of a tariff system and the effective protective rate", *Journal of Political Economy* 74, 221–237.

Corden, W.M. (1976) "The costs and consequences of protection: A survey of empirical work", in: P. Kenen (ed.), *International Trade and Finance* (Cambridge), pp. 51–91.

Denny, M. and M. Fuss (1977) "The use of approximation analysis to test for separability and the existence of consistent aggregates", *American Economic Review* 67, 404–418.

Denny, M. and D. May (1977) "The existence of a real value-added function in the Canadian manufacturing sector", *Journal of Econometrics* 5, 55–69.

Diewert, W.E. (1974) "Applications of duality theory", in: M.D. Intriligator and D.A. Kendrick (eds.), *Frontiers of Quantitative Economics*, vol. II (Amsterdam: North-Holland), pp. 106–171.

Diewert, W.E. (1976) "Exact and superlative index numbers", *Journal of Econometrics* 4, 115–145.

Diewert, W.E. and A.D. Woodland (1977) "Frank Knight's theorem in linear programming revisited", *Econometrica* 45-2, March, 375–398.

Dixon, P.B., B.R. Parmenter, G.J. Ryland and J. Sutton (1977) *ORANI, A General Equilibrium Model of the Australian Economy: Current Specification and Illustrations of Use for Policy Analysis* (Canberra: Australian Government Publishing Service).

Evans, H.D. (1972) *A General Equilibrium Analysis of Protection* (Amsterdam: North-Holland).

Gamaletsos, T. (1973) "Further analysis of cross-country comparison of consumer expenditure patterns", *European Economic Review* 4, 1–20.

Goldberger, A.S. and T. Gamaletsos (1970) "A cross-country comparison of household expenditure patterns", *European Economic Review* 1, 357–400.

Gregory, R.G. (1971) "United States imports and internal pressure of demand: 1948–68", *American Economic Review* 61, March, 28–47.

Hall, R.E. (1973) "The specification of technology with several kinds of outputs", *Journal of Political Economy* 81, July, 878–892.

Helpman, E. (1976) "Solutions of general equilibrium problems for a trading world", *Econometrica* 44-3, May, 547–559.

Hickman, B.G. and L.J. Lau (1974) "Elasticities of substitution and export demands in a world trade model", *European Economic Review* 4, 347–380.

Houthakker, H.S. (1957) "An international comparison of household expenditure patterns, commemorating the centenary of Engel's law", *Econometrica* 25-4, October, 532–551.

Houthakker, H.S. (1965) "New evidence on demand elasticities", *Econometrica* 33, 277–288.

Houthakker, H.S. and S.P. Magee (1969) "Income and price elasticities in world trade", *Review of Economics and Statistics* 51-2, May, 111–125.

Hufbauer, G.C. (1970) "The impact of national characteristics and technology on the commodity composition of trade in manufactured goods", in: R. Vernon (ed.), *The Technology Factor in International Trade* (New York: NBER), pp. 145–231.

Kohli, U.R. (1978) "A gross national product function and derived demand for imports and supply of exports", *Canadian Journal of Economics* 11-2, May, 167–182.

Kohli, U. (1981) "Nonjointness and factor intensity in US production", *International Economic Review* 22-1, February, 3–18.

Lage, G.M. (1970) "A linear programming analysis of tariff protection", *Western Economic Journal* 8-2, June, 167–185.

Lau, L.J. (1974) "Applications of duality theory: Comments", in: M.D. Intriligator and D.A. Kendrick (eds.), *Frontiers of Quantitative Economics*, vol. II (Amsterdam: North-Holland), pp. 170–199.

Leamer, E.E. (1974) "The commodity composition of international trade in manufactures: An empirical analysis", *Oxford Economic Papers* 26, 350–374.

Leamer, E.E. and R.M. Stern (1970) *Quantitative International Economics* (Boston: Allyn and Bacon).

Leontief, W.W. (1953) "Domestic production and foreign trade: The American capital position re-examined", *Proceedings of the American Philosophical Society* 97. Reprinted in J. Bhagwati (ed.), *International Trade* (Penguin, 1969).

Leontief, W.W. (1956) "Factor proportions and the structure of American trade: Further theoretical and empirical analysis", *Review of Economics and Statistics* 38, November, 386–407.

Leontief, W.W. (1964) "An international comparison of factor costs and factor use", *American Economic Review* 54-4, June, 335–345.

Lluch, C. and A. Powell (1975) "International comparisons of expenditure patterns", *European Economic Review* 5, 275–303.

Minhas, B. (1962) "The homohypallagic production function, factor-intensity reversals, and the Heckscher–Ohlin theorem", *Journal of Political Economy* 70, April, 138–156.

Parks, R.W. and A. Barten (1973) "A cross-country comparison of the effects of prices, income and population composition on consumption patterns", *Economic Journal* 83-331, September, 834–352.

Shoven, J.B. and J. Walley (1974) "On the computation of competitive equilibrium on international markets with tariffs", *Journal of International Economics* 4, 341–354.

Stern, R.M. (1976) "Testing trade theories", in: P. Kenen (ed.), *International Trade and Finance* (Cambridge), pp. 3–49.

Taylor, L. and S.L. Black (1974) "Practical general equilibrium estimation of resource pulls under trade liberalization", *Journal of International Economics* 4, 37–58.

Woodland, A.D. (1977) "Estimation of a variable profit and of planning price functions for Canadian manufacturing, 1947–70", *Canadian Journal of Economics* 10-3, August, 355–377.

Woodland, A.D. (1978) "On testing weak separability", *Journal of Econometrics* 8, 383–398.

Yeung, P. and H. Tsang (1972) "Generalized production function and factor-intensity cross-overs: An empirical analysis", *Economic Record* 48-123, September, 387–399.

Zellner, A. (1962) "An efficient method of estimating seemingly unrelated regressions and tests for aggregation bias", *Journal of American Statistical Association* 57, 348–368.

CHAPTER 13

TRADE AND GROWTH: A STATIC APPROACH

13.1. Introduction

Over time the production possibilities set for a nation will change because of changes in the endowments of the factors of production and because of changes in the state of technical knowledge. The labour force may increase due to the natural increase in the size of the population. The capital stock may increase as a result of deliberate plans on the part of producers. Improved knowledge about production processes may occur as a result of the researches of scientists, or of learning by doing. In any case, the production possibilities set changes and so the equilibrium solution for prices, productions, consumptions and trades will be affected.

The task in this chapter is to analyse the effects of changes in technical knowledge and factor endowments within a static framework. The technique of analysis is comparative static and the changes in endowments and technology are taken to be exogenous. In a subsequent chapter attention will be given to a dynamic model of trade in which capital formation and technical change are endogenous.

13.2. Growth, the terms of trade, and welfare

Let the production possibilities set be written as $Y(v, a)$, where v is the vector of factor endowments and a is a vector which describes the "state of technology". This formulation is very general and several special cases will be considered in subsequent sections. For example, a can be a vector of indices of factor augmenting technical change, or of product augmenting technical change. Also, we can let $a \equiv v$, in which case changes in a are really changes in the endowment vector.

The GNP function is now written as $G(p, v, a)$. A change in a will cause production plans, and hence the complete equilibrium solution, to alter. Of particular concern is the effect that the change in a will have upon the prices of traded goods and upon the welfare of the residents of each of the trading nations. To analyse these effects the equilibrium conditions are written as

$$X(p,a) \equiv x(p,v,a) + x^*(p,v^*,a^*) = 0,$$ (1)

where x^* is the vector of foreign excess supply functions, which for the home nation is

$$x(p,v,a) \equiv G_p(p,v,a) - \phi(p, G(P,v,a)),$$ (2)

where $\phi(p,m)$ is the vector of demand functions. Again, we assume that aggregation of the consumption sector is possible. Because of the balance of trade conditions, only $M - 1$ of the M equations in (1) are independent. Also, p is only determined up to a factor of proportionality. Accordingly, the first equation is dropped and the normalization $p_1 = 1$ is used. As in previous chapters we define $p_2 = (p_2, ..., p_M), X_2 = (X_2, ..., X_M)$, etc.

Applying the standard comparative statics procedure to (1) we obtain that

$$dp_2 = - X_{22}^{-1} X_{2a} da,$$ (3)

where $X_{22} \equiv \partial X_2(p,v,a)/\partial p_2$ and $X_{2a} \equiv \partial X_2(p,v,a)/\partial a$ using standard derivative notation. The term X_{2a} indicates the effect of a change in a upon world excess supplies for goods at fixed prices, while X_{22}^{-1} represents the effect of these excess supplies on the equilibrium prices. The former is

$$X_{2a} = x_{2a} = G_{2a} - \phi_{2m} G_a,$$ (4)

and is the effect of a upon the net export vector for the home nation under fixed prices, e.g. for a small open economy. If $G_a > 0$, meaning that an increase in each element of a raises GNP (growth) and no good is inferior (which is assumed), then the consumptions of all goods increase. However, it is not necessary that the net supplies increase by the same amounts and, indeed, some net supplies must fall. The general restrictions imposed on the change in net exports and production levels at fixed product prices are $pG_{pa} = G_a$, which follows from the homogeneity of G in p, and $pX = px = pG_{pa} - p\phi_m G_a = G_a - G_a = 0$. Thus, growth at fixed prices may cause all output levels to rise, some to rise and others to fall or some (but not all) output levels to fall, and will cause the net exports of some goods to fall and some to rise.

In the general case of M goods no clear answers seem possible. Consider, therefore, the case where $M = 2$ and a is a scalar. Then the stability condition for the world market is $X_{22} > 0$. In this case the effect of da upon dp_2 depends solely upon the sign of X_{2a}. If, for example, $G_{2a} < 0$, then $X_{2a} < 0$ and hence $dp_2/da > 0$. Here an increase in a causes the output of good 2 to fall at initial prices so that the home nation's net exports of good 2 fall. Thus, a rise in the price of good 2 is required ro re-establish equilibrium. Only if G_{2a} is sufficiently positive to outweigh the consumption effect will X_{2a} be positive requiring a decrease in the price of good 2. Suppose, for example, that good 2 is being exported. Then the above results show that an export biased growth ($G_{2a} > 0$) may or may not cause a deterioration in the terms of trade, while an import biased growth ($G_{2a} < 0$) will certainly cause an improvement in the terms of trade (p_2).

Can growth harm the home nation? Bhagwati (1958) showed the result, at first glance perhaps rather surprising, that growth could cause a sufficiently large deterioration in the terms of trade to cause the level of utility to fall. This he termed "immiserizing growth". The utility level is $\mu = V(p, G(p, v, a))$, where V is the indirect utility function, hence the change in utility is given by

$$d\mu/V_m = x_2 dp_2 + G_a da, \qquad V_m > 0. \tag{5}$$

If the prices remained constant, as in a small open economy, then growth would indeed raise utility since it is assumed that $G_a > 0$. However, for a large economy account has to be taken of the terms of trade effect given by the Laspeyre's price index $x_2 dp_2$.

The second term in (5) represents the direct income effect of growth, which is positive. If the terms of trade move against the home nation ($x_2 dp_2 < 0$), then it seems possible that utility could fall. To check this, (3) and (4) may be used to eliminate dp_2 from (5). This yields:

$$d\mu/V_m = [G_a - x_2 X_{22}^{-1} X_{2a}] da = [(1 + x_2 X_{22}^{-1} \phi_m) G_a - x_2 X_{22}^{-1} G_{2a}] da, \tag{6}$$

where

$$X_{22} = (S_{22} + S_{22}^*) + (\phi_{2m}^* - \phi_{2m}) x_2, \tag{7}$$

and S_{22} and S_{22}^* are the second derivative matrices of $S \equiv G(p, v, a) - E(p, \mu)$ and $S^* \equiv G^*(p, v^*, a^*) - E^*(p, \mu^*)$ with respect to p_2.

Is there anything which prevents the expression in square brackets on the right-hand-side of (6) from being negative? The terms G_a and G_{2a} refer to the effect of a upon the GNP function, whereas the remaining terms refer to income and price effects in production and consumption. While it is true that $pG_{pa} = G_a$, since G_a is linearly homogeneous in p, nevertheless G_a and G_{pa} can be chosen to make the right-hand side of (6) negative if G_{2a} is sufficiently large. We conclude, therefore, that "immiserizing growth" is possible.

In the case where $M = 2$ and a is a scalar, it was shown above that growth will cause the terms of trade (p_2 if good 2 is being exported) to fall if $X_{2a} > 0$, i.e. exports of good 2 increase at initial prices. This requires that growth be sufficiently export biased. In this case, if the bias causes a big increase in the net exports of good 2 and this induces a large fall in the price of good 2, then utility may fall. The reader may wish to construct a diagram illustrating this possibility. If $X_{2a} < 0$, then $dp_2 > 0$ and so immiserizing growth is not possible. Of course, the utility level for the foreign nation depends solely upon how its terms of trade are affected. If p_2 falls, then the foreign nation which imports good 2 will gain, whereas if p_2 rises it will suffer a loss in utility.

When $M = 2$ and a is a scalar (6) reduces to

$$\frac{d\mu}{V_m} = \frac{G_a}{X_{22}} \left[(S_{22} + S_{22}^*) + x_2 \left(\phi_{2m}^* - \frac{G_{2a}}{G_a} \right) \right] da$$

$$= \frac{G_a}{p_2 X_{22}} [p_2 (S_{22} + S_{22}^*) + x_2 (c_2^* - q)] da, \tag{8}$$

where c_2^* is the marginal propensity to consume good 2 abroad and $q \equiv p_2 G_{2a}/G_a$ is the increase in GNP due to product 2 consequent upon an increase in a. If good 2 is exported, then $c_2^* < q$ is a necessary, but not sufficient, condition for immiserizing growth.

The preceding argument was thought to represent a possible difficulty for developing nations. If growth was strongly biased towards the export sector, then there would be a substantial glut of the export good on the world market. If, furthermore, the demand by industrial countries was very inelastic, then there would result a large fall in export prices which could reduce welfare, or at the very least mitigate the welfare inducing effects of growth. The export goods of developing nations, typically primary or resource based, were thought to have an inelastic demand.

If the nation experiencing growth is large enough to influence world prices, then it is certainly large enough to be able to use trade taxes to manipulate the terms of trade in its favour. That is, it can raise welfare by exercising its monopolistic power on the world market. If it chooses an optimal trade tax strategy against a passive foreign nation, then it can be shown that growth cannot be immiserizing. To see this, note that its optimizing problem may be written as

$$\max_{p} V(p, G(p, v, a) + R(p, v^*, a^*)), \tag{9}$$

where $R(p, v^*, a^*) \equiv \max_{x^*} \{px^* : x^* \in X^*(v^*, a^*)\}$ is the tariff revenue function and $X^*(v^*, a^*)$ is the foreign nation's net offer set whose boundary is the offer curve. If a increases causing G to increase for any given p, then V is higher for any given p and, consequently, the maximum level of utility attained cannot fall. Thus, immiserizing growth is not possible for a nation employing an optimal trade tax policy.[1]

This argument holds for a nation of many consumers in the sense that growth will not cause the utility possibility set to contract under an optimal trade tax policy. The utility possibility set is

$$\{\mu : E(p, \mu) = G(p, v, a) + R(p, v^*, a^*)\}, \tag{10}$$

where $E(p, \mu) = \sum_{\ell=1}^{L} E^{\ell}(p, \mu^{\ell})$. Clearly, the right-hand side of the equality is increased by an increase in a, thus expanding the utility possibility set.

We now proceed to examine some special types of growth that can occur.

13.3. Sources of growth

13.3.1. Technical change

Technical change alters the production possibilities of firms. Economists have developed many different characterizations of technical change each of which restricts the manner in which the production possibility sets alter. For example, technical change may be factor augmenting or product augmenting. It may be embodied in a factor or disembodied. It may be neutral or biased. In the following the two cases of product and factor augmentation are considered.

---

[1] See Chapter 9, section 9.6, for this formulation of the optimal trade tax problem. Alternatively, the optimizing problem is

$$\max_{z} \{u(z) : z \in Y(v, a) + X^*(v^*, a^*)\}.$$

An increase in a which causes the production possibility set Y to enlarge causes the whole constraint set to enlarge and hence the maximum level of utility cannot fall.

13.3.2. Product augmenting technical change

In this case the transformation frontier is $t(y, v, a) = t^+(y^+, v) = 0$, where $y^+ \equiv A^{-1}y$ and $A = \text{diag}(a)$, i.e. $y_j^+ = y_j/a_j$. Thus, if a_j increases, then y_j can increase proportionately keeping the production of all other goods fixed.[2] The GNP function is

$$G(p, v, a) \equiv G^+(p^+, v), \tag{11}$$

where $p^+ \equiv Ap$, i.e. $p_j^+ \equiv a_j p_j$. Thus, an increase in a_j acts just like an increase in p_j. The function $G^+(p^+, v)$ is a GNP function expressed in terms of the "effective prices", p_j^+, for the "effective outputs", y_j^+. Since $G^+(p^+, v)$ is linearly homogeneous in p^+, a proportional increase in a will increase GNP proportionately. Outputs will also increase proportionately since $G_p = AG_p^+$ and G_p^+ is homogeneous of degree zero in p^+. This is the case of neutral product augmenting technical change.

In the case of $M = 2$ it can be shown (see problem set) that if only a_2 changes then q in (8) is given by

$$q = 1 + \frac{\partial y_2}{\partial p_2} \frac{p_2}{y_2}, \tag{12}$$

i.e. one plus the own-price supply elasticity. If good 2 has a very elastic supply, then an increase in a_2 will cause a large increase in the output of that good leading to the possibility of a loss in welfare.

13.3.3. Factor augmenting technical change

In this case the transformation frontier is $t(y, v, a) = t^+(y, v^+) = 0$, where $v^+ = A v$ and A is defined as before. The term $v_j^+ = a_j v_j$ is the "effective input" of factor j, and an increase in a_j acts just like an increase in v_j. The GNP function is now

$$G(p, v, a) \equiv G^+(p, v^+). \tag{13}$$

---

[2] One difficulty with the concept of product augmenting technical change of this multiplicative form is that if $y_j < 0$ (j is an input), then an increase in a_j implies that a *greater* input of j is needed to produce given outputs of other goods.

Since $G^+(p, v^+)$ is linearly homogeneous in v^+, a proportional increase in a will increase GNP proportionally by increasing the net outputs of all goods proportionally. This is the case of neutral factor augmenting technical progress, which is clearly identical, in a formal sense, to neutral product augmenting technical progress under constant returns to scale.

Consider the special case where $M = 2$ and a_2 is increased. Then q in (8) is given by

$$q = \frac{\partial y_2}{\partial v_2} \frac{p_2}{w_2} = \frac{\partial w_2}{\partial p_2} \frac{p_2}{w_2} , \tag{14}$$

where w_2 is the price of factor 2 and the reciprocity conditions have been used. Thus, q is the Stolper–Samuelson elasticity. If the Stolper–Samuelson elasticity is greater than unity (industry 2 is factor 2 intensive in a final-good model, for example), then the second term in (8) is negative, and if sufficiently large can cause utility to fall as a result of technical progress. Here technical progress which increases the efficiency of factor 2 will, at fixed prices, cause the output of good 2 to rise more than consumption. This will require a fall in the price of good 2 to clear the market large enough to outweigh the direct improvement in welfare, so that welfare falls.

13.3.4. Product specific factor augmenting technical change

If factor augmenting technical change is limited to some products, then the technologies of the individual products have to be dealt with directly.

The case where factor augmentation in industry j is neutral is, however, equivalent to product augmentation in industry j in view of the assumption of constant returns to scale. If factor augmentation is not neutral then the analysis is more complicated. The appropriate characterization in terms of cost functions, ruling out joint products and intermediate inputs for simplicity, is to write the unit cost function as

$$c^j(w, a) \equiv c^{+j}(w^j),$$

where $w_i^j \equiv w_i/a_{ij}$. Thus, w_i^j is the price of an "effective unit" of factor i in industry j. To obtain the GNP function $G(p, v, a)$ note from eq. (3.9) that it is the minimum factor payment consistent with non-negative factor prices and non-positive profits. By utilizing this result the derivatives of $G(p, v, a)$ and hence an expression for q in (8) can be obtained. This calculation is left for the problem set.

In the preceding discussion very simple characterizations of technical change have been briefly considered. Other more general forms may be envisaged. For example, factor augmenting technical change might be embodied, in which case a factor would have to be distinguished by its vintage. In this case the time profile of the past history of technical change and the profile of additions to the stocks of inputs are needed to determine the effect on units of input in the current period.

It has also been assumed that technical change comes to the economy exogenously. An alternative view is that it is due to the conscious choice of agents in the economy based upon the anticipation of profits. The topic of endogenous technical change will be taken up in a later chapter in the form of a model of learning by doing.

13.3.5. *Changes in factor endowments*

Changes in factor endowments can be dealt with by letting $a \equiv v$ in the analysis of section 13.2 above. Indeed, factor augmenting technical change and changes in factor endowments are equivalent. Thus, for example, if $M = 2$ and the endowment of factor 2 increases, then in (8) q is given by (14). Since this expression has already been discussed, it will not be pursued further.

For a small open economy (5) implies that the increase in utility due to a one unit increase in v_j is proportional to $w_i = \partial G/\partial v_i$, the price of factor i. Also, (4) may be rewritten as

$$\frac{\partial x_j}{\partial v_i} = \left(\frac{\partial w_i}{\partial p_j} \frac{p_j}{w_i} - c_j \right) \frac{w_i}{p_j} \tag{16}$$

making use of the reciprocity (symmetry) conditions. The first term is the Stolper–Samuelson elasticity while the second is the consumption effect given by the marginal propensity to consume good j, c_j. If the Stolper–Samuelson elasticity exceeds unity and good j is not superior $(c_j \leqslant 1)$, then net exports of good j will increase if the supply of factor i is increased.

One important remark concerning the effect of changes in endowments upon the level of utility for a one-consumer economy, or the utility possibility set for a many-consumer economy, is that the preceding analysis has assumed that preferences are independent of factor endowments. If the factor in question is labour, this assumption is suspect since for an individual the amount of labour supply can be expected to enter the utility function. Consider the case where the economy consists of many individuals with identical linearly homogeneous utility functions and identical endowments of factors. An endowment increase occurs by the addition of one more person with the same tastes and endowments as the others. There has been a proportional increase in the endowments of all factors so that, at given product prices, GNP has increased by the same proportion. Clearly, utility per person has not changed even though GNP has increased, contrary to the result in (5). Of course, this case can be dealt with by defining a per capita indirect utility function as a function of per capita income. Other cases are not as easily dealt with, and so the preceding analysis has to be modified appropriately. The reader may wish to derive an expression to replace (5) for the case of a single consumer whose utility depends upon v.

13.4. Foreign ownership of factors

The production possibility set for a nation can expand or contract because of changes in factor endowments caused by their movements from one nation to another. The case that will be of direct concern here is where capital is internationally mobile. The production possibility set for the receiving (host) nation expands, while that of the investing nation contracts. On the other hand, part of the host nation's value of domestic production is repatriated to the investing nation as income for the services of capital. In this section a model of foreign investment is formulated and analysed.

If there is foreign ownership of factors, a distinction has to be made between the input vector and the ownership vector in each nation. Let the *input* vector be partitioned as $v = (L, K)$, where L is a vector of N_L factors which are not internationally mobile and which are owned by domestic residents only, and K is a vector of N_K factors which are internationally mobile. The endowment (*ownership*) vector for the latter is C, so $K - C$ is the net amount of ownership of these domestic factors by foreigners. As usual, the foreign variables are denoted by asterisks (∗). Let

$$K^W \equiv K + K^* \equiv C + C^* \tag{17}$$

be the world endowment vector. Evidently,

$$(K - C) + (K^* - C^*) \equiv 0. \tag{18}$$

In the case where L and K have just one element each, they may be thought of as labour and capital. For concreteness these labels will be used for the case of vectors, although the analysis obviously applies irrespective of the names chosen.

A distinction also has to be made between gross national product (GNP) and gross domestic product (GDP). The latter is the value of domestic production, whereas the former is the income of domestic residents, the difference arising from the income earned on net foreign ownership of capital. Thus, $G(p, L, K)$ is now interpreted as the GDP function, while GNP is $G(p, L, K) + G_K^*(p^*, L^*, K^*)$ $(C-K)$ if the home nation is a net owner of foreign capital and $G(p, L, K) - G_K(p, L, K)(K-C)$ if the foreign nation is a net owner of domestic capital.

If capital is freely mobile, then the owners, who are assumed to remain in their home nation, will employ their capital where the rental is highest in order to maximize their incomes. The search of capital for the highest rental thus ensures that, in equilibrium, the rentals will be equal in the two nations (if capital is used in both nations) if there are no taxes on the foreign earnings of capital and rentals are measured in the same unit of account. In the following model allowance is made for taxes on the foreign earnings of capital and on trade, but it will be assumed that only the home nation imposes such taxes. If g is the tax vector imposed by the home nation upon the net foreign earnings of capital then the relationship between the home and foreign rental rates implied by the free mobility of capital is

$$G_K(p, L, K) = G_K^*(p^*, L^*, K^*) - g, \tag{19}$$

where G_K and G_K^* are the home and foreign rental vectors. The income received by domestic residents from their ownership of foreign capital is equal to the gross earnings $G_K^*(K^* - C^*)$ since the tax paid to the government is assumed to be redistributed.

The budget constraint for the foreign nation is

$$S^*(p^*, \mu^*, L^*, K^*) + G_K^*(p^*, L^*, K^*)(C^* - K^*) = 0, \tag{20}$$

where $S^*(p^*, \mu^*, L^*, K^*) \equiv G^*(p^*, L^*, K^*) - E^*(p^*, \mu^*)$. This equation may be solved for the level of utility $\mu^* = H^*(p^*, L^*, K^*)$ and then the excess supply function for goods obtained as

$$x^*(p^*, K^*) \equiv S_p^*(p^*, H^*(p^*, L^*, K^*), L^*, K^*), \tag{21}$$

ignoring C^* and L^* since these are fixed.

The home nation has a trade balance function $S(p, \mu, L, K) \equiv G(p, L, K) - E(p, \mu)$ which yields its net export vector as $x = S_p(p, \mu, L, K)$. Hence, the market equilibrium condition may be written as

$$S_p(p, \mu, L, K) + S_p^*(p^*, \mu^*, L^*, K^*) = S_p(p, \mu, L, K) + x^*(p^*, K^*) = 0. \qquad (22)$$

The home nation is permitted to impose trade taxes which yield net revenue of $(p^*-p)S_p(p, \mu, L, K)$. In addition, there are the gross foreign earnings of capital. The budget constraint may therefore be expressed as

$$S(p, \mu, L, K) - (p - p^*)S_p(p, \mu, L, K) +$$
$$+ G_K^*(p^*, L^*, K^*)(K^* - C^*) = 0 \qquad (23)$$

or, using the identity $pS_p = S$, as

$$p^*S_p(p, \mu, L, K) + G_K^*(p^*, L^*, K^*)(K^* - C^*) = 0. \qquad (24)$$

If the tax rates for capital (g) are given, then (19) determines K^* as a function of p, p^* and g. If the tax rates for goods are given, then p is a function of these rates and p^*. Then p^* and μ are determined by (22) and (23). Thus, the model is complete. The solution for K^* determines the amount of foreign investment $K^* - C^*$. There will be foreign investment if the foreign nation's rental exceeds the home nation's rental plus the tax, the rentals being those without foreign ownership. The extent of foreign ownership will depend on the response of rentals to the employment of capital and upon the effect of capital upon trade and product prices and hence upon rentals.

13.4.1. Effects of foreign ownership

To obtain a better understanding of the structure of the model consider the effect of a movement of capital from the home to the foreign nation upon the utility levels in each nation. Differentiation of (20) yields the effect upon the utility level for the foreign nation

$$-S_\mu^* d\mu^* = [S_p^* - (K^* - C^*)G_{Kp}^*] dp^* - (K^* - C^*)G_{KK}^* dK^*. \qquad (25)$$

To obtain the effect on the utility of the home nation which takes account of the market equilibrium condition, (22) is substituted into (23) and differentiated to obtain:

$$-S_\mu d\mu = (S_p + x^*)dp + [(p - p^*)x_p^* - x^* + (K^* - C^*)G_{KK}^*]dp^* \qquad (26)$$
$$+ [(p - p^*)x_K^* + (G_K^* - G_K) + (K^* - C^*)G_{KK}^*]dK^*.$$

Since $-S_\mu^*$ and $-S_\mu$ are positive the signs of (25) and (26) indicate the direction of change in μ^* and μ. The addition of (25) and (26) yields:

$$-S_\mu^* \mathrm{d}\mu^* - S_\mu \mathrm{d}\mu = (S_p + x^*)\mathrm{d}p + (p - p^*)x_p^* \mathrm{d}p^* +$$
$$+ [(G_K^* - G_K) + (p - p^*)x_K^*]\mathrm{d}K^*. \tag{27}$$

If the market equilibrium condition $S_p + x^* = 0$ holds, the first term vanishes. If, in addition, $p = p^*$, then (27) becomes:

$$-S_\mu^* \mathrm{d}\mu^* - S_\mu \mathrm{d}\mu = (G_K^* - G_K)\mathrm{d}K^*. \tag{28}$$

Consider now the effect of a movement of capital $\mathrm{d}K^*$ upon the utility levels when there is free trade in goods, so $p = p^*$. The right-hand side of (28) will be positive in general if capital moves in the direction of the highest rental. Hence, it is possible for both nations to gain from capital mobility and certainly both cannot lose. Clearly, the reason for the potential gain is that the world production possibility set is enlarged by capital mobility.

Assume that, in addition to free trade, the initial situation is one of no foreign ownership ($K^* = C^*$). Furthermore, ignore for the present any product price effects. Then as can be seen from (25) and (26) there will be no gain to the foreign nation from a marginal movement of capital, but there will be a gain to the home nation since the right-hand side of (26) reduces to $(G_K^* - G_K)\mathrm{d}K^*$. This is positive if capital moves in the direction of higher rentals. The asymmetry in these results is due to the assumption that the home nation taxes the foreign earnings of capital while the foreign nation is passive. Thus, in the case of a single capital input, for example if $G_K^* > G_K$, then $\mathrm{d}K^* > 0$ and this foreign investment yields a rental higher than it could obtain at home. There is a clear gain in income. If, however, $G_K > G_K^*$, then $\mathrm{d}K^* < 0$ and the foreign nation invests in the home nation. In this case an additional unit of capital raises the home GNP by G_K, but only G_K^* is repatriated to the lending country since the difference is taxed by the home nation. Hence, the home nation gains.

If the movement of capital continues beyond the marginal unit but the assumption that prices are equal and fixed is maintained, the gain in utility to the foreign nation is proportional to $-(K^* - C^*)G_{KK}^* \mathrm{d}K^*$. If the foreign nation is in the interior of its diversification cone, then rentals are not affected by small changes in the capital stocks, $G_{KK}^* = 0$, and hence the change in utility vanishes. There are other special cases where the foreign nation gains. For example, if $\mathrm{d}K^* = \alpha(K^* - C^*)$, where α is a positive scalar, then the change in utility is proportional to $-\alpha(K^* - C^*)G_{KK}^*(K^* - C^*)$, which is non-negative since G_{KK}^* is a negative semi-definite matrix. Thus, if there is an equi-proportional change in foreign ownership the foreign nation gains. The reason for this is that such a movement of capital alters the rentals in the foreign nation in a way which decreases the net repatriation to the home nation of earnings on the existing (intra-marginal) foreign-owned capital. If the home nation invests in the foreign nation, rentals are reduced, so that the amount repatriated to the home nation falls; if the foreign nation increases its investment in the home nation, the rentals are increased and thus the earnings repatriated to the foreign nation increase. A special case of this result occurs when there is one capital input and specialization occurs, in which case $G^*_{KK} < 0$. In general, the gain that accrues to the foreign nation is a loss to the home nation.

The preceding discussion has assumed that prices are fixed. The reader may wish to use the market-clearing conditions to solve for $dp \equiv dp^*$, up to a factor of proportionality, and hence obtain expressions for $d\mu$ and $d\mu^*$ in terms of dK^* which take account of the price effects of the international movements of capital. This exercise treats the movement of capital as an exogenous phenomenon. The *equilibrium* amount of foreign ownership is, however, determined by the condition that the net rentals in the two nations be equalized as in (19). This is depicted in fig. 13.1, where K^*_e is the equilibrium capital stock in the foreign nation. The curves shown describe the rentals on capital in the two nations as functions of the capital stock. They are flat for capital stocks in the cone of diversification and downward-sloping functions of the capital stocks elsewhere.

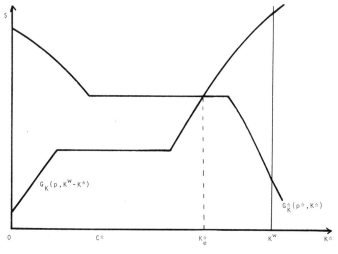

Figure 13.1

13.4.2. Optimal tax policy

The preceding model permits the home nation to impose taxes on the international trade of goods and the foreign earnings of capitalists. The home nation can, of course, choose these tax rates and it can pursue an optimal tax policy. In what follows the optimal policy is characterized and discussed. Concern is with the case of full optimization with respect to both sets of tax rates. Consideration will be given later to the case where one set of taxes is fixed exogenously at non-optimal levels, and the home nation can only choose a second-best policy.

The constraints facing the home nation are its budget constraint (23) and the market equilibrium condition (22). Combining these into a single constraint yields:

$$S(p, \mu, L, K) + (p - p^*)x^*(p^*, K^*) + G_K^*(p^*, L^*, K^*)(K^* - C^*) = 0,$$

(29)

which implicitly defines the indirect utility function $\mu = H(p, p^*, K^*)$. The problem is to choose p, p^* and K^* to maximize utility.

The first-order conditions for a solution are (29) and

(a) $1 + \lambda S_\mu = 0$ $\hspace{3cm}$ (μ),

(b) $H_p = \lambda[S_p + x^*] = 0$ $\hspace{2.3cm}$ (p), $\hspace{1cm}$ (30)

(c) $H_{p^*} = \lambda[-x^* + (p - p^*)x_p^* + (K^* - C^*)G_{Kp}^*] = 0$ $\hspace{0.5cm}$ (p^*),

(d) $H_{K^*} = \lambda[(G_K^* - G_K) + (K^* - C^*)G_{KK}^* + (p - p^*)x_K^*] = 0$ $\hspace{0.3cm}$ (K^*),

where λ is the Lagrange multiplier associated with the constraint. Condition (30, a) simply shows that λ is the marginal utility of income, $-1/S_\mu$, assumed to be positive. Eq. (30, b) is the market equilibrium condition, and eqs. (30, c) and (30, d) characterize the optimal tax structure. Eq. (30, c) may be cast into a more familiar form by differentiating the foreign budget constraint, $p^*x^*(p^*, K^*) - G_K^*(p^*, L^*, K^*)(K^* - C^*) \equiv 0$, with respect to p^* to obtain the relation

$$p^*x_p^* = -x^* + (K^* - C^*)G_{Kp}^*,$$

(31)

and substituting it in (30, c) to obtain:

$$H_{p^*}/\lambda = px_p^* = 0.$$

(32)

This is the familiar characterization of the optimal trade tax vector which is that the domestic price vector is orthogonal to the foreign offer curve, conditional upon the optimal level of K^*. It should be noted that $x_p^*(p^*, K^*)$ incorporates all of the effects of p^* not directly captured by K^*. Eq. (30, c) shows each of these effects: the usual terms of trade effect, $-x^*$; the effect of a change in p^* upon the tax trade receipts, $(p - p^*)x_p^*$; and the effect upon the earnings of foreign capital ownership, $(K^* - C^*)G_{Kp}^*$.

An alternative characterization is obtained by differentiating the identity $x^*(p^*, K^*) \equiv S_p^*(p^*, H^*(p^*, L^*, K^*), L^*, K^*)$ to obtain:

$$x_p^*(p^*, K^*) = S_{pp}^* + \phi_m^*[(K^* - C^*)G_{Kp}^* - x^*], \tag{33}$$

which may be used in (30, c) to obtain:

$$H_{p*}/\lambda = (p - p^*)S_{pp}^* + \iota^*[(K^* - C^*)G_{Kp}^* - x^*] = 0, \tag{34}$$

where $\iota^* \equiv p \, \phi_m^*$, which is positive if there are no inferior goods.[3]

Condition (30, d) is a characterization of the optimal amount of foreign ownership or, equivalently, the optimal tax structure on the earnings of foreign capital. The transfer of a unit of capital (treat K as a scalar for expositional purposes) from the home to the foreign nation will have the following effects upon disposable income. There will be a loss of income of G_K at home but a gain of G_K^* from abroad. In addition, the extra capital abroad will cause rentals there on all capital employed, not just the marginal unit, to change (fall) by G_{KK}^*, which causes foreign capital earnings to change by $(K^* - C^*)G_{KK}^*$. Finally, the additional capital will alter the net export vector by x_K^* which will cause trade tax receipts to change by px_K^*. The optimal choice of K^* is that which makes the marginal change in disposable income zero, taking into account all three sources of income.

Alternative characterizations of the optimal capital tax are obtained as follows. Differentiation of the foreign budget constraint with respect to K^* yields:

$$p^*x_K^* - G_K^* - (K^* - C^*)G_{KK}^* = 0, \tag{35}$$

which may be used to rewrite (30, d) as

$$H_{K*}/\lambda = px_K^* - G_K = 0. \tag{36}$$

---

[3] See the problem set. Use has been made of the identity $p^*\phi_m^* \equiv 1$. Eq. (34) can be simplified by noting that $p^*S_{pp}^* \equiv 0$, but it is convenient to leave the first term as $(p - p^*)$ S_{pp}^* rather than pS_{pp}^* since $t \equiv p - p^*$ is the optimal tax vector. Also note that non-inferiority is sufficient but not necessary for ι^* to be positive.

This states that the optimal level of K^* equates the marginal gain in trade tax revenue with the rental at home. Another characterization is obtained by differentiating the identity $x^*(p^*, K^*) = S_p^*(p^*, H^*(p^*, L^*, K^*), L^*, K^*)$ with respect to K^* yielding:

$$x_K^*(p^*, K^*) = G_{pK}^* + \phi_m^*(K^* - C^*)G_{KK}^*, \tag{37}$$

which may be used in (30, d) to obtain:

$$H_{K^*}/\lambda = (G_K^* - G_K) + (p - p^*)\, G_{pK}^* + \iota^*(K^* - C^*)G_{KK}^* = 0. \tag{38}$$

13.4.3. Optimal tax formulae

Conditions (30,c) and (30,d), or (32) and (36), or (34) and (38), characterize the optimal taxes on goods and capital. They can be used to obtain "optimal tax formulae". Let $t \equiv p - p^*$ be the tax vector for goods and let $g \equiv G_K^* - G_K$ be the tax vector for capital. One tax normalization is permitted, so we set $t_1 = 0$. Also, one price can be normalized, so p_1^* is fixed and the first equation in (34) can be ignored. If $t_2 \equiv (t_2, \ldots, t_M)$ and so on, as is our custom, (34) may be "solved" for t_2 as

$$t_2 = \iota^*[S_{22}^*]^{-1}\,[x_2^* - (K^* - C^*)G_{K2}^*], \tag{39}$$

while (38) may be "solved" for g as

$$g = -\,[t_2 G_{2K}^* + \iota^*(K^* - C^*)G_{KK}^*]. \tag{40}$$

Care must be taken in the interpretation of these "solutions" which are not reduced-form solutions since the taxes appear implicitly on the right-hand sides. They merely express relationships which must exist at the solution to the optimal tax problem. Moreover, they are obtained from some, but not all, of the necessary conditions.

13.4.4. Special case

To illustrate the use of the optimal tax formulae, consider the special case of trade in $M = 2$ products and one capital service. In particular, interest is centred on the signs of t_2 and g.

First, it is noted that $S_{22}^* > 0$, while $G_{KK}^* \leq 0$ with equality to zero if the foreign nation is diversified in production. $G_{K2}^* = G_{2K}^*$ is positive if industry 2 is capital intensive, and negative otherwise. The remaining terms, x_2^* and $K^* - C^*$, have signs depending upon the pattern of trade and direction of capital flows. Evidently, the sign of t_2 depends upon the sign of $[x_2^* - (K^* - C^*)G_{K2}^*]$. Sufficient conditions for this to be positive are $x_2^* > 0$ (we import good 2), $(K^* - C^*) > 0$ (we export capital services) and $G_{K2}^* < 0$ (good 2 is labour intensive). In this case the tax on the imports of good 2 will cause the price to fall abroad and this will raise the foreign rental on capital. Thus, both the usual terms of trade effect and the effect on foreign earnings are positive. In this case (40) shows that $g > 0$. Hence, the optimal policy involves a tax on capital earnings abroad, restricting the amount of ownership of foreign capital and so raising its rental.

If $K^* - C^* > 0$, as above, but now good 2 is exported and is capital intensive, then $t_2 < 0$. This means, however, that exports are taxed so, again, the optimal policy is to restrict trade. Again, $g > 0$ implying that foreign ownership is discouraged. This raises the rental abroad, as does the increase in the price of good 2 abroad. This is another case where both taxes work in harmony.

Consider the case where $K^* - C^* > 0$, good 2 is imported ($x_2^* > 0$) and is capital intensive ($G_{K2}^* > 0$). From (39) it is clear that the sign of t_2 is ambiguous depending on the relative sizes of $x_2^* > 0$ and $(K^* - C^*)G_{K2}^* > 0$. Here there is a conflict. As can be seen from (34), with initial free trade, $p = p^*$, an increase in p_2^* will cause utility to fall since good 2 is imported, but will cause utility to rise since the resulting increase in the foreign rental on capital will cause foreign earnings to rise. Thus, utility may rise or fall if p_2^* is increased, and so the sign of t_2 is ambiguous. If $t_2 < 0$, then (40) shows that $g > 0$. On the other hand, if $t_2 > 0$ so imports are taxed, then g has an ambiguous sign since $t_2 G_{2K}^* > 0$, while $\iota^*(K^* - C^*)G_{KK}^* \leq 0$. The ambiguity is removed if $G_{KK}^* = 0$, which occurs if the foreign nation is in the interior of its diversification cone, in which case $g > 0$.

The results concerning the signs of t_2 and g may be conveniently summarized by:

$$t_2 \gtrless 0, \text{ as } x_2^* - (K^* - C^*)G_{K2}^* \gtrless 0;$$

$$\text{if } t_2 > 0, \text{ then } g \lessgtr 0 \text{ as } G_{2K}^* \lessgtr 0 \text{ under diversification;}$$

$$\text{if } t_2 < 0, \text{ then } g \gtrless 0 \text{ as } G_{2K}^* \gtrless 0 \text{ under diversification;} \qquad (41)$$

$$\text{if } t_2 > 0, G_{K2}^* < 0 \quad \text{or} \quad t_2 < 0, G_{K2}^* > 0, \text{ then } g > 0 \text{ when } K^* - C^* > 0;$$

$$\text{if } t_2 < 0, G_{K2}^* > 0 \quad \text{or} \quad t_2 > 0, G_{K2}^* < 0, \text{ then } g < 0 \text{ when } K^* - C^* < 0.$$

The case where the foreign nation is diversified has been discussed already. If specialization occurs, then $G_{K2}^* = 0$ if specialization is in good 1, while $G_{K2}^* = G_K^*/p_2^*$ if specialization is in good 2. Consider the case of specialization by the foreign nation in good 1. The formulae reduce to

(a) $t_2 = \iota^*[S_{22}^*]^{-1} x_2^*,$

(b) $g = -\iota^*(K^* - C^*)G_{KK}^*,$

$$\text{(42)}$$

so t_2 has the sign of x_2^*, meaning that trade is taxed and hence discouraged, while g has the sign of $K^* - C^*$. Thus, exports of capital services are taxed, and imports of capital services are subsidized. Notice that the foreign nation cannot export both good 2 and capital services, however, since good 1 is exported. This means that $g < 0$ and $t_2 > 0$ is not a feasible combination.

If specialization is in good 2, then the formulae reduce to

(a) $t_2 = -\iota^*[S_{22}^*]^{-1} p_1^* x_1^*/p_2^*,$

(b) $g = -[G_K^*(t_2/p_2^*) + \iota^*(K^* - C^*)G_{KK}^*],$

$$\text{(43)}$$

where use has been made of the foreign budget constraint. (See problem set.) Here t_2 has the sign of $-x_1^*$ so that if the foreign nation imports good 1 and capital services, then $t_2 > 0$, meaning that the home nation taxes imports of good 2. In this case the sign of g is ambiguous. If the foreign nation exports both goods and imports capital services, then $t_2 < 0$ and $g > 0$, meaning that the home nation subsidizes imports of good 2 and taxes exports of capital services.

13.4.5. *Alternative formulation of foreign investment*

In the preceding model, capital and goods were treated asymmetrically. While this treatment is natural given the standard model formulation and while it corresponds to that discussed in most of the literature, it hides the fact that trade in goods and foreign ownership are formally identical phenomena. In this section they are treated symmetrically as in Kemp (1969).

Capital is a durable commodity, but its services are perishable as, according to our model formulation, are goods. A nation that produces more of a good than it demands will export it. Similarly, a nation which "produces" more capital services than it demands (for production of goods) will export them. How are capital services exported? In the current model, capital moves from one nation to another but ownership does not change and the income earned is returned to the owner. Thus, one can think of the owner of capital simply selling the services of capital in the foreign nation. Looked at in this way, trade in goods and capital services are the same.

Let

$$\Pi(p, r, L) \equiv \max_{y, K} \{py - rK : y \in Y(K, L)\} \tag{44}$$

be the revenue function where r is now defined to be the rental vector for capital. This is similar to the GDP function except that the rental bill is subtracted. Clearly, $\Pi_p(p, r, L)$ is the supply function for goods, $-\Pi_r(p, r, L)$ is the demand function for capital, and Π_L is the wage vector for labour. The consumption sector's expenditure function is $E(p, \mu) - rC$, where $E(p, \mu)$ is the expenditure function for goods and $-rC$ is the "expenditure" on capital services provided.[4] Setting expenditure equal to income m yields the indirect utility function $\mu = V(p, m + rC)$. The demand functions for goods are $\phi(p, m + rC) \equiv E_p(p, V(p, m + rC))$, while those for factors are $-C$.

The foreign nation has no taxes, so $m^* = \Pi^*(p^*, r^*, L^*)$. Its excess supply functions are therefore

(a) $\quad x^*(p^*, r^*) \equiv \Pi_p^*(p^*, r^*, L^*) - \phi^*(p^*, \Pi^*(p^*, r^*, L^*) + r^*C^*),$

$$\tag{45}$$

(b) $\quad \xi^*(p^*, r^*) \equiv \Pi_r^*(p^*, r^*, L^*) + C^*,$

which satisfy the balance of payments condition

$$p^*x^*(p^*, r^*) + r^*\xi^*(p^*, r^*) \equiv 0. \tag{46}$$

For the home nation

$$\Sigma(p, r, \mu, L) \equiv \Pi(p, r, L) - [E(p, \mu) - rC] \tag{47}$$

is the excess of income over expenditure ignoring taxes. If taxes on trade of goods and capital services are permitted, then the budget constraint may be written as

$$\Sigma(p, r, \mu, L) + (p - p^*)x^*(p^*, r^*) + (r - r^*)\xi^*(p^*, r^*) = 0. \tag{48}$$

[4]   It is assumed for simplicity that C does not enter the utility function.

The second term is the net tax revenue from goods, while the third is the net tax revenue from capital earnings abroad, i.e. from capital services traded. Notice that $\xi^*(p^*, r^*) \equiv C^* - K^*$, where $K^* = -\Pi_r^*(p^*, r^*)$.

The above treatment emphasizes the equivalence, in a formal sense, between trade in goods and in capital services. The only difference in the treatment is that capital is assumed to have a fixed supply whereas goods have demands depending upon prices and income. This gives $\xi^*(p^*, r^*)$ and $\Sigma_r(p, r, \mu, L)$, simpler structures than $x^*(p^*, r^*)$ and $\Sigma_p(p, r, \mu, L)$, which can be exploited.

The optimal policy is obtained by maximizing μ subject to (48) by an appropriate choice of p, p^*, r and r^*. The solution must satisfy the conditions

(a) $\quad -x^* + (p - p^*) x_p^* + (r - r^*) \xi_p^* = 0,$

$$(49)$$

(b) $\quad -\xi^* + (p - p^*) x_r^* + (r - r^*) \xi_r^* = 0,$

which, in view of (46), become (see problem set)

(a) $\quad px_p^* + r\xi_p^* = 0,$

$$(50)$$

(b) $\quad px_r^* + r\xi_r^* = 0.$

An alternative characterization is obtained by explicitly calculating the derivatives of x^* and ξ^* and substituting them into (50) to obtain:

(a) $\quad t\Sigma_{pp}^* - g\,\Pi_{rp}^* - \iota^* x^* = 0,$

$$(51)$$

(b) $\quad t\Pi_{pr}^* - g\,\Pi_{rr}^* - \iota^* \xi^* = 0,$

where $t \equiv p - p^*, g \equiv r^* - r$ and $\iota^* \equiv p\phi_m^*$ (see problem set).

If the tax on good 1 is set equal to zero and the foreign price of good 1 is fixed, (51) can be solved for (t_2, g). In the special case where there are two goods and one capital, the solution is

(a) $\quad t_2 = \dfrac{\iota^*}{\Delta}\, [x_2^* \Pi_{rr}^* - \xi^* \Pi_{r2}^*],$

$$(52)$$

(b) $\quad g \;\; = \dfrac{\iota^*}{\Delta}\, [x_2^* \Pi_{2r}^* - \xi^* S_{22}^*],$

where

$$\Delta \equiv \Sigma_{22}^* \Pi_{rr}^* - \Pi_{2r}^* \Pi_{r2}^* = - E_{22}^* \Pi_{rr}^* + [\Pi_{22}^* \Pi_{rr}^* - \Pi_{2r}^* \Pi_{r2}^*] > 0,$$

since E is concave and Π is convex in prices. It is known that $\Pi_{rr}^*, \Sigma_{22}^* > 0$ so, apart from the trade pattern, the only remaining term to sign is $\Pi_{r2}^* = \Pi_{2r}^*$. This is the effect of a unit change in r^* upon the supply of good 2, which is equal to the effect of a unit change in p_2^* upon the "net supply" of (negative of demand for) capital. It can be shown, in general, that $\Pi_{pr}^* = G_{pK}^* [G_{KK}^*]^{-1}$, so that in the special case under consideration $\Pi_{2r}^* = G_{2K}^* [G_{KK}^*]^{-1}$ has the opposite sign to G_{2K}^* and so is an indicator of whether industry 2 is capital intensive. The analysis of (52) and its relation to (39) and (40) is left to the reader.

13.5. Migration of labour

If individuals move from one nation to another they take their labour services, and possibly other factors, with them and consume in their new country of residence. In this respect the migration of labour is different from foreign ownership of capital as dealt with in the previous section, since owners of capital were assumed to remain in their native country. Consequently, special treatment of migration is warranted.

Migration is a very complicated topic and only a simple model will be dealt with here. Some of the complications ignored here are as follows. It is possible that the preferences of migrants change towards those of their adopted country. Also, they may bring with them factors other than labour. There may be factors which enter utility functions other than the consumption of goods, such as "a way of life" or scenery or weather. Finally, they may return some of their earnings to their home country, to relatives for example.

To simplify the model it is assumed that preferences of individuals are identical and homothetic throughout the world. This is more than sufficient for aggregation of the consumption sector, and avoids the question of whether preferences remain the same or change as a result of migration. Only labourers, who own no capital but supply one unit of labour, are allowed to migrate. The home nation is allowed to impose taxes on trade of goods, but the foreign country imposes no taxes.

An individual will move from one country to another if his utility level is thereby raised. If $E(p, \mu) = e(p)\mu$ is the expenditure function (common to everyone), the utility level of an individual living in the home country is $\mu_L = V(p, m_L) = m_L/e(p)$, where m_L is his disposable income and $e(p)$ can be interpreted as the "cost of living" index. His utility level in the foreign nation is $\mu_L^* = V(p^*, m_L^*) = m_L^*/e(p^*)$, where m_L^* is his disposable income there and p^* is the foreign price vector. The equilibrium condition for free migration is that $\mu_L = \mu_L^*$. In the foreign nation there are no taxes so his disposable income is $m_L^* = G_L^*(p^*, L^*, K^*)$. At home it is

$$m_L = [G_L(p, L, K) + \alpha\{(p - p^*)x^*\}], \tag{53}$$

where x^* is the foreign net export (equal to the home net import) vector, and α is the proportion of taxes redistributed to each labourer.

The equilibrium conditions for a trading world with labour migration and trade taxes are

$$S_p(p, \mu, L) + x^*(p^*, L^*) = 0, \tag{54}$$

$$S(p, \mu, L) - tS_p(p, u, L) = 0, \tag{55}$$

$$\mu_L^* = G_L^*(p^*, L^*, K^*)/e(p^*) =$$
$$= [G_L(p, L, K) + \alpha\, t\, x^*(p^*, L^*)]/e(p) = \mu_L, \tag{56}$$

$$L + L^* = L^w, \tag{57}$$

$$p = p^* + t, \tag{58}$$

where L^w is the given world supply of labour. The foreign net export functions are defined by

$$x^*(p^*, L^*) \equiv S_p^*(p^*, G^*(p^*, L^*, K^*)/e(p^*), L^*), \tag{59}$$

and $S(p, \mu, L) \equiv G(p, L, K) - E(p, \mu)$ with a similar definition for the foreign nation. System (54)–(58) consists of $2M + 3$ equations in $2M + 3$ unknowns, namely p, p^*, μ, L and L^*. The variable μ can be shown to be $\mu \equiv L\,\mu_L + K\,\mu_K \equiv [G(p, L, K) + \alpha tx^*(p^*, L^*)]/e(p)$, the simple sum of utilities of labourers and capitalists, and is the real income of the home nation. Eqs. (54) and (57) are the market equilibrium conditions for goods and labour. The budget constraint is given by (55). Eqs. (56) and (58) are the pricing or "zero profit" conditions for trade in goods and labour migration.

The model can be reduced in size by using (55) to eliminate μ, (57) to eliminate either L or L^*, and (58) to eliminate p or p^*. Also, it can be written in terms of $w \equiv G_L(p, L, K)$ and $w^* \equiv G_L^*(p^*, L^*, K^*)$ rather than L and L^*.

If there are no trade taxes, then it is clear than an individual will move to-wards higher wage rates and hence the equilibrium condition for migration (56) is that wages be equal in the two countries. If there are taxes, then the individual has to consider the cost of living, wages and the taxation distribution. Suppose, for example, that $\alpha = 0$, meaning that none of the trade tax revenue is returned to labour. Then (56) states that $w/e(p) = w^*/e(p^*)$, i.e. real wages have to be equal. This implies that $e(p/w) = e(p^*/w^*)$ but this does *not* imply that $p/w = p^*/w^*$. In other words, it is not necessary that the real wages in terms of each good are the same in the two countries, only that *the* real wage, defined in terms of the proper cost of living index $e(p)$, be the same in the two countries.

13.5.1. Effects of migration

Before dealing with the complete model, consider the case of an exogenous move-ment of labour from the foreign to the home nation. In this exercise (56) is ig-nored, and it is further assumed that $\alpha = 0$ for simplicity. We will obtain the ef-fects of this migration upon the terms of trade, and upon real incomes.

The market equilibrium conditions may be rewritten as

$$X(p^*, L, t) \equiv x(p, L, t) + x^*(p^*, L^*) = 0, \tag{60}$$

where

$$x(p, L, t) \equiv \{x: x = S_p(p, \mu, L), S(p, \mu, L) - tx = 0\} \tag{61}$$

is the net export function for the home nation, and $p = p^* + t$. As usual, one of the equations in (60) is redundant and the price vectors may be normalized. If the first good is the numeraire and $dt = 0$, then

$$dp_2 = dp_2^* = X_{22}^{-1}(x_{2L}^* - x_{2L})dL, \tag{62}$$

where, as usual, $p_2 = (p_2, ..., p_M)$ and

$$x_{2L}^* - x_{2L} = (G_{2L}^* - \phi_{2m}^* G_L^*) - (G_{2L} - \phi_{2m} G_L). \tag{63}$$

In the special case where there are only two goods, the condition for stability of the goods market for fixed labour endowments is $X_{22} > 0$. The effect of migra-tion upon the terms of trade therefore depends upon the sign of (63). If the home nation specializes in good 1 and the foreign nation specializes in good 2, then $G_{2L}^* = 0$ and $p_2 G_{2L}/G_L = 1$, so that $x_{2L}^* < 0 < x_{2L}$, if inferior goods are ruled out, and hence $x_{2L}^* - x_{2L} < 0$. In this case immigration to the home nation unambiguously reduces p_2^*, meaning that the terms of trade improve. If the reverse pattern of specialization occurs, then p_2^* rises so again the terms of trade for the home nation improve.

Suppose now that complete specialization does not occur. If there are only two factors and no joint production, then x_{2L} and x_{2L}^* will be positive or negative according to whether industry 2 is labour or capital intensive. Thus, a sufficient condition for a determinant sign for (63) is that there be a factor intensity reversal between the two nations. In this case the terms of trade of the home nation will improve if it exports the capital intensive good. More labour at fixed prices will reduce home exports but will raise foreign imports thus creating an excess demand and hence an increase in price for home exports. If there is no factor intensity reversal the effect upon the terms of trade depends upon the sign of $x_{2L}^* - x_{2L}$. This will be positive if the home nation specializes in good 1, and good 2 is labour intensive, or if the foreign nation specializes in good 1 and good 2 is capital intensive.

What is the effect of migration upon real incomes? In this model there are capitalists, who do not migrate, and labourers, who can migrate. The effects upon their (per capita) utility levels are

(a) $e \, \mathrm{d}\mu_L = (G_{L2} - \phi_{2m} G_L)\mathrm{d}p_2 + G_{LL} \mathrm{d}L,$

$$(64)$$

(b) $e \, \mathrm{d}\mu_K = (G_{K2} - \phi_{2m} G_K)\mathrm{d}p_2 + G_{KL} \mathrm{d}L,$

if $t = 0$, with similar expressions for foreign labourers and capitalists. The wage rate may fall ($G_{LL} \leq 0$) due to immigration at constant prices. Price changes will affect the wage rate and the cost of living. In the standard two-sector model immigration will reduce the utility levels of home workers if the first term in (64,a) is negative, i.e. if the price of the labour intensive product falls. This cannot occur if both nations are specialized in production, but will occur, for example, if the home nation produces both goods, the foreign nation specializes in good 1, and good 2 is labour intensive.

The aggregate real income or utility per worker is $\mu/L = [G(p, L, K) + tx^*(p^*, L^*)]/e(p)L$, which has significance if capital earnings and tax revenue are distributed equally among resident labourers. The change in aggregate utility per worker is given by

$$eL \, \mathrm{d}(\mu/L) = px_p^* \mathrm{d}p^* + [G_L - tx_L^* - (G + tx^*)/L]\mathrm{d}L, \qquad (65)$$

made up of the terms of trade effect and migration effect.

13.5.2. Optimal tax policies

In the previous section on foreign investment the taxes on trade in goods and foreign earnings of capital which maximized home nation utility were character-ized. The case of labour migration is more complicated since the population is endogenous. To simplify the problem suppose that all individuals are labourers, and that capital is collectively owned by domestic residents and its earnings are shared equally. In such a case all residents are identical and distributional prob-lems do not exist. The optimal policy for the home nation might be regarded as one which maximizes utility per capita for its residents. This objective gives no weight to current residents who may emigrate as a result of the policy undertaken.

   An expression for the effect of migration upon utility per worker is given by (65) above. It is, in fact, the total derivative of utility per worker with respect to independent changes in L, p^* and p, although dp does not appear since its coef-ficient is zero due to the market equilibrium condition for goods. Thus, the op-timal policy may be obtained by requiring the right-hand side of (65) to be zero for all dp^* and dL. The characterization of the optimal policy is therefore

(a) $\quad p\, x_p^*(p^*, L^*) = 0,$

$$\text{(66)}$$

(b) $\quad G_L(p, L, K) - tx_L^*(p^*, L^*) - [G(p, L, K) + tx^*(p^*, L^*)]/L = 0,$

where $L + L^* = L^w$. The first expression is the usual characterization of the op-timal trade tax vector, which is that p^* is chosen to maximize the tax revenue given the optimal choices of p and L. The second gives the optimal choice of L, i.e. that which maximizes disposable income per person given the optimal choices of p and p^*.

   By using (59) we obtain that

(a) $\quad x_p^* = S_{pp}^* - \phi_m^* S_p^*,$

$$\text{(67)}$$

(b) $\quad x_L^* = S_{pL}^* - \phi_m^* S_L^*.$

Hence an alternative characterization to (66) is

(a) $\quad p\, x_p^* = tS_{pp}^* - \iota^* S_p^* = 0,$

(b) $\quad G_L - (G + tx^*)/L = tx_L^*(p^*, L^*) =$

$$\text{(68)}$$

$$= t(S_{pL}^* - \phi_m^* G_L^*) = tS_{pL}^* + (1 - \iota^*)G_L^*,$$

where $\iota^* \equiv p\phi_m^*$ and $G_L^* = S_L^*$. If t is normalized so that $t_1 = 0$, then we may "solve" (68,a) for $t_2 = (t_2, ..., t_M)$ as

$$t_2 = \iota^* S_2^* (S_{22}^*)^{-1}. \tag{69}$$

The optimality condition for L is a balance between two contributions to average income for home residents. More workers in the home nation means that average income from production sources falls, since $G(p, L, K)$ is concave in L whence G_L is less than G/L. The optimality condition is that this reduction must be matched by an increase in average tax receipts. If the increase in average tax receipts is greater than the loss of average production income, then immigration should be encouraged; if less, then it should be discouraged.

Consider now the special case of the standard two-sector model with no joint production. In this case it is clear from (69) that the optimal policy is to tax trade, since S_{22}^*, $\iota^* > 0$. If good 2 is imported by the home nation $S_2^* > 0$, so $t_2 > 0$, whereas if it is exported $S_2^* < 0$ and $t_2 < 0$, meaning that exports are taxed. The condition on L becomes

$$G_L - G/L = t_2 x_2^*/L + t_2(S_{2L}^* - \phi_{2m}^* G_L^*). \tag{70}$$

The left-hand side of (70) is negative while $t_2 x_2^* > 0$, as explained above. Thus, a necessary condition for optimality is that $t_2(S_{2L}^* - \phi_{2m}^* G_L^*)$ be negative, which is the case if and only if the foreign nation's import good is labour intensive and export good is capital intensive. The required condition can be rewritten as

$$t_2 \left[\partial \ln G_L^* / \partial \ln p_2^* - c_2^* \right] = (G_L - G/L) - t_2 x_2^* < 0, \tag{71}$$

where $c_2^* \equiv p_2^* \phi_{2m}^*$ is the marginal propensity to consume good 2. If good 2 is exported by the foreign nation, then $t_2 > 0$ and (71) indicates the required condition on the Stolper–Samuelson elasticity in relation to c_2^*.

13.6. Notes on the literature

The modern literature on the effects of improvements in technology and growth in factor endowments upon a trading economy dates back to the pioneering work of Hicks (1953). Extensions and refinements were carried out by many others including Johnson (1955) and Findlay and Grubert (1959). The latter paper deals systematically with neutral and factor biased technical progress in the context of the standard two-product, two-factor model. Bhagwati (1958) established the possibility of immiserizing growth.

The effects of capital mobility and foreign ownership were discussed by Mac-Dougall (1960). More extensive treatments were given by Kemp (1962, 1966) and Jones (1967). See also Kemp (1969). Chipman's (1972) treatment makes use of duality theory and has influenced the presentation in the present chapter. Most emphasis has been on optimal trade policy in the presence of trade in goods and capital services. However, there has been some treatment of comparative static questions, such as the effects of changes in tariffs, in the above-mentioned references. See also Das and Lee (1979) and Woodland (1981). For the implications of the presence of foreign-owned factors of production in the evaluation of the welfare effects of changes, such as in world prices or the movement to free trade, see Bhagwati and Brecher (1980) and Svensson (1980).

There is less literature on labour mobility. Mundell (1957) and others were concerned with the possibility that factor mobility could be a substitute for trade, in the same way that trade is a substitute for factor mobility under factor price equalization. Rodriguez (1975) extends the Mundell model to allow for many products and factors.

Amano (1966) deals with the terms of trade effects of both capital and labour mobility, while Chipman (1971) and Uekawa (1972) deal with the conditions for incomplete specialization in production when one factor is perfectly mobile. Neary (1980) uses duality theory to provide a general treatment of perfect factor mobility and then derives results for a sector specific factor model.

Problems

1. Illustrate a case of immiserizing growth on a diagram. Also, illustrate the proposition that growth cannot be immiserizing if optimal trade taxes are always imposed.

2. (a) Prove that product neutral growth and homothetic preferences imply that the trade vector expands at fixed world prices.
   (b) If there are just two goods show that the terms of trade must deteriorate, and hence that the foreign nation gains.
   (c) Can such growth be welfare reducing for the home nation?

3. (a) Show that $-S_\mu d\mu - S_\mu^* d\mu^* = S_a da = G_a da$ in equilibrium, where $S \equiv G(p, v, a) - E(p, \mu)$, so growth cannot make all nations worse off. If there are just two goods and good 2 is exported show that
   (b) both nations will gain from growth in the home nation if $c_2^* > q > c_2$, and
   (c) the foreign nation loses and the home nation gains if $c_2 > q$.

4. (a) Derive eq. (6).

(b) Derive eqs. (11) and (12).

(c) Derive eqs. (13) and (14).

5. Consider a two-product, two-factor model of production with (biased) factor augmenting technical change in one industry. In particular let $c^1(w_1, w_2)$ and $c^2(w_1, w_2/a)$ be the unit cost functions.

(a) Describe the nature of technical change defined by a change in a.

(b) Write down the first-order conditions for the solution of the minimum factor payments problem $G(p, v, a) \equiv \min_w \{wv: c^j(\cdot) \geqslant p_j, j = 1, ..., M; w \geqslant 0\}$.

(c) Use these to calculate G_a as $G_a = p_2 y_2 \theta_{22}/a$ and hence $q \equiv \partial \ln G_a/\partial \ln p_2 = \partial \ln(p_2 y_2)/\partial \ln p_2 + \partial \ln \theta_{22}/\partial \ln p_2$, where $\theta_{22} \equiv w_2 c_2^2/p_2$ is the cost share of factor 2 in industry 2.

(d) Derive $\partial \ln \theta_{22}/\partial \ln p_2 = \theta_{12}(1 - \sigma_2) \partial \ln(w_2/w_1)/\partial \ln p_2$, where σ_2 is the elasticity of substitution between factors in industry 2 and $\theta_{12} = 1 - \theta_{22}$.

(e) Using (d) and noting that $\partial \ln p_2 y_2/\partial \ln p_2 = \partial \ln y_2/\partial \ln p_2 + 1$, establish conditions for the foreign nation to gain from an increase in a, and for the home nation to gain.

6. Under what conditions on the technology is neutral factor augmenting technical change in industry j equivalent to product augmenting technical change in industry j?

7. In the case of trade in two goods and one capital service, the optimal tax formulae are often expressed in ad valorem elasticity form as in Kemp (1966), Jones (1967) and Chipman (1972).

(a) Use (30,c) to obtain (for the case where $t_1 = 0$) the formulae $\tau_2 \equiv t_2/p_2^* = (1 + \epsilon_2^*)/\xi_{22}^*$ and $\rho \equiv (G_K - G_K^*)/G_K^* = - (\tau_2 \gamma_2^* + \iota^* \delta^*)$, where $\gamma_i^* \equiv G_{Ki}^* p_i^*/G_K^*, \delta^* \equiv (K^* - C^*)G_{KK}^*/G_K^*$, and $\epsilon_i^* \equiv - (K^* - C^*)G_{Ki}^*/x_i^*$.

(b) Express the optimal taxes in ad valorem form based upon domestic rather than foreign prices.

(c) Interpret these formulae.

(d) Express (39) in ad valorem elasticity form as $\tau_2 = \iota^*(1 + \epsilon_2^*)/\bar{\xi}_{22}^*$, where $\bar{\xi}_{ij}^* \equiv S_{ij}^* p_j^*/S_i^*$.

8. Consider the situation in problem 7.

(a) Show that $x_{ij}^* = S_{ij}^* - \phi_{im}^* [x_j^* - (K^* - C^*)G_{Kj}^*]$ (eq. (33)).

(b) Jones (1967, p. 7) claims that $\xi_{22}^* < 0$ and hence $x_{22}^* > 0$ if $x_2^* < 0$ (foreign nation imports good 2) and no good is inferior. Use the expression in (d) for x_{ij}^* to evaluate this claim (which is true if $K^* = C^*$ as in the standard model with no foreign ownership).

(c) Chipman (1972, p. 236) claims that $x_{22}^* > 0$ if $x_2^* < 0$ and preferences are homothetic (so $\phi_{im} m/\phi_i = 1$). Evaluate this claim (also true when $K^* = C^*$).

(d) Use the results in (a) and (d) of problem 7 to show that *under the optimal tax structure* $\xi_{22}^* < 0$ if $x_2^* < 0$ and $\iota^* \equiv p\phi_m^* > 0$ (a sufficient condition for which is that no good is inferior).

9. In the alternative treatment of optimal taxes with trade in goods and capital services use was made of the functions $\Pi(p, r, L)$ and $\Sigma(p, r, u, L)$ defined by (44) and (47), whereas the original treatment used $G(p, L, K)$ and $S(p, u, L, K)$. Show that their second derivatives are related by

(a) $\Sigma_{rr} = \Pi_{rr} = -G_{KK}^{-1}$;

(b) $\Sigma_{pr} = \Pi_{pr} = G_{pK}G_{KK}^{-1}$;

(c) $\Pi_{pp} = G_{pp} - G_{pK}G_{KK}^{-1}G_{Kp}$;

(d) $\Sigma_{pp} = \Pi_{pp} - E_{pp} = S_{pp} - S_{pK}S_{KK}^{-1}S_{Kp} = S_{pp} - G_{pK}G_{KK}^{-1}G_{Kp}$ if G_{KK}^{-1} exists.

10. (a) Use (46) to rewrite (49) as (50).

(b) Derive (51).

(c) Use the results of problem 9 to show the equivalence between (52) and (39)–(40) for the case of trade in two goods and one capital service.

11. (a) Derive the effect of an exogenous increase in foreign investment upon the terms of trade for the investing nation in a model of free trade in two goods.

(b) What is the stability condition in this model?

(c) For what situations is the effect of the change in foreign investment upon the terms of trade unambiguous.

(d) Calculate the effect upon the utility of the investing nation from an initial situation of free trade in capital services.

(e) Hence, consider the optimal strategy if trade taxes on goods are not permitted, but if taxes on foreign capital earnings are allowed.

12. (a) The optimal tax problem with trade in goods and capital services may be expressed as $\max_{p, p^*, K} \{u(G_p(p, L, K) + x^*(p^*, K^W - K))\}$, where $u(z)$ is the direct utility function. By solving this problem derive (32) and (36).

(b) The optimal tax problem with trade in goods and labour mobility may be expressed as $\max_{p, p^*, L} \{u((G_p(p, L, K) + x^*(p^*, L^W - L))/L)\}$. By solving this problem derive (66).

13. Consider free trade in two goods and capital services in a model without intermediate or joint outputs and two factors, labour and capital, both of which are necessary in production of each good.

(a) Write down the profit maximization and factor (two labour and one capital) market clearing conditions in both nations in terms of unit cost functions.

(b) Suppose that world prices for goods are given. Is it likely that both nations are diversified?

(c) Suppose both nations are diversified in production and all factors are positively priced. Show that the factor market equilibrium conditions are a set of three linear equations in four unknown output levels. Then show that if $\Delta \equiv a_{11}a_{22} - a_{12}a_{21} \neq 0$ or $\Delta^* \equiv a^*_{11}a^*_{22} - a^*_{12}a^*_{21} \neq 0$ (where a_{ij} is the output of factor i per unit of output j) that the world production possibility set for goods is linear over a range (i.e. output levels are nonunique) (Chipman, 1971).

References

Amano, A. (1966) "International factor movements and the terms of trade", *Canadian Journal of Economics and Political Science* 32-4, November, 510–519.

Bhagwati, J. (1958) "Immiserizing growth: A geometric note", *Review of Economic Studies* 25, 201–205.

Bhagwati, J.N. and R.A. Brecher (1980) "National welfare in an open economy in the presence of foreign-owned factors of production", *Journal of International Economics* 10-1, February, 103–115.

Chipman, J.S. (1971) "International trade with capital mobility: A substitution theorem", in: J.N. Bhagwati, R.W. Jones, R.A. Mundell and J. Vanek (eds.), *Trade, Balance of Payments and Growth* (Amsterdam: North-Holland), pp. 201–237.

Chipman, J.S. (1972) "The theory of exploitative trade and investment policies: A reformulation and synthesis", in: *International Economics and Development* (New York: Academic Press), pp. 209–244.

Das, S.P. and S.-D. Lee (1979) "On the theory of international trade with capital mobility", *International Economic Review* 20-1, February, 119–132.

Findlay, R.E. and H. Grubert (1959) "Factor intensities, technological progress and the terms of trade", *Oxford Economic Papers* 11-1, February, 111–121.

Hicks, J.R. (1953) "An inaugural lecture", *Oxford Economic Papers* 5, June, 117–135.

Johnson, H.G. (1955) "Economic expansion and international trade", *The Manchester School of Economic and Social Studies* 23-2, May, 95–112.

Jones, R.W. (1967) "International capital movements and the theory of tariffs and trade", *Quarterly Journal of Economics* 81-1, February, 1–38.

Kemp, M.C. (1962) "Foreign investment and the national advantage", *Economic Record* 38-81, March, 56–62.

Kemp, M.C. (1966) "The gain from international trade and investment: A neo-Heckscher–Ohlin approach", *American Economic Review* 55-4, September, 788–809.

Kemp, M.C. (1969) *The Pure Theory of International Trade and Investment* (Princeton: Prentice-Hall).

MacDougall, G.D.A. (1960) "The benefits and costs of private investment from abroad: A theoretical approach", *Economic Record* 36-73, March, 13–35.

Mundell, R.A. (1957) "International trade and factor mobility", *American Economic Review* 47, June, 321–335.

Neary, P. (1980) "International factor mobility, minimum wage rates and factor price equalization: A synthesis", unpublished paper, July.

Rodriguez, C.A. (1975) "International factor mobility, nontraded goods, and the equalization of prices of goods and factors", *Econometrica* 43, 115–124.

Svensson, L.E.O. (1980) "National welfare in the presence of foreign-owned factors of production: A note on the dual approach", Seminar paper 150, Institute for International Economic Studies, University of Stockholm.

Uekawa, Y. (1972) "On the existence of incomplete specialization in international trade with capital mobility", *Journal of International Economics* 2, 1–22.

Woodland, A.D. (1981) "Stability, capital mobility and trade", forthcoming in *International Economic Review*.

CHAPTER 14

TRADE AND GROWTH: A DYNAMIC APPROACH

14.1. Introduction

The model that has been used in previous chapters is static in the sense that no treatment is given to the passage of time. The endowments of factors were held fixed, or were allowed to vary as a function of various economic variables within the period. Only in the preceding chapter did changes in basic endowments occur and these were exogenously given or not related to time. Thus, even there the approach was static. Attention is now turned to changes which take place through the passage of time and directly as a result of economic forces. The interaction between international trade and economic growth is the main concern.

Over time there are many aspects of the economy which may change. The most obvious is that there may be changes in the endowments of labour and capital. In most growth models the growth of the labour force is usually taken to be given exogenously by demographic forces. However, it may well be that decisions regarding procreation are based upon economic factors, an idea which is at the heart of Malthus' theory of population. In addition, the amounts of different types of labour (such as unskilled, skilled, scientific) may be determined by prior decisions on education and these may be influenced by economic factors. That is, there may be investment in human capital. The same is true of physical capital. The current level of capital stock depends upon previous investment decisions by firms. The state of technology may also change. Typically, technological change is treated as an exogenous phenomenon, but it seems evident that it is partly, if not completely, the result of conscious decisions to invest in research. Finally, there may be changes in the preferences of consumers as the result of advertising, demonstration effects, or exogenous factors.

Economic dynamics is concerned with the changing structure of the economy over time. In this and the following chapter we will focus upon the dynamics as a consequence of capital formation, but some attention will also be given to the case where there are technological improvements. The endowments of capital may increase as a result of decisions to divert part of current productive capacity to the production of capital. The willingness of consumers to allow such a reduction in current consumption, depends upon their recognition that consumption may be higher in future periods as a result of having larger endowments of capital then. Thus, it is the saving decision of consumers that is the crucial determinant of how fast the capital stock is increased (or decreased). In the following section we will assume that consumers have perfect foresight in making current decisions and that they have a very long horizon. In the absence of uncertainty, this is the intertemporal counterpart of the static utility maximization hypothesis used in previous chapters.

14.2. Capital accumulation and trade

In what follows attention is focused on an economy which trades competitively in the world market, and which can alter its capital stock by foregoing some current consumption and diverting that expenditure to the purchase of newly produced capital goods. These may be purchased from local producers or from the world market. The accumulation of capital will shift the production possibility set outward and hence result in a different production mix and a different trade vector. It is possible that the pattern of trade might change. Certainly, the product price vector will change as will decisions about consumption, saving and investment. The economy thus evolves over time, and it is this evolution which we wish to examine. It is also of interest to examine the long-run solution or "steady state" if it indeed exists. The effects of trade taxes upon the steady-state solution and upon the dynamic path to that solution are also of interest.

14.2.1. The model

Let the endowment vector be partitioned as $v = (L, K)$, where K is the capital stock and L is a vector of non-capital endowments, which will be referred to as "labour".[1] Clearly, the capital stock might include human capital, and labour might include other inputs such as land, but the terms "capital" and "labour" will be maintained nevertheless. Let outputs be partitioned as $y = (y_1, y_2)$ with

---

[1]   Extension of the model to include several capital goods is straightforward but the exposition is simpler if attention is restricted to one capital good. The following chapter deals with heterogeneous capital goods.

y_2 being the production of capital goods. The production price vector is $p = (p_1, p_2)$ and the gross national product function is denoted $G(p, K) = G(p_1, p_2, K)$, where explicit reference to the labour input vector is ignored since it is assumed to remain constant.[2] Each variable has a time profile written, for example, as $K(\tau)$, $y(\tau)$, $p(\tau)$, etc. Sometimes it will be convenient to drop explicit reference to time, but the dependence on time should be remembered.

Capital accumulation occurs if gross investment exceeds depreciation. In what follows it is assumed that capital is subject to an exogenously determined geometric rate of depreciation, δ. If $z_2(\tau)$ denotes gross capital formation, then net investment or the change in the capital stock is given as

$$\dot{K}(\tau) \equiv dK(\tau)/d\tau = z_2(\tau) - \delta K(\tau), \tag{1}$$

where the dot above a variable denotes a time derivative. If $z_2(\tau)$ were known for all $\tau \geqslant 0$, eq. (1) together with an initial stock $K(0)$ would determine the time profile for capital $K(\tau)$. Of course, $z_2(\tau)$ is endogenous and has to be explained by economic behaviour.

The consumer receives income $G(p, K)$ and has to decide how to allocate it among the various consumer goods and capital. This raises several possible formulations of the model. One approach is to assume some ad hoc saving rule based upon current variables. For example, a common assumption is that saving is a fixed proportion s of total income. In this case saving is $S(\tau) = s\, G(\tau)$, where $G(\tau) = G(p(\tau), K(\tau))$, and so gross investment is simply given by

$$p_2(\tau)\, z_2(\tau) = S(\tau). \tag{2}$$

This saving rule thus determines $z_2(\tau)$ and hence the time profit $K(\tau)$. However, this approach ignores the possible influence of economic variables upon the saving rate, and they only influence the course of the economy via the GNP function. Also, it assumes that consumers are not utility maximizers. Accordingly, an alternative approach is followed.

The approach used here assumes that consumers maximize an intertemporal utility function subject to an intertemporal budget constraint. The consumer makes his current saving decision based upon how it will affect the complete time profile of his consumption vector $z_1(\tau)$. This profile determines his level of utility, which he wants to maximize. If he saves nothing today, then future income and hence consumption possibilities will be lower. If he saves all his current income, then there will be no present consumption but future income and

---

[2] The extension to exogenous growth in L is straightforward.

hence consumption will be higher. Thus, the consumer needs his intertemporal utility function to evaluate these different consumption profiles. Also, he needs to know the consequences of his actions. That is to say, he needs to know the complete profile of consumer goods' prices, $p_1(\tau)$, and of income $G(\tau) = G(p(\tau)$, $K(\tau))$. The latter depends, of course, on his saving decisions. In short, it is assumed that the consumer follows an optimal or "rational" saving policy. This is the intertemporal counterpart to the static utility-maximizing consumer.

To simplify the model it is assumed, as is customary in the literature, that the intertemporal utility function is of the "additive form":

$$U(\{z_1(\tau)\}) = \int_0^\infty e^{-\rho\tau} u(z_1(\tau))\,d\tau, \tag{3}$$

where $\{z_1(\tau)\}$ denotes the complete time profile of $z_1(\tau)$. In (3) $u(z_1)$ is the instantaneous utility function and ρ is the rate of time preference which, if $\rho > 0$, gives a geometrically declining weight to utility obtained further into the future. The consumer chooses a consumption profile $z_1(\tau) \geqslant 0$ and the gross investment profile $z_2(\tau) \geqslant 0$ to maximize (3) subject to the budget constraint

$$p_1(\tau) z_1(\tau) + p_2(\tau) z_2(\tau) = G(p(\tau), K(\tau)) \tag{4}$$

and the capital accumulation, eq. (1). Notice that (4) rules out borrowing from abroad to finance expenditure, meaning that a zero balance of trade is assumed. New capital goods can be imported or exported, but once installed as capital stock they cannot be traded internationally.

The assumption that the utility functional is maximized over an infinite horizon requires some comment. The difficulty that arises if the time horizon T is finite is that the optimal solution will have a zero capital stock at time T, unless it is fixed at some arbitrary positive level or a positive value is placed upon it in the objective function. The infinite horizon model avoids this arbitrariness and, indeed, yields an optimal value for capital at any time t. Moreover, the infinite time horizon can be justified if it is supposed that the utility of each generation depends upon the utility of the following generation in addition to its own consumption vector. This means that the utility functional is recursively separable, a condition required for planning to be intertemporally consistent.[3] The functional (3) has this property, being "additive" in current and future utility, the

---

[3]   For a discussion of the notion of intertemporally consistent plans and their relationship to recursively separable utility functions, see Blackorby, Primont and Russell (1978, ch. 10).

latter being weighted by $e^{-\rho\tau}$. It is further noted that all generations are assumed to have the same instantaneous utility function.

The consumer's consumption–saving problem as formulated above is an optimal control problem which may be solved using Pontryagin's "maximum principle".[4] The (present value) Hamiltonian for this problem is

$$H(\tau) = u(z_1(\tau)) + \lambda(\tau)\,[z_2(\tau) - \delta K(\tau)], \tag{5}$$

where $\lambda(\tau)$ is the "co-state" variable in present value terms. The maximum principle states that a necessary condition for the controls $z_1(\tau) \geqslant 0$ and $z_2(\tau) \geqslant 0$ to be optimal is that there exists a $\lambda(\tau)$ such that the controls maximize the Hamiltonian at each point in time τ, subject to (4). This is equivalent to choosing $z_1(\tau) \geqslant 0$ and $z_2(\tau) \geqslant 0$ subject to (4) to maximize

$$U^*(z_1(\tau), z_2(\tau); \lambda(\tau)) \equiv u(z_1(\tau)) + \lambda(\tau)\,z_2(\tau). \tag{6}$$

This is an ordinary (static) utility-maximizing problem which can be solved in the usual manner, yielding ordinary demand functions for consumer goods and the investment good at each instant. The role of $\lambda(\tau)$ is now evident. It represents the value of a unit of an investment good in terms of the *future* utility that it will yield. Knowing $\lambda(\tau)$ the consumer can decide on the allocation of his current budget.

Let the indirect utility function corresponding to (6) under constraint (4) be $V^0(p_1, p_2, G; \lambda)$ and let $W(\lambda, K; p) \equiv V^0(p_1, p_2, G(p, K); \lambda)$. Of course, this function has a special structure due to the additive nature of (6). This may be exploited by a two-step budgeting procedure as follows. Define expenditure on consumer goods $E(\tau)$ by

$$E(\tau) + p_2(\tau)\,z_2(\tau) = G(\tau). \tag{7}$$

Then $u(z_1)$ can be maximized subject to $p_1 z_1 = E$ and $z_1 \geqslant 0$ which yields the indirect utility function $V(p_1, E)$. Having optimally allocated expenditure among consumer goods, the problem reduces to one of finding the optimal total expenditure. Thus, an alternative definition of $W(\lambda, K; p)$ is

---

[4] The primary reference is Pontryagin et al. (1962). For an introduction to the mathematics of dynamic optimization theory see Intriligator (1971). A convenient survey of theorems on optimal control is provided by Long and Vousden (1977).

$$W(\lambda, K; p) \equiv \max_{z_2} \{V(p_1, G(p,K) - p_2 z_2) + \lambda z_2 :$$
$$0 \leqslant p_2 z_2 \leqslant G(p,K)\}, \tag{8}$$

where (7) has been used to eliminate E. This yields the demand function for investment goods $z_2 = z_2(\lambda, K; p)$. The first-order conditions defining this function are

(a) $\quad V_E(p_1, G(p,K) - p_2 z_2) = \lambda/p_2, \quad 0 \leqslant z_2 \leqslant G(p,K)/p_2,$

(b) $\qquad\qquad\qquad\qquad\qquad > \lambda/p_2, \quad z_2 = 0, \tag{9}$

(c) $\qquad\qquad\qquad\qquad\qquad < \lambda/p_2, \quad z_2 = G(p,K)/p_2,$

where $V_E(p,E) \equiv \partial V(p,E)/\partial E$. Condition (9) allows for corner solutions. More details regarding the investment function will be provided below.

The maximized Hamiltonian may be expressed in terms of W as

$$H^0(\lambda, K) \equiv W(\lambda, K; p) - \lambda \delta K. \tag{10}$$

The necessary conditions for a solution to the optimal control problem are completed by adding the equations of motion

$$\dot{K}(\tau) = H^0_\lambda(\lambda(\tau), K(\tau)) = W_\lambda(\lambda(\tau), K(\tau)) - \delta K(\tau) \equiv \theta(\lambda, K) \tag{11}$$

and

$$\dot{\lambda}(\tau) = \rho\lambda(\tau) - H^0_K(\lambda(\tau), K(\tau)) = (\rho + \delta)\lambda(\tau)$$
$$- W_K(\lambda(\tau), K(\tau)) \equiv \psi(\lambda, K), \tag{12}$$

together with the initial and transversality conditions

(a) $\quad K(0) = K_0,$

(b) $\quad \lim_{\tau\to\infty} e^{-\rho\tau}\lambda(\tau) \geqslant 0; \quad \lim_{\tau\to\infty} e^{-\rho\tau}\lambda(\tau)K(\tau) = 0. \tag{13}$

Condition (13,a) is simply that the economy begins with capital stock K_0. Condition (13,b) is the infinite horizon counterpart of the finite time horizon (T) condition that $e^{-\rho\tau}\lambda(T) = 0$ if there is no utility attached to the terminal stock $K(T)$.

Equations $(11)-(13)$ determine the time paths of $K(\tau)$ and $\lambda(\tau)$. By solving them we obtain $\lambda_0 = \lambda(0)$, which can then be used instead of $(13,b)$ to plot the paths of K and λ and all the control variables. That is to say, since $\lambda(0)$ depends on the complete future the whole optimal path has to be solved backwards to obtain $\lambda(0)$. Once known, then the forward solution of the same path can be characterized. This is the essential aspect of the optimal saving decision, and which makes the analysis of growth models complicated. It should be contrasted with the case of an ad hoc constant saving ratio model in which the future is irrelevant to the saving decision and which may therefore be solved forwards.

14.2.2. Properties of W and z_2

To consider (11) and (12) further, the derivatives of $W(\lambda, K; p)$ are needed. It is easily shown that

$$W_\lambda(\lambda, K; p) = V_\lambda^0(p_1, p_2, G; \lambda) = z_2(\lambda, K; p), \tag{14}$$

$$W_K(\lambda, K; p) = V_G^0(p_1, p_2, G; \lambda) G_K(p, K) = [V_E(p_1, E) + \kappa] G_K(p, K), \tag{15}$$

where $E \equiv G(p, K) - p_2 z_2(\lambda, K; p)$ and $\kappa \equiv \max\{0, \lambda/p_2\}$, but the demonstration is relegated to the problem set. Thus, the investment function is found by simply differentiating W with respect to λ. The net export functions, X, can be obtained almost as simply by applying Roy's identity to obtain:

$$X(\lambda, K; p) = W_p(\lambda, K; p)/V_G^0(p, G; \lambda). \tag{16}$$

The nature of the investment function is of interest for the analysis below. It is convenient to first define the three regions in (λ, K) space corresponding to the three possible solution types for z_2 indicated in (9). The boundary (A) between regions (a) and (b) occurs when $z_2 = 0$ is a solution to $(9,a)$. The boundary (B) between regions (a) and (c) occurs when $z_2 = G(p, K)/p_2$ is a solution to $(9,a)$. Formally, these boundaries are sets of (λ, K) for which

(a) $V_E(p_1, G(p, K)) = \lambda/p_2$, A,

(b) $V_E(p_1, 0) = \lambda/p_2$, B. $\tag{17}$

It is noted that B and hence region (c) do not exist if $V_E(p_1, 0) = \infty$, as is often assumed. Curve B, if it exists, is parallel to the K axis, while A is downward-sloping, as illustrated in fig. 14.1.

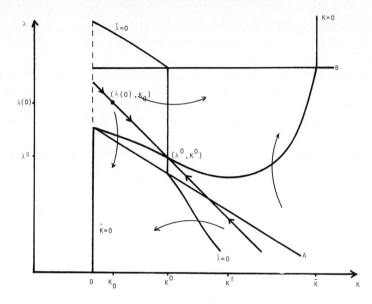

Figure 14.1

The derivatives of $z_2(\lambda, K; p)$ are given by

$$W_{\lambda\lambda} = z_{2\lambda}(\lambda, K; p) = \begin{cases} 0, & \text{in regions (b) and (c),} \\ (-p_2^2 V_{EE})^{-1}, & \text{in region (a);} \end{cases}$$ (18)

$$W_{\lambda K} = z_{2K}(\lambda, K; p) = \begin{cases} 0, & \text{in region (b),} \\ G_K(p, K)/p_2, & \text{in regions (a) and (c).} \end{cases}$$ (19)

(See problem set.) Also,

$$W_{KK} = \begin{cases} V_E G_{KK} + G_K^2 V_{EE}, & \text{in region (b),} \\ V_E G_{KK}, & \text{in regions (a) and (c),} \end{cases}$$ (20)

while $W_{K\lambda} = W_{\lambda K}$ and is therefore given by (19).

It is assumed that $V(p_1, E)$ is strictly concave in E (diminishing marginal utility of income) so $V_{EE} < 0$ and, of course, that $V_E > 0$. $G(p, K)$ is concave in K, but not necessarily strictly so.

14.2.3. Phase diagram

These results may be used to obtain a phase diagram which illustrates the nature of the solution to (11)–(13). At this point it is assumed that the exogenous variables are constant through time. In fig. 14.1 boundaries A and B have been drawn. Also drawn are curves indicating the loci of (λ, K) points for which $\dot{K} = 0$ and $\dot{\lambda} = 0$. Consider each region in turn. Region (a) is the area between A and B in which there is an interior solution for z_2. Here $V_E = \lambda/p_2$ so (12) may be written as

$$\dot{\lambda}(\tau) = [\rho + \delta - G_K(p_1, K(\tau))/p_2] \lambda(\tau), \tag{12'}$$

which is zero if $\lambda(\tau) = 0$ or if $\rho + \delta = G_K(p, K)/p_2$. For the latter case let K^0 be the solution. The $\dot{\lambda} = 0$ curve is vertical at $K = K^0$. The slope of the $\dot{K} = 0$ curve is

$$\left.\frac{d\lambda}{dK}\right|_{\dot{K}=0} = \frac{\delta - G_K(p, K)/p_2}{z_{2\lambda}(\lambda, K; p)}, \quad \text{region (a)}, \tag{21}$$

where $z_{2\lambda} > 0$ using (18) and the assumption that $V_{EE} < 0$. If the capital stock for which the numerator in (21) is zero is K^δ, then the $\dot{K} = 0$ curve has a minimum at K^δ. (The numerator is positive for $K > K^\delta$ if G_K falls with K, as is assumed in fig. 14.1.) Notice that $K^\delta > K^0$ unless $G(p, K)$ has kinks.

In region (b) $z_2(\lambda, K; p) \equiv 0$, so $\dot{K} = -\lambda K = 0$ only at $K = 0$. The slope of the $\dot{\lambda} = 0$ curve is

$$\left.\frac{d\lambda}{dK}\right|_{\dot{\lambda}=0} = \frac{V_E G_{KK} + G_K^2 V_{EE}}{\rho + \delta} < 0, \quad \text{region (b)}. \tag{22}$$

The difference between the slopes of $\dot{\lambda} = 0$ and A curves is

$$\left.\frac{d\lambda}{dK}\right|_{\dot{\lambda}=0} - \left.\frac{d\lambda}{dK}\right|_A = \frac{V_E G_{KK} + p_2 V_{EE} G_K G_K/p_2 - (\rho + \delta)}{\rho + \delta}, \tag{23}$$

which is non-positive for $K \geqslant K^0$. Thus, the A curve is flatter than the $\dot{\lambda} = 0$ curve in this region.

In region (c) $z_2(\lambda, K; p) \equiv G(p, K)/p_2$, so

$$\dot{K}(\tau) = G(p, K(\tau))/p_2 - \delta K(\tau), \quad \text{region (c)}, \tag{24}$$

which is zero for some $\bar{K} > K^{\delta}$, irrespective of the value of λ. The slope of the $\dot{\lambda} = 0$ curve is

$$\left.\frac{d\lambda}{dK}\right|_{\dot{\lambda}=0} = \frac{V_E G_{KK}}{\rho + \delta} \leqslant 0, \quad \text{region (c)}. \tag{25}$$

This completes the derivation of the $\dot{\lambda} = 0$ and $\dot{K} = 0$ curves in fig. 14.1. Also shown are arrows indicating the direction of movement of (λ, K).

Of particular interest is the steady-state solution where $\dot{\lambda} = 0$ and $\dot{K} = 0$ occur simultaneously. Fig. 14.1 shows the steady-state point (λ^0, K^0) to be in region (a). Since $K^0 < \bar{K}$, the intersection of the curves cannot take place in region (c). Also, if $K^0 > 0$ (it can be zero), then the intersection cannot take place in region (b). The optimal path leading to (λ^0, K^0) is shown in fig. 14.1. If $K(0)$ is the initial stock of capital, then $\lambda(0)$ is the appropriate value of λ at $\tau = 0$. With $\lambda(0)$ and $K(0)$ the forward solution to (11) and (12) takes the economy to (λ^0, K^0). Any other choice for $\lambda(0)$ would put the economy on a path which would veer away from (λ^0, K^0) and eventually result in a zero capital stock or a capital stock of $\bar{K}$ which is maintained by devoting all income to investment with zero consumption.

The optimal path towards K^0 is intuitively plausible. If the capital stock is below K^0, then a high value, λ, is placed upon saving to encourage the growth of capital. Conversely, if the stock is above K^0, a low value is placed upon saving and current consumption is encouraged.

14.2.4. Special cases

It was assumed in the preceding analysis the $V(p_1, E)$ was strictly concave in E so that $V_{EE} < 0$. However, if the instantaneous utility function is linearly homogeneous, then $V_{EE} \equiv 0$. In this case $V_E(p_1, E) = \bar{V}_E(p_1)$ is a constant and so the solution for z_2 in (9) will belong to region (a) for only one value of λ, namely $p_2 V_E(p_1)$. In this case the solution for z_2 is not unique but is the complete interval $[0, G(p, K)/p_2]$. The A curve becomes horizontal at $\lambda = p_2 \bar{V}_E(p_1) = \lambda^0$ and is coincident with B. That is, region (a) shrinks to the line A. Along A in the interval $[0, \bar{K}]$, K is not unique. One possibility is to set $\lambda(0) = \lambda^0$ and arbitrarily choose z_2 to eventually get to K^0. Another is to set $\lambda(0) > \lambda^0$ and devote all income to investment until K^0 is reached in the case where $K(0) < K^0$. If $K(0) > K^*$, then one could set $\lambda(0) < \lambda^0$ and consume all income until K^0 is reached. Once K^0 is reached, $z_2 = \delta K^0$ is chosen to maintain a constant capital stock.

If the economy consists of separate industries there arises the possibility that

$G_{KK} = 0$, which occurs in the cone of diversification. This means that $G_K(p, K)$ is a constant in the interval $[K_1, K_2]$ describing the diversification cone. Hence, a special configuration of exogenous variables is required to have K^0 in this interval, and if it is, then the solution for K^0 is the whole interval. If this is the case, then $\lambda = 0$ for any $K \in [K_1, K_2]$ and hence the $\dot{\lambda} = 0$ curve becomes a region here. There is then an infinity of steady-state solutions. If $K(0)$ is not in this interval, then production specialization will occur in the steady-state. If $K(0)$ is in this interval, then the optimal policy is to choose $\lambda(0) = \lambda^0$ so that the capital stock remains constant. There is no incentive to change the stock of capital since the future utility gain equals the present utility loss. Of course, it may occur that K^0 is not in the interval $[K_1, K_2]$ in which case specialization will occur irrespective of the initial capital stock.

The reader may wish to fill in the details of the preceding discussion by drawing the appropriate phase diagrams. What happens if $G_{KK} = 0$ in an interval $[K_1, K_2]$ *and* $V_{EE} \equiv 0$?

14.2.5. Comparative statics of the steady state

What are the long-run consequences of changes in the exogenous variables? For example, if the world price of investment goods increases permanently, what will happen to the stock of capital, the level of consumption of consumer goods, and the level of investment once all adjustments to the change have taken place? To answer questions such as these a comparative statics analysis can be applied to the steady-state solutions.

The steady-state solutions in region (a) are defined as solutions to

$$z_2(\lambda, K; p) - \delta K = 0, \tag{26}$$

$$(\rho + \delta) - G_K(p, K)/p_2 = 0, \tag{27}$$

where $z_2(\lambda, K; p)$ is defined by

$$V_E(p, G(p, K) - p_2 z_2) = \lambda/p_2. \tag{28}$$

Consider first the effects of a change in ρ and δ. It is evident from (27) that an increase in either requires G_K to rise and this can only be achieved by a fall in the capital stock K. (Note that if $G_{KK} = 0$, then the steady-state solution is not unique and hence a comparative static analysis can only indicate the effects on the range of solution.) The solutions are

$$dK/d\rho = dK/d\delta = p_2/G_{KK} < 0 \tag{29}$$

and

$$d\lambda/d\rho = [G_K/p_2 - \delta]/\Delta > 0; \quad d\lambda/d\delta = K/z_{2\lambda} > 0, \tag{30}$$

where $\Delta \equiv -z_{2\lambda} G_{KK}/p_2 > 0$ is the Jacobian for (26) and (27). Thus, an increase in δ or ρ increases the steady-state solution for λ. The effects upon gross investment, z_2, are

$$dz_2/d\rho = \delta p_2/G_{KK} < 0; \quad dz_2/d\delta = (G_K - KG_{KK})/G_{KK} < 0. \tag{31}$$

While it is obvious from (29) and (26) that z_2 must fall when ρ increases, it is not obvious that z_2 must fall when δ increases. However, (31) shows that the fall in K outweighs the rise in δ so that z_2 falls. Even though the depreciation rate increases, the actual level of depreciation falls.

Of more interest is the effects of an increase in the world price of investment goods, p_2. The effects are

$$dK/dp_2 = -[G_{K2}p_2/G_K - 1]G_K/p_2 G_{KK}, \tag{32}$$

$$d\lambda/dp_2 = -[G_{KK}z_{22} + (\delta - G_K/p_2)G_{K2}]/z_{2\lambda} G_{KK}, \tag{33}$$

where

$$z_{22} = [V_E/V_{EE} p_2^2 - (G_2 - z_2)]/p_2. \tag{34}$$

The term in square brackets in (32) is Diewert's (1974, p. 145) "elasticity of intensity" minus unity. In the case of a two-sector model with only final goods, for example, this elasticity of intensity will be greater than unity if investment goods are capital intensive and negative otherwise. Thus, an increase in p_2 will raise the steady-state capital stock if, and only if, investment goods are capital intensive. In this case the increase in p_2 raises the rate of return to capital, $G_K(p, K)/p_2$, and hence encourages capital formation. If investment goods are non-capital intensive, an increase in p_2 will reduce the rate of return to capital and discourage capital formation.

The effect of an increase in p_2 upon gross investment mirrors that of capital since $dz_2 = \delta dK$ in the steady-state. The effect on λ is ambiguous, but it will rise if $z_{22} \leqslant 0$ and $G_{K2} > 0$. The first term in (34) is the pure substitution effect of a change in p_2 and is negative, while the remaining income effect may be of either sign depending upon the direction of trade in investment goods. z_{22} will be negative if investment goods are exported or if imported in sufficiently small quantities. If this is the case, and investment goods are capital intensive, then an increase in p_2 will raise λ.

The effect upon E, expenditure on consumer goods, is

$$
\frac{dE}{dp_2} = x_2 + \left(\frac{G_K}{p_2 - \delta}\right) p_2 \frac{dK}{dp_2}
$$

$$
= x_2 - \frac{G_K p_2^2}{G_{KK}} (G_K/p_2 - \delta)(G_{K2} p_2/G_K - 1) \tag{35}
$$

which is positive if investment goods are capital intensive and are exported. In this case an increase in p_2 leads to a higher capital stock and a higher level of steady-state consumption. If no investment goods are traded ($x_2 = 0$), then E increases as a result of an increase in p_2 if and only if $G_{K2} p_2/G_K > 1$, i.e. if and only if investment goods are capital intensive.

14.2.6. Effects of trade taxes

Suppose that investment goods are imported and that the government imposes an import duty on investment goods imports. What will be the steady-state effects?

With trade taxes there is a difference between domestic and foreign prices and between domestic income and expenditure. To take account of trade taxes the preceding model is amended by treating p as the domestic price vector, and replacing income $G(p, K)$ in (7)–(9) by $G(p, K) + R$, where R is tax revenue given by

$$
R \equiv -tx, \tag{36}
$$

$t \equiv p - p^*$ is the trade tax vector and x is the net export vector. The solution to (9) for z_2 and the function W given by (7) will now depend upon t. The time path of the economy will also depend upon t, including the steady-state to which the economy converges.

For convenience the amended versions of (8) and (9) are recorded as

$$
W(\lambda, K; p, R) \equiv \max_{z_2} \{V(p, G(p, K) + R - p_2 z_2 :
$$

$$
0 \leqslant p_2 z_2 \leqslant G(p, K) + R\}, \tag{8'}
$$

$$V_E(p_1, G(p,K) + R - p_2 z_2) = \lambda/p_2, \quad 0 \leqslant z_2 \leqslant (G+R)/p_2,$$

$$> \lambda/p_2, \quad z_2 = 0, \tag{9'}$$

$$< \lambda/p_2, \quad z_2 = (G+R)/p_2.$$

In (8') and (9') R is treated as an exogenous variable. That is, the competitive consumer does not realize that R will be affected by his saving decision. The solution to (9') for z_2 is written as $z_2(\lambda, K; p, R)$.

The steady-state in region (a) is described by

$$z_2(\lambda, K; p, R) = \delta K, \tag{37}$$

$$G_K(p, K)/p_2 = \rho + \delta. \tag{38}$$

The effect of a change in the trade tax vector upon K can be obtained from (38) since it does not depend on λ.

Let the sole trade tax be on the investment good whose price rises. Then $dp_2 = dt_2 > 0$, with $dp_1 = 0$, and so $dK/dt_2 = dK/dp_2$ which is given in (32) above. The steady-state capital stock increases if good 2 is capital intensive in the sense that $G_{2K} p_2/G_K > 1$, and decreases if it is non-capital intensive. This result assumes that $G_{KK} < 0$.

If we consider a two-sector model, then $G_{KK} = 0$ and K is not unique if diversification occurs. If it does, then a small increase in p_2, due to the trade tax increase, will cause specialization in product 2 in the new steady-state. This is illustrated in fig. 14.2(a), where good 2 is capital intensive, in which case the new steady-state capital stock is $K = K_2$ and production is specialized in good 2. An increase in p_2 has caused industry 1 to disappear. In fig. 14.2(b) good 2 is capital intensive and the rate of return to capital increases, except where only good 2 is produced, and the new steady-state capital stock is $K = K_2$, where the rate of return to capital is as before. Fig. 14.3 illustrates the relationship between p_2 and K in (p_2, K) space for the case where product 2 is non-capital intensive.

The effect upon steady-state expenditure on consumer goods is

$$\frac{dE}{dt_2} = -t_2 G_{22} + [G_K - \delta p_2 + t_2(\delta - G_{2K})] \frac{dK}{dt_2}$$

$$\tag{39}$$

$$= (G_K - \delta p_2) \frac{dK}{dt_2}, \quad \text{at } t_2 = 0.$$

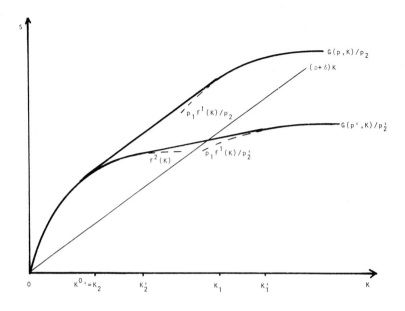

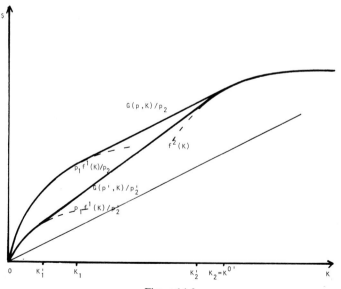

Figure 14.2

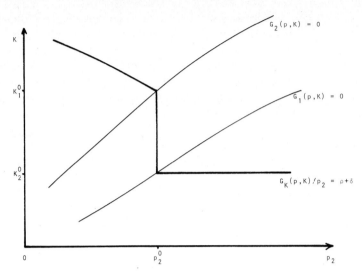

Figure 14.3

Thus, if initially the tax is zero, the imposition of a small positive tax will cause steady-state consumption expenditure E to rise if and only if the capital stock increases. The latter increases if and only if investment goods are capital intensive when $G_{KK} < 0$.

14.2.7. Net export functions

At each instant the net exports of each good are equal to the supplies minus demands. The demands depend upon the saving decision, which depends upon $\lambda(\tau)$. Let $\lambda(\tau) = \Lambda(K(\tau))$ denote the optimal path of λ as a function of K. Then

$$\dot{K}(\tau) = \theta(\Lambda(K(\tau)), K(\tau)) \equiv \Phi(K(\tau)) = z_2(\Lambda(K(\tau)), K(\tau)) - \delta K(\tau) \quad (40)$$

is the "reduced form" equation of motion of the capital stock. Also, the net export vectors may be written as

$$x(\{p(\tau)\}, K(\tau)) \equiv X(\Lambda(K(\tau)), K(\tau)); p(\tau)). \quad (41)$$

These functions express net exports as a function of $K(\tau)$ and $\{p(\tau)\}$, taken to mean the entire time path of p beginning at τ, and hence take account of the fact that $\lambda(\tau)$ is an endogenous variable whose value depends upon the current capital stock and the entire time path of the exogenous variables. The X function has all the usual properties of a static net export function, since it is in fact a static net export function derived from a utility function depending on $\lambda(\tau)$. The properties of $x(\{p(\tau)\}, K(\tau))$ will depend upon the relationship between the optimal path and $\{p(\tau)\}$ and $K(\tau)$. Consider, for example, an increase in a particular price at τ. For given $\lambda(\tau)$ this has the usual effects. However, this change will alter the optimal path and hence alter $\lambda(\tau)$ which, in turn, affects the level of net exports. That is, there is a shift in X which must be taken into account.

14.3. A dynamic model of a trading world

The previous section was concerned with a small open economy which faced exogenously given product prices. In the present section the model is extended to allow for the determination of product prices in the world market.

14.3.1. Dynamic equilibrium

Suppose that the foreign nation has net export functions $x^*(\{p^*(\tau)\}, K^*(\tau))$ at time τ, defined in a similar manner as for the home nation. Then the market equilibrium conditions are

$$x(\{p(\tau)\}, K(\tau)) + x^*(\{p(\tau)\}, K^*(\tau)) = 0, \qquad \tau \geqslant 0. \tag{42}$$

That is, at each instant τ the world markets must clear. The time path of $p(\tau)$ is then no longer arbitrary, but endogenous. Beginning at $\tau = 0$ with stocks $K(0)$ and $K^*(0)$, the consumers in each nation solve their optimal control or intertemporal utility-maximizing problems based upon an exogenously given time path for $p(\tau)$. A *full dynamic equilibrium* occurs when these paths are compatible with market equilibrium, implying that the consumers' consumption and saving plans are realized at each instant in time.

An alternative approach is to assume that somehow each consumer forms expectations of future prices, calculates the optimal solution and puts the plan into action at $\tau = 0$. A *temporary equilibrium* is then defined as a price vector $p(0)$ which ensures that (42) holds at $\tau = 0$ only. The compatibility of future plans is irrelevant to a temporary equilibrium. At the next instant the optimal solution is recomputed and the plan put into action and again an equilibrium price is established. In this way the economy evolves through time with continual replanning by the consumers, taking into account new information and possibly revising expectations. However, the model needs an explicit formulation of the mechanism by which expectations are formed. The full dynamic equilibrium model may be viewed as a special case where expectations are always fulfilled – a case of perfect foresight.

The full dynamic equilibrium model of world trade determines the equilibrium time paths for $p(\tau)$, $K(\tau)$ and $K^*(\tau)$, and hence also for the other economic variables in the model, given initial capital stocks $K(0)$ and $K^*(0)$ together with the technologies and preferences (including the rates of depreciation and time preference). The analysis of the previous section showed that a price-taking economy facing a fixed price vector would converge to a steady-state. Let us suppose that in the present model there is a convergence to a steady-state or long-run equilibrium. In this equilibrium all prices are constant and the steady-state capital stocks are maintained by a constant flow of investment. The saving ratio is constant as is the income level in each nation.

14.3.2. Steady-state

Formally, the steady-state is described by

$$\dot{K} = z_2(\lambda, K; p, R) - \delta K = 0, \tag{43}$$

$$\dot{\lambda}/\lambda = (\rho + \delta) - G_K(p, K)/p_2 = 0, \tag{44}$$

for the home nation;

$$\dot{K}^* = z_2^*(\lambda^*, K^*; p^*, 0) - \delta^* K^* = 0, \tag{45}$$

$$\dot{\lambda}^*/\lambda^* = (\rho^* + \delta^*) - G_K^*(p^*, K^*)/p_2^* = 0, \tag{46}$$

for the foreign nation; and the market equilibrium conditions are

$$x + x^* = 0, \tag{47}$$

where x and x^* are defined by

$$\begin{aligned}
x_1 &= G_1(p, K) - \phi(p, G(p, K) - tx - p_2 z_2), \\
x_2 &= G_2(p, K) - z_2(\lambda, K; p, R),
\end{aligned} \tag{48}$$

$$x_1^* = G_1^*(p^*, K^*) - \phi^*(p^*, G^*(p^*, K^*) - p_2^* z_2^*),$$
$$x_2^* = G_2^*(p^*, K^*) - z_2^*(\lambda^*, K^*; p^*, 0),$$

(49)

and ϕ and ϕ^* are the ordinary demand functions for consumer goods. These equations determine the endogenous variables λ and λ^*, K and K^*, and p and p^* which are connected by $p = p^* + t$, where t is the trade tax vector. As is usual, p and p^* are only determined up to a factor of proportionality, and one of the equations in (47) can be ignored.

Consider the effects of a change in the trade tax vector upon the steady-state solution. These effects are more difficult to obtain than in a static model, since the capital stocks and the saving rates are endogenous to the steady-state model. For given capital stocks, K and K^*, and for given λ and λ^*, eqs. (47)–(49) determine product prices as a function of t as in a static model. It is well known that in a two-product model a positive trade tax will improve the terms of trade for the home nation but that the effect upon domestic prices is ambiguous. The "normal" effect is for a tax on imports to raise the domestic price of importables, but Metzler (1949) showed that it is possible for the domestic price of importables to fall if the terms of trade effect is strong enough. For given λ's and K's the same results apply to the present model. But this is not the end of the story since the λ's and K's are endogenous. That is, a change in t will influence both the saving behaviour and the capital stocks. These, in turn, will affect the market equilibrium conditions and hence the commodity prices.

In the case where there are two products with only product 2 taxed, the steady-state equations may be simplified by using (43) and (45) to eliminate z_2 and z_2^* functions (hence λ and λ^*), and retaining only the market equilibrium condition for investment goods. The model becomes

$$\rho + \delta = G_K(p, K)/p_2,$$

(50)

$$\rho^* + \delta^* = G_K^*(p^*, K^*)/p_2^*,$$

(51)

$$G_2(p, K) + G_2^*(p^*, K^*) = \delta K + \delta^* K^*,$$

(52)

where $p_2 = p_2^* + t_2$. These equations determine p_2, p_2^*, K and K^*, whence λ and λ^* can be obtained from (43) and (45). The first two state that the rate of return on capital must just cover the depreciation and interest (ρ), while the third condition is that product markets must clear.

A change in the trade tax on good 2 will alter product prices and hence alter the rate of return to capital in each nation. This causes the capital stocks to change to re-establish the rates of return at the original levels. The effects of a change in t_2 upon p_2, p_2^*, K and K^* when $t_2 = 0$ initially are

$$\frac{dp_2}{dt_2} = \frac{Q^*}{Q + Q^*}, \tag{53}$$

$$\frac{dp_2^*}{dt_2} = \frac{-Q}{Q + Q^*}, \tag{54}$$

$$\frac{dK}{dt_2} = \frac{G_K/p_2 - G_{K2}}{G_{KK}} \cdot \frac{dp_2}{dt_2}, \tag{55}$$

$$\frac{dK^*}{dt_2} = \frac{G_K^*/p_2^* - G_{K2}^*}{G_{KK}^*} \cdot \frac{dp_2^*}{dt_2}, \tag{56}$$

where

(a) $\quad Q \equiv G_{22} + (G_{2K} - \delta)(G_K/p_2 - G_{K2})/G_{KK},$

(b) $\quad Q^* \equiv G_{22}^* + (G_{2K}^* - \delta^*)(G_K^*/p_2^* - G_{K2}^*)/G_{KK}^*.$ $\tag{57}$

The term Q is the effect on the excess supply of good 2 at home of an increase in its price taking into account the consequent change in the capital stock required to maintain the equality in (50). Although $G_{22} > 0$, it is not necessary in general for Q to be positive. It is easily shown that if either (i) $G_{K2} - G_2/p_2 > 0$ or (ii) $G_{K2} < 0$, then $Q > 0$, but that if (iii) $0 < G_{K2} < G_K/p_2$, then $G_{2K} - \delta$ and hence Q can be of either sign. In the standard two-sector model with no joint production only situations (i) and (ii) are possible, and they correspond to the cases where industry 2 is capital intensive and non-capital intensive, respectively. In any case, Walrasian stability of the product market, taking into account perfect adjustment of capital stocks, requires that world excess supply of good 2 be an increasing function of its price, i.e. $Q + Q^* > 0$.

Suppose that Q and Q^* are positive and $G_{KK}, G_{KK}^* < 0$. Then (53)–(56) indicate that a tax on the imports of good 2 (or a subsidy on exports of good 2) will raise the domestic price and reduce the world price of that good. If investment goods are capital intensive at home ($G_{K2} > G_K/p_2$), then the steady-state capital stock will also rise. This is because the increase in p_2 raises the return to capital inducing a higher capital stock. If industry 2 is also capital intensive in the foreign nation, the capital stock there will fall. If investment goods are non-capital intensive, then the reverse argument applies and home stocks fall while foreign stocks increase. Thus, trade taxes have a clear effect on the steady-state allocation of resources.

In the standard two-sector model the steady-state solution defined by (50)—(52) is not unique if both countries are diversified. To see this consider what happens if such a solution is perturbed. Let K increase and K^* decrease to maintain market equilibrium for product 2 at unchanged prices. Since G_K and G_K^* are independent of K and K^* while diversification is maintained, eqs. (50) and (51) continue to hold. Therefore the solutions for K and K^* are not unique if both countries are diversified.

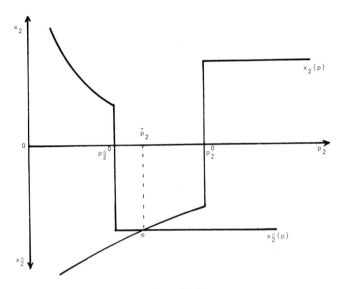

Figure 14.4

Figure 14.4 illustrates the steady-state equilibrium for the case where industry 2 is non-capital intensive, using the concept of a steady-state excess supply curve. This supply curve, for the home nation, is defined by

$$x_2(p) \equiv G_2(p, K) - \delta K, \tag{58}$$

where K is determined by (50). Fig. 14.3 shows the relationship between K and p_2 given by (50). If $p_2 = p_2^0$, then K is any point in the interval $[K_2^0, K_1^0]$, and so x_2 is any point in the interval $[-\delta K_1^0, G_2(p_2^0, K_2^0) - \delta K_2^0]$. If $p_2 > p_2^0$, the economy specializes in product 2 with capital stock K_2^0. An increase in p_2 does not alter the capital stock so the exports of good 2 remain constant. If $p_2 < p_2^0$, the economy specializes in product 1. Reductions in p_2 cause the capital stock to rise thus increasing the demand for investment goods which are fully imported. Therefore the steady-state excess supply curve for good 2 is as indicated in fig. 14.4.

The foreign nation also has a steady-state excess supply curve such as that drawn in fig. 14.4 (note the change of axis). The steady-state free trade equilibrium is where the curves cross since at this point the world market for good 2 clears. In fig. 14.4 the equilibrium is at $\bar{p}_2$, where the home nation imports investment goods and specializes in the production of consumer goods. Noteworthy is the fact that specialization by at least one nation will occur almost always. Also, the only possibility of diversification in one nation is for an intersection on the vertical portion of one of the excess supply functions. This implies that the free trade steady-state equilibrium price is equal to the closed steady-state equilibrium price. This situation is reminiscent of the static Ricardian model of trade in two goods with one factor of production. The similarity occurs because both models have a straight-line production possibility frontier, one static and the other dynamic, taking into account the adjustment of the capital stock.

Now consider the effect of a tariff upon the steady-state solution for the model depicted in fig. 14.4. The tariff imposed by the home nation on good 2 puts a wedge between p_2 and p_2^*. A small tariff will have no effect upon p_2 but will reduce p_2^* by the full amount of the tariff since the foreign nation has a zero elasticity of supply in the neighbourhood of e. If the tariff is increased the foreign supply becomes perfectly elastic so p_2^* stops falling and p_2 begins to rise. Eventually, the tariff would force p_2 up to p_2^0 and so, with $p_2^* = p_2^{*0}$, both nations would be on the vertical portions of their excess supply curves. There exists an infinity of solutions for the trade vector, including zero trade.

Is there an optimal steady state tariff? This is the tariff that will maximize the steady-state consumption of the consumer good. Evidently, a small tariff is beneficial in the steady-state sense since domestic prices and capital stock do not change while tariff revenue increases. Once $p_2^* = p_2^{*0}$, the tariff causes p_2 to rise and K to fall, so consumption may not continue to rise. The derivation of the condition for an optimal tariff is left to the reader.

14.3.3. Alternative models

The model outlined in this section assumes that each nation is a price-taker and maximizes its intertemporal utility function over an infinite horizon. Previous studies of trade in a dynamic context have treated the foreign nation in a different manner. Ryder (1967) and Bruce (1977), for example, have assumed the existence of time variant (apart from a constant growth factor) excess supply functions (or, alternatively, offer curve) for the foreign nation. In addition, the offer curve is assumed to be elastic, concave and differentiable. This is a great simplification of the model and is regarded by Ryder as his model's greatest weakness.

The model in the papers by Ryder and Bruce may be regarded as simple extensions of the small open economy model with fixed world prices to allow for world prices to depend upon the trade vector. The optimal solution obtained by Ryder involves an optimal tariff at each instant in time since the foreign offer curve is not perfectly elastic. Bruce assumes price-taking behaviour and obtains the parametric change in the tariff rate, assuming diversification in the home nation. The steady-state equilibrium in the Bruce model can be depicted as in fig. 14.4 for the case where good 2 is non-capital intensive, but with the foreign excess supply curve smoothly downward-sloping. A tariff will not affect domestic prices but will have a full impact on the terms of trade.

The effects of a tariff on the steady-state solutions in the Bruce model can be obtained as follows. From the market equilibrium condition that $\delta K - G_2(p,K) = x_2^*(p^*)$ it follows that

$$\frac{dK}{dt_2} = \frac{x_{22}^* \, dt_2}{G_{2K} - \delta} \, , \tag{59}$$

when $dp_2 = 0$ and $dp_2^* = -dt_2$. In the standard two-sector model $G_{2K} - \delta \gtrless 0$ according to whether investment goods are capital intensive or not. If $x_{22}^* > 0$, as is assumed by Bruce, then the capital stock rises or falls depending on whether investment goods are capital intensive or not when t_2 is increased.

From the budget constraint $E = G(p, K) + t_2 (\delta K - G_2(p, K)) - p_2 \delta K$ it follows that

$$\frac{dE}{dt_2} = (G_K - p_2 \delta) \frac{dK}{dt_2} - px_{p2}^* \, , \tag{60}$$

where $px_{p2}^* = t_2 x_{22}^* - x_2^* = 0$ is the characterization of the optimal tariff for given K. As Bruce shows, this standard characterization occurs at each instant of time if the economy exercises its market power when maximizing its intertemporal utility function. If the economy follows such a policy, then in the steady-state $px_{p2}^* = 0$ and so (60) indicates how E is affected by moving t_2 away from its optimal level. Since $G_K/p_2 = \rho + \delta > \delta$, the effect on E hinges on whether K rises or falls. But we have already dealt with the effect on K. Thus, an increase in t_2 from its "optimal level" (where $px_{p2}^* = 0$) will raise the steady-state consumption of consumer goods if the imported investment good is capital intensive and reduce it if investment goods are non-capital intensive.

14.4. Gains from trade

In the model of trade and growth of an economy facing exogenously given product prices it was shown that a trade tax on the investment good will raise the steady-state consumption level if investment goods are capital intensive and reduce it if investment goods are non-capital intensive. In the static trade model it was shown that the optimal policy for a price-taking country is to impose no trade taxes. Is there a difference, therefore, in the models which cause free trade to be optimal in the static model and suboptimal in the dynamic model? The answer is "no". In fact, the dynamic model with competitive behaviour is formally no different from the static model and the same theorems regarding the gains from trade and Pareto optimality of free trade apply to both.

The fact that the steady-state consumption of goods can be increased by introducing a trade tax does not imply that free trade is suboptimal for a price-taking economy. As Smith (1979) points out, a comparison of steady-state solutions is irrelevant to the issue of whether free trade is optimal. What is important in a dynamic model is whether the utility possibility set for the nation is enlarged or contracted by the introduction of trade taxes. In a one-consumer model, such as formulated in this chapter, the question is whether the level of total utility obtained over the whole time period under discussion is greater or lower under trade taxes. A comparison of steady-state solutions would be relevant only if the economy adjusted immediately to the steady-state. When the entire period is considered, it can be shown that there are (a) gains from free trade and (b) free trade is optimal for a price-taking nation. One way to establish these results is to recognize that the dynamic model can be cast into the static model by distinguishing commodities by the date at which they are consumed or produced. In a continuous time framework there is a continuum of commodities which alters the formal similarity with the static model, but in a discrete time model with finite horizon the number of commodities remains finite. This is the way Debreu (1959) dealt with time.

Two-period model

Rather than proceed with the details regarding the equivalence of the dynamic and static models, an alternative approach is taken. This approach is to consider a simple two-period model of trade and growth, with which the essence of the gains from trade are easily illustrated. At the beginning of the first period the economy inherits capital stock K^1 and chooses production $y^1 = (y_1^1, y_2^1) \in Y(K^1)$ and consumption–investment $z^1 = (z_1^1, z_2^1)$. In period 2 the capital stock is $K^2 = (1-\delta)K^1 + z_2^1$ and vectors y^2 and z^2 are chosen. At the end of period 2 the economy has capital stock $(1-\delta)K^2 + z_2^2$. Since only two periods are considered, the utility function for the single consumer can be written as $u(z_1^1, z_1^2)$, which is assumed to possess the standard properties of a utility function.

Under autarky the consumption possibility set is

$$Z^a \equiv \{(z_1^1, z_1^2): (z_1^t, z_2^t) \in Y(K^t); K^{t+1} = (1-\delta)K^t + z_1^t, t = 1, 2\}. \quad (61)$$

This is the set of consumptions which are feasible given the technology (assumed independent of time, but this is not necessary) and the initial capital stock K^1. This is analogous to a two-sector economy in which some goods (here investment goods) are pure intermediates being produced in one sector (period 1) and used in the other (period 2). The consumer's problem is to maximize $u(z_1^1, z_1^2)$ on the consumption possibility set.

Under free trade the consumption possibility set depends upon the prices of the traded goods and is defined by

$$Z^f \equiv \{(z_1^1, z_1^2): p_1^t z_1^t + p_2^t z_2^t \leq G(p^t, K^t); K^{t+1} = (1-\delta)K^t + z_2^t,$$
$$t = 1, 2\}. \quad (62)$$

The consumer's problem is to maximize $u(z_1^1, z_2^2)$ on this set. To establish the gains from trade independently of the particular nature of the utility function, it suffices to show that Z^a is a proper subset of Z^f, i.e. that Z^f is larger than Z^a. This is easily established. By definition $G(p^t, K^t) \geq p_1^t y_1^t + p_2^t y_2^t = p^t y^t$ for all $y^t \in Y(K^t)$. Thus, in period 1 the autarky consumption and investment vectors are available under free trade. Thus, under free trade the economy can choose to have the autarky capital stock in period 2. In this period the autarky choices are again feasible. Thus, any (z_1^1, z_1^2) which is feasible under autarky is also feasible under free trade and hence $Z^a \subset Z^f$. Indeed, at each t there will generally be production vectors which yield greater GNP than the chosen autarky production vectors, so the free trade economy can (but may not, of course) choose to have more consumption and more investment so that present consumption and future consumption can exceed that available under autarky.

The preceding argument clearly shows that the consumption possibility set under free trade contains the autarky consumption possibility set as a subset.

Consequently, the consumer will be no worse off under free trade than under autarky, and will be better off in most cases. This does not mean, however, that the consumer will necessarily consume more goods in each period under free trade, although he can do so if he wishes. He chooses the entire profile of consumption to attain greatest satisfaction and, depending upon the circumstances, this may involve greater consumption in some periods and less in others than would have been chosen under autarky.

What is the nature of the argument if there is not one consumer but many consumers? In the static model the compensation principle is used to show that, with lump-sum redistributions, it is possible for free trade to be Pareto superior to autarky. Application of the compensation principle to the intertemporal framework may require that some consumers receive lump-sum income payments, while others have their incomes reduced in order that each consumer's intertemporal utility is no lower than attained under autarky and is higher for at least one consumer.

The simple two-period model can also be used to show that free trade is optimal for a nation that faces exogenously given prices for traded goods. In period 1 trade taxes will lower GNP, evaluated at international prices, and hence make smaller the set of (z_1^1, z_2^1) possibilities. In period 2, since the set of possible capital stocks is reduced, the production possibilities are less. For any given capital stock in period 2, a trade tax will reduce GNP at international prices. Thus, the set of possible consumption vectors (z_1^1, z_1^2) is reduced under tariffs at exogenously given world prices, and so trade taxes are suboptimal from an intertemporal viewpoint. Again, this is not to say that consumption in each period is necessarily lower under tariffs, but simply that the consumption profile necessarily yields less utility under trade taxes. A tariff might encourage capital formation in period 1 thus enabling higher consumption in period 2 than actually takes place under free trade. The preceding argument shows, however, that the gain in utility in the second period cannot outweigh the first period's loss.

14.5. Growth and trade with fixed saving ratios

Much of the literature on growth has assumed that saving is a fixed proportion of income, whereas the model dealt with above makes the saving ratio an endogenous variable depending upon the entire profile of the economy. The simpler assumption of a fixed saving ratio makes the model much simpler and hence allows a clearer examination of the dynamics of trade and growth.

14.5.1. Model

With constant saving rates and just two goods, an investment good and a consumer good, the paths of the two economies in a freely trading world are described by

$$\dot{K} = s\, G(p, K)/p_2 - \delta K \equiv \theta(K, p_2; s), \tag{63}$$

$$\dot{K}^* = s^*\, G^*(p^*, K^*)/p_2^* - \delta^* K^* \equiv \theta^*(K^*, p_2^*; s^*), \tag{64}$$

$$s\, G(p, K)/p_2 - G_2(p, K) + s^* G^*(p^*, K^*)/p_2^* - G_2^*(p^*, K^*) = 0, \tag{65}$$

where $p = p^*$ and s and s^* are the constant saving rates. The first two equations describe capital accumulation while the third is the market equilibrium condition for investment goods. By fixing p^* and ignoring (65), (63) then describes the dynamic small open economy. Tariffs can be introduced without difficulty. If the economies begin with stocks $K(0)$ and $K^*(0)$, (63)–(65) determine the entire profile of p_2 (p_1 is normalized), K and K^*. Clearly, the pattern of production, consumption and, hence, trade can then be deduced.

14.5.2. Nature of the temporary equilibrium

Consider, first, the response of net investment to changes in K and p_2. For the home nation (similar expressions are obtained for the foreign nation) these are

(a) $\theta_K = s\, G_K/p_2 - \delta < 0$,   at $\theta = 0$,

(b) $\theta_2 \equiv \partial\theta/\partial p_2 = s\,[G_2 p_2 - G]/p_2^2 \lessgtr 0$,

$$\tag{66}$$

where the sign condition in (a) follows from the concavity of $G(p, K)$ in K. Secondly, the effects of K and p_2 upon the net export function $x_2(p_2, K) \equiv s\, G(p, K)/p_2 - G_2(p, K)$ are

(a) $x_{2K} \equiv \partial x_2/\partial K = G_{2K} - s\, G_K/p_2 = (G_{2K} p_2/G_K - s)\, G_K/p_2$,

(b) $x_{22} \equiv \partial x_2/\partial p_2 = G_{22} - \theta_2 \geq 0$.

$$\tag{67}$$

The effect of K upon x_2 is ambiguous, depending upon the capital intensity of good 2. However, unlike the usual static model the price effect is quite unambiguous: net exports never fall when p_2 increases.

In the two-sector model some special features should be noted:

(a) $G_1 = 0$ implies $G_{2K} p_2 / G_K = 1,$ $G_{1K} = 0,$

(b) $G_2 = 0$ implies $G_{2K} = 0,$ $G_{1K} p_1 / G_K = 1,$

(c) $G_1, G_2 > 0$ implies $G_{2K} p_2 / G_K > 1,$

$\qquad G_{1K} < 0;$ or $G_{2K} < 0,$ $G_{1K} p_1 / G_k > 1.$

$\hfill (68)$

Thus,

(a) $G_1 = 0$ implies $x_{2K} = (1 - s) G_K / p_2 > 0,$ $\theta_2 = 0,$

(b) $G_2 = 0$ implies $x_{2K} = -s \, G_K / p_2 < 0,$ $\theta_2 = -s \, G / p_2^2 < 0,$ (69)

(c) $G_1, G_2 > 0$ implies $x_{2K} > 0;$ or $x_{2K} < 0,$ $\theta_2 < 0.$

The first alternative in (68,c) and (69,c) occurs when industry 2 is capital intensive, while the second occurs if it is labour intensive.

14.5.3. Steady-state

The steady-state solution may be described in the same manner as used in section 14.2 for the optimal saving model. That is, steady-state net export functions $X_2(p_2) \equiv x_2(p_2, K(p_2))$ can be defined where $K(p_2)$ denotes the solution for K from $\theta(K, p_2; s) = 0$. The slope of this function is

$$X_{22} = x_{22} + x_{2K} K_2, \hfill (70)$$

where $K_2 \equiv \partial K / \partial p_2 = -\theta_2 / \theta_K \leq 0.$ The sign of X_{22} is ambiguous since x_{2K} given by (67,a) is ambiguous in sign. Let the model be the standard two-sector model. Then if industry 2 is always labour intensive, $G_{2K} p_2 / G_K \leq 0$ and $x_{2K} < 0$ implying that $X_{22} \geq 0$ for all prices. If the same is true for the foreign nation the equilibrium price for good 2 will be unique. On the other hand, if industry 2 is always capital intensive, $G_{2K} p_2 / G_K \geq 1$ and $x_{2K} > 0$ and X_{22} cannot be signed in general. Since the net export functions are not monotonic the equilibrium solution may not be unique and the question of market stability is raised. The reader may wish to draw the net export functions and compare the diagram with fig. 14.4.

14.5.4. *Dynamic paths of capital stocks*

Let us return to consideration of the dynamic behaviour of the world economy described by (63)–(65). The aim is to eliminate p_2 and to examine behaviour in (K, K^*) space as in Oniki and Uzawa (1965), Kemp (1969), Bardhan (1965) and others. The "reduced form" dynamic equations are

$$\dot{K} = \theta(K, P_2(K, K^*, s, s^*), s) \equiv \psi(K, K^*; s, s^*), \tag{71}$$

$$\dot{K}^* = \theta^*(K^*, P_2(K, K^*, s, s^*), s^*) \equiv \psi^*(K, K^*; s, s^*), \tag{72}$$

where $p_2 = P_2(K, K^*, s, s^*)$ denotes the solution to (65) for p_2. The equations $\dot{K} = 0$ and $\dot{K}^* = 0$ define curves in the phase diagram in (K, K^*) space, determining the steady-state solution and helping graphically to obtain the dynamic paths from any initial point. The slopes of ψ are

(a) $\quad \psi_K = \theta_K + \theta_2 P_{2K}$,

$$\tag{73}$$

(b) $\quad \psi_{K^*} = \theta_2 P_{2K^*}$,

where θ_K and θ_2 have been discussed. Similar expressions are obtained for ψ_K^* and $\psi_{K^*}^*$. The effects of K and K^* upon the equilibrium price, p_2, are

(a) $\quad P_{2K} = -x_{2K}/(x_{22} + x_{22}^*)$,

$$\tag{74}$$

(b) $\quad P_{2K^*} = -x_{2K}^*/(x_{22} + x_{22}^*)$,

where $(x_{22} + x_{22}^*)$ is assumed to be strictly positive implying stability of the temporary market equilibrium.

The differential equation system is locally stable in the neighbourhood of the steady-state if, and only if, the Routh–Hurwitz conditions

(a) $\quad \psi_K + \psi_{K^*}^* < 0$,

$$\tag{75}$$

(b) $\quad J \equiv \psi_K \, \psi_{K^*}^* - \psi_{K^*} \, \psi_K^* = \left[\frac{dK^*}{dK} \bigg|_{\psi=0} - \frac{dK^*}{dK} \bigg|_{\psi^*=0} \right] \psi_{K^*} \, \psi_{K^*}^* > 0$

are satisfied. It is evident from an examination of the expressions for ψ_K, ψ_{K^*}, ψ_K^* and $\psi_{K^*}^*$ that the slopes of the $\dot{K} = 0$ and $\dot{K}^* = 0$ equations and the expressions in (75) depend upon the relative factor intensities and upon whether the economies are specialized in production.

To proceed, assume that good 2 is always non-capital intensive. In this case

(a) $G_1 > 0$ implies $\theta_2 < 0$, $P_{2K} > 0, \psi_K < 0, \psi_K^* = \theta_2^* P_{2K} \leqslant 0$,

$$\text{(76)}$$

(b) $G_1 = 0$ implies $\theta_2 = 0$, $P_{2K} < 0, \psi_K < 0, \psi_K^* = \theta_2^* P_{2K} \geqslant 0$,

with a similar set of relationships for the foreign nation. Note that it is always the case that $\psi_K < 0$ (in the neighbourhood of $\psi = 0$) so that, for given K^*, the steady-state solution for K is locally stable. Using (76) and the corresponding relationships for the foreign nation, it may be established that

$$\left.\frac{dK^*}{dK}\right|_{\psi=0} = -\frac{\psi_K}{\psi_{K^*}} = -\frac{\theta_K + \theta_2 P_{2K}}{\theta_2^* P_{2K^*}} = \begin{cases} <0, & \text{if } G_1, G_1^* > 0, \\ \infty, & \text{if } G_1 = 0 < G_1^*, \\ >0, & \text{if } G_1 > 0 = G_1^*, \end{cases} \quad (77)$$

and

$$\left.\frac{dK^*}{dK}\right|_{\psi^*=0} = -\frac{\psi_K^*}{\psi_{K^*}} = -\frac{\theta_2^* P_{2K}}{\theta_K^* + \theta_2^* P_{2K^*}} = \begin{cases} <0, & \text{if } G_1, G_1^* > 0, \\ >0 & \text{if } G_1 = 0 < G_1^*, \\ 0 & \text{if } G_1 > 0 = G_1^*. \end{cases} \quad (78)$$

The difference in the slopes of the $\dot{K} = 0$ and $\dot{K}^* = 0$ curves is

$$\left.\frac{dK^*}{dK}\right|_{\psi^*=0} - \left.\frac{dK^*}{dK}\right|_{\psi=0} = -\frac{[\theta_K(\theta_K^* + \theta_2^* P_{2K^*}) + \theta_K^* \theta_2 P_{2K}]}{\theta_2 P_{2K^*}(\theta_K^* + \theta_2^* P_{2K^*})} < 0,$$

$$\text{if } G_1, G_1^* > 0. \quad (79)$$

There are three possible production patterns for the steady-state solution. In each of these the local stability condition (75) is satisfied, as may be verified by referring to (76)–(79). That is, ψ_K and $\psi_{K^*}^*$ are both negative so the trace condition (75,a) is satisfied, and the $\dot{K}^* = 0$ and $\dot{K} = 0$ curves have the correct relative slopes so condition (75,b) is satisfied. Fig. 14.5 illustrates the possible situations.

The complete phase diagram may be obtained by noting some additional features of the model. In particular, the region of the (K, K^*) space for which $G_1 = 0$ can be obtained by solving $G_1(p, K) = 0$ and the market equilibrium condition (65) for K in terms of K^*. The slope of this function is therefore

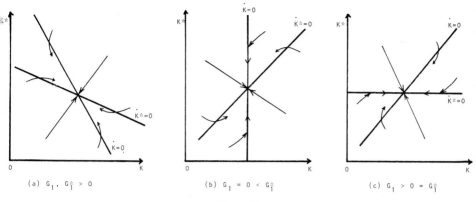

Figure 14.5

$$\frac{\mathrm{d}K}{\mathrm{d}K^*} = -\frac{G_{12}P_{2K^*}}{G_{12}P_{2K} + G_{1K}} > 0. \tag{80}$$

The positive sign occurs because $G_1 = 0$ implies $P_{1K} < 0$ and $G_1^* > 0$, which in turn implies $P_{2K^*} < 0$, and because $G_{12} < 0 < G_{1K}$. A similar expression occurs for the case where $G_1^*(p, K) = 0$. Fig. 14.6 shows these curves in (K, K^*) space.

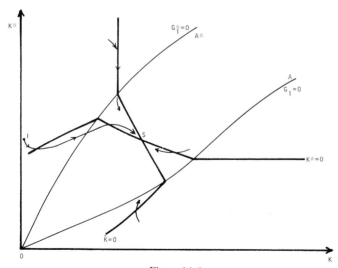

Figure 14.6

Also shown are the $\dot{K} = 0$ and $\dot{K}^* = 0$ curves drawn such that the steady-state solution is in the $G_1, G_1^* > 0$ region. The various dynamic paths are illustrated, all leading (eventually) towards the steady-state solution, which is therefore globally stable. All sorts of possible paths emerge depending upon the initial point. For example, consider the initial point I where the foreign nation specializes in good 2. Along the path from I to S the home nation accumulates capital, whereas the foreign nation reduces its capital stock initially then accumulates capital and eventually decumulates capital until S is reached. The precise paths will depend upon the technologies and savings rates as well as the initial capital stocks.

It has been assumed in the preceding analysis that industry 2 is always non-capital intensive. If industry 2 is always capital intensive, then the analysis becomes more complicated and so a detailed treatment will not be given here. Instead, some indications of why the analysis is more difficult are given. First, note that P_{2K} is now negative when $G_1 > 0$. Hence ψ_K is not necessarily negative, and similarly for $\psi_{K^*}^*$. The result is that the expressions in $(77)-(79)$ are no longer unambiguously signed. Secondly, the lines OA and OA^* in fig. 14.6 will no longer be monotonic. Thus, the possibilities of multiple steady-state solutions and instability are raised. Local stability is assured only in the case of complete specialization by both nations in the steady-state. For example, if $G_1 = 0$ and $G_2^* = 0$, then $\psi_K = \theta_K < 0$, $\psi_{K^*} = 0$, $\psi_K^* = \theta_2^* P_{2K} > 0$ and $\psi_{K^*}^* = \theta_K^* + \theta_2^* P_{2K^*} < 0$ since $P_{2K} < 0 < P_{2K^*}$. The phase diagram is similar to that in fig. 14.5(b).

14.6. Notes on the literature

Most of the literature on trade and growth is based upon the fixed saving ratio assumption. The first rigorous treatments are those of Oniki and Uzawa (1965) and Bardhan (1965, 1966a) who examine the full dynamic paths of trading economies. Other treatments include Stiglitz (1970), Kemp (1969) and Khang and Kemp (1973) who deal with the case of unequal rates of growth of labour. Inada (1968) considers the question of factor price equalization in a growth context. Models with special features include Bardhan (1966b) dealing with vintage capital, Khang (1969) dealing with intermediate inputs, and Bardhan and Lewis (1970) dealing with imported intermediates and imported capital goods. An exposition of the two-sector, fixed saving ratio, growth model for an open economy is provided by Johnson (1971).

The gains from trade within a dynamic context have been discussed by Kemp (1973), Samuelson (1975) and Smith (1979).

There is much less literature on the optimal saving model and on taxes. Stiglitz (1970) devotes some attention to the optimal saving model while Ryder

(1967) obtains the optimal policy for a nation facing a stationary foreign offer curve. Bruce (1977) deals with taxes in the Ryder framework.

Problems

1. (a) Derive eqs. (14) and (15) of the text – the first derivatives of $W(\lambda, K; p)$.
   (b) Derive eqs. (18), (19) and (20) – the second derivatives of $W(\lambda, K; p)$.
2. Derive a characterization of the trade tax vector that maximizes the steady-state consumption of the consumer good in the dynamic model of trade as formulated in section 14.3.
3. Consider the Ryder–Bruce model of trade in two goods in which there are given foreign net export functions $x_i^*(p^*)$. The home nation maximizes an intertemporal utility functional as in section 14.2 except that it now takes $x^*(p^*)$ as given, not p^*.
   (a) Write down the home nation's problem using the indirect utility function and GNP function.
   (b) Obtain a characterization of the solution (via the maximum principle and the canonical equations).
   (c) Hence, show that the home nation imposes optimal trade taxes at each instant – i.e. there is a profile of optimal trade taxes.
   (d) What are the steady-state conditions?
   (e) Will the steady-state optimal trade taxes maximize the steady-state (instantaneous) utility level?
4. Consider the discrete time utility maximizing problem for a small open economy expressed as

$$\max\left\{ \sum_{\tau=0}^{\infty} u(z_\tau)(1+\rho)^{-\tau}: y_\tau \in Y(K_\tau), K_{\tau+1} = \iota_\tau - \delta K_\tau, p_\tau(z_\tau + \iota_\tau - y_\tau) = 0, \right. $$
$$\left. \tau = 0, 1, ... \right\},$$

where K_1 is given, as is $\{p_\tau\}, \rho$ and δ.
   (a) Show that this problem is equivalent to the problem

$$\max\left\{ \sum_{\tau=0}^{\infty} V(p_\tau, G(p_\tau, K_\tau) - p_\tau \iota_\tau): K_{\tau+1} = \iota_\tau - \delta K_\tau, \tau = 0, 1, ... \right\}.$$

   (b) Form the Lagrangian $L = \sum_{\tau=0}^{\infty} L_\tau (1+\rho)^{-\tau}$, where $L_\tau \equiv V(p_\tau, G(p_\tau, K_\tau) - p_\tau \iota_\tau) + \lambda_\tau(\iota_\tau - \delta K_\tau - K_{\tau+1})$. Maximize with respect to $\iota_\tau, \tau = 0, 1, ...,$ to get $L^* = \sum L_\tau^*(\lambda_\tau, K_\tau; p_\tau)(1+\rho)^{-\tau}$. (Discrete version of the maximum principle.)

(c) Obtain the equations of motion by maximizing L^* with respect to (λ_τ, K_τ), $\tau = 1, 2, \ldots$.

(d) Interpret these equations of motion.

(e) Obtain the steady-state condition for the case where p_τ is a constant vector, and relate them to those obtained from the continuous time model.

5. (a) Draw the steady-state net export functions for a two-good model of trade with fixed saving ratios. Compare your figure with fig. 14.4.

(b) Verify that (76)−(79) imply that the local stability condition (75) is satisfied for each possible production pattern. (These apply for the case where good 2 is non-capital intensive in production.)

6. Consider a model of trade between two nations. Let the saving function (in each nation) take the classical form $S = sKG_K(p, L, K)/p_2$, where p_2 is the price of the investment good, there are only two goods and s is the constant saving ratio out of capital income. Derive the condition for stability of the model of trade and growth (Bardhan, 1965).

7. Suppose that, in the model of section 14.2, there are two goods − one good a pure intermediate and the other capable of being consumed or used to add to the capital stock.

(a) Reformulate the model.

(b) Does this change in the model lead to substantial changes in the analysis?

References

Bardhan, P. (1965) "Equilibrium growth in the international economy", *Quarterly Journal of Economics* 79-3, August, 455–464.

Bardhan, P. (1966a) "On factor accumulation and the pattern of international specialization", *Review of Economic Studies* 33-1, January, 39–44.

Bardhan, P. (1966b) "International trade theory in a vintage-capital model", *Econometrica* 34-4, October, 756–767.

Bardhan, P. and S. Lewis (1970) "Models of growth with imported inputs", *Economica* 37, November, 373–385.

Blackorby, C., D. Primont and R.R. Russell (1978) *Duality, Separability and Functional Structure: Theory and Economic Applications* (New York: North-Holland).

Bruce, N. (1977) "The effects of trade taxes in a two-sector model of capital accumulation", *Journal of International Economics* 7, 283–294.

Debreu, G. (1959) *Theory of Value* (New York: Wiley).

Inada, K. (1968) "Free trade, capital accumulation and factor-price equalization", *Economic Record* 44-107, September, 322–341.

Intriligator, M.D. (1971) *Mathematical Optimization and Economic Theory* (Englewood Cliffs, N.J.: Prentice-Hall).

Johnson, H.G. (1971) "Trade and growth: A geometrical exposition", *Journal of International Economics* 1, 83–101.

Kemp, M.C. (1969) *The Pure Theory of International Trade and Investment* (Englewood Cliffs, N.J.: Prentice-Hall).

Kemp, M.C. (1973) "Trade gains in a pure consumption-loan model", *Australian Economic Papers* 12-20, June, 124–126.

Khang, C. (1969) "A dynamic model of trade between the final and the intermediate products", *Journal of Economic Theory* 1-4, December, 416–437.

Khang, C. and M.C. Kemp (1973) "International trade and investment between countries with different natural rates of growth", *Metroeconomica* 25-3, 215–228.

Long, N.V. and N. Vousden (1977) "Optimal control theorems", in: J.D. Pitchford and S.J. Turnovsky (eds.), *Applications of Control Theory to Economic Analysis* (Amsterdam: North-Holland).

Metzler, L.A. (1949) "Tariffs, terms of trade, and the distribution of national income", *Journal of Political Economy* 57, 1–29.

Oniki, H. and H. Uzawa (1965) "Patterns of trade and investment in a dynamic model of international trade", *Review of Economic Studies* 32, 15–34.

Pontryagin, L.S., V.G. Boltyanskii, R.V. Gamkrelidze and E.F. Mischenko (1962) *The Mathematical Theory of Optimal Processes* (New York: Interscience).

Ryder, H.E. (1967) "Optimal accumulation and trade in an open economy of moderate size", in: K. Shell (ed.), *Essays on the Theory of Economic Growth* (Cambridge: M.I.T. Press).

Samuelson, P.A. (1975) "Trade pattern reversals in time-phased Ricardian systems and intertemporal efficiency", *Journal of International Economics* 5, 309–363.

Smith, M.A.M. (1979) "Intertemporal gains from trade", *Journal of International Economics* 9, 239–248.

Stiglitz, J.E. (1970) "Factor price equalization in a dynamic economy", *Journal of Political Economy* 78-3, May/June, 456–488.

CHAPTER 15

TRADE AND GROWTH:
DYNAMICS OF TECHNOLOGY AND INVESTMENT

15.1. Introduction

This chapter continues the analysis of trade and growth from a dynamic view-point. First, the process of learning by doing, which is at the heart of the infant-industry argument for tariff protection, is examined. The second topic concerns heterogeneous capital goods which have received increasing attention recently, usually within the context of time-phased models. Finally, some attention is devoted to the dynamics of trade, growth and foreign investment.

15.2. Endogenous technical change: the infant-industry argument for protection

15.2.1. The basic argument

The infant-industry argument has long been regarded as the major argument for tariff protection which is valid on economic grounds. The argument originated with early economists such as Hamilton, Say, List, Mill and Bastable, but it is only recently that it has come under close scrutiny.

Kemp (1964) provides an excellent account of the infant-industry argument in terms of technical progress through "learning by doing". Kemp's account may be illustrated as in fig. 15.1. Under free trade the price vector, p, and production possibility set, $Y(v)$, are such that production of good 2 is not profitable. In each period the production point is y and the consumption point is z. The infant-industry argument is that, if (and only if) producers could be induced to produce good 2, then they would learn more about the technological possibilities and hence, in some future period, the production possibility set would shift outwards to $Y'(v)$. This learning by doing could be induced by an import tariff, which could be removed once the infant had "grown up", i.e., when positive production of good 2 is profitable at the free trade world price vector. In fig. 15.1 production is y^t and consumption is z^t under the tariff, and becomes y^f and z^f once tariff protection is removed.

That the infant must eventually be profitable is Mill's argument. Bastable added the requirement that the losses in the early years must be outweighed by the future gains, appropriately discounted.

Kemp (1964, 1974) has argued that the economies created by learning by doing must be external to the firm. If the economies were internal to the firm, then it would be profitable for the firm to borrow funds to cover the losses in the early years since the future gains would accrue to it alone. On the other hand, if the economies are external to the firm, the knowledge gained becomes freely available to all potential producers and hence an individual firm cannot profit by being the learner.

It is important to note that the economies referred to are dynamic economies *not* static economies of scale. Experience in production, which can only take place with the passage of time, is the essence of the infant-industry argument for intervention with the free market. In addition, as pointed out above, these economies must be dynamic external economies. It is well known, of course, that one of the main arguments for intervention with the free market is provided by exter-

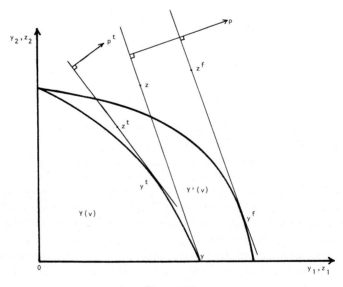

Figure 15.1

nalities. Hence, the infant-industry argument is a special case of this more general argument, relying as it does upon externalities which are dynamic in nature.

It is also important to note that the mere existence of learning by doing is not sufficient for intervention, as Mill and Bastable were aware. The gains must outweigh the losses. If current consumption has to be forgone to reap future consumption benefits, then we must have an intertemporal utility function to enable an evaluation of the infant-industry policy. Given an intertemporal utility function, the nature of the learning by doing, and the time horizon, a particular infant-industry policy can be evaluated and compared with a free trade policy. Also, alternative intervention policies can be compared and the optimal one chosen. This is the task of the remainder of the section.

15.2.2. A two-period model

For simplicity let there be just two periods, the present and the future, denoted by subscripts 1 and 2, respectively. The analysis is easily extended to many periods. In period 1 the production possibility set is $Y(v, 0)$ and in period 2 it is $Y(v, q)$, where q is a vector of "experience", which is taken here to be the production vector in period 1, y_1. Thus, the production possibility set in period 2 depends upon the production vector in period 1. The exact nature of the dependence is not specified at this point, so the analysis is very general. The GNP function is $G(p, v, 0)$ in period 1 and $G(p_2, v, q) = G(p_2, v, G_p(p_1, v, 0))$ in period 2.

Let it also be assumed that consumption decisions can be aggregated with preferences given by an intertemporal utility function $u(z_1, z_2)$ and corresponding expenditure function $E(p_1, p_2, \mu)$. The aggregate consumer is assumed to maximize utility subject to this intertemporal budget constraint. In the absence of any intervention by the government the budget constraint is

$$E(p_1^*, p_2^*, \mu) = G(p_1^*, v, 0) + G(p_2^*, v, G_p(p_1^*, v, 0)) \qquad (1)$$

where p_1^* and p_2^* are world price vectors.

With the intertemporal production externality it is not necessarily the case that the right-hand side of (1) represents the maximum intertemporal GNP that is feasible. Thus, at fixed world prices it may be possible to obtain a greater value of production and hence the utility level could be increased. This argument requires that consumers face the constant world prices and hence that the shift in production is obtained by production taxes. It will be demonstrated that such a policy is, in fact, optimal. If world prices are not fixed, then the optimal policy will also involve trade taxes.

The optimization problem is to maximize the level of utility subject to the market equilibrium conditions:

$$E_1(p_1^d, p_2^d, \mu) - G_p(p_1^s, v, 0) = x_1^*(p_1^*, p_2^*),$$

$$E_2(p_1^d, p_2^d, \mu) - G_p(p_2^s, v, G_p(p_1^s, v, 0)) = x_2^*(p_1^*, p_2^*),$$

(2)

by choosing world prices p_i^*, producers prices p_i^s and consumer prices p_i^d. Assuming differentiability the first-order conditions include

(a) $1 + \sum_{i=1}^{2} \lambda_i E_{i\mu}(p_1^d, p_2^d, \mu) = 0$ (μ)

(b) $\sum_{i=1}^{2} \lambda_i E_{ip}(p^d, \mu) = 0$ $(p^d = (p_1^d, p_2^d))$

(c) $\sum_{i=1}^{2} \lambda_i x_{ip}^*(p^*) = 0$ $(p^* = (p_1^*, p_2^*))$

(3)

(d) $[\lambda_1 + \lambda_2 G_{pq}(p_2^s, v, G_p(p_1^s, v, 0))] G_{pp}(p_1^s, v, 0) = 0$ (p_1^s)

(e) $\lambda_2 G_{pp}(p_2^s, v, G_p(p_1^s, v, 0)) = 0$ (p_2^s),

where λ_1 and λ_2 are vectors of Lagrange multipliers associated with the market equilibrium conditions (2). The homogeneity properties of E and G may be used, in a now familiar argument, to show that (3,b) and (3,e) imply that $\lambda_1 = p_1^d$ and $\lambda_2 = p_2^d = p_2^s$.[1] Thus, condition (3,c) is the usual characterization of optimal trade taxes expressed in an intertemporal framework with goods distinguished by period. Condition (3,d) shows that $p_1^s = \lambda_1 + \lambda_2 G_{pq}(p_2^s, v, G_p(p_1^s, v, 0))$, i.e.

$$p_1^s = p_1^d + p_2^s G_{pq}(p_2^s, v, G_p(p_1^s, v, 0)) = p_1^d + G_q(p_2^s, v, G_p(p_1^s, v, 0)),   (4)$$

the right-hand expression following from the homogeneity properties of G. This shows that the price vector facing producers in period 1 should contain a subsidy of $s_1 \equiv G_q(p_2^s, v, G_p(p_1^s, v, 0))$. The amount of the subsidy to each product depends upon the contribution of its current output to the increase in GNP in the next period. In the next period the subsidy is removed, since the learning is complete.

[1] See theorem (11.16).

It should be noted that the optimal policy with respect to the dynamic externality involves production subsidies, not trade taxes. The optimal policy includes trade taxes but these would be present even if there was no externality. Of course, the presence of the externality affects the values of all the variables and hence influences the values of the optimal trade taxes, but the decision to impose trade taxes arises from the market power of the nation, not the externality. If the nation has no market power, $\lambda_i = p_i^*$ and the optimal policy with respect to the externality remains one of imposing production subsidies. The reason why production subsidies are optimal is fairly obvious. The source of the externality is learning by producing and hence the tax which directly influences production is a production tax. A trade tax could generate the same production prices in period 1, but consumer prices would also be distorted creating an unnecessary welfare loss.

15.2.3. Dynamic internal economies

Kemp (1964, 1974) has argued that there is no justification for protection of an industry experiencing dynamic internal economics, a proposition challenged by Negishi (1972) and Ohyama (1972). Kemp (1974) argues that justification for protection under dynamic internal economies is really based upon the optimal tariff argument or upon myopic behaviour of firms and not upon any form of infant-industry argument.

To see this consider the two-period model developed above. Let p^0 be the free trade price vector and p^1 be the world price vector under a *production* tax-subsidy scheme at home, with other variables superscripted in the same way. Define

$$U^i \equiv \{(z_1, z_2): u(z_1, z_2) \geqslant u(z_1^i, z_2^i)\} \tag{5}$$

as the set of consumption vectors which are at least as good as (z_1^i, z_2^i). If (z_1^1, z_2^1) $\in \text{int} U^0$, then it is superior to (z_1^0, z_2^0). But for this to occur it is necessary that $\Sigma_t p_t^0 z_t^1 > \Sigma_t p_t^0 z_t^0$, since otherwise (z_1^1, z_2^1) would have been feasible under free trade and hence chosen, which it was not. Since $z_t^i = y_t^i - x_t^i$, where y_t^i is the production and x_t^i is the export vector, it follows that for $(z_1^1, z_2^1) \in \text{int} U^0$ it is necessary (but not sufficient) that

$$\sum_t p_t^0 (x_t^0 - x_t^1) > \sum_t p_t^0 (y_t^0 - y_t^1). \tag{6}$$

If firms maximize intertemporal profits then $\Sigma_t p_t^0 y_t^0 \geqslant \Sigma_t p_t^0 y_t^1$, in which case (6) requires that $\Sigma_t p_t^0 (x_t^0 - x_t^1) > 0$, i.e. since $\Sigma_t p_t^0 x_t^0 = 0$ under an intertemporal balance of trade, $\Sigma_t p_t^0 x_t^1 < 0$. This means that the Laspeyre's quantity index for net exports must fall. If, in addition, the nation is small, then $p_t^1 = p_t^0$ and hence the required inequality is impossible.

These observations show that for protection to be justified it is necessary that either firms are myopic or the terms of trade can be altered. In the former case, justification rests upon the government being able to recognize intertemporally profitable production while firms cannot, or that firms do recognize this but cannot borrow the necessary funds. There may, of course, be more efficient ways of dealing with this case such as improving the loans market. In the latter case, the justification is really that of the optimal trade tax to take advantage of monopolistic market power. These situations are not related to the infant-industry argument.

15.2.4. The dynamics of infant-industry protection

The preceding two-period model is useful in presenting the essentials of the infant-industry argument. However, it is more convenient to use a continuous time model in examining the dynamics of infant-industry protection. Dynamic treatments have been provided by Clemhout and Wan (1970) and Bardhan (1971) whose model provides the basis for the present discussion.

The GNP function remains as $G(p, v, q)$ and the time change in q is given by

$$\dot{q} = G_p(p, v, q) - \delta q, \tag{7}$$

where δ is a diagonal matrix of "rates of forgetfulness". Thus, q represents net accumulated experience. The intertemporal utility function takes the additivily separable form

$$\int_0^\infty e^{-\rho t} \mu \, dt = \int_0^\infty e^{-\rho t} u(z(t)) \, dt \tag{8}$$

used in the previous chapter. Suppose, for simplicity, that the world price vector is fixed and that trade balances at each instant

$$p^*[E_p(p^d, \mu) - G_p(p^s, v, q)] = 0. \tag{9}$$

The problem is to choose p^d, p^s, q, and μ at each instant in time to maximize the discounted integral of instantaneous utility. The Hamiltonian is

$$H = e^{-\rho t} \{\mu + \kappa\, p^* \left[G_p(p^s, v, q) - E_p(p^d, \mu) \right] +$$
$$+ \lambda [G_p(p^s, v, q) - \delta q]\} \tag{10}$$

which, by the maximum principle, is to be maximized with respect to p^d, p^s and μ. The solution requires therefore that

$$p^d = p^*; \quad p^s = p^* + \lambda/\kappa, \quad \kappa > 0, \tag{11}$$

implying that the optimal policy is to impose the production subsidy vector $s \equiv \lambda/\kappa$. It is easily shown that the maximized Hamiltonian may be written as

$$H(q, s) = e^{-\rho t}\, V(p^*, G(p^s, v, q) - s\delta q), \quad p^s = p^* + s, \tag{12}$$

where $V(p, m)$ is the indirect utility function corresponding to the direct utility function $u(z)$. The canonical equations describing the dynamic paths of q and s are

(a) $\quad \dot{q} = G_p(p^* + s, v, q) - \delta q,$

$\tag{13}$

(b) $\quad \dot{s} = s(\rho I + \delta) - G_q(p^* + s, v, q) - s\, \dot{V}_m/V_m.$

(See problem set.) The subsidy s is interpreted as the value (in money terms) of the experience vector, and if the dynamic learning was internal to firms it would be the equilibrium price of experience with G_q the equilibrium rental value. Eq. (13,b) says that the capital gain ($\dot{s}$) plus the rental (G_q), plus the instantaneous increase in marginal utility equals the interest (ρ) plus depreciation (forgetfulness) (δ) costs.

The model is very general and requires some additional structure and simplifications to establish concrete results and to aid the exposition. Thus, it is assumed that preferences are homogeneous of degree one making $\dot{V}_m = 0$. Also, only one industry (the first, say) experiences learning by doing so that $s_j = 0$, $j > 1$. Suppose also that $\delta = 0$, meaning that experience once obtained is never forgotten. Further assumptions are made below.

Note that, under these assumptions, $q_1 = G_1(p^* + s, v, q)$ is positive when ever good 1 is produced. According to the infant-industry argument, $G_1(p^*, v, 0) = 0$, meaning that the industry cannot survive in the free market given the initial experience $q = 0$. In general we may solve for the maximum s_1 for which $G_1(p^*, v, \dot{q}) = 0$ as $s_1(q_1)$. This is the subsidy which puts industry 1 on the verge of production, and it is a non-increasing function of q_1 if $G_{1q} \equiv \partial G_1/\partial q_1 \geq 0$. If $s_1 \leq \bar{s}_1(q_1)$, then $q_1 = G_1 = 0$, and if $s > \bar{s}_1(q_1)$, then $\dot{q}_1 = \dot{G}_1 > 0$.

What matters for the economy is not whether q_1 is increasing, but whether a higher q_1 leads to higher GNP by shifting out the production possibility frontier. Suppose that learning ceases to increase GNP after a critical level of experience $\bar{q}_1$, but does increase it, at a decreasing rate, before this level is reached. Then $G_q > 0$, $G_{1q} > 0$, $G_{2q} < 0$ for $q_1 \leqslant \bar{q}_1$, and are zero thereafter. Thus, $\dot{s}_1 = 0$ requires that $s_1 = 0$ for any $q_1 \geqslant \bar{q}_1$. For $q_1 \leqslant \bar{q}_1$, if $\dot{s}_1 = s_1 \rho - G_q(p^* + s, v, q) \equiv \psi(q_1, s_1)$, then $\psi_s = \rho - G_{q1}$ and $\psi_q = -G_{qq} > 0$. Where $\dot{s}_1 = 0$ we have that $\psi_s = G_q/s_1 - G_{q1} = (1 - G_{q1}s_1/G_1) G_q/s_1 = (1 - \partial \ln G_q/\partial \ln s_1)$. It is assumed that $\partial \ln G_q/\partial \ln s_1 < 1$, i.e. that the elasticity of the "rental value of experience" with respect to the "price of experience" is less than unity. This ensures that the $\dot{s} = 0$ curve is downward-sloping for $q_1 \leqslant \bar{q}_1$.

The phase diagram is illustrated in fig. 15.2. It is drawn such that $\dot{s}_1 = 0$ and $\dot{q}_1 = 0$ cannot simultaneously occur. This simply means that $\bar{q}_1$, the level of experience at which learning ceases, exceeds $\hat{q}_1$, the minimum level of experience needed for industry 1 to survive without a subsidy. To obtain the optimal path it is necessary to establish the direction of motion from any initial point. Various paths are shown, including the "stable arm", the path that leads to a quasi-stationary state in which $\dot{s}_1 = 0$. For example, if $q(0) = 0$ is the value of initial experience then $s_1(0) > 0$ is the optimal subsidy which is sufficient to establish positive production of good 1. The subsidy gradually reduces to zero at the instant when q_1 reaches $\bar{q}_1$; thereafter the subsidy stays at zero, meaning that the infant has "grown up". Experience continues to increase since production of good 1 is

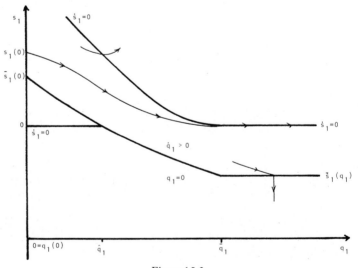

Figure 15.2

positive but, under the assumptions made, it does not shift the GNP function.

Bardhan (1971) analysed this model under a special assumption regarding learning, namely that the production function for good 1 could be written as $y_1 = \ell(q_1)f^1(x_1)$, where $\ell(q_1)$ is the learning function. In fact, he assumed that $\ell(q_1) \equiv q_1^n$, where $0 < n < 0$, n being the elasticity of ℓ with respect to q_1. It can be shown (see problem set for details of this and the following assertions) that $G(p, v, q) \equiv G^+(p^+, v)$, where $p_1^+ = p_1 \ell(q_1)$, $p_j^+ = p_j$ for $j > 1$, and $G^+(p^+, v)$ is a valid GNP function. In this case, if we define $\dot{q}_1 = G_1(p^* + s, v, q) - \delta q_1 \equiv \theta(q_1, s_1)$ and $\dot{s}_1 = s_1(\rho + \delta) - G_q(p^* + s, v, q) \equiv \psi(q_1, s_1)$, then

(a) $\theta_q = G_{1q} - \delta = [n(1 + e_1) - 1]\delta + (G_1/q_1 - \delta)n(1 + e_1),$

$$(14)$$

(b) $\theta_s = G_{11} > 0,$

and

(a) $\psi_q = -G_{qq} = [1 - n(1 + e_1)]q_1/G_q,$

$$(15)$$

(b) $\psi_s = (\rho + \delta) - G_{q1} = \rho + \delta [1 - n(1 + e_1)] -$
$\quad - (G_1/q_1 - \delta)n(1 + e_1),$

where $e_1 = \partial \ln G_1/\partial \ln p_1$ is the own-price supply elasticity for good 1. The first expression in (14) and (15) is general, the second being the case for the Bardhan learning function model. It can be shown that $\partial \ln G_1/\partial \ln q_1 = n(1 + e_1)$. If this "output elasticity of learning" is less than unity, then $\psi_q > 0$ and, where $\dot{q} = 0$ and hence $G_1/q_1 = \delta$, it also follows that $\theta_q < 0 < \psi_s$. Thus, the $\dot{q}_1 = 0$ curve is upward-sloping in (q_1, s_1) space and the $\dot{s}_1 = 0$ curve is downward-sloping at the point where $\dot{q}_1 = 0$. Also, the $\dot{s}_1 = 0$ curve is downward-sloping when $\dot{q}_1 < 0$, but when $\dot{q}_1 > 0$ it is downward-sloping only if $\psi_s = \rho + \delta - n(1 + e_1)G_1/q_1 > 0$.

The phase diagram presented in fig. 15.3 assumes that $\psi_s > 0$ everywhere, for ease of exposition. The stationary state is at (q_1^0, s_1^0), where

(a) $q_1^0 = G_1(p^* + s^0, v, q^0)/\delta > 0,$

$$(16)$$

(b) $s_1^0 = G_q(p^* + s^0, v, q^0)/(\rho + \delta) > 0.$

Thus, in the Bardhan model the subsidy to industry 1 goes on for ever, even though the industry might be able to survive without a subsidy (as in fig. 15.3 where $q_1^0 > \hat{q}_1$). This is because the externality is a permanent one.

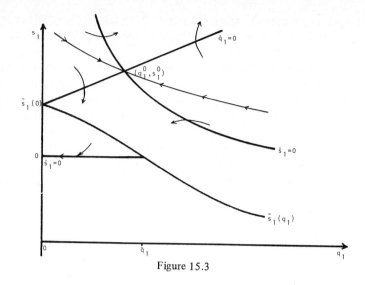

Figure 15.3

15.2.5. Remarks on the infant-industry argument

The infant-industry argument for protection is based upon the existence of dynamic production externalities arising from "learning by doing". It is, indeed, a valid argument for government intervention in the free market. However, it has been shown that the optimal intervention is to impose a set of production subsidies (and taxes possibly) since the source of the learning is the act of production. While trade taxes may be used to improve welfare they are suboptimal.

Also, there is nothing in the theory which prevents the export industries from "learning by doing", so the optimal policy may be to protect these export industries. Moreover, if learning is permanent, the optimal subsidy may always be positive, even though the industry could survive without protection. While the figures above showed the case where the optimal subsidy falls over time towards its steady-state value, this is not a necessary result since, in Bardhan's model for example, ψ_s could not be signed unambiguously in the region where $\dot{q}_1 > 0$.

These results are consistent with those obtained by Clemhout and Wan (1970), who also consider learning in more than one industry and various special learning functions in a model with a fixed horizon. Bardhan also considers learning by both nations. At a less theoretical level Baldwin (1969) questions the effectiveness of tariffs in accomplishing a more efficient allocation of resources. His argument applies also to protection by production taxes, and is, essentially, that these may be too blunt as a policy instrument if the learning is based not directly upon production or if there are extra costs associated with the learning. For example, if the externality arises through the training of workers who are free to switch to other firms, the optimal policy will be to subsidize the training of workers. A production subsidy will encourage production but will not encourage the training of workers by the firm. As another example, there may be costs associated with the evaluation of advances in knowledge acquired which the firm is reluctant to make if that knowledge becomes freely available to other firms. A direct subsidy to new entrants is suggested.

Perhaps the main difficulty with the infant-industry argument in practice is that of identifying the existence and nature of the learning process and establishing that it involves an externality.

15.3. Heterogeneous capital goods and steady-state theorems

Attention is now turned to a consideration of the case of heterogeneous capital goods, and to an analysis of the steady state for a small open economy.

Let the (instantaneous) production possibility set be $Y(K, L)$, where $K = (K_1, ..., K_M)$ is a vector of capital stocks and L is a vector of non-capital inputs, called labour for convenience. The output vector $y = (y_1, ..., y_M)$ is the same length as K and $y = z + \iota + x$, where z is the consumption vector, ι is the (gross) investment vector and x is the net export vector. The optimal saving problem is

$$\max \left\{ \int_0^\infty e^{-\rho t} \, V(p, G(p, K, L) - p\iota) dt : \dot{K} = \iota - \Delta K, \right.$$

$$\left. p\iota \leqslant G(p, K, L), \iota \geqslant 0 \right\}, \tag{17}$$

where the time dependence of p, K, L and ι has been suppressed and Δ is a diagonal matrix of depreciation rates. The maximum principle states that ι is chosen (at each instant) to solve

$$W(K, \lambda; p, L) \equiv \max_\iota \left\{ V(p, G(p, K, L) - p\iota) + \right.$$

$$\left. + \lambda \iota : \iota \geqslant 0, p\iota \leqslant G(p, K, L) \right\}. \tag{18}$$

The Kuhn–Tucker conditions for a solution to (18) are

(a) $\lambda - [V_E(p, E) + \kappa] \, p \leqslant 0 \leqslant \iota,$

(b) $E \equiv G(p, K, L) - p\iota \geqslant 0 \geqslant \kappa,$ (19)

where κ is the Lagrange multiplier for the upper bound on $p\iota$. The second-order conditions are satisfied if indirect utility is concave in E, i.e. $V_{EE} \leqslant 0$. It can be shown that

$$\kappa = \max \{0, \lambda_1/p_1 - V_E(p, 0), ..., \lambda_M/p_M - V_E(p, 0)\}. \qquad (20)$$

The investment–expenditure choice may be expressed in terms of $q \equiv \max \{\lambda_1/p_1, ..., \lambda_M/p_M\}$, the maximum ratio of present value to asset price for capital goods. If $q \leqslant V_E(p, G(p, K, L))$, then no feasible investment is as beneficial as current consumption so $\iota = 0$ and $E = G(p, K, L)$ is the solution. If $V_E(p, G(p, K, L)) < q < V_E(p, 0)$, then $\iota \geqslant 0$ and $0 < E \equiv G(p, K, L) - p\iota < G$. In both these cases expenditure is positive, $\kappa = 0$ and hence the Kuhn–Tucker conditions reduce to $\lambda - V_E \, p \leqslant 0 \leqslant \iota$. The third case is where $q > V_E(p, 0)$ and hence $\kappa = q - V_E(p, 0) > 0$. In this case $E = 0$ and $\iota \geqslant 0$.

In short, the following procedure may be used to obtain the investment pattern. If $q < V_E(p, G(p, K, L))$, then $\iota = 0$. If $q > V_E(p, G(p, K, L))$, then $\iota \geqslant 0$ such that $\iota_j \geqslant 0$ for $\lambda_j/p_j = 1$ and $\iota_i = 0$ for $\lambda_i/p_i < q$.

The canonical equations are

$$\dot{K} = W_\lambda(K, \lambda; p, L) - \Delta K,$$

$$\dot{\lambda} = \lambda \, [\rho I + \Delta] - W_K(K, \lambda; p, L), \qquad (21)$$

where $W_\lambda(\cdot) = \iota(\cdot)$ is the optimal investment vector and $W_K(\cdot) = [V_m(p, G(p, K, L) - p\iota(\cdot)) + \kappa] \, G_K(p, K, L)$.

15.3.1. The steady state

In the steady state $\dot{K} = 0$ and $\dot{\lambda} = 0$. If $\iota > 0$ and $E > 0$ in the steady state, then

(a) $\dot{K} = 0$ implies $W_\lambda(K, \lambda; p, L) = \Delta K,$

(b) $\dot{\lambda} = 0$ implies $R_K(p, K, L) \equiv P^{-1} G_K(p, K, L) = 1 \, [\rho I + \Delta],$ (22)

where R_K is the own gross rate of return vector, 1 is a vector of ones, and $P = \text{diag}$

(p). These equations determine the steady-state values for K and λ for constant p and L. The first equation states that gross investment equals depreciation, so net investment is zero. The second states that the gross rate of return for capital goods equals the rate of time preference, ρ, which may also be interpreted as the equilibrium interest rate, plus the rate of depreciation. For capital good j

$$R_j(p, K, L) \equiv G_{K_j}(p, K, L)/p_j = \rho + \delta_j, \qquad j = 1, ..., M. \tag{23}$$

This model is quite general and contains various special cases. For example, in the previous chapter we dealt with a model with one capital good and several consumer goods, a special case of the present model. Also of interest is the case where intermediate inputs and joint outputs are ruled out. Then conditions (23) can be expressed in terms of industry cost functions. Let the unit cost function for good j be $c^j(r, w)$, where r is the rental vector and w is the wage vector. Since $r = G_K(p, K, L) = P1 \, [\rho I + \Delta] = p \, [\rho I + \Delta]$ condition (23) may be expressed as

(a) $\quad c^j(p(\rho I + \Delta), w) = p_j, \qquad j = 1, ..., M,$

(b) $\quad \sum_j c^j_w(p(\rho I + \Delta), w) y_j = L.$
$$\tag{24}$$

This has been used by Burmiester (1978) for example.

The exogenous variables in (22) are p, ρ, Δ and L, while K and λ are endogenous. It is of interest to consider the effect of changes in the exogenous variables upon the steady-state solution. Consider, for example, the effects of a change in p upon the capital stock, output and net exports. These are summarized as

(a) $\quad \mathrm{d}K = G_{KK}^{-1}[\rho I + \Delta - G_{Kp}]\mathrm{d}p = G_{KK}^{-1}[\mathrm{diag}(R_K) - G_{pK}]\mathrm{d}p,$

(b) $\quad \mathrm{d}y = G_{pp}\mathrm{d}p + G_{pK}\mathrm{d}K = [(G_{pp} - G_{pK}G_{KK}^{-1}G_{Kp}) + G_{pK}G_{KK}^{-1}(\rho I + \Delta)]\mathrm{d}p,$
$$\tag{25}$$

(c) $\quad \mathrm{d}x = \mathrm{d}y - \Delta \mathrm{d}K = [G_{pp} - (G_{pK} - \Delta)G_{KK}^{-1}(G_{pK} - \Delta) +$

$\qquad + \rho(G_{pK} - \Delta)G_{KK}^{-1}]\mathrm{d}p,$

if G_{KK}^{-1} exists. The effect of p upon K clearly depends upon the matrix G_{Kp}, whose sign structure indicates the capital intensity of the products, but also upon ρ and Δ, or R_K.

If the price of good j increases, will the net output of that good increase as in the static model? In general this result does not hold unless special assumptions are made, as is now shown. In (25,b) the component $G_{pp}\,dp$ is the static effect for given K, while $G_{pK}\,dK$ indicates the effect on y of the change in K that occurs. The matrix $G_{pp} - G_{pK}G_{KK}^{-1}G_{Kp}$ is positive semi-definite, the proof being left to the problem set. If $G_{pK}G_{KK}^{-1}\,(\rho I + \Delta)$ were also positive semi-definite, then the whole matrix would be positive semi-definite and so the effect of p upon y would be similar to that in the static model. However, this is not the case in general.

If $G_{pK}G_{KK}^{-1} \geqslant 0$, then it is easily seen that $G_{pK}G_{KK}^{-1}\,(\rho I + \Delta) \geqslant 0$ and hence $\partial y_j/\partial p_j \geqslant 0$, so the own-price output response is non-negative. What about the cross-price effects? In the case of just two goods it can be shown that $\partial y_i/\partial p_j \leqslant 0$ for $j \neq i$. This occurs because the net supply functions are homogeneous of degree zero in p, whence $\Sigma_j\, p_j(\partial y_i/\partial p_j) = 0$. In general, the homogeneity property implies that if p_j changes, then some output will increase and some will decrease.

The assumption $G_{pK}G_{KK}^{-1} \geqslant 0$ needs to be interpreted. If

$$\Pi(p,r,L) \equiv \max_{y,K} \{py - rK: y \in Y(K,L)\},$$

than it can be shown that $\partial y/\partial r = \Pi_{pr} = G_{pK}G_{KK}^{-1}$, where $r = G_K$, or equivalently, $K = -\Pi_r$. Thus, the assumption is that $\Pi_{pr} = G_{pK}G_{KK}^{-1} \geqslant 0$, which means that capital and goods are "substitutes" in the sense that an increase in any rental will increase the net output of all goods for a given vector of labour endowments. A sufficient condition for this is that $G_{pK} \leqslant 0$ and that G_{KK} has non-negative off-diagonal elements, the latter condition ensuring that $G_{KK}^{-1} \leqslant 0$. Thus, the sufficient condition is that all capital inputs are substitutes in the technical sense that an increase in any one stock will raise the rental on all other stocks, and that an increase in any stock will reduce the output of all goods, meaning that no good is capital intensive.

In general the effect of a change in p upon net exports is ambiguous. The first two terms in (25,c) form a positive semi-definite matrix so they show that net exports of a good increase in response to an increase in it price. The third term depends on the sign structure of $G_{pK} - \Delta$ if it is assumed that $G_{KK}^{-1} \leqslant 0$. If in addition, however, $G_{pK} \leqslant 0$, then this matrix is non-negative and so exports increase in response to an increase in their own price.

What is the effect of a change in the rate of time preference? The results are as follows:

(a) $dK = G_{KK}^{-1} p \, d\rho,$

(b) $dy = G_{pK} G_{KK}^{-1} p \, d\rho$

(c) $dx = (G_{pK} - \Delta) \, dK = (G_{pK} - \Delta) G_{KK}^{-1} p \, d\rho,$

(d) $dw = G_{LK} G_{KK}^{-1} p \, d\rho.$

$$(27)$$

An increase in the rate of time preference raises the rate of return to all capital goods requiring a reduction in the capital stock by some measure. Since G_{KK}^{-1} is negative definite it follows that

$$p \, dK/d\rho = p G_{KK}^{-1} p < 0, \qquad (28)$$

so the asset value of the capital stock falls as ρ increases.

Under what conditions will an increase in the interest rate reduce every wage rate? A sufficient condition is that $G_{LK} \geq 0$ and G_{KK} has non-negative off-diagonal elements, meaning that all factors are substitutes in a technical sense, for then $G_{KK}^{-1} \leq 0$ and hence $dw/d\rho \leq 0$. It is of some interest to note that (27,d) gives the slope of the factor price frontier with respect to ρ. The factor price frontier is defined as

$$\{(w, \rho): w = G_L (p, \kappa (\rho; p, \Delta), L), \rho \geq 0\}, \qquad (29)$$

where $K = \kappa (\rho; p, \Delta)$ is the solution for K from (23).

If ρ increases, net exports will all rise if $G_{pK} \leq 0$ and $G_{KK}^{-1} \leq 0$, conditions which have previously been discussed.

The above results indicate that the steady-state model with capital contains features which distinguish it from the static or atemporal model. The steady-state model is akin to the static model with endogenous factor supplies or non-traded goods. Indeed, the distinguishing feature is that capital stocks are endogenous, adjusting in the steady state to ensure equal (net) rates of return on all capital types and zero capital gains. If a product price increases, it is possible that net output of that good might not increase, since the change in capital stocks will shift the production possibility set. This is precisely the same situation that occurred in the static model with endogenous factor supplies, an observation which should contain little surprise.

15.3.2. The steady state and the theorems of international trade

There has been considerable interest in recent years in establishing conditions under which standard static theorems continue to apply in the steady state. Attention has been focused upon the Rybczynski, Stolper–Samuelson, factor price equalization, and Heckscher–Ohlin theorems, as well as the net output–price relationship discussed above. Most of the discussion has taken place using a so-called "time-phased" model which is briefly outlined below, but the present model formulation can serve as a vehicle for discussion.

In examining these theorems in the steady state much depends upon how one wants to interpret them. One way is to treat capital like goods, in fact as an intertemporal intermediate commodity, and have these theorems relate to the fixed factors. Then we ask, for example, whether an increase in the endowment of one factor causes, at fixed product prices and interest rate (ρ), the output of one good to rise while that of other falls – the Rybczynski result. This requires at least two primary factors. This is the approach in Kemp (1973), Steedman and Metcalfe (1977), and Kemp and Khang (1974).

Let (24) be written in matrix form as

(a) $C(r, w) = p,$

$$\text{(30)}$$

(b) $C_w(r, w) y = L,$

where $r = Dp$, $D \equiv \rho I + \Delta$ and y is a vector of gross outputs. For fixed p and ρ (and Δ) this looks exactly like a static model, so the Rybczynski theorem relating L to y applies directly. If p changes such that (30,a) continues to hold and there are equal numbers of goods and fixed factors, we have

$$dw = C_w^{-1} [I - C_r D] dp, \qquad (31)$$

which is just like the case of intermediate inputs of Chapter 5. In the case of two factors and two products the sign structure of (31) for a productive ecomomy is such that there is an ordering of factors for which an increase in the price of good i will raise w_i and reduce the other factor reward. In fact, the real reward to i will increase in terms of either good and, of course, the other factor loses real income. The reasoning is as in Chapter 5. Consider now the factor price equalization theorem. If the technology is the same in two countries, the depreciation and interest (time preference) rates are the same, both countries produce all goods, and the L endowments are in the same diversification cone, then the price vector w will be the same in both nations. Again the reasoning is as in Chapter 5.

Steedman and Metcalfe (1977) also examine the validity of the HOS theorem in this model and conclude that it continues to hold in its quantity form but not in its price form.

An alternative procedure is to continue to treat capital as a factor. Since the quantity of capital is endogenous, theorems such as Rybczynski's lose their meaning or, at least, have to be reinterpreted very carefully. In this vein Ethier (1979) considers a two-product, one-labour, two-capital model in which he defines an aggregate factor "capital" and establishes that all of the basic theorems of the static model apply to the steady state. In terms of the current framework (Ethier used the "time-phased" framework) the quantity of capital is defined by

$$K_0 \equiv pC_r y = pK \tag{32}$$

as the current value of the capital stock. The cost vector $C(r, w)$ may be written as $C((\rho I + \Delta) p, w) = C^0(\rho, w; p, \Delta)$, where $C^0_\rho = pC_r$ is the input vector for aggregate capital. The equilibrium conditions then read

(a) $C^0(\rho, w; p, \Delta) = p,$

$$\tag{33}$$

(b) $C^0_w y = L,$

with K_0 determined as

$$K_0 = C^0_\rho y. \tag{34}$$

By using this aggregation procedure, the model as written in (33) and (34) looks just like a static model with one capital good with rental price ρ. Note that K_0 depends upon prices, so it is not a consistent quantity aggregate. Ethier's approach is to look at the basic theorems in terms of this model (with two products and one labour), and shows that the Rybczynski, Stolper–Samuelson, factor price equalization and HOS theorems continue to hold. He treats ρ as if it were an endogenous variable and K_0 as if it were an exogenous variable. The conclusion reached is that "all four theorems are impervious. The inference is that the standard model's assumption of two homogeneous timeless factors, and consequent neglect of the nature of capital, is quite harmless, as far as the four basic theorems are concerned". He argues that difficulties found in proving these theorems are due to the introduction of other features, such as the introduction of more factors than goods or of non-traded goods, not to the introduction of capital as such.

However, there is the question of how the Ethier results should be interpreted.

What does it mean to keep K_0 fixed when p is changing, for example? Or to change K_0 and observe the effect upon ρ? In our formulation of the steady state ρ is given by consumer preferences while K, and hence K_0, is endogenous. In this light, what Ethier has established is that relationships contained in the four theorems hold in the steady state. For example, if K_0 were kept fixed, then an increase in p_1 must be associated with a fall in the real income of capital and a fall in the real income of labour if product 1 is capital intensive in the sense of having the highest value of capital per worker. Since K_0 is not fixed but ρ is, the result applies to a hypothetical experiment, not one that is of direct interest. It is left to the reader to interpret the other results. If ρ is given by preferences and p by the market, then w and K_0 are endogenous, reinterpreting them as indicating relationships which hold in steady-state equilibrium. Thus, ρ is treated as if it were an endogenous variable and K_0 as if it were an exogenous variable, but that is for the purpose of obtaining relationships in the usual way. The results should be interpreted as follows. In the Rybczynski case an increase in the capital stock K_0 is associated with an increase in the output of the product which is intensive in its use of "capital" (in the sense that the value of capital used per worker is higher than in the other product).

15.3.3. Time-phased models

Reference was made above to "time-phased" models of steady-state growth, which are now briefly considered but not analysed. The models are based upon discrete time and are cast in terms of an intermediate-good model. All activities use primary factors whose price vector is w, and inputs of goods produced last period. The latter are paid for at the beginning, while the primary factors are paid at the end of the current period. If the interest rate is ρ, then the cost of the "time-phased" intermediate inputs is $q \equiv (1 + \rho)p$, where p is the steady-state price vector. The cost function for the unit production of good j is $c^j(q, w)$ and is equal to p_j in steady-state equilibrium if good j is produced. If all goods are produced this condition can be written in matrix form as

$$C(q, w) = p \quad \text{or} \quad qC_q + wC_w w = p. \tag{35}$$

Here C_q is the Leontief-type input–output matrix and C_w denotes input–output coefficients for primary factors. The net output vector is $y = [I - C_q]g$, where g denotes the activity (gross output) vector. Finally, the factor market equilibrium condition is that $C_w g = v$.

The model is very general and contains various special cases. The direct interpretation is where capital is of the "circulating" variety. Current production requires the input of goods produced in the previous period plus current inputs of primary factors. The capital vector is $C_q g$. Other interpretations are possible, as Smith (1976) demonstrates.

To see the connection with the model of fixed capital used in this chapter, let it be supposed that our capital vector is simply a vector of goods produced last period and used up fully this period. Then the depreciation rates are all unity $(\Delta = I)$ and hence the rental vector in (30) is $r = (\rho I + \Delta)p = (1 + \rho)p$, which coincides with q in (35). Thus, our model formulation encompasses the "time-phased" formulation.

15.4. Foreign investment

Consideration is now given to the dynamics of trade and investment when foreign ownership of capital is permitted. In Chapter 13 a static model of perfect mobility of capital was dealt with in some detail. There the amount of capital owned by each consumer (nation) was given and the world stock was allocated so as to equate the rentals in each nation. This is a simplistic view of the process of foreign investment, and so we now try to make it more realistic by embedding it in a dynamic framework in which the amounts of capital owned are also chosen.

Two approaches seem possible. First as in Chapter 13, one can assume that capital is perfectly mobile throughout the world. In this case the world stock is allocated by the forces of competition so as to equate rentals in each nation. Free trade in the services of capital, like free trade in goods, equates market prices. But this assumes a great deal. Alternatively, one can assume that newly produced capital (investment goods) is internationally mobile, but that once installed as capital within a nation is immobile internationally. One could take this formulation to its logical conclusion and assume that it is immobile between industries within each nation, but we will continue to assume perfect mobility intranationally. In this second approach there need not be an equality of rental rates on capital since there is no international mobility statically. Dynamically there is, however, since consumers, in addition to choosing how much capital stock to acquire, choose where to locate new investment. Clearly, profit-seeking consumers will locate it where the return is highest and so let stocks fall through depreciation where it is lowest. Thus, permanent differences in rental rates cannot be maintained. Given time for investments to alter capital stocks sufficiently, the rentals will be equated internationally. Then the model will be like that postulated in the first-mentioned approach. Evidently, the time paths followed by the economy differ according to which assumption is made.

In previous sections of this chapter, trade in investment goods was permitted but the domestic stock of capital could only be increased, and was limited, by domestic saving. In a world of free foreign investment the world capital stock is increased, and limited, by world saving. The domestic capital stock (installed and used for production) depends on investment decisions in both countries, not just the home country. Consider now how the investment decisions are made.

Suppose there are two countries each containing an (aggregate) consumer, and that capital and labour are used to produce a pure consumer good and an investment good (new capital). Let the saving decisions be made and consider the allocation of that saving. The international price vector is $p = (p_1, p_2)$, where p_2 is the price of investment goods. The asset price of capital is q in the home, and q^* in the foreign country. The rental rates are $r \equiv G_K(p, K, L)$ and $r^* \equiv G_K^*(p, K^*, L^*)$.

15.4.1. The investment process

The investment process formulated by Hori and Stein (1977) is as follows. The asset price q is interpreted as an equity price, the price for a share in the ownership of a unit of the home nation's capital stock. These prices are determined to equate the rates of return on equities, i.e.

$$G_K/q = G_K^*/q^*. \tag{36}$$

Moreover, the rate of return on new investment equals the rate of return on equities, so

$$\max \{G_K/p_2, G_K^*/p_2\} = G_K/q = G_K^*/q^* \quad \text{or} \quad \max \{q, q^*\} = p_2. \tag{37}$$

It is assumed that savers buy new equity in the home nation alone if $p_2 = q > q^*$, i.e. if $G_K > G_K^*$. Conversely, if $p_2 = q^* > q$, i.e. if $G_K^* > G_K$, then savers buy new equity in the foreign nation. Thus, all saving is directed towards the nation with the highest current rental on capital.

Eventually the rental rates will be equalized (except in the case where the capital stock in one nation reduces to zero) as will equity prices. Then the savers are indifferent as to where their saving is directed. However, equal rental and equity prices should be maintained by the saving allocation. If each nation is in its diversification cone, then the capital stocks, and hence the allocation of investment, are not unique. This is the indeterminacy of capital stocks pointed out by Fischer and Frenkel (1972). Hori and Stein (1977) solve the problem of indeterminacy by assuming specialization in production and hence forcing $G_{KK} < 0$. Fischer and Frenkel solve it by introducing costs of adjustment which can be obtained by supposing a transformation function of the form $T(y, K, L, \dot{K} - \delta K) = 0$. That is to say, putting new capital in place shifts the production possibility set for goods inwards and therefore involves a cost in addition to the purchase price. Again, $G_{KK} < 0$ results. Alternatively, one could assume no trade in investment goods, which is somewhat unrealistic, as in Frenkel (1971). Finally, $G_{KK} < 0$ can be obtained by supposing that there are more factors than products. In the two-product case this means having three (or more) factors such as capital and a specific factor in each industry.

15.4.2. The Hori–Stein model

Hori and Stein complete their model by assuming that both nations have a common constant saving rate s. If the home nation specializes in the investment good then $G_2(p, K, L) = F_2(K, L)$, while $G_1^*(p, K^*, L^*) = F_1^*(K^*, L^*)$ if the foreign nation specializes in the consumption good, where F_2 and F_1^* denote the production functions. World demand for good 1 is $(1 - s)[p_1 F_1^*(K^*, L^*) + p_2 F_2(K, L)]$, which equals production $F_1(K^*, L^*)$ in equilibrium. If p_1 is normalized to unity, this determines p_2 as

$$p_2 = sF_1^*(K^*, L^*)/F_2(K, L)(1 - s), \tag{38}$$

whence

$$\xi(K, K^*) \equiv \frac{s}{1 - s} \frac{F_1^*(K^*, L^*)}{F_2(K, L)} \frac{F_{2K}(K, L)}{F_{1K}^*(K^*, L^*)} =$$

$$= p_2 \frac{F_{2K}}{F_{1K}^*} = \frac{q}{q^*} = 1 \tag{39}$$

defines the set of (K, K^*) for which equity prices are equal. This yields the explicit relationship $K = \psi(K^*)$ which is maintained if $\dot{K} = \psi_K(K^*)\dot{K}^*$, and this relationship determines the allocation of investment between the two nations.

The equations of motion are

(a)
$$\left.\begin{array}{l} \dot{K} = F_2(K,L) \ - \delta K \\[2mm] \dot{K}^* = \qquad\quad - \delta K^* \end{array}\right\}, \qquad q > q^*,$$

(b)
$$\left.\begin{array}{l} \dot{K} = \qquad\quad - \delta K \\[2mm] \dot{K}^* = F_2(K,L) - \delta K^* \end{array}\right\}, \qquad q < q^*, \qquad (40)$$

(c)
$$\left.\begin{array}{l} \dot{K} = \psi_K (1 + \psi_K)^{-1} \, [F_2(K,L) - \delta(K + K^*)] \\[2mm] \dot{K}^* = (1 + \psi_K)^{-1} \, [F_2(K,L) - \delta(K + K^*)] \end{array}\right\}, \qquad q = q^*.$$

This formulation is actually more general than that of Hori and Stein. They assume that $a \equiv KF_{2K}/F_2$ and $a^* \equiv K^*F_{1K}^*/F_1^*$ are constants so that $\xi(K, K^*)$ is linear in (K, K^*), whence $K = bK^*$, where $b \equiv sa/(1 - s)a^*$. In this case (40,c) becomes

(c')
$$\left.\begin{array}{l} \dot{K} = \theta\, F_2(K,L) - \delta K \\[2mm] \dot{K}^* = (1 - \theta)\, F_2(K,L) - \delta K^* \end{array}\right\}, \qquad q = q^*, \qquad (40)$$

where $\theta \equiv sa/(sa + (1 - s)\, a^*)$ is a constant fraction. The equations of motion (40) together with (39), which gives q/q^*, determine the paths of K and K^* through time. The paths for p_2, q and q^* can then be derived from (36)–(38). The paths converge to a steady state where $q = q^*$.

The net ownership of foreign capital is $Q \equiv C - K$ for the home nation and the amount of the net foreign investment is $\dot{Q} = \dot{C} - \dot{K}$. If $Q > 0$, then the home nation consumers accumulate capital faster than it is demanded by home producers. Home income is

$$m \equiv G(p_1, K, L) + \begin{cases} G_K^* \, Q, & Q > 0, \\[2mm] G_K \, Q, & Q < 0. \end{cases} \qquad (41)$$

If $q = q^*$, then $G_K = G_K^*$ is the common rental on capital. Hence

$$m = G(p, K, L) + G_K(p, K, L)\, Q = p_2 F_2(K, L) + p_2 F_{2K}(K, L)\, Q$$

irrespective of the sign of Q and

$$\dot{C} = s\left[F_2(K,L) + F_{2K}(K,L)\,Q\right] - \delta C. \tag{42}$$

Thus,

$$\dot{Q} = \dot{C} - \dot{K} = \left[sF_{2K}(K,L) - \delta\right]Q + (s - \theta)F_2(K,L) \tag{43}$$

describes the time path of Q in terms of the time path of K.
  In the steady state $\dot{Q} = 0$, implying

$$Q = -(s - \theta)F_2(K,L)/\left[sF_{2K}(K,L) - \delta\right]. \tag{44}$$

Also, $\dot{K} = 0$, implying $\theta F_2 = \delta K$ and

$$sF_{2K}(K,L) - \delta = saF_2(K,L)/K - \delta = \left[sa + (1 - s)\,a^*\right]\delta < 0, \tag{45}$$

since $a \equiv KF_{2K}/F_2 < 1$ if $F_2(K,L)$ is strictly concave in K, and similarly $a^* < 1$.
  The denominator in (44) is therefore negative, so Q has the same sign as $s - \theta$.
That is,

$$Q = C - K \gtrless 0, \quad \text{as } s - \theta = \frac{s(1 - s)\,(a^* - a)}{sa + (1 - s)a^*} \gtrless 0.$$

If $s > \theta$, then $Q = C - K > 0$ and the home nation is a net creditor in the steady state, i.e. it owns capital abroad. If $s < \theta$, then $Q = C - K < 0$ and the home nation is a net debtor, with some of its capital stock owned by foreigners. Thus, whether a nation ends up as a net debtor or creditor depends upon the technologies, the saving rate and the labour supplies. If the technologies are identical, $a = a^*$, then $s - \theta = 0$ and net indebtedness is zero. If $a^* > a$, then $s - \theta > 0$ and hence the home nation will be a net creditor.

  Hori and Stein examine the time path described by (40). They conclude that even in such a simple model with considerable structure it is not possible to be definite about the sequence of "stages of the balance of payments" that are often postulated in the literature. The advantage of their model is that it nicely presents the essentials of the process of capital accumulation and foreign investment in a simple framework.

  It is often assumed that there is just one good produced which can be used for both consumption and investment purposes, whereas Hori and Stein assume two goods and specialization. Also, it is customary to assume different saving rates, but the assumption of a common saving rate allows great simplifications since then capital accumulation does not depend upon the income distribution.

Also, most studies consider a small open economy for which prices and foreign rentals are exogenous.

15.4.3. *An optimal saving model*

We now consider a model of foreign investment based upon optimal saving programs rather than the assumption of fixed saving rates.

The home nation consumer takes all prices, including the rentals on capital at home and abroad, as given and maximizes his intertemporal utility function. His problem is

$$\max \left\{ \int_0^\infty e^{-\rho t} V(p_1, E)dt: \dot{C}_d = \iota_d - \Delta C_d, \dot{C}_f = \iota_f - \Delta^* C_f, \right.$$

$$\left. E + p_2(\iota_d + \iota_f) = m \equiv G_L L + G_K C_d + G_K^* C_f, (E, \iota_d, \iota_f) \geqslant 0 \right\}. \tag{47}$$

Here C_d is the domestic capital stock owned by the home consumer, C_f is the amount of the foreign capital stock he owns, and ι_d and ι_f are the investment vectors. The price vector is partitioned as $p = (p_1, p_2)$ into subvectors for consumer and investment goods. The problem is a special case of optimal growth with heterogeneous capital goods. Here each type of investment good can be used to add to the domestic or foreign capital stocks. The conditions for a solution correspond to those set out in section 15.3.

The Hamiltonian for (47) is

$$H = V(p_1, E) + \lambda_d(\iota_d - \Delta C_d) + \lambda_f(\iota_f - \Delta^* C_f) \tag{48}$$

which, by Pontryagin's maximum principle, is to be maximized with respect to the control variables as in

$$H^0(\lambda_d, \lambda_f, C_d, C_f) \equiv \max \{H: E + p_2(\iota_d + \iota_f) = m, (E, \iota_d, \iota_f) \geqslant 0\}. \tag{49}$$

The Kuhn–Tucker conditions are

(a) $\lambda_j - [V_E(p_1, E) + \kappa] p_2 \leqslant 0 \leqslant \iota_j, \quad j = d, f,$

(b) $E = m - p_2(\iota_d + \iota_f) \geqslant 0 \leqslant \kappa,$
$$\tag{50}$$

where κ is a Lagrange multiplier. Clearly (50) allows for corner solutions for E, ι_d and ι_f. Consider, for example, the case where there is just one capital good and $E > 0$ ($\kappa = 0$). Then (50) says that all investment is directed to domestic capital if $\lambda_d = V_E p_2 > \lambda_f$ since in this case $0 = \lambda_d - V_E p_2 > \lambda_f - V_E p_2$ which implies $\iota_d \geqslant 0$ and $\iota_f = 0$. Thus, for $\iota_d, \iota_f > 0$ it is necessary that $\lambda_d = \lambda_f$. In general the solutions to (50) are written as $\iota_j = \iota_j(\lambda, m, p) = \iota_j^0(\lambda, C)$ and $E = m - p_2(\iota_d + \iota_f) = E(\lambda, m, p) = E^0(\lambda, C)$, where $\lambda = (\lambda_d, \lambda_f)$ and $C = (C_d, C_f)$.

The equations of motion are

$$\dot{C}_d = \iota_d^0(\lambda, C) - \Delta C_d = \partial H^0(\lambda, C)/\partial \lambda_d,$$
$$\dot{C}_f = \iota_f^0(\lambda, C) - \Delta^* C_f = \partial H^0(\lambda, C)/\partial \lambda_f, \tag{51}$$

and

$$\dot{\lambda}_d = \rho \lambda_d - \partial H^0(\lambda, C)/\partial C_d,$$
$$\dot{\lambda}_f = \rho \lambda_f - \partial H^0(\lambda, C)/\partial C_f, \tag{52}$$

where

$$\partial H^0(\lambda, C)/\partial C_d = \Delta \lambda_d - (V_E + \kappa) G_K,$$
$$\partial H^0(\lambda, C)/\partial C_f = \Delta^* \lambda_f - (V_E + \kappa) G_K^*, \tag{53}$$

and

$$\kappa = \max \{0, P_2^{-1}(\lambda_d - V_E(p_1, 0)p_2), P_2^{-1}(\lambda_f - V_E(p_1, 0)p_2)\} \tag{54}$$

is the Lagrange multiplier from (50).

The preceding describes the decisions taken by the home nation, the foreign nation being assumed to follow a similar policy. The model is completed by imposing the equations of motion for capital stocks and the market equilibrium conditions for goods. The former are

(a) $\dot{K} = (\iota_d + \iota_f^*) - \Delta K,$

(b) $\dot{K}^* = (\iota_f + \iota_d^*) - \Delta^* K^*,$
$\tag{55}$

and the latter are

(a) $G_1(p, K, L) + G_1^*(p, K^*, L^*) - \phi(p_1, m) - \phi^*(p_1, m^*) = 0,$

(b) $G_2(p, K, L) + G_2^*(p, K^*, L^*) - (\iota_d + \iota_f + \iota_d^* + \iota_f^*) = 0.$

$$(56)$$

At any point in time K, K^*, C and C^* are given. The consumers choose E, E^*, $\iota_d, \iota_f, \iota_d^*$ and ι_f^* in accordance with the maximum principle. These choices determine K, K^*, C and C^* and so the economy evolves through time. The profiles of commodity prices adjust to clear markets at each instant. A steady state occurs when all variables cease to change.

Consider the steady-state solution. Suppose that $E, E^* > 0$ ($\kappa, \kappa^* = 0$) always, that $K, K^* > 0$ and $C \geqslant 0$ and $C^* \geqslant 0$. Then

$$\iota_d + \iota_f^* = \Delta K > 0; \quad \iota_f + \iota_d^* = \Delta^* K^* > 0, \tag{57}$$

and

$$\iota_d = \Delta C_d; \quad \iota_f = \Delta^* C_f,$$
$$\iota_d^* = \Delta^* C_d^*, \quad \iota_f^* = \Delta C_f^*, \tag{58}$$

and

$$(\rho I + \Delta) \lambda_d = V_E G_K; \quad (\rho I + \Delta^*) \lambda_f = V_E G_K^*, \tag{59}$$

and

$$(\rho^* I + \Delta) \lambda_f^* = V_E^* G_K; \quad (\rho^* I + \Delta^*) \lambda_d^* = V_E^* G_K^*. \tag{60}$$

To facilitate the exposition suppose there is just one capital good. Then (57) indicates that four patterns of investment are possible. If both ι_d and ι_f^* are positive then the Kuhn–Tucker conditions require that $\lambda_d = V_E p_2$ and $\lambda_f^* = V_E^* p_2$ which, from (59) and (60), require that $\rho + \delta = G_K/p_2 = \rho^* + \delta^*$. Thus, both ι_d and ι_f^* are positive only if $\rho = \rho^*$, i.e. both nations have equal rates of time preference. If $\rho > \rho^*$, then it is easy to show that $\iota_d > 0 = \iota_f^*$. The home nation invests at home but the foreign nation does not. Moreover, $\rho > \rho^*$ implies that $V_E p_2/\lambda_f > V_E p_2/\lambda_d^*$ and hence that $\iota_f > 0 = \iota_d^*$. Thus, the nation with the greatest rate of time preference owns all the world's capital in the steady state!

To see why, it is noted that $\rho = G_K/p_2 - \delta = G_K^*/p_2 - \delta^* \equiv i$, the world interest rate, while $\rho^* = (V_E^* p_2/\lambda_d^*) G_K^*/p_2 - \delta^* = (V_E^* p_2/\lambda_f^*) G_K/p_2 - \delta < i$. Thus, the world interest rate, i, which is equal to the maximum net rate of return to capital, exceeds the rate of time preference for the foreign nation. The foreign nation therefore finds the interest rate too high to warrant the allocation of current income to investment. All income, which is derived from non-capital sources, is devoted to consumer goods.

Since in this case the home nation invests in both countries there is an element of indeterminacy in ι_d and ι_f. This is precisely of the same origin as the indeterminacy discussed previously, and can be resolved in the same ways.

If rates of time preference are indeed equal then there is a further indeterminacy since ι_d, ι_f, ι_d^* and ι_f^* can all be positive. This suggests that the values of C_d, C_f, C_d^* and C_f^* might be non-unique. But it also raises the question of whether the intertemporal equilibrium conditions might resolve or partially resolve these indeterminacies since, while the static choices are non-unique, they will influence the future course of the economies. This question is left open.

Away from the steady state the model is even more difficult to analyse. Note that since the saving choice is optimal it is based upon the complete profile of the economy which is captured by the λ's. These determine the allocation of current income between consumption and saving and the allocation of saving to domestic or foreign capital. The λ's give the present value of a unit of the capital good in question, and the present value is compared with the current asset price and the value of current consumption. The reader may wish to compare the nature of the investment choice with that formulated by Hori and Stein in which the future plays a limited role.

15.4.4. Concluding comments

The foreign investment problem is one of investment with heterogeneous capital goods, distinguished by nationality. Investment will be directed to where it yields the highest rate of return and this process will force an equality of rates of return internationally. Eventually, in the steady state, a situation of no change in real economic variables occurs in which in general there exists foreign ownership of capital. The time profile of the amounts of foreign investment and the accompanying repatriation of rental earnings depends upon the initial conditions, the technology and consumer preferences. There are two interrelated processes: the saving decision and the allocation of saving amongst the alternative (foreign and domestic) capital goods. The analysis of Hori and Stein (1977) showed no definite pattern of foreign investment and ownership, although their model had considerable structure. In the steady state their model implies that the nation with the highest ratio of marginal to average product will be a net creditor. In the optimal saving model the nation with the highest rate of time preference ends up owning all the capital and is hence a net creditor, irrespective of the technology.

15.5. Notes on the literature

The primary references on the infant-industry argument for protection are Kemp (1964) and Negishi (1965). The dynamics of various learning-by-doing models of the infant-industry argument have been spelt out by Bardhan (1971) and Clemhout and Wan (1970). Kemp (1974) has a clear statement of the inappropriateness of the infant-industry argument in the case of dynamic internal economies, while Baldwin (1969) has a critique of the effectiveness of taxes in achieving dynamic external economies. The present chapter has dealt only with the infant-industry argument based upon learning by doing. However, Chipman (1970) has made a first attempt at formulating a model of trade with endogenous technical change based upon Kennedy–Kamien–Schwartz lines. In this model the amounts of resources devoted to the acquisition of knowledge are determined by economic considerations. This approach offers interesting possibilities of integrating product-cycle theories with the general equilibrium trade model.

The heterogeneous capital model has been analysed in detail recently. Most discussions are based upon the time-phased production model, ignore the consumption side of the economy, and focus attention upon the steady-state solution. Most examine whether theorems obtained from a static model continue to apply in the steady state. Steedman and Metcalfe (1977) consider the validity of the HOS theorem, Kemp (1973) looks at the Rybczynski and Stolper–Samuelson theorems, Kemp and Khang (1974) examine the net output price relationships, and Burmeister (1978) considers the factor price equalization theorem. Other related papers are Acheson (1970) on capital aggregation, Findlay (1978) on interest rate equalization in an "Austrian" model, and Petith (1976) on vintage models. Ethier (1979) argues that the standard theorems apply in the steady state if capital is aggregated and they are applied properly. Samuelson (1975), especially the mathematical appendix, provides a very useful survey of the time-phased models.

The literature on foreign investment has concentrated upon the fixed saving ratio model. Models with trade in more than one good have been developed by Fisher and Frenkel (1972), based upon costs of adjustment, and by Hori and Stein (1977), who assume specialization. Other studies which use a single-good model include Negishi (1965), Long (1973), Manning (1975) and Ohyama (1978), who deal with the optimal tax on foreign investment in a dynamic context. See also Negishi (1972, ch. 9). Gale (1974) examines the steady state of a model of trade and investment and argues that trade imbalance (foreign ownership) is the rule rather than the exception. Bardhan (1967) considers the optimal policy for a country facing an upward-sloping foreign supply curve for capital. Ruffin (1979) compares steady-state solutions obtained under the polar assumptions of no capital mobility and perfect capital mobility under fixed saving rates.

Problems

1. For the continuous time infant-industry model of section 15.2:
   (a) Show that the maximized Hamiltonian can be written as (12).
   (b) Derive the equations of motion for experience q and the optimal rate of production subsidy s as in (13).
   (c) Show that if the instantaneous utility function is linearly homogeneous, then $\dot{V}_m = 0$ for given world prices.

2. Consider the continuous time model of learning by doing of section 15.2. Assume that learning only occurs in industry 1, whose production function is $y_1 = \ell(q)f^1(x_1)$, where the scalar q is "experience".
   (a) Show that $G(p, v, q) = G^+(p^+, v)$, where $p_1^+ = p_1\ell(q)$, $p_j^+ = p_j, j > 1$. That is, an increase in q acts like an increase in p_1.
   (b) Hence, show that $G_1 = G_1^+\ell(q)$ and $G_q = G_1^+p_1\,\ell_q$.
   (c) If $\ell(q) \equiv q^n$, where $0 < n < 1$, as in Bardhan (1971), we have that $\ln G_q = \ln G_1^+ + \ln p_1 + (n - 1)\ln q + \ln n$. Show that (i) $e_1 \equiv \partial \ln G_1/\partial \ln p_1 = \partial \ln G_1^+/\partial \ln p_1^+$ and (ii) $\partial \ln G_1/\partial \ln q = n(1 + e_1)$. Hence, $G_{qq} < 0$ if and only if the "learning elasticity of output of good 1" is $\partial \ln G_1/\partial \ln q = n(1 + e_1) < 1$.
   (d) Do these results generalize to the case where $\ell(q)$ is increasing and concave, and not simply of the constant elasticity form considered in (c)?

3. Suppose that, in the case of the Bardhan (1971) constant elasticity learning function, the rate of forgetfulness $\delta = 0$. What effect, if any, does this have upon Bardhan's results?

4. Consider the heterogeneous capital goods model of section 15.3.
   (a) Derive expression (20) for κ.
   (b) Derive the steady-state responses of capital stocks, outputs and net exports to a change in the world price vector as in (25).
   (c) Prove that $G_{pp} - G_{pK}G_{KK}^{-1}G_{Kp}$ is positive semi-definite.
   (d) Derive the steady-state effects of a change in the rate of time preference as in (27).

5. Consider the optimal saving model of foreign investment in section 15.4.
   (a) Derive eqs. (51)–(54).
   (b) Show that, in the steady state, if $\rho > \rho^*$, then $\iota_d > 0 = \iota_f^*$ and $\iota_f > 0 = \iota_d^*$.
   (c) How might the model be amended to allow for both nations to invest in the steady state, without forcing preferences to be identical?

6. Suppose that capital is perfectly mobile internationally at every instant of time, contrary to the Hori–Stein model of section 15.4 in which only currently produced capital moves across international boundaries. Suppose, furthermore, that there is just one good produced at unit price and each nation

has a fixed, but possibly different savings—income ratio.

(a) Derive the equations of motion $\dot{C} = \psi(C, C^*)$ and $\dot{C}^* = \psi^*(C, C^*)$, where C and C^* are the home and foreign nations' ownership of capital.

(b) If ψ_C, $\psi_{C^*}^* < 0$, show that the steady-state equilibrium is locally stable.

(c) Prove that the steady-state solutions for income and capital stocks (owned) are higher under free trade in the single good and capital services than under autarky in both.

(d) Prove that the wage rate is lower and the rental rate is higher under capital mobility for the nation that exports capital services (Ruffin, 1979).

References

Acheson, K. (1970) "The aggregation of heterogeneous capital goods and various trade theorems", *Journal of Political Economy* 78-3, May/June, 565–571.

Baldwin, R.E. (1969) "The case against infant-industry tariff protection", *Journal of Political Economy* 77, May/June, 295–305.

Bardhan, P. (1967) "Optimal foreign borrowing", in: K. Shell (ed.), *Essays in the Theory of Optimal Economic Growth* (Cambridge: M.I.T. Press), pp. 117–128.

Bardhan, P. (1971) "An optimum subsidy to a learning industry: An aspect of the theory of infant-industry protection", *International Economic Review* 12-1, February, 54–70.

Burmeister, E. (1978) "An interest rate and factor price equalization theorem with non-traded commodities", *Journal of International Economics* 8, 1–9.

Chipman, J.S. (1970) "Induced technical change and patterns of international trade", in: R. Vernon (ed.), *The Technology Factor in International Trade* (New York: Columbia University Press), pp. 95–127.

Clemhout, S. and H.Y. Wan (1970) "Learning-by-doing and infant industry protection", *Review of Economic Studies* 34-1, January, 33–56.

Ethier, W. (1979) "The theorems of international trade in time-phased economies", *Journal of International Economics* 9, 225–238.

Findlay, R. (1978) "An 'Austrian' model of international trade and interest rate equalization", *Journal of Political Economy* 86-6, December, 989–1007.

Fischer, S. and J.A. Frenkel (1972) "Investment, the two-sector model and trade in debt and capital goods", *Journal of International Economics* 2, 211–233.

Frenkel, J.A. (1971) "A theory of money, trade and the balance of payments in a model of accumulation", *Journal of International Economics* 1-2, 159–187.

Gale, D. (1974) "The trade imbalance story", *Journal of International Economics* 4, 119–137.

Hori, H. and J.L. Stein (1977) "International growth with free trade in equities and goods", *International Economic Review* 18-1, February, 83–100.

Kemp, M.C. (1964) *The Pure Theory of International Trade* (Englewood Cliffs, N.J.: Prentice-Hall).

Kemp, M.C. (1973) "Heterogeneous capital goods and long-run Stolper–Samuelson theorems", *Australian Economic Papers*, 12-21, December, 253–260.

Kemp, M.C. (1974) "Learning by doing: Formal tests for intervention in an open economy", *Keio Economic Studies* 11-1, 1–7.

Kemp, M.C. and C. Khang (1974) "A note on steady-state price output relationships", *Journal of International Economics* 2, 187–197.

Long, N.V. (1973) "On a paradox in the theory of international capital movements", *Economic Record* 41, September, 440–446.

Manning, R. (1975) "Attitudes to international capital movements in the long run: The case with neoclassical savings in the foreign country", *Economic Record* 51, June, 242–248.

Negishi, T. (1965) "Foreign investment and the long-run national advantage", *Economic Record* 41, December, 628–632.

Negishi, T. (1972) *General Equilibrium Theory and International Trade* (Amsterdam: North-Holland/American Elsevier).

Ohyama, M. (1972) "Trade and welfare in general equilibrium", *Keio Economic Studies* 9-2, 37–73.

Ohyama, M. (1978) "Reconsideration of some paradoxes in the theory of optimal foreign investment", *Economic Record* 54, 346–353.

Petith, H.C. (1976) "The Stolper–Samuelson theorem, the Rybczynski theorem, and the pattern of trade in neoclassical and vintage capital trade and growth models", *International Economic Review* 17-1, February, 57–75.

Ruffin, R. (1979) "Growth and the long-run theory of international capital movements", *American Economic Review* 69-5, December, 832–842.

Samuelson, P.A. (1975) "Trade pattern reversals in time-phased Ricardian systems and intertemporal efficiency", *Journal of International Economics* 5, 309–363.

Smith, M.A.M. (1976) "Trade, growth and consumption in alternative models of capital accumulation", *Journal of International Economics* 6, 371–384.

Steedman, I. and J.S. Metcalfe (1977) "Reswitching, primary inputs and the Heckscher–Ohlin–Samuelson theory of international trade", *Journal of International Economics* 7, 291–208.

CHAPTER 16

FURTHER TOPICS IN TRADE THEORY

16.1. Introduction

International trade theory encompasses a wide range of individual topics. Those that are at the core of international trade theory have been dealt with in varying degrees of detail in the preceding chapters. Many other topics could be taken up in detail but are not, since they are more peripheral to the essential aspects of international trade theory than those already covered. Indeed, there may be considerable disagreement on which additional topics are of greatest importance and hence most worthy of inclusion. Possible additional topics include integration of real and financial models of trade, monopolistic behaviour, disequilibrium models, factor market distortions, externalities, models with a continuum of goods, a more extensive coverage of endogenous technological change including the development of new products, the role of transportation and space in trade theory, trade with exhaustible resources, international commodity agreements, and so forth.

Rather than devote additional chapters to each or some of these or to ignore them altogether, the present chapter is devoted to a very brief introduction to a few of these topics. The purpose is simply to put the chosen topics into the perspective of this book and to indicate directions for further reading. We shall deal with the general topic of distortions, uncertainty, and trade with exhaustible resources. These topics involve a departure from the standard analysis covered in preceding chapters so it is important to indicate the nature of this departure.

16.2. Distortions

The competitive model of trade consists of three sectors — the production, consumption and foreign sectors. Distortions can be introduced into the model in two different forms, given this triad. The first type of distortion is the introduction of different prices for the three sectors. This can arise, for example, by imposing a set of trade taxes which create a wedge between foreign and domestic prices, consumers and producers both facing the latter. Alternatively, a set of production taxes creates a wedge between producers' prices and market prices which apply to both consumers and foreigners. Consumption taxes create a distinction between consumer prices and market prices faced by producers and foreigners. Production, consumption and trade quotas have equivalent price effects in the competitive model. This type of distortion has, of course, been dealt with in detail in preceding chapters.

The second general type of distortion causes the production and/or consumption decisions to be non-optimal. Production distortions cause actual GNP to differ from the maximum GNP that can be attained given product prices and factor endowments. That is,

$$py < G(p, v), \tag{1}$$

where y is the production vector under the distortion. Similarly, a consumption distortion occurs when expenditure exceeds the minimum needed to attain the actual utility vector. That is,

$$pz > E(p, \mu), \tag{2}$$

where z is the production vector under the distortion and μ is a vector of utilities.

There are, of course, many reasons why (1) and (2) may occur and these form the subject-matter of the general topic of distortions. Most researchers have concentrated upon production distortions with very little attention being devoted to those arising in the consumption sector. The main form of consumption distortion would occur if preferences were interdependent, a type of externality. As an example, suppose that person 2 is indifferent to person 1's consumption choice but that person 1's welfare is affected by person 2's consumption choice. Then the utility functions are $\mu^1 = u^1(z_1, z_2)$ and $\mu^2 = u^2(z_2)$ while the minimum expenditure functions are $E^1(p, \mu^1, z_2)$ and $E^2(p, \mu^2)$. The vector $\partial E^1 / \partial z_2$ will have elements which are positive or negative according to whether higher consumption by person 2 raises or lowers the minimum expenditure needed by person 1 to attain utility level μ^1. It is easy to show that

$$E(p, \mu) \equiv \min_{z_1, z_2} \{p(z_1 + z_2): u^1(z_1, z_2) \geqslant \mu^1, u^2(z_2) \geqslant \mu^2\}$$
$$= \min_{z_2} \{E^1(p, \mu^1, z_2) + pz_2: u^2(z_2) \geqslant \mu^2\}$$
$$< E^1(p, \mu^1, E_p^2(p, \mu^2)) + E^2(p, \mu^2). \tag{3}$$

The latter expression is the total expenditure when each consumer separately minimizes his own expenditure, and this exceeds the minimum expenditure needed to attain vector μ when the externality is taken into account. Thus, this is a distortion which causes inefficiency in the consumption sector in the sense of (2).

In short, distortions of the second type alter our analysis which has been based upon optimal behaviour from the production and consumption sectors' viewpoint. In what follows some effects of certain types of production distortions are developed to illustrate the type of problems created by their existence.

16.2.1. Factor market distortions

Production distortions may take many forms. The most studied distortion arises through the factor markets and occurs if there is a difference in the factor price vector between industries. This prevents an efficient allocation of resources among industries and so results in a lower level of GNP than would occur without the distortion. The model of the production sector becomes

(a) $\quad c^j(w^j) - p_j \geqslant 0 \leqslant y_j, \qquad\qquad j = 1, ..., M,$

(b) $\quad \sum\limits_{j=1}^{M} c_w^j(w^j)y_j - v \leqslant 0 \leqslant w,$ \hfill (4)

(c) $\quad w^j = w + t_j = w(I + T_j), \qquad j = 1, ..., M,$

where w^j is the factor price vector in industry j, t_j may be interpreted as the (per unit) tax vector in industry j, and $T_j = \mathrm{diag}\,(\tau_j)$, and $\tau_{ij} \equiv t_{ij}/w_i > -1$ is the ad valorem rate of tax on factor i in industry j. The interpretation of t_j as a tax vector is convenient, but it could be the result of factor price rigidities due to institutional factors or of monopolistic behaviour on the part of labour unions. In any event the factor prices are forced to be different among industries.

Unless $t_j = 0$ for all j (or more accurately $\tau_{ij} = k$ for all i and j) it is no longer true that (4) constitutes the Kuhn–Tucker conditions for the maximization of GNP on the production possibility set since this requires the same factor price vector in each industry. To obtain comparative static results (4) has to be analysed directly. Thus, the effect of a change in p, v and $t = (t_1, ..., t_M)$ upon y and w (hence w^j) can be obtained by differentiating (4).

It is readily verified that if the t_j are fixed, then the effect of p and v upon y and w is exactly the same as in a model without distortions (qualitatively, but not quantitatively the same). If, however, the τ_j are given, then the results are affected. The comparative static results for the case where there are equal numbers of products and factors are given by

$$
\begin{bmatrix} dw \\ \\ dy \end{bmatrix} = \begin{bmatrix} (\bar{A}^{\,T})^{-1} & 0 \\ \\ -A^{-1}C_{ww}(\bar{A}^{-1})^{T} & A^{-1} \end{bmatrix} \begin{bmatrix} dp \\ \\ dv \end{bmatrix}, \tag{5}
$$

where $\bar{A} \equiv [a_j(I + T_j)]$, $\bar{C}_{ww} \equiv \sum_j y_j c^j_{ww}(w^j)(I + T_j)$ and $A \equiv [c^1_w, ..., c^M_w]$.

Notice that the effect of v upon y is the same as in a model with no distortions so the previous results concerning the Rybczynski effects apply without change. The effect of p upon w depends upon $\bar{A}$ rather than A. Since $1 + \tau_{ij} > 0$ is assumed, $\bar{A}$ and A have the same sign structure so the Stolper–Samuelson results derived previously apply here. In terms of percentage changes we have that $\partial \ln w / \partial \ln p = \theta^{-1}$, where $\theta = [\theta_{ij}]$ and $\theta_{ij} \equiv \bar{a}_{ij} w_i / p_j = a_{ij} w^j_i / p_j$ is the cost share of factor i in industry j. This shows that the Stolper Samuelson results continue to apply without change. Since there is a distinction between A and $\bar{A}$, however, the reciprocity condition $\partial w / \partial p = \partial y / \partial v$ does not hold. Finally, the effect of p upon y is no longer given by a positive semi-definite matrix. The matrix $\bar{C}_{ww}$ is positive semi-definite but its pre- and post-multiplicands are not the same, so positive semi-definiteness of $\partial y / \partial p$ is not assured. Consequently, it is possible that $\partial y_i / \partial p_i$ is negative, meaning that an increase in the price of good i causes a reduction in its supply.

When there are just two products and two factors the sign structures of $A, \bar{A}$ and $\bar{C}_{ww}$ imply

$$
\frac{\partial y}{\partial p} = -A^{-1}\bar{C}_{ww}(\bar{A}^{-1})^{T} = \begin{bmatrix} + & - \\ - & + \end{bmatrix} \Big/ |A| \cdot |\bar{A}|. \tag{6}
$$

It is noted here that $\bar{a}_{ij} \equiv a_{ij}(1 + \tau_{ij}) \geqslant 0$ since $a_{ij} \geqslant 0$ and $(1 + \tau_{ij}) > 0$ by assumption, and that c^j_{ww} has negative diagonal and positive off-diagonal elements. Clearly, $\partial y_i / \partial p_i > 0$ if and only if $|A| \cdot |\bar{A}| > 0$. The sign of $|A|$ indicates the relative factor intensities defined in quantity terms. On the other hand,

$$
|\bar{A}| = (\theta_{11}\theta_{22} - \theta_{12}\theta_{21})c^1 c^2 / w_1 w_2 = |\theta| c^1 c^2 / w_1 w_2. \tag{7}
$$

When there are no distortions $|A|$ and $|\bar{A}|$ are equal and have the sign of $|\theta|$, but the presence of distortions allows $|A|$ and $|\bar{A}|$, hence $|\theta|$, to have opposite signs. Thus, industry 1 may be factor 1 intensive in the quantity sense ($|A| > 0$)

but factor 2 intensive in the cost share sense ($|\theta| < 0$). It is this situation that causes an increase in p_1 to cause output of good 1 to fall and that of good 2 to rise.

In the general case it is no longer true that p is orthogonal to the distorted production possibility frontier (defined by solving for y in (4) for all choices of p) whence $p\,\partial y/\partial p \neq 0$. Consequently, the change in utility $\mu = V(p, py)$ due to a change in world prices is proportional to

$$d\mu/V_m = (y - z) + p\,\partial y/\partial p, \tag{8}$$

where $z = \phi(p, m) = -V_p/V_m$, $m = py$. It is possible that an increase in the price of an exported good j could reduce welfare if $p\,\partial y/\partial p_j$ is sufficiently negative, in contrast to the case of no distortions.

Most of the literature is concerned with pointing out how many of the standard results of international trade theory may become invalid and that many "perverse" results may occur when factor market distortions are introduced. Also discussed are the effects of altering the amount of the distortion. For details the reader is referred to the survey by Magee (1973), Pearce (1971), who has a detailed examination of $\partial y/\partial p$ when $M = N > 2$, Bhagwati and Srinivason (1971), and Batra and Pattanaik (1971), who examine the effect of changes in distortions upon the terms of trade and welfare. Neary (1978) argues that if certain stability conditions for the factor market are taken into account the possibility of perverse results is reduced considerably.

The discussion of factor market distortions now concludes with several observations. First, while most of the literature has focused upon factor market distortions, similar distortions also occur if there are taxes imposed on outputs (or inputs) of intermediate goods. Then the price received by the producer is different from that faced by a user of the intermediate good and inefficiency arises again. Secondly, the reasons for the distortions in factor markets are seldom made clear. The distortions are usually made exogenous rather than the result of explicit optimizing (or other) behaviour of groups such as labour unions. Thirdly, there is an alternative approach to factor market distortions which fixes the prices of one of more factors in terms of some product price or price index, and allows for unemployment of these factors. See, for example, the treatment by Brecher (1974), and the generalization by Schweinberger (1978) and Neary (1980), who makes use of the GNP function.

16.2.2. Externalities and increasing returns to scale

Another type of distortion in production is due to increasing returns to scale. Our analysis has assumed constant returns to scale throughout. Decreasing returns can, however, be accommodated by defining a fictional factor, maintaining constant returns to scale over all (including the fictional) factors. The earnings of the fictional factor are the profits earned. Increasing returns to scale are not handled so easily. In fact, once internal increasing returns to scale are introduced, monopolistic behaviour must also be allowed. One way of modelling increasing returns to scale while maintaining competitive behaviour is to assume that the scale economies are external to the firm. This leads to the more general problem of externalities.

Externalities may be modelled by

(a) $c^j(w, y) - p_j \geqslant 0 \leqslant y_j, \qquad j = 1, ..., M,$

(b) $\displaystyle\sum_{j=1}^{M} c_w^j(w, y) y_j - v \leqslant 0 \leqslant w,$

$\qquad\qquad\qquad\qquad\qquad\qquad\qquad\qquad\qquad\qquad\qquad (9)$

where the *average* cost function for industry j is $c^j(w, y) \equiv C^j(w, y)/y_j$ and $C^j(w, y)$ is the industry's total cost function. The cost functions depend upon all outputs. If there are economies of scale which are external to firms and internal to each industry, then only y_j enters as an argument in the cost function. Increasing returns to scale occur where average costs $c^j(w, y)$ fall with increases in output y_j. The formulation in (9) is general enough to allow for the typical U-shaped average cost curve exhibiting initial increasing returns and eventual decreasing returns to scale. If there are externalities between industries, then the general formulation of (9) applies.[1] Thus, the cost function for industry j may depend upon the output of industry k, with $\partial C^j / \partial y_k$ being negative if the externality is beneficial and positive if it is detrimental to industry j.

Equation (9, a) is the zero profit condition in the presence of scale effects. The difficulty created is that y appears on the left-hand side of (9, a) in contrast to the constant returns to scale case. Once again the price vector will in general not be orthogonal to the production possibility set and GNP is not maximized at the competitive solution (to (9)), as is well known. Comparative statics results for the effect of changes in p and v upon w and y can be obtained by total differentiation of (9). For treatments of the variable returns to scale case see Jones

---

[1]   This is only one type of externality. Alternatively, the cost function for industry j may depend upon the input of some factor in industry k.

(1968), Panagariya (1980) and Mayer (1976), who assumes a homothetic production function implying a cost function of the form $C^j(w, y) = \gamma^j(w)h^j(y)$.

16.2.3. Monopolistic behaviour

Monopolistic behaviour, with or without internal economies of scale, may constitute a distortion. In modelling monopolistic behaviour there arises the question of how extensive the monopolist perceives that his power spreads. However, the important point is that the monopolistic firm will not price according to marginal cost. Hence, the price vector will (apart from exceptional cases) not be orthogonal to the production possibility frontier and GNP is not a maximum at the monopolistic equilibrium prices. For treatments of the monopolistic case see Melvin and Warne (1973), Krugman (1979) and Dixit and Norman (1980).

16.3. Uncertainty

Our analysis has assumed that all behaviour is based upon certainty regarding all variables. This is a convenient assumption but is likely to be violated in many instances. Particularly in agriculture, where weather plays an important role, there may be stochastic components to production. Market prices may be unknown at the time when production decisions are being made. The certainty assumption is particularly suspect in the analysis of the dynamics of trade and growth. The perfect foresight assumption neglects the uncertainty of the future.

In recent years the role of uncertainty in international trade has received increasing attention. Not unexpectedly, there is considerable variety in the way in which uncertainty is modelled and, consequently, in the type of results obtained. Because of this and because there exists a recent review of the area by Pomery (1979), the present section will not attempt a comprehensive coverage of the area but will simply point out some of the issues raised in the context of some simple models.

Let us restrict attention to the "full knowledge" case where the model is known by the agents. That is, they know the probability distribution for the stochastic variables — there is no ignorance. Uncertainty can arise through stochastic elements in production or consumption. If no decisions are made until the uncertainty is resolved (i.e., the stochastic variables have been determined and are known) then the equilibrium conditions are those for a certainty model. If some decisions have to be made before the uncertainty is resolved then the decision-maker has to take account of the stochastic nature of his economic environment. Accordingly, the equilibrium conditions differ from those in a certainty model so that the theorems of international trade theory developed for a certainty model may not continue to hold. Moreover, the introduction of uncertainty leads to new questions that can be asked.

To illustrate the role played by uncertainty consider the case of a small open economy facing world prices which are stochastic. Presumably the uncertainty is due to stochastic elements in foreign production or consumption. Models differ in the choice of the division of decisions into those made before and those made after the uncertainty is resolved, and the choice of who bears the risk. Suppose that the allocation of capital among industries is chosen before the uncertainty is resolved but all other decision in the economy are made afterwards. Assume also that the economy behaves as if it maximizes expected utility. Then the problem of the consumer–producer may written as

$$\max_{K_1, \ldots, K_M} \left\{ E\, V(p, G(p, L, K_1, \ldots, K_M)\colon \sum_{j=1}^{M} K_j \leqslant K, K_j \geqslant 0, \right.$$

$$\left. j = 1, \ldots, M \right\} \tag{10}$$

where E is the expectations operator and $G(p, L, K_1, \ldots, K_M)$ is the GNP function with K_j being the allocation of capital to industry j.[2] Here p is a random vector with known probability distribution. The solution to (10) must satisfy the first-order conditions:

(a) $\quad E\, V_m G_j - \lambda \leqslant 0 \leqslant K_j$,

(b) $\quad \displaystyle\sum_{j=1}^{M} K_j - K \leqslant 0 \leqslant \lambda$, $\tag{11}$

where λ is a Lagrange multiplier and $G_j \equiv \partial G / \partial K_j$.

Under certainty about p, (11) indicates that the allocation of capital is such as to equal the marginal value product of capital in each industry. Under uncertainty the expected marginal utility of capital is equated in each industry. The allocation of capital will be different as a result of uncertainty.

The interpretation of the decision process is as follows. The consumer–producer maximizes expected utility by solving (11) for $K_1, \ldots, K_M$. After these are chosen the uncertainty in p is resolved and a particular price vector is faced by the economy. The production sector becomes identical to the industry-specific

---

[2] If x is a continuous stochastic variable defined on the set X with density $f(x, \theta)$, where θ is a vector of parameters, then $Ex = \int_X x f(x, \theta)\,dx$.

factor model dealt with in Chapter 4. There the amounts of capital allocated to each industry were arbitrarily given, whereas here the allocation is based upon expected utility-maximizing behaviour. Ex-post the choice may be suboptimal (from a certainty viewpoint) but is optimal ex-ante (i.e. under uncertainty). Given p, output and the allocation of labour are chosen to maximize GNP which is then spent by the consumption sector to maximize utility. Thus, the trade vector is determined as in a certainty model, but depending upon the allocation of capital determined in a state of uncertainty.

The above model (used by Eaton, 1979) is just one of many that can be postulated for the case of price uncertainty. One variation is to assume that the producer maximizes expected GNP. Another is to assume that actual output levels and the allocations of all factors are chosen before uncertainty is resolved. Then the expected utility maximization problem is

$$\max_{y} \{ \mathrm{E}\, V(p, py) \colon y \in Y(v), \text{ i.e. } t(y, -v) = 0 \} \tag{12}$$

with first-order conditions

(a) $\quad \mathrm{E}\, V_m p - \lambda\, t_y(y, -v) = 0$

(b) $\quad t(y, -v) = 0.$

$$\tag{13}$$

This shows clearly that in general p will not be orthogonal to the production possibility set. However, $\mathrm{E}\, V_m p$ will be. If preferences are linearly homogeneous $V(p, m) = m/e(p)$, where $e(p)$ is the unit expenditure function, then $V_m = 1/e(p)$ is independent of income m (the case of risk neutrality).[3] In this case $\mathrm{E} p/e(p)$ is orthogonal to $Y(v)$ at the solution y. If, instead of (12), the problem is to maximize expected GNP, then the solution requires that $\mathrm{E} p$ be orthogonal to the production possibility set at the solution for y. The model given by (12) is a generalization of that used by Turnovsky (1974) and Ruffin (1974), who assume a Ricardian production model.

There are different approaches that can be used in analysing uncertainty models such as those outlined above. One approach is to take the uncertainty (i.e. the probability distribution) as given and to ask questions about the effect of changes in exogenous variables upon the equilibrium solution. For example, will an increase in the endowment of labour cause an increase in the output of the labour intensive product in model (12), or in the expected output of that prod-

---

[3] The consumer is said to be risk neutral if $V_{mm} \equiv \partial^2 V/\partial m^2 = 0$, risk averse if $V_{mm} < 0$, and a risk lover if $V_{mm} > 0$.

uct in model (10)? Will there be factor price equalization under certainty? Are there gains from trade under uncertainty? A second approach is to examine the effects upon the equilibrium solution of a change in the distribution of world prices. For example, what is the effect of increasing the amount of uncertainty? Usually, increasing uncertainty is defined to be some specific spread in the distribution which preserves the mean (arithmetic or geometric). Much of the literature is concerned with comparing solutions obtained under certainty (the probability distribution is degenerate with probability of one attached to the mean) and uncertainty (non-degenerate probability distribution with the same mean). For example, Turnovsky (1974) considers a Ricardian production model and shows that it may be optimal to specialize in the production of the good that would not be produced if the expected price vector held with certainty. As another example, many authors, such as Anderson and Riley (1976), Batra (1974) and Eaton (1979) have obtained conditions under which a mean-preserving spread will raise expected utility.

While a detailed treatment of uncertainty models is beyond the scope of this section, let us briefly consider the question of the gains from free trade for a small open economy facing stochastic prices. Since in the above models certain production decisions are made before uncertainty is resolved, there is the possibility that the actual level of utility attained under free trade is lower than that attained under autarky. This is in contrast with the certainty model (abstracting from distributional considerations). However, it is easy to show that expected utility is higher (strictly no lower) under free trade at random world prices than under autarky. This is now demonstrated for model (12), but the same argument can be applied to (10). Define $H(p, y) \equiv V(p, py)$ as an indirect trade utility function (introduced in Chapter 6), where y takes the role of the "factor endowment". Let y^f be the solution to (12) and let p^a and y^a be the (non-stochastic) autarky price and output vectors. Then

$$\mathrm{E}\, H(p, y^f) \geqslant \mathrm{E}\, H(p, y^a) \geqslant H(p^a, y^a). \tag{14}$$

The first inequality occurs because $y^a \in Y(v)$ is a feasible output vector under free trade and y^f is chosen to maximize expected utility. Since any price vector yields a utility level at least as great as the autarky utility level given the same production possibilities (Chapter 9), it follows that $H(p, y^a) \geqslant H(p^a, y^a)$ when y^a is the set of productions available. Thus, $\mathrm{E}\, H(p, y^a) \geqslant H(p^a, y^a)$, which is the second inequality in (14). Thus, (14) holds indicating that there are expected gains (strictly no losses) from trade under uncertain world prices. The reader will recognize the strong resemblance of this argument to that provided in Chapter 9.

The preceding discussion has been confined to uncertain world prices. Price uncertainty is studied by Anderson and Riley (1976), Eaton (1979), Ruffin (1974) and Turnovsky (1974) among others. Another section of the literature deals with uncertainty in the production functions. See, for example, Turnovsky (1974), Batra (1974) and Kemp and Ohta (1979). Indeed, in a general equilibrium framework even random prices must be due to randomness in production or consumption. An important contribution which introduces international trade in equities as well as goods is by Helpman and Razin (1978, 1980), an approach taken up by Dumas (1980). Helpman and Razin develop a model in which product prices and the technology are random, firms maximize their net market values, individuals make consumption choices after the resolution of uncertainty, and choose their portfolios of equity in firms to maximize expected utility. They demonstrate that the failure of the standard theorems of international trade theory (such as the Stolper–Samuelson theorem) to remain valid upon the introduction of uncertainty is due to the implicit assumption that there is no trade in real equities. If free trade in real equities is permitted, then these theorems continue to hold. More generally, the introduction of markets for real equities by Helpman and Razin helps free the literature from its "commodity" orientation. For a detailed survey of the literature see Pomery (1979).

16.4. Exhaustible resources

The analysis of the dynamics of trade in Chapters 14 and 15 can be extended in several (non-exclusive) ways. One way is to eliminate the perfect foresight assumption by introducing savings decisions based upon currently available information, and perhaps involving expectations formation. Another is to introduce uncertainty about the future explicitly into the model. Another area for concern is the absence of a treatment of the special problems created by exhaustible resources. In our analysis capital stocks could grow by devoting resources to the production of new capital. However, exhaustible resources require special treatment since their stocks can only be depleted.

A number of studies of trade in exhaustible resources have appeared in recent years, partly in response to the "oil crisis" and the concern that current rates of extraction will soon use up known stocks of many exhaustible resources. Here a simple model is postulated for comparison with those of Chapters 14 and 15, and to introduce the literature on exhaustible resources. Let $y = (y_1, y_2)$ be the production vector, where y_2 is the extraction of a resource and y_1 is a vector of other net outputs. The production possibility set is $Y(R)$, where R is the stock of the resource. The resource stock is depleted by extraction as $\dot{R} = -y_2$ (y_2 being gross and net production for simplicity). If the trade must be balanced, then the budget constraint for a small open economy is $pz = py$, where z is the consumption vector and p is the world price vector. The model is completed by assuming that the economy maximizes the present value of the utility stream. Thus, the problem is

$$\max\left\{\int_0^T e^{-\rho\tau} u(z)\mathrm{d}\tau : y \in Y(R), \dot{R} = -y_2, pz = py\right\}, \tag{15}$$

where T is the time horizon, ρ is the rate of time preference, and y, z and R are implicitly time dependent with the initial resource stock R_0 given. The problem is to determine the rate of extraction and hence the rate of depletion of the resource stock.

The solution to (15) proceeds by forming the Hamiltonian and applying the maximum principle. The maximized Hamiltonian may be written as

$$H(\lambda, R) = V(p, G(p^s, R)), \tag{16}$$

where $V(p, m)$ is the instantaneous indirect utility function, $p^s = (p_1, p_2 - \lambda^s)$, $\lambda^s = \lambda/V_m$, $G(p^s, R)$ is the GNP function, and λ is the multiplier associated with the depletion equation $\dot{R} = -y_2$. The variable λ^s is interpreted as the rental value of the resource. The optimal policy therefore requires that producers be charged a royalty or tax of λ^s for each unit of the resource extracted, or that firms themselves impute a price of λ^s for use of the resource.

The changes in R and λ through time are given by

(a) $\dot{R} = H_\lambda = -G_2(p^s, R),$

(b) $\dot{\lambda} = \rho\lambda + H_R = \rho\lambda + V_m G_R,$

$$\tag{17}$$

where the subscripts denote derivatives. Along with the initial and terminal conditions (17) can be solved for the time profiles of λ and R, hence all the endogenous variables. The rate of change in the royalty of the resource is $\hat{\lambda}^s \equiv \dot{\lambda}^s/\lambda^s$ $= \rho - \hat{V}_m - G_R/\lambda^s$.

Evidently, the solution depends upon the nature of the technology, preferences, and the initial conditions. The above model is a generalization of that of Vousden (1974) who deals with one non-resource product and assumes that the production possibility set is independent of R except when $R = 0$. Vousden examines the nature of the solution in detail and shows that if the initial R is sufficiently large and T is sufficiently small, then the optimal tax rate λ^s is zero. Otherwise a positive tax is required.

Kemp and Long (1979) consider a variation on this model by assuming that extraction of the resource is costless, and that two final goods are produced using labour and the resource. The GNP function is $G(p, L, E)$, where E is the extraction rate and $\dot{R} = -E$. Unlike in Vousden's model the resource is not traded but the goods are. They show that the nation specializes, and that if there is an increase in the initial resource stock the production of the resource-intensive good increases at each instant of time for which it is produced. They call this a generalized Rybczynski theorem.

The preceding discussion has focused on a central problem of resource depletion, namely of determining the optimal profile for the tax rate on the extraction of the resource. This is the fundamental problem of all dynamic optimization problems. The exhaustible resource model has the feature, however, that a steady state will not exist except in the trivial case where the extraction rate is zero (as it must be if the resource is exhausted). The nature of the solution depends crucially upon possibilities of substituting away from the exhaustible resource in both production and consumption as the stock is depleted.

Another important aspect of exhaustible resources is that of the saving decision. Some authors, such as Long (1974), Dasgupta, Eastwood and Heal (1978), Calvo and Findlay (1978), and Harris (1978), have permitted international capital flows as a means of providing resources for resource extraction and/or providing future income for the resource-owning nation. In these papers international borrowing and lending can occur and so the budget constraint is defined over the whole time horizon. None of these deals with a full general equilibrium model of world trade and investment, but Dixit (1981) does so using a two-period model.

References

Anderson, J.E. and J.G. Riley (1976) "International trade with fluctuating prices", *International Economic Review* 17-1, February, 76–97.

Batra, R.N. (1974) "Resource allocation in a general equilibrium model of production under uncertainty", *Journal of Economic Theory* 8, 50–63.

Batra, R.N. and P.K. Pattanaik (1971) "Factor market imperfections, the terms of trade, and welfare", *American Economic Review* 61-5, December, 946–955.

Bhagwati, J. and T.N. Srinivason (1971) "The theory of wage differentials: Production response and factor price equalization", *Journal of International Economics* 1, 19–35.

Brecher, R.A. (1974) "Minimum wage rates and the pure theory of international trade", *Quarterly Journal of Economics* 88, 98–116.

Calvo, G. and R. Findlay (1978) "On the optimal acquisition of foreign capital through investment of oil export revenues", *Journal of International Economics* 8-4, November, 513–524.

Dasgupta, P., R. Eastwood and G. Heal (1978) "Resource management in a trading economy", *Quarterly Journal of Economics* 92-2, 297–306.

Dixit, A.K. (1981) "A model of trade in oil and capital", Princeton University.

Dixit, A.K. and V. Norman (1980) *Theory of International Trade* (J. Nisbet/Cambridge University Press).

Dumas, B. (1980) "The theorems of international trade under generalized uncertainty", *Journal of International Economics* 10, 481–498.

Eaton, J. (1979) "The allocation of resources in an open economy with uncertain terms of trade", *International Economic Review* 20-2, June, 391–403.

Harris, R. (1978) "Trade and depletable resources: The small open economy", Discussion Paper no. 289, Queen's University.

Helpman, E. and A. Razin (1978) "Uncertainty and international trade in the presence of stock markets", *Review of Economic Studies* 45-2, June, 239–250.

Helpman, E. and A. Razin (1980) *A Theory of International Trade Under Uncertainty* (New York: Academic Press).

Jones, R.W. (1968) "Variable returns to scale in general equilibrium theory", *International Economic Review* 9-3, October, 261–272.

Jones, R.W. (1971) "Distortions in factor markets and the general equilibrium model of production", *Journal of Political Economy* 79, June, 437–459.

Kemp, M.C. and N.V. Long (1979) "International trade with an exhaustible resource: A theorem of Rybczynski type", *International Economic Review* 20-3, October, 671–677.

Kemp, M.C. and H. Ohta (1979) "Some implications of uncertainty in a small open economy", *Economic Record* 55, December, 354–358.

Krugman, P. (1979) "Increasing returns, monopolistic competition and international trade", *Journal of International Economics* 9, 395–410.

Long, N.V. (1974) "International borrowing for resource extraction", *International Economic Review* 15-1, February, 168–183.

Magee, S.P. (1973) "Factor market distortions, production and trade: A survey", *Oxford Economic Papers* 25-1, March, 1–43.

Mayer, W. (1976) "A small open economy with more produced commodities than factors", *Econometrica* 44-3, May, 561–573.

Melvin, J.R. and R.D. Warne (1973) "Monopoly and the theory of international trade", *Journal of International Economics* 3, 117–134.

Neary, J.P. (1978) "Dynamic stability and the theory of factor-market distortions", *American Economic Review* 68-4, September, 671–682.

Neary, J.P. (1980) "International factor mobility, minimum wage rates and factor price equalization: A synthesis", unpublished paper, Trinity College, Dublin, July.

Panagariya, A. (1980) "Variable returns to scale in general equilibrium theory once again", *Journal of International Economics* 10, 499–526.

Pearce, I. (1971) "The theory of wage differentials: The $n \times n$ case", *Journal of International Economics* 1, 205–214.

Pomery, J. (1979) "Uncertainty and international trade", in: R. Dornbusch and J. Frenkel (eds.), *International Economic Policy: Theory and Evidence* (Johns Hopkins), ch. 4.

Ruffin, R.J. (1974) "Comparative advantage under uncertainty", *Journal of International Economics* 4, 261–273.

Schweinberger, A.G. (1978) "Employment subsidies and the theory of minimum wage rates in general equilibrium", *Quarterly Journal of Economics* 92, 361–374.

Turnovsky, S.J. (1974) "Technological and price uncertainty in a Ricardian model of international trade", *Review of Economic Studies* 41-2, April, 201–218.

Vousden, N. (1974) "International trade and exhaustible resources: A theoretical model", *International Economic Review* 15-1, February, 149–167.

AUTHOR INDEX

SUBJECT INDEX